Management for Engineers

DATE DUE

NOV 0 8 1998		
APR 04 2000		

Demco, Inc. 38-293

WITHDRAWN

Management for Engineers

Andrew C. Payne
John V. Chelsom
Lawrence R. P. Reavill
City University, London, UK

JOHN WILEY & SONS
Chichester • New York • Brisbane • Toronto • Singapore

Other Wiley Editorial Offices

John Wiley & Sons, Inc., 605 Third Avenue,
New York, NY 10158-0012, USA

Jacaranda Wiley Ltd, 33 Park Road, Milton,
Queensland 4064, Australia

John Wiley & Sons (Canada) Ltd, 22 Worcester Road,
Rexdale, Ontario M9W 1L1, Canada

John Wiley & Sons (SEA) Pte Ltd, 37 Jalan Pemimpin #05-04,
Block B, Union Industrial Building, Singapore 2057

Library of Congress Cataloging-in-Publication Data

Payne, Andrew C.
    Management for engineers / Andrew C. Payne, John V. Chelsom,
Lawrence R. P. Reavill.
        p.   cm.
    Includes bibliographical references and index.
    ISBN 0-471-95603-1 (pbk. : alk. paper)
    1. Engineering — Management.   I. Chelsom, John V.   II. Reavill,
Lawrence R. P.   III. Title.
TA190.P39   1995
658′.002462 — dc20
                                                        95-30725
                                                        CIP

British Library Cataloguing in Publication Data

A catalogue record for this book is available from the British Library

ISBN 0-471-95603-1

Typeset in 10/12pt Times by Dobbie Typesetting Ltd, Tavistock, Devon
Printed and bound in Great Britain by Bookcraft (Bath) Ltd
This book is printed on acid-free paper responsibly manufactured from sustainable forestation,
for which at least two trees are planted for each one used for paper production.

Contents

Preface

Why should engineers study management? One reason is that engineers, like most specialists, spend more of their working life 'managing' than directly practising their specialism. Engineers, however, have the advantage that their disciplined and analytical training equips them better than most for the tasks of management — provided they can see the parallels between engineering systems and business systems.

This book, in the early, scene setting chapters, aims to identify the parallels, not by reducing management decisions to formulae or calculations, but by showing that businesses are systems, with structures and processes that in many ways are similar to engineering systems. Business systems, like engineering systems need some form of inequality to make them function, and similar terms are often used in the two different fields: 'power differential', 'market pull', 'science push'. Organizations exhibit resistance to change, and inertia, rather like physical entities, and some observers see an inevitability in the pattern of growth, maturity and decline in organizations which is similar to the phases of life systems. Also, like an engineering system, a business has to be designed to operate in an environment subject to change. Measurements of change and information feedback can be applied to monitor, maintain or improve business performance and continual attention to variations in external and internal forces is as important to management of a company as it is to the performance of a machine or plant, or the safety of a bridge or a building. Training as an engineer can, therefore, be complementary to an introduction to management.

In part, the value of an engineering education as a basis for a managerial role explains the presence of so many engineers in top management positions, even in Britain. A survey among the UK's top ten companies (by sales volume) for the 1992 Walmsley Lecture at City University, showed that between 10 and 30% of the most senior positions were filled by chartered engineers who did not have the word 'engineer' in their job title. This included a vice-president treasurer, and a vice-president personnel. However, the engineer needs more management skills than the traditional UK university degree has provided, and many of those top managers have had to supplement their early training with further studies. Engineers who bemoan that the corporate high ground is dominated by lawyers and accountants, and that there are not more top management with a technological background, have to recognize that this is largely a result of their own shortcomings. It is also the result of the other professions' more vigorous and persistent efforts to recruit and develop the best graduates from many disciplines, including engineering. Engineering skills alone do not meet the market requirements; they have to be supplemented by management training. Engineering and science graduates from the 1980s and earlier may need special management diploma courses or suitable MBA programmes to retrofit themselves with management skills. Undergraduates in the 1990s are more fortunate — engineering courses are being updated to include an introduction to such skills. *Management for Engineers* stems from this development. It has its origins in "The Voice of the Customer" — with students and employers, whom the authors see as customers, making themselves heard. There have been calls from UK industry, and recommendations from numerous committees for changes in the training of engineers in higher education [1–3]. The changes are needed to produce graduates who have, in addition to some specialist engineering knowledge:

- good communication skills
- analytical problem solving abilities
- experience of team and project work.

These views are endorsed by one of Britain's top engineering managers, who has said: '. . . engineers have got to come out from behind their drawing boards and take a hand in the companies where they work, and take an interest in the society in which the company operates. . . . The whole engineering profession, the education system and the professional bodies should set out to train engineers as managers' [4].

The response at City University, London, has been its Engineering Management Programme which offers all of its undergraduate engineers[1] portable management skills and presents them with the most recent management concepts and related issues.

The programme is taught by staff from the Department of Systems Science all of whom have practical management experience in engineering industries. The authors have converted the course material for the BEng and MEng programmes (applying some of their own 80+ years' experience in senior management positions) to form the basis of this book. This has been supplemented by sections drawn from other management courses taught by the Department of Systems Science — in particular from the unique MBA in Engineering Management which is exclusively for experienced postgraduate engineers, and from the highly successful BSc in Management and Systems, which is one of the few undergraduate management courses whose teaching is rated 'Excellent' by the Higher Education Funding Council for England.

The book is in two parts: Part I is a series of chapters on management applications and concepts, starting with basic issues such as 'What is a business?'

---

[1]City University's School of Engineering has made recruitment of greater numbers of female students one of its key objectives, and has achieved some welcome success. However, the male students continue to form the vast majority, as in most UK universities and in the profession. In this preface it has been possible to use the non-sexist terms 'engineer', 'student' and 'undergraduate', but in the major part of the text we found that the persistent use of his/her, him/her etc became very clumsy, and we abandoned it. With apologies to female readers, please understand 'he', 'his', 'him' etc to mean 'he/she', 'his/her', 'him/her' etc.

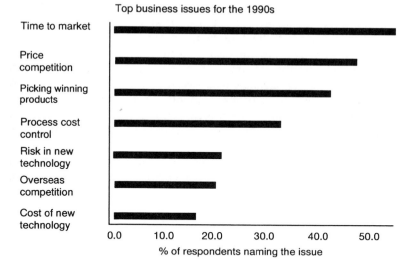

Figure P.1   Top business issues

and 'What is management?', continuing through management of quality, materials and new product development, and concluding with examples of successful companies who provide models of good enginering management.

Part II starts with chapters on human resources management (HRM), and communication, and goes on to provide some tools and techniques, such as critical path networks, discounted cash flow, and inventory control — with exercises and worked examples. These examples relate to large organizations, but the lessons apply also to small and medium enterprises. 'Know your customers' is good advice for any company, and large companies, directly or indirectly, are the customers of small companies. Some of the mysteries of activities such as finance, marketing and purchasing are unveiled — a greater understanding of these functions is a precondition for greater cooperation with them.

To assist those who may wish to pursue a particular subject further, references and bibliographies are provided throughout. These make specific recommendations for further reading, identifying useful chapters and passages or outlining the contents of the referenced material.

We hope the book will be useful to students and to teachers, that it will be occasionally enjoyable as well as informative, and that it may inspire and assist many young engineers to become successful engineering managers. There are opportunities vacant.

The *Sunday Times* (13 June 1993) said: 'British management's biggest defect is its lack of technocrats: managers combining technical know-how with financial acumen.' This defect is not peculiar to Britain, and wherever it occurs well-trained engineers can help put it right.

The need for such technocrats is endorsed by a survey of major UK companies whose bosses were asked to identify the three top business issues of the 1990s [5].

Figure P.1 shows that 'time to market' was named by over 50% of respondents as a 'top issue', and over 40% named 'picking winning products'.

'Time to market', 'picking winning products', 'process cost control', 'risks of new technology', are all clearly technology related. 'Price competition' and 'overseas competition' are two other areas where engineers can make vital contributions. Again, these major issues are not peculiar to the UK — they apply to almost every industrialized country, and many of the newly industrialized countries. In each of these countries the objectives of business are similar, and the need for managers with an understanding of engineering and technology is growing.

This may mean that the engineer's day has come! It is hoped that this book will help to equip and encourage young engineers to meet the challenge.

REFERENCES

1. Parnaby *et al. The Engineering Doctorate* (1990). Report to the SERC.
2. *Robbins Report on Higher Education* (1963). HMSO Cmnd 2154.
3. *Swann Report on Postgraduate Training* (1968). HMSO Cmnd 3760.
4. Yates, I. (1991) *Engineering British Economic Success*. The 1991 Walmsley Lecture, City University, London.
5. Bone, S. (1992) *Chief Executives' Attitudes to Innovation in UK Manufacturing Industry*. PA Consulting, London.

Acknowledgments

This book began when Andrew Slade, a representative of John Wiley, visited City University in 1992 to discuss textbook requirements for our Engineering Management Programme. There was no book which satisfied our needs. Our Engineering Management Programme for all engineering undergraduates at the University had been successfully designed and run for several years under the direction of David Hobbs (now retired) and developed by his successor Lawrence Reavill. It was this course which has provided the structure for this book.

We are especially grateful to two Visiting Lecturers, Diane Campbell, a very busy Chartered Accountant, and David Telling of the Council for Legal Education at the Inns of Court Law School for providing Chapters 14 and 23 respectively. Our long search for relevant expertise in Marketing eventually led to a delightful rail journey from London to Plymouth where Tony Curtis of the Plymouth Business School committed himself to providing Chapter 22. We are most indebted to him. After academic review we decided to introduce a chapter on Maintenance Management and this was provided with his customary and exemplary speed by Fred Charlwood, Head of our Department of Systems Science.

We are indebted to Graham Clewer for his persistence in chasing up so many references, and for his stylish illustrations.

We would like to acknowledge help from the following organizations:
ABB (Asea Brown Boveri); BAe (British Aerospace), British Steel; Chrysler Corporation; Ford Motor Company; IBM; Ingersoll Milling Machine Co. USA; Lamb Technicon; Nissan; the Office of Official Publications of the European Community; PA Consulting Group; Siemens AG; the Institution of Chemical Engineers; the Institution of Electrical Engineers.

We acknowledge the support of the staff of the Department of Systems Science throughout the writing of this book and, in particular, Joyce Banier who has forborne our eccentricities and our occasional ill humour with her usual grace and charm.

Part I

Business Basics

Business basics

1.1 INTRODUCTION

This chapter identifies the basic business functions, and shows how they relate to each other to form a 'system' that leads from the idea — the concept of a product or service — to satisfying the customers for that idea. It identifies the need to find funds, that is, money, to get the business started, and to generate more funds by operating the system so that the business can be sustained and expanded. The first part of the chapter describes 'management', and the various roles of managers. The basic business functions are then introduced, and the way they relate to each other to form the 'business chain' or business system is outlined. The chapter concludes with a description of some of the ways in which the performance of business systems may be measured.

1.2 ABSOLUTE BASICS

In absolutely simple terms, businesses, and many other organizations, are concerned with obtaining reward from an idea. How this is done is the task of management, as shown in Figure 1.1.

What is management? This question can be answered by considering first what it is that managers manage — that is, the inputs to the business system — and secondly the roles of managers as they help to transform the inputs to outputs, products or services, through the business process.

So, what are the inputs? Through the 19th century it was normal to consider three inputs to a business system:

- land
- labour
- capital

This has its roots in the agriculture-based economies, where the capital was used to provide tools for the labour to work the land, plus 'material' in the form of livestock, feed and seed. As economies became more industrialized, the emphasis moved away from land, and capital became a more important element, to provide more equipment for the labour, as well as a wider range of material inputs. Even in manufacturing, labour was the most important cost element from the late 19th century until the mid 20th century. At this point, mechanization was supplemented

Figure 1.1   From the idea to the rewards — management's task is to find the most efficient, most effective route

by automation, and labour's share of total costs fell rapidly. Mechanization had increased labour productivity through devices such as the moving assembly line which was introduced in the automotive industry in 1913 by Henry Ford I, initially for the assembly of magnetos in the Highland Park plant in Detroit, and subsequently for the assembly of the complete vehicle. Automation, through numerically or computer-controlled machines for cutting, shaping and joining materials, through materials handling equipment, and through reprogrammable universal transfer devices (UTDs) — better known as robots — has accelerated this decline in labour's share of cost. As a result, material and equipment costs have become progressively more significant.

Managing materials and equipment requires a lot of data about them, and about the companies that supply them. Managers also need to know what is going on inside their organization, and about what is happening outside in the market place and general environment. So, by the 1980s a new input became a vital part of many businesses: information.

Thus there are now four inputs or factors to be managed — but what does it mean, 'to manage'?

From the 1950 edition of *Chambers' Dictionary*, 'to manage' means: 'To have under command or control; to bring round to one's plans; to conduct with great carefulness; to wield; to handle; to contrive; to train by exercise, as a horse,' or the intransitive form, 'To conduct affairs.'

Some of these terms are rather militaristic or dictatorial, but most of the elements of later definitions of management are there. Note that the manager has

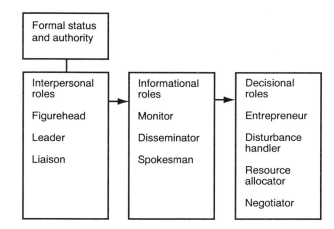

Figure 1.2   Mintzberg's three roles of management

'plans', and brings others round to them, and that 'training' is included. These are elements that have grown in importance.

The 1993 edition of *Chambers* adds: 'to administer, be at the head of; to deal tactfully with; to have time for; to be able to cope with; to manipulate; to bring about.' This suggests that the world outside business and industry has detected little change in management in more than 40 years, and still sees it as a form of constraint or control. Some authorities closer to the action share this view. Stafford Beer, a deep thinker and prolific writer on the subject describes management as 'the science and profession of control' [1]. As shown briefly below, and in more detail in Chapter 3, these definitions are too restrictive — good management entails more positive features, such as initiative and leadership.

Mintzberg [2] quotes a definition from 1916 by a French industrialist, Henri Fayol, who said the manager 'plans, organizes, coordinates and controls', but goes on to show that managers actually do rather different things most of the time. Mintzberg defines a manager as a 'person in charge of an organization or one of its subunits'. From his own observations and from studies by others in the US and the UK, Mintzberg concludes that managers spend their time in ways that can be grouped into three separate roles: interpersonal, informational and decisional. Elements of each role are shown in Figure 1.2.

While some of the old dictatorial terms from the dictionary definition are still there in Mintzberg's analysis — 'figurehead', 'monitor', 'handler', 'allocator' — there are some important softer additions — 'disseminator', 'negotiator' and most important 'leader' and 'entrepreneur'.

Within the role of leader, Mintzberg notes 'Every manager must motivate and encourage his employees, somehow reconciling their individual needs with the goals of the organization.' This is more like the style that most organizations aim for today. It recognizes that employees are individuals, with needs that may sometimes conflict with corporate goals and that corporations do have goals. Setting corporate goals, and encouraging and enabling all employees to share them, and work towards their achievement is one of top management's major tasks.

Mintzberg also states 'As entrepreneur, the manager seeks to improve his unit, to adapt it to changing conditions in the environment...is constantly on the lookout for new ideas...as the voluntary initiator of change.' Many organizations are still striving to realize this image of the manager at all levels, and to create a working environment where constant improvement and new ideas are encouraged by involvement and empowerment of all employees, not just managers, to the limits of their abilities.

So, today's manager is enabler, coach and counsellor, as well as leader, entrepreneur, communicator, planner, coordinator, organizer and controller. The manager performs these roles within the business system, and in some cases in setting up the business system.

1.3   THE BUSINESS SYSTEM

The manager performs within an environment, and manages resources to achieve some end, or objective. Whatever the resources and the objective, there are some features common to the route from the idea or concept to the end result. The sequence of processes and the functions to be performed are similar whether the product is a dynamo or a doughnut, a piece of software or a symphony, a car or a cure. A chart showing the major business functions is shown in Figure 1.3.

What the organization does (i.e. what is to be produced, where it is to be sold, where the facilities are to be located) is largely determined in the 'corporate' box.

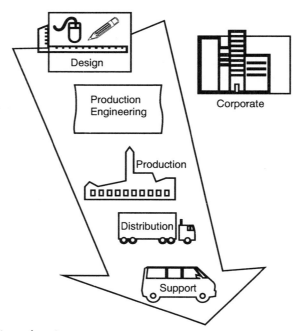

Figure 1.3   Business functions

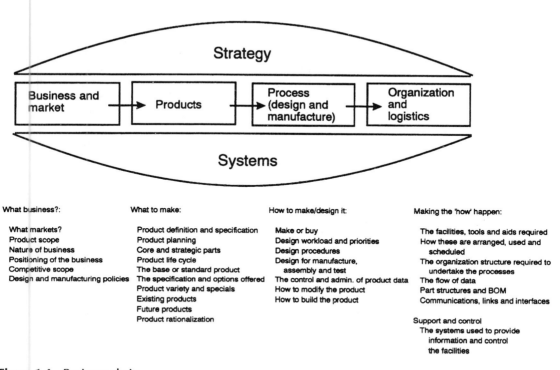

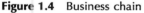

Figure 1.4   Business chain

'Design' is concerned with what the product or service or system contains, what its dimensions are, what it is made from and how it performs to meet the market requirement. Production engineering is concerned with developing *how* — how the components of the product or service or system are made and assembled. The production, distribution and support functions are concerned with *when* operations are performed — when is material, labour or information brought in, when are production, distribution and service activities performed. A more detailed list of the decisions and actions in each of these groups of functions is shown in Figure 1.4.

The collection of processes and functions can be regarded as a system, or a business or a business system, through which the idea is turned into a design, which is turned into a product, which is made, sold, distributed, serviced and eventually replaced and scrapped or recycled. Figure 1.5 represents such a system.

Within the system, the core functions of design, sales and production are supplemented by analysts, advisers and score keepers concerned with financial, legal and personnel matters. In Figure 1.3 these are contained in the remote 'Corporate' box, which is sadly realistic — one of the most difficult management tasks is to close the gap between advisers and monitors in one group, and 'doers' in other parts of the organization.

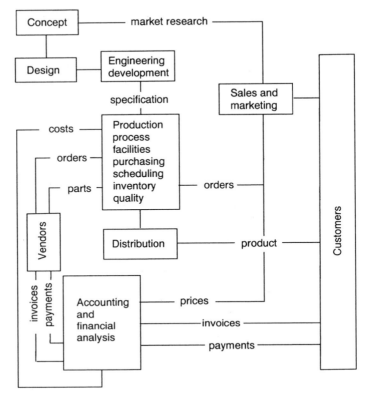

Figure 1.5   A corporate system

1.4   HOW THE SYSTEM WORKS

The entrepreneur, or research team, with the brilliant idea, may find that a great deal of waste is avoided if the appeal of the idea is checked first with potential users or buyers. This may be done by market research through specialists, or by the entrepreneur, or by the organization's own sales and marketing activity. This is not an infallible process. One of the most famous market failures of recent times was the Ford Edsel, a car introduced for the US market in the 1950s, which was also one of the most expensively researched. As at election times, what the pollsters think the public say they will do is not always what they do do. Internal committees may be no better — the video cassette recorder was invented in the Victor company of the USA, but its management thought it had no market. The idea was only brought to market by Matsushita, through their ownership of the Japanese Victor Company (JVC). The Sony Walkman, on the other hand, was the result of logical and lateral thinking rather than third party market research, and was enormously successful.

Market tested or not, the idea will need design and development, to turn it into something fit for production. The production processes have to be developed,

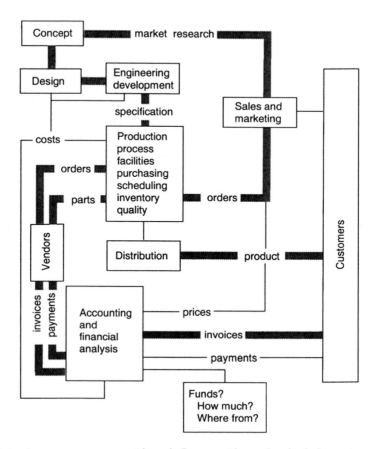

Figure 1.6 A corporate system with cash flow out (shown by shaded areas)

production personnel put in place with any necessary equipment, materials procured, and the completed product delivered to the customer. The customer in most cases has to be charged, and suppliers of goods and services paid. Some products need support or service after they have been sold and taken into use, and disposal or recycling at the end of the product life have to be considered.

Many of these activities have to be performed, and paid for, before payments are received from customers, so the idea needs backing with money to bring it to market or into use. This may be the entrepreneur's own money, or it may be borrowed — in which case the lender will require a return in the form of interest — or it may be subscribed in exchange for a share in the business. Shareholders will require either interest payments, or dividends, that is a share of profits, as reward for risking their capital. In Figure 1.6, the shaded lines represent flows of information, product or funds, or actions that have to be completed before money starts to flow into the organization as payments from customers.

The first few months in the life of any business are critical, as the owners wait for the inflow of payments for sales to overtake the outflow of payments for costs.

These 'cash flows' of course have to be carefully considered at all times, not just at start up.

For short-term success, the entrepreneur has to meet all the organization's costs from sales of the product, and have something to spare to make it all worthwhile. Longer term, the something to spare has to cover continual generation of more and better ideas, the maintenance and renewal of facilities, development of personnel, and reaction to competitors and other external factors. Long term success comes from doing all these things better than other organizations in the same or a similar business — that is better than the competition.

The more successful the original idea turns out to be, and the more successful the company becomes, the greater the likelihood that competitors will appear.

1.5   MEASURING PERFORMANCE

Managers need to measure several aspects of company performance, and where 'other people's money' is involved, those other people will want to know how 'their' company is doing.

Some measures come from the financial accounts which most companies are required by law to keep. The accounts comprise two major elements — the profit and loss (P&L) accounts, and the balance sheet (described in more detail in Chapter 14).

A very simple indication of what appears in P&L and balance sheets is shown below. The P&L accounts show revenues — the value of sales — and the costs incurred in making those sales. The difference between revenue and costs is the profit (if revenue exceeds costs) or loss (if costs exceed sales revenue). The trend of profit or loss in successive accounting periods is one important performance measure.

The balance sheet shows the company's assets on one side, and its liabilities on the other. The total value of the assets equals the total of the liabilities — hence the name 'balance sheet'. Growth in the balance sheet total is normally seen as 'a good thing', but much depends on why the figure has grown, and what use has been made of the investment or assets.

Two of the most common performance measures that can be derived from the accounts and which give an indication of how well the assets have been used are: return on capital employed (ROCE) and return on sales.

Return on capital employed is calculated as

$$\frac{\text{profit before tax}}{\text{capital employed}}$$

The normal target is 10% or more.

Return on sales, calculated as

$$\frac{\text{profit before tax}}{\text{sales revenue}}$$

The normal target is 5% or more.

Some of those terms may need explanation: *profit before tax* (PBT) is the difference between sales revenue and costs. The following simple P&L account shows £5m PBT.

Sales revenue (£m)		100
Costs (£m)		
Labour	10	
Material	60	
Overhead	25	
		95
Profit before tax (£m)		5

'Overhead' includes (but may not be limited to):

- Depreciation — the portion of fixed assets written off each year, recognizing that they wear out and will need to be replaced,
- Utilities — the costs of gas, electricity, fuel oil, water,
- Rates — taxes on property paid to local government,
- Central staff etc. — these costs are usually allocated to 'operations', so much per employee in each operating unit.

'Assets' comprise:
  Fixed assets
  such as land, buildings, machinery, equipment

Current assets
      cash and near cash (e.g. bank balances)
      debtors (amounts owed to the company)
      inventory
less
      creditors (amounts the company owes its suppliers)
      short-term loans (e.g. overdrafts)

'*Total assets*' are the sum of fixed assets and current assets.

It is easy to understand why companies wish to make more than 10% annual return on their assets — the money could earn almost as much as 10% invested in government bonds. This is a lot easier and, for most governments' bonds, less risky than creating and running a business.

Another performance measure normally available from the accounts is 'sales per employee'. This is a rather crude indicator of labour productivity, and not very helpful for inter-firm comparisons. It can be useful to indicate productivity changes over successive accounting periods, but, as already stated, labour is a reducing element of cost, and there are other more powerful indicators of a company's overall performance.

For manufacturing, one such indicator is 'inventory turnover', which is the ratio of total cost of materials during a year to average stock or inventory. This measures the frequency of inventory 'turns' in a year. In the very simple P&L account above, material costs were £60m for the year. If average inventory was £6m, it would have 'turned over' ten times a year. This is a fairly typical rate, but not a good one. Manufacturers such as the car producers Nissan Manufacturing UK, and General Motors Saturn company in Tennessee claim turnover rates of 200 times a year — that is, not much more than one day's stock. Such rates can only be achieved with 'perfect' quality within the plant and from suppliers, plus balanced production facilities, well-trained labour, and careful management of incoming suppliers' material and distribution of the assembled product. That is why inventory turnover is such a good business performance indicator.

Another powerful measure is the percentage of sales derived from products less than two years (or one year) old. This shows how innovative the company is, and can be applied to many types of business. As shown in the Preface, new product 'time to market', or innovativeness, is the top business issue of the 1990s. This measure cannot be derived from the financial accounts, but some progressive companies are including such information in their reports. It is an *output* measure, and therefore a better indicator of the effectiveness of a company's Research and Development (R&D) effort than the alternative *input* measure, R&D expenditure as a percentage of sales, which may be high because R&D is inefficient or misdirected.

These financial and non-financial performance indicators are very much measures of management performance, and should be seen as a package to be used together, rather than as separate indicators for shareholders or managers. This was neatly expressed by one of the UK's most successful managers, Gerry Robinson. His summary of the overall aim of businesses, and the role of managers is:

'You are in business to manage the corporate affairs of the company in which people put their money. I have never seen a dilemma between doing what shareholders want and what is good for the company and the people in it. The two go hand in hand.' [3]

1.6 SUMMARY

In this chapter a general form of business system has been described, and an indication given of the major elements or functions that make up the system, and the processes that turn inputs to the system into outputs. Changes in the relative importance of the land, labour, and capital inputs were indicated, and the new, significant input — information — was mentioned. Some definitions of 'management' and the manager's task were given, including a reference to Minzberg's 'three roles of management' — interpersonal, informational and decisional. The chapter concluded with outlines of some of the ways in which the performance of the business and its managers is measured by managers themselves, and by outside observers and analysts.

1.7 REFERENCES

1. Beer, S. (1959 and 1967) *Cybernetics and Management*. Unibooks. English Universities Press.
2. Mintzberg, H. (1975) *The Manager's Job: Folklore and Fact*. Harvard Business Review July/August 1975.
3. Quoted in *The Times*, December 1992, during an interview following his appointment as head of Granada Television. Robinson was a millionaire by the time he was 40 as a result of leading Compass, the corporate catering group after their management buy-out from Grand Metropolitan. He is not an engineer but an accountant — with an approach that engineers can learn from!

2

The business environment

2.1 INTRODUCTION

As soon as a business is established, it creates its own contacts with the business environment through its customers, employees and suppliers. The more successful it is, the more contacts it makes — competitors appear, 'authorities' become interested, and new products and markets have to be explored. Soon, the company is involved in the 'business game', surrounded by other players on a huge pitch that covers the globe, all governed by common factors — the rules: economics, demographics, politics, technology, ecology — and all affected by and contributing to change. Surprisingly, even at the start, in its own corner of the field, the new company is influenced by events and developments on the other side of the pitch — or, realistically, as far as the other side of the world. This chapter reviews the major elements or factors that make up the business environment, and considers how their effects may be grouped into *opportunities* or *threats* to influence the strategy of business organizations seeking competitive advantage.

Variations in the significance of the external factors, depending on the type of business and its location in *the supply chain* are described. Common business objectives are set against this background of external factors, and the ways in which the objectives interact with each other and with the environment are shown, with special reference to the role that engineers can play in achieving each objective.

2.2 BUSINESS OBJECTIVES — THE GAME

Almost all companies and organizations have the same objectives:

- greater customer satisfaction
- higher quality products and services
- lower operating costs
- lower capital costs
- shorter lead times — quicker to market

and of course, particularly now, in the 1990s

- survival.

For businesses, an implicit, superordinate objective is to make profit. This is essential for survival, and will follow from lower costs, greater customer satisfaction and the other objectives listed.

These objectives are being pursued in a business environment which features:

- slow economic growth
- relentless cost competition
- government and consumer pressures
- changing consumer expectations
- increasing market complexity
- faster technological change
- globalization of key industries.

Managers who have trained as engineers are uniquely well equipped to help companies succeed in achieving these aims in this environment, but before considering the ways in which engineers can contribute, two more influences on the engineer's role are introduced. Different business functions, such as design, manufacturing, distribution and service, which all involve engineers in different ways, have already been mentioned. The two further influences on the engineer's tasks to be reviewed here are:

(1) location of the organization in the 'supply chain,'
(2) the type of organization (product or project based).

2.3 THE SUPPLY CHAIN

The requirement for a particular management skill, the importance of particular objectives, and the influence of particular external factors, depend somewhat on where the manager's organization is located in the supply chain (Figure 2.1). Environmental factors may be more important to extractive industries which supply basic raw materials, and to process industries, such as power generation or oil refining. Demographic factors, that is the size and age structure of populations, may be more important to service or assembly industries with relatively high labour requirements.

The supply chain stretches from holes in the ground or sea bed where metals, minerals, fuels and feedstuffs are extracted from mines, quarries, and boreholes, through refining of basic materials, the processing and forming of parts and components, the stages of sub-assembly, final assembly, distribution, service and maintenance, and, eventually, disposal — possibly into more holes in the ground or sea bed. Along the way, all manner of services and equipment are required. At every stage there are supplier/customer relationships — internally, between different functions within the organization, and externally, between the organization and its suppliers and customers. It is these internal and external relationships that occupy most of a manager's time. They may also be the source of an engineer's first business experience, through participation in preparation of an offer to supply a product or service, or through helping to review and analyse such an offer from within the receiving organization, or through 'chasing' a

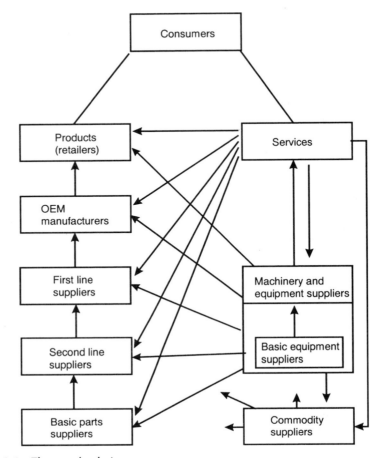

Figure 2.1 The supply chain

supplier organization to expedite delivery of information or the product or service.

2.4 PRODUCT BASED COMPANIES AND PROJECT BASED COMPANIES

2.4.1 Product based companies

A product based company is one that makes a range of products such as hardware, light fittings, motor cars or television sets, which are designed to meet a general market need. A series of models and options may be necessary to cover the majority of customers' requirements, and together with a mix of technologies, this can result in a high level of complexity in designing, manufacturing and

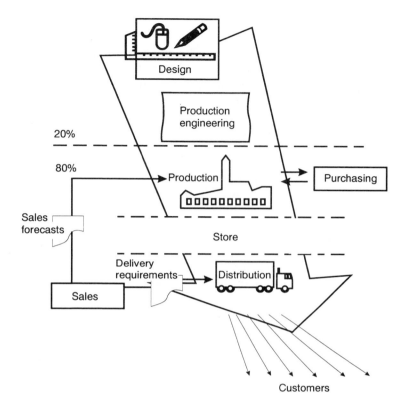

Figure 2.2   The product based company

distributing the product. The products are made in relatively high volumes, which leads to a high percentage of management and engineering effort being devoted to manufacturing and distribution. This is illustrated in Figure 2.2.

The figure indicates that production schedules for product based companies are based on sales forecasts, which is still generally the case. Some product based companies, though, particularly in the car industry, are seeking to become more responsive in their manufacturing operations and to supply within a few weeks or even days, to fill specific orders. Another change affecting product based companies is the growing emphasis on design and production engineering. This stems from the realization that manufacturing concerns to improve quality and increase responsiveness are often better resolved in these early phases of the business cycle. In turn, this means that suppliers, and hence purchasing are also more involved in the design stages than solely with production as shown in the illustration. The figure was provided by PA Consultants in 1991, immediately after it had been used in a workshop for a leading UK engineering company. It has been reproduced as then used to make the point that many aspects of engineering and business are continually changing.

2.4.2 Project based companies

Project based companies design and manufacture complex items such as aircraft or locomotives in relatively low volumes, or design and construct such things as bridges, processing plant, ships or oil rigs, which may be unique, one-off projects. Some of these products, such as aircraft, have extended working lives of 20 years or more, so that after-sales support such as maintenance, servicing and upgrading are more important than for product based companies. A greater proportion of management and engineering effort is therefore absorbed by such support functions. Equally, more effort goes into design and production or construction engineering compared with product based companies (Figure 2.3).

Selling and buying a 'project' is a more complicated task than selling or buying a product like a domestic washing machine, and is done by teams rather than individuals. The teams contain engineers of many kinds, who have to work together with other professionals such as lawyers, accountants and buyers to secure the best contract for their company. Learning to work as a member of a team is particularly important for engineers in project based companies, and is increasingly important for engineers in product based companies. Project based or product based, the companies and teams have to work in a business environment with similar external factors.

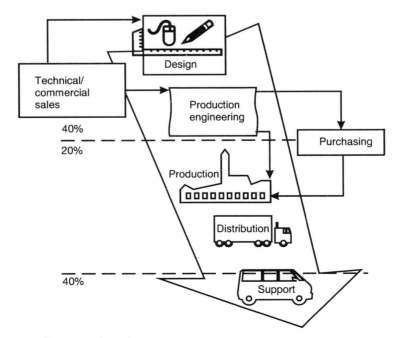

Figure 2.3   The project based company

2.5   EXTERNAL FACTORS

To determine a business strategy, or any other strategy, it is necessary to consider the environment within which the manager's unit is performing. This consideration should identify the 'OT', *opportunities* and *threats*, of 'SWOT' analysis arising from the external factors which are considered below. ('SW' stands for *strengths* and *weaknesses*, which are identified by internal review to determine how the organization is placed to handle the opportunities and threats.) SWOT analysis is useful at any level in business (see also Chapter 22, section 22.6), and in many other aspects of life — such as preparing for a sporting encounter, or an unsporting encounter, so engineers will benefit in many ways if they use the approach. Like most management tools, it is not new — a much cheaper version with a different mnemonic, 'SMEAC' was used at the very low level of the British infantry section at least 50 years ago. It may be easier to remember and use than SWOT analysis. SMEAC covers:

S — Situation.	What is the operating environment?
M — Mission.	What are we aiming to do?
E — Execution.	How are we going to do it?
A — Administration.	What do we need to get it done?
C — Communication.	Who needs to know what? when? how?

A review of the situation or business environment, to identify the factors that are important to the organization's mission, and the ways in which the mission is to be pursued, is the initial management task. This applies whether the unit being managed is a small team within an office, or a whole department, or a manufacturing plant, or an entire company.

External factors can be classified in two ways:

(1) Groups of people, sometimes labelled *stakeholders* such as shareholders, suppliers, customers, competitors, unions, the media, governments, financial institutions. (These are not separate groups!)
(2) Abstract concepts, such as economics, politics, technology, ecology, culture. (Again, the borders overlap.)

Figure 2.4 illustrates the way in which these factors 'surround' the organization, with the stakeholders in the inner ring having more direct, short-term influence than the factors in the outer ring.

In this chapter, only the outer general or global factors will be considered. Some of the stakeholders and inner factors are covered elsewhere — suppliers in Chapter 21, and competitors in Chapter 22 for example.

Some factors coming from the outer group that affect many managers are as follows.

Economics — worldwide economic growth, measured by Gross National Product (GNP) was slow in the 1980s, and is likely to be even slower in the 1990s — probably less than 2% annually over the decade. Even the 'driver' economies of Japan, Germany and the USA slowed in the first few years of the 1990s.

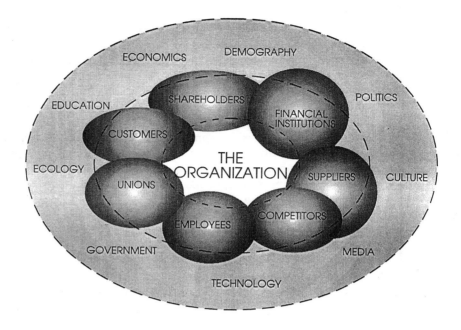

Figure 2.4　External factors influencing the organization

Japan became used to double-digit growth rates from the 1960s, and has been shocked to find herself struggling with annual rates of 3 or 4% in the early 1990s — the sort of increase that many western economies would be glad to reach. Germany consistently grew at 4 or 5% for many years, but has been struggling since re-unification at the levels around two or three which are more

Table 2.1　Real GDP % change per annum in G7 countries

	1991	1992	1993	1994	1995	1996
US	−0.7	2.6	3.1	3.9	3.1	2.0
Japan	4.0	1.3	0.1	1.0	2.5	3.4
France	1.7	1.9	−1.1	2.8	2.8	3.5
Germany	0.7	1.4	−1.0	2.2	3.1	3.2
Italy	1.3	0.9	−0.7	2.2	2.7	2.9
Britain	−2.2	−0.5	2.0	3.5	3.4	3.0
Canada	−1.7	0.7	2.2	4.1	4.2	3.9
G7	0.4	1.8	1.4	3.0	3.0	2.7
Total OECD*	0.5	1.7	1.3	2.8	3.0	2.9

*The Organization for Economic Cooperation and Development (OECD) countries comprise over 20 of the world's more advanced economies. They are dominated by the seven largest 'free-world' economies of the 'G7' countries; USA, Japan, Germany, France, UK, Italy and Canada.

familiar to Britain, Italy and France. From 1994, both Japan and Germany face the possibility of growth rates close to zero (see Table 2.1).

This slow growth has led to surplus capacity in many industries — automotive, aerospace, shipbuilding, steel etc. Despite the surplus, new capacity has been added as part of national or company policy, and the effectiveness of existing capacity has been increased by efficiency improvements. This has led to intense competition, with national and company efforts enhanced or frustrated by fluctuating exchange rates. For example, the value of the Japanese yen doubled versus the dollar in the 1980s, completely changing the economics of shipping products from Japan to the USA. Japanese companies therefore set up assembly plants in the USA for motorcycles, televisions, copiers, cars and more, and their major suppliers followed. Some of the American states with limited industrial development, such as Tennessee, came up with their own economic policies to attract this investment, and became alternative sources for the US market. With further exchange rate changes in the 1990s, and partly due to political influences, these new, efficient, low-cost, high-quality American assembly plants are in some cases being used as a base for exporting to Europe, or back to Japan.

Demography — changes in the age structure of populations — is having important effects. Figures 2.5 and 2.6 (taken from an internal Ford publication distributed in 1985) show projections of the age structure of the populations of the USA and Western Europe. These projections were made in 1985, but this is one area where forecasts are very reliable and it can be expected that the projections

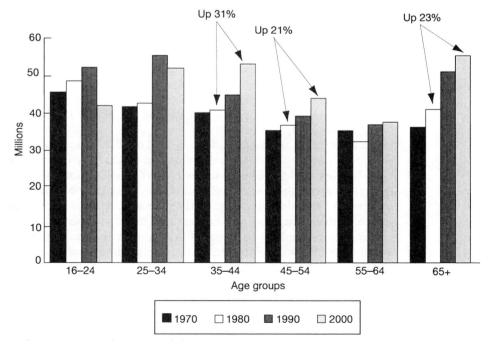

Figure 2.5　Population age shifts — Europe

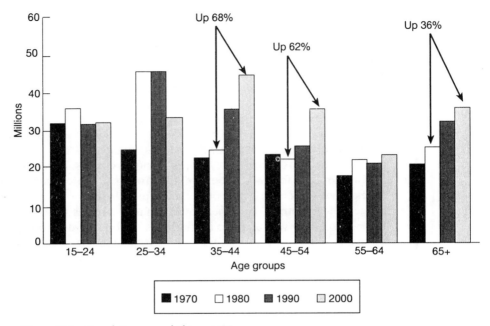

Figure 2.6 Population age shifts — USA

will hold good. The chart shows, for example, that the number of Americans in the 35 to 44 age group was expected to increase by 68% between the years 1980 and 2000.

In both Europe and North America there is a middle age bulge (not an anatomical feature, but an increase in the proportion of the population, and the absolute numbers in the 35 to 55 age range). There is also a growing old age tail, as life spans increase with better diet, better health care and better education and, in Europe particularly, as the effects of loss of lives in World War II diminish.

The way these expanded middle age and old age groups use their relatively high disposable income has a profound effect on the demand for services and consumer goods. They tend to be better informed and more demanding customers, and their priorities and values are changing compared with their counterparts 20 or even 10 years ago. This shifts the edge of the intense competition generated by economic factors into quality and product features, and convenience as well as cost. These older groups tend to be impatient, so they want the improved products and services NOW, which introduces time competition — shorter times from idea to availability, and shorter times from order to delivery. So, products become more complex, and tailored to segments of the market, and production and delivery systems have to be adjusted to deal with this complexity.

Governments — local, national and supra-national all take on greater responsibilities in areas such as health, safety, care for the environment, consumer protection and much else. Keeping up with the resultant legislation, and complying with it, is an increasing part of a manager's job. Designers and researchers in the pharmaceutical, automotive and aircraft industries in particular, need to be aware of existing and expected legal requirements affecting the content, production and use of their industries' products in all the countries where they are to be made and used. Managing the associated information is almost an industry in itself, and complying with the laws is an important driver of technological change.

Technological change — the pace of technological change continues to increase. Information technology and electronics are two of the fastest changing areas, and these changes themselves generate more potential for change by putting powerful tools at the disposal of designers. A complete car, aircraft or oil refinery can be designed and shown in three dimensions on screen in sufficient detail to 'sit in' or 'walk through', and components or processes can be tested by computer simulation in a fraction of the time it would take to build and test a model or a prototype. Materials with new properties are being developed, bringing the possibility of new products and processes — and new competition. Bringing these new materials and technologies to market ahead of competition is becoming, or has become, the most important source of competitive advantage (see Chapter 22).

Globalization — because of the huge costs of developing new products in many industries, such as aerospace, pharmaceuticals, computers and cars, it is becoming increasingly common for design to take place in one centre only, and manufacturing or assembly facilities to be established in several locations to minimize production and delivery costs. Readily transportable products, like aeroplanes can be built wherever the necessary skills are available and flown or floated to the customer, but products like cars and consumer electronics (TV and hi-fi for example) tend to be assembled closer to major markets. Centralized design and dispersed production of 'end products' by the OEMs (original equipment manufacturers) has implications all the way down (or is it up?) the supply chain.

A more complete picture of the external factors at work in the business environment is shown in Figure 2.7, from the Department of Trade and Industry's book *Manufacturing in the 1990s* [1]. It is worth spending time looking at the threats and opportunities, and considering how they work their way through to the strategies of companies close to home — wherever that may be.

At first it may be difficult to see the links between, say, the expanding Pacific Rim countries, exchange rate fluctuations, etc. and the affairs of, say, a small UK supplier to one of the long-established European vehicle companies. However, such a supplier has to consider the effects of the arrival of the Japanese as vehicle producers in Europe (because currency movements and political pressures preclude reliance on continued growth in the shipment of cars from Japan). Will the UK supplier's present customer lose a large part of its market share to the Japanese? Will the customer perhaps even go out of business? Will they be demanding price cuts as part of their battle to survive? Should the supplier begin to court the newly-arrived producers? If they do, what will be the reaction of their present major customer? What do the Japanese expect from their suppliers? Will this mean new equipment, retraining of staff, and involvement with designers in Japan? Suddenly, what is happening on the other side of the world becomes an

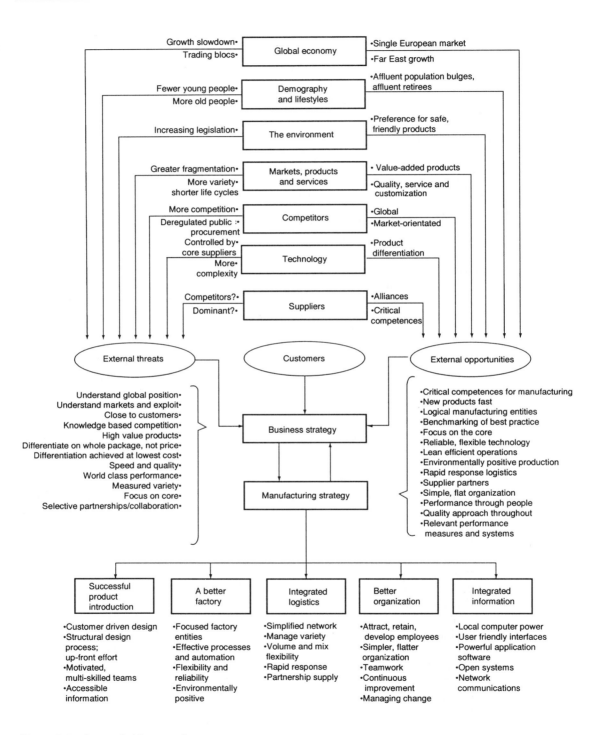

Figure 2.7   External drivers or factors

important factor in the development of the UK supplier's business plan, and they have to review their strengths and weaknesses (the internal factors) to determine their response.

2.6 THE OPPORTUNITY FOR ENGINEERS

2.6.1 Natural strengths

Engineers probably have better basic strengths than any other professional group to handle the pursuit of those common business goals listed at the start of this chapter, against the background of external factors described above. This can be inferred from a look at the corporate objectives from an engineer's point of view. They are considered in turn below.

2.6.2 Greater customer satisfaction

Think about customers in the internal sense. The major internal customer and supplier functions are engineering activities, so it should be the case that engineers in the supplier functions will readily understand the needs of engineers in the customer functions, and will be motivated to satisfy them.

In the wider, external context, customers — as shown in figures 2.5 and 2.6 — are getting older. This is unavoidable and should not depress young engineers. We all get older one year at a time, which means that from a population's present age structure it is possible to predict its future age structure with some precision. This is one case where making predictions, even about the future, is not so dangerous. By combining the expected age structure with some rather less secure forecasts about social and income patterns it is possible to outline customer profiles some years ahead. Figure 2.9 shows such a forecast of age and income distributions in the USA.

It can be seen that potential customers were expected to become richer. This is not so certain as the prediction of their life expectation, but the general trend should be an encouragement to young engineers. The chart reflects an expected increase in real affluence. From a mid 1980s base when $40 000 p.a. was a comfortable level of earnings, it was expected that the 35 to 54 age group earning more than $40 000 would increase from 19 to 30% of the population by the year 2000. The increased number of middle aged Europeans can probably expect a similar comfortable state of affluence.

So customers are getting older and wealthier. Maybe they are getting wiser, but engineers should not rely on it. They are also becoming better educated, more discerning and more demanding.

In both senses, internal and external, customers are changing, and their requirements are changing. This is where engineers can score, because engineers are used to dealing with change. Change results from potential difference, temperature difference, or a force. Inertia and impedance slow down change. A control system listens, measures, adjusts so that the desired performance or result is achieved despite variations. The same analytical approach can be used to

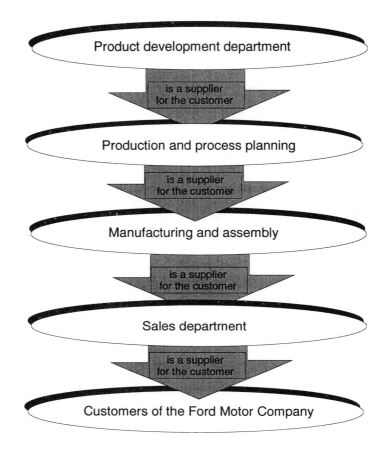

Figure 2.8 The internal customer chain

	Under $40k				Over $40k			
	1985	2000	PP change		1985	2000	PP Change	Total PP Change
Under 25	9%	6%	−3		2%	1%	−1	−4
25–34	19	11	−8		9	9	0	−8
35–44	10	9	−1	19% {	11	17	} 30% 6	5
45–54	6	7	1		8	13	5	6
over 55	17	14	−3		9	13	4	1
Total	61%	47%	−14		39%	53%	14	0

Figure 2.9 Increasing real affluence — USA. Source: DRI population trends applied to NNCBS age/income distribution

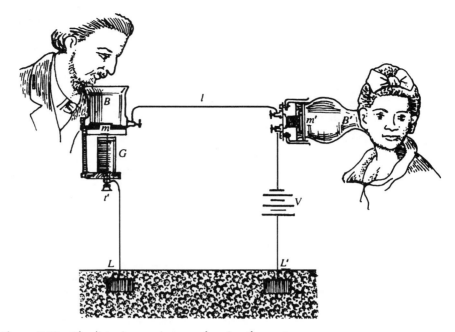

Figure 2.10   The listening engineer — hearing the customer

recognize the forces creating change, and the obstacles to change in business, to measure and hear 'The voice of the customer', which is the key to quality, and the start of new product and process development.

2.6.3   Higher quality

Customer satisfaction and improved quality are inseparable. Compliance, performance, reliability, durability, availability, disposability are all aspects of quality that affect customer satisfaction.

Engineers meet all these quality aspirations through design both of the product and the process. At the same time, they can, by using tools such as QFD, FMEA, Pokayoke and the concept of the internal customer, resolve the 'design dilemma'. (See Chapter 4 for an explanation of these tools and Chapter 6 for an illustration of the design dilemma.)

2.6.4   Lower operating costs

The key to lower operating costs is higher quality, doing things right first time every time. Redoing things, sorting, dismantling, correcting, scrapping, replacing, compensating, inspecting, checking, chasing are all unnecessary wasteful activities that add 20% or more to cost. (See Chapter 4.)

Engineers can eliminate these wasteful activities, through design for quality, design for manufacture, design for assembly, design for maintenance — design for customer satisfaction and delight. They are therefore key people in the drive for lower operating costs.

2.6.5   Lower capital costs

Quality is again the key to lower capital costs. Capacity utilized in making defects is lost capacity. The way this can be changed by engineers is illustrated by achievements in Ford's paint shop at Halewood which at one time had a first time OK rate of about 65%, meaning that 35% of painted bodies needed rework before they met the levels of quality required for the next phase of production. With problem solving techniques, minor investment and improved labour relations this has been raised to over 90% — similar to the best European and Japanese paint shops, and equivalent to almost 50% more capacity, with a similar increase in labour productivity. Production control, maintenance planning and other activities for which engineers are responsible can have similar effects — but to influence investment levels, these aspects have to be considered in the planning phases, and included in the QFD analysis — another province of engineers. This is the sort of thing that cuts investment costs, rather than 'squeezes' by accountants.

Another spectacular example of savings that engineers can achieve in this field also comes from the motor industry. A 12 year old transfer line for machining engine blocks was *the* bottleneck in production of the engine whose availability was restricting sales. For every extra engine produced, another car could be sold. The line ran only just over 50% of the time. One engineer, working with the shop floor operators, using simple analytical methods, found out why, (the main reason was waiting for parts) and devised ways to increase production by over 50%, and at the same time reduce manning levels by 22 employees per shift. The changes in the way the line was managed were valid for other lines — including the next transfer line of that type, which could be designed with 20% fewer stations — at a saving of more than £3m.

An example which is not from the motor industry, but from close to it, is the British Steel Llanwern works. It is reckoned that their total quality performance programme helped raise plant utilization from 80 to 90%, saving £20m a year. However, it is not clear whether this success can be claimed by engineers alone — in fact, like all successful quality programmes, it was the result of involvement of the whole workforce (which includes many engineers!).

2.6.6   Shorter lead times

The main cause of programme delays is change — design change leading to component change, process change and equipment change. The next most important cause is the development process itself, including the sourcing of bought-out materials, parts and equipment, which generates a series of delays if performed sequentially.

Engineers may argue that they are not the source of changes but innocent victims of the whims of the customer or senior management. This is not very persuasive — it is really an admission of poor communication and an inadequate new product development process for which they themselves are largely responsible.

By working together in teams, using the simultaneous engineering approach to new product development (see Chapter 6), and seeking to satisfy internal customers as described in section 2.6.2, engineers can eliminate, or at least reduce by significant margins, such as 80%, the changes to product and process that cause delay in new product development. They are the drivers of 'faster to market'.

2.6.7   Government, pressure groups and technological change

This review of the engineers' natural strengths in relation to business objectives has mentioned most of the global influences that were listed, but rather understated the engineer's role in:

- government and consumer pressures
- technological change.

The first always translates into new or modified products or processes — engineers' territory, and the second is generated largely by engineers, so handling it is also their responsibility.

Government and consumer pressures are most keenly felt in the areas of health and safety, and in environmental protection. Most developed countries have legislation relating to Health and Safety at Work, as well as safety in the home, in all forms of transportation, in public buildings, and in connection with products such as foods and pharmaceuticals. These all have important implications for engineers. It is a small step from product safety to product quality and consumer protection. The consumer movement probably began with a safety issue raised by Ralph Nader in the USA in his book *Unsafe at Any Speed* [2], which criticized the design of some of the then recently introduced cars. Now there are regulations on product liability that go beyond safety, to function and durability, and on to environmental effects in use and after use. Processes, too, may be required to comply with standards relating to noise, emissions, effluents and residues, and meeting all these standards involves engineers. Environmental issues were highlighted by Rachel Carson in 1963, in her book *The Silent Spring* [3]. A wide range of environmental pressure groups has built up since — some private, some funded by governmental bodies like the United Nations. Recognition of public concerns as expressed by such bodies can have an influence on corporate image, and for this reason alone the environmental lobby is yet another factor for engineers and managers to consider.

There is an example of government and consumer pressures in Appendix 1, which deals with the Single European Market, and Chapter 6 touches on technological change as part of product innovation.

2.7 SUMMARY

This chapter identified in very general terms the business objectives that are being pursued by almost all organizations, and the major factors in the external business environment that have to be considered by managers working towards achievement of these corporate goals. The concept of 'the business chain' was introduced, followed by a classification of engineering companies into product based and project based organizations. Together with the business functions described in Chapter 1, this should give some idea of the wide range of business roles for engineers. The chapter concluded with an indication of the outstanding opportunities for engineers in all of these roles to contribute to the achievement of corporate objectives, and to respond to the threats and opportunities in the global business environment.

REFERENCES

1. *Manufacturing in the Late 1990s*. (1993) Written by PA Consulting for the Department of Trade and Industry. HMSO. London.
2. Nader, R. (1965) *Unsafe at Any Speed*. Grossman, New York.
3. Carson, R. L. (1963) *The Silent Spring*. Hamilton, London.

3

Management styles: from Taylorism to McKinsey's 7Ss

3.1   INTRODUCTION

This chapter describes the major changes in the ways that successful organizations have been managed in the 20th century. It shows how today's successful companies have come to practise a style of management designed to maximize the contribution of individual employees who, at the same time, work as team members rather than isolated stars. Terms such as *participative management* and *employee involvement* are introduced, which are aspects of this new style of management behaviour. Attention is drawn to the coincidence between early 1980s findings by McKinsey from analysis of successful American companies and the search for explanations of the spectacular success of the Japanese in many Western markets. Both found the same emphasis on teamwork, respect for the individual, shared values and goals. An earlier, transitional period is described, when most successful companies were those with the best financial controls and marketing skills. The chapter starts with a look at management styles when attention was concentrated on labour productivity and manufacturing systems, and notes that, even then, product innovation was a key success factor.

3.2   LABOUR DAYS

The major engineering companies that grew from the Industrial Revolution were typically in heavy industry — mining, steelmaking, shipbuilding, railways, chemicals, textiles etc. — requiring huge sites, huge investments and huge labour forces. Technical skills were important for product and process development, but the dominance of labour in the cost structure drove management's attention to labour productivity or low wage rates as the key to success. Table 3.1, taken from an article by Nyquist [1] shows how direct labour cost (that is, the wages of employees directly concerned with production), as a proportion of total cost, has declined from about half at the end of the 19th century to one-tenth by the 1980s.

Table 3.1 Cost structure models

	1890–1920	1920–1980	1980–1990	Forecast 2000
Direct labour	0.50	0.30	0.10	0.01
Materials	0.30	0.45	0.60	0.70
Overhead	0.20	0.25	0.30	0.29
Cost of goods	1.00	1.00	1.00	1.00

It is easy to see why so much effort went into reducing labour costs, and to see why management attention should now be focused on other aspects of cost and performance. It is not necessary to agree with Nyquist's forecast for the year 2000, but it is worthy of consideration.

Early efforts to cut labour costs in manufacturing concentrated on the performance of the individual. Some payment systems were devised to make employees work harder by tying their pay to the number of pieces produced, called 'piecework'. Alternatively, workers were paid an hourly rate. Under both systems, work simplification and standard rates of performance for each task were seen as ways to increase output. Adam Smith in 1776 [2] noted the benefits of specialization: 'the division of labour' in a pin factory. He observed that when operations such as 'cut to length', 'form point', 'form head', were performed separately, operators developed specialist skills and dexterity, and production soared. More sophisticated versions of the same approach were the basis of 'work study', 'time and motion study', and 'industrial engineering', developed by Taylor, Gilbreth and others in the USA. This analysis of operator actions, and speeding up of production through more efficient workplace layout, and the development of individual manual skills, somehow acquired the label 'scientific management'. Although highly regarded at the time, it is now less admired, and has been accorded the somewhat dismissive labels of 'Taylorism', (after Frederick Taylor its main proponent)[1], or 'Fordism', as a result of Henry Ford I applying Taylor's methods in his manufacturing and assembly plants in the early half of the century. Even towards the century's end, some faint effects are still discernible in Ford plants and management attitudes.

Management structures in the 19th and early 20th centuries were hierarchical and militaristic, reflecting the social structures of the day. Employees were expected to obey orders, particularly in manufacturing where most of them worked. They had few rights, so there was little need for an elaborate personnel function, nor much need for other staff. Financial work was little more than bookkeeping, and sales, particularly for the railway and shipbuilding industries, was almost a branch of diplomacy or government. Engineering and manufacturing were the pillars supporting these huge companies.

Some of the most significant changes in manufacturing processes, and eventually in management, were first developed in the automotive industry

---

[1]See Chapter 12, Section 12.1

around the beginning of the 20th century. After the spread of Taylorism, another of these significant changes, with effects still being felt, was the introduction of the moving assembly line. This was an early example of the power of lateral thinking, being introduced in 1913 by Ford for the assembly of magnetos as a result of seeing carcass processing in the Chicago meat factories, where the operators had their work brought to them on the hooks of overhead conveyors.

Frederick Taylor's methods were applied to each task on the assembly line, and their effectiveness was enhanced by the improved precision of machining operations. This meant that successive parts from the machine shops were interchangeable and could be fitted into assemblies without further attention from skilled workers. The effect of the moving assembly line on productivity was so enormous that its use quickly spread through the automotive industry and outside. However, it did little for engineering management, other than to reinforce the emphasis on high volume, the deskilling of labour and the subordination of employees to the needs of the production line. Companies continued to be monolithic, hierarchical, and, the dominant ones, highly integrated — that is they processed, or even extracted their own raw materials, made their own parts and sub-assemblies, and managed their own distribution channels. In the case of railways, where development peaked in the 19th century, it is possible to detect a form of integration that is being reintroduced and seen as novel in the late 20th century — design, build, operate and maintain (DBOM) contracts. (See Chapter 19.)

Where outside suppliers were involved, their role was, like that of the labour, subordinate to the production line. The accident of history and geography that concentrated the motor industry on Detroit had a profound effect on this aspect of management. The scale of assembly operations, the importance attached to volume, the priority given to keeping the assembly line going, and the dominance of the Michigan peninsular by the car companies, led to another set of master/servant relationships — the car company's buyer was the master, and suppliers, however big, were the servants.

Other early events in the motor industry sowed the seeds of a style of engineering management that prevailed for almost 60 years. In 1917, DuPont bought 24% of General Motors (GM), and began to introduce their financial management expertise. In 1918, GM bought the United Motors Corporation, a conglomerate of suppliers headed by Alfred P. Sloan who became a GM director. Sloan and the DuPont financial control systems proved a formidable combination. By 1921 he was beginning to dominate the company, which was suffering 'conflict between the research organization and the producing divisions, and . . . a parallel conflict between the top management of the corporation and the divisional management' [3]. Sloan's solutions to these conflicts shaped the future of General Motors. He became chief executive officer and president in 1923, and implemented plans that he had developed in the prior two years. He had already introduced a technique that is still one of the key marketing tools — market segmentation — by focusing effort on six 'grades' of cars. (See Chapter 22 for more details of segmentation and other marketing concepts.) He labelled these a to f, by price range: $450–$600, $600–$900 etc. (The prices have changed, but the grades are still used in the car industry — for example Micras, Fiestas and Clios are 'B Class'; Escorts, Astras and Golfs are 'C Class' etc.). Sloan developed these grades as part of an overall plan to rationalize GM's range of cars, in order to reduce development complexity and increase component volume by sharing sub-assemblies between different end products. The rationalization enabled GM to enter the low cost segment of the market, which until then had been dominated by Ford to such an extent that Ford took more than 50% of the total US market. Sloan's plan was to differentiate the GM product in each grade, and to charge premium prices for products that were relaunched each year with novel features. Segmentation, premium pricing and annual model change were all new marketing practices when GM introduced them in the early 1920s. Combined with instalment buying (hire purchase) and the concept of the trade-in, these practices were a response to changed consumer needs. These needs were no longer being met by Ford's policy of supplying only one model at ever lower prices — a policy that had been enormously successful for 19 years, thanks to the perfect fit of the original, innovative 1908 Model T with the market requirement of that time, and to the subsequent labour-saving assembly line methods.

The change to market-led rather than supply-led product and production policies was a turning point in the evolution of modern management, but though GM's contribution to marketing management was remarkable, it was their (or Sloan's) general approach to the management of large businesses that was most significant. The key features are decentralized organization, and financial controls.

'It was on the financial side that the last necessary key to decentralization with co-ordinated control was found. That key, in principle, was the concept that, if we had the means to review and judge the effectiveness of operations, we could safely leave the prosecution of those operations to the men in charge of them.' [3]

The basic elements of financial control by which the operations were reviewed and judged were cost, price, volume and rate of return on investment. Control of these elements is still a good way to run a business, as long as control does not stifle initiative. It was a doctrine in General Motors that 'while policy may originate anywhere, it must be appraised and approved by committees before being administered by individuals' [3]. This doctrine recognizes the possibilty of an individual originating new ideas, as well as the role of individuals in implementing policy decisions, so that, like many of Sloan's ideas from the 1920s, it is consistent with late 20th century views of good management practice. It is also worthy of note that GM's four control elements: cost, price, volume and rate of return do not specifically mention labour productivity. Sloan's approach saw the beginning of the end of labour as the prime concern of management.

According to Sloan, this type of organization — coordinated in policy and decentralized in administration — 'not only has worked well for us, but also has become standard practice in a large part of American industry.' He could have said 'world industry'.

Since Sloan wrote those words in the 1960s his wonderful concept has become less effective. One reason for this is that personal success has become almost independent of corporate success.

Within companies managed on these lines, the reward systems related status and benefits to the number of levels controlled and the number of 'direct reports' (people) coordinated. This encouraged complex structures and systems — by adding levels of supervision, managers became directors and directors became vice-presidents. It also encouraged the growth of separate divisions held together only by the centrally exercised financial controls, with the exercise of those controls becoming more dominant than the divisions' efforts to run their businesses. Also, the numerous committees became very powerful, and an individual's performance as a member of, or standing before one of these committees had implications for his/her career. Consequently, great effort went into preparing for committee meetings, and staff reviews and pre-meeting meetings added to the growth of bureaucracy.

For a long time this was not all bad: Sloan retired as CEO of the world's biggest and most profitable organization. He was, at that time, described as the world's highest paid executive.

3.3   THE GIANT KILLERS

In the years following World War II, i.e. after 1945, many companies managed in the GM style achieved great success. Ford deliberately copied GM, and became the world's second largest company. International Telephone and Telegraph (ITT) under Harold Geneen earned a reputation similar to GM's, and it is only in recent years that Geneen's appreciation of the importance of quality has been put alongside his skills in financial control. American companies dominated many of the most important industrial sectors, such as automotive, aerospace, oil and petrochemicals, and computers. In almost every part of the world, and in almost every industry, overwhelming influence was exercised by financially-controlled, committee-managed business giants.

Again, it was events in the automotive industry that demonstrated that another significant change in corporate management had been taking place. The oil crises of the 1970s accelerated realization that US automotive companies were not competitive with the Europeans or Japanese in terms of price, quality or economy in use. The Japanese had already captured shipbuilding, motorcycles, cameras, copiers, TV and radio, but their invasion of the US car market was a blow to American national pride. It may have been this that prompted the search by McKinsey for 'excellence' among 62 of America's largest and most successful companies, though they track it back to a seminar on Innovation that they ran for Royal Dutch/Shell in Europe. McKinsey [4] found that the most successful US companies put more emphasis on what they called the *four soft Ss* — *style, skills, staff* and *shared values* (or *goals* in some versions), than the *three hard Ss* — *strategy, systems* and *structure*. In total there are seven factors, all interrelated, all with the initial letter 'S', so a diagram linking them became known as 'McKinsey's 7S Framework'. (The framework is shown in Figure 22.4.) This framework had been developed in the late 1970s, and was used as an analytical tool in the 'Search for Excellence'. The originators claim that each factor has equal weight, but many practising managers believe that 'shared values' is more significant than the others. A brief explanation of the four soft Ss is given below, based on the introduction to Peters' and Waterman's *In Search of Excellence* [5].

Shared values — these were originally called 'superordinate goals' — represent the set of values or aspirations which underpin what a company stands for and believes in. It is only when these goals are known and shared throughout an organization that individual and sectional efforts support each other. The concept should be familiar to electrical engineers from Ewing's experiment with electromagnets. (In this experiment, dozens of small pivoted magnets are set out in rows on a table with a magnetic field passing underneath. Initially, the magnets align themselves in groups, but each group points in a different direction. As the strength of the field is increased, the groups come more and more into line, until eventually they are all pointing in the same direction. The magnets retain this alignment even when the field is later reduced or removed.) Shared values are like the superimposed field — they bring everyone's efforts to bear in the same direction.

Style — is the pattern of top management action which establishes the corporate culture. The style in the most successful companies was found to be participative — that is, employees and junior managers were involved in making changes and decisions that affected them or the performance of their job.

Staff — obviously the 'people' part of organizations, but, less obviously, includes their development as individuals and as more effective contributors to corporate goals.

Skills — the company's core competences, vested in individuals and departments, and sustained by learning and training.

These four soft Ss are vital to the encouragement of personal initiative and responsibility, which, combined with teamwork and customer focus, underpin excellent quality and rapid product development.

By a completely different route, several western companies found the same key characteristics in successful Japanese companies. The different route was through study of competitors or associates in Japan. Teamwork between product development and manufacturing, and between producers and their suppliers, was identified as a significant difference between the Japanese and the visiting companies from the USA and Europe. This was the main reason for the Japanese companies' more rapid development of new products, and in part the explanation of the product's superior quality. The other part of the quality explanation was customer focus — really understanding what the customer wanted or would want. The greater effectiveness and efficiency of the Japanese companies was generally ascribed to the way they involved employees and suppliers in pursuit of shared goals.

Drawing these two sets of conclusions together resulted in 'action plans' in those giant companies that had seen their dominant market positions eroded. Those plans that were based on the hard Ss were in some cases still being actioned ten years later. Good new systems and sensible new structures were not the answer without the support and commitment of all employees, and these do not come without attention to the soft Ss. Even those companies that realized this had great difficulty undoing the influence of years of bureaucracy and complex control systems, and the persistence of low cost as an overriding objective.

In later chapters covering management of quality (Chapter 4) and product innovation, (Chapter 6), the importance of employee involvement will be yet more apparent. However, involvement in learning or management is not a new idea, as the following quotation shows:

'TELL ME . . . I'LL FORGET
SHOW ME . . . I'LL REMEMBER
INVOLVE ME . . . I'LL UNDERSTAND'
    K'ung Fu Tze (551–479 BC)

There was one marked difference between the characteristics of McKinsey's selection of excellent American companies and most of the successful Japanese companies studied in Japan.

McKinsey's excellent companies concentrated on their core businesses, from which McKinsey concluded that, to be successful, companies should 'stick to the knitting' [5] and grow organically rather than by acquisition of companies in different fields of business. Acquisitions, mergers and diversification were widespread in the USA and Europe during the 1960s and 1970s. For example, ITT expanded in automotive components and plumbing fittings, Gulf and Western added film studios and machine tools to their oil interests, British American Tobacco moved into insurance and Ford and GM bought into aerospace. An example from the construction industry is the UK firm Beazer, who bought local companies such as M.P. Kent and French-Kier (itself a merger), followed by a major acquisition in the USA, and was itself bought by Hanson, a diverse holding company. In retrospect, many of these actions have been criticized as short-termism and in the 1990s some conglomerates have been selling off their non-core businesses. (Beazer, for example, was a management buy out from Hanson.)

In contrast, many of the successful Japanese companies were, and still are, members of huge corporations or business houses (Keiretsu) with subsidiaries sometimes closely linked as buyers and suppliers, but in other cases having little obvious connection. Mitsubishi, for example, makes motor cars and car components, machinery, electrical and electronic products for domestic and industrial use, has a metals and minerals division concerned with materials extraction, processing and development, and is Japan's biggest brewer. Toyota makes cars, car components and machinery, and has links that provide financial, shipping and marketing services. Sony has widely applied its skills in electronics and miniaturization, and has 'vertically integrated' into film production to secure raw material for its range of video products.

For students of engineering management, the significance of the contrast is that what appear to be similar strategies can be criticized in one environment, and praised in another. This calls for an explanation. One possible explanation is that in the unsuccessful mergers and acquisitions there were insufficient transferrable management skills, and a mismatch between the management and technological expertise required to run the parent and the purchased companies. Poor research, which failed to identify the skills gap, may have contributed to some of the unsuccessful acquisitions. The experience of ITT, which continues to prosper, supports this — the company has sound *management systems*. Another possible explanation is that there were insufficient financial resources, in that some of the American mergers were funded on the basis of projected earnings from the acquired or diversified company which did not materialize. An explanation that was offered in the 1970s is that Japanese successes, and their inter-firm cooperation are based on their domestic environment and 'culture'. This has been disproved by many examples of overseas investment by Japanese companies, such as the 'transplant' car, TV and electronics factories in the USA and the UK, using local labour and, to an increasing extent, local suppliers. These counter-examples support the first possible explanation given above, and reinforce the McKinsey findings: an effective balance of the seven Ss will lead to successful management in many different industries in many different environments.

REFERENCES

1. Nyquist, R. S. (1990) Paradigm shifts in manufacturing management. *Journal of Applied Manufacturing Systems*, **3**, (2) Winter, University of St Thomas, St Paul, Minnesota USA.
2. Smith, A. (1776) *The Wealth of Nations*.
3. Sloan, Jr A. P. (1967) *My Years With General Motors*. Pan Books, London.
4. Waterman, R. H., Peters, T. J. and Phillips, J. R. (1980) (All McKinsey employees at the time) Structure is not organization. *Business Horizons*, June 1980.
5. Peters, T. and Waterman, R. (1982) *In Search of Excellence*. McGraw-Hill, New York.

BIBLIOGRAPHY

Managing people: lessons from the excellent companies, an article by Julien R. Phillips in the *McKinsey Quarterly*, Autumn 1982, gives several examples of the '7Ss of Management' in practice.

Leadership, management and the seven keys, an article by Craig M. Watson in the *McKinsey Quarterly*, Autumn 1983 describes the differences between leadership and management, using the 7Ss.

Management of quality

4.1 INTRODUCTION

The concept of 'Quality' has changed enormously in the past 40 years, from one which meant compliance with a specification to versions which cover the whole design, production, sales, distribution, use and disposal cycle. Management of quality has similarly changed — in an active way to spread the new ideas, and in a reactive way because of the demands of the new concepts, and the use of quality as a competitive weapon. Immediately after World War II, the term 'quality' usually meant compliance with a specification, and often allowed a 'small' percentage of non-compliance. Responsibility for compliance was assigned to specialists who checked quality by inspection. This was costly and, worse, it was ineffective. Major changes began (mainly in Japan) with the work of people like W. Edwards Deming and Joseph Juran (both Americans) who spread the ideas of *defect prevention* through control of production and business processes, and elimination of causes of major variation to bring *never ending improvement*. Some causes were found to be in the design of the process or product itself, so preventive actions moved back in the product cycle to the design phase. By the 1980s, in most industries and markets, quality had become whatever the customer perceived it to be, so customer needs were considered at the design phase, and a range of new 'tools' was developed to take account of these needs. Internal customers were included in these reviews and their quality requirements were recognized, creating '*total quality*' throughout the organization and beyond — forward into sales and service activities, and backwards through the supply chain.

Now, in the 1990s, 'Total Quality is about total business performance . . . It is about turning companies around, and achieving step change improvement' [1].

This chapter traces the changes in quality concepts and quality management, and introduces some of the tools and techniques for improvement.

4.1 QUALITY BY INSPECTION

Immediately after World War II, and into the 1950s, there was such demand for consumer goods in the western economies that almost anything could be sold. In Britain, for example, there were two year waiting lists for cars, and one year after delivery the car could be sold second-hand for more than its new price. As a

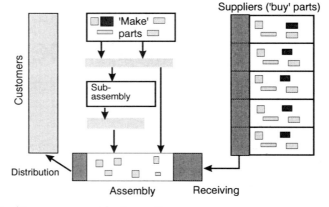

Figure 4.1   Quality management by inspection

result, production quantity was more important than quality in the eyes of most managers.

Control of quality was by mass inspection, and inspectors were under pressure to pass a product as good enough to sell or use. End customers, who are the final inspectors, were often so grateful to get the product that they put up with less than perfect quality.

Mass inspection was extremely inefficient. Every item in every batch made or received was checked against its specification, at several stages of production (see Figure 4.1). In consumer goods manufacture, such as vehicles or refrigerators, this meant that inspection departments, often known as 'receiving inspection' at goods inward, where parts from suppliers were received, had to keep up-to-date records of the specifications of hundreds, or thousands, of components and the procedures for testing them. These procedures required a wide range of gauges and test equipment, and a correspondingly wide range of skills to use them. Not surprisingly, inspectors were an elite, highly paid group, and there were lots of them. It was not unusual for companies, even Japanese companies, to boast that 'One in ten of our employees is an inspector — this is your guarantee of quality'. Of course, it was not a guarantee at all — defects still got through. In addition to the costs of the army of inspectors and their extensive records and expensive equipment, there were huge costs in inventory. Material and components could not be used until they were inspected, and assemblies could not be shipped until they had been checked. The stages of production where inspection took place, and where delays could occur, are shown in Figure 4.1.

The figure shows inspection taking place at suppliers prior to despatch to the assembler, and being repeated on receipt by the assembly company. Later, the assembled product was inspected before despatch to the customer who completed a more rigorous inspection by putting the product to use.

These practices took a long time to die out. For example, in the early 1970s, managers from Ransome, Sims and Jeffries (RSJ) a leading supplier of agricultural equipment, visited Ford to exchange ideas about the use of computers

Action required	Where the fault was found					
	As a part	In sub assy	In assy	In transit	At sale	In use
Inspect	X	X	X	X	X	X
Sort	X	X	X	X	X	X
Return	X	X	X	X	X	X
Disassemble		X	XXX	XXX	XXX	XXX
Rework	X	XX	XXX	XXX	XXX	XXX
Scrap	X	XX	XXX	XXX	XXX	XXX
Reschedule	X	XX	XXX	XXX	XXX	XXXX
Replace	X	XX	XXX	XXX	XXXX	XXXX
Compensate					XXXX	XXXX

Figure 4.2 The escalating cost of non-quality

in materials management. Probing for explanations of RSJ's low inventory turnover rates revealed that the *average* time material was held in receiving inspection was one month! Even then it was known that Japanese producers had turnover rates above 12 times a year i.e. *total* inventory of less than one month. In another example from the late 1970s, British Leyland (BL), to reassure customers about the quality of a new car, announced proudly that 20 000 square feet of factory space had been allocated for final inspection and rectification. Today, Rover (BL's successor) having learnt from their partner and competitor, Honda, are at the forefront of total quality management, and would not tolerate such wasteful use of facilities — they have eliminated the need for it.

The costs of space and inventory carried by firms like RSJ and BL were not the end. What happened when a fault was found? If it was found by the inspectors in receiving, it meant that the whole batch had to be sorted, or sent back to the supplier for sorting, rework and replacement, which generated a whole series of other costs for accounting, record adjustments, shipping and handling. A defect found during or after assembly would in addition require an interruption of the assembly process while the defective part was extracted and replaced. If a defect was not found until the product was in use, there were further costs under warranty (guarantee), plus, possibly, other actions to pacify the customer, and the immeasurable cost of lost sales as the word spread that the product was faulty.

The way in which costs pile up, according to when a fault is found, is shown in Figure 4.2. The number and size of the 'x' gives an indication of the relative cost of rectifying the defect. While the value of each 'x' is unknown to most producers, it is generally reckoned that the total cost of quality defects is in the range of 15 to 30% of turnover.

The pressure of all these costs led to some helpful changes in quality control, but the system still relied on end-product inspection. One change was to move the inspection process back down the supply chain. If suppliers made more thorough checks prior to shipment, fewer defects reached receiving, and some of the costs there were avoided, along with the costs of returning and replacing batches containing defective parts. Another change was the introduction of sample inspection. If checking a 10% sample revealed no faults it might be assumed (sometimes wrongly) that the whole batch was OK. If one or two faults were found, another 10% sample would be taken. If this was OK, the batch might be accepted. If not, the batch would be returned — or if there was an urgent need for the part, the batch would be 100 per cent checked and the faulty parts returned.

Practices such as these throughout manufacturing might still result in defect rates around 5% in the end product, and this may have been accepted indefinitely had it not been for the quality revolution in the Far East — led by Americans. Engineers faced with an inspection-based quality system should do all they can to spark a similar revolution, and move to defect prevention through process control, rather than partial defect detection by inspection.

4.3   QUALITY BY PROCESS CONTROL

Deming and Juran, are generally recognized as the leaders of the quality revolution. It is not surprising that their philosophies have much in common, since they both worked for Western Electric Company in the late 1920s, and were influenced by that company's approach to people management, as well as its quality management. The common elements of their views of quality management are:

- At least 80% of defects are caused by 'the system', which is management's responsibility, not by operators.
- Quality is defined by the customer.
- Quality improvement can be continuous and is never-ending.
- Quality improvement involves everyone in the organization.

A third American, Philip Crosby, shares many of Deming and Juran's views, but his approach is based on the cost of quality — or non-quality, since he maintains that 'Quality is Free' [2].

During World War II, Deming applied his expertise to the American manufacturing base to increase output through defect reduction. After the war he offered his services to individual companies, but they were so busy concentrating on volume to meet pent up demand that he was rejected, and became a government employee as a statistician with the US Census. It was in this capacity that he was sent to Japan in 1950. His presence became known to the Japanese, and he was invited to present his ideas about quality management to a group of top industrialists. He was soon in demand to address audiences of thousands, which launched the quality revolution. His role in transforming the Japanese car industry was so significant that he became sought after by US car companies to help combat the surge of Japanese imports. Ford, who had earlier rejected him, retained Deming as a consultant in 1980 at a daily rate higher than his monthly pay had he been hired in 1950.

Deming's work stressed most strongly the reduction of variance in processes as the key to continuously improving quality, using what he called 'simple statistical tools'. The most important tool is statistical process control (SPC), based on the fact that, once 'special' causes of variation are removed, variation will follow the

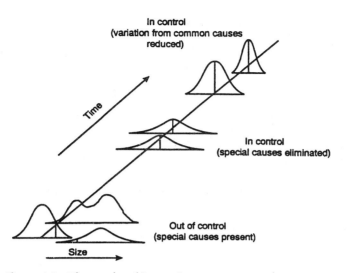

Figure 4.3 The results of improving process control

normal, or Gaussian, distribution. Figure 4.3 shows some distributions before and after removal of special causes.

In metal cutting, a skew distribution might be due to faulty tool setting; a bimodal distribution might be caused by drawing raw material from two sources and the normal distribution would be achieved when all such special causes of variation have been removed.

The search for special causes, or root causes of faulty output can be made in a systematic way, using cause and effect analysis, illustrated in Figure 4.4.

Measurement of output data may indicate a defect, and the need to take action to sort and correct faulty product, and to take action on the process to prevent further defects. But what action? On which input? Headings under which the search should be made are shown in the box labelled 'the process' in Figure 4.4. For example, is the material to specification? Is the operator fully trained? Is the equipment working properly? The answer No leads to further study, and to 'twigs' on the input 'branches'. As the questions and answers are entered on the chart, it takes a form that many people prefer to call a 'fishbone diagram'.

However, it is not necessary to wait for a defect to identify the need for action on the process. For each key parameter of the process it is possible to measure the range (R) within which acceptable variations are likely to fall, and to establish upper and lower control limits (UCL and LCL) either side of the mean (x-bar). By continuously sampling the key parameters and plotting the mean value of each sample on a chart, (called an x-bar/R chart) trends can be detected, indicating that a defect is likely to occur if the process is not adjusted. Figure 4.5 shows a control chart for a process at a British Steel plant.

The point outside the UCL on the chart would normally mean that corrective action was necessary, but in this particular case it was the result of changing the target value of the parameter for a different customer. The four values for the

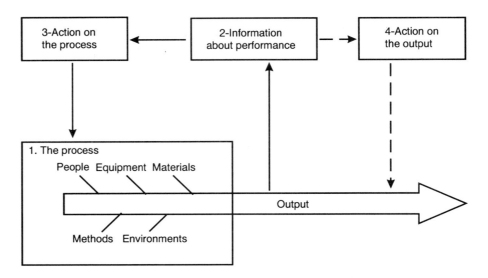

Figure 4.4   A process control system

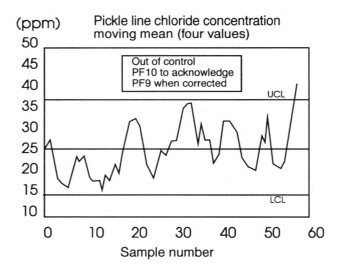

Figure 4.5   A process control chart from British Steel

moving mean indicates that four readings of the variable are made in each sample. (This may be a BS productivity improvement measure, as the general practice is to sample five values.) The screen messages to the process controller in the box headed 'Out of control' flash when the graph crosses a limit. The operator then has to touch the PF10 key to acknowledge that the condition has been noted.

Corrective action would then be taken according to a set of instructions, and completion of this action would be confirmed by touching the PF9 key.

At their integrated works at Llanwern and Port Talbot, British Steel have SPC monitors at every operation from unloading materials at the dockside, through the sinter plant to the blast furnaces, the continuous casting process, the rolling mills, coiling, annealing, packing and despatch. Control charts are displayed at consoles in the plants, and each of them can be viewed in the central SPC room. The displays in the plants show corrective action messages if adverse trends are detected, and the x-bar plot changes to red if it strays outside the control limit. This degree of automation cannot always be justified, and there is much to be said for manual completion of the control charts as a way of engaging operators more deeply in quality management. (This is what British Steel did at the outset, as part of the training programme.) British Steel's use of SPC has helped to make them fully competitive on quality, and one of the world's lowest cost producers. Despite their dedication to quality, British Steel still have a sign at the entrance to their Llanwern Works that reads 'Cost Quality Delivery'. Ford tried for years to have them put quality first on the sign as they do in their operations. The sign has acquired the status of a war memorial, and maybe serves to remind everyone entering Llanwern just how far BS have gone down the quality road. A paper by Dr Bernard Hewitt entitled *'Total Quality at Port Talbot Works'* gives an account of their introduction of SPC [3].

The importance of involving all employees in SPC is becoming widely recognized. One of the best examples in the UK is at Nissan Manufacturing's unit shop (the engine plant) at Washington, near Sunderland. A display, about four feet high, spells out the merits of SPC, as well as the steps to implement it. This is reproduced in Figure 4.6.

Process control can be taken beyond the x-bar/R chart to consider the capability of the process. A process which has been well designed and implemented will result in only small variations in results, and the average (mean) result will be close to the centre of the tolerance range. Capability considers both the spread of results, and their relation to the specification range. The usual measure of spread is six standard deviations (sigmas). This covers 99.73% of the normal distribution i.e. less than three items in a thousand can be expected to fall outside this range. Dividing this measure of variation by the tolerance gives an indication of the process potential, labelled Cp. The formula is:

$$Cp = \frac{\text{specification width}}{\text{process width (six sigma)}}$$

By relating the position of the distribution of parameter values to the centre of the tolerance range, a capability index Cpk is calculated. This is done by comparing half the spread (from the mean to the upper or lower three sigma value) to the distance to the nearer of the UCL or LCL. The formula is:

$$Cpk = \frac{\text{distance from the mean to nearest specification limit}}{\text{half the process distribution width (i.e. three sigma)}}$$

Illustrations of process potential and process capability are shown in Figure 4.7.

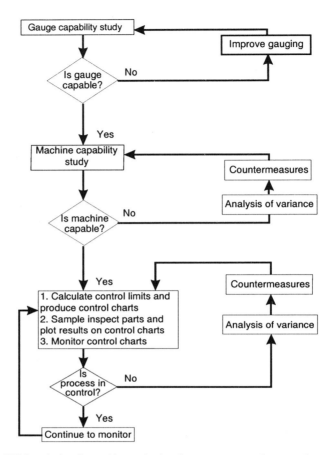

The flowchart contains the following elements:

Gauge capability study → Is gauge capable? — No → Improve gauging (loops back to Gauge capability study)

Is gauge capable? — Yes → Machine capability study

Machine capability study → Is machine capable? — No → Analysis of variance → Countermeasures (loops back to Machine capability study)

Is machine capable? — Yes →
1. Calculate control limits and produce control charts
2. Sample inspect parts and plot results on control charts
3. Monitor control charts

→ Is process in control? — No → Analysis of variance → Countermeasures (loops back to step 1)

Is process in control? — Yes → Continue to monitor (loops back to step 1)

SPC in unit shop is used by production dept. as a means of progressive process improvement

Production and its TPQC dept. control and monitor the SPC functions while VQA dept. performs an advisory role in its application

Advantages of SPC

Fewer rejects and rework–reduced operating costs
Less down time–increased productivity
Improved performance–fewer customer complaints
Continued measurable improvements in production and products
Trend monitoring–highlights problem areas
Process control charts–identify problem areas for corrective action
Improve image

Figure 4.6   Implementation of SPC in Nissan's Sunderland unit shop

In the first chart, there is a fairly tight distribution of the measured parameter, with the six sigma spread equal to half the width of the specification range. The capability potential Cp is therefore 2.0. However, the distribution is centred towards the upper end of the specification range, and the process would generate an unacceptable level of defects.

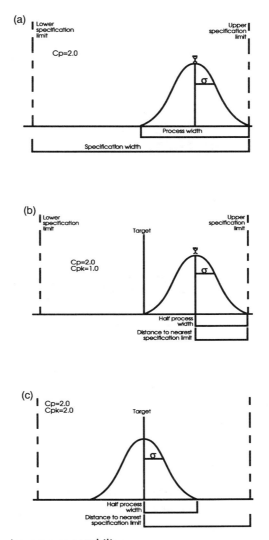

Figure 4.7   Improving process capability

In the second chart, the distribution is shown relative to the target (the middle of the specification range). In this case, the distance of the distribution mean from the nearest specification limit (in this instance the upper limit) is equal to half the process width (i.e. three sigmas), so the process capability index Cpk is 1.0. This is not an acceptable value, and corrective action would be taken, such as adjusting the position of a fixture, to centre the process spread closer to the target.

The third chart shows the process distribution mean on target. The distance to the nearest specification limit is now double the three sigma value, so the Cpk is 2.0.

The value of Cpk can be increased by continuously reducing the variations in the process, and by moving the centre of the spread closer to the centre of the

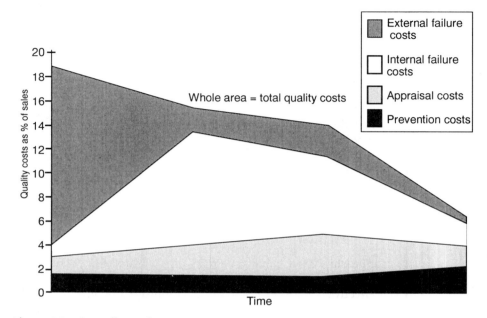

Figure 4.8   Cost effects of TQM

tolerance. Cpk can also be increased by widening the tolerance, which is sound practice if the greater tolerance is the result of robust design (see Chapter 6). Increasing the tolerance just to get a bigger Cpk is pointless, but is not unknown when plants are judged by the percentage of processes with Cpks greater than 2.0. Many manufacturing processes aim for a Cpk value greater than 2.0 — which means that only a few parts per million (ppm) will be outside the tolerance. So, by controlling the process, defects can be prevented, and inspection of the output becomes unnecessary.

With in-process gauging and computer control, Cpk, like x-bar/R, can be calculated and displayed automatically, but again it is preferable to start with manual calculation to aid understanding, and to secure involvement of the operators.

Whether performed manually or automatically, defect prevention by process control is a far more effective way of assuring the quality of output. Costs of appraisal and prevention will be higher than with inspection-based attempts at quality control, but total costs will be reduced dramatically. Figure 4.8 shows the sort of relationship that generally applies, with total cost reductions in the range 10–15%. The initial extra attention to appraisal and prevention results in an increase in internal failure costs, as more faults are found in-house. These higher internal failure costs are more than offset by lower external failure costs, as less faulty product reaches customers. As process control becomes more effective, defects are prevented, and internal failure costs also fall dramatically. Such cost reductions go straight to the bottom line — that is the profit of the organization — or can be used to reduce prices to gain a competitive advantage without reducing profit margins.

Cause and effect analysis can be used for process improvement as well as problem solving, until a point where the process, the equipment or the design has to be changed to make the next advance in quality performance. Such changes are extremely costly once a product or service is in use. The later in the product cycle that a change is made, the higher the cost will be.

For example, the design of an aircraft's doors was changed for safety reasons some years after the plane entered commercial use. The cost of the design change included lost revenue, as all the planes of that design were grounded until modifications were made, and future sales of planes and flights may have suffered because of damage to the plane builder's and airlines' quality reputations.

To avoid such changes late in the product cycle, the concept of defect prevention therefore has to be taken further back — to the design phase.

4.4   QUALITY BY DESIGN

The shift from quality control, using inspection to detect defects, to quality assurance by defect prevention, was a gradual one. So was the movement to more effective defect prevention through improved design management. There were two forms of delay in the spread of both these changes. One delay was from assemblers and end producers, the so-called 'original equipment manufacturers' (OEMs), to their suppliers; the other was from East to West. Figure 4.9, derived from a Ford engineer's trip report of his visit to Japan, illustrates how the new concepts spread through the Japanese automotive industry. Introduction and development of the ideas in the western automotive industry followed between five and ten years later, so that in some cases it was still going on in the early 1990s.

The cost incentive to 'design it right' is enormous. For example, in the early 1980s, Ford of Europe introduced a new engine (known as the DOHC, because it was their first high volume Double OverHead Camshaft engine), which suffered so many design changes in the run up to production that over $40m had to be spent to modify the three major pieces of production equipment. These were obvious costs, but even greater penalties were incurred through delays in market introduction and lost sales. This is not a unique experience — the pattern is repeated in other companies and other industries. Figure 4.10 shows an assessment by British Aerospace of the way opportunities to make changes declines, and the cost of making changes increases at each stage of their product cycle [4]. This aspect of design management is covered more fully in Chapter 6, but the significance of design change and subsequent process change for quality management should be noted — each change creates a risk to quality. The later in the product cycle that the change is made, the greater the risk, since the effects of the change may not be fully evaluated under pressure to get the product to market, or to keep it there.

To minimize late changes, techniques have been developed to assess risks to quality while the product is still being designed. One of the most effective is potential failure mode and effect analysis (FMEA), which can be applied to the design itself or to production or operating processes. Examples of design FMEA

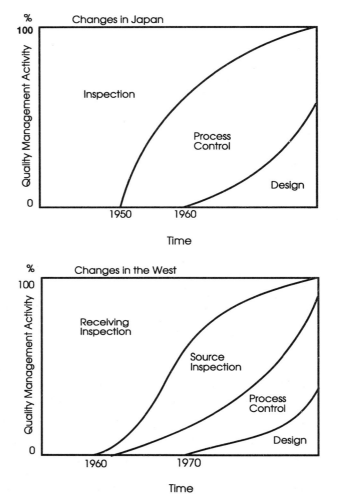

Figure 4.9   A comparison of changes in quality management between Japan and the West

are shown in Appendix 2, and a complete book on the subject is published by the SMMT [5].

The essential steps of FMEA are to:

- Identify every conceivable failure mode.
- Consider the consequences of failure for each failure mode and assign a severity index on a scale 1 to 10. (Lethal would be 10, insignificant would be 1.)
- Assess the likelihood of occurrence, again on a scale of 1 to 10. (Almost certain would be 10, just possible 1.)
- Assess the likelihood that the failure would be detected before the product is in use, using the same scale. (Almost sure to be spotted would be 1, very hard to detect 10.)

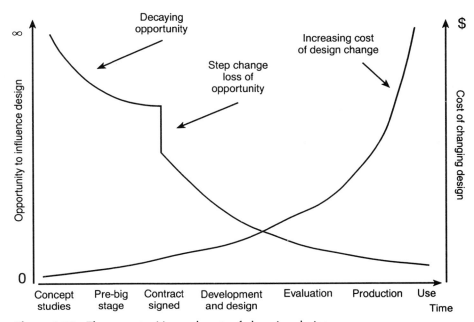

Figure 4.10   The opportunities and costs of changing design

- Calculate a risk priority number (RPN) as the product of the three indexes (The RPN is sometimes shown as Severity × Occurrence × Detection. Maybe this is the origin of 'Sod's Law' — what can go wrong, will go wrong.)

The RPN can range from 1 to 1000, and is used to prioritize the designer's actions to reduce risk. If the significance of failure is rated high, say 7, 8, 9 or 10, the design or process would be changed to lower the occurrence level and to increase the likelihood of detection. Reducing occurrence (prevention) is always preferred, since detection processes (inspections) are always fallible.

Other techniques to 'design in' quality, such as design of experiments (DOE), and quality function deployment (QFD) are covered in Chapter 6.

By the time that the importance of design for quality was recognized, the definition of quality had changed from 'meeting specification' to something much wider. The three 'gurus', (Crosby, Juran and Deming), changed their own definitions from time to time, but they can be roughly summarized as:

- conformance to requirements — Crosby
- fitness for purpose — Juran
- predictable degree of uniformity and dependability, at low cost and suited to the market — Deming

These differing views reflect the variety of pressures on the designer, from the external customer and from a range of internal customers. This set of sometimes conflicting demands has been labelled 'The design dilemma' and is covered in Chapter 6, but some idea of the range of demands can be obtained from Figure 4.11.

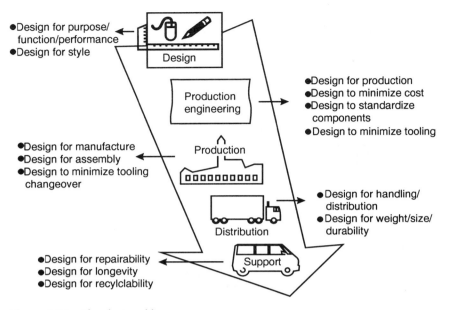

Figure 4.11 The design dilemma

The designers have to first consider quality in use, where customer experiences which determine new product features can be fed back directly or through dealers and sales organizations. They also have to ensure that the design: assists producers and distributors to develop reliable processes; simplifies service and maintenance actions; and does not give rise to concerns about disposal and recycling. By minimizing complexity, the designer can even help the salesforce to do a better job — simplifying the task of finding the right product to meet a customer's needs in a brief phone call or showroom visit.

So far, this section on quality by design has dealt with defect prevention through consideration of the needs of internal and external customers. There is, however, the possibility of an even greater contribution to quality at the design stage. This is through the anticipation of customer needs, and the designing-in of features that will surprise and delight the customer. Oddly, one or two pleasant surprises can lead to a customer forgiving and overlooking some shortcomings. This was dramatically illustrated when Ford introduced the Taurus car range in the USA. As with all new car introductions, great care had been taken to identify the 'things gone wrong' (TGW) with the outgoing model, and to aim to put them right by improved design and manufacturing processes. (TGWs per thousand vehicles during the first three months and the first 12 months in service are one of the principal ways of measuring vehicle quality. The score reflects not only how well the vehicle was designed, but also how well it was put together. Producers benchmark themselves against other makers' TGW scores through syndicated market research.) Although delayed by over two years to modify design features that gave rise to manufacturing concerns, the new car disappointed the producers by scoring more TGWs than targeted in the design brief. Yet it was a huge success. The 'European' styling and other features so delighted customers that they reported very favourably on their ownership experience. The 'things gone right' greatly outweighed the 'things gone wrong', and the cooperation between designers and producers in the two years' delay became something of a legend, under the name Team Taurus. The car might have been even more successful had it been developed in the five years originally targeted, and designed right first time.

4.5 QUALITY MANAGEMENT SYSTEMS

To ensure that good quality management practices are applied consistently, most organizations have a quality system. In the defence, health, aerospace and automotive industries, most organizations have their own systems designed to comply with extensive legislation and regulation, as well as driving to meet their own quality objectives. The existence of so many private systems can be very demanding on suppliers, who may have to comply with several different sets of requirements. There have been attempts to introduce generally applicable systems, but so far these have had severe limitations.

One of the most widely used is known as BS 5750/ISO 9000. (Minor changes were made to BS 5750/ISO 9000 in 1994, and the revised version was renamed BS/EN/ISO 9000.) This is the UK standard, widely copied and adopted by less developed countries (LDCs), and used by over 30 000 UK companies. It has its origins in military quality control systems, and this shows in its rather bureaucratic style and emphasis on consistency rather than improvement.

The British Standards Institute defines BS 5750 as: '. . . a quality assurance system geared to producing goods and services of consistent quality'. It is in three parts which cover some or all of an organization's activities. Part 1 is the most comprehensive. It details requirements for design and development, production, installation and servicing when requirements are specified by the customer in terms of how they must perform. Part 2 covers the supply of goods or service to a published specification or to the customer's specification. Part 3 is a system to be used in final inspection and test procedures.

Requirements are prescribed under 20 headings, such as management, system principles, contract review, etc. These are summarized in Appendix 2, and the whole system is described in a DTI booklet *BS 5750/ISO 9000* [6].

The system's strengths are that it provides a framework for quality management, and it requires attention to quality throughout the organization. Its weaknesses are that it does not actually ensure that a product or service meets customers' quality requirements, and that it assumes static levels of performance, rather than constant improvement. This conflict led one MBA student to list in a company strengths and weaknesses analysis:

The company's No.1 strength: it has BS 5750
The company's No.1 weakness: it has no quality culture.

A supplier was quoted in the *Financial Times* [7]: 'We have BS 5750 but the Japanese just weren't interested.' This attitude of 'the Japanese' is typical of big user companies, who prefer their own systems. One fairly representative system is one of the oldest, which has been updated and adapted for use worldwide — Ford Q101, a quality system standard for Ford plants and suppliers.

This is in five sections:

- planning for quality
- achieving process and product quality
- documenting quality
- control (delta) items
- system and sample approvals.

The emphasis is on planning and prevention, with much use of SPC. It is written for easy reading, to promote partnerships and encourage never ending improvement. There is a wide range of supporting literature and training support, backed up by a performance rating and reward system. Systems such as Q101 start early in the sense of 'early in the supply chain'. Thus, when a producer plant does not already supply products, so the user will conduct a system survey prior to awarding a contract, to evaluate the quality systems, to review the use of statistical methods, to examine system and performance records, and to verify the quality of outgoing products. It is also early in the sense of 'early in the product development process'. There are separate guidelines for assisting in the production of quality prototypes, and for using this experience to start quality planning for volume production. Involvement of producers at the design stage is a significant change in relationship, and is fairly recent for many products. Producers must be responsible for prototype production to get the full benefit of this change.

Supplier rating is an important part of Q101 type systems. Reaching an acceptable score in the survey is a first stage, but a typical rating system will go on to evaluate:

- supplier management awareness and commitment (SMAC)
- quality of delivered products.

The Ford system weights these: survey 30%, SMAC 20%, delivered quality 50%. For each element there is an extensive scoring process which provides continuous monitoring.

Producers gaining sufficient scores on all three counts get an award — the Q1 award — which is presented with due ceremony, and publicized in the national press. Not every big company behaves this way. Rank Xerox, for example, believes that continued business is sufficient reward for satisfactory supplier quality.

The scope of BS 5750 and Q101 type systems is similar. Both are aimed at compliance — with specifications, and with regulations. The difference is that Q101 style systems measure performance, and aim for never ending improvement. There were signs in 1994 that the huge task of reconciling the international standard, ISO 9000, and some of the major private schemes was being tackled. The 'Big Three' US car producers — GM, Ford and Chrysler — came up with a unified quality management scheme closely aligned to ISO 9000. If this spreads through the whole automotive industry worldwide, and is followed by other industries, suppliers will find that demonstrating their quality capability has become much less difficult. However, much modern quality management goes

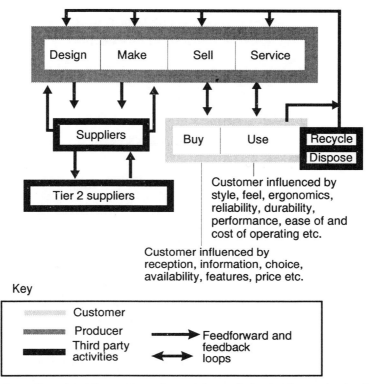

Information about the customer's experience during buying and using the product is fed back to the sales and service activities and to the manufacturing organizations, and on to suppliers. This information is used to improve the 'buy, own and use' experience on current products, and to build up a list of customer needs for new products. New products and process ideas are fed forward by suppliers to the producer, and are implemented or logged for future use. Feedback is also obtained from recycling and disposal agencies, which may also influence current and future products.

The producer takes care of customers' concerns from the time they think about buying, through purchase and delivery, use and service to disposal — and to their next purchase.

Figure 4.12   Total customer care

beyond both BS 5750/ISO 9000 and Q101/Q1 type systems, and uses such a system as only a part of total quality management (TQM).

4.6   TOTAL QUALITY MANAGEMENT

The consideration of the customers' needs from concept, through design, production, distribution, use, service and disposal can be labelled 'total customer care'. Figure 4.12 illustrates the scope of this quality concept.

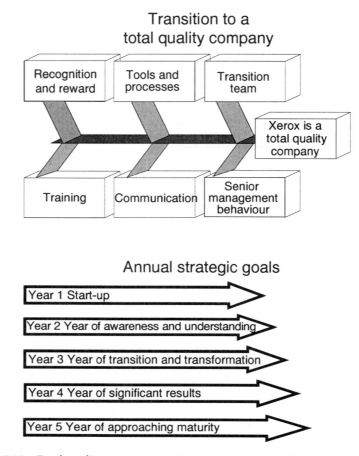

Figure 4.13   Total quality management: Xerox's attempts to achieve it

The way in which a company deals with its customers or potential customers, and with its suppliers, and with the business and wider community is all part of its quality performance. The involvement, motivation and training of employees in all of these areas requires participation of all managers, not just those in quality control.

The way in which people behave as members of a team, or how they care for their customers — the designer for the 'customer' process engineer; the process engineer for the 'customer' production manager etc. is also part of quality. This is the result of the treatment of staff, the provision of skills, the company's style and its shared values, as well as its systems, structure and strategy — all the 7Ss defined by McKinsey.

The actions of all the people in every function, and in every customer contact, all contribute to quality performance, and managing them is 'total quality management' (TQM).

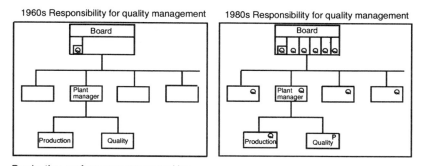

Production performance measured by adherence to schedule.

Quality performance measured by adherence to specification.

Figure 4.14   Quality management responsibility

Some organizations have dropped the 'management' from the name of their programmes to introduce the TQM concept, because it can be interpreted to mean that the programme is management's task alone. This is just one way to stress the significance of 'total', which implies that everyone is involved and responsible for their own contribution to quality performance.

TQM does start with management, but it is a philosophy or style of behaviour that has to permeate the whole organization to be effective. When Xerox Corporation determined that they had to become a total quality company they set themselves a five year programme, summarized in Figure 4.13. This covered every aspect of their operations, every employee, and every supplier. The programme involved training each employee in the Xerox quality 'system' — both training and system are essential elements of TQM.

Xerox set out to change every aspect of corporate behaviour, in order to meet their business objectives. This made quality management everyone's responsibility, and helping their staff to exercise that responsibility was part of every manager's task.

Organization charts showing management's quality responsibility 40 years ago and currently might look something like Figure 4.14. In the 1960s chart, quality appears as part of the assignment of one board member, and the whole of the assignment of one department in the production plants. In the plants there was conflict between the production volume objectives of the plant manager, and the quality objectives of the quality control manager. In the later chart, everyone shares the quality goals, and the quality manager in the plant — if there still is one — may even have an interest in supporting the production goals.

4.7   SUMMARY

The most important points in this chapter were:

- the changes in the meaning of 'quality' from compliance with a specification (most of the time) to meeting or exceeding customers' changing expectations (on time, first time, all the time),

- the shift of responsibility for quality management from specialists to every employee,
- quality improvement by defect prevention instead of defect detection.

The influence of design on quality in all of the later stages of the product cycle was stressed, and some of the tools and techniques of quality management, such as statistical process control, and potential failure mode and effects analysis, were described.

REFERENCES

1. Kooger, J. (1993) Operations Director, Du Pont Europe. From the promotion material for PERA International *Briefing Programme — Making Quality Pay*. PERA publish an illuminating summary of case studies in Total Quality Management.
2. Crosby, P. (1979) *Quality is Free*. McGraw Hill, New York.
3. Hewitt, B. (1990) *Total Quality at Port Talbot Works. ISATA Conference Proceedings*, International Symposium on Automation in the Automotive Industry, Wiesbaden.
4. From a DTI publication *The Case for Costing Quality*, available from DTI, c/o Mediascene Ltd. PO Box 90, Hengoed, Mid-Glamorgan CF9 9YE.
5. *Failure Mode and Effect Analysis,* Society of Motor Manufacturers and Traders, Forbes House, Halkin Street, London.
6. BS 5750/ISO 9000 published by the DTI, available free from Mediascene Ltd., PO Box 50, Hengoed, Mid-Glamorgan CF9 9YE.
7. 'Supplying the Japanese'. *Financial Times*, 21 May 1991.

Materials management and the engineer

5.1 INTRODUCTION

A knowledge and understanding of the characteristics, uses and business impact of materials at every stage of the product life cycle is essential to every engineering discipline. Engineers are concerned with the selection of materials during the design phase, with the processing of materials into components and sub-assemblies, with the assembly of processed materials, with materials handling and storage, with servicing and maintenance of products, and possibly with recycling or disposal of products and their constituent materials.

Data about the availability and performance of materials and components are critical inputs for the design engineer. What the design engineer does with this information can determine up to 80% of costs throughout the rest of the product cycle. So the designers' outputs are of interest to process engineers, construction engineers, layout engineers, safety engineers, quality engineers, materials handling engineers and service engineers — and others who may not be engineers. Availability, on time, of perfect quality parts, assemblies and materials is vital to successful production or construction, and is greatly influenced by the decisions of engineers. Materials in one form or another make up a high percentage of operating costs, and in the form of stock can be a major element on the balance sheet.

Their management therefore has a significant impact on a company's financial performance. Component quality, combined with the quality of assembly processes, determines total product quality to a large extent. Supplier performance is therefore one of the major influences on user company performance in both quality and financial terms. The sourcing process is increasingly a team activity, and engineers thus have an opportunity to share in materials management from the earliest stage. The engineers' interaction with suppliers in manufacturing plants, and on building and construction sites continues this involvement, and influences the user/supplier relationship just as much as the work of the purchasing department.

This chapter indicates the scope of materials management, its influence on operating costs and the balance sheet, and hence its dual effect on profitability.

Some of the interactions of engineers with other functions also involved in materials management are described, showing how engineers have become part of the decision-making team for materials and supplier selection.

The growing significance of new materials and associated technologies is covered in Chapter 6, and inventory management, purchasing and logistics are dealt with in more detail in Chapters 20 and 21.

5.2 MATERIALS SELECTION

The choice of material by the design engineer has an influence right through the product cycle and deep into the supply chain. This is illustrated in the next three sections, which give examples from three engineering industries.

5.2.1 An example from the electronics industry

The following paragraph is an extract from a Siemens publication [1].

'At the design engineering stage, materials are normally selected according to functional, production-specific, aesthetic and financial criteria... Electrical engineering and electronics owe their technical and economic success in no small measure to the use of custom-made and design-specific materials.... Until recently, the development and application of materials has been dictated by technical and economic considerations, with little attention being paid to the possibility of retrieving and reutilizing waste materials... This situation is, however, changing rapidly in leading industrial nations as the "throw away society" makes way for an economy based on avoiding, minimizing and recycling waste, as well as environmentally compatible waste disposal.'

5.2.2 An example from the automotive industry

In the automotive industry, if a body design engineer decides that to improve corrosion resistance, a door inner panel should be made from steel coated on one side with zinc/nickel (Zn/Ni), it has a series of effects:

- the *body stamping engineer* has to review the stamping process, die design and die life;
- the *body construction engineer* has to review welding processes;
- the *paint engineer* may have to review pre-paint and paint processes;
- the *component engineer* has to inform purchasing that new supply contracts will be needed, with revisions to scheduling and materials handling;
- the *materials handling engineer* needs to note that special scrap has to be segregated;
- *service engineers* have to check whether dealer body repair processes need to be changed.

If the panel is on a vehicle produced in large quantities, say a few hundreds or even thousands a day, there may be an impact on sourcing decisions — for example, coating capacity may be limited at the present supplier. If the panel is on a product to be made in a number of different locations, say in Europe and North America, the availability of Zn/Ni coated steel might have even more serious implications. The American industry favours Zn/Zn and discussions with several suppliers in both continents may be necessary to secure supplies.

Life-cycle costing would have to take account of all these factors, as well as the forecast trends of zinc, nickel and other commodity prices.

5.2.3   An example from the construction industry

In Germany, environment protection laws have led to a ban on window frames, doors and other building products made from uPVC, which has created surplus capacity in some parts of the plastics processing industry. Elsewhere in Europe uPVC products may still be used, and German extruders have vigorously marketed their products in these countries, where selection of uPVC window frames, doors, fencing or fittings by designers would set up a transaction train crossing national borders and stretching from petrochemicals to landfill.

5.2.4   Advanced materials

Developments in materials sciences have importance for engineers of all disciplines. Their significance is indicated in the following extract from the introduction to a report for the *Financial Times* by Lakis Kaounides [2]:

'Advanced materials have now emerged as a major new technology upon which further progress, innovation and competitive advantage in high technology and the rest of manufacturing industry increasingly depend. The materials revolution is irreversible, is gathering momentum and its reshaping of the map of world industry will accelerate from the late 1990s onwards.'

The implications for new product development are described in Chapter 6, but other implications are summarized in a note by P. Dubarle of the OECD [3].

'Advanced materials are increasingly the result of conventional materials blending, associated with various types of mechanical and chemical treatment. Such a materials mix is more and more designed at the molecular level. It therefore reflects the growing integrated and horizontal nature of materials innovations. This new pattern of materials design and fabrication technologies calls for new skills and especially multidisciplinary knowledge among firms and laboratories, engineers and R&D staff, and even among technicians and supervisory personnel involved.'

These quotations emphasize the need for engineers to learn to work with other professionals, and to take a holistic view of the implications of their materials selection.

5.3   ENGINEERS AND THE SUPPLY SYSTEM

In the early 1970s 'The supply concept' was thought to cover everything to do with materials, components and bought out sub-assemblies 'from womb to

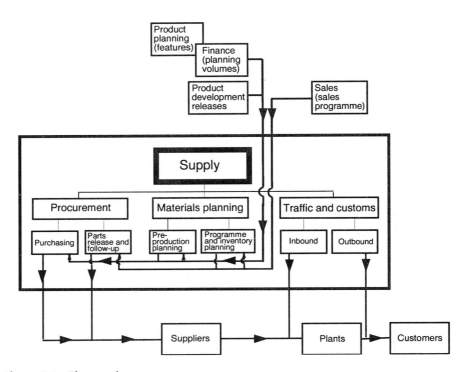

Figure 5.1   The supply concept

tomb' — from release of individual parts by the design engineer to delivery of the end product to the customer. In the 1990s, many industries have extended the scope of materials management to coordination of the research and development phases prior to 'conception' of parts or sub-assemblies, and beyond the 'tomb' of sale and use, to disposal or recycling.

Nevertheless, a description of the earlier supply concept can be used to identify some of the downstream involvement of engineers following their selection of materials and development of designs and specifications.

Figure 5.1 shows the 'supply' activities within the heavily outlined box. It is these activities that have the 'womb to tomb' materials management responsibility. There are three closely linked areas. *Procurement* organize the purchasing and issue delivery schedules to suppliers and follow-up to make sure that suppliers deliver on time. *Material planning* set up and maintain the records of each part used in each plant and determine target inventory levels, and hence delivery frequency. *Traffic and customs*, are responsible for movement of materials at every stage — from suppliers to the production plants (sometimes called 'inbound logistics'), between plants, and from plants to the outside customer (sometimes called 'outbound logistics'). Linking these three functions together in a single organization, and so eliminating duplication of activities and conflicting goals in materials management, became fairly widespread in the late 1960s/early 1970s. This is an early example of fitting an organization to a horizontal process or series of related processes, rather than having the separate elements of supply report upwards within separate organizational chimneys. This approach later became fashionable under the 'business process re-engineering' banner. ('Business process re-engineering' (BPR) is a term used to describe radical change of organizations and processes — 'breaking the mould' or 'starting with a clean sheet' — as opposed to incremental change or improvement. See Chapter 8 for details of BPR at Chrysler Corporation.) Although this organizational grouping of supply activities improved liaison between each element, and between them and the company's suppliers, it sometimes led to supply being another chimney, separated from the manufacturing and product development activities (other chimneys) in a way which was an obstacle to constructive dialogue between designers, buyers, producers and suppliers. Further developments of supply systems, and their integration with product planning, design, production, distribution and sales and marketing, are dealt with in Chapters 6 and 21.

Information was fed into the system shown in Figure 5.1 in two phases. First the system was primed (shown by the arrows from finance and engineering into the supply box) by taking each engineering release as an input to establish:

- bills of materials (BOMS) for each end product, and each producer location,
- lead times for each commodity group in the BOM (greatly influenced by the designers' specification),
- sources (suppliers) for each item (which often involved the design engineers, who may have designated 'approved' sources),
- shipping modes, inbound and outbound (involving materials handling engineers),
- target inventory levels for each item (involving production engineers),
- databases for scheduling, material control and accounting.

All these data would have to be changed at every point in the system where they were recorded if a component specification were changed. Changes could be made as a reaction to concerns raised

- by customers, fed back through sales or service, or
- from production or construction difficulties in plants or on sites, or
- from materials handling and transportation.

They could also be made by

- designers seeking to improve performance or reduce cost.

Most of these sources of change are problems, or obstacles to the achievement of separate functional goals, and so are likely to bring user engineers and suppliers' engineers or sales people into contact in situations likely to produce conflict, which could adversely affect user/supplier relationships.

In the second phase, once the system was primed, information was fed in to make it 'run' (shown by the arrows from sales). This information was based on customer orders, and was input to establish:

- plant build schedules
- supplier delivery schedules
- end product shipping schedules.

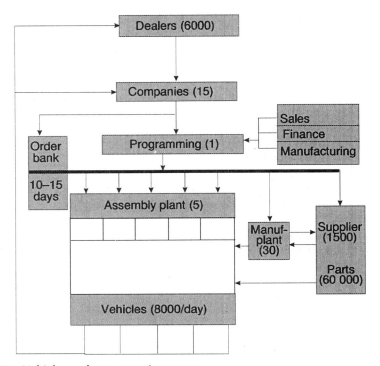

Figure 5.2   Vehicle producer operating system

This second phase is illustrated in another representation of a supply system in Figure 5.2, where the scope is extended to show dealers and suppliers. The numbers of the various groups of players (for example, 6000 dealers) have been shown in brackets for a typical European vehicle producer.

The overall process is similar for most manufacturing industries. The materials management task starts with the gathering of orders from the 6000 dealers, through the 15 national sales companies, and arranging these orders to form a production programme for each of the five assembly plants. It continues with 'exploding' the orders into production and delivery schedules for 60 000 parts from 1500 outside suppliers and the company's own 30 manufacturing plants, and planning the delivery of the 8000 finished vehicles each day to the 6000 dealers. Deriving schedules for the manufacturing plants from the overall production programme, and preparing the plants to meet them, is often called manufacturing requirements planning (MRP II), and calculation to derive schedules for suppliers is called materials requirements planning (MRP I). There are several standard software packages designed to perform MRP I and II, but most companies find it necessary to modify them for their own circumstances, or to develop bespoke systems. Using such a supply system, any one of the six major European car and truck producers, processes about 100 m materials related transactions a day. Turnover (the value of materials moving through the system) for one producer is in the order of £35 m a day, and production material inventories held within the system have historically been in the range of £200 m to £400 m. These figures suggest a high level of activity, and vehicle production plants are in fact very busy places. Despite this, the time lapse from the dealer placing an order and delivery of the vehicle to the customer has been in the region of two to three months for the major European producers.

Reduction of inventory, and of the time to fill a customer order are two tasks of materials management, and the historical values quoted above do not represent 'world class' performance. Greater attention to these tasks has resulted in major improvements in the 1990s. For example, in October 1994, Ford announced a trial scheme at its Dagenham plant which would reduce delivery times for UK customers from two months to two weeks. Customer orders which could not be met from dealer stocks would go straight from the dealer to the plant, where more flexible production and scheduling systems had been introduced — by teams that included engineers.

On top of the daily sales and production activities, more materials management tasks arise from the implementation of design changes. Stocks of a superseded part or material have to be exhausted if the designer gave a 'stocks use' disposition, or removed from the system immediately if there is a quality or safety implication. The exact timing of the change has to be recorded for each plant, each process and each product that is affected. It has been estimated that each change involves administrative costs in the region of £10 000, and a vehicle production system as shown in Figure 5.2 historically suffered about 20 000 changes a year.

With the volumes and values of material movements, the numbers and costs of transactions involved, and their impact on product quality and customer satisfaction, materials management systems such as those described above were among the first candidates for change in response to increasing competitive pressures in the 1970s.

To simplify the process by reducing input transaction volumes, as a precondition for reducing inventories, and developing a more responsive system, the first step would be to reduce the number of suppliers and the number of parts being scheduled and handled. The most effective way of doing this is through designing and specifying at a higher level of assembly — e.g. complete seats from one supplier, instead of 28 seat parts from eight, nine or ten suppliers. To make this change, a materials management strategy is required. This would have to be developed and implemented jointly by designers, producers and buyers.

The level of assembly specified by the designer also impacts on materials management in industries other than vehicle production. For example, a building can be designed with bathrooms that can be put in place as a single unit, which creates a materials management task quite different from that for a building where tiles, taps, toilets and toothbrush holders have to be bought, delivered, stored and handled separately. Similarly, the construction or production process also affects the 'supply' task. Fabrication on site of roof sections, structural steelwork, or bridge spans creates quite different materials management tasks compared with off-site prefabrication and sequenced delivery. The Lloyd's building in London provides an example of higher level assembly design and new production methods — the toilet blocks are attached to the outside of the

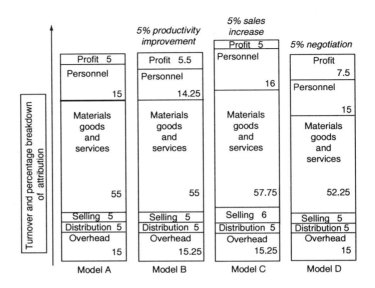

Figure 5.3   Corporate cost models

structure as complete 'pods', and can be removed (with suitable warning) as a complete unit.

Engineers' actions at the design stage also influence another important aspect of materials management — timing. In setting up bills of material (BOMS) for each unit of production, and for each location where the product is to be made, long lead time items have to be identified so that action is taken early enough to ensure that the items are there at the appropriate time in the production or construction process. In fact, the lead time for *all* items has to be reviewed with the purchasing and scheduling activities in order to set up the project control system. Ideally, this review should take place before design starts, so that the choice of some exotic material or unusual fabrication can either be avoided or built into the timing plan.

The BOM multiplied by the number of units to be built determines quantities to be made or bought in total. The production plan determines the rate of delivery and capacity required — capacity to make, store, handle, assemble, inspect, deliver and service. Planning these capacities involves engineers of many kinds.

Even with the use of computers, or especially with the use of computers, the task of controlling data and physical product becomes complex and error-prone when every component part is designed, specified and released by the producer's own design activity. Quality management and materials management tasks can be greatly simplified if a higher level of assembly is specified, and there are fewer sources with whom to discuss quality, delivery and cost issues.

Improved materials management therefore starts at the design stage, with cooperation between the designers, producers, buyers and schedulers to identify materials and components and suitable sources of supply, that support the design intent without compromising cost and timing objectives.

5.4   COST INFLUENCE OF MATERIALS MANAGEMENT

In Chapter 3 it was shown that 'material' constitutes about 60% of total cost in manufacturing. Material is also an important element in construction costs, ranging from 30 to 35% of total costs for dams and civil works, through 40 to 45% for housing, to over 50% for industrial, commercial and public buildings [4].

It follows that a 5% cut in materials costs can have a greater effect on profit than a 5% increase in sales, or a 5% improvement in productivity. It may also be less difficult to achieve, for, as shown in Chapter 4, total quality management can cut costs by between 15 and 30%. So a 5% material cost reduction is well within the range of savings that can be achieved through early cooperation between user and supplier to improve quality.

Figure 5.3 shows, in the first column, Model A, a simplified corporate cost model for a typical manufacturing company, with total sales of 100 units, and profits of five units after deducting costs of 95 units. The effect of various management actions to improve profit is shown in the other three columns.

As shown in the second column, Model B, a 5% improvement in labour productivity does not affect the costs of materials, services, selling or distribution, but may lead to a small increase in overhead if capital investment in new equipment is required. Profit increases from 5 to 5.5% of sales, a welcome improvement, but not a transformation in business performance.

The third column, Model C, shows the likely effects of a 5% sales increase. This would lead to a 5% rise in materials and services costs (ignoring volume discounts), and would probably entail higher selling costs, including special discounts, increased advertising and promotional campaigns, as well as higher personnel costs for extra hours worked — possibly at premium rates. Distribution costs might be unaffected if this part of the system were less than 100% loaded at previous sales levels. Costs rise by the same amount as sales, and profit remains at about five units (or to be unreasonably precise, increases to 5.25 units), which is poor reward for the extra effort.

However, a 5% reduction in the cost of materials, goods and services, illustrated in the right hand column, Model D, does not increase any of the other costs, and goes directly into profits, which rise to seven and a half units — a 50% increase.

The cost and profit effects described above would appear in the company's profit and loss (P&L) accounts, and hence in the numerator of the return on capital employed (ROCE) formula. (See Chapter 14 for further information on the construction of P&L accounts, a balance sheet and the ROCE formula.) Materials management also has a major impact on the denominator in the ROCE formula. In the balance sheet, materials and components appear as inventory or stocks under the 'current assets' heading. Inventory can be as much as 20% of total assets, and the absolute sums involved mean that a 20% reduction in inventory could fund a whole new product programme or a new manufacturing complex! Ford's worldwide accounts for 1989, for example, showed stocks valued at $8 billion, and ABB's 1991 accounts showed that they held inventories valued at $7 billion.

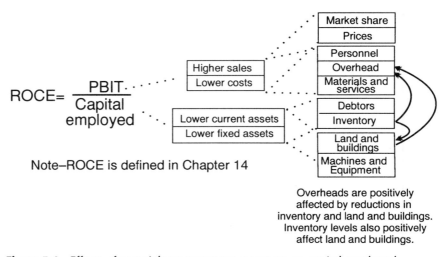

Figure 5.4 Effects of materials management on return on capital employed

Inventory also affects the balance sheet through the capital cost of buildings in which to store it. The importance of this was brought home forcibly to teams from the West who visited Japan in the 1970s. They found that only about 10% of factory floor space was used for storage, compared with 40% back home. With building costs at that time in the region of £60 per square foot, that had serious cost implications — and still does.

Inventory carrying costs, such as depreciation of the costs of floorspace, heat and light for the storage area, and interest on the money tied up, are P&L items. Therefore, inventory reductions improve financial performance both by reducing assets and by cutting operating costs. An elaboration of the ROCE formula illustrating these linked effects is shown in Figure 5.4.

Combined with the sort of material cost reductions described in section 5.2, inventory reductions can change ROCE performance figures significantly. Some examples of theoretical material cost reduction and inventory reduction are shown in Table 5.1 for a selection of engineering companies.

5.5 INVENTORY MANAGEMENT

Inventory is likely to build up in four parts of a production system, and in similar ways in construction:

- on receipt
- in process
- on completion
- in repair, maintenance and non-production material stores.

Table 5.1   The profitability effects of reductions in materials costs and inventory

Company	Sales	Cost of sales (COS)	COS as % of sales	Net capital employed (NCE)	Stocks	Stocks as % of NCE	Operating profit	Return on capital employed	Return on capital employed (2)
BBA	1322.6	1028.6	78%	372.8	245.7	66%	77.6	21%	40%
T&N	1390.1	1017.5	73%	535.0	281.3	53%	90.7	17%	30%
VICKERS	718.5	589.4	82%	206.6	153.1	74%	12.6	6%	24%
600 GP	98.5	73.9	75%	58.3	39.2	67%	−1.7	−3%	4%
LUCAS	2252.7	2168.1	96%	743.2	437.1	59%	58.3	8%	25%
GKN	1993.5	1857.8	93%	814.9	306.9	38%	125.9	15%	29%
APV	947.5	732.6	77%	149.8	142.4	95%	16.8	11%	44%
TI	1149.3	1038.0	90%	279.3	250.7	90%	111.3	40%	71%
SMITHS	635.3	428.6	67%	330.0	114.6	35%	93.5	28%	37%
CMB (FF)*	24830	21286.0	86%	25375.0	3534.0	14%	2454.0	10%	14%
IMI (1991)	968	889.8	92%	364.4	256.3	70%	78.2	21%	39%

*Figures for CarnaudMetalBox shown in French Francs, otherwise all figures shown in Sterling.
ROCE (2) assumes 5% COS reduction and 20% reduction in inventory.
All figures calculated from 1992 company reports, except where shown.

In manufacturing there may also be a fifth type of inventory in transit from suppliers to the producer/assembler, and possibly in transit or storage from the producer to the customer. Material belongs to the producer, and hence appears in the producer's inventory, from the moment it is bought, (which may be ex-suppliers' works), until the moment it is sold as part of the end product (which may be after it has passed through a distribution system and has been held by the retailer waiting for a customer). This is illustrated in Figure 5.5.

Inventory is held on receipt to allow administrative processes to be completed, which may include inspection, and to provide protection of the production process from interruption due to late delivery, or the delivery of the wrong or faulty items.It may also be held to allow a short-term increase in the production rate. In other words, stock is held to guard against uncertainty in usage or availability, or while information is processed. Reduction of stocks at this stage depends on several factors, which can involve engineers, such as supplier quality performance, inbound logistics, and on the design of information and materials handling systems.

Work-in-process (WIP) inventories held during processing are unavoidable, but can be reduced by faster processing. WIP is held between processes for the same reasons as inventories are held on receipt — uncertainty and poor information flow — and for other reasons. If output from one stage of production is unreliable, stocks may be held after that stage to protect later stages. They may build up before a process if it is interrupted or slows down, or simply because it is not known that the material is there ready to be used — or perhaps it needs to be inspected. Additionally, WIP may be held because of mismatches in process capacity, or competing demands for the same equipment — which could be handling or process equipment — or because of poor layout that requires

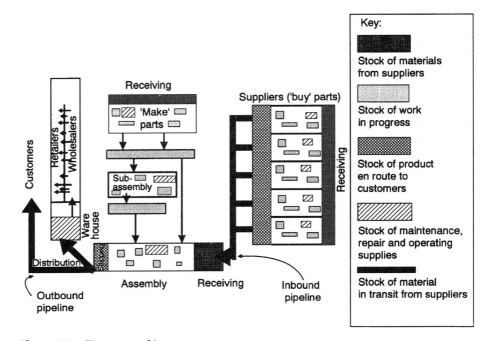

Figure 5.5   Five types of inventory

material to be moved around the site between processes. In some businesses such as machine tools, civil engineering, shipbuilding, and aerospace, WIP can amount to almost 100% of total project value, so completion on time and prompt handover are vital to profitability, even if the supplier's burden is lightened by stage payments. If interest charges are 1% a month, and other inventory carrying costs are a further 1% monthly, a few months' delay can wipe out the profit margin. Thus the true cost of a missing component or a quality concern in the last stages of completion could be thousands of times its nominal cost.

Reduction in WIP depends on machinery and equipment reliability, capacity planning, plant layout, process capability (i.e. quality), and information and materials handling systems, which again are the concerns of engineers.

Completed, finished goods, or end of line inventory may be held because the goods are not in fact finished — there may be more inspection, or packaging operations. They may also be held for consolidation with other material prior to delivery, or for collection (poor information processing, again, is a possible stock generator). On the other hand, they may have been completed sooner than required, or they may be on time and demand has reduced. This form of inventory can be reduced by responsive (flexible) production processes, process capability (quality), outbound logistics, and information and materials handling systems, which means that engineers of various kinds may again be involved.

Maintenance, repair and operating supplies (MRO) or non-production material inventory has a habit of growing through neglect. It consists of such things as spare parts or wear parts for equipment, tooling, cleaning materials, lubricants, fuels, protective clothing or workwear, paint, timber, metals, building materials for small works or maintenance, and packaging materials. Spare parts and tooling are often bought before production starts, and are sometimes kept after production ceases or a change makes them obsolete. This is one class of inventory that really is the direct responsibility of engineers, and can be reduced by arrangements made for them, or by them, with suppliers — for example to hold emergency spares, fuels, industrial gases and other stocks on consignment at the producer's site. The time to make such arrangements is before orders are placed for facilities or services. This requires a team effort between engineers, buyers and suppliers at the product or project planning stage.

Ways of reducing or eliminating (i.e. managing) these four types of inventory are described in Chapter 20. Even at this stage, however, it should be apparent that inventory reduction, like other aspects of materials management, involves cooperation between engineers of many kinds at an early stage of planning.

5.6   SUMMARY

This chapter indicated the importance of materials management to business success. It showed how engineers' selection of materials and their designation of levels of assembly can affect the scope and scale of the materials management task, with ramifications throughout the production, construction and supply system. The effectiveness of materials cost reduction and inventory reduction in raising return on capital employed was shown to be greater than that of other actions to improve profitability. Four categories of inventory were described, and for each category it was shown that engineers can contribute to inventory reduction. It was emphasized that simplification of the materials management task, materials cost reduction, inventory reduction and lead time reduction all start with teamwork in the conceptual and planning phase of a project or product programme.

REFERENCES

1. *Towards a Comprehensive Materials Balance* (1993) Siemens Review R&D Special. Fall.
2. Kaounides, L. (1995) *Advanced Materials: Management Strategies for Competitive Advantage*. Management Report for the *Financial Times* London. See also: Kaounides, L. (1994) *Advanced Materials in High Technology and World Class Manufacturing*. UNIDO, Vienna.
3. From correspondence with Lakis Kaounides in preparation of the *Financial Times* Management Report.
4. Cassimatis, P. J. (1969) *Economics of the Construction Industry*. National Industry Conference Board Inc., USA.

Managing design and new product development

6.1 INTRODUCTION

Earlier chapters have shown how, throughout the world, all engineering companies face similar challenges — ever more demanding customers, rapid technological change, environmental issues, competitive pressures on quality and cost, and shorter time to market with new product features. They operate against a background of common external factors — slow growth, excess capacity, increasing legislative control, demographic changes, market complexity and increasing globalization of industries.

Responding to these challenges against this background leads to focusing on the product development process:

'Three familiar forces explain why product development has become so important. In the last two decades, intense international competition, rapid technological advances and sophisticated, demanding customers have made "good enough" unsatisfactory in more and more consumer and industrial markets.' [1].

The chapters on materials management and quality described how efforts to achieve step-change improvements in performance in these areas have led to multifunctional teamwork in the design phase as the key to success. It is also the key to shorter development times and greater customer satisfaction. However, multifunctional teamwork was not the style of product development practised in western industries until competitive pressures forced them to change, starting in the mid 1980s.

This chapter describes the transition to collaborative new product development. It starts with the design dilemma, first mentioned in Chapter 4, and proceeds through a summary of the pressures for change to conclude with an outline of Simultaneous (or Concurrent) Engineering, which provides a resolution to the design dilemma.

6.2 THE DESIGN DILEMMA

The design dilemma was introduced in Chapter 4, Management of Quality, since many of the 'design for' objectives are aspects of quality. The 'design to'

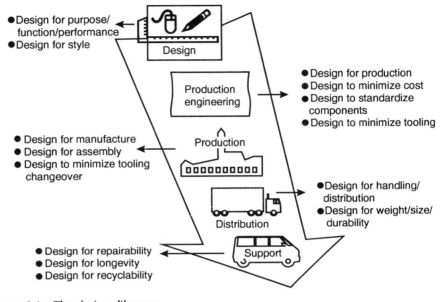

- Design for purpose/
  function/performance
- Design for style

Design

- Design for production
- Design to minimize cost
- Design to standardize
  components
- Design to minimize tooling

Production
engineering

- Design for manufacture
- Design for assembly
- Design to minimize tooling
  changeover

Production

- Design for handling/
  distribution
- Design for weight/size/
  durability

Distribution

- Design for repairability
- Design for longevity
- Design for recyclability

Support

Figure 6.1   The design dilemma

objectives are among the corporate objectives shown in Chapter 2. The designers'
dilemma is the reconciliation of their own objectives with those of the production
engineering, production, distribution, and support activities. The illustration of
the design dilemma is reproduced in Figure 6.1.

Not shown in the figure are some other important business issues that need to
be considered as part of the management of design. These include time to market,
picking winning products, risk in new technology and the cost of new
technology — which should all have a familiar ring from reading the Preface.

Many attempts to resolve the design dilemma, and to handle the major business
issues, founder when new product development is handled in a sequential way. If
design for manufacture and design for assembly, or design for 'buildability' are
tested by sequential trial and error, time is wasted and design work has to be
repeated. This approach is illustrated in Figure 6.2. FMEA, (failure mode and
effect analysis) was mentioned in Chapter 4 and worked examples are shown in
Appendix 2. 'DFA' is design for assembly.

The diagram shows how some infeasibilities can be identified by analysis at the
process planning stage, but others only show up as a result of physical trials in
manufacturing or assembly. (The word 'alternation' in the figure is a word coined
by a German engineer. It is fit for its purpose here, combining alteration and
alternate.)

The trial and error approach to testing the effectiveness of designs can be
extended beyond manufacturing to the customer — the ultimate inspector.
Performance in the market place and in use will show whether a product really
has been designed for performance, function, repairability and longevity.

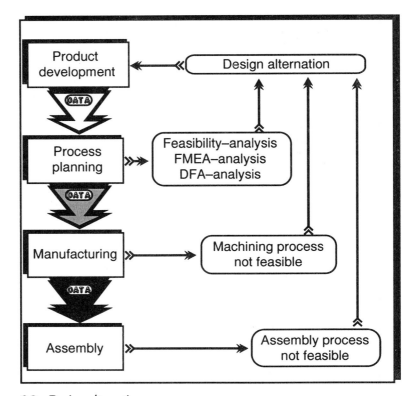

Figure 6.2 Design alternation

This expensive, unsatisfactory way to evaluate designs has been labelled 'over the walls' engineering, (OTW) illustrated in Figure 6.3. In over the walls engineering, product planning information (features and timing) is drip fed to the designer who, in the privacy of his/her own cell prepares a design and starts to test it. Before tests are complete, timing pressures lead to design information being released (over the wall) to production or construction engineers and buyers so that they can make their own studies and enquiries. Some of these feasibility studies by suppliers and manufacturers will reveal potential problems, and lead to requests for design change (back over or under the wall). The designer may already be making changes as a result of his/her own testing of the first design. Meanwhile, timing pressures dictate that procurement of facilities and long lead items must proceed. The concerns about feasibility and quality lead to design changes which in turn lead to process and facility changes. Evaluation of these changes may not be fully completed when the time comes for engineering sign off (ESO). ESO is given in the hope that the product will be 'good enough'. The customer will probably decide that it is not, and this information comes back to confirm the internal final test results. Sales fall below objectives.

Living through one programme managed in this fashion is enough to persuade any intelligent engineer that there must be a better way. There is, and it is called 'simultaneous engineering' (SE). It is also known as 'concurrent engineering'.

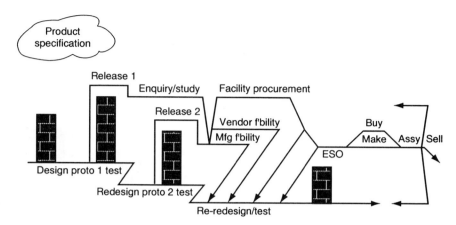

Figure 6.3   Over the walls engineering

Poor business performance as a result of OTW engineering is a powerful reason for adopting SE, but there are others, which may be the root causes of the poor business performance. The most important of these are:

- quality management
- cost management
- time management
- customer requirements
- the impact of new technologies.

These reasons for adopting SE are described in Sections 6.3 and 6.4. Simultaneous engineering is described in Section 6.5.

6.3   PRESSURES TO CHANGE

6.3.1   Pressure from quality management

In Chapter 4, cause and effect analysis, with its fishbone diagrams was described as a tool for identifying and removing causes of variation and so improving process control. This produces diminishing returns — smaller and smaller improvements from more and more analysis. A point will be reached where a step change in quality performance requires a change to the process itself, possibly involving a change to equipment and a change in design [2]. It was also shown in Chapter 4 that the cost of making such changes increases exponentially when production or construction is under way. Clearly, there would be advantage in identifying these process, equipment or design changes at an earlier stage, but this requires some way of envisaging or simulating production or construction conditions. Ways exist, but they require input from the production or construction experts at the design stage — that is the formation of a design team with the knowledge to define alternatives, the skills to evaluate them and, ideally, the authority to

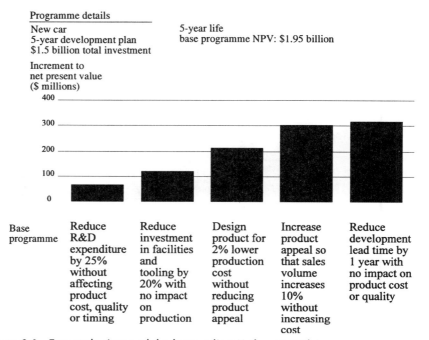

Programme details
_____

New car
5-year development plan
$1.5 billion total investment

5-year life
base programme NPV: $1.95 billion

Increment to
net present value
($ millions)

Base programme	Reduce R&D expenditure by 25% without affecting product cost, quality or timing	Reduce investment in facilities and tooling by 20% with no impact on production	Design product for 2% lower production cost without reducing product appeal	Increase product appeal so that sales volume increases 10% without increasing cost	Reduce development lead time by 1 year with no impact on product cost or quality

Figure 6.4   Fast cycle time and the bottom line (Arthur D. Little)

implement the jointly agreed optimum solution. Establishing such teams, and vesting them with authority will normally require a corporate culture change.

6.3.2   Pressure from cost management

It is not just changes made to improve quality that cost more to implement later in the product cycle. All changes cost more the later they are made, and the costs impinge on all parties. It is a mistake to believe that contractors or suppliers profit from changes — they make more profit from doing things right first time, on time. For manufacturers, some idea of the waste resulting from specification changes can be derived from Chapter 5, Section 5.3. There it was stated that a typical major European vehicle producer would process about 20 000 component changes a year, at a cost of about £10 000 for each change. That means there is a £200 m prize for the elimination of these changes.

6.3.3   Pressure from time management

Time to market for consumer goods, and time to build for construction projects, are important competitive factors. In the Preface it was shown that UK business leaders considered time to market *the* top issue of the 1990s. The principal reason for this is the impact of reduction in development time on profitability over the total product life. This was demonstrated by the Arthur D. Little Company's research published in 1990, (described in [3]) and summarized in Figure 6.4.

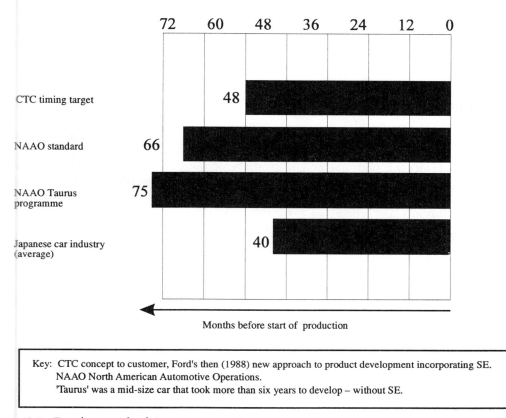

72   60   48   36   24   12   0

CTC timing target   48

NAAO standard   66

NAAO Taurus   75
programme

Japanese car industry   40
(average)

Months before start of production

Key: CTC concept to customer, Ford's then (1988) new approach to product development incorporating SE.
NAAO North American Automotive Operations.
'Taurus' was a mid-size car that took more than six years to develop – without SE.

Figure 6.5   Development lead time — competitive comparison

The chart shows that the $1.95 billion net present value (NPV) of a project requiring an investment of $1.5 billion would be increased by $0.06 billion if R&D expenditure were reduced by 25%. It would also be increased by $0.12 billion if facilities costs were cut by 20% etc. But the biggest impact on NPV (an increase of more than $0.3 billion) would result from a reduction in the new product development time from five years to four years. See Chapter 15 for an explanation of NPV.

The gap between US and Japanese performance in consumer goods product development timing in the mid 1980s is illustrated in Figure 6.5. The example is for car programmes, but the relationship was similar for home entertainment products, cameras, copiers, communications equipment and others. In many industries, US and European performance was similar — they lagged behind their Japanese counterparts.

Compression of product introduction or project completion timing spans can be achieved by doing things faster, possibly by the use of advanced information technology. However, improvements by this method are small compared with the time savings from doing things right first time, and doing several things in parallel rather than sequentially. Chapter 17 describes ways of achieving parallelism in implementation, and such methods have been widely used in the West as well as in Japan for more than 40 years. The difference in performance between these groups in the 1980s was found to be in the planning, design and sourcing phases prior to implementation. SE introduces parallelism to these phases.

6.3.4   Pressures from customers

'Picking winning products' was another top issue identified by UK business leaders, and would certainly feature in similar lists elsewhere in the world. The history of personal and domestic entertainment equipment provides several examples of 'nearly right' products — audio and video tape systems that came second in the competition to be the industry standard; alternative compact disc formats and satellite TV receivers. Whatever happened to digital audio tape (DAT) and high definition television (HDTV)?

In the European motor industry, some producers pursued 'lean-burn' engine technology as their way of meeting expected emission control legislation, but their efforts were wasted when three-way catalytic converters became the mandatory specification. They had picked the wrong product option.

Making the right choice, and accurately forecasting consumers' perceived or latent requirements is obviously difficult, but the choice has to be made at the start of design. Masatoshi Naito, head of design at Matsushita, the Japanese electronics group whose brand names include National Panasonic, JVC and Pioneer stated the task in the following way:

'Design is not just a shape or a form but realising what a consumer needs and making a product that meets those needs. Consumer needs have to be the starting point rather than just seeking to differentiate a product superficially.' [4]

Consumer needs can only be incorporated in designs if designers are well informed about those needs, and have techniques to reflect them in designs that recognize material and process capabilities. Capturing and using the necessary information is part of SE.

6.4   THE IMPACT OF NEW TECHNOLOGIES

The continually increasing rate of technological change is both a threat and an opportunity. At consumer level, rapid changes in products such as personal computers and audio equipment render obsolete, within months, equipment that has been touted as 'state-of-the-art'. Buyers who see the value of their purchase halved when scarcely out of its packaging become resistant to the next wonder product. At producer level, the pressure to be first in the market place, or first in the factory, with the latest material, machine or method calls for new ways of evaluating the alternatives in order to avoid costly mistakes. The French politician Francois Mitterand has been credited with the assertion that:

'There are three ways of losing money — women, gambling and technology. Women is the most pleasurable way, gambling is the fastest, and technology the most certain.'

There is no published research to support this statement, but examples of unsuccessful investment in new technologies feature regularly in the press. This does not make them representative. On the other hand, since most organizations do not willingly publicize failure, the reported cases may only be the tip of an iceberg.

For example, there have been reports, separated by more than ten years, of two new international airports whose opening or full operation was delayed by several months by problems with their automated baggage handling systems. In the earlier case of Schipol, the interim solution was allegedly to hire circus acrobats to scale the racking and retrieve luggage. In recent years, two new high-speed train services had inauspicious launches. One, from Munich to Hamburg, suffered 'a spate of breakdowns, including the electric engines, the super flush toilets and the microwave ovens and beer cooler in the restaurant car' [5]. The other was the London–Paris Eurostar link which suffered rolling stock failure on its first two days of operation in October 1994. This was a minor embarrassment compared with problems which had been foreseen in 1991. At that time it had been expected that the Channel Tunnel would be open for business in June 1993, but that the trains would not be available until December, causing a loss of revenue of more than £100 m. This expectation was due to 'changes to the design of the tourist shuttles . . . insisted on by the Intergovernmental Commission after its rejection of the proposed size of the wagons' fire doors.' [6] Completion of the tunnel itself was in fact delayed, and blame for the loss of revenue was placed elsewhere.

These examples indicate the need for thorough testing of the product prior to public availability. With new materials and processes this means that producers have to reach down the supply chain to involve the developers of the new materials and methods in their own design and test programmes. It also means that the producers have to evaluate the new technologies in partnership with their materials, component and equipment suppliers in conditions representative of volume production and customer use. Failure to do this can delay and diminish the benefits of innovation at great cost in lost market opportunity and idle facilities.

In some industries, such as air transportation and pharmaceuticals, the evaluation requirements are determined by government authorities, but even here simultaneous engineering can help. Boeing's development of the 777 aircraft is an example of 'total system' SE within such regulatory constraints [7]. A research programme to reduce development lead times in the UK pharmaceutical industry was launched in 1994 as part of the government's Innovative Manufacturing Initiative. It is understandable that this should be a national priority, since evaluation of a new medicine within the regulatory framework can take 12 years of the 20 year patent protection period. The phases of development are shown in Figure 6.6, which is reproduced from a Confederation of British Industries publication [8].

Something not shown in Figure 6.6 is the task of the industry's process engineers. Traditionally, starting late in the clinical development phase, when the likelihood of success is emerging, the process engineers have had to devise production methods that retain the integrity of the laboratory processes used in the discovery and small-scale production phases. The engineers' proposals for scaling up production also require approval by the regulatory authorities, which

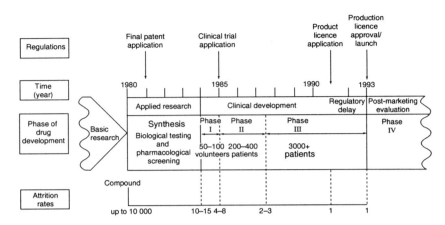

Figure 6.6   Pharmaceuticals development timing

can result in delays to marketing the new product. The engineers' earlier introduction to the development team will be an important part of any plan to reduce overall new product development lead times.

The benefits of saving time in new product development and the faster introduction of new technologies have been demonstrated by success stories in the automotive industry, computer peripherals, aircraft and electronics. In most instances, the time saving is between 20 and 30%, which equates to a year on a typical car project — worth over $300 m according to *A. D. Little 1990* (see Figure 6.4 above). Several case studies from a variety of industries are given in a special report *Concurrent Engineering*, by Rosenblatt and Watson [9].

6.5   SIMULTANEOUS ENGINEERING — RESOLVING THE DESIGN DILEMMA

6.5.1   The aims of simultaneous engineering

In 'over the walls' engineering, what the external customer really wanted, and what the internal customers would have liked to have, is eventually provided through application of downstream expertise to resolve problems. This results in late changes which endanger quality, cost and timing. The aim of SE is to avoid the changes, and remove the dangers.

This can be done by bringing the downstream expertise of process engineers, service engineers, machine operators, materials and component suppliers, equipment suppliers, sales people and even financial analysts, to bear at the same time, and early enough to resolve design and manufacturing concerns before production requirements of components and equipment are ordered.

6.5.2   Simultaneous engineering teams and processes

Although the SE process was developed in manufacturing industry, its general applicability has been increasingly recognized. For example, by the early 1990s

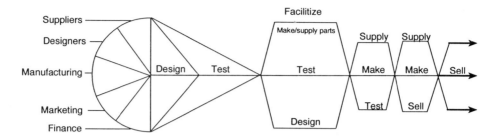

Figure 6.7   The team process of simultaneous engineering

there were pleas for its introduction to civil engineering. In the construction industry, SE is achieved by what is known as 'fast-track' construction in which construction operations are in parallel with, but slightly behind design. *The Latham Report 1994* [10] identifies two factors which are significant in the success of this approach:

(1)   the degree of involvement of the client/owner: clients should be more involved than in the past;
(2)   the degree of coordination between design and construction; design processes all too often exclude any construction expertise.

The *Latham Report* challenges the UK construction industry to reduce its costs by up to 30% by improving relationships between clients, designers, contractors and subcontractors. Chapter 17 includes further discussion of SE in construction and civil engineering.

The following steps reflect SE's origins, or revival, in a programme to introduce a new car engine, but can be adapted and adopted for use elsewhere.

The stages of SE are:

• form a team
• agree objectives
• agree working methods
• establish control and information systems
• work together on the design
• stay together through the implementation.

The process is illustrated in Figure 6.7.

The team consists of representatives from marketing: to provide input of customer needs, from design: to translate those needs into product features, from manufacturing and suppliers (of materials, components and equipment): to realize those features, and from finance: to provide assistance in the evaluation of alternatives — not to control costs, which is part of the team responsibility. The inputs from the team members are not spontaneous thoughts, but the documented results of learning from experience and from internal and external customer feedback. See Chapter 4, Figure 4.12.

Selection of individual team members has to be on the basis of their technical skills. In theory, team performance would be improved by incorporating the right mix of personalities to perform the allegedly different team roles. In practice, teams have to be formed from the talent that is available. If the team members' companies have paid due attention to the soft Ss of management (see Chapter 3), all the members will have the interpersonal skills and shared values needed to contribute willingly to the team effort. If some of the companies have neglected the soft Ss, the team leader has an additional task: to create a 'microclimate' of style and shared values that will extract the full potential of the shy, lazy, selfish or obdurate members.

In the early phase, when the team focuses on developing and testing designs, the design engineer is the team leader — the chosen alternative must reflect the design intent. As the project progresses towards production it may be appropriate for leadership to move to the manufacturing engineer or the manager responsible for production, and, towards market launch, Marketing may take the lead in setting priorities for the product mix and sequence.

At every phase, the task of the team leader is to harness the expertise required to dissolve problems and concerns. Only a small part of the expertise will be available within the producer company — which is why there are supplier members of the team. Since more than 60% of materials and about 90% of production equipment comes from outside the company, in manufacturing industries it follows that this is where most of the expertise lies. The same logic applies to other industries.

An important early step is recognition of this outside capability by the internal experts, and to move from the stage where SE is seen merely as cooperation between design and manufacturing to stages where inputs are contributed by the whole external supplier base, and by customers — simultaneously, and in a spirit of partnership. These stages are shown in Figure 6.8.

The spirit of partnership has to be created, both at corporate level and at the personal level. This entails breaking down barriers between functions and between companies, which will not happen until sales people share their access to customers, purchasing staff share their access to suppliers, and physical and mental barriers between groups of engineers are removed. For many companies this requires a complete change of corporate culture or style, which may take years to achieve. Figure 6.9 (a) and (b) illustrate the change.

Robert Lutz, chief operating executive of the Chrysler Corporation describes the situation in Figure 6.9(b) as 'the extended enterprise', where there are no boundaries between the company and its supply base, nor between the company and its dealers [11]. In such a company, the organizational location of the SE team would not be a major concern. However, in the more common hierarchical bureaucracies of western industry there has been extensive debate about the choice between:

- lightweight programme management — where the programme manager has use of the services of team members who remain in their organizational location;
- heavyweight programme management — where members are withdrawn from their organizational location and work for the programme manager;

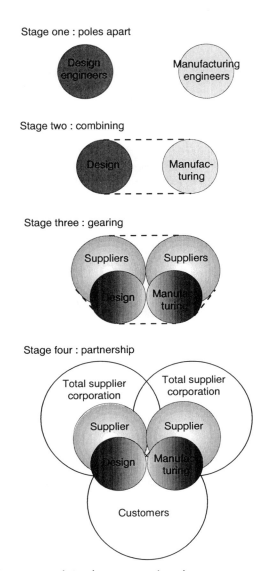

Figure 6.8   The four stages of simultaneous engineering

- independent business units — where a self-contained unit is set up with its own support services and structure.

There are examples of success and failure for each arrangement, and there is no universal 'right' choice. There is, however, a universally wrong choice, which is to superimpose a project management structure on top of the operating functions to coordinate, to gather progress reports, and to second guess decisions made by the line managers. For effective SE, the team has to be the people who do the design

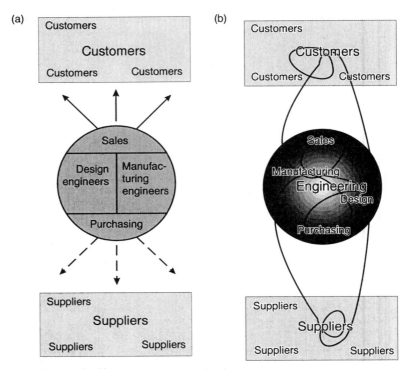

Figure 6.9   Removal of barriers to communication

and process engineering, the buying and the supplying, and they should be given authority to make decisions within clear guidelines.

When the team has formed, and has been briefed on the corporate objectives, targets can be developed and expressed in the team's own terms. Figure 6.10 shows (verbatim) the targets set by the team that rediscovered SE for Ford of Europe in 1986 on the Zeta engine programme.

The abbreviations in Figure 6.10 are part of the car industry's jargon. Their translation is:

- DQR — durability, quality and reliability
- NVH — noise, vibration and harshness
- P&E — performance and economy.

For each of these characteristics, evaluations of competitors' engines provided benchmarks of 'best in class' values. 'Performance feel' is harder to translate, but there is something about the responsiveness of an engine which can be detected in the first moments of driving, and this term aims to describe it.

Having agreed their targets in terms they all understood, the ZETA team then developed a simple algorithm to express their design optimization strategy, which is shown in Figure 6.11. It may appear from this abbreviated account that the ZETA team went straight to the 'norming' stage of team behaviour described in

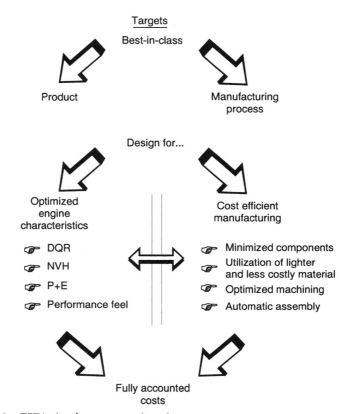

Figure 6.10   ZETA simultaneous engineering team targets

Chapter 10. In fact they had their share of 'storming' — at the first meeting of what was then a task force rather than a team, half the design engineers wanted to disband because they had been called together too soon. The other half thought they had come together too late. The task force leader and some members had the sense and skills to keep the group together. Other teams have developed other ways to proceed, but all the successful teams have had an agreed method and style of working.

The algorithm indicates that the team's starting point was a design that met the product objectives (best in class for DQR, NVH etc.). They then sought ways of making the design a 'design for manufacture' by eliminating machining or assembly operations, or, if that was not possible, simplifying operations, until they had a design that was both 'product and manufacturing oriented' — it would meet the product objectives and would be easier to produce with consistent process quality and both piece cost and capital cost would be within the cost objectives.

Having agreed their targets and strategy, the team's next task is idea generation. By pooling their individual knowledge and experience, and by tapping the knowledge base of their 'home' organizations, the team can compile a list of

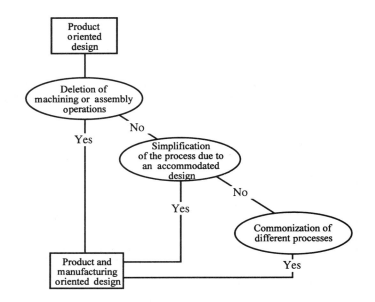

Figure 6.11   Design optimization strategy

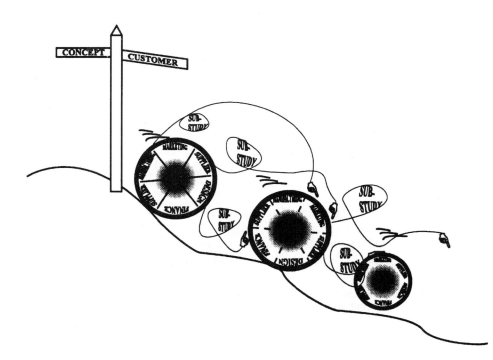

Figure 6.12   The team rolls on, helped by sub-studies by satellite teams

opportunities — ways in which the targets may be met. The core team will not be able to handle the evaluation of all the opportunities themselves, and sub-studies will have to be spun off to other *ad hoc* satellite teams, coordinated by core team members.

Figure 6.12 is a representation of the way the emphasis of the team's activity changes as the project progresses, (illustrated by the changes in the function at the top of the wheel), and the way in which sub-studies are spun off and their results fed back.

Barriers that may have existed when the team was formed are removed by shared experiences and team leadership (shown by gradual removal of the spokes in the wheels).

The work of the core team and the satellite sub-study teams has to be managed. Tasks and timing have to be set, results evaluated and decisions made. A control format for this purpose is shown in Figure 6.13, which is another of the ZETA team's ideas.

The table in Figure 6.13 is headed 'design for competition' which itself shows a change in focus of the team's thinking — they have a common overriding goal instead of a series of 'design for' statements. The first column in the table, which is headed 'design feature', lists all the opportunities that came out of the idea-generation or brainstorming sessions. There were about 20 ideas, some of which

1992 ZETA Engine Programme Design for Competition Cylinder Head

Number	Design feature	Advantage	Disadvantage	Piece cost effect	Investment effects ($000 max)	Action Responsibility Timing	Concurred as prime programme
1 i	Oil drain holes cast finished	-Machining operations reduced -Tool cost reduction	-NAAO comment-increased fingers on oil jacket core which may result in increased core breakage -Montupet state no change in cost	TBE	(400) x2	Oil drain holes on exhaust cast or machined may result in water circulation problems around exh. port -PDG to review	YES TBA
ii	Self-contained hydraulic tappets	-Machining operations reduced -Minute cost reduction -Product improvements claimed by tappet supplier	-Tappet design not fully developed (DQR concern) -Piece cost increase -Longer assy leakdown required -May require additional squirt holes between tappet and valve stem. -No fallback route in the case of failure if oil hole machining is not protected		(4000)* x2	Action plan established -Resource and facilities to be established -EAO/NAAO joint testing	
iii	Delete camshaft lubrication holes in half bore	-Machining operations reduced -Tool cost reductions		TBE	(600) x2		TBA
iv	Delete machined oil gallery system by casting the oil gallery and	-Machining and assembly operations deleted	-External system for CAM bearing lube required DQR -Piece cost increase	TBE	(4000)* x2	-Design study to be established -Build prototypes for test	TBA
2	Delete machining	Machining and		TBE	(1200) x2	Series I heads will be made to new level	Montupet YES NAAO

Figure 6.13 Sample of ZETA control format

(a) • Six areas of opportunity identified:

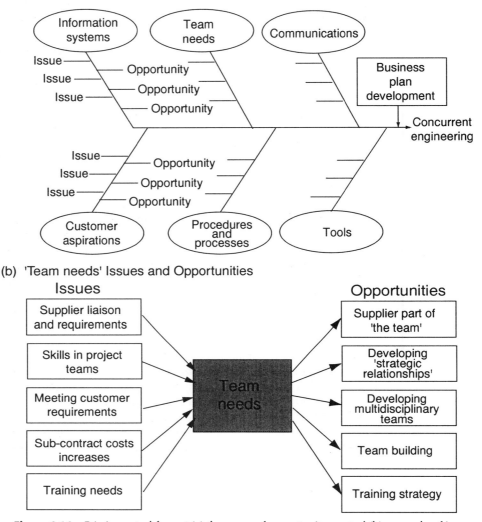

(b) 'Team needs' Issues and Opportunities

Figure 6.14   BAe's control format (a) the areas of opportunity control (b) example of issues and opportunities control

were mutually exclusive — hence the asterisk identifying investment costs that could only be deleted once. The advantage, disadvantage and cost columns are almost self-explanatory. The key control information is shown in the action/resposibility/timing column, which names the core team member (by organization) who will coordinate the feasibility and evaluation study, and summarizes the agreed scope of the study. The last column shows whether the idea has been accepted by the whole team. The technical terms and processes mentioned are not important to understanding the role of the document, and engineers not familiar with them should not be distracted by them or worry about them.

The control format used by the ZETA team, like the other examples of their documents, was something developed by the team as they went along. In later programmes these simple hand-drawn sketches or typed tables were replaced by more sophisticated media, and more formalized management structures were put in place. Figure 6.14 shows a project control structure developed by British Aerospace plc, which reflects the same principles of delegation and monitoring as the ZETA team's simple charts.

British Aerospace (BAe) used the term 'concurrent engineering project' (CEP), when introducing the SE concept. Their 'fishbone' chart, shown in Figure 6.14 (a), identifies six areas of opportunity, and Figure 6.14 (b) is an example of how they listed issues and opportunities under one of the six headings.

Control of information can be greatly assisted by setting up a shared computer database, enabling all participants to have access to current data. All the powers of information technology (IT) can be harnessed for this purpose, including computer-aided design (CAD), computer-aided manufacture (CAM), and computerized data exchange (CDX). Rosenblatt and Watson [9] describe a range of research programmes in the USA aimed at greater use of IT for communication between geographically separated groups within SE teams. However, IT has its limitations. Some are technical, such as the very real difficulties of CDX between different CAD systems. Some are geographical, such as the limited working hours overlaps between countries and continents. Some are psychological — screen to screen communication is no substitute for face to face communication, does not allow full debate and discussion, and is slow to create a sense of shared purpose and teamwork. All SE teams therefore need to meet regularly face to face in the same room, even if it means some of them flying half way round the world. *Business Week* [12] reported that Honda, the Japanese car company, brought nearly 60 production engineers and their families to Japan to make sure that the car designers paid as much attention to the manufacturing needs of the US plants as they did to those of the Japanese plants.

When the team does get together it is important that they follow some house rules for communication. One team built up the following list of 'Dos' and 'Don'ts' over the first few months of working together (shown verbatim):

DO	DON'T
Let one talk, all listen	Talk forever
All contribute	Dominate
Open your mind to all options	Interrupt
Begin and end on time	Tell lengthy anecdotes
Be prepared	Use jargon
Be brave	Confine comment to your own discipline
Be a team player	Patronize or be sarcastic
Share facilitization	Make personal attacks
Set an agenda	Conceal vested interests or constraints of home organization
Reach consensus (try!)	
Check the process	Be a star
Record agreements	Create unnecessary paper
Gather facts; analyse; reach decision; let the facts speak	

Figure 6.15   Communication methods (a)

A parallel group used the illustration in Figure 6.15 to show what they were trying to achieve.

In retrospect, they wished they had illustrated their new approach as shown in Figure 6.16, where there is no 'we' and 'they', and there is only one speaker at a time.

For all SE teams, in addition to their own house rules, there are generally applicable tools and techniques that they can employ. Some of these are described in the next section.

Figure 6.16 Communication methods (b)

6.5.3   SE tools and techniques

The most powerful SE technique is quality function deployment (QFD), developed originally in Mitsubishi's Kobe shipyard in the early 1970s. It is a systematic way of considering customer requirements, turning them into product features, and developing specifications, manufacturing processes and production plans. Three stages of QFD are shown in Figure 6.17. It is possible to continue the process to a fourth stage covering production requirements, and a fifth stage covering service requirements, but three stages are enough to illustrate the technique.

The whole SE team is involved throughout QFD to provide expert input and to reach balanced decisions. At the first stage, customer requirements are listed in everyday terms, such as better economy, or more occupant protection and translated into design requirements. One of the design measures to improve economy might be weight reduction, and a measure to protect the occupants might be improved resistance to side impacts. At the second stage, design requirements are turned into part characteristics. A part characteristic to reduce weight could be an engine part made from aluminium instead of cast iron, and a characteristic to resist side impacts could be additional spars of high strength alloy steel between the inner and outer door panels. In the third stage, the manufacturing requirements to implement the part characteristics are developed. At each stage the interaction of the various inputs is noted, and identified as a positive or a negative relationship. The added door spars to improve safety would have a negative relationship with measures to reduce weight aimed at improved economy. The team has to consider such conflicts, and make trade-offs — which

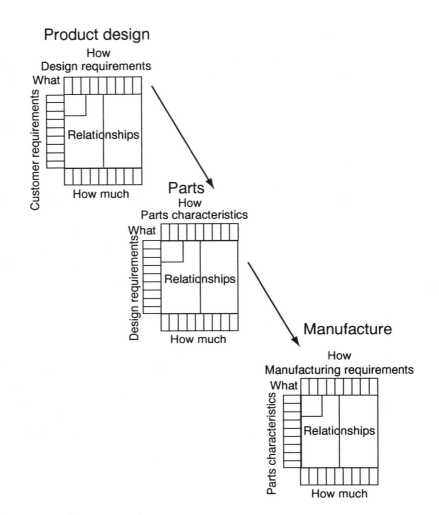

Figure 6.17   Three stages of QFD

are all recorded on the QFD charts. Rankings are assigned to each input to determine priorities and likely return for engineering effort. Comparisons with competitor products can be built in as another factor in determining priorities. The end result is that the most important customer requirements are incorporated in the product in the most cost-effective, quality assured way.

QFD was first applied in the Japanese shipbuilding industry, but is now most widely used in the automotive industry. For those who wish to pursue the subject further, a worked example can be found in the *Harvard Business Review* [13].

Potential failure mode and effects analysis (FMEA) is another powerful tool that helps to prioritize engineering effort. The two forms — design FMEA and process FMEA — were introduced in Chapter 4 and a worked example is shown in Appendix 2.

Team effort can be focused by identifying for each part or system the *critical characteristics* — which affect safety or compliance with legislation — and *significant characteristics* — those which affect customer requirements. Using FMEA, designs and processes can be made sufficiently 'robust' to ensure that these characteristics are always within specification. Advanced planning of robust designs and processes can start by review of existing production methods and process capability for 'surrogate' parts, similar to the new parts.

In some organizations, including the US Defense Procurement Executive, SE teams use a suite of decision support tools known as interactive management (IM) [14]. The three phases of IM are idea generation, nominal group technique (which synthesises the team's ideas), and interpretive structure modelling (which establishes a hierarchy of relationships between factors leading to the group objective).

The workload and time required to evaluate alternative designs and processes can be dramatically reduced by another tool, design of experiments (DOE). Factorial design of experiments to measure the effects of varying each of several factors dates from the work of A. L. Fisher in the 1930s. More recent developments by the Japanese statistician, Genichi Taguchi, allow variation of several parameters simultaneously to provide reliable results with fewer iterations. Lipson and Sheth [15] provide more details.

Pre-sourcing, the selection of suppliers by ongoing assessment rather than competitive bidding, is another time-saving technique that can reduce new product development times by many months, for example six to nine months in a 24 month lead time. Pre-sourcing is necessary in any case, since SE requires the involvement of key suppliers during product design. This means that the old ways of buying, which entail issuing detailed specifications and soliciting competitive bids, cannot be used. Pre-sourcing cuts out the enquiry/quote/evaluate/order cycle, and uses team assessment of suppliers to select partners to join the SE team. How this is done is described in Chapter 21, section 21.5.

6.5.4   Benefits of SE

In general terms, it can be said that SE:

- reduces time from design concept to market launch by 25% or more,
- reduces capital investment by 20% or more,
- supports total quality with zero defects from the start of production, and with earlier opportunities for continuous improvement,
- supports Just-in-Time production with total quality supplies, and advanced planning of inbound logistics,
- simplifies after-sales service,
- increases life-cycle profitability throughout the supply system.

In short, it resolves the design dilemma, and helps to achieve all the fundamental business objectives.

Rosenblatt and Watson [9] describe extensive research into the application of information technology to simultaneous engineering (or concurrent engineering, as they prefer to call it), but they also quote Roy Wheeler of Hewlett Packard:

'What tools does an engineer need to get started in CE? Pencil, paper, some intelligence, and a willingness to work with peers in other functional areas to get the job done. Computer based tools can be added as the budget permits.'

Wheeler makes a good point — open minds are more important to SE than open systems.

6.6 NEW DIMENSIONS TO SIMULTANEOUS ENGINEERING

Rapid technological change and advanced materials offer new opportunities to the designer. This brings a new challenge to SE — having reduced the time from design to market launch, the new task is to close the gap between basic research and its application. The reach of the SE team has to be extended to participation of the science base, and the range of possibilities evaluated has to be extended in two dimensions. One is to broaden the coverage of the team's studies to include revolutionary new materials and new processes, not just incremental change. The other is to lengthen the time horizon so that the implications of using new materials are considered through to disposal and recycling.

SE teams have been doing design FMEAs and process FMEAs in many industries and many parts of the world since the early 1980s. In considering the use of advanced materials, they now have to perform something akin to life-cycle FMEAs, and will need new analytical and control tools. An example has been provided by Siemens AG, the German electrical and electronics company, where scientists and engineers developed a decision support system for their work on printed circuit board design [16]. Their decision support wheel for selection of plastic materials is shown in Figure 6.18.

The designer starts in the material production sub-division of the manufacturing sector, to identify raw materials and their polymerization, and proceeds in a clockwise direction to cover formulation and supply, before moving to processing, utilization, recycling and disposal. This is a comprehensive system!

Getting R&D closer to the market can be assisted by actions within companies, but is even more dependent on relationships between companies.

An example of action within companies is Nestlé's restructuring in 1991–92, which established an independent business unit (IBU) for each product group, and assigned an R&D person to each IBU [17]. This type of action is likely to be more effective if the whole company is alert to the need to encourage the passage of new developments horizontally through the organization, without having to refer up and down functional chimneys (see Chapter 7). Pralahad and Hamel emphasize this in a way that links technology management with two of the soft Ss of management, style and skills:

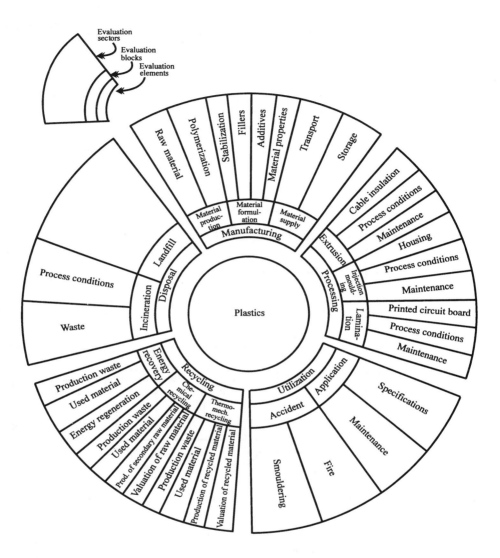

Figure 6.18   Siemens life-cycle decision support wheel

'Technology can be narrowly held by a group of experts, but the competence to utilize it as a way of improving the performance of . . . products . . . requires many people across the company to understand the potential and *the skills* to integrate it in new product development' [18].

Outside the company, simultaneous engineering of new designs, new processes and new materials requires new alliances. The science base for new materials is down in the supply chain among the basic materials suppliers and in academic

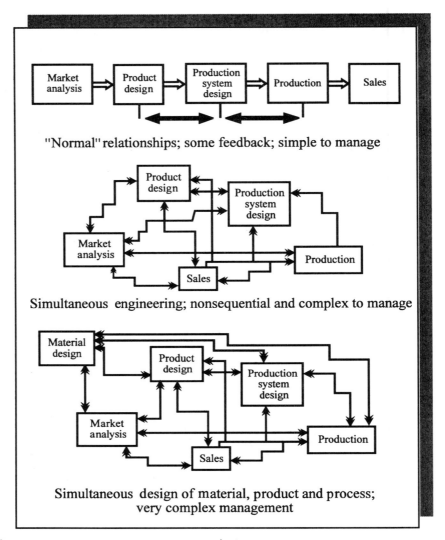

Figure 6.19 Increasing management complexity

institutions which are outside the normally accepted scope of the supply chain. Application of the science base output may be at intermediate stages of the chain, at the levels of component and sub-assembly suppliers. End-product manufacturers, constructors or assemblers, therefore, have to set up complex, market-driven alliances between themselves, their suppliers, their suppliers' suppliers and the science base. If these organizations are to work concurrently, in the style of SE, the concept of the supply chain has to be set aside, and replaced by the supply system. Managing this system, with its multiple interfaces within an SE framework is a complex task. This is illustrated in Figure 6.19.

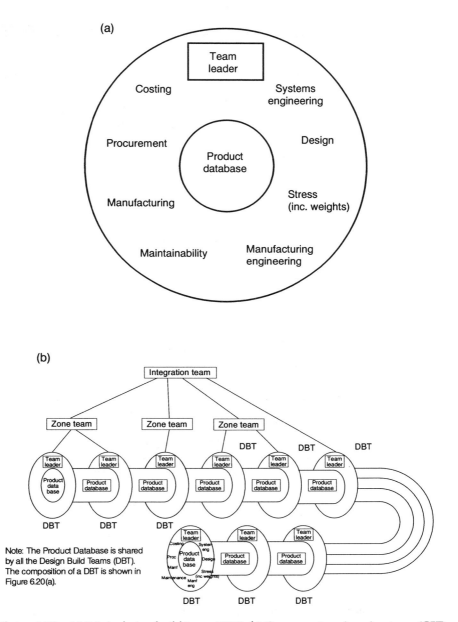

Figure 6.20   (a) BAe's design build team (DBT) (b) Concurrent engineering team (CET)

In the 'normal' linear process of new product development, there is some feedback from production to the production system designers, and from them to the product designers. This is 'over the walls' engineering — ineffective and inefficient, but fairly simple to manage. In SE the multifunctional team is generally trying to make incremental improvements to known products and processes. Because design is by a team, relationships between individuals and between organizations become more complex, and are more difficult to manage. When revolutionary new materials and technologies also have to be considered, the design team have to think in terms of radical change, and possibly the complete replacement of processes rather than their improvement. Members of the team may have to be drawn from different industries, and from academic or government institutions not familiar with the industrial and business worlds. Management of these new partners in a new environment may become very complex.

The importance of such collaborative alliances for new product development has been recognized at national level in the USA and in Japan, where 181 state-sponsored projects were launched in 1993, to hit world markets early in the next century [19]. At corporate level, too, new product development programmes of this complexity are being successfully managed.

The European Fighter Aircraft (EFA) is an example of a complex project, both in terms of the product and in the extent of the collaborative alliances involved. The EFA was being designed and built in the late 1980s–early 1990s by teams in Germany, Italy, Spain and the UK. The UK partner, British Aerospace, used SE (or CE in their terms), through a series of design build teams (DBT) coordinated into zone teams, which were coordinated further by integration teams. Figure 6.20(a) shows the composition of a DBT, with a core product database. Figure 6.20(b) shows how the DBTs were coordinated, linked by an organizational structure and by the shared database.

Ford's CDW27 car programme, which produced the Mondeo in Europe, and the Mystique and Contour in the USA is another example of a complex programme. The key to its success was identified at the first briefing of the 300 or so pre-sourced suppliers from all over the world: a huge majority (about 70%) voted 'communication' as the most important issue.

The implication for engineers and technologists is that they too must be able to communicate if they are to contribute effectively to collaborative new product development, and to work in teams, with other teams.

6.7 SUMMARY

This chapter described how the new product development process has become the key to achieving the universal business objectives of customer satisfaction, continuous improvement of quality, operating cost reduction, capital cost reduction and reduced 'time to market'.

It was shown that to meet all these objectives 'over the wall' sequential development has to be substituted by simultaneous engineering, performed by teams that include materials suppliers, component suppliers, equipment suppliers, internal experts, and, possibly, experts from the science base. Pre-sourcing, rather than competitive bidding to a detailed specification is necessary to identify the supplier members of the SE team.

Corporate cultures and individual training must be conducive to cross-functional and inter-company partnerships and team working, and the teams need tools and techniques that enable them to contribute their specialist expertise. Some of the tools and techniques were described.

The need to expand SE to facilitate early application of new materials and processes was described, with its implications for collaborative alliances embracing the science base. This led to substitution of the 'supply system' concept for the 'supply chain' if all participants are to work concurrently. Management of the resultant complex relationships was shown to require engineers with interpersonal and communication skills, as well as technical expertise.

REFERENCES

1. *Harvard Business Review* (1990). 4th Quarter
2. Box, G. (1994) 'Statistics and quality improvement'. *Journal of the Royal Statistical Society*, 157 part 2. This article describes the removal of process disturbances as 'statistical process control' and the step-change to compensate for disturbances as 'engineering process control'. This is rather kind to engineers. The same article gives some interesting views on the education of engineers and statisticians.
3. Dussauge, P., Hart, S. and Ramanautsun, B. (1993) *Strategic Technology Management*, John Wiley & Sons, Chichester.
4. Leadbeater, C. (1991) Design-led change: from quantity to quality. *Financial Times* 14 August.
5. Murray, I. (1991) Bonn's rail jewel is crown of thorns. *The Times*, 11 April.
6. Bond, M. (1991) Design delays will cut income for Eurotunnel. *The Times*, 9 April.
7. An article entitled 'Triple Seven' in the May 1993 issue of British Airways' BA Engineering house journal describes the scope and benefits of SE on this project. A shorter article 'Boeing, Boeing' in BA's *Business Life* December/January 1993/4 in-flight magazine provides similar information. A more accessible article, Genesis of a giant, by Guy Norris appeared in *Flight International* 31 August–6 September 1994.
8. *Pharmaceutical Successes* (1993) CBI Manufacturing Bulletin No. 5 September. The article gives a brief profile of the UK pharmaceutical industry.
9. Rosenblatt, A. and Watson, G. (editors) (1991) *Concurrent Engineering*. Spectrum magazine of the IEEE, New York, July 1991. The report also gives a list of terms and techniques and a bibliography.
10. *Constructing the Team* (1994) Sir Michael Latham, HMSO, London.
11. Lutz R. A. (1994) *The Re-engineering of Chrysler*. Hinton Memorial Lecture. Royal Academy of Engineering. London, October.
12. A car is born, *Business Week* 13 September (1993) describes Honda's development of the 1994 Accord. The article gives some insights into Honda's new product development and corporate strategies. It mentions that 33 Japanese and 28 American suppliers were involved, who between them provided 60 to 70% of the car's value.
13. Hauser, J. R. and Clausing D. (1988) The house of quality. *Harvard Business Review*, May–June.
14. IM is described in 'Interactive Management' by Hammer, K. and Janes, F. R., in the *Journal of Operational Research Society* OR *Insight*, 3, 1, Jan–March 1990.
15. Lipson, C. and Sheth, N. J. (1973) *Statistical Design and Analysis of Engineering Experiments*. McGraw-Hill.
16. Towards a Comprehensive Materials Balance. *Siemens R&D Review* Fall 1993.
17. Research comes back to the nest (1992) *Financial Times* 14 July 1992
18. Pralahad, R. and Hamel, G. (1990) Core competence and the concept of the corporation. *Harvard Business Review*.
19. Kaounides, L. (1995) Advanced Materials Technologies: Management and Government Strategies in the 90s. *Financial Times Management Reports*, London.

BIBLIOGRAPHY

Concurrent Engineering — Concepts, Implementation and Practice, edited by C. S. Syan and U. Menon, Chapman & Hall London 1994, gives an overview of the history, tools and techniques of Concurrent Engineering. Chapter 2, *The Ford Experience* by J. V. Chelsom describes two examples of concurrent engineering from the European automotive industry and compares management of these new product programmes with similar programmes without CE.

Simultaneous Engineering — the Executive Guide 2e, Hartley J. and Mortimer J., Industrial Newsletters, Dunstable 1991, with contributions by J. V. Chelsom, provides many examples of automotive industry practice, and explanations of some of the SE/CE tools.

7

Organizations

7.1 INTRODUCTION

The development of organization structures has proceeded along lines similar to early attempts to improve labour productivity. Activities became more and more specialized, and at the same time there were increasing efforts to measure and control the performance of the specialists. The main debate was about centralization or decentralization of management control, with general acceptance of a broad division between 'staff' and 'line' functions. These divisions of labour, combined with personal reward systems and status linked to numbers of personnel controlled, led to the growth of bureaucratic hierarchies ill-equipped to deal with changing customer requirements and social developments.

Various alternatives to staff and line were attempted, with much attention being paid to organizational change in the hope of achieving faster development of new products. Where western manufacturers have modelled their organizations on successful Japanese companies the results have often been disappointing — because the changes have not been accompanied by fundamental changes of attitude and corporate culture. To be competitive in quality, cost and innovation, it is necessary to remove internal barriers to communication and teamwork, and to give the new product design teams direct access to external customers, who may be the best source of new product ideas, as well as to team members from suppliers who may be the best source of new process ideas.

A major reason for the internal barriers and lack of teamwork in western engineering organizations is the widespread adoption of the structures and control systems introduced at General Motors Corporation of the USA, in the early 1920s. Centralized control of these western companies has often been dominated by the finance function, which, as a result of consistently recruiting and training the best graduates, was staffed by very talented people who were able to out-debate engineers, even in engineering matters. Manufacturing and engineering people have not only been out-debated, they have been outstripped in the promotion stakes as a result of their lack of business and communication skills.

This chapter examines the development of organizations from simple structures designed to assist management, through a stage where centralization provided effective management control, and a further stage where organizational complexity became an obstacle, until the present day when efforts are being made to recreate simplicity and responsiveness.

7.2   GROWTH OF THE HIERARCHIES

The original divisions between staff and line were simple enough: line were the doers — product designers, producers, and sellers and service people — staff were enablers — they kept the accounts, handled personnel matters, interpreted the law, etc. Organizations were correspondingly simple, as shown in Figure 7.1.

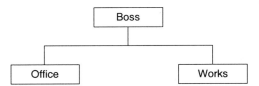

Figure 7.1   The first stage of organizational development

In this first stage of development, the boss employed an office manager to take care of everything in the offices, and a works manager to take care of everything in the works.

As the business grew, the division of labour principle was applied to the offices as well as the works, and the organization became more complicated. The boss acquired a grander title, such as chief executive officer (CEO). This is shown in Figure 7.2.

Then the organization became more complicated still, with sales becoming sales and marketing, accounts becoming accounting and financial analysis, personnel becoming labour relations, organization planning, training and recruitment, management development, etc.

Complexity bred complexity, and financial analysis developed into project analysis, budget analysis, manufacturing cost analysis, purchase cost analysis, analysis cost analysis (!) and many more. Then, with the setting up of separate product divisions, or regional divisions, the whole structure was replicated at

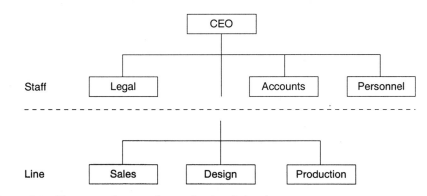

Figure 7.2   The second stage of organizational development

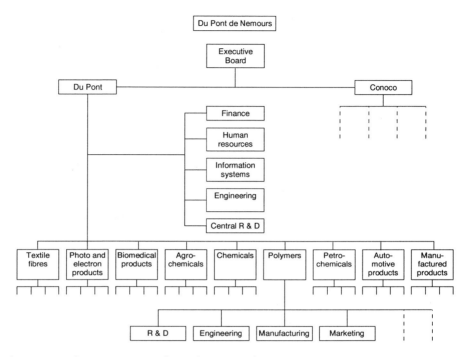

Figure 7.3   The organization chart of Du Pont de Nemours

lower levels and the original staff activities were elevated to a new 'corporate staff' status — see for example the chart for Du Pont in Figure 7.3.

The chart in Figure 7.3 shows some of the structure for the polymers division, with some duplication of the central staff functions — engineering and R&D, for example. Similar structures exist in the other product divisions. What the chart does *not* show is the extent to which the polymers division is allowed to act independently, or to what extent its management is controlled by the executive board or central staff. The difference is a matter of corporate *culture* or *style,* rather than one of *organizational structure*, a very important distinction. If the divisions are fully empowered, with delegated authority to manage their own affairs, they can be regarded as separate or strategic business units (SBUs), which are discussed later in this chapter. If the divisions are centrally controlled, they are just part of the total Du Pont bureaucratic hierarchy, and will behave in a completely different way from an SBU.

The growth of such hierarchies in many western engineering companies provided wonderful career opportunities, particularly if combined with a job evaluation or grading system that gave credit for the number of employees supervised. Three or more analysts doing similar work would be coordinated by a senior analyst, and a section of nine or ten analysts with three senior analysts would acquire a supervisor. The need to coordinate three or four supervisors would lead to the appointment of a manager to manage them, and four or five managers would be headed by a director. Directors might be exalted to the status

Engineering staff

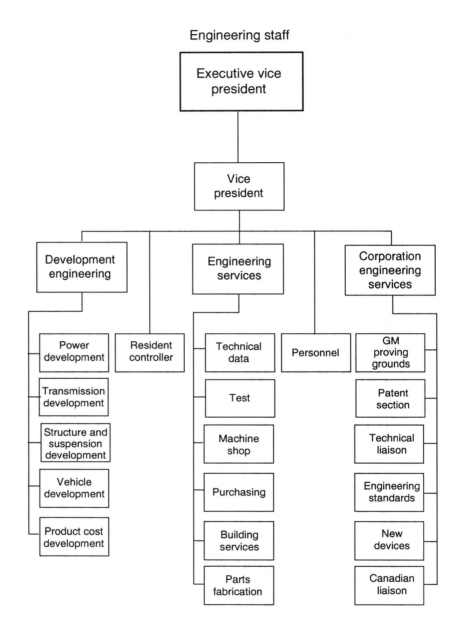

June 1963

Figure 7.4 Engineering and manufacturing organizational structure at General Motors

Manufacturing staff

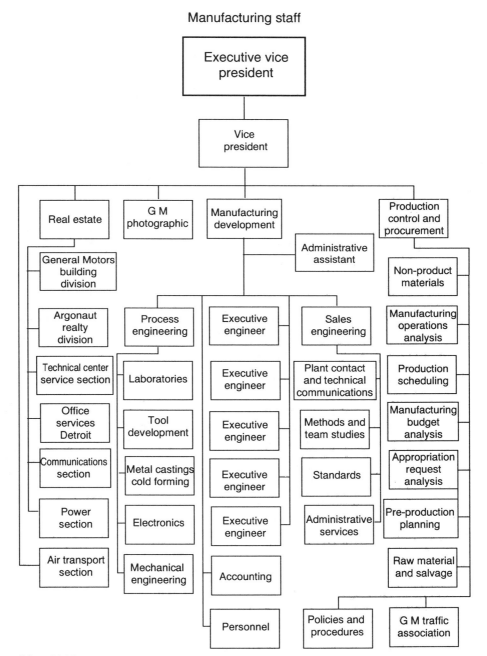

May 1963
©1963 by Alfred P. Sloan, Jr. © renewed 1991 by Alfred P. Sloan
Foundation. Reprinted by permission of Harold Matson Company
Inc.

of executive director, and enough of these would generate their very own vice-president, or even an executive vice-president.

These organizational developments are part of the problems of growth (doing more of the same thing) and development (doing something different), which sooner or later lead to the business becoming too big for the owner/manager or small generalist team. Hence the 'division of labour' in the offices as well as on the shop floor.

The dangers of monolithic structures — slow reactions, stifled initiative, poor communication etc., were recognized by many companies, and for a long time the most effective response was some form of decentralization. One of the most successful examples was General Motors (GM), which grew by acquisition over a period of less than ten years from one car producer to a raft of vehicle and component companies, too complex to be managed by the original entrepreneur, William C. Durant. It took the systems of Du Pont, who bought a major shareholding in GM, and the genius of Alfred P. Sloan, who came to GM with one of their acquisitions, to establish the pattern of central financial control and decentralized operations that provided the model for many other successful organizations. From the early 1920s, when Sloan became head of GM, the combination of his skills and Du Pont's financial control systems enabled GM to become by 1962 the world's largest industrial company. But by the 1970s, Sloan's creation was beginning to prove inadequate for the changed customer requirements of that decade. Some of the GM organization charts from 1963 are shown in Figure 7.4.

It is possible to get some idea from the charts in Figure 7.4 of the bureaucracy that weighed GM down, but there were even more barriers than the charts can display. The chart 'engineering division divisions' in Figure 7.5 hints at these barriers.

The product development division is shown divided according to the length of time separating the subdivision's work from its application to the product. The manufacturing division is divided according to the type of engineering function performed. In an automotive company there would be further vertical divisions by vehicle type or by manufacturing activity, as shown in Figure 7.6.

There is no way to illustrate the barriers caused by personal attitudes within and between these divisions, but the most frequent analogy is the 'organizational chimneys' — as illustrated in Figure 7.7.

Information or an idea had to go all the way up one chimney, say the product development chimney, (with wider and wider gaps to bridge between levels of

Product engineering	Manufacturing engineering
Vehicle engineering System engineering Component engineering Advanced engineering Development engineering Research engineering	Process engineering Industrial engineering Tooling engineering Safety engineering Quality engineering Plant engineering

Figure 7.5 Engineering division divisions

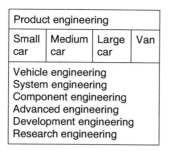

Product engineering			
Small car	Medium car	Large car	Van
Vehicle engineering System engineering Component engineering Advanced engineering Development engineering Research engineering			

Manufacturing engineering		
Power train	Body and assembly	Component plants
Process engineering Industrial engineering Tooling engineering Safety engineering Quality engineering Plant engineering		

Figure 7.6 More engineering division divisions

organization within the chimney) before it could cross to, say, the manufacturing chimney down which it had to make its way to the expert who could provide a sensible response. The response had to follow the same tortuous route in reverse. In many companies, this crossover at the top of the chimneys was complicated by conflict between the two functions.

The finance activity, which had responsibility for providing management with the means to exercise central control, was often blamed for fostering this conflict. They had become disablers rather than enablers, allocators of goals and blame, rather than providers of advice and assistance.

Companies with strong finance activities and with 'divide-and-rule' policies were common in North America, and their management style was widely copied in the West until the 1980s. The strength of the finance departments stemmed from three factors:

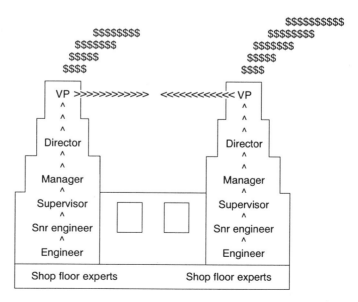

Figure 7.7 Organizational chimneys

(1) their location at the top centre of organizations
(2) the role of 'controllers' assigned to them by 'Sloanism'
(3) their policy of recruiting the best graduates

Hayes [1] in a chapter entitled 'The Making of a Management' describes Ford's recruiting policies in the USA as follows:

'The top three graduates from Carnegie regularly went to Ford year after year. By 1969 the company's remarkable hiring offensive had recruited twelve hundred executives with MBA degrees, and twenty two hundred with undergraduate degrees in business administration. Half of the MBAs had engineering degrees as well. Most of them were in finance . . . Neither Manufacturing nor Engineering placed the same emphasis on the calibre of its recruits . . . It was not surprising that they were so often out-debated in their own specialty by finance men.' [1]

Not only were the manufacturing and engineering people out-debated, they were also outstripped in the promotion stakes as a result of their inability to shine in discussions, and their lack of business skills.

Placed in corporate staff at the top of organizations divided into functional chimneys, talented people like those recruited by Ford finance became one of the major inhibitors to teamwork and rapid new product development. Halberstam quotes Hal Sperlich, who was vice-president of product development at Ford, and later at Chrysler to illustrate this:

'One of the worst things about being in a finance-driven company was that it took the men from manufacturing and product, men who should have been natural allies, and made them into constant antagonists.' [2]

The organization, recruitment and personal development policies of Japanese engineering companies enable them to avoid this divisiveness. Promising engineers are given the opportunity of education in management, and are placed in a variety of functions within the company. As a result, there are people in sales, finance, personnel and corporate planning with technical and business skills.

Two charts in Figures 7.8 and 7.9 illustrate (for fictitious companies) the differences in organizational location of engineers and technologists in Japanese and western engineering companies.

The shaded areas in the charts represent engineers and technologists. In the Japanese company these people are dispersed throughout the organization, and they form the majority in the upper echelons. In the western company, the engineers and technologists are shown to stay in R&D, product development and manufacturing — the functions to which they were recruited — and to be outnumbered in the upper echelons.

7.3 TEAM TIME

It was the early 1980s before most of the megalith organizations recognized the need to change, and in particular to change their new product development process and their attitude to employees. Teamwork and employee involvement became the order of the decade.

Penetration of management hierarchy by staff with technical background

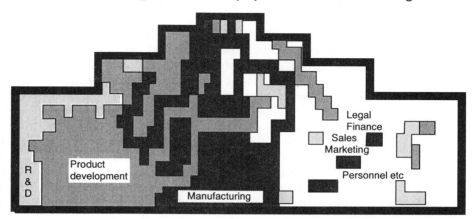

Figure 7.8 Typical Japanese Engineering Company

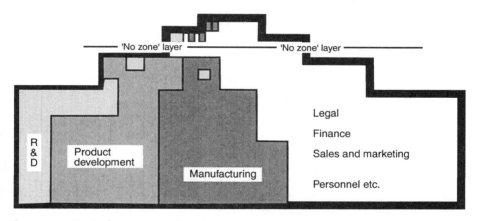

Figure 7.9 Typical western engineering company

In the late 1970s and early 1980s, (as described in Chapter 3) two separate sets of studies came to similar conclusions. One set was conducted by the wave of westerners going to Japan to try to identify reasons for the success of so many Japanese companies in export markets. The other — in some ways a deliberate counter to the first — was an examination of US and European companies by the management consultants McKinsey and Co., which came up with their 7Ss of management, and subsequently the 'search for excellence' in American companies, using the 7S structure as an analytical tool. (The work was popularized by Peters and Waterman in their book *In Search of Excellence* [3] and in Peters' road show and videos.)

The conclusions included the view that teamwork was essential for rapid new product development and for continuous improvement of quality and, hence, productivity. Since then, several organizational schemes designed to encourage cross-functional cooperation have been developed, and many programmes to change corporate cultures have been started.

General Motors, for example, in 1982, began a restructuring of their product development and manufacturing staff [4]. Instead of being in two separate chimneys, product design engineers and manufacturing process engineers were brought together in two huge teams. One was concerned with existing products, called 'current engineering and manufacturing services'; the other, dealt with longer term projects and was named 'advanced product and manufacturing engineering'. At the same time, the whole of the North American GM operations embarked on programmes to promote employee participation, under the heading 'quality of worklife'. Ten years later they were still working on it.

The main reason for this, and other changes mentioned below, not being pursued to completion was a dramatic recovery in the US car market in the mid 1980s. This enabled GM and Ford to make record profits by doing what they had done in the past: sell big cars and small trucks and to benefit briefly from their partly implemented programmes.

Ironically, Alfred P. Sloan the long-time head of GM had warned of this 'danger of success'. In 1963 he wrote:

'Success may bring self satisfaction. In that event the urge for competitive survival, the strongest of all economic incentives, is dulled. The spirit of venture is lost in the inertia of the mind against change. When such influences develop, growth may be arrested, caused by a failure to recognize advancing technology or altered consumer needs, or perhaps by competition that is more virile and aggressive'. [5]

GM also initiated a change to 'programme management', so that new car development programmes were each directed by one senior manager, with their own teams of product engineers, production engineers, stylists, market researchers, finance people and materials management etc., and responsibility from product concept through to the start of production. This type of structure is often called 'heavy programme management' (see for example Dussauge, Hart and Ramanautsen [6]). A similar style, where the specialists participate in the team effort, but remain part of their parent function is known as 'lightweight programme management'.

Both of these styles are western versions of something seen in successful Japanese companies, but they have rarely been successfully copied. The teams have instead become another part of the bureaucracy, watchers and reporters rather than doers.

However, the Chrysler Corporation has developed a successful form of programme management that is *not* copied from the Japanese. In 1990, faced with disastrous business performance and the prospect of bankruptcy, Chrysler embarked on a complete 're-engineering' of the company, which included the introduction of what they call the 'platform team organization'. Robert Lutz, President of Chrysler has said:

'We did indeed study, and learn from, many companies, including — yes — some Japanese companies. And, tough as it was to do, we also said "Rest in peace" to the "old Chrysler" and left it to die.' [7]

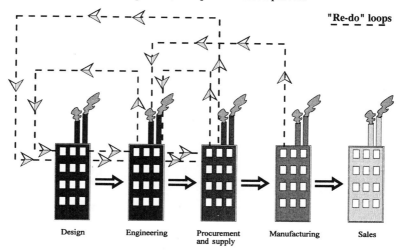

Figure 7.10 Traditional vehicle development process at Chrysler

Lutz describes how Chrysler moved from development of new products by 'traditional, vertically-oriented functional departments' (shown in Figure 7.10), which had become '. . . little bureaucratic empires . . . just chock-full of "re-do loops" — mis-communications, false starts, doubling back to do again what should have been done right the first time . . . because nobody really worked together as a team'.

Lutz also describes why Chrysler changed its methods and organization:

'. . . this system did indeed serve Detroit fairly well for decades. But in this new era of intense global international competition, products simply weren't being developed fast enough, inexpensively enough, or — truth be told — *good* enough.' [7]

Chrysler introduced four 'platform teams', named after the basic underpinnings, or 'platform' of any given vehicle type, as shown in Figure 7.11.

Each of Chrysler's platform teams is headed by a truly empowered leader. The success of these teams is due in large part to the fact that the leaders are not empowered by top management — the leaders *are* top management. Each leader is also an operating vice-president, as shown in Figure 7.12. According to Lutz:

'What this does is create a natural interdependency among and between our key people and their organizations. For instance, our team leader for large cars — who's also our Vice-President for Procurement and Supply — is motivated to help our team leader for minivans in any way he can. That's because he, in turn, needs the help of the minivan leader — who's also our Executive Vice-President for Sales and Marketing — when it comes to *marketing* his large cars. [7]

Chrysler's re-engineering of their entire organization produced a turnround in their business performance within three years. A description of the transformation of Chrysler's business performance is given in Chapter 8.

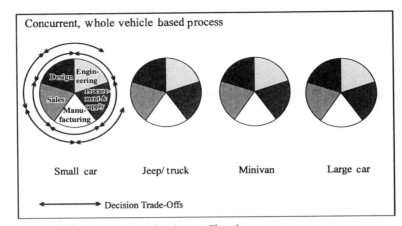

Figure 7.11 Platform team organization at Chrysler

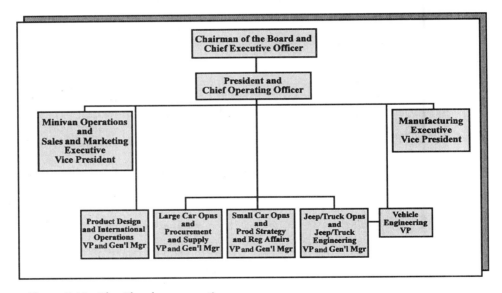

Figure 7.12 The Chrysler corporation

Another American automotive industry example of organizational change has been slower to benefit total corporate performance, but, nonetheless, shows recognition of the need to change from functional chimneys to a team-based organization.

The example comes from GM who embarked on another dramatic effort to shake off the burden of bureaucracy: they formed a completely new company, the Saturn Motor Co., entirely separate from the rest of the corporation — separate geographically, financially and psychologically.

This is the first all-new GM company since 1918, and is providing a sort of test bed for new ways of managing just about everything — from production to procurement, and design to distribution. It is an expensive test: the cost of the new facilities in Nashville Tennessee was about $17 billion — but it may point the way to GM's salvation. The Saturn Car Company has already achieved a great deal, though the experience has not yet been used to change GM's overall organization or practices. Saturn's successful Just-in-Time or 'lean' manufacturing is used as an example in Chapter 20, at the end of section 20.4.2.

The Saturn Car Company is a separate (or strategic) business unit (SBU). Dividing a company into a series of SBUs is another of the organizational alternatives for companies seeking the same results as heavy or light programme management: that is, closer contact with customer needs, closer links between R&D and the production process, better communication, greater employee participation.

Pralahad and Hamel [8] argue that SBUs have a number of disadvantages:

- no SBU feels responsible for maintaining a viable position in core products, nor able to justify the investment required to build world leadership in a core competence;
- resources can become 'imprisoned' in an SBU;
- world-class research can take place in laboratories without it impacting any business of the firm.

The Nestlé food and confectionery company restructured in 1990 in an attempt to overcome this gap between research and the rest of the business, while securing the benefits of SBUs. Each SBU has a representative of R&D assigned to it as a sort of research sales representative, since research is expected to treat the SBUs as clients [9]. Nestlé's recognition of the need to exert 'market pull' on its R&D activities is an example that engineering managers should follow, even though a Swiss chocolate company may seem to be rather different from their own. However, there is a fine example of an engineering organizational innovation from Switzerland which is described in the next section.

7.4   THINK GLOBAL, ACT LOCAL

The phrase 'Think global, act local' summarizes the strategy of ASEA Brown Boveri (ABB), probably the most successful example of another organizational style known as 'matrix' management.

The usual matrix organization has products on one axis, and functions on the other, as illustrated in Figure 7.13. In the matrix organization each product has a product manager, who draws on the specialist functional resources to handle implementation of their plans. This is not far distant from the lightweight programme manager concept, or the brand manager approach of companies such as Procter & Gamble or Unilever, where the Brand Manager has responsibility for design, manufacture, marketing and distribution of a washing powder, a food product etc.

Matrix organizations can be effective on a national scale, to help multi-product companies coordinate the use of resources that are required for the design and manufacture of more than one of the products. The most common, and most

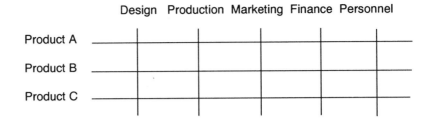

Figure 7.13 The matrix organization

effective, application of matrix organizations, however, is when they are used to manage resources on a global scale.

Electronics and electrical companies such as Korea's Samsung, and Japan's Matsushita and Sony, as well as the Japanese automotive companies Toyota, Nissan and Honda have global strategies of designing a product in one place only and manufacturing it in several places geographically 'close to the customer', but generally their organizations are not in the matrix form. The Dutch electrical company, Philips, as well as IBM and Ford have organizations which are somewhere between the Korean/Japanese pattern and the matrix form. Their variation involves setting up 'centres of excellence' or 'centres of responsibility', which have global or regional responsibility for designing or making one product line for which the centre has special skills. Without firm direction from corporate management, however, such centres will find their work being redone or duplicated on the grounds of 'not invented here'.

Where ABB has differed from most companies using the matrix structure, and from those using the centres of excellence approach, is in the use of local, national heads, who have shared responsibility for all ABB products in that country — shared with product line managers who have global responsibilities. Up to 1992 the ABB product lines were organized into eight groups, as shown in Figure 7.14.

The national CEOs were coordinated in five regional groups: Europe EC; Europe EFTA; North America; Latin America/Africa; Asia/Australia.

In 1993, ABB simplified their organizational superstructure by consolidating into four product segments, plus financial services, and three regions: Europe, The Americas and Asia/Pacific. Their central staff in Switzerland was reduced to less than 100 employees. The revised structure is shown in Figure 7.15.

At the same time, ABB strengthened local capabilities by establishing about 5000 independent profit centres around the world. Each profit centre had about 50 employees and complete delegated responsibility for running their part of the business. (This kind of delegation is called 'empowerment'. It should be preceded by training in decision making, so that the employees are able to use their newly-delegated power.) Some of the coordinating levels of management were removed, so that there are only two levels of management between the employees in the profit centres and the executive committee in Zurich. These two levels are the 5000 profit centre heads, and the 250 business area/country managers. (This removal of supervising and coordinating management has been widely practised in the West,

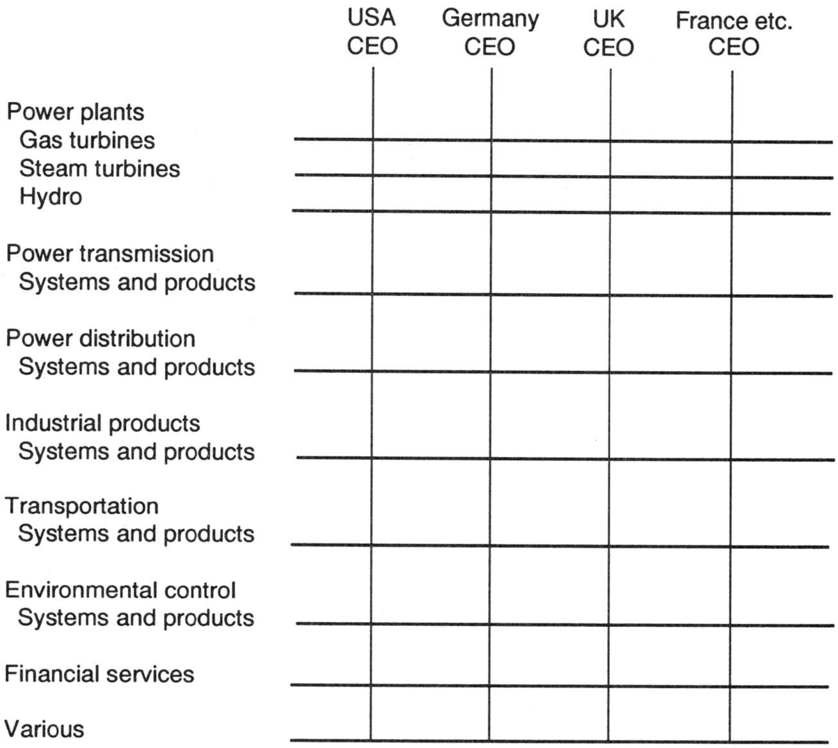

	USA CEO	Germany CEO	UK CEO	France etc. CEO
Power plants Gas turbines Steam turbines Hydro				
Power transmission Systems and products				
Power distribution Systems and products				
Industrial products Systems and products				
Transportation Systems and products				
Environmental control Systems and products				
Financial services				
Various				

Each of the product divisions – power plants, power transmission etc., had its own design, production, marketing and other activities shown for product A, product B etc. in Figure 7.13.

Figure 7.14   ABB's product line/national matrix

and has been described as 'delayering'.) The flat, decentralized organization is shown in Figure 7.16.

Having started a customer focus programme in 1990, ABB shifted management efforts away from the reshaping of organizational entities to concentrate on improving business processes as the route to improved quality, faster completion of orders and all the other business objectives that lead to customer satisfaction, (listed in Chapter 2). As a result of focusing on business processes and meeting customer needs, ABB have dismantled the hierarchies of the original ASEA and Brown Boveri companies that were merged in January 1988 to form ABB, and have significantly improved their business performance.

As ABB have concluded, organizational structures are really secondary to business processes. It can be argued that with the right attitudes, any organization can be made to work. Equally, with the wrong attitudes, no form of organization will work. To get the right attitudes, the right processes and the right

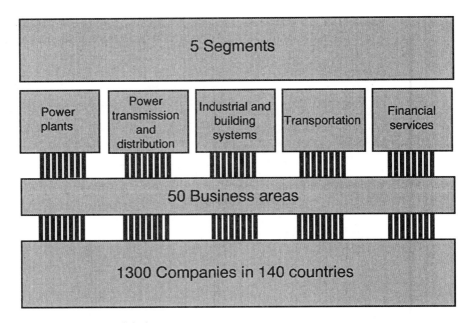

Figure 7.15 ABB global structure

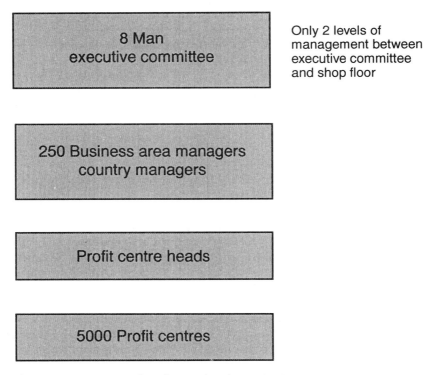

Figure 7.16 ABB — a flat, decentralized organization

organization, requires a holistic approach to business management. Chapter 8 gives some examples of companies that have managed to succeed in this respect.

7.5 SUMMARY

This chapter has traced the development of organization structures from a simple means of sharing management responsibilities and tasks into a series of boundaries that divide companies:

- vertically — into functional 'chimneys', and
- horizontally — into 'staff' and 'line' activities.

It was noted that organizations with hierarchical structures resulting from the management style of A. P. Sloan Jr, with their centralized financial control of separate operating divisions, were unable to respond to the challenges of the 1970s. Despite having been successful at General Motors for 50 years and serving as a model for many other engineering companies, these structures had become obstacles to communication and inhibitors to rapid response to customer needs.

Some alternative organizational arrangements were described, such as heavy and light programme management, separate or strategic business units and matrix management.

The special form of matrix management organization developed by ABB was given as an example of the 'delayering' of hierarchies, and the benefits of focusing first on process improvement, then on organization, rather than the other way round.

REFERENCES

1. Hayes, W. (1990) *Henry — A Life of Henry Ford II*. Weidenfeld and Nicholson, London.
2. Halberstam, D. (1986) *The Reckoning*. William Morrow & Co, New York. This 751 page book compares and contrasts the development and management of Nissan and Ford. Chapter 17, 'Deming Finds an Audience' reveals the basic differences in corporate culture between American and Japanese car companies.
3. Peters, T. and Waterman, R. (1982) *In Search of Excellence: Lessons from America's Best-run Companies*. Harper & Row, New York. Tom Peters has changed his mind about what the lessons were, and some of the 'excellent' companies have suffered in the market place since the book was written. Nevertheless, they were successful for many years, and the lessons are there to be considered.
4. Will success spoil General Motors? *Fortune Magazine* 22 August 1983.
5. Sloan, A. P. Jr (1963) *My Years with General Motors*. Pan Books, London.
6. Dussauge, P., Hart, S. and Ramanautsen, B. (1993) *Strategic Technology Management*, Chapter 8. John Wiley & Sons, Chichester.
7. Lutz, R A. (1994) *Re-engineering the Corporation for the '90s*. The 1994 Christopher Hinton Lecture, delivered to The Royal Academy of Engineering 4 October 1994.
8. Pralahad, R. and Hamel, G. (1990) Core competence of the Corporation. *Harvard Business Review*, May–June issue, **90311**.
9. Research comes back to the nest. An article in the *Financial Times* on 14 July 1991, describes Nestlé's reorganization of their R&D activities to bring them closer to the market place.

BIBLIOGRAPHY

The logic of global business (an interview with ABB Chief Executive, Percy Barnevik) *Harvard Business Review*, March/April (1991) describes Barnevik's vision of ABB's development.

Resetting the clock and ABB managers strip for action also give information about ABB's restructuring. These articles appeared in the *Financial Times* on 10 February 1993 and 25 August 1993 respectively.

8

Managing to succeed

8.1 INTRODUCTION

This chapter draws together the separate themes of Chapters 1–7. It starts with a general diagnosis of the shortcomings of many western engineering companies, but shows that there are companies that have managed to succeed against a background of changing customer requirements and a changing business environment.

Earlier chapters have shown that technological change is going to be the most demanding management challenge of the 1990s and the early years of the next century. Zero defects quality and Just-in-Time (JIT), or 'lean manufacturing' are going to be the performance base from which excellent companies build their lead in customer care through technological advances in materials, products and processes.

Engineers and technologists will be the key players in creating that performance base, and managing the new technological developments, through *teams* containing in-house and supplier and customer members. In these teams, engineers not only have to work with other engineers in new cooperative ways, they also have to work with economists, sociologists, accountants and lawyers.

This chapter looks for models of the organizations, methods, skills and style that will typify the excellent companies of the next century. By learning from these examples of companies that have 'managed to succeed' potential engineering managers can prepare for a role in the development or creation of other successful companies. There are also lessons to be drawn from companies that have not kept up with competition and change, and the chapter includes some of these.

8.2 SLOWLY SINKING IN THE WEST

There are some general explanations for the widespread failures of western engineering management in the past decade. The inability of many companies to respond to the changed needs of their customers can be attributed to five major weaknesses.

8.2.1 Western weakness number 1

Application of 'Taylorist' specialization, and 'Sloanist' divide-and-rule policies created bureaucratic, top-heavy organizations which have:

- obstructed internal communication
- created warring internal 'empires'
- destroyed cooperation and teamwork
- focused attention on internal conflicts rather than the outside customer.

The narcissistic style of large corporations has been copied by some small and medium sized enterprises too, who, far too soon, turned themselves from 'Stepfoot and Son' into 'The Stepfoot Group of Companies', complete with executive directors or vice-presidents.

Consequently, in large and small companies, employees have been placed in organizational *boxes*, with restricted responsibilities. They have been invited to leave their brains and initiative behind when they come to work.

To overcome this weakness, engineers, and other specialists, have to rise above the rim of their boxes and look downstream to their customers — internal and external — and upstream to their suppliers, also internal and external. They have to ensure that they understand their customers' needs, and that their own needs are understood by their suppliers.

8.2.2   Western weakness number 2

Performance measurement and reward systems in many companies have encouraged employees to concentrate on demonstrating their individual abilities, or, at best, the abilities and strengths of their own department, rather than working in cooperation with other company activities, and with customers and suppliers. For design engineers or manufacturing engineers to seek or accept advice (particularly from suppliers) has been regarded as a sign of weakness, or even a sign of incompetence. Dictatorial management styles, combined with divisive organizational structures and individual-focused performance measurement, have led many engineers to adopt confrontational *attitudes*, and to have a self-regard verging on arrogance.

To rectify this, when they do come out of their boxes, engineers need to listen and learn, to communicate and cooperate.

8.2.3   Western weakness number 3

The third weakness is *success*: something which Sloan [1] warned could bring:

- self-satisfaction,
- dulling of the urge for competitive survival,
- loss of the spirit of venture in the inertia of the mind against change,
- arrested growth or decline, caused by failure to recognize advancing technology, or altered customer needs, or competition that is more virile and aggressive.

General Motors itself, as well as IBM, Xerox and Pan-Am Airlines have all been blinded by their own success, and suffered in the way that Sloan predicted.

'Benchmarking', the practice of comparing a company's performance with that of successful companies in other industries, or with the company's most successful competitors, has similar risks. If the company making the comparisons finds that it performs better than the industry average, or that some parts of their company are 'world-class', there is the same danger of self-satisfaction and reduced spirit of venture.

The dangers of success can be avoided by embracing the policy of never-ending improvement. As soon as one success is looming, engineers should be working towards the next success, and the next after that.

8.2.4   Western weakness number 4

The fourth weakness is *imitation*. Too many western companies have identified what they believed to be the practices, policies, strategies or structures that generate superior performance by their competitors, particularly Japanese competitors, and have sought to copy them. When this has been done without complete understanding of why and how these practices, policies etc., work the attempts at imitation have been detrimental rather than beneficial.

Robert Lutz, President of the Chrysler Corporation has said that Chrysler has learned from studying the Japanese, but warned against superficial attempts to copy them. He uses an analogy to make his point. This is taken from a discussion following the 1994 Christopher Hinton Lecture:

'A four year old child wants to learn how to swim. The child's father takes the child next door where they have a pool, and encourages his child to watch the neighbour's four year old swimming up and down the length of the pool. After ten minutes father asks 'Have you got the idea?' The child says 'Yes', so the father throws the child in and it drowns.'

Attempts to introduce total quality management, Just-in-Time materials management or simultaneous engineering without first providing employee and supplier training in the new philosophies, or without management belief in and understanding of the philosophies can be almost as disastrous as the swimming lesson.

Engineers should make sure they fully understand what they observe, add their own expertise to adapt what is beneficial to their own circumstances, and practise the new methods on a limited scale until their local applicability is proven.

8.2.5   Western weakness number 5

The fifth weakness is the inability to recognize, foresee and manage *change*. This is particularly damaging when combined with the dangers of success. Sloan [1] actually lists it as one of the dangers of success. Sloan explained GM's replacement of Ford as leader of the US car market by saying of Henry Ford I: 'The old master has failed to master change'.

It was change in market requirements that Henry Ford I failed to master. The same can be said of IBM, Xerox, British Motor Corporation (BMC) and most of the European automotive component producers. In the later guise of British Leyland, BMC plus its acquisitions repeated the mistake.

It is not only market place changes that need to be managed. All the external factors listed in Chapter 2 have to be carefully monitored. These include technology, legislation, exchange rates, demography, political, educational and sociological trends, as well as internal factors such as employee aspirations and abilities.

Most companies can react successfully to dramatic change, such as a factory burning down or being flooded. Such disasters receive focused attention, and often generate a strong team spirit among the whole workforce in their efforts to recover the situation.

It is the slower, more fundamental changes that are not well managed. Senge [2] borrows an analogy from Tichy to illustrate this management weakness. With apologies to animal lovers and environmentalists it is as follows:

'Attempts to boil a frog by dropping it into boiling water fail because the frog reacts to the dramatic change by jumping out of the pot. However, if the frog can be lured into the pot with a few flies and a lily pad, and the water is gradually warmed, the result is different. The frog may feel more comfortable as the water warms, and not notice until it is too late that the water is boiling, and end up dead.'

Engineers should be constantly alert to changes in their own working environment and in their company's environment to avoid a comfortable, but premature curtailment of their careers.

8.2.6 Forward to BASICS

The five weaknesses can be overcome by BASIC behaviour. The 1990s BASICS for engineers is as follows:

- Boxes   — get out of them to listen and learn with your customers and suppliers.
- Attitudes — be team players, not stars; seek cooperation not confrontation; consider the other point of view; accept that there are experts other than yourself.
- Success   — don't be blinded by it. Remember Sloan's advice.
- Imitation — what works for others may not work for you. 'It is no use simply to take on board the latest flavour of the month such as quality circles, . . . only to find that these concepts cannot be successfully transported to an environment which remains alien to it.' [3] Listen, learn, but add your own magic.
- Change   — don't be a boiled frog.

If an 'S' is required, be 'Systemic' — take a holistic view and work on management of people, quality, materials, new products and new technologies, and customer and supplier relationships concurrently. That is what the successful companies do. Who some of them are, and how they do it are covered in the balance of this chapter.

8.3   DOES ANYBODY KNOW THE WAY? SIGNS FROM THE 1980s

What should be examined, and who should be followed to find the way to succeed?

There is no point in looking at organization structures, they tell us nothing. It is the way people behave within, between and outside their organizational boxes that makes the difference. So are there models of successful behaviour from which general rules can be derived?

The two long-time models and longer-time largest industrial corporations in the world, General Motors and Ford, are both struggling with the same issues of inadequate quality, bureaucracy, long lead times, and uncompetitive costs and are trying to recover from record breaking losses. Ford's solution (a plan, labelled Ford 2000, to create a truly global corporation) has not yet been tested, and GM has been slow to develop a solution. Where else can we look?

From the top European companies, Royal Dutch/Shell may give one of the best leads towards the way to succeed. They have moved from being one of the marginal members of 'The Seven Sisters' (as the world's leading oil companies were known in the 1970s) to being the largest company in Europe, ahead of BP, and consistently one of the most profitable oil companies. One of the management actions contributing to this improvement is a process which Shell has called 'planning as learning' [4]. This involved all the senior managers in 'What if?' business games — such as 'What would Shell do if the price of crude oil increased fourfold?'. The resultant plans, which had been developed jointly by the top managers, were filed, and when one of the apparently unlikely events actually happened Shell were much faster to respond than their competitors. The planning-as-learning process also helped Shell's performance by changing managers' perceptions of themselves, their jobs, their markets, the company and their competitors. This gives three interesting characteristics of a successful company and its management:

- a dramatic performance shift
- a built-in learning process
- a change in management outlook.

There are others who have done something similar. Two who had a dramatic performance shift forced upon them are Xerox and IBM, and their responses are described below.

Having lost their world dominance of the plain paper copier market to the Japanese, Xerox used to be the case study example of American business downfall, but they are now used as a benchmark company that has turned itself around from loser to winner.

They embarked on a five-year programme to become a total quality company, after a six month study by a 25 strong task force. The key elements of the Xerox transition process, and the five stages of their 'leadership through quality' plan are shown in Chapter 4. Aspects of the Xerox recovery strategy that are generally applicable in managing to succeed, and therefore relevant to this chapter, are:

- quality was identified as 'the basic business principle';
- Xerox developed a universal quality process (see chart in Figure 8.1);

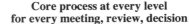

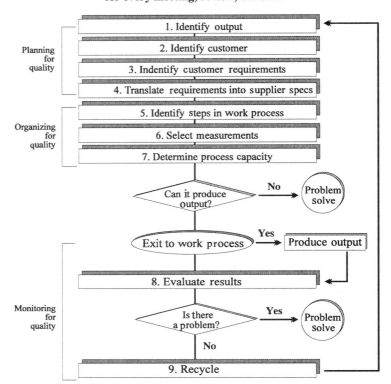

Figure 8.1   Xerox's quality improvement process

- Xerox went beyond customer care or customer focus to 'customer obsession';
- cooperation was encouraged throughout the supply chain by what was called 'team Xerox' — members were all customers, all employees, all suppliers (but the plan involved reducing the Xerox supply base from 5000 to 400 suppliers worldwide);
- benchmarking, looking out, not in at Xerox;
- business unit teams, not functional structures;
- new attitudes to employees and suppliers.

The Xerox quality improvement process illustrated in Figure 8.1 includes two features that are particularly important for improving business performance: customer focus (steps two and three) and continuous improvement (step 9). However, the heading is even more important for young engineers: use of the process at every level, for every meeting, every review and every decision is not confined to Xerox. Every engineer can use it.

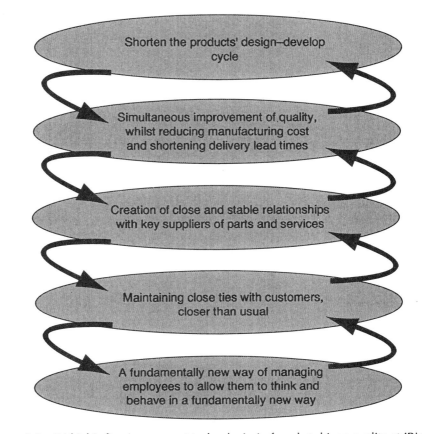

Figure 8.2   Fridrich's five 'component technologies' of market driven quality at IBM

Xerox did not fully recover their market dominance by the end of their five-year plan, but they managed to reverse their decline, which is a major step towards managing to succeed.

IBM were seen to be in deep trouble in the early 1990s, but were already planning corrective action before the full extent of their difficulties was made visible in the press. Their decline was rapid: in 1979 IBM were one of the Peters and Waterman's 'excellent' companies, and from 1982 to 1985, *Fortune* magazine's 'most admired' American company. By 1989 they were 45th in the *Fortune* list! Like Xerox and GM they were victims of their own success (remember Sloan's warning), and of the habit of introspection. As a result of looking inwards, and backwards, at themselves, IBM believed they were leaders in quality, and felt some pride in their achievement of almost halving product defects every two years, but when they looked outwards they found that competitors had passed them to set new quality standards. They also thought they were cost leaders, but found their costs were 20% above their main competitors. Through the 1980s, IBM had attempted various piecemeal improvement programmes, but by 1990 they realized that they had to change their whole view of competitiveness,

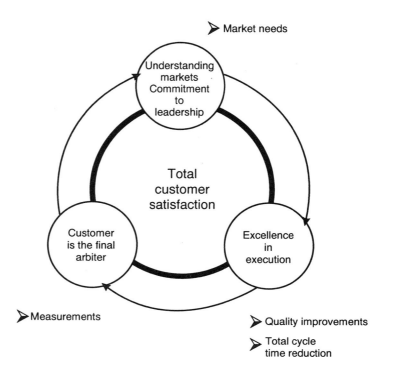

Figure 8.3   IBM's market driven quality circle

and set out to achieve total customer satisfaction through 'market-driven quality'. This programme was described in a lecture by Heinz K. Fridrich of IBM, from which the following material has been drawn [5].

The IBM research in preparation for their own recovery programme identified five characteristics of world-class companies which are shown in Figure 8.2.

The five 'component technologies', as Fridrich called them, have to be practised simultaneously as a single strategy. In terms of the McKinsey 7S structure (see Chapter 3), the last three are 'soft' S requirements: person to person interactions with customers, suppliers and employees.

The starting point of IBM's programme was an understanding of the market, and the end point was the customer, as shown in Figure 8.3.

To implement their programme, IBM simultaneously pursued the twin goals of quality improvement and total cycle time reduction. This is illustrated in Figure 8.4. (It was pursuit of the goals that was expected to generate the improvements shown — for example, cycle time reduction does not itself reduce defects, but striving for reduction may have this effect.)

Like Xerox, IBM did not recover their dominance of world markets, and had to recognize that the structure of the industry had changed. However, they have shown that they, too, can change. They have introduced new products faster, they have improved quality and reduced cost, and they have returned to profitability

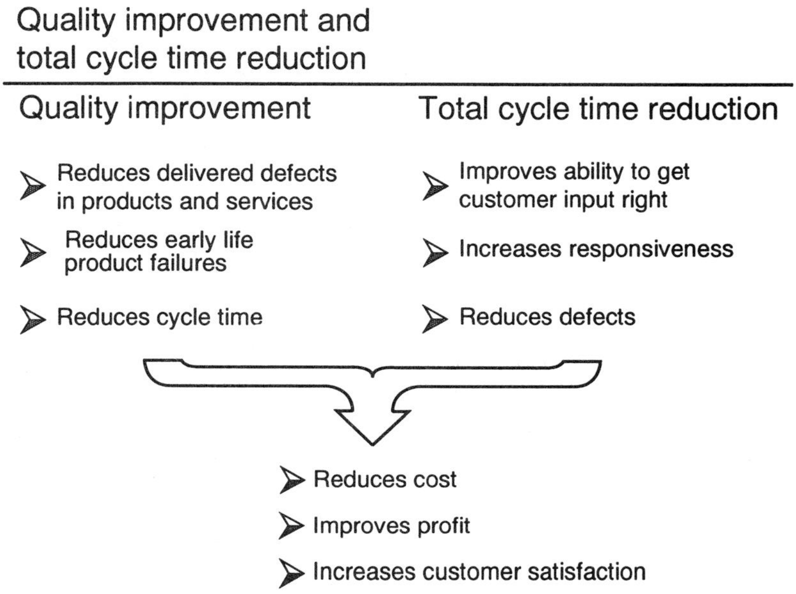

Quality improvement and total cycle time reduction

Quality improvement	Total cycle time reduction
➤ Reduces delivered defects in products and services	➤ Improves ability to get customer input right
➤ Reduces early life product failures	➤ Increases responsiveness
➤ Reduces cycle time	➤ Reduces defects

➤ Reduces cost

➤ Improves profit

➤ Increases customer satisfaction

Figure 8.4   IBM's twin goals

(having briefly held the world record for making the largest one-year operating loss).

There are elements common to the Xerox and IBM programmes. They are both striving to:

- consider the customer (to the point of obsession),
- change the way they manage people (so that *all* are involved),
- simultaneously improve quality, cost and delivery time (by orders of magnitude, not by the 'old' target of 5% a year),
- include customers and suppliers in close and lasting relationships ('cooperative contracting' Xerox call it),
- concurrent design of product and process by teams that include suppliers,
- improve execution by shared learning from past mistakes.

There is another company that does all these things, is outstanding in managing technological change, and has not been forced to do so by near-disaster. This company, which has been consistently successful, is Hewlett-Packard (H-P). Phillips [6] described some of the successful H-P practices which are summarized below.

Communication is informal — H-P invented the term and practice of 'management by wandering around'. Information is exchanged freely between people at different levels and in different functions, helping them to behave 'more as a team than as a hierarchy'.

Goals are achievable — with effort. This gives everyone the chance to be a winner, and people share in each others' success: 'you don't have to embarrass a loser to be a winner'. Stretch goals are regarded as '. . . bad motivationally, and they also lead to organizational self-deception, as people begin misrepresenting what is really going on, in an ultimately futile effort to hide the infeasibility of stretch targets.'

Learning is built in: H-P give overwhelming attention to training and development, not just to enhance the value of human assets, or make employees happy, but for two other reasons:

(1) H-P believe they are dependent on the initiative and judgement of the individual employee; it therefore follows that they should do everything possible to instil in the employee the values and expectations — and the capabilities — that will enable him or her to do what is best for the company. (If that can be done there is no need for the cost-generating controls that typify most cost reduction programmes.)

(2) They believe that they must continually adapt to a changing environment and therefore must create a climate of continual learning within the company.

The H-P annual planning reviews illustrate how learning is part of the regular management process:

'These are full day affairs, attended by corporate management and top divisional managers. They are structured conversations . . . with few charts or numbers . . . used to seek a common understanding about how to develop the division's business . . .

About 20% of the time is devoted to reviewing the history of past product development programmes and major investments — seeking to learn . . .

The next third is devoted to new product plans . . . shaped on the basis of careful study of past lessons . . .

About 15% is spent discussing a special theme . . .

20% on the management by objectives programme — not more than three or four critical things that just have to be done . . .

Only about 10% is devoted to next year's financials — if they get the rest of it right, the financials will follow.'

Reviews are shared — when divisional managers review performance with their boss, the other managers are there, to stimulate and learn from each other.

Development is on the job — learning from assignments, membership of task forces, and maybe from a course to provide a special skill.

This section has described how some outstanding companies have survived, avoided decline, or recovered in the 1980s, and are now leading the way.

There is no guarantee that their solutions will apply elsewhere, but there does seem to be a general indication that centralized, heavily structured organizations, with command and control styles of management, cannot respond to customer needs changing at the rate they did in the 1980s and are changing in the 1990s. The final section of this chapter looks at two companies that have more recently managed to succeed.

8.4   LEADING IN THE 1990s: TWO WAYS TO SUCCEED

Two engineering companies, one American and one European, have demonstrated leadership and examples of excellent management in the early 1990s. They are the Chrysler Corporation of the USA, and Asea Brown Boveri (ABB). Chrysler, like Xerox and IBM, had greatness thrust upon them by the prospect of extinction. ABB, like Hewlett-Packard have steadily acquired greatness, or maybe they were born great. Chrysler's achievement is described first.

8.4.1   Re-engineering Chrysler for the 1990s

The achievements of Chrysler in the early 1990s can be measured by extracts from two articles in *The Economist*.

An article in the 14 April 1990 issue asked 'Are America's carmakers headed for the junkyard?' and advised 'One wise move would be for the Big Three to embrace Japanese partners still more closely . . . And if Chrysler were taken over, nobody should weep.' The article also stated: 'The only way to save America's car industry is to leave the present one to die. Detroit, rest in peace.'

An article on 17 April 1993 headed 'Japan spins off' told a different tale. It stated that 'America has changed its methods of making cars' and 'Chrysler is emerging as a star after narrowly escaping its second brush with bankruptcy. The firm is winning sales from the baby-boomers, a group that had been a keen buyer of imported cars.' It also speculated '. . . sales look so good that Chrysler could be the most profitable car company in the world this year.'

Chrysler was *not* taken over, and it *was* the most profitable car company in 1993, measured by profit per vehicle. How did they make such big changes so fast?

There were five major steps:

(1) a dramatic change from vertically-oriented functional departments to 'vehicle platform' teams;
(2) a complete change in the way Chrysler dealt with suppliers;
(3) a lot of progress in bringing teamwork and empowerment to the shop floor;
(4) after achieving one level of success Chrysler determined to 'shoot for more' by adopting a mindset of continuous improvement;
(5) a new employee evaluation system that relies 50% on the attainment of performance goals, and 50% on behaviours.

	Viper	LH Sedans	Ram Pickup	Neon	Cirrius/ Stratus
Development time (mo's)	36	39	32	31	35
Development costs (US$bn)	0.08	1.6	1.2	1.3	0.9
Team size	85	850	700	740*	592

*Includes other small car platform products

Figure 8.5 Chrysler 'getting better all the time'

The re-organization into 'platform teams' was described in Chapter 7. The result of the re-organization was 'lots of teamwork and innovative thinking'. In turn, this led to a flood of new products that were affordable, different and well received by the market. One model, the 'Vision', was named by the press 'Automobile of the Year' in the USA, and Number One among family saloons by *Consumer Reports* magazine. That was the first time in 12 years that the magazine had named a domestic US car as Number One. The new products were brought to market faster, and with fewer resources than before the re-organization. The new levels of performance are shown in Figure 8.5.

According to Lutz, Figure 8.5 'shows that, with true teamwork, success is not only repeatable, but that it can even be improved upon.' [7]

Chrysler's new relations with suppliers involved treating them as 'true extensions of our company — as an integral, creative link in the value-added chain, just as we ourselves are merely a link.' Chrysler called this the 'extended enterprise' concept, which is shown in Figure 8.6.

Chrysler stuck to their new style of relationships with suppliers even when the competitive cost pressures of the early 1990s drove some other automotive companies to revert to type, and to seek short-term savings by transferring business to less-qualified suppliers or by threats to do so. By their consistency, Chrysler retained the trust of their supply base, and their continued willingness to participate in the early supplier involvement (ESI) programme. Chrysler regard ESI as an essential part of simultaneous engineering (SE), and SE as an essential part of their faster new product development. Moreover, it is already clear that

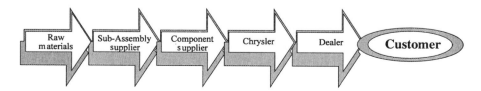

Figure 8.6 The 'extended enterprise' concept

Supervisors to hourly workers

> Past: 1:25

> Present: 1:50

> Future: 1:70

Figure 8.7   Empowerment on the factory floor

Chrysler's approach to cost reduction is more effective than the old '5% off everything' approach. Chrysler reckon that their SCORE (*s*upplier *co*st *r*eduction *ef*fort) programme has generated nearly 9000 cost-reducing ideas, worth more than $1 billion annually. The rate of saving has been increasing — from $250 m in 1993, to $500 m in 1994, and a planned $750 m in 1995. This has not been achieved at the expense of suppliers' profit margins, but by the elimination of waste, including waste in the Chrysler link of the extended enterprise. (More information about Chrysler's purchasing policies and performance is given in Chapter 21, section 21.4.2.) Suppliers reacted favourably to Chrysler's new methods: Chrysler were rated a close third to Nissan and Toyota in terms of 'partnership', and ahead of Honda, Saturn, Ford, Mazda and GM in that order.

Empowerment on the factory floor has also involved radical change. One change is the reduction in numbers of supervisors, as shown in Figure 8.7.

Reduced supervision is possible because 'self-directed work teams' have been introduced. These teams develop their own work assignments, schedule their own vacations, solve productivity and process problems, and train other team members.

The mindset of continuous improvement has demonstrated itself in the new product introductions and cost reductions already described. Another example is the reduction in 'order-to-delivery' time, as shown in Figure 8.8. From the 37 days achieved in 1994, Chrysler planned further improvement to 25 days.

The new employee evaluation scheme was designed to institutionalize the principles behind the other changes. The scheme gives equal weight to achievement of goals and to the behaviour of employees. Behaviour includes teamwork, empowerment and innovation, and is judged by several people in the work group as well as the employee's boss. The aim is to reward 'the champions *and* the foot soldiers of constructive change' rather than 'the person who meets his own goals only at the expense of others.'

While these changes have been concentrated on Chrysler's North American activities, the company has not neglected the long-term potential of the European

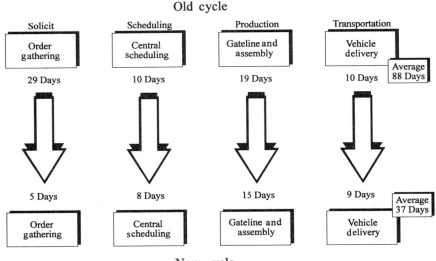

Figure 8.8   Continuous improvement in the Chrysler order-to-delivery process

market which they re-entered in 1988. At that time, all Chrysler's European sales came from vehicles built in the USA. Since 1992, however, Chrysler have been assembling minivans in Austria for sale in Continental Europe, and in 1994 assembly in Austria was expanded by the addition of 'luxury sports-utility' Jeeps. Austria's accession to the European Union in January 1995, and the introduction of right-hand drive vehicles to the Austrian built range, will continue this expansion. Chrysler's low manufacturing costs in the USA allow them to export saloon cars to sell profitably in Europe.

Summarizing the re-engineering of Chrysler, Lutz [7] said:

'If there's one overriding lesson from our experience, I think it's that there are indeed great rewards for organizations that pay as much attention to the engineering going on in the so-called "soft" side of their business as the "hard" side.'

Chrysler's balance between hard and soft aspects of management, and their use of development and delivery time compression as competitive weapons, are mirrored in the final example in this chapter, which relates to ABB.

8.4.2   ABB at the threshold: Ready to 'go for growth'

ABB, Chrysler, and almost all engineering companies have been pursuing the business goals listed in Chapter 2. ABB's strategy for achieving these goals differs from Chrysler's in the extent of its response to the external factors influencing the business environment, which were also listed in Chapter 2. ABB have given the same sort of attention as Chrysler to customer satisfaction through new technologies, faster delivery and higher quality at competitive prices. They have gone somewhat further in reducing management structure and empowering employees. They have gone much further than Chrysler in extending their operations on a global basis to position themselves to use external factors to their own advantage.

The difference of approach between ABB and Chrysler derives from Chrysler's concentration on only one of what Eric Drewery, Chief Executive of ABB UK called 'the two fundamental changes in the international environment for multinational corporations' [8]. The two changes are:

(1) 'An unprecedented wave of restructuring measures in the business world (which) has been called the "third industrial revolution" (and) has to do with all the processes of management aiming at producing the best, most innovative products and services, in the shortest amount of time, at the lowest price . . .

(2) . . . (the realization that) today the "world economy" comprises the whole world . . . a new world with new growth poles in China, Central and Eastern Europe, India, the Middle East, Brazil and Mexico.'

ABB in China

➤ 11 joint venture companies—more in the pipeline

➤ ABB China Business School established

➤ 1000 managers a year to be trained in business administration

➤ Employees will increase to 10 000 by end of decade

ABB in Central and Eastern Europe

➤ 61 majority owned joint venture companies

➤ 25 000 employees in 16 countries

➤ Enormous production and design potential—will become a major competitor to Western Europe

Figure 8.9 ABB's moves into emerging markets

ABB have not merely observed the second change — they are participating in it. Figure 8.9 summarizes ABB's actions in two of the 'growth poles' at a time when they were reducing their total, worldwide employment levels (by 47 000, or about 25% in the western world).[4]

ABB's activities in the developing regions of the world have also helped them to benefit from what other companies see mainly as a threat: long-term trends in currency exchange rates (as opposed to daily or monthly changes). The 1993 ABB Annual Report stated:

'About one third of ABB's total value-added is in countries where currencies have significantly depreciated against those of their major trading partners. The increased overall competitiveness of the products, parts and projects from those countries will support growth as well as defend our domestic market positions.'

Another thing that ABB does more extensively than Chrysler is to use its financial services division as an integral part of its marketing strategies. This enabled ABB to supply a 'turnkey' paint plant for a US automotive company, a combined heat and power plant in Scandinavia, and rolling stock to London Underground in the UK. (Chrysler do have a customer finance arm, but its offerings are just like other car purchase finance schemes, while ABB's schemes are innovative and distinctive in their markets.)

ABB have done more than Chrysler to confirm their 'good corporate citizen' role in their management of environmental issues. This goes beyond the development of 'cleaner' power plants: ABB have made environmental protection management a top corporate priority. They signed the International Chamber of Commerce Business Charter for Sustainable Development in 1991, and set out a five-year programme of internal and external actions to establish environmental management systems. In many other respects the two companies have performed at similarly outstanding levels.

ABB's customer focus programme started in 1990, and was aimed at responsiveness and continuous improvement worldwide. The faster throughput times and materials management actions resulting from this programme enabled ABB to halve its inventories between December 1990 and December 1993, from $7.3 billion to $3.6 billion. ABB also contributed to its customers' inventory reductions by providing 'fast, comprehensive and reliable equipment maintenance and service' and by introducing services such as 'short time no stock' (STNS) deliveries. An STNS system in Scandinavia delivers cable in any length the customer needs, directly from the factory to the construction site, in many cases within three days.

---

[4]Under the heading 'Corporate Unity', ABB's *Missions and Values* booklet explains such variations in regional employment trends as follows: 'Optimizing our worldwide resources to serve our local and global customers will require strategic re-orientation and major structural changes in local companies. Overall improvement of the Group's competitiveness is the most important criterion for making such changes. We will strive for the best possible and equitable solution from a Group perspective, even if this should result in uneven distribution of hardship among the countries or locations involved.' Also, the company's 1993 accounts show that expansion into new markets in China and Eastern Europe has had a mitigating effect on employment reductions by increasing exports from Western Europe and North America.

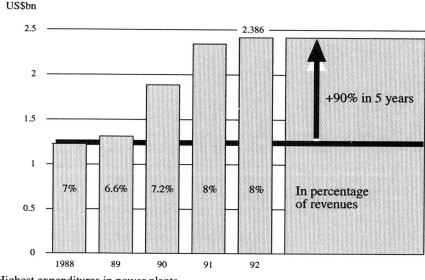

> Highest expenditures in power plants
> Major productivity improvements, shorter cycle times
> Strengthened global coordination

Figure 8.10   ABB research and development

ABB almost doubled its R&D investment over a five year period while eliminating overlapping work in different R&D centres — see Figure 8.10. This R&D was customer driven, and enabled the product divisions to make more than 50% of their 1993 sales from products developed in the previous four years.

ABB's 'delayering' and 'employee empowerment' actions have been described in Chapter 7. They are comprehensive and sustained, like Chrysler's.

Suppliers do not feature strongly in ABB's public statements. They are explicitly involved in ABB's environmental management plans, and implicitly must be involved in ABB's quality and JIT programmes since purchased materials account for over 40% of ABB sales, and other purchases push the total 'buy' beyond 50% of sales. ABB's lesser emphasis on suppliers is a major difference from Chrysler, IBM, Xerox and the other models of successful engineering management.

In total, ABB's internal restructuring and outward customer focus have enabled them to sustain modest growth in sales and profits during the 1991–3 period, which saw the deepest recession in the OECD countries. Their long 'reach' in geographical terms and in planning horizons has put them in a strong position to take advantage of the expected recovery in the OECD countries and the forecast strong growth in emerging countries in the decade from 1995. Percy Barnevik, ABB's President describes this period as 'the third phase in ABB's short history, the expansion phase', and says that the company is well-positioned to 'go for growth'.

8.4.3 Why Compare and Contrast?

ABB is primarily an electrical engineering company that is also a world leader in process engineering, and is based in Europe. Chrysler is an automotive industry company, based in the USA. The reason for comparing them is that they have both been successful in recent years, and it is possible to identify factors common to their success. These factors are:

- removal of organizational barriers to fast communication and decision making,
- use of the simplified organization to motivate all employees to focus on their customers, and to pursue never-ending improvement,
- use of speed as a competitive weapon — speed of new product development and speed of order execution,
- balanced management of 'hard' and 'soft' issues.

The reason for contrasting them is that '... mere rationalization and restructuring are not enough to safeguard the future. Much more is needed today to differentiate a company, because most companies are restructuring successfully' [8].

Chrysler have differentiated themselves in their industry by their concept of 'the extended enterprise' and their cooperation with their supply base. They have differentiated themselves in global terms by the speed of their restructuring, and the extent of their turnround in profitability.

ABB have differentiated themselves by the extent of their planning horizons, the extent of their delegation and empowerment, and the extension of their offering to their customers.

ABB have not needed the sort of turnround that Chrysler achieved, because they never sank to the low levels of performance that Chrysler suffered. This can be construed as 'better' management, but there is little point in trying to determine who is 'best'. Both companies are examples of excellent engineering management.

In June 1994, ABB was rated equal first with the UK retailer Marks & Spencer in terms of commitment to their customers, shareholders and employees, in a survey by the *Financial Times* and Price Waterhouse that questioned 2000 executives of the largest organizations in nine countries. In September 1995 the survey put ABB first on their own, while Marks & Spencer fell back to fifth place [9].

In December 1994, Chrysler was named by Alex Trotman, Chairman of Ford Motor Company, as Ford's most dangerous competitor in North America. For over 80 years previously that accolade had gone to General Motors.

8.5 SUMMARY

The chapter started with a list of BASIC weaknesses of western engineering management: organizational boxes, antagonistic attitudes, satisfaction with a single success, ineffective attempts at imitating the Japanese and inability to manage change.

Companies that had overcome these weaknesses in the 1980s have been examined, and the common factors in their formulae for success have been identified.

Two companies, ABB and Chrysler, which have been outstandingly successful in the early 1990s, were considered in more detail. The internal restructuring, or re-engineering, of these companies was found to have much in common, but it was noted that, on its own, restructuring would not be sufficient to secure success in the future. To succeed in the next decade, engineering companies have to match or beat their competitors in quality, innovation and customer satisfaction, but additionally they have to find ways to differentiate themselves. ABB do this by their intense forward look down the value-added chain. Chrysler do it by an equally intense look in the other direction: backwards, up the value-added chain.

REFERENCES

1. Sloan, A. P. Jr (1963) *My Years with General Motors*. Pan Books, London.
2. Senge, P. (1990) *The Fifth Discipline*. Century Business Books, Boston, USA.
3. Robinson, P. (1990) *Innovation, Investment and Survival*. Institution of Mechanical Engineers Conference. 4 July 1990.
4. de Geus, A. P. (1988) Planning as Learning. *Harvard Business Review* March/April 1988.
5. Fridrich, H. K. (1992) *World Class Manufacturing*. The 1992 Lord Austin Lecture at the Institution of Electrical Engineers, London.
6. Phillips, J. R. (1982) Managing people. *McKinsey Quarterly* Autumn.
7. Lutz, R. A. (1994) The 1994 Christopher Hinton Lecture, delivered by R. A. Lutz, President of the Chrysler Corporation, to The Royal Academy of Engineering on 4 October 1994, and private correspondence with T. T. Stallkamp, Vice President — Procurement and Supply and General Manager — Large Car Operations provided the basis of section 8.4.1.
8. Drewery, E. (1994) Address of the Department of Systems Science Research Colloquium, City University, London.
9. Europe's Most Respected Companies. *The Financial Times* 27 June 1994, 19 September 1995.

BIBLIOGRAPHY

'Resetting The Clock — Asea Brown Boveri is transforming its factories by slashing lead times', *Financial Times* 10 February 1993, gives some background to ABB's Customer Focus programme.
'ABB Managers Strip for Action' — The Swiss engineering group's streamlining, *Financial Times* 25 August 1993, reports ABB's 'delayering' of its management structure.

Part II
Managing Engineering Resources

Human resource management — the individual

9.1 INTRODUCTION

This chapter and Chapter 10 provide an introduction to the management of human resources in organizations. The human workforce is arguably the single most important resource of any organization. The human being is also the most complex and perhaps the least predictable of all organizational resources. All engineering activity involves people, and no engineer can be successful in his career without an understanding of human behaviour. These two chapters give an introduction to some basic aspects of human behaviour. The logical place to start is with the individual, the basic building block of groups and organizations. This is followed by a study of interactions between individuals and then the dynamics of group behaviour. A study of organizations has already been provided in Chapter 7.

In this chapter the behavioural sciences are briefly described and explained, the issues of motivation explored and the theories of Maslow and Herzberg outlined. The latter part of this chapter is concerned with individuals in pairs, and the relationship between individuals is examined using transactional analysis. However, some general aspects of the behavioural sciences, and their relationship to engineering, are considered first.

Adopting the differentiation frequently used in systems science between 'hard' and 'soft' complexity, engineering is found in the 'hard complexity' area. Engineering is a complex subject, but most of its problems are quantifiable. There is a basis of science from which engineering laws are developed. These laws may be derived from a mathematical basis, or may be established empirically by observation and experiment. A mathematically derived theory may be shown by experimentation or by empirical observation to be true, and the linkage will give understanding to the phenomenon under examination.

Consider two examples. In engineering, the study of the behaviour of fluids or materials starts from a mathematical base. It is possible to derive a mathematical model for the flow of fluids from the Navier-Stokes equations. The model can be verified by experimental observation. Similarly, a mathematical representation can be derived for the bending of a beam by consideration of the physical characteristics of the system such as the beam length, the force applied and the modulus of elasticity. This can also be checked by experiment. Conversely, in any area of applied science an experiment can be performed and a hypothesis proposed to explain the results obtained. This is the empirical approach. By reiteration between such empiricism and theory a complete understanding of the phenomenon under consideration can eventually be obtained.

Students who train as engineers generally do so because their aptitudes and inclinations are compatible with the scientific basis of their profession and its practical aspects. The further training of engineers tends to reinforce the understanding of the relationship of theory and practice, and the dependability of the results that can be obtained by the application of established engineering knowledge. Engineers are comfortable with the way in which practical aspects can be represented in a 'hard', i.e. quantifiable way. The performance of a machine or a structure can be assessed, hard data generated, and the whole condensed in the form of definitive equations which are known to have a sound basis in theory as well as to work in practice. This is comforting for the engineer, who can predict with reasonable confidence the outcome of the application of engineering skills.

Unfortunately, there is no fundamental theory derived from a scientific basis for the behaviour of the human being. People are individual, complex and sometimes unpredictable. Professional engineers frequently work in teams with other engineers and with other professions. Many engineering organizations, and organizations which employ engineers, are large and have many people with whom engineers have to relate. Little if anything is achieved in the world without human effort, so it is essential that the engineer should have a basic understanding of the way people behave. We need to know what makes people tick.

Studies in this area are known as behavioural studies or behavioural sciences, though students of sciences with a mathematical basis might argue about the use of the term 'science' for investigations of human behaviour. Even so, much effort has been put into the study of human behaviour and a mass of evidence collected, giving a body of information which constitutes what is known about the behaviour of human beings, individually and in groups. Some engineering students may find their first encounter with behavioural science a little strange, because it does not have the same scientific basis that underpins engineering and other technologies, and uses an unfamiliar terminology. The individuality and complexity of the human being does not allow a hard theoretical basis for human behaviour. As people from the North of England might comment, 'there's now't so strange as folk'!

Though the subject may appear woolly and intangible when contrasted with the certainties of engineering, behavioural scientists have brought order and structure to their study of the human race. Their method has similarities with the empirical approach to engineering mentioned earlier. Human behaviour is observed, individually and in groups, and common characteristics noted. Theories are advanced to explain the behaviour of individuals or groups of individuals in various situations. These theories are better described as hypotheses or models, in that they are constructs based on observation, which suggest a basis for the behaviour, or a common thread in the observations. The hypothesis or model may help towards an understanding of human behaviour, and therefore help in the management of human resources.

Publication of these hypotheses allows discussion and further evaluation on a wider basis. The system is similar to the publication of papers on scientific subjects. As work progresses, some models of human behaviour are developed, and are accepted as a helpful indication of behaviour. Such models, once they gain acceptance, constitute the theory of the behavioural sciences. Some of the more generally accepted theories, hypotheses or models will be discussed in the next chapters, but it must be remembered that these constructs are a guide to, and frequently a simplification of, the very complex reality of human behaviour.

Human resource management contains many elements which could be considered as 'soft', i.e. not easily quantified. Soft issues are those which involve value judgements, have no right or wrong solution, are difficult to define precisely, and which may be interpreted differently by many people according to the principles and priorities which they hold. Such issues are clearly difficult to quantify, and readers more familiar with 'hard' data may experience some discomfort, as the phenomena do not slot neatly into boxes, or generate equations which will produce 'right answers'. There are, quite often, no right answers to human resource management problems; just better or worse solutions.

Just as good engineering relies on a sound basis of theory and practice, so good human resource management relies upon a sound knowledge of the theory and practice of human behaviour. No matter how technically brilliant an engineer may be, success and progress will depend on an ability to work with, motivate, influence and manage other people. Even the most sophisticated computer systems and robotic production facilities are designed and controlled by people. Professional engineers are likely to spend the majority of their lives working in organizations with a variety of people; individuals, groups of individuals, and the amalgamation of groups which forms the organization. Ability to interact effectively with these individuals and groups will be of primary importance to the career of the professional engineer, so it is of very great value to the engineering student to acquire knowledge and skills in the area of human resource management.

9.2   THE BEHAVIOURAL SCIENCES

Behavioural science is an interdisciplinary collective term for the three elements of social science interested in the study of the human species. It involves the study of psychology, sociology and anthropology, but is often taken to apply specifically to aspects of human behaviour related to organization and management in the working environment. It is therefore very relevant to the circumstances in which engineers perform their duties.

Psychologists are concerned with human behaviour, individual characteristics, and the interaction of individuals in small social groups. Attention is focused on the 'personality system', the characteristics of the individual, such as attitudes, motives, and feelings.

Sociologists are concerned with social behaviour and the relationships among social groups and societies, and the maintenance of order. Attention is focused on the 'social system' the interrelationship of individuals in social structures.

Anthropologists are concerned with the study of mankind and the human race as a whole. Their attention is focused on the 'cultural system', the values, customs and beliefs, which influence the emphasis people put on various aspects of behaviour.

The interrelationship of psychology, sociology and anthropology forms the interdisciplinary study area of behavioural science.

9.3   THE INDIVIDUAL AND THE ORGANIZATION

The approach taken in this introduction to human resource management is to consider initially the individual, pairs of individuals, then individuals in groups, groups in organizations, and finally organizations within the environment. Leavitt [1] adopted a similar approach in his book *Managerial Psychology*, considering people as individuals, in pairs, in groups of three to 20, and in organizations of hundreds and thousands. He also considered the ways in which people are similar, and the ways in which they are different. It is perhaps from an understanding of the similarities and differences, the way people interact with one another, and the way they work in groups, that an appropriate start can be made to human resource management.

For the *individual*: consideration will be given to personality, attributes and skills, attitudes and values, and expectations and needs. For *individuals*: (in pairs and in relation to groups) personal interaction, influence, authority, leadership and manipulation, will be considered, but communication will be discussed in Chapter 12. For the *group*: functions and structure, informal organization, role relationships, and group influences and pressures, will be discussed in Chapter 10.

These aspects will be related to the achievement not only of organizational performance and effectiveness, but also satisfying the needs of the individuals in the organization. By the use of good human resources management, the goals of the organization are achieved, and the needs of the employees are satisfied. At the same time, a climate is created in which the employees will work willingly and effectively.

9.4   THE INDIVIDUAL

9.4.1   The concept of self

The way in which a person behaves in the working environment depends on the 'self', the internal psychology of the individual. Part of this the individual understands, but much of it is unconscious. The 'self-concept' is that part of the self of which the individual is aware. The major part of the self is the 'unconscious self'. An individual also has a 'self ideal', the self that person would like to be. The self ideal is quite separate from the self, and the individual continually compares the self concept with the self ideal. Another important element of the self is self-esteem, how good an individual feels about himself or herself. The individual tries to increase self-esteem whenever possible.

The self is formed as a result of the complex interaction of expectations, inhibitions and preferences which individuals experience as children and adolescents. Personal growth involves the enlargement of self-awareness, i.e. becoming consciously aware of more of the self, and thus enlarging the self-concept. The self develops and changes with time.

Here are some definitions:

- *Self*: The total set of beliefs, values and abilities within the individual, including those not yet realized.
- *Self-concept*: The pattern of beliefs, values and abilities of which an individual is aware. This excludes the unconscious component.
- *Unconscious self*: The pattern of beliefs, values and abilities of which an individual is unaware. This excludes the conscious component.
- *Self-ideal*: The set of beliefs, values and abilities towards which an individual aspires.
- *Self-esteem*: The value placed by individuals on their beliefs, values and abilities.

9.4.2   Psychological energy

Psychological energy is present in all individuals, and is variable but not limited. The quantity of psychological energy varies with the psychological state of the individual. Its individual expression can never be permanently blocked. If its expression is frustrated, some alternative form of expression will be found. Psychological energy is largely beyond an individual's control, and finding how to inspire, enthuse, 'turn-on' or 'psych-up' oneself is very important. In a leadership or managerial role, it is just as important to be able to perform the same function of inspiring and enthusing the team members or the employees under managerial control. Competitive sports players are now well aware of the need for psychological energy. International sports players, particularly in one-to-one competitive sports such as tennis, may have a psychological coach as well as a physiological one.

An individual will be happy to contribute energy to an activity if it is anticipated that by so doing, an increase in self-esteem will result. Self-esteem will be increased if a measure of 'psychological success' is achieved in the activity. The judgement of the measure of psychological success will depend on the self-concept and the conditions associated with the activity. There are two broad criteria which will determine whether self-esteem is enhanced by an activity. Firstly, the individual should feel 'comfortable' with the activity. It should feel right or fit the subconscious self. If this is not the case, the individual will not feel happy, however successfully the activity has been performed. The activity should seem important to the individual. Secondly, the individual should perceive success in the activity, the success being measured according to the individual's own criteria, not those of any other person.

Self-esteem is enhanced in two major ways. The first way is by growth. The individual may try something new. As a result, the individual's self concept will be enlarged, and the individual will value himself or herself more. With increased confidence, the individual will be encouraged to try more new activities, which will develop that person yet further. The second most important process for increasing a person's self-esteem is dealing competently with the problems of his or her environment. If the person can attribute the resolution of personal, domestic or work problems to his or her own efforts, skills or abilities, self esteem will increase. It is essential that the individual can see a direct connection between his/her own efforts and the resolution of the problem.

To summarize, the self-esteem of an individual will increase as: the individual is better able to define the goals; the goals relate to his/her basic values and needs; and he/she is able to select the means to achieve those goals. Thus it is important when dealing with people in a working environment to be aware of their need for self-esteem. People will be more responsive and more willing to help or to carry out a manager's wishes, if they are allowed some autonomy. The manager may not be able to allow them to select the goal; this is most likely to have been decided already by higher authority, but the manager can be sensitive to the needs and values of subordinates, and allow them as much freedom as possible in the way they do their jobs.

9.5   BEHAVIOUR, MOTIVATION AND WORK

Why should engineers be interested in the psychological basis of human behaviour? Why should they need to understand what motivates people?

All organizations consist of complex interrelationships of individuals and work functions. In most cases, individuals can be subjected to hard (i.e. quantifiable) analysis of their intelligence, skills or work output, but on their level of motivation (their enthusiasm for the job) will depend the performance, efficiency and ultimate success of the organization. Thus a manager needs to understand the behaviour and motivation of those who work in the organization. The individual also needs to know how to motivate himself or herself to give a better performance, for the good of self-esteem, or perhaps to enhance career progress. The manager needs to motivate subordinates, convince peers and persuade superiors.

There are many views on the principal factors which motivate people. An individual may be motivated by personal gain, or by concern for the good of others; by a desire for security, or a need for excitement; by physical gratification or intellectual stimulus. A person may experience all of these motivations at different times. Studies of the psychology of the individual has identified three elements of behaviour which can be applied to all [1]:

(1)   behaviour is caused
(2)   behaviour is motivated
(3)   behaviour is goal directed.

These elements can be related by a simple model, Figure 9.1.

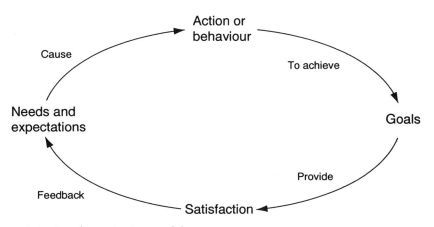

Figure 9.1 Simple motivation model

The model has a feedback loop, and engineers will recognize it as a control model. A simple example might be the feeling of hunger. This need would motivate an appropriate behaviour or action, which could be the opening of a can of soup or the booking of a table at a restaurant. Either might achieve the desired goal of a satisfied stomach, and the choice, which is by no means restricted to the examples given, would depend on many things, the most significant being the time and money available. Having consumed the soup or the restaurant meal, the individual might or might not have resolved the need for sustenance or achieved the goal of satisfaction. The feedback loop will allow for further action if required.

This physiological example is a very easy one. Satisfaction of one's psychological needs may be a little more complex and a little more difficult to define. They will certainly be more variable from individual to individual than the hunger example which will apply to all people at some time. Such psychological needs as safety, friendship, recognition, and perhaps achievement come to mind, and apply to most people. These will be examined in more detail later.

Before moving to consider human psychological needs, the simple motivational model needs to be examined a little more. All is well if the desired goal is achieved. The feedback loop will identify that the need or expectation has been fulfilled, and therefore no further action is required. It could be that the goal is only partially fulfilled, and further action is required, but in this case one can assume perhaps that the progress made will encourage further effort to achieve fully the required goal.

However, what if the person is completely obstructed in achieving the goal? There are a number of possible results. The barrier or blockage to achieving the goal could be considered as a problem which requires resolution, and various means could be sought to resolve the problem. The problem solving method might be successful, and the goal would then be achieved. By a somewhat longer and more complex route we arrive at the same situation given in the earlier model. The action taken would be regarded as constructive behaviour. Seeking an alternative

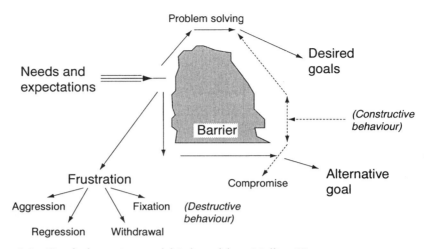

Figure 9.2   Simple frustration model (adapted from Mullins [6]

acceptable goal would be another example of constructive behaviour. This might involve some element of compromise; the original goal might now be perceived as unrealistic in the circumstances, and a less difficult goal substituted. If the alternative goal can be accepted, and can be achieved, the result will be satisfactory, though some residual minor frustration might remain.

If the required goal, or an acceptable substitute, is not achievable, the needs and expectations are unfulfilled, and frustration is the result. This can be very damaging psychologically, and a number of possible non-constructive, negative, and defensive behaviour patterns can emerge. These include aggression, regression, fixation, and withdrawal, and the response to the obstruction may involve combinations of these reactions.

Aggression could be in the form of a physical or verbal attack on the cause of the obstruction. If the cause happens to be the boss, and career preservation suggests that violence in that direction is unwise, the aggression may be displaced in other directions, such as abusing subordinates or kicking the cat. *Regression* is reversion to a childish form of behaviour, such as sulking or throwing a temper tantrum. *Fixation* is persisting with the action or behaviour, and disregarding the obvious failure and likelihood of continuing failure. *Withdrawal* is giving up, not just with the action or behaviour which has been the basis of the frustration, but with all aspects of the situation in which the problem occurred. The frustrated individual can become generally apathetic, and may lose totally the will to continue with the activity. A model of frustration is given in Figure 9.2.

Frustration will occur in some form and to some degree in most jobs and in engineering as in other professions. It is therefore the function of the manager or team leader to minimize the extent to which these naturally occurring problems de-motivate the team. The manager needs to be aware of the frustration potential within any job, and to assess how important this element is to the team member. This will depend on such factors as the personality of the individual, the nature of the obstruction, and how intensely the individual desires the goal. The manager can help the situation generally by sound guidance and leadership, particularly by good communication, good work organization, and perhaps by adopting a participative style of management.

9.6   PERSONALITY

9.6.1   Individuality

Even within the areas considered so far in the search for commonality in human behaviour, it is evident that only partial success has been achieved. Some general similarities in human behaviour have been identified, but they all tend to be hedged about by implied deviation; some individuals may be an exception to the generalizations put forward. Leavitt [1] moves quickly from a short chapter headed 'People are alike: some basic ideas' to a much longer evaluation commencing in his second chapter headed 'People are different: the growth of individuality'. This could imply that the differences are greater than the similarities, or that they should be given more consideration; it does not matter which, provided the significance of individuality is understood.

We are all different, and most of us are conscious and proud of our individuality. No one can get to the stage of commencing a university course without being aware of differences in personality. Friends at home and school display personality differences. Even close relatives near in age such as brothers and sisters can be quite different in personality and sons and daughters differ from their parents in many ways. In the last two examples, common inherited characteristics would suggest some similarities. Similar experiences of brothers and sisters and closeness of age might make for greater likeness than between children and parents, where age and experience disparity might cause greater differentiation.

When encountering another person for the first time, perhaps the characteristics noticed initially are physical ones such as sex, age and physique. The other person, for example, is a tall slim teenage girl or a short stocky middle-aged man. Greater acquaintance will reveal other aspects of the person, such as abilities, motivation and perhaps attitude. An even greater knowledge of the individual might be needed before the perceptions and the cultural and social aspects of that person are established. If the initial meeting was in a social setting rather than a work environment, the cultural and social aspects of personality might become apparent earlier.

With the exception of sex, most characteristics will change during a person's lifetime. Of course, most people have physical characteristics which remain with them throughout life, such as a propensity towards slimness or plumpness, but even such characteristics are known to change in the long term. Many people who were slim in their adolescence and early adult period have encountered the phenomenon known colloquially as 'middle age spread'.

So what aspects influence an individual's personality? There will be hereditary characteristics that will be derived from the person's parents. These will probably influence such elements as intelligence and specific abilities such as those concerning, for example, music or mathematics. Early experience in the family will have a profound effect and will bring social and cultural influences. Later, experience in the working environment will influence the personality which has been formed in childhood and adolescence. The roles taken, and the successes achieved, will influence the personality, and develop further attitudes and perceptions. However, the debate continues as to which of the two main components is the most significant, the inherited characteristics or those acquired from experience.

9.6.2   Personality studies

As early as the fourth century BC, Hippocrates identified four types of personality: sanguine; melancholic; choleric; and phlegmatic. In modern psychology, there are two different approaches to the study of personality, the nomothetic and the idiographic. The *nomothetic* approach assumes that personality is largely inherited and consistent; social and environmental influences are minimal, and the personality is resistant to change. The *idiographic* approach regards personality as a developing entity, subject to the influence of interactions with other people and the environment. Though an individual is unique, the self-concept (see section 9.4.1) of each one will develop with time.

It is not appropriate in an introductory text on management for engineers to consider in any depth studies of human personality. However, some studies, notably those of Cattell [2] and Myers-Briggs [3], have enabled tests to be developed which give an indication of the characteristics of individuals, and which are generally referred to as personality tests. Some companies use these in their assessment of potential recruits, and for internal promotions, and it is in the first of these examples which the young engineer is most likely to encounter.

The *Cattell 16PF Questionnaire* assesses personality on the following factors:

Outgoing	— Reserved
Abstract Thinker	— Concrete Thinker
Emotionally Stable	— Emotionally Unstable
Dominant	— Submissive
Optimistic	— Pessimistic
Conscientious	— Expedient
Adventurous	— Timid
Tender-minded	— Tough-minded
Suspicious	— Trusting
Imaginative	— Practical
Shrewd	— Ingenuous
Insecure	— Self-assured
Radical	— Conservative
Self-sufficient	— Group Dependent
Controlled	— Casual
Tense	— Relaxed

The *Myers-Briggs (MBTI) Test* assesses personality on the following four scales:

Introvert (I) — (E) Extrovert
Sensing (S) — (N) Intuitive
Thinking (T) — (F) Feeling
Judging (J) — (P) Perceiving

This Myers-Briggs classification provides a 4 × 4 matrix of personality types, with 16 possible combinations designated by the letters of the four characteristics which predominate. It is interesting to note that there is a preponderance of ISTJ and ESTJ types among managers in UK organizations.

Students will recognize many of the characteristics mentioned in these tests, and may be able to attribute some of them to themselves or their friends. Experience will also tell you that personalities with combinations of these characteristics occur, and may result in individuals having personalities which are compatible or incompatible with others, or complementary or non-complementary to others. When people work in teams, this can be most important, but that is a subject which will be discussed in Chapter 10, which considers people in groups.

So what should the engineer learn from this very short section on personality, or the differences between people? Perhaps nothing more than that although human beings have many characteristics in common, everyone is different. Each has strengths and weaknesses in a wide spectrum of capabilities. The better the manager knows these characteristics and capabilities, the better he or she will be able to manage and motivate the team.

9.7 GENERAL THEORIES OF HUMAN MOTIVATION

9.7.1 Introduction

What motivates the human being is of great interest to the manager, and to the behavioural scientist. In the former case, the interest is caused by a desire to obtain more productive performance from members of the workforce at all levels. A highly motivated and enthusiastic workforce can be a major asset to a company, and contribute substantially to its progress and profitability. A demoralized and uninterested workforce can have a debilitating effect on an organization. It is a major objective of managers, supervisors and group leaders to achieve high levels of motivation from the subordinates under their control.

The study of human motivation has occupied the time of behavioural science research workers for decades, and many theories and models have been proposed, criticized, modified, accepted or rejected, according to the help they provide in understanding the subject. A totally acceptable model has yet to be found, but two of those which have gained a measure of acceptance will be discussed, together with the criticisms made of them.

The theories or models which will be discussed will be those of:

- Maslow — Hierarchy of Human Needs [4]
- Herzberg — Two Factor Theory [5]

9.7.2   Maslow — hierarchy of human needs

Maslow's model identifies five levels of human need, which are in ascending order:

- physiological
- safety
- social
- esteem
- self-actualization

Figure 9.3 illustrates these five levels.

The principal elements of Maslow's model are as follows:

- *Physiological needs:* The most important is homeostasis, the body's automatic system for maintaining its normal functions. These include the need to breathe, eat, drink and sleep, and to maintain a reasonable temperature. Also included are activity, sensory pleasures and sexual desire.
- *Safety needs:* These include safety and security, protection from danger and physical attack, protection from pain or deprivation, and the need for stability.
- *Social needs:* These are also defined as love needs, and include friendship, affection, love, social activities, and interaction with other people.
- *Esteem needs:* These are also defined as ego needs, and include self-respect and the respect of others. This involves strength, independence and achievement; appreciation, status and prestige.

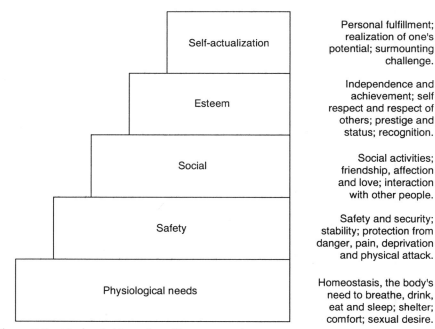

Figure 9.3   Maslow's hierarchy of human needs

- *Self-actualization needs:* This is the fulfilment of one's potential, of achieving all one is capable of achieving, and becoming whatever one is capable of becoming.

Maslow maintained that people generally fulfilled these needs in the order given, but there were many exceptions, and there might in some special circumstances be a reversal of the order. Reversal of the social and esteem elements in the hierarchy is the one most frequently encountered. To some people, esteem assumes a greater importance than the social elements, such as love. Some managers may accord greater value to the respect of their associates, rather than their affection.

Individuals who have experienced continual deprivation may never aspire to the higher level needs. The peoples of many famine-stricken and disaster-prone areas of the world may regard attainment of modest elements of the safety and social levels as a happy achievement. The permanently unemployed may be willing to settle for any job and its attendant security.

People with high levels of motivation, such as idealists and creative artists, may be little concerned with the lower level needs such as food, shelter and security, provided they can achieve the objective to which they are dedicated. The artist starving in a garret is willing to accept the absolute minimum of lower order needs, providing he can continue to paint. However, those minima must be available so that he can remain dedicated to his art. Martyrs, in the most extreme example, are prepared to give up life itself for the sake of their cause, showing that for a few, self-actualization even transcends homeostasis.

Maslow claims that the hierarchy is universal across different cultures, but that there are some differences between the individual's motivational content in a particular culture. He adds that it is not necessary for an individual to be fully satisfied at one level before having needs at a higher level. Requirement for satisfaction at a particular level will vary from individual to individual.

Maslow's model has been much evaluated, and some criticisms have been made of it. If the extent to which individuals vary in their requirements for satisfaction at each level is unclear, so too is the time element. How long does it take for a higher level need to emerge, or are they all present to some degree, latent in our personalities? We may all have needs for self-actualization, but to many, working to pay the mortgage and provide food for the family may take precedence. The differences in personality briefly mentioned earlier in this chapter may have some influence. Those with timid, insecure and pessimistic characteristics might value security highly, and be willing to work in a safe but tedious job. An optimistic, self-assured and adventurous individual might feel more suited to an exciting high risk, high prestige, post. An aspect which the manager should bear in mind is that the employee does not fulfil all his aspirations in the workplace. The home, social activities, organizations outside the workplace, all provide means for the individual to fulfil his or her needs. It is advantageous for a manager to have some knowledge of the employee's life outside the workplace to understand what needs are fulfilled in Maslow's terms.

9.7.3 Herzberg — two factor theory

Herzberg's original investigation involved interviews with some 200 engineers and accountants. They were asked to identify those aspects of their jobs which made them feel exceptionally good or exceptionally bad. Consistent responses were obtained, indicating two sets of factors which affected motivation, and led Herzberg to propose his two factor theory.

One set of factors was identified which, if absent, caused dissatisfaction. These were related to the context of the job, and were called hygiene or maintenance factors. The other set of factors are those which motivate the individual to superior performance. These are related to the content of the job, and were called 'motivators' or 'growth' factors.

Herzberg extended his analysis to other groups of workers, and found that the two factors were still present. Components of jobs which fall into each category are indicated below:

Factor name	Motivators	Hygiene factors
Alternative name:	Satisfiers	Dissatisfiers
Concerning:	*Growth*	*Maintenance*
	Job content	*Job context*
Factors:	Challenging work	Status
	Achievement	Interpersonal relations
	Growth in the job	Supervision
	Responsibility	Company policy
		and administration
	Advancement	Working conditions
	Recognition	Job security
		Salary

There are two major criticisms of Herzberg's theory. One is that it has limited application to people in jobs which are monotonous, repetitive and limited in scope. Some studies undertaken subsequently showed that some groups of manual workers were primarily concerned with pay and security, and regarded work as a means of earning money to satisfy outside demands and interests. However, studies of other groups of manual workers tended to support Herzberg's view.

The other major criticism is that the results obtained were influenced by the methodology. Studies conducted without asking the employee to identify aspects of the job which caused good or bad feelings tended to give different results and there was a possibility that Herzberg's results might be subject to interviewer bias.

It should be noted that the hygiene factors of Herzberg correspond roughly to the lower level needs in Maslow's hierarchy, as shown in Figure 9.4.

9.7.4 Other theories of motivation

There are many other theories of human motivation, and a detailed account of many of these is given in *Human Resource Management* [6]. Many of the factors included in the models of Maslow and Herzberg are included in models proposed by Alderfer and by McClelland. Alderfer [7] has proposed a three factor model incorporating: existence needs (Maslow's two lowest levels of physiological and

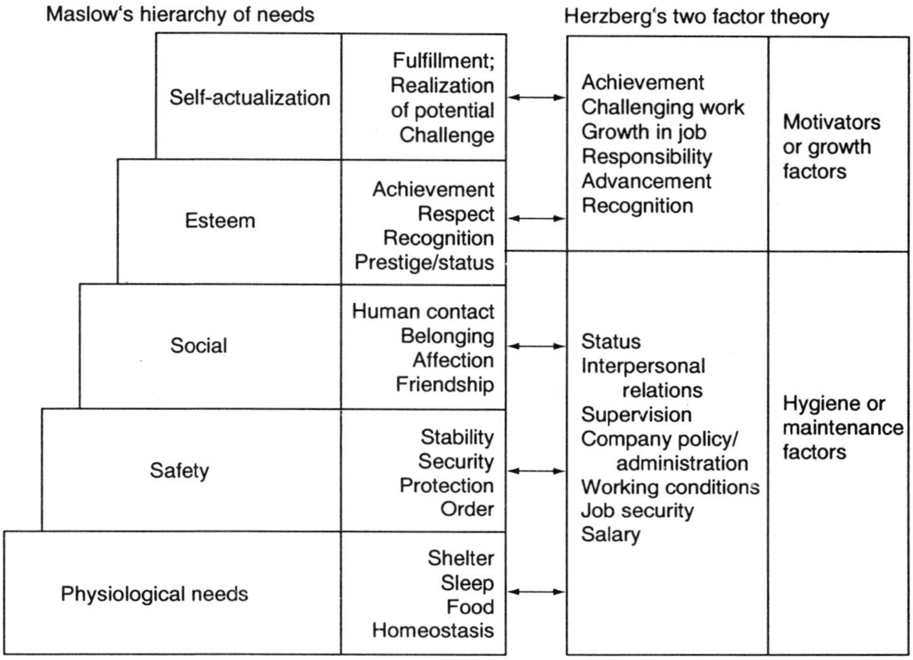

Maslow's hierarchy of needs   Herzberg's two factor theory

Self-actualization	Fulfillment; Realization of potential Challenge	Achievement Challenging work Growth in job Responsibility Advancement Recognition	Motivators or growth factors
Esteem	Achievement Respect Recognition Prestige/status		
Social	Human contact Belonging Affection Friendship	Status Interpersonal relations Supervision Company policy/ administration Working conditions Job security Salary	Hygiene or maintenance factors
Safety	Stability Security Protection Order		
Physiological needs	Shelter Sleep Food Homeostasis		

Figure 9.4   Maslow/Herzberg comparison

safety needs); relatedness needs (Maslow's third level social needs) and growth needs (Maslow's top two levels of esteem and self-actualization needs). McClelland [8] has proposed an achievement/motivation theory, which has four classifications of motives. Three of them: affiliation; power; and achievement; approximate to Maslow's: social needs; esteem needs; and self-actualization needs. The fourth class is avoidance motives.

9.8   INDIVIDUALS IN PAIRS

9.8.1   The importance of personal relationships

Some of the most enjoyable and enriching experiences and also some of the most annoying, frustrating and distressing experiences for people in all walks of life occur on a one-to-one basis. In the workplace, relationships are usually more formal, less close, yet can have a powerful influence on the lives of the people involved and on others. A good relationship between a young engineer and his/her supervisor might lead to rapid promotion within the company. The synergy of a good relationship between two engineers working on the same project might lead to a greater interest in their work, a more creative design, and a more successful outcome to the project. A relationship of shared confidence and trust between the engineer and the client might result in more commissions for that engineer from the client, as well as recommendations to other clients.

A key to successful relationships is good communication. Even in the most formal situations, and even where the personal feelings of the parties toward each other need to be suppressed in order to achieve an effective working relationship, good communication between the parties is essential. (This chapter should be read in conjunction with Chapter 11, which begins with an examination of the processes of communication, and then considers ways in which engineers and managers can improve their ability to communicate with others by the most appropriate means.) The remainder of this chapter deals with the *psychology of personal relationships*.

9.8.2   Development of relationships

Close relationships start very early in life. The human baby's first and most critical relationship is with its mother. The bond that is made during the nine months of pregnancy is the precursor to the maternal instincts which encourage a mother to feed and protect her offspring. This is fundamental behaviour which is found throughout the animal species, with few exceptions.

The father is perhaps a shadowy figure in the early stages of the life of a new baby. His role in its procreation, short but enjoyable, is well removed in time from the birth of the baby. In most cases, however, 'daddy' will be the second person with whom the infant has a unique relationship. Often, 'mummy', and 'daddy', are the first words a baby will learn. This brings us to another fundamental in human behaviour, the desire and need to communicate with other individuals. The very important activity of *one-to-one communication* provides a major part of the later material on communication.

As the child develops, so do other relationships. Interactions with family members: brothers and sisters; grandparents; the wider members of the family. At school, relationships develop with teachers and particularly with other children. These relationships may be formal, as with the teacher, or friendly (most of the time) with other pupils.

With the onset of puberty, a need arises for closer relationships. The human being is one species with a tendency to 'bond for life'. There are others, swans for example. With some species, the bonding is only for one breeding cycle. The increasing incidence of divorce in the more highly developed countries might suggest that life bonding is decreasing, or that the ability to make an accurate choice is deteriorating. However, most human adults have a need for a special relationship with another person, and although the phrase 'a meaningful relationship' has become a cliché, the phenomenon it describes is still important.

Special relationships sometimes occur in the working environment, and when they do, they can cause problems as well as benefits. Relationships at work are basically formal. There is work to be done; each person has a job function and a role to perform. Ideally, friendly relationships exist in the work place, but this does not always occur and in some instances the reverse is true. Technically it is not necessary for there to be friendship between co-workers. Some bosses may opt for a relationship with subordinates where there is an element of fear. 'You don't have to like me, you have to do what I say' observed the boss of one of the authors, when as a young engineer he unwisely expressed disagreement with a decision.

At work, the engineer tends to interact with a wide spectrum of colleagues, and needs to establish a viable working relationship with each and every one of them. If this can be friendly, so much the better, and you may even socialize after work with some of your colleagues. This can be a helpful, but not essential, element; you need only to establish a practical relationship for the duration of working hours. The key to this is communication.

9.9   INTERPERSONAL PSYCHOLOGY

9.9.1   Transactional analysis

In Part I of this book, teamwork was identified as a positive factor helping to enhance engineering performance, and confrontational attitudes were cited as an obstacle. Effective teams depend upon transactions between individuals, and a person's manner or the words chosen in the early stages of a dialogue can strongly influence the transaction. It is therefore important for engineers to be aware of the ways in which transactions between individuals can be 'managed', to improve communication and elicit cooperation.

Personality dynamics

The following is the introduction to an article by John Martin [9] on personality dynamics:

'Interpersonal work relationships display the complete spectrum of possibilities; cooperative and competitive, loving and hateful, trusting and suspicious and so on. Most individuals would like to improve some of their work relationships so as to make their job easier or more rewarding or more effective. The problem is that although we can all recognise relationships that aren't right, only a few know how to improve them. Often attempts to improve relationships are based on analyses of what the other person is doing wrong. Such an approach never works, and usually makes things worse.

There are three requirements to improving relationships. The first is to have a well-tried framework for thinking about and understanding what goes on in relationships — a theory. The second is to apply the theory to oneself so as to discover how one elicits the responses one gets and why these are unsatisfactory. The third is to use the theory and one's self-understanding to set about doing something different, i.e. relating to others in a different way. Experience in all sorts of management training, relating workshops, therapy groups, training groups and so on has demonstrated that such an approach can work; individuals who follow the above steps do find their relationships improving. One of the theoretical frameworks used in this sort of exercise is the Transactional and Structural Analysis developed by Eric Berne.'

A better understanding of personality dynamics can be obtained from transactional analysis (TA), and the basic principles of TA will be considered in the rest of this chapter. For an excellent analysis of the main features of TA, refer to the article by John Martin [9]. For further reading, the original works of Eric Berne [10] should be consulted.

The simple theoretical model

TA is all about interactions between people. The interaction is normally limited to two people, and concerns the *transactions* which pass between them. These are frequently in the form of a conversation, but can be by other forms of communication, such as body language, gesture and physical contact. Eric Berne calls these interchanges *strokes*. A remark by one person which elicits a response from another will be a two-stroke transaction.

The theoretical framework assesses the psychological state in which the participants find themselves during the transaction, and relates this to the psychological development of the individual from infancy. Three major *ego states* or sub-personalities are identified, which coexist in every individual over the age of five years. They are parent, adult and child, as shown in Figure 9.5.

The child is the biologically driven subsystem which provides emotions, feelings and energy (pleasure, sadness, excitement, curiosity, etc.). Almost all the basic components are there at birth, and a stable configuration is achieved by four or five years of age which remains unchanged until the emergence of adult sexuality at puberty.

The parent subsystem is established in the child during the first few years of life by copying and relating to its parents and immediate environment. Cultural background is assimilated by this process, and desirable and undesirable behavioural patterns are passed on from generation to generation.

The adult subsystem is the computer-like part of behaviour, which collects data, makes estimates and deductions, attempts rational judgements, and tries to make the individual behave in a logical manner. The adult ego state is present in the small child, but it is the part of the individual which 'grows up' as that person gets older, whereas the other two states are formed very early in life and remain

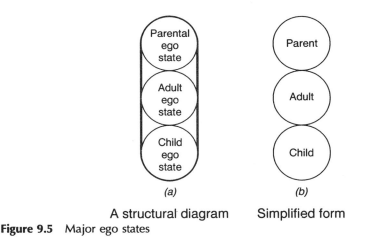

(a)   (b)

A structural diagram   Simplified form

Figure 9.5   Major ego states

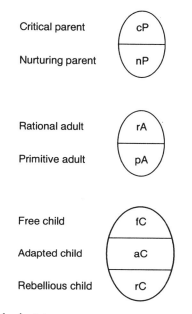

Critical parent — cP
Nurturing parent — nP

Rational adult — rA
Primitive adult — pA

Free child — fC
Adapted child — aC
Rebellious child — rC

Figure 9.6 Subdivision of sub-states

substantially unchanged. Even when the child and the parent ego states appear to be in control, the adult state can regain control if necessary.

John Martin suggests a simple method of distinguishing the major substates by the phrases used while in those states. The key adult phrase is 'I think I could do...'; the key parent phrase is 'I ought to do...'; and the key child phrase is 'I want...'. Other words frequently used which are indicative of the three states are listed in Figure 9.7.

The extended model

There are subdivisions of the three main states. The parent state can be subdivided into the two parts of the parental role, the nurturing parent, who comforts and supports, and the critical parent, who makes demands and sets standards.

Although it is not usual to subdivide the adult ego state in transactional analysis, it is possible to make a division into the primitive adult for the intuitive problem-solving abilities possessed even by young children, and the rational adult for the ego state which develops as the child's linguistic and conceptual skills increase.

The child starts as the free child, expressing simple and immediate needs, and becoming angry if these are not obtained. The free child soon has to compromise, and the adapted child, and its converse the rebellious child, develop.

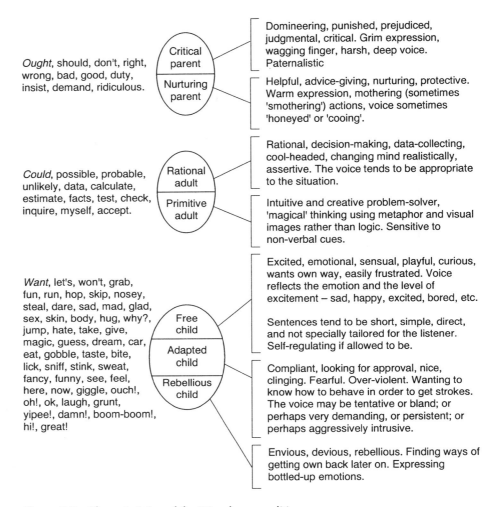

Ought, should, don't, right, wrong, bad, good, duty, insist, demand, ridiculous.

Critical parent

Nurturing parent

Domineering, punished, prejudiced, judgmental, critical. Grim expression, wagging finger, harsh, deep voice. Paternalistic

Helpful, advice-giving, nurturing, protective. Warm expression, mothering (sometimes 'smothering') actions, voice sometimes 'honeyed' or 'cooing'.

Could, possible, probable, unlikely, data, calculate, estimate, facts, test, check, inquire, myself, accept.

Rational adult

Primitive adult

Rational, decision-making, data-collecting, cool-headed, changing mind realistically, assertive. The voice tends to be appropriate to the situation.

Intuitive and creative problem-solver, 'magical' thinking using metaphor and visual images rather than logic. Sensitive to non-verbal cues.

Want, let's, won't, grab, fun, run, hop, skip, nosey, steal, dare, sad, mad, glad, sex, skin, body, hug, why?, jump, hate, take, give, magic, guess, dream, car, eat, gobble, taste, bite, lick, sniff, stink, sweat, fancy, funny, see, feel, here, now, giggle, ouch!, oh!, ok, laugh, grunt, yipee!, damn!, boom-boom!, hi!, great!

Free child

Adapted child

Rebellious child

Excited, emotional, sensual, playful, curious, wants own way, easily frustrated. Voice reflects the emotion and the level of excitement – sad, happy, excited, bored, etc.

Sentences tend to be short, simple, direct, and not specially tailored for the listener. Self-regulating if allowed to be.

Compliant, looking for approval, nice, clinging. Fearful. Over-violent. Wanting to know how to behave in order to get strokes. The voice may be tentative or bland; or perhaps very demanding, or persistent; or perhaps aggressively intrusive.

Envious, devious, rebellious. Finding ways of getting own back later on. Expressing bottled-up emotions.

Figure 9.7   Characteristics of the TA subpersonalities

The major substates, and their subdivisions are shown in Figure 9.6. The ego states, their characteristics, and the words often associated with them, are summarized in Figure 9.7, from John Martin's article [9].

Complementary transactions

In order to maintain a satisfying transaction, it is important that the initial transaction and response are in the same ego state, or a compatible one. Clearly if one person talks to another in an adult ego state, that person will not be kindly disposed to a critical parent response, still less to a rebellious child response. Also, if an individual wishes to complain about current difficulties, (on a rebellious child

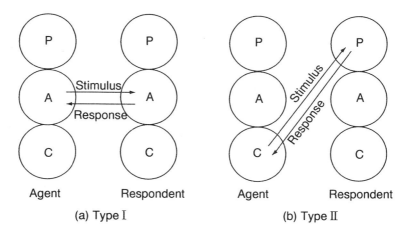

Figure 9.8   Complementary transaction

basis), a rational adult response precisely analysing the problems may not really be what the individual is looking for.

Berne analyses such transactions as follows: The comment or action which initiates the sequence of transactions is termed the *stimulus*, and the reply (again a comment or action) is termed the *response*. The simplest transactions are those between individuals in the same ego state, adult to adult for example, or child to child. Also satisfactory are transactions in compatible states such as parent to child. Berne designates these as *complementary transactions*, and differentiates them as Type 1 and Type 2 (see Figure 9.8). Each response is in turn a stimulus, so the interaction can continue almost indefinitely, or as long as it is worthwhile for the participants, provided the ego states remain compatible, and the transactions therefore complementary.

Crossed transactions

Disruptive to useful interaction and communication is the *crossed transaction* and it is this which causes social and communication problems, in both personal and working relationships. Berne comments that the problems caused by crossed transactions provide work for psychotherapists. He defines two types, see Figure 9.9. The stimulus could be adult to adult: 'Do you know where my pocket calculator is?', expecting to elicit an adult to adult response such as: 'It is under that pile of drawings'. If the response is: 'Don't blame me, I haven't borrowed it!' (a child to parent response), this is a crossed transaction. Another response could be: 'Why don't you look after your things properly?', which is also crossed (parent to child), and just as unhelpful.

If someone encounters a situation involving a crossed transaction, the first aspect to realize is that the transaction will have no useful outcome if it remains crossed. Therefore, the first reaction must be to find a way of uncrossing it, and there are two.

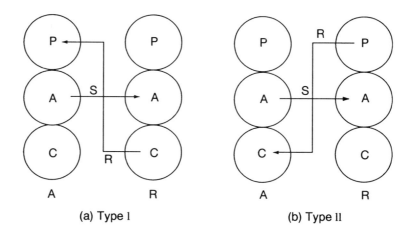

(a) Type I   (b) Type II

Figure 9.9   Crossed transactions

One is to try to reactivate in the respondent the ego state wanted originally, i.e. adult in the example given. The other is to find an ego state which is compatible with that of the respondent. If the respondent is in the child state, then a parent response (preferably nurturing parent) would be appropriate. If the respondent is in the parent state, a child response would be suitable, preferably adapted child.

On the simple and un-subdivided model of parent, adult and child, Berne analyses the possible combinations of transactions. The 3 × 3 matrix gives nine combinations, as shown in Figure 9.10. Berne identifies three complementary transactions between 'psychological equals': 1–1, 1–1 (parent/parent);5–5, 5–5 (adult/adult); and 9–9, 9–9 (child/child). These are transactions in which both participants are in the same ego state, and are perhaps the most fruitful. Three more complementary transactions are identified: 2–4, 4–2 (parent/adult); 3–7, 7–3 (parent/child); and 6–8, 8–6 (adult/child). All other combinations are crossed transactions. John Martin [9] gives some examples using the extended and subdivided model, and identifies that in most cases the person initiating the transaction assumes a preferred ego state in the respondent, and the best result is a reply in that ego state. The response may be from another acceptable ego state (complementary) or it may not (crossed). An acceptable response to the adult enquiry concerning the whereabouts of the calculator could be: 'I have not seen it, you can borrow mine.' (nurturing parent to adult). A crossed response would be: 'If you were more careful and put it away in your desk drawer, you would not waste time looking for it!' (critical parent to child).

Ulterior transactions

Berne has identified *ulterior transactions*, those in which the transaction occurs simultaneously at two levels. A transaction, often a spoken one, occurs at the social level. However, another transaction also occurs at the same time, and unspoken, at the psychological level. Berne has defined two types of such ulterior

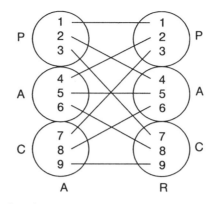

Figure 9.10 A relationship diagram

transactions, the *angular transaction*, which involves three ego states and the *duplex transaction*, which involves four. These ulterior transactions are shown diagrammatically in Figure 9.11.

The angular transaction is illustrated by Berne with a salesman's gambit, ploy or 'game'. The salesman comments to the customer: 'This one is better, but you probably can't afford it'. The transaction is ostensibly adult to adult, and the adult to adult response should be: 'No, that one is too expensive, but I can afford the cheaper model'. The psychological transaction is adult from the salesman, aimed at the customer's child ego state, which responds (unspoken): 'Though I can't afford the purchase, I'm not having that arrogant fellow making my decisions for me, I'm as good as any of his customers'. The sale of the more expensive unit is made, three ego states are involved, and one of the parties is being manipulated.

The duplex transaction can be illustrated by the behaviour of two adults in the later stages of a 'date'. The ostensibly adult to adult enquiry: 'Would you like to come up for some coffee?' may elicit the adult to adult response: 'Yes, I would love to see your flat'. The unspoken ulterior transaction is: 'I fancy you!', and again: 'I'm interested if you are !' We are now into a flirtation or seduction game. Either both parties are being manipulative, (adult to child), or some more fundamental instincts are taking over (child to child).

Rituals

There are many stereotyped and often meaningless procedures we adopt before the real transaction starts. These include greetings such as: 'How do you do'; 'Good morning'; 'How are you?'; 'Nice weather for the time of year'; and so on. Unlike the duplex transmission where two sets of interactions proceed in parallel, in the ritual very little is happening. It often provides a starting point for later transactions of more substance.

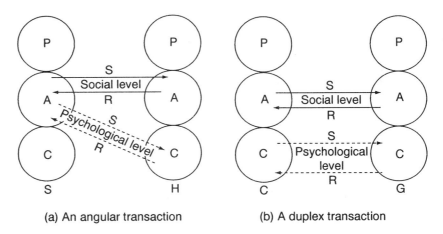

(a) An angular transaction   (b) A duplex transaction

Figure 9.11   Ulterior transactions

Games

Almost everyone needs to interact with other human beings; only hermits appear not to have such needs. Almost all people need 'strokes', and often behave in such a way as to encourage other people to 'stroke' them. The person chosen to be the partner in this activity will also need to be stroked, and will behave in a way that fulfils this need. Berne gives many detailed examples of such *games*, and the way people obtain the stroking that is essential for psychological wellbeing. Harris [11] also gives many examples of game plays, and it should be noted that use can be made by the unscrupulous of an understanding of 'games' to manipulate other people. The 'gamesman' may end up appearing wiser, more knowledgeable or more distinguished, and gain a spurious elevation of self-esteem. It can provide some mildly amusing entertainment when dealing with acquaintances, or people the 'gamesman' dislikes. The temptation to practise on one's friends should be resisted; it will cause a rapid decline in their number!

Conclusion

An understanding of transactional analysis allows individuals to be aware of the ego state they find themselves inhabiting, and to recognize it in others. It is possible thereby to respond more appropriately to the needs of the other person, and so perhaps achieve better understanding and cooperation. Recognition of a crossed transaction will allow the interaction to be modified so that a fruitful outcome can be achieved. An understanding of ulterior transactions enables an individual to understand the more subtle inferences of a seemingly simple interchange. An understanding of games will ensure that the individual can resist being manipulated to his or her disadvantage. It is best to aim for an adult/adult interaction in most situations that the young engineer will encounter, though there are some instances when other complementary relationships may be appropriate, for example the nurturing parent and adapted child mode of many superior and subordinate relationships.

9.10 SOME GENERAL CONCLUSIONS ON INTERPERSONAL RELATIONSHIPS

Many of the problems of life are concerned with achieving good relations with other people. This can be on a personal, domestic, social or work basis. The key to this is an ability to communicate, and an ability to understand something of the workings of the mind of the other person. In one-to-one relationships the objective is often simple, to obtain understanding of one's views and requirements, and to solicit the cooperation of the other person. The method is also simple, but not always easy to achieve. It involves communicating at all times in a clear and appropriate way, (see Chapter 12), and being aware, as much as possible, of the perspective of the other individual.

9.11 SUMMARY

This chapter has indicated the difference between the hard systems base of engineering, and the soft systems base of behavioural studies. The methods used by behavioural scientists have been discussed, and similarities noted with the empirical approach used by scientists and engineers. The roots of behavioural studies in psychology, sociology and anthropology were described. The basis of the psychology of the individual was briefly discussed, and the way individuals seek to achieve personal goals considered. Individuality, or the difference between people was discussed, and two methods of assessing this were summarized. The discussion of individuals concluded with an analysis of human motivation, and discussed two examples of models of human motivation which are regarded as helpful to the understanding of individual behaviour.

The psychological state of individuals during interaction was then considered. Personality dynamics was discussed on the basis of transactional analysis. A simple and an extended theoretical model was introduced, together with the concepts of complementary, crossed and ulterior transactions. Other aspects of transactional analysis such as rituals and games were discussed. The importance of awareness of the other person in any one-to-one interaction was stressed in the conclusions.

REFERENCES

1. Leavitt, H. J. (1964) *Managerial Psychology*. Second edition, University of Chicago Press, Chicago.
2. Cattell, R. B. and Kline, P. (1977) *The Scientific Analysis of Personality and Motivation*. Academic Press, London.
3. Myers-Briggs, I. (1987) *Introduction to Type*. Oxford Psychologists Press, Oxford.
4. Maslow, A. H. (1987) *Motivation and Personality*. Third edition, Harper and Row, London.
5. Herzberg. F. *et al* (1959) *The Motivation to Work*. Second edition, Chapman and Hall, London.

6. Mullins, L. J. (1993) *Management and Organisational Behaviour*. Third edition, Pitman, London.
7. Alderfer, C. P. *Existence, Relatedness and Growth*. Collier MacMillan, London.
8. McClelland, D. C. (1988) *Human Motivation*. Cambridge University Press, Cambridge.
9. Martin, J. (1984) in *Organisations: Cases, Issues, Concepts*, Eds Paton, R., Brown, S., Spear, R., Chapman, J., Floyd, M. and Hamwee, J., Harper and Row, London.
10. Berne, E. (1964) *Games People Play*. Grove Press, New York. Also published by Andre Deutsch, London (1966).
11. Harris, T. A. (1975) *I'm OK — You're OK*. Pan, London.

BIBLIOGRAPHY

Open University T244 Course 'Managing in Organisations'
Weihrich, H. and Koontz, H.   (1993) *Management*. Tenth edition, McGraw-Hill, Maidenhead.

10

Groups of people

10.1 INTRODUCTION

In the old joke, a psychologist is defined as a man who goes to the Folies Bergère, and looks at the audience. Those who attend entertainment such as theatres or sports matches, and who observe the crowd as well as the spectacle, will testify that the behaviour of a crowd differs in many respects from the behaviour of individuals. People will take actions as members of groups which they would not consider doing as individuals, and are sometimes swayed by the influence of others to actions which are inconsistent with their normal behaviour. It is therefore not surprising that psychologists have devoted great interest and much study to the behaviour of groups.

Since, in the world of work, much activity is undertaken by people in groups, and most organizations are set up with teams, committees, sections, departments and other agglomerates that could be broadly classified as 'groups', the industrial psychologists' use of their time in the study of group behaviour is worthwhile. Engineering is done in the main by engineers of various disciplines and experience working in teams. Managers are believed to spend about 50% of their time working in groups, and senior managers may spend more than 80% of their time working in groups. Thus engineers who aspire to management roles have a particular need to understand the purposes for which groups are established, how they function, and how the characteristics of the group members impact upon the group.

There is another old saw which defines a camel as a horse designed by a committee. This implies that something put together by a group of people may be an uncoordinated product, containing a hotch-potch of features acceptable to the majority, and other features included to keep individuals happy. It might also imply adverse criticism of the way committees operate. If this is so, why do people spend so much of their lives in groups? Perhaps because performing a task with a group of people can often be a very efficient way of achieving the objective, or because it is difficult to see how a task of substantial size could be achieved without using large numbers of people. The completion of the Channel Tunnel, or getting a man on the moon are examples of tasks which needed vast resources of money and people, and the coordination of such activity was a major management activity.

For individualists, groups and committees tend to be inhibiting. More gregarious 'team' people enjoy working in groups, and want the involvement and participation of everyone. The manner of operation of project teams with a well defined task is usually easier to comprehend than the operation of committees, where more complex personal interactions tend to occur. In this chapter, the workings of some of the most frequently encountered groups will be studied, together with the way the individual group member relates to the group.

10.2   TYPES AND PURPOSES OF GROUPS

10.2.1   Introduction

There are many types and purposes of groups. Some may be established in organizations in the form of semi-permanent formal work groups, such as sections, departments, divisions, and so on. Another system of group organization is the project team, which has a specific task and exists only for the period necessary to complete that task. The status, importance and power of the group can vary from the board of directors of an organization, which will have statutory responsibilities, to an informal (*ad hoc*) discussion group, which has no power and is significant only to its members. The purpose of the group is usually a major factor influencing its type, structure and characteristics. The basic purposes for which groups are formed will now be considered.

10.2.2   Organizational purposes

Work groups may be assembled within an organization for any of the following purposes:

- distribution of work,
- to bring together skills, talents and experience appropriate to a particular task,
- to control and manage work,
- problem solving and decision making,
- information and idea collection,
- to test and ratify ideas,
- coordination and liaison,
- negotiation and conflict resolution,
- inquest and enquiry into past events.

10.2.3   Individual's purposes

An individual may join a group for one or more of the following purposes:

- to satisfy social and affiliation needs, to belong or to share,
- to establish a self-concept, in relation to others in a role set,
- to gain help and support,

- to share in common activities,
- to gain power, promotion or political advantage.

10.3 GROUP EFFECTIVENESS

10.3.1 General

Groups utilize the abilities, knowledge and experience of the individual members, to a greater or lesser degree of efficiency. Groups tend to produce less ideas than the sum of the ideas which the individuals might produce working separately. However, the ideas produced are likely to be better because they are more thoroughly evaluated, and have the benefit of the greater collective knowledge of the group during this evaluation. Groups tend to take greater risks in decision making than the individual members might make on their own because the responsibility is shared. People behave in a more adventurous way in a group, because of the safety of numbers.

How effective a group might be depends on many things, some of which are inherent in the purpose, structure, membership etc., of the group (the 'givens'); another is the maturity of the group, which changes during the life of the group. The performance of a group can be enhanced by education in group behaviour and training in teamwork skills.

10.3.2 Givens

Group size

The larger the group, the greater the diversity of talent, skills and experience, but the less the chance of individuals participating to their full capability and making a useful contribution. The optimum group size is usually considered to be about five, six or seven.

Member characteristics

People with similar characteristics tend to form stable groups. The groups have homogeneity, but tend to be predictable and not particularly innovative. Groups with members having dissimilar characteristics exhibit higher levels of conflict, but are often more innovative and more productive.

Individual objectives and roles

If all group members have similar objectives, the group effectiveness is much enhanced. However, some group members may have specific objectives of which the rest of the group are unaware ('hidden agendas'). These can include such activities as covering up mistakes, scoring points, making alliances, paying off old scores, etc. When this occurs, group effectiveness can be much reduced.

Nature of the task

Effectiveness will vary with the nature of the task; whether it is urgent; whether the result can be measured in terms of time and quantity; how important the particular task is in terms of the objectives of the individual; and how clearly the task is defined.

10.3.3   The maturity of the group

The way a group performs will change radically during its existence. When the individuals who are to constitute the group first come together they may have no knowledge of one another. They may not know at the outset the skills, abilities and experience that the other members possess. They may not know how to cooperate and coordinate with each another. They are at the bottom of the learning curve.

As time progresses, so the group will develop and with effort (and perhaps a little luck), will become a coordinated working unit. How this happens has been the subject of much study, and a number of theoretical models have been proposed. Here are two examples:

Tuckman's model of group development

Tuckman [1] suggested that there were four stages in the development of a working group: forming, storming, norming and performing.

Forming: The group members meet for the first time. They are a set of individuals. They may not know each other, or much about each other. They need to establish what is the group purpose, who is to lead the group, who is to be influential in the group. Each individual wishes to establish a personal identity.

Storming: This is the conflict stage. More than one individual may feel a desire to lead the group. Leadership may be challenged. Interpersonal hostility may develop. Hidden agendas may become apparent. The successful handling of these problems by the group will lead to the formulation of realistic objectives.

Norming: Norms of group behaviour are established. Greater knowledge by group members of the skill resources available within the group allows appropriate work practices to be established. Greater trust and understanding by group members of other group members allows realistic decision-making processes to be set up.

Performing: The group is fully mature. It works in an efficient and coordinated way. There is open behaviour by group members, with mutual respect and trust.

Bass and Ryterband model

Bass and Ryterband [2] also suggest a four stage model:

Developing mutual acceptance and membership: Members initially distrust each other, and fear personal inadequacies. They are defensive, and limit their behaviour to conformity and ritual.

Communication and decision making: Members learn to accept each other, and to express their feelings. Norms of procedure are established. Members develop some sense of acceptance of each other. Open and constructive behaviour develops.

Motivation and productivity: Members are now involved with the work of the group. They cooperate rather than compete. Members are motivated, and productivity rises.

Control and organization: Work is allocated by agreement according to members' abilities. Members work independently, and the group organization is flexible and adaptable.

Although there are some minor differences of definition and emphasis between these two models, there is a great deal of similarity and a large measure of agreement on the key elements of the learning process.

10.3.4 Behaviour of mature groups

A mature group, one which is long established and which perhaps has an ongoing task, will exhibit a different pattern of behaviour. One model of this is the 'creative cycle' [3]. This also has four phases.

Nurturing phase: The members meet. There may be social discussion. Perhaps coffee or tea is served. Late arrivals may be sought. Papers are circulated, minutes of previous meetings may be discussed.

Energizing phase: The meeting proper starts. Discussions relevant to the group's purpose commence. Input is made and the required decisions are identified.

Peak activity phase: Interaction between members is high. Important matters are evaluated. Conflict may occur, and be resolved. Decisions are made.

Relaxation phase: All important business is complete. Participants begin to 'wind down', and consider their next activity or appointment. This is not the time to introduce significant new matters.

An example of the application of the creative cycle model would be the regular meetings of a management team, or an engineering project design team. These meetings might be monthly in the first case, or weekly in the second example. The purpose in both cases would be to review progress against schedule, and to resolve any problems that had occurred since the previous meeting, but could include other activities. Since the meeting is employed frequently as a means of communication and decision making, it will be considered in some detail.

10.4 MEETINGS

10.4.1 Introduction

The meeting format is much used in the working environment, many would argue that it is too much used, for it can be a very inefficient means of conducting business. Many managers spend a major part of their working time in meetings, of greater or lesser productivity, either as the chairperson or leader of the meeting, or as a participant. The efficiency and effectiveness of the meeting is critically dependent on the way it is run by the chairman, and on the behaviour of the meeting members. Engineers will encounter meetings with increasing frequency during their careers, and therefore would be wise to learn about their characteristics. Section 11.6 gives more details about meetings.

10.4.2   Types of meeting

Meetings can be generally classified according to their size, frequency, composition and motivation:

Size

Meetings can be placed in three broad categories according to size:

(1) Large — the 'mass meeting', with perhaps 100 or more people, divided into speakers and listeners;
(2) Medium — the 'council', with speakers, listeners, questions and comments;
(3) Small — the 'committee', with a maximum of about 12 people and a free range of discussion and interaction.

Frequency

Four groupings for meetings according to frequency are suggested:

(1) Daily — people liaising as part of their work;
(2) Weekly or monthly — meetings such as formal review meetings, or the coordination and decision meetings of functional heads in organizations;
(3) Annual — the type of meeting which is required by statute or some other governing ordinance, such as the annual general meeting of a public limited company involving the directors and the shareholders. These meetings tend to be very formal;
(4) *Ad hoc* — meetings of an irregular nature, occasional and usually called to deal with a special problem or situation.

Composition

In this case we can categorize according to the commonality of the activities of the participants:

● Same activity — engineers, nurses, doctors, accountants;
● Parallel activities — managers of sections of a production plant, leaders of sections of a project, regional sales managers of a marketing company;

- Diverse — a meeting of strangers of diverse interests, united only by one interest, which is the reason for the meeting.

Motivation

This category relates to the purpose of the gathering, which could be business or social, active or recreational:

- Common objective — process improvement task force, product design group, senior citizens club, football team, pressure group;
- Competitive — subsidiary company managers within a conglomerate discussing resource allocation.

10.4.3 Functions of a meeting

The most obvious functions of a meeting are communication and decision making, but the meeting also fulfils a rather broader spectrum of functions for the group. The meeting *defines* the team, the group, the section or the unit. An individual's presence at the meeting signifies full membership of the group, and allows identification with the other members of the group. Group members are able to share *information*, authority and responsibility, and to draw upon the knowledge, experience and judgement of the other members. The meeting enables each individual to understand the collective *objectives* of the group, and the way each member can contribute to the attainment of those objectives.The activities of the meeting create a *commitment* to the objectives and decisions of the group. The concept of 'collective responsibility' is generated. The meeting allows the group leader, (whether so designated or titled chairman or manager), to *lead and coordinate* the whole team. The meeting allows each individual to establish a *status* within the group, and the group membership can confer a status on the individual within the organization.

10.4.4 Managing a meeting

There are a number of training videos which give guidance on the correct procedure for managing a meeting. Two also demonstrate what can go wrong if the established guidelines are not followed [4]. In these, a demonstration is given of inept chairmanship which renders the meeting totally ineffective, (group members confused, essential decisions not taken), and inefficient (group members' time wasted). It is suggested that the five essentials to getting the meeting to operate well are, (with alliteration to assist easy memorizing): planning; pre-notification; preparation; processing and putting it on record.

Planning

It is worthwhile considering the objectives of the meeting at the outset. Is a meeting the best way to achieve these objectives? The chairman should be clear precisely what the meeting is intended to achieve by the time of its conclusion.

Pre-notification

All the other members of the group need to be informed about the meeting and its purpose. The time, place and duration need to be conveyed to the members, and these should be realistic to accommodate the known or anticipated commitments of the group members. Sufficient notice should be given to allow members to attend without having to cancel other engagements, and to acquire whatever information is needed to make a contribution to the meeting. Occasionally, a manipulative chairman or secretary may arrange the meeting at a time and place that ensures that certain members of the group cannot be present!

Preparation

To some extent, preparation runs in parallel with pre-notification. The matters to be considered need to be arranged in a logical sequence. The amount of time needed to consider each item should be assessed. The relative importance of the items should also be considered. Care should be taken that items that seem urgent should not take too much time, time that might better be spent considering longer term matters of greater importance. There is merit in an agenda which allows some quick decisions to be made on urgent but less important items at the start of the meeting, allowing more time for more detailed consideration of weightier matters for the greater part of the meeting. Group members need to know the agenda of the meeting in advance so that they can come fully prepared and able to contribute to the discussion and decision-making process.

Processing

The management of the meeting itself requires considerable skill, and it is surprising how often this skill is lacking in the people who chair meetings. The discussion of each item needs to be structured. Members need to be brought back to the point when they wander into subjects outside those scheduled for consideration (diversion), or attempt to revisit subjects already discussed (reversion). Loquacious members need to be gently but firmly restrained (repetition), so that the contributions of the more reticent members can be obtained. Attempts to have private discussions, or to have a mini-meeting within the meeting (diversion), should be firmly resisted. A skilled chairman can deal positively with any disagreements that arise during the meeting, and steer the group to a consensus. However, the chairman should not impose his view arbitrarily, a fault which often occurs when the chairman is significantly more senior than the other members of the group. To do so renders the meeting pointless, the same result could be achieved more efficiently by the chairman sending written instructions to each member. Members should be aware that the chairman may need their compliance to endorse his actions, and should not commit themselves to a course of action that they believe to be wrong.

Putting it on record

There is a need to summarize as the meeting progresses, and record the decisions made, their principal justification, what actions are to be taken, and by whom. This ensures that at a later date, perhaps the next meeting if there is one, the 'story so far' is clear, and progress can be reviewed without wasting time on establishing what was intended to be done. The notes may be taken by the chairman, by one of the members designated to do so permanently, or on rotation, or by a minute taker or secretary brought into the meeting for that purpose. The latter option has advantages as a member of the group can participate less if he or she also has to concentrate on keeping an accurate record of the proceedings. It is often helpful if the conclusions, decisions and action points are recapitulated at the end of the meeting to ensure that all members are clear about the outcome and committed to the decisions taken, before the meeting disbands.

10.5   DIVISION OF WORK

10.5.1   Introduction

Groups come together to form multiple groups, which in turn come together to form organizations. Examination of an established organization will show that it is composed of groups and sub-groups, and this system forms the organizational structure. There are many ways that these structures can be formed, and organizations frequently revise their structures in a search for the most efficient way of achieving their objectives. Here are some of the more common methods of division of work.

10.5.2   Major purpose or function

This is the most common basis. The group is formed according to its specialization, professional expertise, primary activity etc. Engineering would be an example, as would accounting, safety or medical services. In a large engineering organization, there may be subdivisions of more detailed engineering expertise, differentiating between civil, mechanical or electrical engineering. In very large engineering organizations, there may be further differentiation, for example, civil, structural, etc.

10.5.3   Product or service

This is common in large diverse organizations. The grouping is on the basis of activities associated with a large production line. An example would be a car production facility or a chemical plant complex for the product based industry, or particular services provided by an insurance company or an engineering consultancy.

10.5.4   Location

It may be more appropriate to group the activities on a location basis. This would apply to country-wide businesses such as multiple retailing, which would be grouped on a geographic area basis, or such organizations as British Rail, whose stations were grouped under the control of an area manager.

10.5.5   Time basis

Processes which have very high installation and depreciation costs, or which cannot easily or economically be started and stopped may be operated on a shift basis. This applies not only to production plants such as steel manufacture, but also to organizations such as police, hospitals, ambulance and fire services. The group may even be named as 'B shift' or 'Red watch'. Those industries which operate complex machinery on a continuous basis normally require an engineering maintenance service, operated on a shift basis.

10.5.6   Common processes

This covers such services which may be provided within an organization due to their general need by other groups within the organization. Examples would be a typing pool, personnel department or computer services.

10.5.7   Staff employed

The grouping is on the basis of the level and type of qualifications and expertise. Examples would include professional engineers, technical draughtsmen and laboratory technicians.

10.5.8   Customers

In organizations devoted to selling a variety of goods to the general public, the grouping may be perceived by market sector or purchasing power. Examples from the UK retailing business could include Woolworths, Marks and Spencer, Harrods, and Fortnum and Mason.

The former pair would provide good quality standard goods at competitive prices, while the latter pair would provide luxury goods at very high prices. The engineering equivalent might be good quality motor products of Ford, General Motors or Rover compared with the very high standard and performance products of Rolls-Royce, Lotus, or Lamborghini.

10.6   LEADERSHIP

10.6.1   Introduction

Any group, even if it is set up with absolute equality of membership, will tend towards a system in which the group has a leader. Of course, many groups are deliberately set up with an officially appointed leader. The England cricket team is selected after the captain has been appointed, and the captain has a role in the selection of the team. In other sports, the team may be selected, and a suitable person appointed captain from the team members by the team manager or controlling committee. There may even be a non-playing captain, or a more democratic approach may be taken, in which team members elect one of their number to be captain. The situation in sport is comparatively simple, as the objective is clear (to win the game), and the philosophy is established that all members of the team will contribute to the full to achieve this objective. Those that do not are unlikely to be selected for the next game. The democratic election of a leader occurs in other groups, particularly where the group members themselves are elected representatives such as parish, borough and county councils in England, or trades unions. In the former case the elected representatives may elect a leader from among their number, and in the latter case, this may also occur. Another option in the case of a trade union is that its rules may require the election of the leader by the total membership.

In the world of work, the leader of a group is usually appointed, by an individual, or by a body of individuals. That person then becomes the manager of the department, the director of the division, the leader of the section or the project leader of the project team. Regardless of the title, the role is that of leadership of that group, be it large or small, and the implication is that an individual can be a leader of a smaller group, or subsystem, and at the same time a member of a larger group or system, of which that subsystem is part. There is much commonality between the roles of leader and manager, though they are not the same. Managers without the ability to lead may become effective administrators, but leaders without management skills may fail.

Even an *ad hoc* group, one which forms casually for a particular purpose such as a discussion, a gossip, or a need to resolve a minor problem, will after a short while show evidence of one or more people attempting to 'lead' the group.

Leadership as a process whereby one person influences other people towards a goal. It may be a function of personality, it is related to motivation, and to communication, and cannot be separated from the activities of groups. Leaders are people who do the right thing to accommodate their team's visions. The leader/follower relationship is a reciprocal one, and to be effective must be a two-way process.

10.6.2   Management and leadership

Leadership and management are closely related. Many definitions of the components of management include leadership, as shown in Chapter 1, where

Mintzberg's description of the manager's role included leadership. Even so, a good leader may not be a good manager, and vice versa.

Management may be defined as the achievement of stated organizational objectives using other people, and is essentially within the organizational structure, or at the interfaces with other organizations. Leadership is based more on interpersonal relationships, and does not need to take place within the structure of the organization.

The components of management were analysed in Chapter 3, but this section concentrates on leadership which can be regarded as the bridge between the group processes and management. According to Hellreigel *et al.* [5], the principal roles of a *leader* are to set vision and direction, to align employees, and to motivate and inspire. The principal roles of a *manager* are to plan and budget, to organize and staff, and to control. Managers who are also leaders will do all of these functions.

Mullins [6] suggests that a leader may be elected, formally appointed, imposed, chosen informally, or may just emerge naturally. Mullins also differentiates between attempted, successful and effective leadership:

- Attempted: an individual attempts to exert influence over the group
- Successful: the behaviour and results are those intended by the leader
- Effective: the leadership helps the achievement of group objectives.

10.6.3   Sources of a leader's power

There are two basic sources of a leader's power. They are:

- Organizational power: Legitimate — Reward — Coercive
- Personal power: Expert — Referent

Organization sources of power

With *legitimate power*, the subordinate perceives that the leader has the right to exercise power. Authority is conferred by position within the organization hierarchy. With *reward power*, the subordinate perceives that the leader has the ability to reward him/her with, for example, pay, privileges, praise, overtime, promotion etc. With *coercive power*, the subordinate fears that the leader has the power to punish him/her, for example by withholding the rewards mentioned previously, and/or giving reprimands, fines, dismissal etc.

Personal sources of power

With *expert power*, the subordinate perceives that the leader has special knowledge or ability or experience which make him/her specially able in a particular area. With *referent power*, the subordinate identifies with the leader who has particular characteristics which the subordinate admires. This could be respect for the leader's values, or admiration for his/her charisma.

Power in the engineering environment

There are no great problems in relating these generalized concepts of power to engineering activity. The director of an engineering division in an organization, the manager of an engineering department in a company, and the leader of an engineering based project are all appointed by the appropriate authority of the organization or company concerned. This authority can replace the individual if it so chooses. While the individual holds the job, he has legitimate power, and the direct subordinates are required by their terms of employment to perform any reasonable instruction given by the leader, within the terms of the job. This is a formal, even a contractual relationship, and the leader is justified in exercising legitimate power. Since the same terms of contract will include arrangements for salary, bonus, and other elements of reward, and also disciplinary procedures, the employment contract will also define some elements of the reward and coercive powers of the legitimate leader. However, the other elements such as praise, blame, the allowance of privileges and the use of criticism will be more directly related to the specific task in hand. A junior engineer may be praised by his leader for a well thought-out design study, but criticized for the imprecise phrasing of the accompanying report.

The young engineer may respect another engineer colleague if this individual has evident talent, skills, qualifications and experience, and will defer to him in areas where these abilities are significant. The colleague therefore has expert power. If the young engineer also respects the ethics, values and principles of the colleague, then any influence exerted by the colleague is derived from referent power. The most successful managers and leaders in engineering activity are very likely to be able to draw to some extent on all the sources of power mentioned previously as they perform their leadership and management function.

10.6.4   Analyses of leadership

Various attempts have been made to examine the basis of leadership. Three aspects are regarded as important by many analysts: *qualities or traits*; *situation*; and *functional* or *group*.

Qualities or traits

This model assumes that leaders are born, not made, and that leadership ability is within the person. Some investigators who have studied acknowledged great leaders of the past have found little correlation of characteristics. Others note the commonality of the traits of intelligence, supervisory ability, initiative, self assurance, individuality, dependability, etc. The subjectivity of this analysis is a major limitation, as is the inability to assess the relative value of the characteristics. It could be suggested that these would vary according to the circumstances in which the leadership was required. This leads naturally to the situation model.

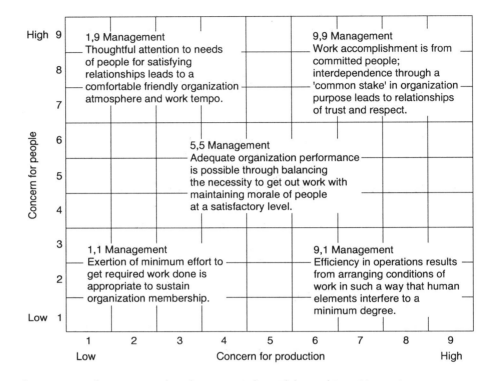

Figure 10.1   The managerial grid (source: Robert Blake and Jane Mouton)

Situation

People with different personalities and from different backgrounds have become successful leaders in a variety of circumstances. Professional knowledge or specific expertise is important, as is the way the leader performs his task. The implication is that training for leadership is possible. However, it seems that knowledge and training do not completely fulfil the requirements. Though professional knowledge, skill and experience would be necessary for the leadership of a high profile, time limited and critical engineering project, and for the management of engineering standards within a large, high-technology organization, the personal characteristics required for these leadership functions would probably be very different.

Functional or group

This model considers the functions of the leader, and how his/her behaviour interacts with the group of followers. Adair [7], identifies three major activities: *task* needs; *team maintenance* needs; and *individual* group member needs. *Task* functions involve: achieving group objectives; defining tasks; work planning; resource allocation; quality control; performance monitoring; reviewing progress.

Team functions involve maintaining team morale; maintaining team cohesiveness; setting standards; maintaining discipline; communication; group training; delegation.

Individual functions involve meeting individual members' needs; sorting personal problems; giving praise; awarding status; reconciling individual/group conflicts; individual training.

Another rather simpler version of the same model was devised many years ago by Blake and Mouton [8], and has been a major element of management thought to the present time. This model differentiates the task elements of leadership, and the people elements, in the form of a two-dimensional matrix. This model does not differentiate, as does the Adair model, between the team people needs and the individual people needs. It is shown in Figure 10.1.

Blake and Mouton apply their model to leadership in an organizational situation, and therefore term it a management grid. Various styles of management are defined on the two-dimensional matrix according to the extent to which the requirements for task management and people management are addressed. They range from a minimal attention to either element, '1/1 or impoverished management', to '9/9 or team management' in which both elements are addressed to the full.

10.6.5 Functions of leadership

Adair [7] suggests three major functions:

(1) Awareness — group process; underlying behaviour;
(2) Understanding — knowing which function is required;
(3) Skill — to lead effectively, which can be assessed by group response.

Krech [9], in an analysis which is similar to that of Mintzberg mentioned in Chapter 3, identifies 14 functions:

(1) Executive — coordinator of activities and policy execution
(2) Planner — ways and means, short and long term
(3) Policy maker — establishes group goals and policies
(4) Expert — source of skills and knowledge
(5) External representative — spokesperson for the group
(6) Internal relations controller — establishes group structure
(7) Rewarder/punisher
(8) Arbitrator/mediator — controls interpersonal conflict
(9) Exemplar — behaviour model for the group
(10) Symbol — provide cognitive focus and entity
(11) Substitute for individual responsibility — relieves individuals of responsibility
(12) Ideologist — source of beliefs, values and standards
(13) Father figure — focus for positive emotional feeling and identification
(14) Scapegoat — 'can-carrier' in the event of failure.

It would take too long to quote examples of the relevance of all these activities in an engineering context, and the detail would not be helpful. Sufficient to say that any manager experienced in leadership in an engineering function would recognize the existence of all of them, and be able to quote many specific examples. The extent to which an individual would be required to exercise leadership will depend on the size and nature of the engineering organization. In a small and highly specialized engineering consultancy, the senior partner may well fulfil most or even all of these functions, even causing some feelings of frustration by other members of the consultancy. In a large engineering organization, the various aspects of leadership may be fulfilled by any number of individuals in various functions within the organization.

10.6.6   Styles of leadership

Here are some styles which have been identified in the literature, with some elements of explanation:

- Authoritarian/autocratic/dictatorial — the leader alone makes all the key decisions;
- Democratic — the leadership function is shared with the members of the group;
- Bureaucratic — the leader takes decisions according to the established organizational mechanisms;
- Benevolent — the leader is motivated by the best interests of the group, and acts as a 'father figure';
- Charismatic — the leader's personality is so strong that the group members follow his/her bidding;
- Consultative — the leader takes the views of the team members into consideration, but makes his/her own decision;
- Participative — the leader accommodates the views of the group members when coming to a decision;
- Laissez-faire — the leader observes the group and allows them to get on with the job as they see fit, but acts as an adviser and is available when help is needed;
- Abdicatorial — the leader lets the group do the job as they see fit, and provides no advice or help. It is arguable that this is the absolute opposite to dictatorial/autocratic leadership, and is zero-leadership and therefore no longer justifies the name.

These tend to lie on a spectrum from authoritarian and dictatorial at one extreme via consultative and democratic to *laissez faire* and abdicatorial on the other. Another way of considering this spectrum of leadership styles is to assign four positions on the continuum, where the leader tells, sells, consults or joins:

- Tells — the leader makes a decision, informs the subordinates, and expects them to expedite the decision.
- Sells — the leader makes the decision, and explains and justifies it to the team.

- Consults — the leader discusses the problem with the team before making the decision.
- Joins — the leader defines the constraints of the problem, and jointly makes the decision with the team.

It is clear that the spectrum of leadership styles is very wide, from the absolute 100% leadership of the autocrat or dictator, to the 0% leadership, (even non-leadership), of the abdicatorial leader. It is difficult to say with certainty where the most appropriate engineering leadership style might be, for the obvious reason that engineering activities vary and the most appropriate leadership style for each activity will be different. It is possible, however, to narrow the spectrum somewhat, to eliminate some extreme options, and to suggest some criteria for style selection.

As the activity is peopled by trained professionals, it is unlikely that the subordinate members of an engineering team would find a dictatorial or autocratic style of leadership acceptable for very long. Also, such a style would not be rational since it would require the leader to be totally expert in all aspects of the subject. If this were so, the expertise of the other members of the team would not be needed, and they could be replaced by less experienced and less well qualified personnel with the attendant saving of cost. Though readers may be aware, as are the authors, of instances where leaders have attempted to follow an autocratic style within an engineering activity, it is rarely successful, and usually proceeds via seething discontent to confrontation.

At the *laissez faire* and abdicatorial end of the spectrum, there is little compatibility with the physical requirements of engineering in the real world, which involves the delivery of a product or service, to cost, to time, and to specification. Neither abdicatorial or *laissez faire* leadership is likely to provide the necessary impetus and coordination to achieve this, though the latter might just cope in the area of engineering research. The most likely area for an effective leadership style is the 'tells' or 'sells' area. The greater or lesser elements of democracy will depend on the personality of the leader and the nature of the task. Since the leader is likely to be established formally in the role by the organization which commissions the task, and will carry the responsibility for the success of the task, it is likely that the style will veer towards the 'tells', rather than the 'sells', particularly when difficulties arise.

10.6.7   Theories of leadership

The contingency theory of leadership

Three key components are identified in this model proposed by Fiedler [10], which considers the influence of the leader/member relationship, and such contingency variables as the task structure, group atmosphere, and position power.

The business maturity theory of leadership

Clarke and Pratt [11] believe that the most appropriate style of leadership may vary according to the maturity of a business:

- Champion — needed for the 'seedling' business;
- Tank commander — growth stage of the business, capture of markets;
- Housekeeper — mature business, keep it running smoothly and efficiently;
- Lemon squeezer — for the business beyond its sell-by date, the need is to squeeze as much out of it as possible.

Leadership theories in an engineering context

The Fiedler model is an integration of components which have been discussed in earlier sections of this chapter, and the comments on the engineering applicability made for the components apply to the integrated version. The Clarke and Pratt model was devised for businesses, and can be related to engineering based businesses. It can also be applied to the embryo, developing, established, and waning elements of the engineering functions within a business. An example of an engineering based business which has followed the Clarke and Pratt model is the UK shipbuilder, Swan-Hunter. An embryo business in 1860, it grew rapidly in the 1870s, and was an established major contributor to Britain's shipbuilding from 1880–1960. Thereafter it waned from 1960–1990. An example of the changes that may befall the engineering function in an organization can be found in those companies manufacturing automatic calculators and cash registers. The early models of both were essentially mechanical devices. The current equipment is mainly electronic. The mechanical engineering function in the companies making such equipment has declined with the change of the basic technology, while the electronic engineering requirements have increased.

10.7   TEAM MEMBERSHIP

10.7.1   Introduction

The team, and being a member of a team, is a concept to which most people are introduced very early in life. The domestic family unit may, with luck, have some of the elements of a team. In pre-school and early school activities, children become members of many teams, usually organized by the teacher. The self-organized group, or 'gang' may not be formal, but it will still have some characteristics of a team. At school, most sport is arranged in the form of team games. Some simple management justification can be found for this. If it is necessary to organize some exercise for a large number of children, what more convenient and economical way of doing this than by a team game of football, netball, cricket or hockey? If rugby football is the chosen sport, 30 children can be exercised simultaneously!

So playing the game, playing for the team, and showing team spirit is a part of the European culture and education, and that of most other countries, almost from the start. The broader concept of team spirit, where the collective good of the team and achieving the objectives of the team, rather than those of the individual, is one of those aspects of education which is believed to be character building. It is soon learned that the individual who wishes to maximize his own achievements; score all the goals, make all the runs, is not the person most desired as a team member. Like the Three Musketeers, there must be an element of 'One for all, and all for one'. It is sometimes possible to create a team of 'star' players, in football for example. Even then, a team with less overall talent, but whose players coordinate better together, may be victorious. In another field, that of music, it is found that the best string quartets are formed from musicians who are very good, but not of international soloist standard. The individualism and bravura of the soloist may not produce as good and as integrated a performance as slightly less brilliant musicians who have practised long together, and therefore work better as a team.

This applies to the selection of teams for engineering activity. The recruitment for an engineering project of a team consisting of 'star' designers of international reputation might not be as successful as its cost would require.

There are jobs to be done in the team, and roles to be taken. These can be specific: an individual cannot be both striker and goal-keeper, bowler and wicket-keeper. They can also be more general: not every member of the team can be the leader, there are other roles or functions which need to be done in the team. In the domestic and social world, people can to a great extent choose the groups or teams they wish to join, and the choice will depend on how the objectives and values of that team or group coincide with their own. At work, the choice of colleagues is rarely available, so it is essential to develop techniques of working with other people to achieve the objectives of the group, team or organization. Engineers in particular have to learn to do this to a high standard of professionalism.

However, it is not only in engineering that the team approach is becoming more prominent. In other technical and even non-technical areas, the use of problem solving teams is increasing. Greater use is being made of project teams for activities within organizations. The simplification of organizational structures, and the introduction of greater flexibility in such structures, which has been one of the outcomes of the 'restructuring' of many companies in response to the recession of the early 1990s, have made it possible for companies to use a project team approach more widely. The need to accelerate the speed of the development of a new concept to a marketable product has encouraged the use of new concepts of multiple interlocking teams such as concurrent engineering. A flexible team approach suited to the operation of long term high technology projects will be discussed later in section 10.7.7.

10.7.2   Motivation

The way in which individuals are motivated was discussed in Chapter 9, and the extent to which group members will be motivated by the activities of the group will depend on a variety of aspects of the group activity. Satisfaction is one of the possible outcomes of group activity, and although a satisfied group is not necessarily a productive group, it generally helps it to be so. Lack of satisfaction will lead to absenteeism by group members, satisfaction is not all that is required for motivation.

An individual will be satisfied with a group if:

- The individual likes and is liked by other group members, i.e. friendship.
- The individual approves of the purpose and work of the group, i.e. task.
- The individual wishes to be associated with the standing of the group, i.e. status.

One or more of these can lead to satisfaction, depending on the *psychological contract*. In the work situation, there is a *formal contract* between employer and employee which states, for example, the task, the hours, and the pay-rate. There is also an *informal contract*, which both parties understand, and which covers the reciprocal needs such as the employees need for time-off for personal reasons and the employers for extra work when the firm is busy. The psychological contract is the often unconscious expectation that the employer and employee, or the group and the group member, have of one-another. It often surfaces only at moments of stress or crisis.

It is important that the group members know what is expected of them, and the standards that they are required to achieve. High standards will give a sense of achievement when attained, and this will contribute to the motivation of the group members. It is also important that the group receive feedback on the results of their efforts. For example, if a team of engineers has designed and built a road, a bridge, a piece of equipment, or a process or production plant, then three major indicators of team performance would be that the new unit was completed to cost, to time, and to specification. The team need to know the extent of their success against these criteria, and to be rewarded in some way or at least praised if they have fulfilled or exceeded the requirements. They also need to know of any shortfall, so that they can learn from the experience and do a better job next time.

Motivation by involvement will only result if the individual perceives that the group and its task are important to that individual. Sometimes it is possible to generate motivation within a group by looking outside the group into the greater organization, or into the environment beyond the organization, and identifying a 'common enemy'. Unfortunately, this can often generate rivalry and conflict between groups within the organization which may be counter-productive to the objectives of the organization.

10.7.3 Characteristics of team members

The seminal work in this area is that of Belbin [12], who studied the performance of teams of management students undertaking a business game. The students were mature people who held senior posts in commerce and industry and the studies continued with many teams over a period of nearly ten years. The objective was to assess what characteristics of the teams and their members made the difference between relative success and relative failure in the management game, which was competitive and designed to simulate real conditions.

The eight role model

Belbin found that there were a number of characteristics which contributed to the success or failure of the team. The ability of the individuals and their general characteristics were measured by various psychometric (personality) tests, but teams with apparent greater ability and with apparently compatible personality characteristics did not perform significantly better than less well endowed teams. Belbin found that the *roles* which individuals undertook in a team were important, and defined eight roles which were significant in team performance: company worker (CW); chairman (CH); shaper (SH); plant (PL); resource investigator (RI); monitor/evaluator (ME); team worker (TW); completer/finisher (CF).

The functions of the team roles are described as follows:

- *Company worker* (CW) Turns concepts and plans into practical working procedures; and carries out agreed plans systematically and efficiently.
- *Chairman* (CH) Controls the way in which a team moves towards the group objectives by making the best use of team resources; recognizes where the team's strengths and weaknesses lie; and ensures that the best use is made of each team member's potential.
- *Shaper* (SH) Organizes the way team effort is applied; directs attention generally to the setting of objectives and priorities; and seeks to impose some shape or pattern on group discussion and on the outcome of group activities.
- *Plant* (PL) Advances new ideas and strategies with special attention to major issues; and looks for possible breaks in the approach to the problem with which the group is confronted.
- *Resources investigator* (RI) Explores and reports back on ideas, developments and resources outside the group; creates external contacts which may be useful to the team and conducts any subsequent negotiations.
- *Monitor/evaluator* (ME) Analyses problems; and evaluates ideas and suggestions so that the team is better placed to take decisions.
- *Team worker* (TW) Supports members in their strengths (e.g. building on their suggestions); underpins members in their shortcomings; improves communications between members and fosters team spirit generally.
- *Completer/finisher* (CF) Ensures that the team is protected as far as possible from mistakes of both omission and commission; actively searches for aspects of work which need a more than usual degree of attention; and maintains a sense of urgency within the team.

Belbin also provides a self perception inventory. The questionnaire allows an individual to determine his compatibility with the various team roles, and his relative preferences, i.e. the most preferred team role, next most preferred, down to those which are least attractive. Thus it is possible to add to the psychometric tests an assessment of most preferred and least preferred team roles. Many years of application of these tests has allowed the prediction of likely success or failure of a particular set of individuals who form a team, though the prediction of failure is easier than the prediction of success. Specifically, Belbin identifies particular combinations of individuals with preferred team roles that are known to cause problems and he indicates ways by which the composition of the team should be adjusted to give a better balance.

Two other general points need to be made. The team may not have as many as eight members, and it would therefore be impossible for each role to be assumed by one team member. For smaller teams, a particular team member may need to assume more than one role. In larger teams, there will be some role duplication. Even in smaller teams, in practice a team member may have to assume a second preference, or 'back-up' role, if there is more than one individual capable of the first preference role. This is termed: 'making a team-role sacrifice'. To give a cricket analogy, if there are two competent wicket-keepers in the team, one may have to field at first slip, or better still at second slip, to avoid role confusion and conflict. In engineering terms, an individual who is familiar with doing the stress analysis of a mechanical design and is happy and comfortable with this function, may have to move to a second string activity, such as pressure vessel design, if the team happens to contain a stress analyst of national standing.

The nine role model

In 1993, Belbin published an up-date on his continuing investigations on the subject of team performance [13]. Two of the team roles were renamed, and a ninth role was added to the model:

'Two of the roles have been renamed, largely for reasons of acceptability. "Chairman" has become "Coordinator", and "Company worker" has become "Implementer". The former term was originally chosen on the grounds of factually referring to the role of the person in the Chair. In the end it had to be dropped for three reasons: its status implications were judged too high for younger executives; in the eyes of some it was "sexist"; and it was liable to be confused with the title that could signify the head of a firm. "Company worker", by contrast, proved too low in status, being especially resented by managing directors who were so described, and the word "Implementer" was eventually substituted.'

The most significant change was the addition of a ninth role: 'specialist'. This role was added after the eight-role theory had been applied in a substantial number of industrial examples. It was found that in project work, (a major user of the team system), relevant professional expertise was significant, and could not be ignored without endangering the objectives of the project. The inclusion of the specialist in the team was also an important element in career development, by widening experience or by encouraging personal growth. This observation correlates with those of one of the authors [14] in balancing the expertise and experience of team members in a long and complex project, while at the same time maintaining continuity.

However, the model needs to be extended further to accommodate the increasing use in engineering related projects of multi-discipline and multi-specialist teams, and the requirement for interlinking or even interlocking teams in some complex projects. Though most engineers will have to adopt one or more of the roles defined in the earlier model on many occasions during their careers, the role of 'specialist' will probably be one of the most frequent. With the increasing use of multi-discipline teams, particularly in the larger, more sophisticated, and more 'high-tech', projects, the majority of the team will be specialists. The specialists, under these circumstances, will need the capability of adopting other roles to facilitate the team activity. Referring back to the Tuckman model, role adoption could take place during the 'storming' phase of the formation of the group, with some role sacrifices being made before the 'norming' phase can commence.

There is growing use within engineering based organizations of *ad hoc* groups, i.e. groups set up with a specific short or medium term objective.

These can be problem solving working groups (PSWGs), quality circles (QCs), quality implementation teams (QITs), departmental improvement teams (DITs), process improvement teams (PITs), team oriented problem solving groups (TOPS), and concurrent engineering groups. The highly interactive nature of such groups, combined with their intermittent meetings and impermanent nature, make understanding of roles and group behaviour even more important if a useful outcome is to be achieved. The contribution of Tuckman and Belbin is very helpful to such understanding. There is growing use of facilitation as a means of helping the group to a successful result. If the facilitator is familiar with the objectives for which the *ad hoc* group has been formed, understands the techniques being used, and is experienced in group behaviour patterns, then he can be a major assistance to the group. In particular, the facilitator can recognize and resolve problem situations, both incipient and actual, which the group members may not be able to recognize due to their heavy involvement in the work of the group.

Since the *ad hoc* group tends to meet from time to time, a need becomes quickly apparent for those good practices identified in section 10.4.4 for meetings, such as advance notice of the gathering, well prepared agenda, notes on progress of activity at the last meeting etc. With an *ad hoc* group, there is perhaps even more need for skilful leadership from the leader or chairman of the group.

10.7.6   Team role behaviour

Belbin identifies six major factors which contribute to behaviour and performance in a team role. These are:

(1) *Personality* — psycho-physiological factors, especially extroversion/introversion and high anxiety/low anxiety. These factors can be assessed by psychometric tests.
(2) *Mental abilities* — high level thought can override personality to generate exceptional behaviour.
(3) *Current values and motivations* — cherished values can provide a particular set of behaviours.
(4) *Field constraints* — behaviour can depend on constraining factors in the immediate environment.
(5) *Experience* — personal experience and cultural factors may serve to conventionalize behaviour, or behaviour is often adapted to take account of experience and conventions.
(6) *Role learning* — learning to play a needed role improves versatility.

In practice, it is seldom the case that there will be a psychologist on hand to assess the personalities of potential team members and to give advice on appropriate selection. However, those who select people to form teams for engineering projects could well consider the factors that Belbin believes underpin role behaviour when considering potential team members. Young engineers who wish to be achieve selection might also give them some thought.

10.7.7   Teams in engineering activity

Belbin tends to use the word 'behaviour' frequently in his analysis of team performance, which is to be expected from a psychologist and behavioural scientist. Teams in engineering activity tend to be judged more on performance, and those who make this judgement are generally those who commission the engineers to perform the task. To the judges, delivery is what matters, the behaviour which assists or impedes this is not their immediate concern.

There are two very significant elements which are relevant to teams of engineers: the importance of experience, and the possibility of role learning. This means that experience of working in teams is helpful. Furthermore, people can be trained in team-working skills. In principle, the available potential team members can be assessed, and the Belbin systems of analysis used to ensure that the requisite role playing skills are represented, and no incompatible combinations are present.

However, a number of factors are significant for the management of teams to undertake engineering activity. The appropriate engineering expertise must be available within the team. Work of one of the authors [14] suggests that there is a need for a variety of specialist expertise to be available throughout a long project, but that continuity needs to be maintained. This continuity is not only necessary in leadership and management, but is also essential for technical reasons. Another practical difficulty is that the 'pool' from which the team is selected is likely to have a limited population, and with the down-sizing of many engineering and technical organizations in the early 1990s, it could be very limited. The 'specialist' role of Belbin's newly revised model is of critical importance in technical and engineering projects, and the specialism is likely to have two components; technical or scientific knowledge or understanding, and practical experience of the application of that knowledge. In some instances, this specialization will be generally available. For example, most major engineering contracting companies can provide experienced personnel over the spectrum of established engineering techniques. However, in the areas of innovation, leading edge technology, and new product and process development, the availability of the essential specialists may be very limited. In any case, the organization may be constrained to use the staff it has, and may be unwilling or unable to recruit extra personnel. In that case it will be necessary to prioritize, and it is recommended that the scarce specializations are given first priority, the other specialisms second and the non-specialist roles third. Whatever flexibility in team selection is then available can be subjected to review to establish any Belbin incompatibilities, and if possible to adjust to give a team as balanced as possible in Belbin terms.

10.8   SUMMARY

This chapter was concerned with people in groups. Initially, the types of group were considered, and then their purpose, both for the individual and for the organization. The relationship between the effectiveness of groups and their size, member characteristics, individual objectives and roles, task, and the maturity of the group was discussed. Some models of group development were presented, together with a model of the behaviour of the mature group. The chapter continued with a discussion of personal interactions within groups. The meeting was considered in some depth, with an analysis of types of meeting, their functions, and how they should be managed. How groups are formed within organizations was assessed by division of work. The next main topic was leadership. The relationship between leadership and management was discussed, together with the sources of the power of a leader, the styles and functions of leadership, and some theories of leadership were introduced. The final topic was teams. Some motivations to become a member of a team were given, and the work of Belbin on team member characteristics was outlined. Two models of team roles were described, and the factors which contribute to team member behaviour summarized. The importance of team building and team roles was considered, particularly that of the specialist, and its importance in engineering projects was emphasized.

REFERENCES

1. Tuckman, B. W. (1965) 'Development sequence in small groups' *Psychological Bulletin*, 63.
2. Bass, B. M. and Ryterband, E. C. (1979) *Organizational Psychology*. Second edition, Allyn and Bacon.
3. Open University Course T244, Block II Work Groups, The Open University Press, Walton Hall, Milton Keynes MK7 6AA.
4. *Meetings, Bloody Meetings*, Video Arts Ltd, (London & Birmingham) 1993, *More Bloody Meetings*, Video Arts Ltd, (London & Birmingham) 1994.
5. Hellreigel, D., Slocum, J. W., Woodman, R. W. (1976) *Organizational Behaviour*. West Publishing, St Paul.
6. Mullins, L. J. (1985) *Management and Organisational Behaviour*. Pitman, London.
7. Adair, J. (1979) *Action Centred Leadership*. Gower, Aldershot.
8. Blake, R. R. and Mouton, J. S. (1985) *The Managerial Grid III*. Gulf Publishing, Houston.
9. Krech, D. *et al.* (1962) *Individual in Society*. McGraw-Hill, Maidenhead.
10. Fiedler, F. E. A. (1967) *Theory of Leadership Effectiveness*. McGraw-Hill, Maidenhead.
11. Clarke, C. and Pratt, S. (1985) 'Leadership's four part progress', *Management Today*. March.
12. Belbin, R. M. (1981) *Management Teams, Why They Succeed or Fail*. Butterworth, London.
13. Belbin, R. M. (1993) *Team Roles at Work*. Butterworth-Heinemann, Oxford.
14. Reavill, L. R. P. (1995) Team management for High Technology Projects, *Management of Technology Conference*, Aston University, April.

11

Communication

11.1 INTRODUCTION

Communication is critically important to the interaction of individuals, to groups of people undertaking a variety of activities, and most particularly to organizations trying to coordinate their work towards a common objective. Engineers are not exempted from the need to communicate clearly and effectively, both to other engineers as part of the team activity that engineering often requires, and to non-engineers, who may be less able to understand the technical concepts on which engineering is based. No matter how skilled an engineer may be, he or she will not succeed without the ability to inform, persuade, instruct, argue with, and convince, other people. The mirror image of this also applies. The engineer needs to be able to receive communication, to understand instruction, and to interpret information.

Young engineers can believe quite correctly that attaining technical competence in engineering science and its practical applications is their first objective. To communicate this acquired competence is of equal importance, and it is for this reason that a substantial chapter of this book is assigned to theoretical and practical aspects of communication directly relevant to engineering activity.

11.2 COMMUNICATION IN THEORY

11.2.1 Theory of one-to-one communication

Communication is a process by which information and data are passed between individuals and/or organizations by means of previously agreed media and channels. Chappell and Read [1] define communication as a process by which information is passed between two units (individuals or organizations) through appropriate channels. Communication can also be defined as any means by which a thought is transferred from one person to another.

So, in the simple situation of communication between two individuals, there are four key elements: the person with the thought or information to communicate, designated the *transmitter*; the person to whom the thought or information is to be communicated, designated the *receiver*; the means by which the thought or information is to be transferred, the *medium*; and the method of connecting the two participants, the *channel*.

11.2.2   The medium

Though the two participants could be individuals, groups or organizations, for the purposes of this chapter, and of establishing the basic principles, two individuals will be considered. The medium can be any form of symbols or code understood by both the transmitter and the receiver, and could include words (both spoken and written), figures, graphs, diagrams, pictures, facial expression, etc. In times past, media such as Morse code were used for international communication, and flag signals (semaphore) were used by ships at sea.

11.2.3   The channel

The word media, (plural of medium), is much used currently as a collective noun for the many means of mass communication such as newspapers, magazines, radio, and television. These are really channels of communication. Each newspaper or magazine will convey information in the form of written words or pictures (media). The newspaper or magazine itself is the channel of communication, the direct link between the writers of the news reports and articles, and the reader. For the radio broadcast, the medium is the spoken word. Other information may be given in the form of 'sound effects'. The channel is the radio station to which you tune your set. In the case of television, the station to which you tune your television set is termed a channel. In the UK currently four 'terrestrial' channels are available in most parts of the country, together with other systems such as 'Sky' and cable television. Provided the appropriate equipment is available, the signals can be received, and the programmes watched. The media used include the spoken word, pictures, and occasionally diagrams or written words. So in this particular example of a major means of public communication, all the terms so far discussed are present: medium and media, channel, transmitter and receiver. However, we cannot be sure that true communication has taken place. Has the receiver understood the message that the transmitter was trying to convey? Has the message even arrived at its intended destination?

11.2.4   Feedback

Transmission is not communication. The other person may not be listening. We need some response from the receiver to know that the person has both received the message and understood it. For successful communication, the response of the receiver must be the one intended by the transmitter. To be fully effective the information must flow both ways, and this return message is termed the *feedback*.

By the nature of the feedback message, the transmitter can judge how well the original message has been understood. It should be noted that in the feedback process, the roles of the two participants have reversed: the original receiver transmits the feedback message for the original transmitter to receive. The feedback message does not necessarily have to be verbal or written, the

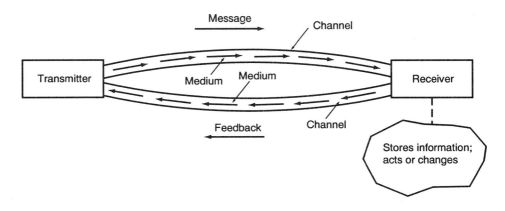

Figure 11.1   The fundamentals of communication

information sent may be stored, i.e. remembered, by the other person, there may be a change of attitude or behaviour, or the receiver may act as intended. Suppose you see someone about to step into the path of a speeding car, and shout 'stop!'. If the person stops, the action is the feedback, and a genuine (and helpful) communication has been achieved. If the person does not hear (channel of communication not established), or does hear but does not understand your instruction (not the response intended), another casualty could be added to the road accident statistics.

A simple conceptual model of communication, relating the elements introduced so far, is shown in Figure 11.1.

11.2.5   Verbal communication

Verbal communication, the conversation of two people together face to face, has a number of advantages. The most significant is the immediacy of the feedback. The receiver of the initiating message can ask questions of the original transmitter to clarify the message, or can supply answers if the original message asked a question. As the conversation continues, new subjects may be introduced by either party, and information will flow in both directions.

11.2.6   Conversation

Not all the information exchange in a conversation is verbal. The message can be attenuated or emphasized by tone of voice (harsh, friendly, jocular), and people sometimes communicate unintentionally by facial expression or posture ('body language'). This will be discussed in a section 11.7.8.

11.3   COMMUNICATION IN PRACTICE

11.3.1   Introduction

The theory of communication suggests a simple process which should work efficiently. All that is required is to formulate the message clearly, select an appropriate medium which will allow easy feedback, and all will be well. Why is it then that our questions receive inadequate answers, our messages are misunderstood, and our clear instructions are not carried out properly? Well, there may be many reasons, but most of them can be traced to poor communication. Though simple in theory, achieving good communication is quite difficult in practice. The more complex the message to be communicated, and the more people involved, the more the difficulty is compounded. Complex communication in large organizations presents particular problems. For the moment, if the basic problems of one-to-one communication can be identified, they will provide the basis for the more complex variations.

11.3.2   Opening the channel

A person has a message to give to another person. How can the channel be established or opened? If the other person is present in the same room, it can be merely a matter of attracting that person's attention, for example by establishing eye-to-eye contact, or making an opening remark: 'Excuse me'. This may elicit a response, perhaps 'Yes, what do you want?', and the channel is open. The message has yet to be passed, but already there is evidence of feedback, in that the other person is at least demonstrating a willingness to listen. The transmitter must ensure that the channel remains 'open'. The would-be listener may be distracted by some other event: the telephone might ring, or the remarks might get so boring that interest fades.

Let us suppose that the other person is not present. A means of communication must be selected. Possibilities include the telephone, the fax, and the postal service. If a letter is sent, the message can be written clearly in a form which the correspondent will understand, but it may take a day or so to reach her. Even if she replies, 'by return of post' it will take some time to learn if the message has been received and understood. She may receive the message and be so convinced that she understands it that it requires no reply. In this situation, information has transferred, but the transmitter does not know that the message has been understood, or even received. Hence the importance of feedback at the most fundamental level. By a system of letter and formal acknowledgement, accurate communication can be achieved, but it can take a long time.

Perhaps it might be quicker to telephone. Once the number is dialled and the telephone receiver is picked up, the channel is established. Well, perhaps it is, if the would-be receiver is at home, and answers the telephone. Maybe there will be no reply as she is not there. There may be an answering machine, so a message can be left, but the transmitter will not know when she will receive it. With ill luck, her father may answer, and the message is definitely not for him!

The fax may present a compromise of speed and accuracy, but still lacks the immediacy of the one-to-one contact. Even the telephone has disadvantages, in that the extra information available visually from your correspondent will not be available. However, the letter and the fax do have the advantage of putting the information on record, which will not be the case with a conversation based exchange, unless one of the participants takes the trouble to record all conversations, like the late US President, Richard Nixon. As another American, the film tycoon Sam Goldwyn commented, 'A verbal contract isn't worth the paper it's written on!' In law, a verbal contract is worth as much as a written one, but proving the verbal contract is more difficult.

11.3.3 Choosing the code

In section 11.2.2, the medium was described as a previously agreed system of symbols or code which is understood by the transmitter and the receiver. The examples mentioned were: words, graphs, diagrams, and pictures. The important factor is that the code or symbols are fully understood by both parties. This might at first sight appear simple, but often it is not.

Consider this example. In England, someone might address a remark to another person in English with a reasonable expectation of being understood. By mischance, the person could encounter in London a first-time visitor from Latvia who understands very little English. An English speaking person, visiting the USA or Australia, could confidently start a conversation in English, as the inhabitants of those countries speak their own version of English. When on holiday in Italy or Greece, an attempt to converse in the language of the country would be recommended. Someone whose Italian or Greek is weak or non-existent might be forced to resort to other means of communication, such as gesture or drawing a picture or diagram. Indeed, there are some messages which might be more easily expressed in these terms. For example, explaining which particular spare part is required for a car repair may be helped by a drawing of the part, or pointing at the appropriate section of an exploded diagram in the car manual.

Thus, at the start of the attempted communication above, a medium was chosen (words), and a code selected (English). The choice might, or might not, be appropriate, and this will soon become clear. If English is not a code understood by both parties, an attempt might be made to identify a common language. The Latvian visitor could be directed to his destination using a few ill-remembered phrases of German, and diagrams drawn on the back of his guide book! The scenario is that a code has been selected, and an attempt has been made to *encode* a message. It has been found that the receiver does not understand the code and therefore cannot *decode* the message, and other codes are tried until a common one is found. To some extent the medium has been changed, i.e. from words to diagrams.

11.3.4 Encoding and decoding

Consider the simplest of situations, in which Smith wishes to give Jones a message. Both are present and speak the same language. The stages in the activity are as follows:

(1) Smith has the content of the message in his mind.
(2) Smith formulates this message into words (encoding).
(3) Smith engages the attention of Jones.
(4) Jones gives Smith his attention (channel open).
(5) Smith enunciates a series of words (transmission).
(6) Jones hears the words (reception).
(7) Jones interprets the meaning of the words (decoding).
(8) Jones now has the message.

Even in this most simple of situations, without feedback it will not be clear that the message has been accurately received and Smith will have to judge from the response of Jones how successful the process has been. Even with a common language, people may interpret the same phrases differently for many reasons.

11.3.5 Barriers to good communication

A surprisingly large number of obstacles stand in the way of good communication, which perhaps accounts for the difficulty in maintaining a good standard in this activity. Here are some of the more significant ones:

Language

As mentioned before, a language must be found which is understood well by both parties. The linguistic *style* must not be too complex for both participants. The linguistic style of an academic may not be appropriate for the shop floor of an engineering factory, or vice versa. If there are specialized components, linguistic short cuts such as acronyms, or technical or other forms of *jargon*, these must be fully understood by both parties.

The *accent* of the speaker may give problems if the listener is unfamiliar with that accent. Most 'Home Counties' English people can cope with the accents of Devon and Cornwall, Wales, Scotland, and Ireland both north and south, and have learnt to understand, perhaps with the help of motion pictures and television 'soaps', American and Australian accents. The metropolitan accents of London, Birmingham, Liverpool, and Newcastle can easily be identified, and accent can often be used to identify geographical origins and social standing within the UK, though not perhaps in the precise detail suggested by G B Shaw's Professor Higgins in '*Pygmalion*'.

Dialect is a different problem, since this usually involves additional vocabulary, regional turns of phrase as well as different pronunciation. People who tend to use dialect expressions in their conversation should remember to eliminate them when talking to someone who is unfamiliar with the expressions.

Culture and education

Culture tends to influence communication largely in the way that information is understood and interpreted, and to some extent the importance and significance attributed to it. *Education* will determine the extent to which the concepts of the conversation are understood by both parties. A technical education will help the understanding of engineering matters and a classical education would help in the literary area. It is helpful to have some knowledge of the culture and education of your communicant, and a few exploratory exchanges, ostensibly for social purposes, can assist business communication. Some Japanese companies, for example, have a stock list of questions aimed at securing information about new business associates.

Personal

People may be selective when receiving a complex communication, or one containing a number of elements. A subordinate in discussion with a superior may give greater emphasis to the more complimentary aspects of the superior's remarks. To an extent, the subordinate may 'hear what he wants to hear'.

In a rather similar example of the superimposition of other mental processes on the simple one of decoding the message, more credence will be given by the receiver to information from someone with status or expertise, or for whom the receiver has great respect. This is called the 'halo effect'. The converse is also true. The information from an individual in whom the receiver has little confidence may be disbelieved, regardless of its true value. A metaphor for this is 'the singer, not the song'. Advertisement creators use this effect to influence buyers. The person advertising the product may wear a white coat, the image being that of a 'scientist', thereby giving the information presented a bogus credibility. When the actor concerned adds a stethoscope to the costume, the even greater credibility of the 'doctor' image is created.

The interpretation of the message is very much dependent on the perception of the receiver, and on that person's frame of reference. Perception is how the individual 'sees' the information and its context, i.e. how it relates to that individual. The frame of reference can be defined as those aspects of our principles, beliefs and experience which go together to make the context against which we judge events. A young single woman who is thinking of leaving her job to get married and live in another area of the country will be little concerned by a message of possible redundancy circulated by her employers. A middle aged married man in the same organization, with a sick wife, a large mortgage and five school-age children, and who had been made redundant from two previous jobs, would probably react entirely differently to the information.

Behaviour of the transmitter

There is much that the transmitter can do to help the communication process. The aim should be accuracy, precision and conciseness. This means that the information sent should avoid the woolly, the vague and the ill-defined, the long winded and the over detailed. The style is also important. A person who presents the information in an enthusiastic and confident manner is much more likely to convince his listener, than one who approaches the communication process in a morose and apologetic fashion.

Behaviour of the receiver

The receiver can do as much to help the process as the transmitter. The major problems to avoid are:

- *Inattention* — The channel is not open, so no messages can flow.
- *Distraction* — The receiver allows himself to be distracted during the transmission of the message, and the channel closes in mid transmission.

Process maintenance

Communication is a process, and like all processes, it requires maintenance, i.e. attention to ensure that it keeps going. The major problems to avoid are:

- *Attenuation* — The system must ensure that part of the message does not get lost.
- *Noise* — Extraneous signals which prevent the receiver from being able to pick up the message, for example background noise during a conversation, must be eliminated or reduced in order that the message can be received.
- *Distortion* — The system must avoid the distortion of the message in transit, or an inaccurate version will be received.
- *Overload* — If the transmitter is sending more information than the receiver can assimilate, then a situation of overload exists. Rate of transmission should not exceed the receiver's capability.
- *Redundancy* — Sending the same information more than once does not always help. The duplication wastes time and may fray the receiver's patience. However, it is noticeable that advertisers, particularly on television, tend to multiple repeats of the name of the product. Their assumption may be that the listener is stupid (or uninterested), or more possibly that they do not have the listener's undivided attention. Repetition is necessary to increase the chance of getting the message through when the channel is open.

A more detailed conceptual model of the communication process is given in Figure 11.2.

11.3.6   A short exercise

Consider the following sentence, which encapsulates many of the problems of poor communication:

'I know that you believe that you understand what you think I said, but I am not sure that you realize that what you heard is not what I meant!'

Try what is called a reductionist analytical approach to the sentence, i.e. break it down into its component parts, and see how many parts can be related to the process and problems outlined so far in this chapter.

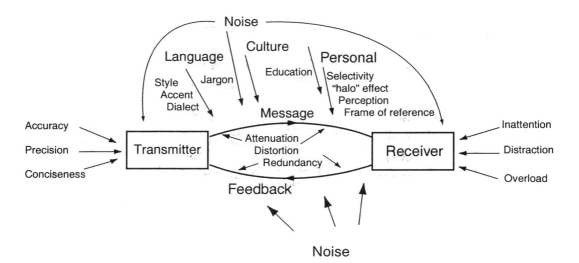

Figure 11.2   Conceptual model of communication

11.4   FORMAL COMMUNICATION SYSTEMS

11.4.1   Interviews

General

An activity which is frequently used in the working environment for communication purposes is the interview. Generally, the interview is on a one-to-one basis, though in certain cases, for example the recruitment or selection interview, the format may involve the interview of one person by a selection panel.

At the workplace, interviews are used for a number of purposes. The most common include the recruitment/selection interview already mentioned, the induction interview, the progress or appraisal interview, the discipline interview, the counselling interview and the termination interview. These will be examined in a little more detail later. Examples of many types of interview can be demonstrated by means of the many excellent training videos currently available [2].

The primary purpose of an interview is the acquisition or exchange of information. There may be other subsidiary purposes such as decision making, but these are usually dependent on the information that has been obtained. All the good general principles which have been considered so far apply to the interview situation, and every effort should be made to ensure good standards of communication or the exercise will be ineffective.

Selection and recruitment interviews

These terms are almost synonymous. We could perhaps differentiate the recruitment interview as the situation where an organization wishes to add to its complement of employees, and recruits externally. Candidates may be found by advertisement, or from agencies, according to the type of job involved. The selection interview might be to fill a post within the company from current employees, either by transfer or by promotion. Here, the candidates would be identified by the personnel department from company records.

The job selection interview is something that a student is likely to encounter in the later stages of a university career. If the student has been interviewed for a place at university, the basics of the exercise are similar. The interviewer will be anxious to discover as much as possible about the candidate, for example: qualifications, experience, aspirations, and potential. The interviewer will have guidelines on the characteristics required by the organization and the particular job. The consequent decision from this information will be whether the candidate is suitable, and if there are a number of candidates, which is the most suitable. The candidate will be equally keen to obtain as much information as possible. He will want to know the conditions of employment, what the duties will be, whether the company will provide an appropriate career and whether he will be happy to work for that organization. Again this may lead to a consequential decision by the potential employee, who may be lucky enough to obtain more than one offer of employment, to select the post which is most suitable.

As in all interview situations, preparation is essential. The interviewer must have a mental or written specification of the job, and clear guidelines on company norms and policies. He will have the details supplied by the candidate on an application form (a documentary communication of information) and should use this as a basis for confirmation and expansion. The candidate should also have done his homework, and obtained details of the company, its policies, and, if possible, the opinions held about it by employees.

The induction interview

This might be considered the second phase of information exchange by the successful candidate. Details of the company's ways of working will be imparted to the new employee. Training plans, company rules and regulations, and other information given only to employees will be discussed at such an interview, and introductions made to site, premises and colleagues.

The progress or appraisal interview

Most organizations with a well developed personnel policy will have a scheme of appraisal interviews. These will normally take place once a year and will involve a representative of the management, usually the employee's supervisor, reviewing the employee's performance and progress. It enables the organization to indicate the areas in which the employee has performed well and those in which performance could be improved. It enables the employee to discuss any problems he may have and how his career is progressing and might progress further.

There are four major activities in an appraisal interview:

- review the case history in advance
- listen to the evidence and agree an analysis
- face up to any problem areas
- agree and review a plan of action.

The discipline interview

In the working environment, discipline is about having a clear and fair framework in which everyone can work; rules on safety, time keeping, standards of work, etc. It is also about ensuring that these rules are kept and standards are maintained, and if they are not, taking action to close the gap between the actual performance and the required performance.

There are three major activities in a discipline interview:

(1) establishing the gap between required and actual performance
(2) exploring the reasons for the gap
(3) eliminating the gap.

The counselling interview

This covers the situation where an employee, a member of a team or department, has a problem. They may come to their supervisor for advice, or the problem may be so evident that the supervisor notices that it is beginning to affect their work. Two possible courses of action which the supervisor may be tempted to take are to disregard the problem (telling the individual 'stop making a fuss, pull yourself together!'), or to impose a solution. Both are doomed to failure. Usually the best action is to help the individual to find his own solution to the problem.

There are four stages in a counselling interview:

(1) setting up the counselling session
(2) encouraging the person to talk
(3) helping the person to think things through
(4) helping the person to find his own solution.

The termination interview

This can incorporate the termination of employment by the employer (dismissal, redundancy), or by the employee (resignation, retirement). In the former case, there may be elements of recrimination. Even so, there still remains information which needs to be transferred, such as terms of compensation, pension entitlement, the address of the Department of Employment, etc. In the case of the resignation of an employee, it provides an opportunity for the organization to establish, if it does not know already, the reason for the departure. Much valuable information may be obtained by the company from the termination interview. It costs substantial sums of money to recruit employees and train them, and a low staff turnover is considered advantageous. It also gives the employee an opportunity to make any comments on the organization and its practices that he feels impelled to do.

Summary

There are four major activities in *any* interview:

(1) The interviewer should always be clear as to the *purpose* of the interview, and what results he wishes to obtain from the interview.
(2) The interviewer must always *prepare* thoroughly for the interview and obtain all the required data beforehand.
(3) Adequate time must be allowed for *performing* the exercise, and privacy assured. Questions must be put clearly and concisely. The interviewee must be encouraged to talk, and attention paid to what is said and left unsaid. Both interviewer and interviewee should use, and note the use of, body language. Notes should be taken as unobtrusively as possible. The next action should be agreed before the interview is ended.
(4) The results of the interview should be recorded, and progress on any agreed actions monitored.

11.4.2 Written communication

Introduction

There is very little that is formal in the short note that is scribbled to a friend, or to let a colleague know of a telephone message. However, the fact that the message or information is written constitutes a record for as long as the 'hard copy' is kept. Even if the message is captured in some other form, for example a computer file, the element of formality exists. A person's word may be their bond, but a piece of paper with a signature is more acceptable to the lawyers.

Here is a comment on the activity of writing from a professional writer, the novelist Simon Raven [3]:

'I enjoyed writing, and it was my pride to render clear and enjoyable what I wrote. A reader, I thought, must pay in time and in money for his reading; both courtesy and equity therefore required, not indeed that one should defer to his possible opinions, but that one should attempt to entertain him while demonstrating one's own. This is a matter of the simplest common sense, but as relatively few aspirant writers ever seem to grasp the point, those that do set out with a distinct advantage.'

The professional engineer, unlike the novelist, will rarely be paid for writing as such, except perhaps for an occasional article in a technical journal, for which the fees are likely to be minimal. Also, unlike the novelist, it is not the duty of the engineer writer to entertain the reader. However, the rest of Raven's comments, and his emphasis on clarity, of getting one's point across, and of doing this in a way which the reader will find acceptable, are germane to our purpose. Focus your attention on the reader. Always have a mental picture of your intended reader when you write a piece. Knowledge of the reader's needs and capabilities are crucial. What is the point of writing anything if it is not read by the intended recipient? Make your material 'user friendly'!

Professional engineers are frequently called upon to communicate their ideas, or report on their work, to others. Similarly, engineering undergraduates are required to write essays and reports during their course of study, to explain the results achieved in laboratory experiments, the bases of design studies, and as a general training for future employment. The following paragraphs give some general guidance on written communication.

Syntax

Your syntax, the grammatical arrangement of words in sentences, must be correct. So must the punctuation and the spelling. There is no excuse for bad spelling. Use a dictionary!

If you have a word processor, establish whether the software package includes a spell-check. Some advanced software packages may include a grammar checking system. Use of the spell-check will eliminate the majority of spelling errors, but not all of them. The spell-check operates by comparing each word you have typed with the computer's data-bank of words. If the system recognizes the word it will pass on to the next. If it does not, it will stop and ask you to check the word. Remember it only checks that the word exists. The computer does not check that you have used the word properly, or that your spelling is correct in the context in which you have used it. Also, the package may have American spelling rather than English. For example the element sulphur (English) is the same material as sulfur (American), and aluminium (English) is the same metal as aluminum (American).

Difficulties arise with grammar and with clarity of exposition because sentences are too long. Short sentences are easier to construct correctly, and easier to understand. An average sentence length of between 25 and 30 words is desirable. Try not to exceed 40 to 45 words. The tense of verbs constitutes another problem. Re-examine sentences and paragraphs to see whether the tense has shifted between past, present, future, conditional, etc., without reason. Another popular error is to mismatch the plural form of a verb with a singular form of subject or vice versa.

The most effective way to eliminate punctuation errors is to read the piece aloud, or get a friend to read it to you. Lack of fluency, hesitation, or breathlessness will indicate any shortcomings.

Content and structure

The engineer must ensure that the content of his writing is clear, correct, concise, and courteous. Every report or essay should have a discernible structure; an introduction, a direction and a conclusion.

Do not use five words when one will do. 'Because' is much simpler than 'due to the fact that'. 'Now' means the same as 'at this present moment in time'. The use of simple words makes for more economical, more easily understood, and often more elegant writing.

Avoid jargon (words the reader might not understand); words which seem impressive, but which you do not understand; or undefined acronyms and meaningless abbreviations.

Resist the use of clichés or hackneyed phrases, such as 'leave no stone unturned', 'free, gratis and for nothing' (five words meaning the same as the first), or 'the acid test'. The latter phrase is a specific term used in assays, and should be avoided in essays. So should weak puns like the last sentence. A cliché should only be used if an original or genuinely witty variant can be found, such as that of the theatre critic who attended a poor variety performance, and returned home to write his review, determined to leave 'no turn un-stoned'.

Essays

Essays are commonly used for the expression and development of ideas. The purpose may be to inform, analyse, explain or persuade. Success will depend on whether the essay is made interesting, whether it is well presented, whether it contains a clear line of argument and whether it is concise.

All essays should have an introduction to tell the reader how the author intends to approach the subject. Where an essay theme is wide ranging or capable of broad interpretation, the writer must define, and possibly justify, the limits of his or her discussion.

Each theme should be discussed in a separate paragraph. Paragraphs having less than eight sentences and 250 words are easier to read than longer ones. Paragraphs and themes should be presented in a logical sequence. Emphasis and balance should be controlled, not arbitrary.

An essay in which a case is argued should reach a conclusion. An essay which discusses a range of inconclusive issues should end with a brief summary of the ideas advanced. An essay which is simply descriptive should, at least, be 'rounded off' so that the reader knows that the end has been reached.

Reports

These are usually more formal than essays. Their objective is to inform and persuade, and they depend more on measured evidence, and less on passion. A report should have an executive summary, introduction, main body, and a conclusion.

The *executive summary* will summarize the findings and conclusions, normally in half a page, and certainly in less than one page. The *introduction* will indicate the purpose of the report and the context, perhaps the background reasons for undertaking the exercise. The *main body* will describe the procedures and methods adopted, and will report on the findings. If the findings consist of extensive tabulation, calculations etc., then they should be summarized in the main body and the bulk placed in appendices. The main body may be divided into sections and subsections for clarity, with suitable headings and sub-headings.

The *conclusions* will state what conclusions the author derived from the findings. Recommendations based on these conclusions may be made, if appropriate. Where the writer is seeking guidance or authority, it is helpful to phrase the recommendations so that the reader only has to sign the document to achieve the required result.

A report which has been commissioned should always begin by stating the terms of reference. If specific facts, figures, conclusions or quotations are made from published material or other sources, this should be acknowledged in the text, and a list of references included at the end of the report. If material is used generally, (but not specifically), from published material, this should be acknowledged in a bibliography at the end of the report.

An undergraduate project report should be arranged as follows:

Title sheet
Contents
Synopsis
Introduction
Main body
Conclusions (and recommendations)
References and/or bibliography
Appendices

Readability

A well known, but rather complex, method of assessing readability is the 'Fog Factor' devised by Gunning [4]. The calculation involves the average sentence length, the number of separate ideas in a sentence, and the number of words with three or more syllables. The answer apparently relates to the number of years of education required to read the passage with ease.

As a check on the readability of a piece of writing, consider the following:

(1)   What is the objective in this communication, and is a written document the best way of achieving it?
(2)   Is the document well orientated towards the reader, both in form and content?
(3)   Does the title explain the relevance of the document to the reader, and does the first paragraph explain this relevance in greater detail?

(4)   Is the document as clear and simple as rewriting can make it?

(5)   Are graphics (pictures, graphs, diagrams, etc.) used to maximum advantage?

(6)   Are signposting devices such as contents lists, headings and sub-headings used as much as possible to make the message easy to follow?

(7)   Are the main points repeated to ensure clear understanding, and are the reactions required of the reader clear or the conclusions he is to accept precisely stated?

Some ways to improve clarity

(1)   Simple declarative sentences are easier to understand than more complex forms; active constructions are easier to understand than passive; positive constructions are easier to understand than negative.

(2)   Many words widely used in industry such as policy, productivity, security, turnover etc., have different meanings for different groups of people. Choose your words with care, be mindful of your intended audience and define every doubtful term.

(3)   Abstruse language often masks fuzzy thinking. When the language is starkly simple, the thought stands out more sharply.

(4)   Paradoxically, a simple style demands more time and effort than a long-winded style.

(5)   Thinking in managerial jargon inhibits new approaches and imaginative solutions to problems. Writing in managerial jargon produces confusion in the minds of both the writer and the reader.

(6)   Jargon can speed communication between people within the same discipline or at the same level, but it causes a breakdown of communication between people of different disciplines and levels.

(7)   Charts, graphs, diagrams, posters etc., offer less scope for misrepresentation than words. It is easy for the reader to visualise information presented graphically, so this is a useful method to communicate technical information to non-technical people.

11.4.3   Summaries and abstracts

Introduction

Frequently in the industrial work situation the young engineer will be attempting to convince a more senior colleague of his views on plans, policies, purchases, technical standards etc. As the colleague is more senior, he will be thankful for saving as much of his time as possible. Crosby [5] refers to the 'elevator speech'. The individual with the point to make enters the elevator or lift, and the senior colleague is already on board. The senior person is trapped for a minute or two, and there is an opportunity for a very short speech in favour of the plan or proposal. The speech is a verbal version of a summary, and summaries or abstracts are very useful forms of written message, particularly if the recipient is known to be very busy.

An *abstract* is an extended title, useful for information storage, and for helping a reader decide if the subject matter of a paper is of interest to him. However, the paragraph at the beginning of a paper or report may be entitled *summary*. This can also be a very short version of a report or paper for a slightly different readership. A *précis* is an exercise in shortening to a specific length, but not reorganizing. As such, it may be useful as a comprehension test, but has no place in informative writing.

Four uses of summaries

For the busy reader a summary is necessary when he or she cannot read the whole document because of lack of time. The summary must present the reader with the main conclusions and recommendations, and the major reasons to support them. This reader will not look at the rest of the report, so the summary must stand alone.

For all readers, a summary helps focus attention on the topic of the paper or report, and its conclusions. The summary does a similar job to a quick flick through the paper itself. It gives readers an overall picture, a sort of map of the paper, which will help them to orientate themselves as they read through the document subsequently.

For the marginally interested reader it acts as an abstract, an extended title, to help the reader decide whether to read the whole paper.

For all readers a summary is a help to memory, a set of notes, to remind them what was in the report itself. This is especially useful when looking back over a paper some time after reading it. The summary acts as a hook to fish out of the recesses of the memory the forgotten details of the report.

Remember the reader

Many readers are prepared to allocate a few minutes to getting a rough idea of what a report is about. This time limit is independent of the complexity of the material. Therefore it is the reader's motivation and needs, rather than the complexity of the report, which will condition the length of the summary. The reader who is given only a few sentences is likely to supplement this by leafing through the paper itself. The writer could better employ the reader's attention with his own deliberate choice of supporting detail. Conversely, if a summary is too long, (more than a page), the reader may skim even the summary, thus defeating its purpose. Thinking about the reader in these terms provides a sense of realism about length.

On style, it is suggested that note form is more difficult and time consuming to read than normal prose.

11.5   GROUP INTERACTIONS

This section will consider how communication occurs within a group. This will affect significantly the performance of the group, and the level of satisfaction obtained by group members. In Chapter 9, communication between individuals was discussed, and the point was made that there needed to be a channel for the communication process. If more than two people are involved, it is possible for interaction to take place between all those involved. With two people, there are two interactions, the message and the response. With three people there will be six possible interactions, with four there will be 12, and with five there will be 20. A mathematical formula can be derived for this relationship, which is:

$$\text{Numbers of interactions } (N) = p(p-1)$$

where p is the number of members of the group.

This is the first and the only instance in this book when it has been found possible to reduce an aspect of human behaviour to an equation.

The increasing complexity of the communication net, as it is sometimes called, is evident with increase in numbers within the group. Between each pair of individuals, there is a communication channel, and with more than two individuals, we have one form of multi-channel communication. However, it is possible to have multi-channel communication between two individuals, so the general subject of multi-channel communication will now be considered.

11.5.1   Multi-channel communication

This can occur in two ways:

In one-to-one communication

There may be one or more channels of communication during an interaction between two individuals. One individual may speak. If the other is listening, one channel of communication is established. The medium of communication is verbal, i.e. spoken words.

Additional channels may be established. The speaker may display a diagram or picture to illustrate his or her remarks. By doing so, a second channel is established if the receiver also pays attention to the visual illustration. The medium of the second channel is graphic. The speaker may make gestures, or display some element of body language which will give information to the receiver if that person is looking, and is perceptive enough to interpret the information. A third channel is established, the medium is visual, but the decoding of the message given by the body language or the gesture could require some skill. In more intimate conversations information may be transferred by touch or physical contact. If all these means are used simultaneously, we have a multi-channel communication with four channels between only two people.

The senses being used in communication discussed so far are sight, hearing and touch. Could communication take place using other senses? The two senses not considered so far are smell and taste. While these senses may seldom be used deliberately for communication, they can provide much useful information. A smell of burning from the kitchen can indicate that the dinner, though unseen, unheard, and untouched, has passed the cooking stage and moved into the incineration stage. A tasting of the product of such an unfortunate accident could indicate the extent to which the food had moved from the uncooked state to the inedible state. Blenders of tea, and buyers of wine, rely heavily on their ability to judge quality by the taste or aroma of a sample of the liquid concerned. An example more likely to be encountered by an engineer would be the product of a water company. Though the quality of drinking water can be tested by chemical analysis, the water is regularly tasted. The smell could be unattractive if some of the chlorine used to treat the water remained when it reached the customer.

The extent to which the various senses are used in the gathering of information has been estimated as follows:

$$Sight = 83\%$$
$$Sound = 12\%$$
$$Smell = 3.5\%$$
$$Touch = 1.5\%$$
$$Taste = 1\%$$

One to 'more than one' communication

In 'one to many' communication, even if only one medium is used, there will be a channel between the transmitter and each receiver. If the transmitter uses more than one medium, verbal and visual means for example, there will be a pair of channels to each receiver who is paying attention.

Multiple (many to many) communication

In a group with high interaction, information is passing between group members by many channels and means (media) throughout the session. All channels are unlikely to be open all the time, and the communication may be intermittent and confused. This is the situation of the 'meeting', and there is a need for some ordering of the discussion, by providing, for example, a chairman, an agenda, a summary of the points made, and the establishment of areas of agreement and disagreement. This will be discussed further in section 11.6.2.

11.5.2 Communication patterns

The pattern of communication that occurs within a group can be quite critical to its efficient functioning. Some theoretical patterns for a simple group of five

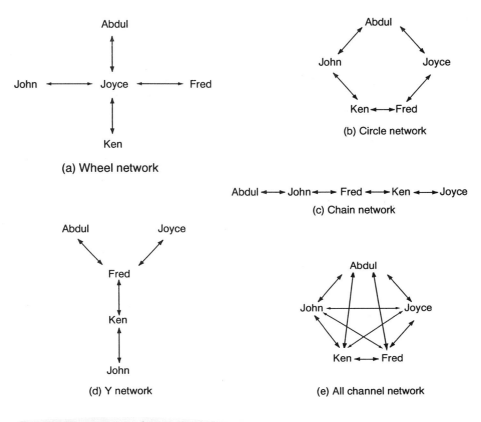

Figure 11.3 Patterns of communciation

people are considered below, but as indicated earlier, the patterns can become much more complex as the numbers in the group increase. Figure 11.3 represents these patterns of communication in diagrammatic form.

Wheel

This mode can occur if there is a formal chairman present who insists on all communication being via the chair, or if one of the group members is very senior or has a dominating personality. The system may be quickest to a solution, but is inflexible to changes of task. The satisfaction of the member at the centre of the wheel is high, but the satisfaction of those at the periphery is low. If the group members are not together and written means of communication are used, the individual at the centre of the wheel is in a very powerful position to influence the decision (see Figure 11.3).

Circle

This is the least satisfactory method in all respects. The system is slow to a solution. Member satisfaction is low. The system is inflexible to task changes. It is most unlikely to occur if the group members are all together. However, it is the practice in some organizations to circulate documents for comment and each individual will receive the information in the document, plus the comments of those who have previously received the document. It eventually returns to the originator. If all members are to be aware of the views of all the other group members, the document needs to be recirculated a second time. This may still not be completely satisfactory, since the comments of those members who received the document late may stimulate further thoughts by those early in the sequence.

Chain

This is also a poor method. The message will take some time to reach the person at the end of the chain, and may become attenuated and distorted in the process. Those who have played the parlour game: 'Chinese Whispers', in which a simple message is passed from person to person, will know how easily this can occur. Member satisfaction is low. There is a possibility of malpractice, in that the intermediate members of the chain may deliberately distort the message to achieve their own goals. Even so, this is a method which is in frequent use in organizations. The views of a director on a particular issue are passed to the divisional manager, then to the department manager, and then to the individual responsible for the issue. The director's views may be subject to some interpretation or distortion on the way.

Branched chain

This is very similar to the chain, except that the individual at the branch point is in a powerful position, in that he can differentiate the way the message is passed to the group members beyond the branch. Information possibly helpful to the career development of people in a particular section of an organization may be passed by a manager to the section head. If the section head decides to pass this information to one member of the section, and not to others, the receiver of the information will have the advantage.

All channel

This system has the potential for the best solution in complex situations. It is highly participative, and therefore has high member satisfaction. The quality of output is high. However, it can disintegrate, or revert to the wheel mode under time pressure. At a distance, and by written communication, an example would be that all information generated by all members of the group is sent to all other members. When the members are present at a meeting, even with the simple example of five people, if everyone attempted to speak at once, there would be pandemonium and no real communication would take place. In practice, and with some discipline, awareness of others' needs, and an element of 'give and take', individuals would listen most of the time and speak only a little of the time, perhaps ideally about one fifth in our simple example.

If the point of discussion were emotive or critically important, there might be a greater need for constraint on all members making their contribution at the same time. Should this happen, one individual might attempt to introduce some order to the proceedings, by leading the discussion, or by moving into a 'chairman' role. The discussion would then have aspects of the 'wheel' model. With the advent of modern communication systems such as video conferences, the possibility of very cost efficient long distance communication becomes a reality, but the requirement for an orderly procedure is enhanced.

The need for good communications not only within groups, but also between groups working on a coordinated project, has been discussed in Chapter 6, and Figure 6.14 shows the inter-group communication requirements in simultaneous engineering. The roles that individuals play in facilitating communication within working groups was discussed in sections 10.6–10.9.

While the theoretical possibilities of communication patterns can be illuminating, the realities of personal style and behaviour, and many other factors, will influence the way the communication pattern develops, particularly if the group is together in a room. As the discussion develops, it may change from a pattern that is represented by one of the models to one similar to another of the models.

Consider the situation where five students are meeting to plan a group exercise. Though all are of equal status, there will probably be natural leaders and natural followers in the group. The initial all-channel communication may develop into a 'chaired discussion' if the initial exchange of information is confused and incoherent. One of the students with a stronger personality may feel a need to take a grip of the random discussion, and focus it on the task in hand. In the professional engineering world, the discussion held by a small group to consider a design point or a problem on a project, is likely to have members with different status, seniority, expertise and responsibility. Other group members will assert their right to comment, or defer to others, according to these factors. If the knowledge, experience, and expertise of all members of the group are to be harnessed to progress the group task, and particularly if the time resources of the group are to used efficiently, there is a need to ensure the best possible ways of communicating within the group. Often, the formal meeting is adopted as a means to achieve this.

11.6   MEETINGS

11.6.1   Introduction

The meeting as an example of a group activity has been discussed in section 9.6, and it is worth repeating that the major objectives of a meeting can include communication and decision making.

11.6.2   Communication at meetings

The comment has been made before that the efficiency and effectiveness of a meeting is critically dependent on the way it is run by the chairman, and on the behaviour of the meeting members. The ordering of the agenda of the meeting helps good communication as the items can be addressed in a logical order. A good chairman will guide the discussion, for example by keeping group members to the point at issue, persuading the more verbose members to be more concise and by eliciting comments from those who are more reticent. The group members themselves can assist the communication process by commenting only when they have something useful to contribute, by avoiding all speaking at once, and more subtly by making supportive comments after other speakers have put forward good ideas and offering constructive criticism of those proposals with which they do not agree. The chairman can assist the communication process by summarizing from time to time in a long discussion and agreeing very carefully with the group the summary and conclusion of each item of discussion. This conclusion can then be committed to paper as one of the 'minutes' of the meeting.

It should be noted that communication in meetings generally follows the 'all channel' model in that all members can both comment and receive information. However, if the chairman is heavy-handed in controlling discussion, and monopolizes most of the speaking time, the 'wheel' model will apply, at least to the transmitting aspects of the communication. Even in this situation, all others present will be able to receive information.

The fact that the major points of the meeting are committed to record as 'minutes' indicates the selection of a different communication technique to allow group members to be able to refresh their memories of the outcome of the meeting, to notify absent members of the results of the discussion and to provide a basis for continued discussion at the next meeting if it happens to be one of a series.

11.7   NON-VERBAL COMMUNICATION

11.7.1   Introduction

The media of communication discussed so far have used words, both written and spoken. The written word is a form of visual communication, but there are many other methods which use visual means. The engineer will be familiar with many of these means; graphs, technical drawings and logic diagrams, for example. The principle in visual communication is the same as in verbal communication: be sure that the receiver understands the code. One engineer can communicate easily with another engineer by means of a technical drawing using the standard conventions, but the same drawing would probably not be easily understood by a company employee with a financial or personnel background, though a simplified version of the drawing might be useful to explain components that will justify expenditure, or space that will be available to accommodate staff.

11.7.2   General

A verbal communication may present difficulty for the receiver if the vocabulary is unfamiliar, the statements are long and complex, and there are too many interrelated clauses to be held in mind. The direct analogy applies to visual means. Difficulty can be caused if the visual vocabulary is unfamiliar, the visual material is voluminous and complex, and too many interrelated elements are presented simultaneously.

11.7.3   Major elements in visual communications

Numbers

Much useful and precise information can be transmitted by numbers, provided they are tabulated clearly, and the interrelationship of the groups of numbers is not too complex. When more complex relationships can be deduced from the numbers, careful tabulation may be required to demonstrate the interesting relationships.

Lines

Lines can be composed into graphs and drawings. Entities can be defined in boxes and circles, and the relationships between such boxes indicated by lines and arrows. The graph indicating the relationship between one variable and another is a simple combination of three lines, but the information conveyed can be very significant.

Words

Tables and diagrams will have no meaning without some words. Many student engineer's reports are submitted with interesting graphs, but with the units of one or both of the variables missing, and sometimes even the names of the variables. It may be obvious to the transmitter, but is sometimes not immediately clear to the receiver. All visual communications deserve a title. Tables of figures need headings, diagrams need captions, graphs require the axes defined and the units of measurement stated, and diagrams need their components annotated. It should be noted that all observers of a visual image may not interpret it in the same way, so it is advisable to give the receiver an indication of what the illustration means.

Shapes

In symbolic charts and drawings, shapes are frequently significant. Many shapes acquire a conventional meaning, often worldwide, for example in road signs and other useful facilities such as public toilets. Representational drawings and photographs convey information by means of a multiplicity of shapes. The well selected picture will certainly save a thousand words, as it conveys multiple information to the eye of the receiver.

11.7.4   Visual cues

Spatial cues

The two-dimensional space available allows the transmitter to incorporate additional information by the method of alignment of figures in rows or in columns, the balance of the elements, and the degree of prominence with which they are presented.

Typographical cues

Information can be conveyed by the size of type, the design and layout of the typography, the use of special typefaces such as capitals and italics, and the weight of type employed.

Colour and shading cues

In a monochrome diagram, meaning can be conveyed by density of shading. With colour, more detailed information can be conveyed, for example the various lines of the London Underground Railway. Colour of print and colour of the background paper can also be made significant.

Ruling

The ruling of lines between elements or groups of figures can help to differentiate between these elements or groups of figures, or relate them to one another, or to indicate common relationships.

11.7.5   Impact

Each visual communication should make a point, usually only one point, but occasionally more than one. The greatest impact is generated if the visual communication is *clear*, *organized* and *uncomplicated*. It is best to give the receiver as much data as is needed to make the point, and to avoid the visual equivalent of waffle. It is worthwhile to use a fresh visual to complement each significant point, and best to resist the temptation to use a diagram or a photograph just because it is impressive or merely available.

11.7.6   Tables

Tables should be arranged in numerical or alphabetical order, should be grouped in a logical sequence, and should accommodate those brought up in the English or

European culture to read from left to right. Units should be quoted in the headings where appropriate. Footnotes may be needed to explain figures which do not follow the trend and the dash which might accompany the absence of a reading may need some explanation.

11.7.7   Charts

There are a great number of different charts, from the simple graph or line diagram to the semi-symbolic diagram. If some measure of time is a component of the illustration, it normally occupies the horizontal axis. Some brief comments on the most frequently encountered types are given here.

Bar charts

Bar charts can be vertical, horizontal or floating. The vertical type may be termed a histogram, and an example would be the monthly rainfall figures for a particular year and location. Horizontal bar charts are used for time-related activities such as the various jobs in a project, can have floating elements if the time of start and finish of a particular job is variable, and may provide input for more complex charts such as PERT (project evaluation and review technique) charts, (see Chapter 18).

Pie charts

The simple circular image of the pie chart is good for indicating the proportions of a particular entity which relate to different contributors. Examples could be the proportion of sales from the five product lines of the company, or the elements of cost attributable to raw materials, labour, overhead and profit. The information is usually recorded in cyclic fashion, starting from 'twelve o'clock', with the segments in descending order of size.

Graphs and line charts

When well presented, these have high visual impact, and numerical accuracy. Scales should be appropriate, and clearly marked, as should the units of any numbers represented. If more than one line or graph is included on the diagram, the significance of each should be clearly labelled. Sometimes space economies encourage communicators to include too many graphs on the same diagram, and it is worthwhile to ponder the inverse relationship between economics and clarity.

Flow charts

The receiver's expectation to read left to right, and downwards should not be forgotten. Some types of flow chart in frequent use have developed standard conventions. Genealogical charts such as family trees have a convention of each succeeding generation occupying a new lower level on the chart (which can create problems for the diagram drafter if the family is prolific) and progeny recorded in birth sequence from left to right. Algorithms show a sequence of decisions and actions. They may incorporate conventions for decision points, information generation and actions.

Semi-symbolic charts

These may involve the use of simple symbols as units in a type of bar chart, for example a motor manufacturer illustrating the monthly output of cars by using rows of car symbols, each equivalent to 100 cars manufactured. A more complex example would be an Ordnance Survey map, where a wide variety of symbols is used. In such cases, a 'key' should be included which explains the symbols to those who are not familiar with them.

Technical drawings

Engineers should have no problem with the sort of illustrative diagram which is a major tool of the profession, the technical or engineering drawing. To this can be added the more specialized drawings of the various disciplines of the engineering profession, such as the wiring diagrams of the electrical engineers, the process flow diagram of the chemical engineer, and the reinforcing steel drawings of the civil engineer. The pitfall here is that familiarity and continual use of such diagrams may tempt the young engineer to assume that most people are able to interpret the information contained within them. If the recipient is an engineer, this assumption is justified. To those not so familiar, the document might well be as meaningful as Egyptian hieroglyphics are to most engineers.

11.7.8   Body language

This is a form of visual communication which is often unwitting, and therefore uncontrolled. An individual may convey information about his or her feelings or views by facial expression, deliberate gestures, nervous movements of the hands or feet, stance or posture, the manner of moving and in many other ways. The poker player may note the gleam of appreciation in an opponent's eye as the other player picks up a strong hand. The experienced poker player will attempt to appear passive at all times; the cunning player may attempt to exude elation when holding a weak hand and gloom when dealt an array of aces and kings. Most people in the interview situations discussed in section 11.4.1 would try to display confidence and calm, but might indicate tension by nervous hand movements or rapid eye movements.

It is impractical in an introductory text such as this to go into detail about body language, but there are a number of specialist texts to which the reader can refer. Study of such texts and, better perhaps, the study of ourselves when attempting to communicate can help to eliminate the more obvious problems of our body language being at variance with our 'official' message. Viewing of a recorded video of ourselves in the act of communication can be enlightening, though sometimes a confidence shaker. Though the real views of the situation might betray individuals when attempting to communicate a message in which they had little faith, the converse fortunately is true. If the belief in the message is strong, and the speaker is committed and enthusiastic about the subject, then body language can reinforce the message and make the speaker more convincing.

11.8 MULTIMEDIA COMMUNICATION

11.8.1 General

The term 'media' is often used to indicate the various means of mass communication which are now available, such as national and international newspapers and magazines, radio, and television. The newspaper will use text, pictures and sometimes graphs and diagrams, for example, for stock-market prices and the weather forecast. More than one medium of communication is used by a newspaper, but there is only one channel, the visual contact between the reader and the newspaper. Radio also uses only one channel, the auditory one between the broadcaster and the listener. Words, music and 'sound effects' are three media that convey information to the listener, who can perhaps imagine the farming activities of the radio programme *The Archers*.

Films, stage musicals, and television are multimedia activities. Many people believe that television is the most powerful means of mass communication. It communicates by both the visual and the auditory channels. We see video and film clips of current events, and the verbal views of commentators as 'voice overs'. Programmes on economics can use graphs and diagrams, the weather forecast presenters can use a sequence of semi-symbolic diagrams, and, at election times, political experts can make assessments supported by tabulated figures and charts. The medium of television has also the immediacy of bringing the 'news', be it the football results or the numbers winning the National Lottery; ministers answering questions, or avoiding answering them, in the House of Commons; or the tragedies of conflict in yet another area of the world; right into our living rooms.

Whereas the young engineer is unlikely to be able to mobilize the communication resources available to the makers of television programmes, there are some basic lessons that can be learned. Use media with which you can cope, and which are appropriate to the message you are trying to project; use both visual and audible media in an appropriate and realistic combination and try for immediacy, strong projection, and close contact with your audience. The situation in which the young engineer is likely to encounter such a problem is the presentation, so the following sections give some advice on how to approach this activity.

11.8.2 Presentations

Introduction

Engineers are required to make presentations with increasing frequency. These may be to customers to explain the technical aspects of an engineering product or service, to senior management to report progress on a project or an area of activity, or to directors to justify budgets or specific items of major expenditure. For the customers and the senior members of the company, the communication method has the major advantage of allowing questions, discussion, feedback and possibly an immediate decision. It may also be preceded by preliminary written information such as a briefing document, and may be followed by a detailed report that the recipients can study and consider at leisure.

It is therefore very important that the young engineer should become competent at making presentations. Ability in this activity is very helpful to a career, since it allows the young engineer to demonstrate ability and make a good impression with influential people. The converse also applies, so the trend towards more frequent presentations has disadvantages for those less able to stand up and communicate well. If one's only exposure to the directors of the company was a totally disastrous presentation, this could be unhelpful for career progress. It is therefore sensible to take every available opportunity to practise making presentations, thereby improving one's technique. The following sections give some tips on how to do it.

Some basic principles

A presentation tends to be a formal occasion, often with little or no audience participation. You will need to work to sustain a good level of interest. Try to avoid turning it into a dreary lecture. Remember that you are not providing entertainment, you want their hearts and minds. Of course, if you can be mildly entertaining at the same time, it helps to maintain attention. The normal attention span is said to be 40–50 minutes. Many members of the audience may have a lesser span of attention. As the audience may not have a chance to ask immediately about a confusing or difficult item, or a missed point, it can be helpful to recapitulate key points. It is helpful to indicate the general subject of your talk at the start, and to summarize at the end. This basic plan can be summarized as: 'tell them what you are going to tell them; tell them what you want to tell them; then tell them what you have just told them'.

Preparation

Decide: what are your objectives; what the title of your talk should be; what the content should be; establish the context, that is the situation in which you have to speak and the audience you expect to address.

Discover: the time available; the characteristics of the audience; the environment in which you have to speak (the room, the equipment in it, the lighting and seating) and adjust the presentation to suit these constraints.

Determine: to avoid unnecessary detail; do not to swamp the audience with information; and do not overestimate their ability to absorb new information.

Design: your presentation to support the conclusions you wish to promote, by introducing the key points or facts in a logical order, demonstrating the linkages between these facts, and using the visual aids to emphasize the important points.

Visual aids

Visual aids provide added impact if well prepared and correctly used. They are excellent for conveying related information such as diagrams and maps by utilizing our parallel visual communication channel. They need to be a focus for the audience's thinking; to be large and clear, to require a minimum of reading and to be left in view long enough to be fully assimilated. Avoid the 'now you see it, now you don't' trick of removing the view-foil before the audience has time to read it. However, it should be removed from view when not supporting the comments of the speaking, as in this situation it can be a distraction. Visual aids may detract from rather than support the speech if they are confusing, hard to read, or sloppily prepared. They are unhelpful if they do not fully relate to the speaker's current comments or if reading and assimilating them removes attention from the content of the continuing speech. They must not contain spelling mistakes, which can be a distraction to some members of the audience.

In most cases, the visual aids will be limited to an overhead projector, a blackboard or a white board, and perhaps a flip chart. If the latter items are available in the presentation room or lecture theatre, it is worthwhile to take chalk, marker pens, and a board rubber, or at least check that these are available. You may need to produce an impromptu illustration in an answer to a question at the end of the presentation. It is therefore worthwhile to have available a couple of blank view-foils and a view-foil pen, for the same purpose.

In these days of high technology, the location for your presentation may have additional facilities such as more than one overhead projector, allowing the projection of more than one image at a time, for example for comparison purposes; television screens or a video projector that would allow you to add video clips to your talk; a slide projector that would allow the use of coloured pictures; a computer facility linked to a 'projection tablet' that sits on the overhead projector, and that will allow you to use computer generated data or diagrams; and audio equipment that would allow music or other sound projection to be used. The important thing to remember is that the more aids you use, the more complex the presentation becomes and the more there is to be controlled. There is also more equipment that can fail at the most inappropriate moment. If you do wish to take advantage of these modern aids, it is well worth training an assistant or assistants to operate the equipment, leaving you free to do the talking, and to perform additional trial runs to ensure that the material is integrated and the exercise is well rehearsed.

The speaker

The speaker should check voice, physical appearance and bearing, and try to avoid nervous or habitual movements. It is helpful to face the audience directly, repeatedly gaining eye-to-eye contact with members of the audience, but avoid permanently addressing one member of the audience, as that person may bask in the special attention, or may become nervous at being the focus of the speaker's performance.

The speaker should attempt to speak clearly at a reasonable speed and loudness, with pauses after key points to allow them to sink in. Try not to speak from a script, which often causes the inexperienced presenter to slip into reading the script and thereby losing contact with the audience. More time should be given to key points, and key words and phrases should be repeated.

The speaker's personality and mannerisms are significant, and the speaker should try to appear confident and enthusiastic. Habits and movements which could distract the audience, such as playing with a pen, chalk or watch should be avoided, as should tendencies to repetitive speech patterns such as 'um', 'ah' and 'you know?'. Small habitual mannerisms such as scratching an ear lobe or, worse still, some more intimate part of the body, are unconscious, so the comments of a frank but kindly friend or colleague can be helpful. The opportunity to see a video recording of the performance is very helpful, if a little damaging to one's self-confidence.

Good practices

Write notes well beforehand so that you can review and correct them. Mark Twain commented 'It takes some three months to write a good impromptu speech'. An early start will allow you to practise the speech several times at the correct volume and speed, to check the timing, and possibly to practise before at least one critical audience. Try to reduce the speech to 'trigger notes' or 'bullet points'. This will give the speech more immediacy, will avoid the trap of reading a script, and the 'bullet point' can be put on the view-foils and on small cards that are convenient to use.

Before you start to speak, check your appearance and that your notes and view-foils are complete and in the right order. Check that the equipment is set up correctly, that the image is the maximum possible for the screen, and that it is in focus. If a microphone is available and necessary, check that it is in working order, and the volume is correct. If you are not introduced, give your name and a short self-description. Then give the title of the talk, and why it is worthwhile for them to give you their attention.

When using an overhead projector, avoid your shadow on the screen, and blocking the view of some members of the audience. Try to ensure that all can see and hear well. To explain or emphasize something, point to the surface of the view-foil with a small pointer or the tip of a pen, not to the screen, otherwise you will tend to turn your back to the audience and your comments will be inaudible. Remember, a finger is a very blunt instrument when used in conjunction with an overhead projector. Place the pointer on the surface of the view-foil if you are nervous and your hand is shaking! It is particularly important not to overrun the time allocated, especially if this occurs in conjunction with a slow and rambling early section and a manic speed-up towards the end.

11.9   SUMMARY

The chapter has considered the importance of communication in the engineering environment. A theoretical framework was given for one-to-one communication, which introduced the concepts of the medium of communication and the channel of communication. The importance of feedback was stressed. Verbal and written communication were discussed, and the use of codes such as a language was introduced, with the procedure of encoding and decoding the message. Some of the problems encountered in achieving good communication were discussed. Formal communication systems such as the various types of interview were defined. Means were suggested of achieving a good standard in such written documents as essays and reports, and uses indicated for summaries and abstracts.

The chapter continued with a discussion of group interactions, particularly the patterns of communication, and different forms of multi-channel communication. A popular form of multi-channel communication, the meeting, was considered. Next, non-verbal communication was addressed, and the use of tables, graphs, figures, diagrams, charts, technical drawings and pictures. Finally, multimedia, the simultaneous use of a number of media, was considered and a detailed guide given of the methods of making a professional presentation.

REFERENCES

1. Chappell, R. T. and Read, W. L. (1984) *Business Communications*. Fifth edition, Pitman, London.
2. *Can You Spare a Minute?* Video Arts Ltd, (London & Birmingham) 1988. *I Want a Word With You!* Video Arts Ltd, (London & Birmingham) 1979.
3. Raven, S, (1961) *The English Gentleman*. Anthony Blond.
4. Gunning, R. (1952) *The Technique of Clear Writing*. McGraw-Hill, Maidenhead.
5. Crosby, P. (1979) *Quality is Free*. McGraw-Hill, Maidenhead.

12

Work study

12.1 INTRODUCTION

Work study derives from the work of F. W. Taylor, *The Principles of Scientific Management* [1] referred to in Chapter 3. 'Taylorism' has been blamed for much that was wrong in the management of large engineering enterprises; for the way in which it led to a fragmentation of labour, the breakdown of jobs into tasks that were reduced to simple movements at set speeds, depriving the workforce of any need for skill or intelligence. This does not mean that the principles of work study should be rejected. Processes in the best run factories can still benefit from studying the sequence and timing of operations, and method study can be of great utility in small factories and workshops, especially if they are complemented by teamworking, delegation and empowerment (see Chapters 7 and 8).

This chapter explains the purposes of *work study*, describing its two parts, *method study* and *work measurement*. Simple examples to illustrate the principles of work study are given.[1]

12.2 OBJECTIVES OF WORK STUDY

British Standard 3138 [3] defines work study as 'the systematic examination of activities in order to improve the effective use of human and other resources'. The proper objective of work study is to ensure that the time and talents of every individual and the operational time of every machine are used effectively. Ideally, this should result in improved productivity and profitability, maintaining employment at higher rates of pay and with greater job satisfaction.

12.3 METHOD STUDY

BS 3138 defines method study as 'the systematic *recording* (sic) and *critical examination* of ways of doing things in order to make improvements'. Therefore, method study can be applied at all operational levels from the narrowly defined interaction between an operative and a machine to, say, a Just-in-Time materials supply system. Method study procedures are defined by the steps below:

---

[1]For those interested in pursuing their studies a little way beyond the principles described in these next few pages, Chapter 11 of Hill, *Production/Operations Management Text and Cases* [2] is recommended.

- *select* the work to be studied
- *record* all the relevant facts
- *critically examine* (analyse) the recorded facts
- *develop* proposals for improved methods
- *choose a solution* from a short list of solutions
- *implement* the solution
- *REPEAT* the procedure as appropriate.

There are similarities between these procedures and those of business process re-engineering (BPR), also known as business process redesign, which sets out to improve the business processes of a company at the highest level. Work study is conducted at the lower operational levels, and the advantages gained can be of only a limited incremental nature, whilst BPR may result in radical change in the company.[2]

Selecting a process for study should not be difficult. Any process in which there is evidence of machinery or operatives being inactive for substantial periods of time will benefit from such a study. Other reasons might be irregular production rates, excessive movement by people, machines or materials, production bottlenecks, low quality, and/or unsafe processes.

It is with the methods of recording and examining the facts that this section will be concerned.

BS 3375 Part 2 [5] provides the following standard symbols for the purposes of recording a task:

O = *operation* (a process which furthers the job or changes the state of the material)

⇨ = *transport* (any form of movement from one position to another)

▽ = *storage* (material in a prescribed storage location)

D = *delay* (some form of interference with the flow)

□ = *inspection*

◎ = main function is inspection but a *process* is also involved

These symbols are used in the tables, charts or diagrams which have been drawn up to represent the task or process. Sections 12.3.1 and 12.3.2 will examine the use of flow process charts and diagrams and multiple activity charts.

12.3.1 Flow process charts and diagrams

A flow process chart shows the sequence of the individual operations which make up the task or process. It should be noted that preparing a flow process chart is a usual first step in any form of process or quality improvement, for all sorts of processes, not just engineering ones.

---

[2]See Hammer M. & Champy J. *Reengineering the Corporation.* Nicholas Brenley Publishing 1994

Table 12.1 Flow process chart

Line 1	Line 2	Line 3	Description
O	O	O	Make elements in workshop
▽	▽	▽	Store elements
⇨	⇨	⇨	Move to assembly point
	O		Assemble unit
	□		Inspect unit
	⇨		Move to insulation bay
	D		Await insulation
	O		Apply insulation
	⇨		Lift to glazing bay
	O		Fit glass
	⇨		Move to inspection bay
	□		Inspect
	⇨		Lift to storage
	▽		Store

Example 12(1)

An aluminium alloy window frame consists of three elements. Assume that the three elements are manufactured in a workshop, that within the same workshop the three elements are assembled and then insulated, after which the glazing is fitted to complete the window. These activities are represented in Table 12.1.

For the sake of simplicity this chart does not show the whole process. Immediately after each inspection there is the possibility of non-acceptance which would lead to an alternative path of rejection or dismantling and some form of re-assembly. These paths are not shown. The flow chart gives rise to two immediate observations: why is there a delay in the insulation bay? Why are there two inspections? Would one suffice or should there be a process to prevent production of components and assemblies of unsatisfactory quality? (See Chapter 4: Management of Quality and the use of statistical process control.)

Figure 12.1 shows a more complex, non-tabulated flow process chart. The actual manufacturing process is not described but it is clear from the chart that three parts are processed separately (two of these include inspection and correction procedures), after this they are assembled (task 13) then inspected. Inspection leads to acceptance or rejection; the rejected assembly is removed to a place of storage; the accepted assembly is stored then moved and after a delay is combined into a larger assembly (task 21) before being placed in final storage.

A flow process diagram provides similar information to the flow process chart except that the flow lines are superimposed upon the layout of the factory or workshop. This is useful where the layout itself is a prime cause of the way/ sequence in which the work is carried out. Figure 12.2 shows how the flow process chart in Figure 12.1 can be drawn as a flow process diagram.

After preparing the chart or diagram, the process is analysed using the questioning technique set out in section 12.3.3. Note: the very act of recording what is actually happening will usually yield some useful information. In this case two delays (D) have been observed before any analysis has been conducted.

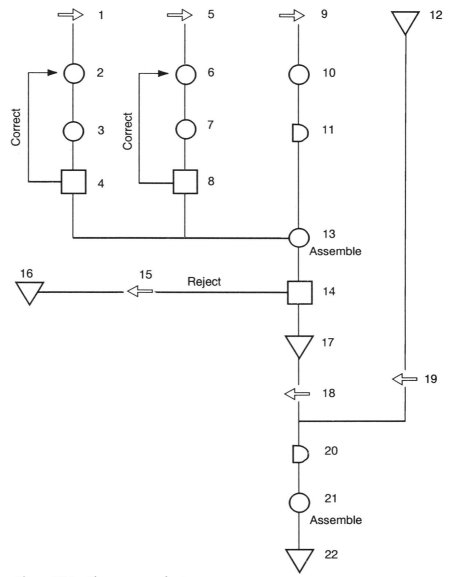

Figure 12.1   Flow process chart

12.3.2   Multiple activity charts

Multiple activity charts examine how processes and movements relate to one another chronologically. The times in which men and machines are operational and non-operational are recorded.

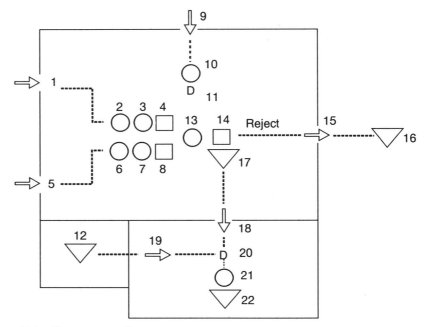

Figure 12.2 Flow process diagram

Example 12(2)

Figure 12.3 represents a materials processing plant in which a mixer is filled from a hopper at Position 1 with material A, moves to Position 2 where material B is added from a second hopper, moves to Position 3 where the contents are discharged, then returns to Position 1 to repeat the cycle. Transportation between stockpile and hopper is by electrically operated barrows.

Time to load material at stockpile A and transport to Position 1	6 min
Time to load material into empty hopper at Position 1	2 min
Time to return barrow to stockpile A	4 min
Time to fill mixer from hopper at Position 1	2 min
Time for mixer to travel to Position 2	2 min
Time to load material at stockpile B and transport to Position 2	12 min
Time to load material into empty hopper at Position 2	2 min
Time to return barrow to stockpile B	6 min
Time to fill mixer from hopper at Position 2	4 min
Time for mixer to travel to Position 3	2 min
Time to discharge mix at Position 3	2 min
Time to return mixer to Position 1	4 min

(a) Draw a multiple activity chart for the process.
(b) Given that 4 m³ of material A is placed in the mixer at Position 1, determine the steady rate of use of material A.

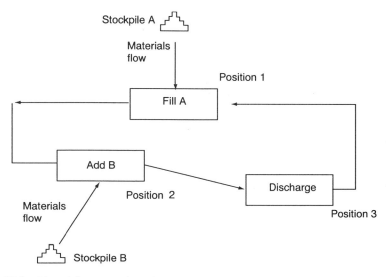

Figure 12.3   Materials processing plant

(c)   Management is interested in speeding up the process. What one small improvement in the speed of operation would have considerable benefits?

Solution

(a)   Figure 12.4 shows the completed chart. Usually at least three operational cycles must be constructed. In this case it becomes clear when constructing the third cycle that the latter elements of the third cycle are identical to those of the second cycle. These, therefore, are not shown.

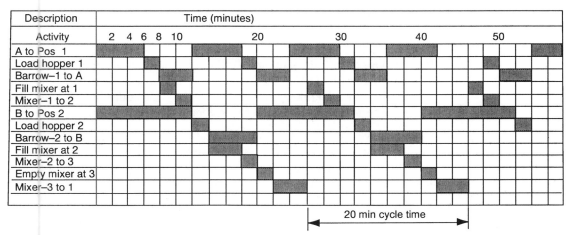

Figure 12.4   Multiple activity chart

In constructing the chart each activity should start at the earliest possible time. So, at the start, both the barrows at A and B are loaded immediately, the materials transported to the mixer location then placed in the hoppers. In the second cycle the barrow at A loads and returns to Position 1 to fill the hopper (completed at *time: 20 minutes*) even though the hopper cannot be emptied until *time: 26 minutes* when the mixer returns to Position 1. The second cycle shows two changes from the first:

(1) **Fill mixer at 1** is delayed 6 minutes, waiting for the mixer to return to Position 1.

(2) **B to Position 1** must await the return of the barrow to stockpile B.

The third cycle shows one change from the second:

(3) the time between the two operations **fill mixer at 1** has increased from 16 to 18 minutes as the return of the mixer from Position 3 is awaited.

The remainder of the third cycle is now identical to that of the second cycle and the regular cycle time of 20 minutes for the operation can be observed from the chart.

The fourth cycle shows the effect of the delayed return of the mixer to Position 1. The hopper at Position 1 cannot be loaded at *time: 42 minutes*, as it has not yet discharged its contents into the mixer. Only between the fifth and sixth cycles does the regular pattern of operations becomes clear: every operation is repeated at 20 minute intervals.

(b) A 20 minute cycle time means three operations per hour, giving a steady usage of materials at stockpile A of

$$3 \times 4 \, m^3 = 12 \, m^3 \text{ per hour}$$

(c) The controlling sequence is

B to Position 2
Load hopper 2
Barrow — Position 2 to B

There are no delays, no waiting for other operations. If this could be reduced by four minutes, the cycle time would be 16 minutes, increasing the average hourly usage at stockpile A to 15 m^3 per hour. This could be achieved, say, by speeding up the operation **B to Position 2** by four minutes.

The chart shows when equipment is operational and when it is not. By the fourth cycle it can be seen that the barrow serving Position 1 works for only 12 minutes out of every 20 and that the mixer is either being filled, moving or being emptied for 16 minutes out of every 20. This shows that the 16 minute cycle advocated in (c) above would be attainable by one change to one operation, namely, **B to Position 2** to take 8, not 12, minutes.

Thus, a multiple activity chart is a simple but effective tool in the analysis of cycles of concurrent and dependent operations.

12.3.3   Interrogative method

This method will usually be used in conjunction with the analysis described in the preceding subsections. The principle is that questions are asked of each activity or task. The questions are:

- WHAT is done?
- HOW is it done?
- WHO carries out the task?

- WHEN is it done?
- WHERE is it done?

and for each of these

- WHY is it done at all, at that time, etc.?

There is always value in questioning what is being done, in taking nothing at face value. By questioning even the obvious it is possible that some fundamental insight might lead to radical change and significant improvement.

Example 12(3)

A yard has been set up for cutting and bending reinforcing steel for a building site. Standard lengths of different diameter steel bars are delivered to the yard by road, unloaded at the roadside, lifted into storage racks from which they are then drawn as demand dictates, cut to length, bent to shape, transferred to a second storage location and eventually transported to site. Table 12.2 below shows a typical interrogative analysis sheet. Only illustrative responses are given in the WHY column.

The responses yield some useful observations.

No. 1, offloading the delivery truck from the road may be less than ideal, possibly unsafe and creating a traffic problem. A slightly wider entrance might ease the problem.

In nos 3, 5, 7 and 9 both the cutter and bender operators have their work interrupted moving materials, is this necessary? Might the addition of one or two unskilled labourers result in a far faster operation?

In no. 6 the benders are slower than the cutters, resulting in an unnecessary temporary storage and probably in double handling. The work rates of the two kinds of machine and numbers available need to be investigated.

This method of analysis is always radical in the sense that it gets to the root of the operation. To be successful it needs to be conducted by someone with an enquiring mind who does not accept things at face value.

12.4   WORK MEASUREMENT

Work measurement is concerned with measuring the times needed for specific tasks. This is essential information for planners and for estimators. It will be equally apparent from the foregoing section that measuring the time taken for selected operations will be important in method study. The objectives of work measurement can be summarized as follows:

Table 12.2 Steelyard analysis sheet

No.	WHAT is done? (a)	WHEN is it done? (b)	HOW is it done? (c)	WHERE is it done? (d)	WHO does it? (e)	WHY?
1	offload steel into racks	weekly, on delivery	by crane	at the roadside	gang from building site	(d) yard entrance is too narrow
2	storage of steel	between delivery and use	in labelled racks	in labelled racks near the roadside		(a) continuous operation needs a stock at the yard
3	move from racks to cutters	on demand by the cutter	sliding by hand	between racks and cutters	cutter operators	(e) no-one else available
4	cutting to lengths	on arrival at cutter	by machine	on power cutters	cutter operators	(a) schedule shows various lengths
5	move steel to temporary storage	after cutting is complete	by hand	from cutters to temporary stack	cutter operators	(a) must be moved out of the way
6	steel awaits bending	between cutting and bending	in small heaps	near the benders		(a) cutting is faster than bending
7	move steel to bender	on demand by bender	by hand to slide into bender	from temporary stack to the benders	bender operators	(e) no-one else to do it
8	bending of steel	on arrival at bender	by hand and machine power	on the bending machine	bender operators	(a) schedule requires different shapes
9	move to storage	after bending is complete	by hand	from benders to storage	bender operators	(e) no-one else to do it
10	steel awaits transfer to building site	between bending and delivery	in marked bays	in bays near to site entrance		(a) and (c) deliveries out are irregular
11	loading of steel onto site transport	on demand from building site	by self-loading truck	at the storage bays	site materials gang	(b) don't want too much stock

- to assist in method study,
- to assist in planning and scheduling of labour, plant and materials,
- to assist in cost control,
- to compare different methods of working,
- to provide a basis for incentive schemes,
- to assist in implementing total quality management.

BS 3138 defines work measurement as 'the application of techniques designed to establish the time for a *qualified worker* (sic) to carry out a *task* at a defined rate of working'.

This is a much more precise definition than might at first sight appear to be necessary to meet the listed objectives. But, for a measured time to have any value, certain criteria have to be met. These are discussed briefly below.

The work must be such that, when carried out by different people and/or plant, it is performed in the same way and under similar conditions. Therefore, there are many operations for which work measurement is inappropriate. Herein lies a difficulty. Engineers may be tempted to rely upon those things that can be measured and to ignore, when making decisions, those things that cannot be measured. Chapter 9 referred to *hard* and *soft* issues. Engineers commonly use hard data in their analyses; this will not suffice in work study. Once the engineer has completed the numerical analysis, careful thought must be given to the soft issues before a decision is made on how the findings should be used.

What is a *task*? The underlying assumption is that any operation can be broken down into a series of finite tasks. Factories, banks and bureaucracies have had occasion to measure the duration of tasks, from the time taken to machine a pipe end to the number of keystrokes per minute made by someone inputting financial data into a computer. If, however, the measurement and summation of these times does not contain provision for the wider needs of people at work, for time to reflect upon what they are doing; for time for discourse and for relaxation; for time to deal with irregular interruptions; then the process of measurement can make work appear mechanistic. This can create all sorts of problems, for people are not machines. Work study and, in particular, work measurement must not be allowed to separate each worker from his or her colleagues. In many work situations, overall performance is improved by teamwork, where the individual's ability to perform a particular task to a specified standard is less important than the combined ability of the team. In this kind of situation work measurement should not be used to compare the performance of individuals but still has a place in determining standard times for an operation. Method study techniques will always be useful in improving performance through joint efforts.

The workers who carry out the work must have the necessary skills and be experienced in the particular operations. Measuring the time it takes for an inexperienced worker, albeit a skilled one, to complete a task would be of little value, as once the worker had become adept at the work it would be performed much more quickly. This simple and obvious lesson is sometimes forgotten when incentive schemes are set up for new operations with which management and workers are unfamiliar; too often the incentive scheme is based on the low initial rate of production during the learning phases, and a few months later extraordinarily high bonus payments are being paid to the workers.

Work measurement is used to establish standard times for jobs. These can be used either for planning or for monitoring of performance. Measurement techniques available range from the simple timing of actual jobs (for example, for constructing multiple activity charts), through time study, in which the actual times are corrected by a performance-rating factor, to various forms of activity sampling synthesis. This chapter will consider briefly the following:

- predetermined motion-time systems
- time study

Although few engineers will be involved in these measuring techniques, they may be required to act on the data provided, so they should be aware of the principles.

12.4.1   Predetermined motion-time systems (PMTS)

PMTS come under the field of work study known internationally as methods-time measurement (MTM). MTM examines the time taken for basic human motions such as to grasp something, or press a key, or bend an elbow. The times taken for these movements are very short and MTM's time measurement unit is 0.00001 hour (0.0006 min.). These systems demand a conjunction of film/video recording and high precision timing methods.[3] Whitmore observes that the time required to analyse a job using the MTM system at its basic level can be as much as 150 times as long as the task takes to perform! Users of MTM systems rely on data tables which provide the times taken for all these 'basic human motions'.[4]

In PMTS a system of synthesis is used. A task under consideration is analysed into its constituent basic human motions and the times for these standard elements are obtained from data tables and aggregated. Underlying the data tables are implicit rates of working for all the classified human movements therein. The principle is that 'the time required for all experts to perform true fundamental motions is a constant' [6]. PMTS data tables have been developed for many areas of employment, from clerical work to maintenance, providing data on higher levels of operation such as inserting a letter into an envelope or changing the wheel of a car. These data tables allow an employer to determine a standard time for any operation selected.

---

[3]No attempt is made in this chapter to describe these methods which in recent years have become capable of measuring very short durations of motion with a higher degree of accuracy. The different approaches to measurement such as consecutive-element timing and selective-element timing are described in *Whitmore D A Work Measurement 2nd edition Heinemann 1987* in Chapters 9 and 17.
[4]These data tables rely on a wide range and large number of measurements. See *Whitmore* Chapter 6 for the mathematics of measurement and Chapter 7 for the process of analysis.

12.4.2 Time study

Time study uses observed times and converts them into standard times. Observed times reflect how well the individual worker applies himself to the task. Consequently, observed times must be adjusted to represent the time the worker would have taken if he had been working at a standard rating. Each measurement of time must be accompanied by an assessment of how much above or below a standard rating the employee is working. Clearly this is a subjective measure and one that is most reliable only where the time study engineers have considerable experience. The principle of assessing a rating for an individual is that if he works at half the standard rating the task will take twice as long. The standard rating assumes that the worker is adequately motivated to do the job. A worker provided with an incentive would be expected to operate one-third faster than his normal rate. In short, the time study engineer, as he times the task, must compare the worker's performance with that of a notional rating that must be held in his mind for the duration of the task.

There are a number of scales in use:

- the 60/80 scale in which 60 represents the standard rating and 80 the 'incentive' rating,
- the 75/100 scale in which 75 represents the standard rating and 100 the 'incentive' rating,
- the 100/133 scale in which 100 represents the standard rating and 133 the 'incentive' rating.

The latter scale is the one recommended by British Standards Institution [7]. In each case the 'incentive' rating is one third higher than the standard rating.

Ratings assessed on the 100/133 scale would normally lie in the range 70 to 160 (ratings in excess of 130 should be rare) for most people are unable to properly assess performances which are very slow or very fast. Ratings should normally be assessed to the nearest 5 points, although an inexperienced observer would be wise to keep to the nearest 10 points. Whitmore [6] recommends that an assessment of rating should include pace, effort, consistency, dexterity and, possibly, job difficulty.

The standard time for an operation is found from the basic mean times of the elements or tasks that make up that operation. Time study engineers will usually subdivide operations into elements of less than one minute's duration. Measurements are usually made in centi-minutes (hundredths of a minute) rather than seconds.

Measurements should be taken over several cycles of the operation and for a sufficient number of workers to provide a statistically representative sample.[5] For each worker completing a task the basic time will be determined (see below) and the mean of all the basic times for the group of workers will be calculated; this is known as the basic mean time.

---

[5]See Chapter 8 of *Dilworth J B* (1992). *Operations Management* [8] for more information and guidance.

For the 100/133 scale:

$$\text{Basic Time (BT)} = \frac{\text{observed time} \times \text{rating}}{100}$$

A slow worker will be characterized by a large observed time and a low rating. A fast worker will be characterized by a small observed time and a high rating, so the basic times for each worker should be similar. Where there are major differences in the BTs for a given task there may well be something wrong with either the observed times or, more probably, the ratings. BTs that are exceptional in some way should not be considered in determining a basic mean time. Either the whole measurement process should be repeated or, where only one or two values are distinctly odd, the exceptional values should be excluded from the calculation.

To calculate the basic mean time the BTs are aggregated and divided by the number of observations.

$$\text{Basic Mean Time (BMT)} = \frac{\sum(\text{BT})}{n}$$

Before the standard time for an operation can be determined allowances must be made for the fact that each cycle of work may have to be repeated many times during the working day. People must be able to relax, sometimes even rest after physical exertion and attend to calls of nature. In addition there will be occasional interruptions which, although unpredictable are not unexpected. Allowances for relaxation etc., are referred to as *relaxation allowances*. Allowances for unexpected interruptions are referred to as *contingency allowances*. Allowances are usually made by adding on a small percentage to the sum of the BMTs. Typical figures for relaxation allowances are from 5 to 10% and for contingency allowances certainly not more than 5%. Other provisions such as for unoccupied time may also have to be made.[6]

The standard time for an operation will be found as follows:

$$\text{Standard Time} = \sum(\text{BMT}) + \text{relaxation \%} + \text{contingency \%}$$

Example 12(4)

Manufacture of a product X involves a single operation which time study engineers have subdivided into three tasks A, B and C. One group of six workers carries out the operation. A time study has been carried out on each of these tasks to determine a standard time for the production of X. The observed times and assessed ratings are tabulated in Table 12.3 (note: in reality, measurement of several cycles for each operation for this group of workers would be carried out).

---

[6]*Whitmore* provides a useful chapter (Chapter 12) on allowances.

Table 12.3

	Task A		Task B		Task C	
Name	Observed time (min.)	Rating	Observed time (min.)	Rating	Observed time (min.)	Rating
Alyson	0.18	110	0.21	80	0.24	90
Anka	0.17	80	0.22	90	0.19	110
Cosma	0.16	110	0.21	100	0.22	90
Josef	0.17	90	0.23	90	0.24	90
Joyce	0.19	100	0.24	80	0.22	90
Kerr	0.16	110	0.22	100	0.25	80

Determine a Standard Time for the manufacture of product X.

Solution

Tabulated in Table 12.4 are the basic times for each worker and each task.

Table 12.4

	Task A	Task B	Task C
Name	BT	BT	BT
Alyson	0.198	0.168*	0.216
Anka	0.136*	0.198	0.209
Cosma	0.176	0.210	0.198
Josef	0.153	0.207	0.216
Joyce	0.190	0.192	0.198
Kerr	0.176	0.220	0.200

For each task the mean time is calculated. However, for each of tasks A and B the BT marked by an asterisk has been eliminated from the calculation; the values are considerably different from all the others and are, therefore, unsafe.[7]

$$BMT_A = \frac{(0.198 + 0.176 + 0.153 + 0.190 + 0.176)}{5} = 0.1786$$

$$BMT_B = \frac{(0.198 + 0.210 + 0.207 + 0.192 + 0.220)}{5} = 0.2054$$

$$BMT_C = \frac{(0.216 + 0.209 + 0.198 + 0.216 + 0.198 + 0.200)}{6} = 0.2062$$

[7]Consideration of the range of performance times is given in section 7.6 of Chapter 7 of Whitmore.

From this the BMT for the whole process is found:

$$BMT_{(A+B+C)} = 0.1786 + 0.2054 + 0.2062 = 0.5902$$

In order to arrive at a standard time, relaxation and contingency allowances should be included. In this case, and in the absence of any further information, the value determined above is multiplied by 1.15. That is a 15% total additional allowance is provided.

$$1.15 \times 0.5902 = 0.6787 \text{ minutes}$$

It would be absurd to give this figure as the standard time. The selection of 15% was arbitrary; it could equally well have been, say, 14% or 16%. Also each rating is a subjective assessment and even with an experienced work study engineer working consistently with his own notional criterion of a standard rating, only an educated estimate is possible. Therefore it would be entirely inappropriate to give the standard time to four decimal places. A realistic standard time would be 40 seconds (0.6667 min.).

Answer: Standard Time = 40 seconds

12.5 SUMMARY

This chapter has provided a brief outline of the principles of work study and described a number of the techniques used in both method study and work measurement. For method study, flow charts and diagrams, multiple activity charts, and the interrogative method have been illustrated. For work measurement, PMTS and time study procedures have been described and illustrated.

REFERENCES

1. Taylor, F. W. (1929) *Principles of Scientific Management*. Harper, London.
2. Hill, T. (1991) *Production/Operations Management Text and Cases*. Second edition, Prentice-Hall, London.
3. BS 3138 (1992) *Glossary of Terms Used in Management Services*. British Standards Institution, London.
4. Hammer, M. and Champy, J. (1994) *Reengineering the Corporation*. Nicholas Brealey Publishing.
5. BS 3375: Part 2 *Guide to Method Study* (1993) British Standards Institution, London.
6. Whitmore, D. A. (1987) *Work Measurement*. Second edition, Heinemann, London (page 144).
7. BS 3375: Part 3 *Guide to Work Measurement* (1993) British Standards Institution, London.
8. Dilworth, J. B. Operations Management, McGraw-Hill International, 1992.

BIBLIOGRAPHY

Jay, T. A. (1981) *Time Study*. Blandford Press. Blandford Management Series, Blandford, Dorset.
Monks, J. G. (1987) *Operations Management*. Third edition, McGraw-Hill, Maidenhead.
Wild, R. (1995) *Production and Operations Management* 5th edition, Cassell, London.

13

Costing and pricing

13.1 INTRODUCTION

Any organization, whether it is a business, a government department or a charitable foundation will eventually fail if costs exceed revenue. Therefore, costs are fundamental to all enterprises including engineering. Engineering businesses must make a profit. This is the business imperative; revenue must exceed costs. This, however, is not the sum total of an engineer's interest in costs. Engineers will often be required to submit cost plans (budgets) for approval, and, once approved, a budget will be used to monitor the engineer's production performance. Engineers often tender for work and/or price their services or products for potential customers; tendering and pricing cannot be achieved successfully without a clear understanding of the principles of costing.

This chapter will examine the nature of costs (*direct* and *indirect* costs, *fixed* and *variable* costs), cost-volume relationships (*break-even*), *budgets*, and *tendering* and *pricing*.

13.2 WHAT IS THE COST OF A PRODUCT?

Consider launching onto the world markets an entirely new product. There are no competitors, nothing like this has been manufactured and sold before. What costs are incurred in the development, manufacture and eventual sales of the product?

Any or all of the following costs might be incurred:

Market research[1]	will people buy this product at what price? what is the potential size of the market?
Design and specification	engineers will specify performance, quality, life; they will carry out calculations and produce drawings and schedules.
Prototype manufacture	one or a small number of the products will be manufactured/built.

---

[1]See chapter 22, section 22.11.1 for the role (and costs) of market research.

Development	the prototype(s) will be tested, modifications may be made to the design and specification.
Tooling	setting up the production line, machine tools, assembly etc., prior to manufacture.
Manufacture	materials will be consumed, labour utilized, fuel/power consumed, etc.
Marketing	publicity and advertising.
Distribution	transportation, etc., to dealers.
Product support	parts and labour for after sales maintenance and servicing.

If the product is a success, the costs of manufacture and distribution will continue, and further expenditure on marketing will be incurred from time to time. The earlier costs must be paid for out of sales revenue. If only 1000 are sold, then the cost of each item sold must include 1/1000 of the total initial costs (market research to tooling), if 1 million are sold, the cost of each item sold could include one millionth of the initial costs. Alternatively, some of these costs may be considered as a company overhead and charged against other products (see section 13.2.3). Whether this is so depends upon how soon and by what means the company wants these initial costs to be recovered. Cost, therefore, is a matter of judgement, not a matter of fact.

Even the cost of manufacture is not straightforward. Certainly there will be an identifiable materials cost and, when operatives work upon that material, direct labour costs are incurred. But there will be other costs; heating and lighting, depreciation in the value of the buildings and equipment, consumables used in maintenance and servicing, salaries of supervisory staff, administration, and so on.

Costs that arise directly from production are known as *direct costs*; those that arise whether production takes place or not are known as *indirect costs*. The allocation of indirect costs is an arbitrary process. In the example given above, the company will be manufacturing other products besides the new one. How should the costs of rent, administration and heating and lighting be assigned to different products? A further question needs to be considered. What would have happened if, during the development stage, a decision had been made to proceed no further? The costs incurred still have to be covered by the revenue earned from selling the company's other products; therefore each product may have to be assigned a proportion of these costs. The subsections which follow will consider the ways in which the costs of *materials* and *components*, of *labour* and of *overhead* (indirect costs) are measured.

13.2.1 Measuring the costs of materials and components

Of all costs, materials costs are the most clearly identifiable as a direct cost. If a production centre uses a material or good then cost is incurred. If production does not take place the material or good is not procured and no cost arises. This suggests that, for a production centre to keep records of its costs, it must buy in the material or good. Most business conscious organizations today comprise a number of *cost centres*. Although actual money is unlikely to flow from one cost centre to another, each cost centre will record the cost of buying in materials, goods or services from either external suppliers or other cost centres, and will charge subsequent suppliers or cost centres for the materials, goods or services provided to them. Therefore, when a production centre draws materials from stock, a clearly defined cost is incurred. But what would be the position if the stock has been supplied by different suppliers at different prices over a period of time? Assuming that the stock is non-perishable, that the time it is kept in stock does not affect its quality so that when drawing from stock the goods are selected at random and not according to, say, chronological order of supply, what is the value of the goods that should be charged to the cost centre? Should it be the cost of the oldest goods in stock? Should it be the cost of the most recently purchased goods? Should it be an average of the values in stock? Before the direct costs of materials or goods can be assigned to production the company must decide, as a matter of policy, a method of stock valuation. The decision will affect two measures; the value of stock in the stockpile at any one time and the cost charged to the production centre.

The two most common methods in use for determining the value of stock are first in first out (FIFO) and last in first out (LIFO).

First in first out (FIFO)

In this case the amount charged to the cost centre will reflect the cost of the earliest items delivered to stock.

Example 13(1)

Stock has been delivered to the stockpile on the first of every month in the quantities and at the prices listed below.

1 February	300 no.	@ £20.00
1 March	400 no.	@ £21.00
1 April	350 no.	@ £20.00
1 May	300 no.	@ £22.00

On the last day of May, 800 items are drawn from stock. What should the production centre be charged? Although there may be no means of determining which stock is the oldest, the charges will be based on the costs of the first in. Thus, the production centre will be charged:

300 no.	@ £20.00 =	£6000.00
400 no.	@ £21.00 =	£8400.00
100 no.	@ £20.00 =	£2000.00
	total cost =	£16 400.00

The value of the remaining stock can also be ascertained:

$$(350-100) = 250 \text{ no.} \qquad @ \text{£}20.00 = \quad \text{£}5000.00$$
$$300 \text{ no.} \qquad @ \text{£}22.00 = \quad \text{£}6600.00$$
$$\text{total value} = \text{£}11\,600.00$$

A consequence of this method of costing and valuation is that the costs charged to the production centre are low relative to the current prices of materials. Is this a sensible policy to adopt? A further consequence of this method is that the value of the stockpile is high, reflecting current prices of buying in materials. A conservative approach to stock valuation will favour a low valuation. For example, the price it might command on the open market, could be lower than the price at which the company buys it from its suppliers.

Last in first out (LIFO)

The alternative is to charge the cost centre at prices which reflect the current prices of buying in stock.

Example 13(2)

The same data will be used as in Example 13(1).
Stock has been delivered to the stockpile on the first of every month in the quantities and at the prices listed below.

1 February	300 no.	@ £20.00
1 March	400 no.	@ £21.00
1 April	350 no.	@ £20.00
1 May	300 no.	@ £22.00

On the last day of May, 800 items are drawn from stock. What should the production centre be charged?

$$300 \text{ no.} \qquad @ \text{£}22.00 = \quad \text{£}6600.00$$
$$350 \text{ no.} \qquad @ \text{£}20.00 = \quad \text{£}7000.00$$
$$150 \text{ no.} \qquad @ \text{£}21.00 = \quad \text{£}3150.00$$
$$\text{total cost} = \text{£}16\,750.00$$

This is a higher cost than would have been charged using FIFO. The value of the remaining stock can now be ascertained.

$$300 \text{ no.} \qquad @ \text{£}20.00 = \quad \text{£}6000.00$$
$$(400-150) = 250 \text{ no.} \qquad @ \text{£}21.00 = \quad \text{£}5250.00$$
$$\text{total value} = \text{£}11\,250.00$$

This is a lower value and therefore might be preferred. However, if this method is adopted a consequence could be that the stock valuation might contain values of small amounts of materials which were purchased many months or even years ago. This would be inevitable if the stockpile were not completely cleared out from time to time.

Other alternatives

Alternatives to FIFO and LIFO include using the average price of the materials bought in, replacement price, and standard costing.

If the average price is used, recalculation is needed whenever more stocks are purchased and/or stocks are issued. In an inflationary situation stock valuation will lag behind market value and costs charged to production centres will lag behind current costs, but not as badly as under FIFO.

Another term for replacement price is next in first out (NIFO). A production centre is charged for goods at the costs of buying in new materials. This ensures that the production centre charges its customers at prices which reflect current prices for goods and materials. Actual stocks will tend to be undervalued.

Standard costs are predetermined estimates (see section 14.2.4), in this case, of material costs. Thus the production centre will be charged the standard cost for the materials provided and the stock will be valued at the standard cost. Records of the variances between the actual costs and the standard costs will be kept and reconciled at the end of an accounting period. This works well when costs are reasonably steady.

To summarize, the way in which material costs are assigned to production is not a matter of fact but a matter of policy. It will become clear that the ways in which labour costs and overheads are determined are equally discretionary.

13.2.2 Measuring the costs of labour

There are two elements within most labour costs:

- time related (hours worked × hourly rates)
- output related (piece-work, incentive schemes).

Hourly rates will also vary with the number of hours worked in a day and in a week. Higher, overtime rates usually must be paid if the hours worked on a given day exceed a prescribed maximum. Working more than, say, 37 hours in a week or working at weekends may also entitle the individual to overtime payments. In some industries there will be extra payments for working with certain tools and/or equipment or for working under certain conditions. Companies often introduce incentive schemes to improve productivity and the incentive payments are later subsumed into pay norms as productivity rises with capital investment. A possible result of this is that over many years a very complex pay structure develops involving an array of so-called special payments which no longer represent the nature and extent of the work done. Companies sometimes experience considerable problems when they try to rationalize pay structures.

The wages bill is only one part of the cost of employing labour. In addition there can be provision for holiday pay, sick pay, national insurance, private medical insurance and pension schemes, redundancy funds, industrial training levies, and possibly travel and accommodation expenses.

When a person is assigned to a specific task, a direct cost arises; the cost of the work must include the cost to the company of employing that individual.

However, it should be clear from the foregoing paragraphs that the actual cost may depend upon the actual hours worked and on the productivity of the individual and includes a number of indirect costs. Therefore, although these costs will provide an historical record of costs incurred in a production process, they will be in a most unsuitable form for immediate entry as current labour costs. What has to be done in order to allocate labour costs against production is to agree a notional labour cost in £ per hour and to monitor regularly how close notional costs are to the recent past historical costs.

In short, a company as a matter of policy, will establish a set of labour rates (for different kinds of work or for different skills) chargeable as a direct cost to customers and/or internal cost centres. These rates will be updated from time to time.

13.2.3 Measuring and allocating overhead

Overhead is the term used for indirect costs (in the USA the term 'burden' is sometimes used). The difficulty lies less in the measurement and more in the allocation of overhead. If a company manufactures a single product then that product must pay for the total overhead of the company. There is no difficulty there! If a company manufactures two products, A and B, how should the overhead (rent, heating and lighting, administration, marketing, even research and development) be allocated? If product A uses the services of ten workers and product B uses the services of 40 workers, one method might be to assign overhead to A and B in the ratio 1:4. If, however, product A benefited from a higher proportion of capital investment then a system relying on a head count would be inappropriate. Another approach might be to use the floor area allocated to production as a basis for distribution of overhead, but, unless these floor areas could be closed down and no charges incurred by the company if there were no production, there is no rationale for this procedure.

The two methods above are actually used; the reason being their simplicity of application. Another method is to allocate overhead on the basis of turnover, where turnover is defined as:

$$\text{number produced} \times \text{selling price per item}$$

Example 13(3)

A company produces 1500 of product A per week which sell for £10 each, and 6000 of product B per week which sell for £6 each. Company overheads amount to £8000 per week. Determine the overhead cost that should be assigned to one unit each of product A and product B.

turnover for product A = $1500 \times 10 = £15\ 000$
turnover for product B = $6000 \times 6 = \underline{£36\ 000}$
              total turnover = £51 000

$$\text{overhead for product A} = \frac{15000 \times 8000}{51000} = £2353$$

$$\text{overhead for product B} = \frac{36000 \times 8000}{51000} = £5647$$

$$\text{unit overhead for product A} = \frac{2353}{1500} = £1.57$$

$$\text{unit overhead for product B} = \frac{5647}{6000} = £0.94$$

This appears to be a clear, rational approach. Overhead could be reassigned, say, annually against production using the previous year's figures for turnover. But what would be the position if product B was in a highly competitive market and its direct costs amounted to £5.25? By adding a unit overhead cost of £0.94 the total cost would be £6.19 and the product would be losing money. If, at the same time, the unit direct costs for product A only amounted to £3.00, then each sale of product A would earn the company a profit of

$$£10.00 - £3.00 - £1.57 = £5.43$$

Both the loss on product B and the profit on product A are illusory, a consequence of an arbitrary distribution of overhead. The facts are as set out below:

```
direct costs of product A = £3.00 × 1500 =    £4500
direct costs of product B = £5.25 × 6000 = £31 500
total overhead =                              £8000
total costs =                               £44 000

total revenue from products A and B =       £51 000
total profit for products A and B =          £7000
```

Which of A or B is responsible for the greater proportion of that profit is a matter of opinion, not a matter of fact. To pursue the matter a little further, an alternative distribution might be to divide equally the overhead between products A and B. In this case the total costs of A would amount to £4500+£4000=£8500 resulting in a total profit for A per week of £6500. The total costs for B would be £31 500+£4000=£35 500 giving a total profit per week for product B of £500. What is evident from this example is that the distribution of overhead can cause a product or cost centre to appear to lose money when in each case the product's sale price exceeds its direct costs. In fact, each product is making money! Perhaps the question that needs to be asked, by the costs centres of their administration, is 'Why are the overheads so high?' It might be that it is the administration which is 'losing money' not the cost centres!

Example 13(4)

A large agro-chemical company has hundreds of distribution centres. Company overhead is £150 m p.a. The annual turnover is £1000 m. A new small distribution centre has been established to serve what is hoped to be an expanding market. Company policy is to distribute central overhead as a direct proportion of turnover. Using the data below for the first year of operation of the new centre, should it be allowed to continue in business for a second year?

Data

	Costs £(k)	Revenue £(k)
annual sales of agro-chemicals		400
costs of importing agro-chemicals	200	
costs of distribution to customers	20	
staff costs	120	
depot overhead	24	
company overhead (15% of sales)	60	
totals	424	400

The new distribution centre is, apparently, losing £24k p.a. Therefore a decision to close it down would not be unexpected. But would that decision make any business sense? If the company overhead is removed from the list of costs, the value of the costs incurred by the new centre is only £364k; so revenue has exceeded costs by £36k. The centre is making money. Since the centre has been located to serve an expanding market, a decision to keep the centre in operation would be far more sensible. Those huge company overheads are so large in comparison with this small operation that they must be absorbed elsewhere, just as they were in the year before opening the new centre.

Overheads must be paid, certainly. If the production centres cannot absorb them then they must be reduced (at head office if necessary!). Engineering managers should be acutely aware that the way in which overheads are assigned to production centres is essentially arbitrary, and therefore should be a matter of discussion not of imposition.

13.2.4   Standard Costs

Managers are required to make decisions on current and future operations on the basis of experience and knowledge of costs. For management to make the correct decisions it must have up-to-date data on costs. By now it should be clear that costing is an imperfect science; yet cost data must be held for the information is needed. In view of this, companies keep records of *standard costs* which are updated at regular intervals. These standard costs are predetermined estimates of the costs of carrying out standard operations under standard conditions. Standard costs can be kept for specific tasks which employ labour, equipment and materials. Standard costs do not usually include overhead; this will be added on at a level decided by management, depending upon the purpose of estimating the costs of the work to be done.

Since the actual costs incurred do not usually correspond to the standard costs that make up the cost plan it will be important to record the differences that arise. These differences are referred to as variances and the engineering manager will be called upon from time to time to examine the findings of variance analyses produced by his cost accountants and to explain any large variances. Large variances may arise when:

- the work is not being carried out under standard conditions,
- productivity is significantly different from that assumed by the standard costing (for reasons known or unknown),
- the standard cost has not been updated.

The objectives of variance analysis are twofold; to ensure that the standard costs held on record are suitable for current and future use and to monitor the performance of the work in hand.

Standard costs will be kept for elements of work on a quantitative or hourly basis depending upon the nature of the work. For example, a garage might apply a single standard cost for an annual service for a vehicle, but an hourly cost for body repair work. A builder might apply a quantitative standard cost for laying asphalt (£ per m²), but a single standard cost for installing a boiler. These standard costs will be kept in the form most suited to the needs of the company.

13.3   MAKING A PROFIT

In order to make a profit revenue must exceed total costs. There will be direct and indirect costs. Direct costs consist of *fixed* costs and *variable* costs. Direct costs will usually be assigned as a variable cost where the cost varies either with time or with production. A fixed cost is one that arises independently of the quantity of goods or materials produced. The cost of bringing in a machine to carry out a task might have two elements to it. Costs arise in transporting the machine to the site, then setting it up, and, after the task is over, removing it and returning it to wherever it came from. The fixed cost for using the machine is the sum of these costs. During production the machine also incurs costs; these could be hire costs, fuel costs or depreciation costs. These are variable costs, that is, they vary with the output, which is determined by time and productivity.

Figure 13.1 shows some of the ways in which costs can vary with production. Figure 13.1(a) shows a fixed cost; the cost does not vary with production. Figure 13.1(b) shows a variable cost in which there is a linear relationship between volume of production and cost, for example, a material cost; double the quantity

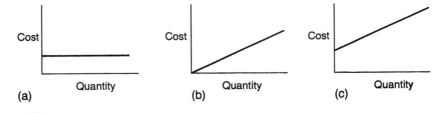

Figure 13.1

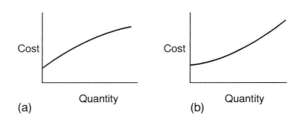

Figure 13.2

means double the material cost. Figure 13.1(c) shows the most common position, in which fixed and variable costs are incurred.

A linear relationship is not going to arise at all times. There are several possibilities. When production rates rise the company might be able to buy materials at a discount, and the materials' unit costs decline as the volume increases; this could give rise to the curve in Figure 13.2(a). On the other hand, to increase production, overtime might be necessary, increasing the direct labour cost; this could give rise to the curve in Figure 13.2(b).

The simplest approach, and one commonly adopted in practice, is to assume a linear cost function. If one then assumes that, once a unit price has been established, it will not vary with the volume sold, a *break-even* chart can be drawn (see Figure 13.3(a)). This linear break-even chart has one break-even point, which is the point at which total revenue equals total costs. Knowledge of the break-even point is most useful, it tells the manager the volume of sales needed before a profit can be made. Further analysis of the position could be carried out. An alternative price would give rise to a different break-even point as shown in Figure 13.3(b) below.

Figure 13.4 below shows a curve obtained by plotting sales price against break-even number. From this curve can be found either the minimum sales that must be achieved for a whole range of price options or the minimum price the company must charge in order to cover its costs if production and sales are limited.

This curve can be plotted from the equation

$$n = \frac{F}{(S - V)}$$

where n = break-even number
F = total fixed costs
S = sales price per unit
V = direct variable cost per unit

(S − V) the difference between the sales price and the variable cost is known as the *contribution*; it is the money available for paying off the fixed costs and, eventually, for providing profit.

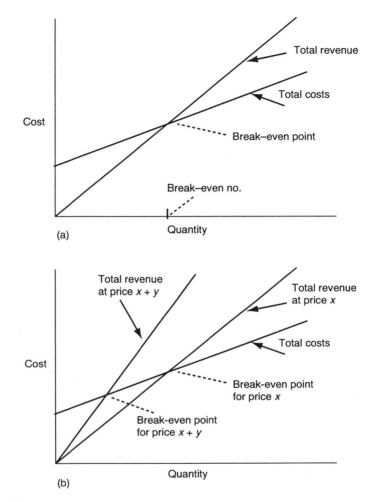

Figure 13.3

Example 13(5)

A factory established to manufacture three products, A, B, C, has fixed costs as below:

	£
salaries per week	7000
heating and lighting per week	100
office supplies per week	100
marketing per week	600
building (lease and taxes) per year	12 000
loan for equipment (repayable over one year)	8000
interest rate on loan 10%	

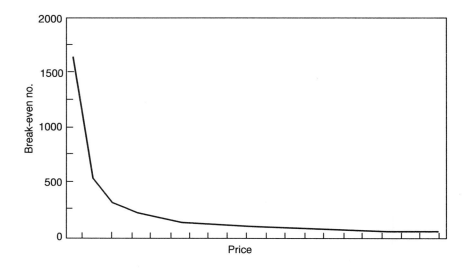

Figure 13.4

Current rates of production are 120 per week for A and 80 per week for B. There is no production of C. The total weekly variable costs are £300 for A, and £440 for B. Sales price for A is £100, sales price for B is £110.

(1)   Find

      (a)   the unit variable cost for each of A and B,

      (b)   the unit contribution for each of A and B,

      (c)   the current total weekly profit.

(2)   Assuming that the fixed costs are distributed to A, B and C in proportion to their turnover (current rate of production × current sales price), determine the break-even number per week for A and B.

(3)   If product C is introduced at 100 units per week, to sell at £150 each, and production rates for A and B are halved, find the new weekly profit. Use a unit variable cost of £15 for C. Should product C be introduced in this way?

(4)   The directors decide to concentrate solely on product C. Find values of the weekly break-even number for C for a sales price ranging from £50 to £150.

Solution

(1)(a)   unit variable cost for A $= \dfrac{300}{120} = 2.50$

unit variable cost for B $= \dfrac{440}{80} = 5.50$

(1)(b)   unit contribution for A $= 100 - 2.50 = 97.50$

unit contribution for B $= 110 - 5.50 = 104.50$

(1)(c)   total weekly profit $= 120 \times 97.5 + 80 \times 104.5 - F$

where $F =$ fixed costs

$$= 7000 + 100 + 100 + 600 + \frac{(12\,000 + 8000 + 800)}{52} = 8200$$

therefore total weekly profit $= £11\,860$

(2)   distributed fixed costs : $A = \dfrac{(120 \times 100)}{(120 \times 100 + 80 \times 110)} \times 8200$

$= 4730.8$

therefore fixed costs: B $= 8200 - 4730.8 = 3469.2$
and

$$\text{break-even no. for A} = \frac{4730.8}{97.5} = 48.5$$

$$\text{break-even no. for B} = \frac{3469.2}{104.5} = 33.2$$

Since the company will be unable to sell a fraction of a product, the break-even numbers should be rounded upwards to 49 no. for product A and 34 no. for product B.

(3)   new weekly profit $= 60 \times 97.5 + 40 \times 104.5 + 100 \times 135 - 8200$
$= 15330$

Since profitability has increased substantially, product C should be introduced in this manner.

(4)   using the formula $n = \dfrac{F}{(S - V)}$

where $F = 8200$ and $V = 15$, the values shown in Table 13.1 are obtained:

Table 13.1   Break-even values for product C

S	50	60	70	80	90	100	110	120	130	140	150
n	234	182	149	126	109	97	86	78	71	66	61

These values have been plotted in Figure 13.5.

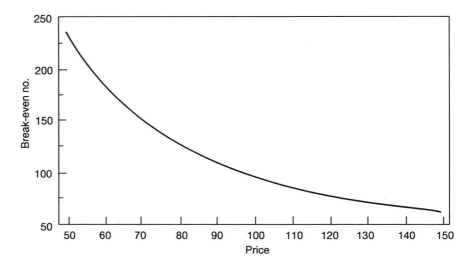

Figure 13.5   Break-even curve for product C

Example 13(6)

A company is planning to produce and sell widgets. Estimated fixed costs are £9000 per week; variable costs are estimated as follows:

£20 each for the first 400 widgets
£40 each for the next 100 widgets
£80 each for the next 100 widgets

A profit margin of at least 10% is desired.
For the weekly production rates below determine an appropriate selling price per widget.

100   200   300   400   500   600

Solution

In this case it is probably easier to apply some commonsense rather than resorting to formulae.
For 100 widgets:
total cost = $9000 + 100 \times 20 = 11\,000$
therefore cost per widget = $11\,000/100 = 110$
therefore sales price per widget = $1.10 \times 110 = £121.00$
similarly, for 200, 300 and 400 widgets, prices of £71.50, £55.00, and £46.75 are obtained
For 500 widgets:
total cost = $9000 + 400 \times 20 + 100 \times 40 = 21\,000$

therefore cost per widget $= 21\,000/500 = 42$
therefore sales price per widget $= 1.10 \times 42 = £46.20$
For 600 widgets:
total cost $= 9000+400 \times 20+100 \times 40+100 \times 80 = 29\,000$
therefore cost per widget $= 29\,000/600 = £48.33$

From the foregoing, the lowest price coincides with sales and production of 500 widgets per week. A problem similar to this is developed a little further in section 13.5.4.

13.4 BUDGETS

A budget is a cost plan. Government departments will work to an annual budget. In the private sector annual cost plans may have to be presented to boards of directors for their approval. For example, a research and development (R&D) department of a company will usually have to obtain approval in advance for its operations; a major element of the departmental plan will be its budget. Even where programmes are instituted to run for several years, the cost plan, when submitted for approval, will break the work down into a series of annual budgets. The purpose of presenting a budget is not merely to obtain approval. Once the programme of work is underway it will be used as the basis for monitoring costs and, possibly, for moving funds within the cost plan (if this is permitted).

An example of a budget for a three year research programme is given in Table 13.2.

Table 13.2 Budget for research programme

Details	Year 1	Year 2	Year 3	Year 4
Personnel nos				
Researcher	2	4	4	2
Technician	1	2	2	1
Secretarial	0.5	0.5	0.5	0.5
Salaries				
@ 18 000	36 000	72 000	72 000	36 000
@ 15 000	15 000	30 000	30 000	15 000
@ 12 000	6000	6000	6000	6000
Consumables	1000	2000	2000	1000
Travel and subsistence	1000	2000	2000	1000
Other costs	500	1000	1000	500
Equipment	2000	500	500	500
Total costs	61 500	113 500	113 500	60 000
Grant income	29 300	54 200	54 200	28 700
Net surplus/(deficit)	(32 200)	(59 300)	(59 300)	(31 300)

13.5   ESTIMATING, TENDERING AND PRICING

There are two determinants of price, they are *cost* and *the market*[2]. If the price is too high the product will not find a market and either production must cease or costs must be reduced.

13.5.1   Tendering

Frequently suppliers and contractors are invited to tender for work. In these circumstances cost will be the major determinant of the tender price. The tender period even for a contract valued at some £100 m may be only a few weeks. The suppliers/contractors may not know who else is competing for the work. In these circumstances the tenderer must, in the first instance, rely on his cost records. Therefore it is essential that companies maintain up-to-date cost records at all times. The basis of the tender will be the standard costs kept by the company. When pricing the work the manager will take the standard costs and add what is often referred to as 'mark up' to cover overhead and profit. This will be at the discretion of the manager or even his board of directors. When work is in short supply mark up will be low, when the company has plenty of work and/or the risk attached to the job is high the mark up will be high. When competition for the work is high and the company is anxious to be awarded the contract, mark up will be low.

13.5.2   Estimating with inflation

In order to price a product, a service, a specific order, or a contract, the costs of that product, service, order, or contract must be estimated. The estimator must be able to convert the recorded standard costs into future costs. Cost price indices, giving figures for materials and labour are published for different industrial sectors and for the national economy. The most commonly quoted index in the UK is the Retail Price Index (RPI) published monthly by the Central Statistical Office. This is based on a range of consumer goods and services, the prices of which are surveyed, averaged across the country and weighted according to a formula. The range of goods and services and the formula weighting are adjusted at intervals of about five or ten years to take into account changes in consumer behaviour. The RPI is used by government and economists to measure the rate of inflation in the UK economy (see also Chapter 15, section 15.8). Price indices can be used to estimate current costs from past costs.

$$\text{Estimated Current Costs} = \text{Past Costs} \times \frac{I_c}{I_p}$$

---

[2]Economists might argue that there is only one determinant of price: the market. However, costs can be considered a determinant of price for two reasons. (1) In markets with few buyers and/or few suppliers the costs of supply are sometimes used as a basis for negotiating prices. (2) Suppliers can only remain in the market if prices exceed their costs in the long term.

where

$$I_c = \text{current index value}$$
$$I_p = \text{index value at time costs were recorded}$$

The estimator may then have to add a further percentage to account for future cost changes during the period of manufacture, installation or construction. During periods of low inflation fixed price contracts (contracts which provide for no change in contract prices as costs of labour and materials change) are common for contracts of up to two years in duration. For longer contracts, fluctuation clauses can be introduced that permit price changes in accordance with a formula associated with an accepted price index (see also Chapter 17, section 17.4.4). In these circumstances the estimator need only consider current costs in his estimate.

13.5.3   Approximate estimates

Estimating is not only carried out by manufacturers and contractors. The recipients of these goods and services will often produce estimates for their own use. Usually the bases for these estimates will be very different from the bases used by the supplier. The bases used by the customer may include:

(1)   comparison with previous prices paid for similar goods and services,
(2)   carrying out a survey of current (published) market prices,
(3)   using an appropriate industrial formula.

An investor in a new powerstation, or theatre, or office building might adopt method (1). An investor in a new fleet of buses or in re-equipping an organization with wordprocessors could adopt method (2). An investor in a new petrochemical plant might adopt method (3).

Unit methods

Three illustrations of the simple unit method of estimating are given in Example 13(7) below.

Example 13(7)

(a)   A 1200 MW powerstation cost £1.8 billion, how much will an 1800 MW powerstation cost?
The cost of the 1200 MW powerstation translates into £1.5m/MW. Therefore the cost of a new 1800 MW powerstation will be:

$$1800 \times 1.5 = \text{£2700m} = \text{£2.7 billion}$$

The simplicity of this formula implies that it should only be used where the two powerstations are of the same order of magnitude.

(b)   A 1000 seat theatre cost £12m, how much will a 1400 seat theatre cost?
In this case the auditorium costs were £8m and the stage and changing room costs amounted to £4m.

The auditorium cost represents £8000 a seat. The stage and changing room costs are not expected to be any different. Therefore the cost of the new theatre will be:

$$1400 \times 8000 + 4.0m = £15.2m$$

(c)   An office providing 2000 m² of floor area cost £2.2m, how much will an office of 2500 m², built to a similar standard, cost?
Building costs are £1100/m². Therefore the new office building will cost:

$$2500 \times 1100 = £2.75m$$

Similar provisos apply to (b) and (c) as were applied to (a).

Elemental methods

A more sophisticated approach is to break the work down into elements and apply unit methods to the elements. For manufacturing, the major elements might comprise flow processes, major equipment and buildings; for an office building, the elements might comprise the separate floors, the roof, and the external walls.

Example 13(8)

Cost data on a recently completed office building (Building A) are provided in Table 13.3. Design data for a proposed new building (Building B) are provided in Table 13.4. Prepare a cost estimate for Building B.

Table 13.3   Cost data

Cost Analysis
Building A 20 m × 10 m × 20 m high (5 storeys)
total floor area: 1000 m²

	Cost data		Cost analysis	
Element description	Element Cost (£)	Element unit qty (m²)	Element unit rate (£/m²)	Element cost per unit floor area of building
Ground floor	300 000	200	1500	300
Upper floors (total)	960 000	800	1200	960
Roof	60 000	200	300	60
External walls	720 000	1200	600	720
Total	2 040 000			2040

Table 13.4   Design data

Building B 40m × 10m × 12m high (4 storeys)	
Design data	
Element description	Element unit qty (m²)
Ground floor	400
Upper floors (total)	1200
Roof	400
External walls	1200

Solution

Table 13.5

Element description	Qty × unit rate	Element cost (£)
Ground floor	400 × 1500	600 000
Upper floors (total)	1200 × 1200	1 440 000
Roof	400 × 300	120 000
External walls	1200 × 600	720 000
Total cost		2 880 000

The estimated cost of Building B is £2 880 000. A degree of accuracy of about 20% should be achievable depending upon the information available.[4]

Industrial Formulae

Examples 13(9) and 13(10) illustrate the application of industrial formulae.

Example 13(9)

De la Mare [2] provides a formula for cost estimating by which the cost of a new plant or process can be estimated using an appropriate exponential cost factor. The relationship between the capital cost of a plant and its design capacity is given by:

$$C = kQ^{\alpha}$$

---

[4]A brief but very useful outline of types and classification of estimates by their degree of accuracy, including the relationship between the number of man hours devoted to developing the estimate and the value of of the project, is given in Chapter 3 of *A Guide to Capital Cost Estimating* 3rd edition, Institution of Chemical Engineers, 1988.

where C = capital cost
$\quad\quad Q$ = production capacity of plant/machine
$\quad\quad k$ = a constant
$\quad\quad \alpha$ = exponential cost factor

Exponential cost factors are available for many processes and for individual pieces of equipment. For an acetylene plant a typical factor of 0.75 is provided. Therefore, if an estimate is needed for the cost of a new acetylene plant, all the estimator needs to do is find the constant k for a similar plant of approximately the same capacity and apply the formula.

Existing Plant A   Cost £50m   Capacity 100 units/week

$$\alpha = 0.75$$

$$50 = k \times 100^{0.75}$$

therefore k=1.58

New Plant B   Capacity 125 units/week
therefore

$$\text{Cost} = 1.58 \times 125^{0.75} = £59.1\text{m}$$

The new plant will cost approximately £59m (if the unit method had been used a figure of £62.5m would have been obtained).

Example 13(10)

The use of installation factors is described in Chapter 4 of *A Guide to Capital Cost Estimating* [3]. One can either use overall installation factors or different installation factors for main plant items. Overall installation factors are often known as Lang factors. These factorial methods are based on an historical knowledge of the relative costs of the various purchases and activities that are necessary to build a plant. The value of each provision (buildings, piping, etc.) is recorded as a percentage of the cost of the purchased equipment delivered. Table 13.6, which is an extract from *A Guide to Capital Cost Estimating*,[5] shows for a fluid processing plant (e.g. a distillation unit) the costs for each item as a percentage of the cost of the purchased equipment delivered.

Thus the total erected cost of a fluid processing plant will be:

$$4.83 \times \text{total cost of purchased equipment delivered}$$

---

[5]See Table 4.4 in A Guide to Capital Cost Estimating.

Table 13.6

Item	Percentage of Delivered Equipment Cost
DIRECT COSTS	
Purchased Equipment Delivered (including fabricated equipment and process machinery)	100
Purchased Equipment Installation	47
Instrumentation and Controls (installed)	18
Piping (installed)	66
Electrical (installed)	11
Buildings (including services)	18
Yard Improvements	10
Service Facilities (installed)	70
Land (if purchase is required)	6
Total Direct Plant Cost	346
INDIRECT COSTS	
Engineering and Supervision	33
Construction Expenses	41
TOTAL DIRECT AND INDIRECT PLANT COSTS	420
Contractor's Fee (about 5% of direct and indirect plant costs)	21
Contingency (about 10% of direct and indirect plant costs)	42
TOTAL ERECTED COST	483
Working Capital (about 15% of total capital investment)	86
TOTAL CAPITAL EMPLOYED	569

The Lang factor for this plant would be 4.83. Lang factors vary between about 2 and 10 depending on the process, the scale of the process, the materials of construction and the location. Lang factors and installation factors for different main plant items should be derived from the historical cost data of the company which owns and operates the installation. The estimator must obtain quotations for purchased equipment delivered from the suppliers.

13.5.4 Pricing for the market

In order to sell engineering products in the market the price must be one which the customers are prepared to pay and, of course, one which compares favourably with the competition. Economists speak of the laws of supply and demand.

As the price of a widely available product falls, more of that product is purchased. This is either a result of existing customers being able to afford more, or a result of new customers buying the product, which previously they could not afford: **demand increases as the price falls.**

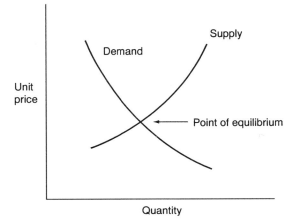

Figure 13.6 Supply and Demand Curves

Further, the higher the price that customers are willing to pay for a product the greater the incentive for companies to provide that product: **supply increases as the selling price rises**.

These two hypotheses are demonstrated in Figure 13.6. The intersection point of the two curves is known as the point of equilibrium. Market prices will tend toward that point. If, for example, the price rises higher than the equilibrium point price, the number of people buying the product will reduce, this will result in the suppliers being unable to sell their stock. Therefore, production will have to be reduced. At the same time prices may have to be reduced to offload surplus stock and prices and quantities will return to equilibrium. There are many reasons why simple economic theory does not always apply in practice but these forces are present in any market economy. The interested reader might find *Economics* by Parkin and King [4] a useful text for further study of the laws of supply and demand. An example of how this theory might apply in practice will conclude this chapter.

Example 13(11)

Company X is planning to produce and sell supa-widgets. Estimated fixed costs are £90 000 per week; variable costs are estimated as follows:

£200 each for the first 400 supa-widgets
£300 each for the next 100 supa-widgets
£600 each for the next 100 supa-widgets

A profit margin of at least 10% is desired.

A market survey suggests that the following sales might be achieved at the prices given.

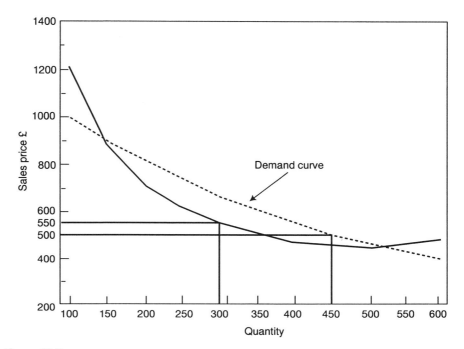

Figure 13.7

100 per week at £1000 each
200 per week at £820 each
300 per week at £660 each
400 per week at £550 each
500 per week at £460 each
600 per week at £390 each

(1) Determine the most profitable rate of production and sales price at which the company should operate.

(2) Company X decides to produce and sell 350 per week at a price of £600 each. Company Y begins to supply 100 supa-widgets per week at a price of £500 each. How can Company X stay in the market?

Solution

(1) First the values of sales price against quantity are determined using a similar method to that given in Example 13(6). These are plotted in Figure 13.7. On the same axes are plotted the market survey data (the demand curve).

If Company X sets its price at the demand-curve price of £660 for production and sales of 300 per week then the profit per unit will far exceed the minimum of

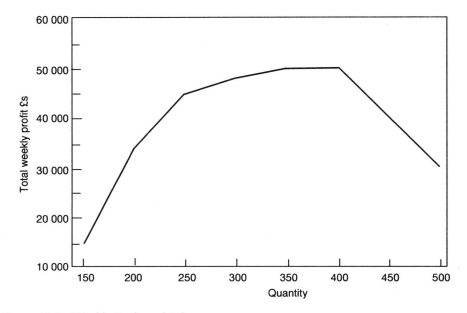

Figure 13.8 Weekly Profit and Sales

10% desired. The maximum profit per unit will be given where the distance on the vertical axis between the demand curve and the price curve is at a maximum. For the curves shown this point is represented by:

production and sales of 250 per week at £740 each

This would give a profit of £180 per supa-widget on unit costs of £560; a 32% profit.

Company X may wish to maximize total profit.

$$\text{profit} = \left(P_d - \frac{P_s}{1.1}\right) \times Q_d$$

where P_d=price on demand curve
P_s=sales price for 10% profit (price curve)
Q_d=quantity on demand curve

Values of profit against Q_d are given in Figure 13.8. Maximum weekly profit is £50 000 for production and sales of between 350 and 400 supa-widgets.

(2) Obviously Company X will have to lower its price otherwise it will quickly lose custom to Company Y. If it reduces its price to £500 will this be sufficient? At a price of £500 the demand for supa-widgets is 450 per week. Now, if Company Y maintains its sales of 150 per week this only leaves a demand of 300 per week for supa-widgets made by Company X. Can Company X sell 300 supa-widgets per week at £500 each and still make a profit? The answer is 'No!' The company

needs to sell at a price of £550 each in order to make a profit of 10%; therefore its break-even price is £500. Therefore, if Company X proceeds to sell 300 per week at £500 each it will only break-even. If, however, it marginally undercuts Company Y (it cannot afford to reduce prices very far as is evident from the curve) then two consequences could flow from this action:

- The sales by Company Y fall as more customers buy from Company X, which means that Company X could move from break-even to a small profit.
- at the lower price the total demand increases such that Company Y continues to produce and sell 150 per week and Company X sells a sufficient number to make a profit too.

In this case it is not possible to give a firm answer because customer preferences for the products of Companies X and Y when prices are equal are unknown, and because there is a strong possibility that Company Y might lower its prices to continue to undercut Company X, which could mean that Company X would be unable to compete and would have to withdraw from the market.

13.6   SUMMARY

This chapter has examined how different costs, direct and indirect, contribute to the cost of a product and the ways in which these costs can be assessed. The concept of break-even has been examined and the two determinants of price (cost and the market) considered. Methods of estimating have been examined and examples provided. Finally, an example was given of how an appropriate market price can be determined using a demand curve and a break-even curve.

REFERENCES

1. de la Mare, R. F. (1982) *Manufacturing Systems Economics*. Holt, Rinehart and Winston, London.
2. Parkin, M. and King, D. (1992) *Economics*. Addison-Wesley, Reading.

BIBLIOGRAPHY

Chapman, C. B., Cooper, D. F. and Page, M. J. (1987) *Management for Engineers*. Wiley, Chichester.
Curtis, T. (1994) *Business and Marketing for Engineers and Scientists*. McGraw-Hill, Maidenhead.
Lanigan, M. (1992) *Engineers in Business*. Addison-Wesley, Reading.
Leech, D. J. (1982) *Economics and Financial Studies for Engineers*. Ellis Horwood, Chichester.

14

Measuring financial performance

14.1 INTRODUCTION

All business managers need to measure the success and performance of their business operations. Engineering managers have exactly the same need. They will want to know how well they have performed relative to their expectations and how well they have performed relative to their competitors.

Some of the most commonly used measures of performance are found in the financial data presented in a set of accounts. It is, therefore, important for engineers to understand the components of a set of accounts, and to be able to analyse and interpret them. In this chapter the basic components are identified and described by examining in detail the *profit and loss account* and the *balance sheet*. The fundamental concepts by which accounts are prepared are briefly outlined. The chapter then examines the *working capital cycle* and shows how data from the primary statements of account can be used by management. Finally the chapter explains how a number of *financial ratios* can be used to analyse and interpret a business's financial position.

14.2 BUSINESS ENTITIES

Business is conducted in a variety of different forms. The most common types of business operations are soletraders, partnerships and limited companies. Sections 14.2.1 to 14.2.3 will examine how these business entities are constituted.

14.2.1 Soletrader

Soletrader is the term used to describe one person engaged in business. It is the simplest business entity, examples of which include corner shop, dentist, farmer and even consulting engineer. The individual is the owner of the business, although he may employ someone to help him. The day to day affairs of the business will be operated independently of the owner's personal affairs and separate accounts will be drawn up. However, from a legal and taxation point of view, the business is part of the individual's personal assets. His liability for business debts is unlimited and all his other personal assets (for example, his home!) are at stake. On the other hand, he is the sole beneficiary of any profits earned by the business.

14.2.2 Partnerships

Partnerships are an extension of the soletrader entity, comprising two or more people engaged in business together. Each partner will have invested capital in the business and will be entitled to a share of the profits. The business therefore has two or more owners. Partnerships are a common form of business entity in the professions. Many small firms of consulting engineers are partnerships.

The share of the profits payable to each partner is normally proportional to the amount of capital each has invested in the business. For example, if three partners contribute capital in the proportions 3:2:1 it is likely that the profits will be shared in the proportions 3:2:1.

In the UK, partnerships are governed by the Partnership Act 1890 which states that partners' liability for business debts is joint and several. This means that the partners are responsible for the debts of the business jointly as a body of partners and also individually (severally). Their liability for the debts of the business is the same as that of a soletrader in that their personal assets may be used to settle liabilities of the business. In addition, a partner's personal assets may be used to settle a debt incurred by the other partners in their business operations if the debt cannot be settled from the funds of the business.

14.2.3 Limited companies

A limited company is often referred to as a corporation. The term 'incorporation' will be explained later. The owners of a limited company are called shareholders. They subscribe capital to the company and in return are issued with shares in the company. Limited companies can be private or public. The difference between the two is that the shares of a public limited company are traded on a stock exchange. Most large engineering businesses are limited companies although not all are public companies.

The term 'limited' is used because the liability of the shareholders is limited. This means that, in the event of the company being unable to settle its debts, the shareholders only stand to lose what they have contributed by way of share capital. Their personal wealth is not at stake. Contrast this with the position of the soletrader or partnership where the individual stands to lose everything. This is probably the most significant advantage of incorporation.

Incorporated companies or corporations are so called because they are regarded in law as separate legal entities which are distinct from their owners, the shareholders. A corporation can enter into contracts in its own right, that is, a contract would be between ABC Company Limited and XYZ Company Limited rather than between the individual shareholders.

The day to day management of a company is carried out by the directors of the company. In smaller private companies the directors and shareholders may, in fact, be the same people. However, in the large public limited companies (plcs in the UK) management is delegated by the shareholders to a board of directors. This is a further element in the separation of the owners of the company from the company itself. The directors have a duty to act in the best interests of the company at all times and their performance is, of course, reviewed by the shareholders at regular intervals. One of the ways in which the shareholders of a company can appraise the performance of its board of directors is by reviewing the annual financial accounts. The accounts are, therefore, very important, and this explains why there can be so much pressure on boards of directors to show a healthy financial position.

Businesses which operate as limited companies are subject to much more accounting regulation than partnerships and soletraders. There are obviously costs associated with this degree of regulation and careful consideration must be given by the owners of a business as to which type of entity would be the most suitable.

Soletraders, partnerships, and companies are also bound by laws covering, for example:

- health and safety at work
- public liability
- employment of individuals
- taxation
- ownership of land and property

14.3   THE FUNDAMENTAL BASES ON WHICH ACCOUNTS ARE PREPARED

Although the different types of business entity are subject to different degrees of regulation, from an accounting point of view, the basic requirements for the different entities have much in common. The level of detail required in a set of financial accounts will be different for each entity, but the methods of preparation and the fundamental accounting concepts are the same. Hence, throughout the remainder of this chapter the term business or company is equally applicable to all types of entity.

14.3.1   Fundamental accounting concepts

All accounts should be prepared with the following fundamental concepts in mind:

The matching principle

Income and costs should be recorded in the accounts of a business in the accounting period in which they arise. This may not necessarily be the same period as that in which the cash is received or paid. In addition, the income and costs should be matched with one another so far as a relationship between them can be established. This concept is discussed more fully in section 14.5.1 when the profit and loss account is examined.

The going concern concept

The assumption is made that the business will continue in operational existence for the foreseeable future unless information is provided to the contrary. There is the further assumption that there will be no significant reduction in the scale of the operation of the company and that debts will continue to be paid when they fall due.

Consistency

This provides for consistent accounting treatment of items that are similar within an accounting period and a consistent treatment of items from one accounting period to the next. For example, there is no reason to treat sales to company A any differently from sales to company B, and one would expect the manner in which these sales are entered in the accounts to remain the same from one period to the next.

The prudence concept

This means that accounts should always be prepared exercising a degree of caution. Profits should not appear in the accounts before they are earned whilst losses should be included as soon as it is known that they will occur.

For example, if a company is engaged in a long term contract and realizes that the costs are escalating to a much higher level than the income which will be received from the contract, then the extra costs should be included in the accounts for the current accounting period rather than when the contract is completed.

This operation of the prudence concept appears to conflict with the matching principle. Where there is a conflict, the prudence concept should prevail. As a result, the loss in the above example will be recognized as soon as it is anticipated.

Thus, the four fundamental accounting concepts are:

- the matching principle
- the going concern
- consistency
- prudence.

In addition, there are a number of measurement rules which are adopted universally. These are described in the next section.

14.3.2 Measurement rules

Units of measurement

The information included in a set of accounts is expressed in monetary units–pounds, dollars, francs, etc. It is therefore impossible to include the value of certain components of a business in its accounts. For example, the value of a skilled workforce would be difficult to quantify in monetary units. The wages paid to them, on the other hand, can be measured easily in these terms.

Historical cost convention

Transactions should be included in the accounts at their original cost. If a machine were purchased for £9000 three years ago, then it will be recorded in the accounts at a cost of £9000 irrespective of what that machine would cost to buy now.

Accounting period

The convention is that businesses will draw up accounts for a period of one year for submission to the taxation authorities and for circulation to the shareholders. This period is usually too long for internal management purposes, therefore, depending upon the size and nature of the business, internal accounts may be produced on a monthly or quarterly basis.

Business entity

For the production of accounts the business entity must be isolated and defined. For a company this is relatively straightforward since the operations of the business tend to be remote from the owners of that business. However, with soletraders and partnerships the process of definition and isolation requires scrupulous attention in order to separate the business operations from personal affairs.

14.3.3   Accounting standards

These concepts and measurement rules ensure that there is consistency and comparability in the financial information provided in the accounts by business entities. This consistency and comparability is further enhanced by the rules and guidelines of the accounting professions and by the legal framework, especially with respect to limited companies.

Most countries have developed their own accounting standards. These standards lay down a basis for the methods of accounting to be adopted in dealing with specific items in the accounts. For example, there is a standard which sets out the basis for valuing and recording stocks.

The International Accounting Standards Committee (IASC) has also developed its own set of accounting standards in order to provide for a reasonable degree of comparability between practices in different countries.

Whilst individual countries tend to draft their own standards to be generally in line with those of the IASC, there are still differences in accounting methods which must be considered when comparing company accounts in different countries.

All standards, irrespective of the country concerned, are drafted to give general guidelines for accounting treatment. Indeed, some guidelines present a number of alternative methods from which to choose. They are, therefore, open to interpretation and allow scope for professional judgement in setting the accounting policies of a company.

14.3.4   Summarizing fundamental practices

In summary, different sets of accounts will always be comparable and will have a lot in common. Accounting standards and the legal framework will ensure that this is so. However, it is important to be aware that accounts will be prepared and interpreted in different ways. This can have a marked effect upon the apparent financial position of a company and this should be taken into account when comparing one company with another, or in appraising a company in which one may wish to invest.

14.4   PRESENTATION OF FINANCIAL INFORMATION

The two most commonly used statements of account are *financial accounts* and *management accounts*. The differences between these are examined below.

14.4.1   Financial accounts

The vast majority of companies in the UK are required by law to produce a set of financial accounts on an annual basis. The contents of these accounts are to a large extent determined by the Companies Act 1985 and by Accounting Standards. The accounts are produced primarily for the shareholders but will also be put on public record and subjected to independent scrutiny by the company's auditors. The readership is thus very wide and a great deal of care is taken to ensure that the financial position of the company is presented in the most accurate and most favourable manner.

As the contents are governed by the regulatory framework, the presentation of published financial statements from different companies will have a lot in common. Each will contain a balance sheet, a profit and loss account, a statement of the accounting policies adopted and notes providing a further analysis of the data provided.

14.4.2   Management accounts

Management accounts on the other hand are an internal document. They may be widely read within the company or even by potential investors but they are not available to the general public. Good management accounts are a very necessary and effective management tool for even the smallest of enterprises. They tend to be produced on a monthly basis and are, therefore, much more up to date than financial accounts.

The level of detail varies greatly from company to company. Typically, management accounts will show the results for the month and the cumulative results for the year to date. These results are then compared with the budget for the year and with the actual results from the previous year, as illustrated in Table 14.1. It is also likely that separate figures will be prepared for each division of the company or even for each product line if the company spends large amounts of money manufacturing a small number of products.

Table 14.1 Campbell Engineering Company. Division D April Management Accounts. Trading and Profit and Loss Account

	Actual		Budget		Prior year		Variance YTD**	
	Month	YTD	Month	YTD	Month	YTD	Budget	Prior year
	£'000	£'000	£'000	£'000	£'000	£'000	£'000	£'000
Sales	2560	11500	2600	11000	2050	9500	500	2000
Direct costs								
Materials	1105	5050	1200	4800	980	4320	250	730
Labour	770	3660	775	3500	515	2740	160	920
Power	130	390	100	400	140	550	(10)*	(160)
Transport	95	350	85	340	95	400	10	(50)
Gross profit	460	2050	440	1960	320	1490	90	560
Indirect costs								
Selling and marketing	27	208	28	112	30	150	96	58
Admin. salaries	115	460	110	440	90	220	20	240
Rent and rates	58	232	58	232	50	210	—	22
Net profit	260	1150	244	1176	150	910	(26)	240

*negative values are shown (. . .). **YTD=year to date.

The company's performance can now be assessed on a monthly basis and compared to the budgets set for the different divisions at the beginning of the year. Comparisons can also be made to the previous year's performance. Large variances will lead to investigation and corrective action taken sooner rather than later. In Table 14.1, the YTD variance for sales is substantial but positive and therefore beneficial; this seems to have resulted in a considerable increase in labour costs in the past year but this was expected as the budget indicates. There has also been a large increase in administrative salaries (possibly something to be watched for the future) but, again, this was anticipated in the budget. These accounts would not give the management serious cause for concern.

The illustration for the Campbell Engineering Company shows the current trading position. Management accounts may also include a balance sheet and a cash flow projection. The latter may be particularly important for companies which have loans to repay or an overdraft facility. The management of working capital will be discussed in more detail later; at this stage it is necessary to understand that it would be almost impossible to manage working capital without management accounts.

14.5 THE PRIMARY STATEMENTS

It should be clear at this stage that businesses prepare accounts for a number of reasons and that there are considerable differences in the ways in which financial information can be presented. However, any set of accounts should always contain a *profit and loss account* and a *balance sheet*. These two primary statements will be examined in detail below.

14.5.1 Profit and loss account

The profit and loss account shows the financial results for the company for a particular period of time, for example, one year. It records the total sales made for the period and the costs incurred over the same period. Sales less costs results in either a profit or a loss. This profit or loss is the company's financial result. An example of a profit and loss account is shown in Table 14.2.

Table 14.2 Roudsari Engineering Limited.
Profit and Loss Account for the year ended 30 June 1995

	£'000	£'000
Sales		900
Cost of sales		(450)
Gross profit		450
Overhead expenses	160	
Finance charges	40	
Depreciation	100	
		(300)
Net operating profit		150
Taxation	40	
Dividends	50	
		(90)
Retained profit for the year		60
Retained profit brought forward		35
Retained profit carried forward(*)		95

(*) carried forward to the balance sheet, see Table 14.4.

Working through the profit and loss account:

(1) Sales for the year ended 30 June 1995 will comprise income arising to the company from all goods and/or services sold for the period from 1 July 1994 to 30 June 1995.

(2) Costs of sales, as the description implies, includes all costs directly attributable to the sales made in the period. Examples of these costs would include production materials, labour, power, storage and delivery costs.

(3) Sales less these costs results in the gross profit. To obtain a true measure of the gross profit for the period it is most important to include all direct costs incurred in making the sales. This is the matching principle discussed in section 14.3.1 The cost of sales figure is therefore calculated as shown in Table 14.3.

Table 14.3   Roudsari Engineering Limited.
Trading Account for the year ended 30 June 1995.

	£'000	£'000
Sales		900
less: *Cost of sales*		
Opening stocks	42	
Purchase of raw materials	260	
	302	
less closing stocks	(54)	
	248	
Direct labour costs	180	
Storage costs	12	
Delivery costs	10	
		450
Gross profit		450

Opening stocks plus purchases made in the year less closing stocks equals the cost of raw materials for the sales made in that year. Opening stocks, which were purchased *last* year form part of *this* year's costs but closing stocks purchased this year do not. This makes sense because the opening stocks at the beginning of the year were sold this year and are included in sales, whilst this year's closing stocks will be part of next year's sales.

(4) From gross profit other expenses are deducted in arriving at the net profit retained for the year. These include overheads, finance charges, taxation and dividends. Taxation is payable on the net operating profit earned, to the Inland Revenue in the UK or its equivalent elsewhere. Finance charges would normally mean interest payments to banks and other financial institutions. Dividends are payments made to the shareholders of the company. They represent a return on the capital which they have invested in the business.

(5) The final profit retained for the year is added to the profits retained in previous years and carried forward to the balance sheet (see section 14.5.3). The majority of companies do not distribute all of their profits to the shareholders. Normally they will retain some of the profit within the business. Retained profits will enable the business to grow, by reinvesting in capital equipment, in new product lines, or in employing extra people.

Without such reinvestment a business would be unlikely to grow significantly or keep up with technological change.

14.5.2   Capital and revenue expenditure

Before examining the balance sheet (section 14.5.3), the differences between capital and revenue expenditure will be explained.

Capital expenditure is accounted for in the balance sheet, and includes purchases of plant and machinery, computers and premises. Capital expenditure is defined as providing a benefit to the business over more than one accounting period. It is, of course, reasonable to apportion these costs over the periods of their use and hence match these costs with the sales generated in each period. This is what is done, and the process is called *depreciation*. Depreciation is examined later in the chapter.

The benefits of revenue expenditure, on the other hand, are normally realized in one accounting period; the payment of rent on the company's premises will be an annual charge for an annual benefit and the sum will be accounted for in the year in which it is levied. Revenue expenditure is accounted for in the profit and loss account as a charge against sales.

14.5.3   The balance sheet

The balance sheet is a statement of the company's assets and its liabilities at a particular point in time. It provides a snapshot of the financial position and is usually drawn up at the end of the year covered by the profit and loss account. The term '**assets**' is used to describe what the business owns and '**liabilities**' means what the business owes to others.

The fundamental equation of any balance sheet is

$$\text{TOTAL ASSETS} = \text{TOTAL LIABILITIES}$$

The assets are balanced by the liabilities, hence the term balance sheet. A typical balance sheet is illustrated in Table 14.4

The equation can be expanded to

$$\text{TOTAL ASSETS} = \text{LIABILITIES TO PROPRIETORS} + \text{EXTERNAL LIABILITIES}$$

The capital invested in the business by its proprietors, whether they be soletraders, partners or shareholders represents long term loans to these businesses, and are, therefore, a liability.

The balance sheet shows how the various categories of assets and liabilities are set out. If this balance sheet were to be represented by an equation it would be as follows:

$$\text{TOTAL ASSETS } less \text{ EXTERNAL LIABILITIES}$$

$$= \text{LIABILITIES TO PROPRIETORS}$$

Table 14.4 Roudsari Engineering Limited.
Balance Sheet at 30 June 1995

	£'000	£'000
Fixed assets		
Tangible fixed assets		700
Intangible fixed assets		20
		720
Current assets		
Stocks	54	
Trade debtors	306	
Other debtors	40	
Prepayments	20	
Cash at bank and in hand	170	
	590	
Current liabilities		
Trade creditors	(175)	
Other creditors (dividends + taxation)	(90)	
Accruals	(25)	
	(290)	
Net current assets		300
		1020
Long term liabilities		
Bank loan		(175)
Net assets		845
Represented by:		
Share capital		750
Profit and loss account		95
		845

This is typical of how balance sheets are drawn up. Note that the top half and the bottom half balance. Effectively this balance sheet shows how the proprietors' investment in the business is represented by assets and external liabilities.

Assets

Let us look first at the assets forming part of the equation above,

$$\text{TOTAL ASSETS} = \text{FIXED ASSETS} + \text{CURRENT ASSETS}$$

Fixed assets

Fixed assets are those assets which are held in the business for the long term and which are used to generate income over a number of accounting periods. These assets would not normally be resold in the course of trade. As noted in section 14.5.2 they represent the capital expenditure of the business. Most fixed assets are tangible assets. Examples of tangibles would be land, buildings, plant, machinery, computers and office furniture. Intangible assets include goodwill, patents, trademarks, etc.

Fixed assets are recorded in the balance sheet at historic cost less depreciation. Historic cost generally equates with the purchase price of the asset, however long ago.

Depreciation

It was stated earlier that fixed assets are recorded at historic cost less depreciation in the balance sheet. This is referred to as *net book value*. In section 14.5.2 it was noted that an annual charge is made to the profit and loss account in respect of depreciation.

All fixed assets have a finite useful economic life and there will come a time when these assets have to be replaced. Examples of this would include photocopiers, concrete mixers and lathes, as well as the very buildings that house them. Depreciation is a measure of the gradual 'wearing out' of these assets. By making an annual charge to the profit and loss account the level of profits available for distribution to shareholders is reduced and the money retained within the business can be used for replacements.

In calculating the annual charge three factors are taken into account:

- the cost of the asset
- the useful economic life
- the estimated residual value.

The only one of these factors that can be stated with any degree of certainty is the cost of the asset. The other two factors involve judgement. This exercise of judgement can lead to very different results and hence it is important to note what depreciation policies a company is adopting so that the impact on declared profits can be appreciated. The effects of exercising judgement are best illustrated by an example.

Example 14(1)

Suppose that two companies purchase identical machines, and the purchase price of each is £81 000.

Company A estimates that the machine will last for eight years and that the residual value will be £1000.

Company B estimates that the machine will only last for five years and its residual value will be £6000.

The annual depreciation charge for company A is as follows:

	£
cost	81 000
less residual value	(1 000)
	80 000

Spread over the machine's economic life, this gives £10 000 p.a. for eight years.

The annual depreciation charge for company B is as follows:

	£
cost	81 000
less residual value	(6 000)
	75 000

Spread over the machine's economic life, this gives £15 000 p.a. for five years.

Company B has an additional £5000 charged against its profits each year and is likely to be reporting lower profits than company A. This method is called the *straight line method* because there is an equal annual charge to the profit and loss account.

An equally common method is the *reducing balance method*. With this method the depreciation charged in the early years of an asset's life is higher than in the latter years. The depreciation charged reduces in each successive year. This method attempts to recognize that the value of most machinery and equipment falls rapidly in the first years of use, and then declines at a much slower rate, and that, as time passes the costs of repairs and maintenance of the asset increase. Depreciation on a straight line basis plus increasing costs of repairs would lead to an escalating charge in the profit and loss account over the life of the asset. Where this might occur the use of the reducing balance method is considered more appropriate. The method is often used for the depreciation of motor vehicles. Similarly, special tooling which has a useful life tied to a particular product is normally written off over a short period using the reducing balance method. This is consistent with the prudence concept described in section 14.3.1.

There are two alternative methods for determining the depreciation charge on the reducing balance basis. These are shown in Examples 14(2) and 14(3).

Example 14(2)

A company purchases a motor vehicle for £13 000. The directors estimate that the vehicle will be used in the business for four years, at the end of which time it will be sold for £2500.

$$\text{annual rate of depreciation} = 1 - \left(\frac{2500}{13\,000} \right)^{1/4} = 33.8\%$$

Charge in year 1 = 0.338 × 13 000	=	4391
Charge in year 2 = 0.338 × (13 000 − 4391)	=	2908
Charge in year 3 = 0.338 × (13 000 − 4391 − 2908)	=	1926
Charge in year 4 = 0.338 × (13 000 − 4391 − 2908 − 1926) =		1275
Total depreciation charge over four years		£10 500

Example 14(3)

For the same conditions as in Example 14(2) the sum-of-the-digits method (widely used in the USA) gives the following charges.

$$\text{Charge for year 1} = (13\,000 - 2500) \times \frac{4}{(4+3+2+1)} = 4200$$

$$\text{Charge for year 2} = (13\,000 - 2500) \times \frac{3}{(4+3+2+1)} = 3150$$

$$\text{Charge for year 3} = (13\,000 - 2500) \times \frac{2}{(4+3+2+1)} = 2100$$

$$\text{Charge for year 4} = (13\,000 - 2500) \times \frac{1}{(4+3+2+1)} = 1050$$

Total depreciation charge over four years
$$= 4200 + 3150 + 2100 + 1050 = 10\,500$$

Figure 14.1 shows the net book value of the vehicle against time for the two methods above and for the straight line depreciation method.

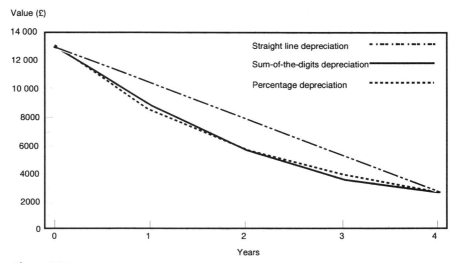

Figure 14.1

A third method of depreciation is the *usage method.* In this method the annual depreciation charge is calculated taking into account the estimated number of units that the asset (machine) will produce in its working life, or the number of hours or miles for which the asset will be productive. This method is commonly used in the depreciation of commercial aircraft.

Example 14(4)

A company purchases an aeroplane for £6.6m. The manufacturer has advised the directors that the plane will fly for up to 40 000 hours during its useful economic life.

The directors estimate that the flying hours over the next three years will be as follows:

	hours
Year 1	5800
Year 2	4700
Year 3	5200

Residual value is estimated at £1.2m

$$\text{Charge for year } 1 = (6.6 - 1.2) \times \frac{5800}{40\,000} = £0.783\text{m}$$

$$\text{Charge for year } 2 = (6.6 - 1.2) \times \frac{4700}{40\,000} = £0.635\text{m}$$

$$\text{Charge for year } 3 = (6.6 - 1.2) \times \frac{5200}{40\,000} = £0.702\text{m}$$

By this means, the depreciation charges will reflect the sales being generated by the machine, or aircraft as in this case. This should provide a better measure of the profitability of operating the asset.

The depreciation policy adopted by a company should be the one which is most appropriate for the type of asset and its use, so that depreciation charges are allocated fairly across accounting periods. The original estimates of the useful economic life of each asset should be periodically reviewed to make sure that, as time passes, they are still appropriate. This is especially important for companies that use equipment at the forefront of technological development, which can so quickly become obsolete and its economic life sharply curtailed.

Net book value

Returning to the net book value of an asset, this is calculated as the asset's cost less the accumulated annual depreciation charge. Consider the aircraft in Example 14(4). These net book values would be recorded in the balance sheet at the end of year 1, 2 and 3 respectively as shown in Table 14.5.

Current assets

Current assets are assets that are retained within the business for a relatively short period of time, usually for less than one year. They are readily convertible into

Table 14.5

| | Cost
£'000 | Cumulative
depreciation
£'000 | Net book
value
£'000 |
|--------|------------|-------------------------------|---------------------------|
| Year 1 | 6600 | 783 | 5817 |
| Year 2 | 6600 | 1418 | 5182 |
| Year 3 | 6600 | 2120 | 4480 |

cash at short notice. Current assets on the balance sheet would usually include the following:

(1) Cash in hand and in bank accounts.
(2) Debtors; that is trade debtors and other debtors.
      Practically all businesses, with the exception of retailers, make their sales on credit. There is therefore a time lag between making a sale to the customer and receiving the cash. During this period the customer becomes a trade debtor. The asset in the books of the company is in recognition of the right to acquire cash from the customer at a later date.
      Other debtors arise from non-trading transactions, for example the sale of a fixed asset at the end of its useful economic life.
(3) Stocks
      Stocks comprise raw materials, work-in-progress and finished goods held for resale. Stocks will be converted into sales and then into cash in the short-term. Repair, maintenance and operating supplies, which may not be converted immediately into sales, are also stocks and are recorded as current assets. Alternative methods of valuing stocks are considered in Chapter 13, section 13.2.1.
(4) Prepayments
      Prepayments are expenses which have been paid by the business in advance and do not relate to the current accounting period. Rent is generally paid in advance and recorded as a prepayment.

Liabilities

Liabilities represent the amounts that a business owes to other parties, both external parties and the proprietors. As with assets, liabilities are subdivided according to a time frame. The parties to whom these amounts are due are known as the creditors of the company.

TOTAL LIABILITIES = LONG TERM LIABILITIES +

CURRENT LIABILITIES

Long term liabilities

These liabilities are due for payment one year or more from the date of the balance sheet. Examples would be bank loans or hire purchase contracts. Long term loans generally require security in the form of a mortgage over the company's assets.

Liabilities to proprietors are also long term liabilities but they are not secured on the assets of the company. These liabilities are normally recorded in the lower section of the balance sheet. Their composition depends upon the type of business.

For partnerships and soletraders the proprietors' liability is represented by a capital account (one for each partner in the case of a partnership). This would include the capital introduced into the business at its establishment plus all retained profits to date.

In the case of a company the liability is represented by share capital plus retained profits. Share capital is also capital introduced by the owners to establish the business.

Any capital subsequently introduced would be added to the capital account for soletraders or partnerships or would increase the share capital of a company.

Current liabilities

These liabilities are due for payment within one year of the date of the balance sheet. Current liabilities include the following:

(1) Trade creditors
    These are amounts owed to other parties for goods or services supplied to the company. For example, a manufacturing company will purchase its raw materials from a number of suppliers on credit terms.
(2) Other creditors
    These include amounts due for taxation and dividends payable to shareholders, all payable within the year.
(3) Bank overdraft
    Overdrafts provide a form of short-term finance for companies. They are arranged in advance with a company's bank to allow for short-term cash shortages. Figure 17.8 in Chapter 17 could be used by a contractor and his bank to plan the overdraft provision for the duration of a project. Technically, bank overdrafts are repayable on demand and must, therefore, be classified as a current liability.
(4) Accruals
    Accruals represent a provision in the accounts for expenses relating to the current accounting period for which an invoice has not yet been received at the time of drawing up the accounts. An example of this is an electricity bill. If the meter is read on the last day of the accounting period there will be a time lag before an invoice is raised by the electricity company and despatched to the user. Where the bill is expected to be substantial it would be sensible to make provision and this is how it is done.

All the major components of a profit and loss account and a balance sheet have now been covered. There will sometimes be other items which have not been discussed in this chapter. The guiding principle is to determine whether an item represents income/costs, or an asset/liability. If it is one of the former it should appear in the profit and loss account, if either of the latter it should appear in the balance sheet.

14.6   BOOK-KEEPING

The profit and loss account and the balance sheet present only a brief summary of the trading performance of a company and an outline of its assets and liabilities. The two statements are in fact a summary of every individual transaction the company has entered into. The process whereby these individual transactions are recorded and then summarized into profit and loss account and balance sheet is called *book-keeping*. Without this systematic recording of every transaction it would be impossible for a company to function and to produce satisfactory results.

Book-keeping involves a process known as double entry whereby every transaction is represented by a debit and a corresponding credit. Detailed instruction in double entry book-keeping can be found in Whithead [1].

Businesses spend large sums of money employing accountants and teams of accounting staff to maintain the accounting records. Indeed, all businesses are subject to some degree of statutory regulation which dictates that accounting records be maintained. The taxation authorities, for example, are concerned that businesses are able to produce accounts which will form the basis for assessing how much they should be taxed.

It is also the case that the owners of a company will want to ensure that a proper account of their enterprise and investment is made available to them at regular intervals. As a result, complex financial reporting systems have to be put in place to safeguard the shareholders' investment. Good financial systems will help to ensure that:

- all stocks sold to customers are recorded as a sale,
- all cash received by the company is banked,
- all fixed assets purchased are secure and can be located,
- staff do not receive pay for more hours than they have worked,
- the possibilities for fraud and other financial loss are minimized.

and so on.

14.7   THE DIFFERENCES BETWEEN CASH AND PROFIT

Before moving on from the detail of the primary statements of accounts, consideration needs to be given to the difference between the cash and profits generated by a business.

Over the entire life of a business total profits will equate to the total increase in cash balances. However, in individual accounting periods cash generated will not equate with profits earned. Consider the sale of a unit of production. As soon as the item is sold to a customer the profit earned on that sale can be recognized in the profit and loss account, but it is unlikely that the cash will be received on that date. As already observed, customers may take some time to settle up, so the corresponding movement in the cash balance will not occur in the same period. In addition, the company may not yet have paid the supplier for the materials used to produce the unit sold.

Example 14(5)

A company sells ten units for £250 per unit during September 1995. The cost of producing each unit during August is £180, comprising £80 of labour costs and £100 of raw materials.

The company's cash balance on 1 August 1995 is £9800. The wages are paid on 30 August 1995 and the supplier is paid on 30 September 1995. The customer pays for the goods in October 1995. The company's cash balance moves as shown in Table 14.6.

Table 14.6

Month	Transaction receipt/payment	£	Cash balance at end of month £	Cumulative movement in cash balance £
August	opening balance	—	9800	—
August	wages paid	(800)	9000	(800)
September	supplier paid	(1000)	8000	(1800)
October	customer pays	2500	10 500	700

The profit on the sale of £700 is recorded in the profit and loss account for September 1995 which has a beneficial effect on the company's result in that month. On the other hand, the cash balance has reduced by £1800 by September 1995, so far as this transaction is concerned. It is not until October 1995 that the profit and cash movements equalize.

Profit is the most common measure of the success of a business, particularly by external parties. However, the generation of cash surpluses, even in the short-term, must not be overlooked. Some very profitable businesses fail because they are so concerned with increasing sales and profits that they run out of cash! This situation can arise as a result of overtrading and frequently results from the poor management of the working capital cycle.

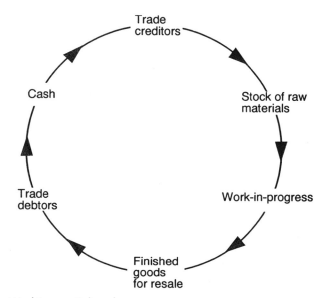

Figure 14.2   Working capital cycle

14.8   THE WORKING CAPITAL CYCLE

The capital introduced into a business can be used to provide fixed assets or working capital. Working capital is essentially the current assets and current liabilities of the business. It comprises cash, stocks, debtors and creditors. These assets and liabilities are short-term and are being continually converted from one into the other. The process is called the working capital cycle and can be represented as in Figure 14.2.

Starting at the top of the cycle and moving clockwise the following occurs. A liability is incurred with the trade creditors of the business in purchasing raw materials. The raw materials are then processed to produce the finished goods which the company will place in stock until an order is received from a customer. When a sale is made on credit to a customer a trade debtor is created. When the customer pays, the trade debtor is replaced with cash which can be used to pay off the trade creditor. The cycle then repeats itself.

A business must have enough cash to pay suppliers, wages and overheads when they are due (Figure 1.6 in Chapter 1 shows the cash flows that must be funded before payments are received from customers.). At the same time there must be sufficient stocks on hand to be able to meet the demand from customers as and when orders arise. (In the case of service companies, such as consulting engineers, the only 'stocks' might be stationery and computer consumables. These stocks have to be funded, and suppliers paid, in the same way as in any manufacturing company.) If the supply of working capital were unlimited these requirements could be met without difficulty. However, a business never has an unlimited supply of working capital. The key to meeting both the need for cash and the need for sufficient stocks is to strike a balance between making profits and retaining enough free cash.

Accountants will give the following advice on the process of managing working capital:

(1) Do not allow stock levels to become too high (see Chapter 20):
   • valuable cash resources are tied up in stock,
   • the stock may become obsolete or perish,
   • warehousing costs can be high,
   • the interest-earning potential of cash is lost.
(2) Do not allow surplus cash to sit in a low-interest bank account:
   • expand the business with it,
   • invest in new plant and machinery,
   • invest in a higher interest earning account or in stocks and shares.
(3) Try to take the same number of days to pay your suppliers as your customers take to pay you:
   • do not act as a source of short-term finance for your customers,
   • encourage early settlement by offering discounts for prompt payment,
   • manage your debtors — invoice promptly and accurately; follow up on overdue payments; use Pareto analysis[1] to find out the major reasons for late payments.

14.9   INTERPRETING ACCOUNTS

The numbers shown in the profit and loss account and balance sheet, to be of some use to managers and/or owners, need to be analysed and interpreted. In section 14.4.2 the use of management accounts in running a business was discussed. The actual results for the period were compared with a budget set at the beginning of the year and with the results of the previous year. This process of reviewing and analysing results is one of the best ways of highlighting the strengths and weaknesses of a business.

Analyses are also carried out on financial accounts, and industry/sector comparisons made; these are of particular importance to the shareholders.

14.10   FINANCIAL RATIOS

Financial ratios are commonly used as a means of analysing and interpreting the financial information provided in accounts. They can be applied to management accounts and to financial accounts, and are used to highlight the strengths and weaknesses in a company's financial position.

Calculation of these ratios is fairly straightforward as shown below. However, they need to be used with care, and there must be a proper basis for comparison. Comparisons of ratios are usually either made within a company to examine

---

[1]In a Pareto analysis the outstanding debts would be listed in order with the highest debts at the top. The top 20% of debtors will probably account for about 80% of the debt; these are the ones to pursue.

performance over different accounting periods or made between companies in the same business sector.

Ratios are calculated on historic data, and so do not necessarily indicate what will happen in the future. Nonetheless, financial ratios can indicate potential cash flow problems or unprofitable business operations that would affect the future of the company.

The most frequently used financial ratios will now be examined.

14.10.1 Operating ratios

Gross profit margin

This measures the percentage of profit earned on every monetary unit of sales made. It is calculated as follows:

$$\text{Gross profit margin} = \frac{\text{gross profit}}{\text{sales}} \times 100\%$$

The margin expected depends upon the industry in which a company operates. In the retail industry the margin is likely to lie between 5 and 10%. The lowest values are particularly true of the supermarket chains where they rely on a very high volume of sales to generate profits. The construction industry with its relatively high volume use of materials shows similar values of gross profit margin. Manufacturing industry on the other hand, which demands a greater investment in capital equipment and in research and development, is characterized by gross profit margins in the range of 10 to 15%.

In any business, however, it is imperative that a gross profit be made in order to meet overheads, finance charges and dividends.

Return on capital employed (ROCE)

ROCE is a very important ratio and is the most commonly used measure of profitability. It is calculated as follows:

$$\text{ROCE} = \frac{\text{profit before interest and tax}}{\text{capital employed}} \times 100\%$$

and

capital employed = share capital + profit and loss reserves + long term liabilities[2]

---

[2]Engineers, who are often concerned with the management of physical things, should remember that 'capital employed' is also equal to fixed assets plus net current assets, as shown in the balance sheet in Table 14.4 section 14.5.3. The way in which ROCE is affected by various aspects of engineering management is shown in Chapter 21, Figure 21.3.

The ratio provides the shareholders of the business with a measure of the return on their capital investment. The shareholders will compare this rate of return with, for example, the rate of interest they could obtain from a building society. In addition, if the investment is perceived as high risk, the shareholders will require a much higher return, and, if the return is not high enough they might sell their shares to invest elsewhere.

Heavy selling of shares will result in a lower share price which will improve the return on new shareholdings, but continuing shareholders will experience a fall in the capital value of their investment.

Asset turnover

This ratio measures the ability of a company to generate sales from its capital base. It is calculated as follows:

$$\text{Asset turnover} = \frac{\text{sales}}{\text{capital employed}}$$

If the ratio is low, intensive capital investment is indicated. If the ratio is high, the investment risk will be low.

The ratio has little value when viewed in isolation. It is the trend over successive accounting periods that is important. A rising trend would indicate that the capital invested is beginning to bring about increased sales. The ratio would also provide a useful comparator within a given industrial sector, a more successful company would expect to show a higher ratio than its competitors. As one would expect there are considerable differences between sectors, for example:

- British Steel plc   = 9.2 (manufacturing)
- Saatchi & Saatchi plc   = 4.7 (advertising)
- J Sainsbury plc   = 1.9 (food retailing)

Figures are for 1994.

Working capital turnover

This measures how quickly working capital is converted into sales. It is calculated as follows:

$$\text{Working capital turnover} = \frac{\text{sales}}{\text{current assets less current liabilities}}$$

The ratio is likely to vary considerably between different industrial sectors as illustrated below:

- British Steel plc   = 3.4
- Pilkington plc   = 6.7 (glass manufacturer)
- Marks and Spencer plc = 14.0 (clothing retailer)

Figures are for 1994.

In the retail industry, the ratio should be relatively high as indicated in the example above. This is a business where sales and hence cash should be generated from stocks much more quickly than in, say, the construction industry. Construction contracts can have a very long working capital cycle, often more than a year, and therefore a low ratio would be expected.

14.10.2   Liquidity ratios

Liquidity ratios measure the ability of a company to pay its debts as and when they fall due. The two most important liquidity ratios are the current ratio and the quick ratio. The latter is sometimes referred to as the 'acid test'.

Current ratio

This indicates how many times the current liabilities of a company are covered by its current assets. It is calculated as follows:

$$\text{Current ratio} = \frac{\text{current assets}}{\text{current liabilities}}$$

In a majority of businesses, current assets will exceed current liabilities, indicating that short-term liabilities are covered by assets that could be readily converted into cash. An acceptable current ratio would be about 2:1 but this is only a guide as some very successful businesses operate on a current ratio of less than this. For a supermarket chain, its stocks and debtors are likely to be low in comparison with its current liabilities (trade creditors), but, because large sums of cash are being collected daily, it is unlikely that it would be unable to meet its liabilities when they fall due. Two examples are:

- J Sainsbury plc   = 0.46: 1
- British Steel plc   = 2.2: 1

Figures are for 1994.

Quick ratio (acid test)

The quick ratio is a more immediate measure of a company's ability to settle its debts. It excludes the value of stock from the calculation, as it may not be as readily converted into cash as trade debtors, for example. It is calculated as follows:

$$\text{Quick ratio} = \frac{\text{current assets less stock}}{\text{current liabilities}}$$

An acceptable quick ratio would be about 1:1. If it is less than that, the company's position warrants careful review as it may have short-term cash flow problems. Some examples are:

- British Steel plc   = 1.5: 1
- Pilkington plc   = 1.0: 1
- Marks and Spencer plc = 1.1: 1

Figures are for 1994.

14.10.3   Working capital ratios

In section 14.8 the working capital cycle was examined and the effective management of working capital was highlighted as an important factor in the success of any business. The following ratios are commonly used as tools in this management process.

Stock turnover ratio

The stock turnover ratio indicates how many times stock is turned over in a year; that is how many times stock is effectively replaced. It can also be adapted to indicate how many days of sales are held in stock. It is calculated as follows:

$$\text{Stock turnover} = \frac{\text{cost of sales}}{\text{average stock level for the period}}$$

and

$$\text{No. of days stock held} = \frac{\text{average stock level for the period}}{\text{cost of sales}} \times 365^3$$

The stock turnover ratio measures how quickly goods are moving through the business. A high ratio implies an efficient operation. A low ratio indicates inefficiencies and the possibility of obsolete goods being held in stocks. The nature of the industry will be a major determinant of this ratio and the industrial sector averages should be used to assess whether a company's ratio is high or low. Some examples of stock turnover ratio are:

---

[3]The latter is a financial measure, and may be calculated from annual accounts, therefore, the full calendar year of 365 days is used. Engineers, managing stocks of materials and components, and using units of measurement such as tonnes, litres or pieces, may prefer to use *working days* to calculate usage per day, and hence the number of days stock.

- British Steel plc   = 5.3
- Pilkington plc   = 6.9
- Marks and Spencer plc = 13.45
- J Sainsbury plc   = 23.0

Figures are for 1994.

The number of days of stock held should be sufficient to cover variations in usage (demand) and in deliveries (supply) plus the number of days required to convert raw materials into finished goods. World-class manufacturing activities hold only a few days stock. A typical UK manufacturer holds between 40 and 60 days of stock. (The significance of inventory management is discussed in Chapter 5. Inventory control methods are covered in Chapter 20.)

Debtors turnover ratio

This ratio measures the number of days it takes to convert trade debtors into cash. It is calculated as follows:

$$\text{Debtors turnover} = \frac{\text{sales}}{\text{trade debtors}} \times 365 \text{ days}$$

In the UK, customers, other than in retailing, generally take anything between 60 and 90 days to settle their invoices. The ratio should, therefore, fall within this range. If it is higher than 90 days the indications are that either the company is not exerting enough pressure on its customers to pay their invoices or that the company is exposed to bad debts. Most companies agree credit terms with their customers. If, for example, invoices are due for settlement within 30 days of receipt of goods, the debtors turnover should be in the order of 30 days, not 90 days. By allowing customers to take longer to pay than the agreed credit period, the company is, in effect, providing its customers with cheap finance (see section 14.8).

Another important point is that this ratio is calculated using trade debtors figures at a single point in time (as shown on the balance sheet). If it were calculated shortly before a large overdue debt was about to be paid there would be a distorted measure of the usual position. It is therefore important to establish a trend in the ratio calculated over a period of time. An upward trend would indicate a deteriorating position which would require action to bring the ratio back down to an acceptable level. Regular (e.g. monthly) review of this ratio is good management practice, especially if accompanied by an analysis of debtors over 30 days, 60 days, 90 days, etc.

Creditors turnover ratio

This ratio indicates the number of days a company is waiting before it pays its trade creditors. It is calculated as follows:

$$\text{Creditors turnover} = \frac{\text{cost of sales}}{\text{trade creditors}} \times 365 \text{ days}$$

It is likely that a company will want to take as long as possible to pay off its creditors so that valuable cash resources are kept within its working capital cycle. However, extending the credit period may mean having to forego valuable discounts for early settlement or incurring premiums for late payments and/or losing the goodwill of suppliers.

The optimum value of the ratio for a company will depend upon the credit terms offered by its major suppliers and should, ideally, be in line with its debtors turnover ratio. An ideal position is reached when cash is collected from trade debtors just ahead of payments to suppliers. Where the trend in the ratio is being reviewed, an increasing ratio indicates potential short-term cash flow problems which might lead to the company being unable to find enough cash to pay its creditors as the payments fall due.

14.10.4   Gearing ratios

Gearing ratios analyse the components of the capital invested in the business by comparing capital that is borrowed with capital provided by the shareholders.

Debt/equity ratio

This ratio is calculated as follows:

$$\text{Debt/equity ratio} = \frac{\text{interest bearing loans} + \text{preference share capital}}{\text{ordinary share capital}}$$

Preference shares carry preferential rights to dividends which must be paid before a company can pay dividends to its ordinary shareholders. If a company has issued 10% preference shares it must pay a dividend on these shares equal to 10% of their capital value, if there are sufficient profits. If that leaves no profits for distribution to ordinary shareholders then so be it. Because preference shares have rights to a fixed rate of return they are treated like loans in calculating the debt/equity ratio.

If the ratio is greater than 1:1 the company has a high proportion of borrowing in its capital base and is described as highly geared. For example, the ratio for Eurotunnel is exceptionally high in the order of about 8:1; for most companies the ratio would be no higher than about 1.5:1. A highly geared company is a more risky company for its shareholders. This is because it must meet all interest payments and preference dividends out of profits before dividends can be paid to ordinary shareholders.

Debt/assets employed ratio

This ratio indicates the proportion of a company's assets that are financed by borrowings. It also highlights the capacity that a company has for obtaining further secured borrowings. It is calculated as follows:

$$\text{Debt/assets employed} = \frac{\text{interest bearing loans} + \text{preference share capital}}{\text{assets employed}}$$

Again a ratio of greater than 1:1 would indicate a high level of gearing. If the ratio is less than this there is potential for more borrowing for further capital investment.

Interest cover

This ratio is used to assess whether profits are sufficient to cover the interest due on borrowings (and preference dividends if applicable). Lenders will pay particular attention to this ratio. It will be almost impossible to obtain finance if profits are insufficient to cover interest payments. The ratio is calculated as follows:

$$\text{Interest cover} = \frac{\text{profit before interest and tax}}{\text{interest payable}}$$

Lenders will require a level of cover which reflects the risk attached to the borrowings; a ratio of 2:1 should be adequate.

14.10.5   Investor ratios

The final set of ratios to be considered are the investor ratios. These ratios are very important for companies quoted on a stock exchange. They will be given careful consideration by investors choosing between companies so they need to be acceptable to attract additional funding.

Earnings per share (EPS)

The EPS measures the amount of profit earned for a year by each share in issue. It is a good indicator of the changes in profitability of a company over a number of accounting periods. For example, the profits of a company could double from one year to the next; this might at first glance appear to be an exceptional result. However, if the company had in issue three times as many shares as it had in the prior period the result would not be perceived to be exceptionally good, and the EPS would demonstrate this. The ratio is calculated as follows:

$$\text{EPS} = \frac{\text{profit after tax and payment of preference dividends}}{\text{number of ordinary shares in issue during the year}}$$

Investors will want to see an upward trend in the earnings per share, as this indicates a growth in profitability.

Price/earnings ratio (P/E ratio)

This ratio expresses the current market price of a share as a multiple of its earnings. It is calculated as follows:

$$\text{P/E ratio} = \frac{\text{current market price per share}}{\text{earnings per share}}$$

P/E ratios are a common means of valuing companies. Indices of P/E ratios for different industrial sectors, compiled by analysts, provide a good indicator of a company's performance. P/E ratios can also be used to appraise a company's investment potential by making comparisons within the same sector.

Example 14(6)

A company has in issue 1.5 million ordinary shares with a nominal value of £1 each. The current market value of the shares is £6.80 each. The latest set of accounts show a profit after interest and preference dividends of £850 000. Calculate the EPS and the P/E ratio for the company.

Step 1: Calculate the EPS

$$\text{EPS} = \frac{850\,000}{1\,500\,000} = 0.57$$

Step 2: Calculate the P/E ratio

$$\text{P/E ratio} = \frac{6.80}{0.57} = 12.57$$

This would then be compared with companies in the same industrial sector to assess how well the company is performing.

14.11   LIMITATIONS ON MEASURES OF FINANCIAL PERFORMANCE

There are limitations to using accounts for assessing the performance of a business.

All accounts are based on historic cost data and can fail to reflect current inflationary pressures. Certain valuable business assets are not taken into account at all. The value of a highly skilled workforce, and/or a prime business location cannot be easily measured using traditional financial criteria.

When depreciation was examined, a degree of choice of method was noted which could affect reported profits. A similar degree of choice exists in measuring and apportioning overheads or evaluating stocks, as described in Chapter 13 section 13.2.

In short, accounts do not provide an absolute measure of performance, but one in which there is room for interpretation. Engineers should not forget this.

14.12 SUMMARY

This chapter began by looking at the different entities used to conduct business and the basic legal framework for each. The accounts of a business were then examined in detail to establish the fundamental concepts and methods of their preparation. The use of accounts as a management tool and for financial analyses was then examined. The aim has been to provide engineering managers with a basic working knowledge of the measures of financial performance. Overall, despite the reservations expressed in section 14.11, the preparation of regular clear management and financial accounts is an essential component in the successful management of any business operation.

REFERENCE

1. Whitehead, G. M. (1993). *Book-keeping Made Simple*. Fourth edition, Made Simple Books.

BIBLIOGRAPHY

1. Chadwick, L. (1993) *Management Accounting*. Routledge and Kegan Paul, London.
2. Dyson, J. R. (1992) *Accounting for Non-Accounting Students*. Second edition, Pitman, London.
3. Glautier, M. W. E. and Underdown, B. (1994) *Accounting Theory and Practice*. Fifth edition, Pitman, London.
4. Glynn, J. J., Perrin, J. and Murphy, M. P. (1994) *Accounting for Managers*. Chapman and Hall, London.

15

Project investment decisions

15.1 INTRODUCTION

Businesses, from time to time, need to make substantial investments in plant, equipment or buildings. It is often the case that the returns from the new investment will be small relative to the size of the investment, such that several years will elapse before the returns can repay the investment. Engineers may be called upon to justify investment in plant and equipment by demonstrating that the benefits exceed the costs. Long term *investment in projects* and *life-cycle costs* of capital assets are the subject matter of this chapter. The ways in which investment decisions of this nature are made and the methods of life cycle costing will be explained. First the notion of *payback* will be briefly considered. The remainder of the chapter is concerned with *discounted cash flow* techniques; the concepts of *present value, annual value, benefit–cost ratio* and *internal rate of return* will be examined and an explanation of how these relate to the underlying problem of *inflation* will be provided.

15.2 PAYBACK

The notion of payback is simple, and, therefore, popular. How long will it take to repay an initial single sum investment? If machine X costs £1000 and earns net annual benefits of £250 per year, the payback period is four years. If machine Y costs £1200 but earns net annual benefits of £400 per year, its payback period is only three years, so, despite the higher price it would appear to be a better investment.

This, of course, is too simplistic; it ignores interest rates. If, in the above example, the interest rates are 10% then, for machine X, the sum of £100 interest (10% of £1000) must be paid out of the first year's benefit of £250. This leaves £150 toward paying back the initial investment of £1000. So, at the end of the first year the sum to be paid back will be £1000 − £150 = £850.

The interest payable in the second year will be 10% of the sum owed, that is 10% of £850 = £85. This leaves £165 available for paying off the initial investment. Table 15.1 shows how this process continues until year six by the end of which the total initial investment has been repaid.

Table 15.1   Payback

Year	Sum owed at start of year (A)	Total benefit=250		Sum owed at end of year (C)−(A)
		Interest (B)=0.1 × (A)	Payback (C)=250−(B)	
1	1000	100	150	850
2	850	85	165	685
3	685	68.50	181.50	503.5
4	503.5	50.35	199.65	303.85
5	303.85	30.39	219.61	84.24
6	84.24	8.42	241.58	(157.34) credit

A similar calculation would show that for machine Y, payback is completed within four years. This suggests again that it is the better investment; but whether this is really so in the long term must depend upon other factors.

Further questions need to be asked:

- Will the earnings for machines X and Y remain at their given levels after the payback period? If they change, X could be the better project in the long term.
- What are the lives of machines X and Y? If X had to be replaced every seven years and Y every five years, X might be better value.
- If X had a higher scrap value than Y, then X might be better value.
- While interest paid out on the investment has been considered, no account has been taken of interest earned on income.
- Would the investment do better if deposited in a bank?

For many managers payback is an invaluable concept; as a matter of policy, if the payback period is short, three years (say) or less, then the investment will be worthwhile. For longer term investments a more sophisticated approach is needed. This is where discounted cash flow should be used.

15.3   DISCOUNTED CASH FLOW

Discounted cash flow (DCF) techniques allow proper consideration of all these questions. These techniques allow rational comparisons to be made between alternative investment projects. The techniques are generally used for long term projects, long term meaning anything from two years to 120 years or more.

If we are to choose between project A, which has an initial cost of £100 and will earn a net annual income of £30 per year for the next ten years, and project B which has an initial cost of £80 and will earn a net annual income of £25 for the next five years then £27 per year for the following five years, DCF will assist us. This will be demonstrated in section 15.3.2.

The underlying premise of DCF is that money will not usually be invested in a project unless that project earns more than if the money were earning steady interest in a bank. A project is said to have negative value if it earns less than if the capital simply earned interest in a bank; a positive value if it earns more. The higher the interest rate the more likely it is that a project will have a negative value.

DCF forms an important part of an investment decision analysis; it does not predict the future! Once a project is underway the outcome may well vary from predictions. It is unlikely, for example, that interest rates will remain constant over the duration of the project; which, amongst other things, makes estimating an interest rate for the DCF analysis so interesting!

15.3.1   Effect of interest rates

If £100 is invested in a bank account now, and the annual interest rate is 12%, then the sum in the bank will grow as follows:

$$\text{end of year 1} \quad £100 \times 1.12 = £112.00$$
$$\text{end of year 2} \quad £100 \times 1.12^2 = £125.44$$
$$\text{end of year 10} \quad £100 \times 1.12^{10} = £310.58$$

Having invested £100 now, the investor would be able to withdraw from the bank the sum of £310.58 after ten years. Returning to the principle of DCF in a business environment, if a company made an investment of £100 in a piece of plant or machinery now, and the annual interest rate were 12%, it would need to be able to demonstrate assets and/or accumulated earnings in year 10 to the value of at least £310.58 for the investment to be worthwhile; otherwise it might just as well have put the money in the bank.

A commercial decision to invest in plant or machinery or even buildings will, therefore, depend on whether the earnings are likely to exceed those provided by the usually more secure option of leaving the money in the bank. The commercial enterprise does not need to concern itself with the absolute value of its earnings but with the value of its earnings relative to the 'do-nothing' policy of leaving the money in the bank. This leads to the idea of equivalence. If interest rates are 12%, and the project investment analysis shows earnings of £310.58 in ten years time, then that sum can be considered equivalent to £100 earned now. £100 is said to be the *present value* of the sum of £310.58 earned at year 10 when the interest rate is 12%. If an investment is made of £100 now and a benefit of £310.58 is earned in year 10 then the *net present value* of the investment is given by:

$$\text{net present value} = \text{present value of benefits} - \text{initial cost} = £100 - £100$$
$$\therefore \text{net present value} = \text{zero}$$

From the foregoing it should be evident that £1.00 earned in year 10 is equivalent to

$$£\frac{1.00}{3.1058} = £0.322$$

earned now. This is the basis of the present value tables provided in Appendix 8. (The use of these tables will be demonstrated later.) In deciding whether to invest in a project or not, the investment analyst determines whether the net present value is greater than zero. If it is, the project should be worthwhile for it provides a better return than the bank.

The method of DCF, therefore, is to discount future cash flows by multiplying each future sum by the factor

$$\frac{1}{(1+i)^n}$$

where

i = rate of interest per unit time (usually per annum)
n = number of units of time (usually years) that must pass before the future sum is realized

This discounted value is the present value (or present worth) of the future sum. It is the sum that would need to be invested now at the given interest rate to attain the value of the future sum after n years.

Note that as interest rates rise the present value of future earnings falls and, therefore, the net present value of any project under consideration will be lower. This is why there is greater reluctance to make capital investments when interest rates are high.

For example, if interest rates are 15%, then £310.58 earned after ten years is equivalent to

$$£\frac{310.58}{1.15^{10}} = £76.77$$

rather than the £100 if interest rates were 10%.

15.3.2 Cash flow diagrams

It is helpful to represent cash flows for investment projects in the diagrammatic form as shown in Figure 15.1. Upward arrows represent net annual income, downward arrows represent costs. Cash flow diagrams for projects A and B described earlier are shown in Figure 15.1. The diagrams show the whole *life cycle* for each project.

Reconsider projects A and B previously referred to at the beginning of section 15.3. The net present value (NPV) of each project will now be calculated.

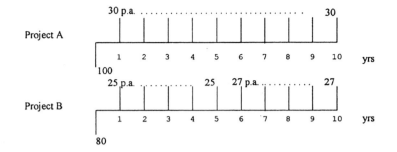

Figure 15.1   Cash flow diagrams

Project A

$$\text{PV of earnings} = \frac{30}{(1.12)} + \frac{30}{(1.12)^2} + \ldots + \frac{30}{(1.12)^{10}} = 169.51$$

Project B

$$\text{PV of earnings} = \frac{25}{(1.12)} + \ldots + \frac{25}{(1.12)^5} + \frac{27}{(1.12)^6} + \ldots + \frac{27}{(1.12)^{10}} = 145.35$$

The two results are summarized below.

Project A   present value of earnings $=£169.51$
Project B   present value of earnings $=£145.35$

If the initial cost of each project is subtracted from the present value of the earnings the NPV of each project is found.

Project A   NPV $= 169.51 - 100$ $= £69.51$
Project B   NPV $= 145.31 - 80$ $= £65.35$

A similar analysis at an interest rate of 4% gives:

Project A   NPV $= 243.33 - 100$ $= £143.33$
Project B   NPV $= 210.09 - 80$ $= £130.09$

A similar analysis at an interest rate of 20% gives:

Project A   NPV $= 125.78 - 100$ $= £25.78$
Project B   NPV $= 107.22 - 80$ $= £27.22$

As interest rates increase, Project B eventually becomes preferable to Project A and both projects decline in value eventually reaching negative values. Project A has zero NPV at an interest rate of approximately 27%; this is known as the *internal rate of return* (IRR) of the project, or the *yield*. The earnings of Project A are equivalent to earning interest at a rate of 27% on the initial investment of £100. There will be more on the concept of IRR later in section 15.4.

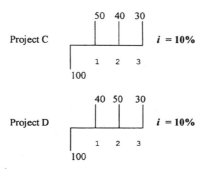

Figure 15.2   Cash flow diagrams

Example 15(1)

The cash flow diagrams in Figure 15.2 show the whole life cycle of each of projects C and D. (Note: in some of the following examples the term net present worth has replaced net present value. NPW=NPV. The purpose behind this is to familiarize the reader with both expressions.)

Project C
Present value of benefits

$$= \frac{50}{1.10} + \frac{40}{1.10^2} + \frac{30}{1.10^3} = 101.05$$

Net present value $= 101.05 - 100 = 1.05$.

Project D
Present worth of benefits

$$= \frac{40}{1.10} + \frac{50}{1.10^2} + \frac{30}{1.10^3} = 100.22$$

Net present worth (NPW)=$100.22 - 100 = 0.22$.
 The same calculations can be made more easily by using the *present value tables* in Appendix 8, as demonstrated below.

Project C

$$NPW = 50 \times 0.9091 + 40 \times 0.8264 + 30 \times 0.7513 - 100 = 1.05$$

the factor 0.9091 is found in the present value tables in the 10% column at row year 1. The factor 0.8264 is found in the present value tables in the 10% column at row year 2. The factor 0.7513 is found in the present value tables in the 10% column at row year 3.

Project D

$$NPV = 40 \times 0.9091 + 50 \times 0.8264 + 30 \times 0.7513 - 100 = 0.22$$

the factors remain the same as for Project C above, only the benefits change.

The only difference between the two projects is the chronological order in which the benefits of 50 and 40 are obtained. It can be observed that bringing forward in time high value benefits increases the net present value.

15.3.3 Annuities

Many investments will result in equal annual benefits for the life of the project. An annuity is a series of equal annual payments. The benefits for Project A above form an annuity. The present value of an annuity can be determined swiftly using the *present value of annuity tables* provided in Appendix 8.

The present value of £1 per annum for n years at $i\%$ interest is given by the formula

$$\frac{1}{(1+i)} + \frac{1}{(1+i)^2} + \ldots + \frac{1}{(1+i)^n} = \frac{1 - (1+)^{-n}}{i}$$

This is the basis of the present value of annuity tables.

Using these tables the net present value of Project A in Figure 15.1 is given by

$$NPV = 30 \times 5.6502 - 100 = 69.51$$

the factor 5.6502 is found in the present value of annuity tables in the 12% column at row 10 years.

Example 15(2)

A project earns £25 000 p.a. for 20 years, determine the present value of these earnings at

$$\text{(a) } i = 5\%$$
$$\text{(b) } i = 15\%$$

where $i =$ interest rate selected for discounting.

(a) PV $= 25\,000 \times 12.462 = £311\,550$
(b) PV $= 25\,000 \times 6.2593 = £156\,482$

Example 15(3)

A project earns £25 000 p.a. for 30 years, determine the present value of these earnings at

$$\text{(a) } i = 5\%$$
$$\text{(b) } i = 15\%$$

(a) PV $= 25\,000 \times 15.372 = £384\,300$
(b) PV $= 25000 \times 6.5660 = £164\,150$

Example 15(4)

A project earns £25 000 p.a. for 50 years, determine the present value of these earnings at $i = 15\%$.

$$\text{PV} = 25\,000 \times 6.6605 = £166\,513$$

Observe how, at the higher interest rate, adding ten or even 30 years to a project's life has very little effect on the present value. Indeed, earning £25 000 p.a. for ever at an interest rate of 15% results in a present value of £166 667 (see section 15.9.2). Analyses which use DCF techniques, particularly at high interest rates, have the unfortunate effect of rendering worthless massive benefits to future generations (see Table 15.2).

Table 15.2 PV of 1 million p.a. for n years

	$n = 40$	$n = 80$	$n = 120$
$i = 3\%$	23.11m	30.2m	32.37m
$i = 5\%$	17.16m	19.60m	19.94m
$i = 12\%$	8.24m	8.33m	8.33m

15.3.4   Equivalent annual value

Large projects operating over many years, which take several years to construct and which require expensive replacement of components (e.g. turbines for a power station) at long intervals are often evaluated in terms of their *Equivalent Annual Value* (EAV) rather than in terms of their NPV. The EAV of a project is found by converting its NPV into a series of equal payments, payable at the end of each year; in other words an annuity.

If £25 000 p.a. for 50 years has a present value of £166 513 at a 15% interest rate, then a payment now of £166 513 has an equivalent annual value of £25 000 over a 50 year period. For large projects, perhaps constructed over two or three years, and for which expensive components may need replacing, say, every 30 years, estimates of the initial capital cost and of the replacement costs can be made, converted into present values then further converted into an *equivalent annual cost* (EAC). This value will represent the minimum net annual revenue necessary to cover these capital costs. The amount by which the net annual revenue exceeds the EAC will be the EAV of the project. In choosing between alternative hydro-electric power schemes, for example, EAV is more likely to be used than NPV.

Individuals are more likely to encounter the concept of EAV when arranging a mortgage. An annual mortgage repayment is simply the EAV of the sum borrowed. Mortgage lenders set the interest rates at an appropriate level to cover costs and profit. The *annual value tables* in Appendix 8 show the equivalent annual value of a single payment now of £1.00 for a range of interest rates and project durations. The values in the annual value tables are the reciprocal of the values in the present value of annuity tables.

Example 15(5)

(1) I intend to take out a mortgage for £80 000; determine the annual repayments if the period of the loan is
   (a) 25 years
   (b) 30 years
   and the interest rate is 7%.
   (a) annual repayment = EAV = £80 000 × 0.0858 = £6864 the factor 0.0858 is found in the annual value tables in the 7% column and the 25 year row.
   (b) annual repayment = £80 000 × 0.0806 = £6448 the factor 0.0806 is found in the annual value tables in the 7% column and the 30 year row.

(2) I intend to take out a mortgage for £80 000; determine the annual repayments if the period of the loan is 25 years and the interest rate is 14%.

   annual repayment = £80 000 × 0.1455 = £11 640

   Observe how my mortgage repayments have almost doubled with the doubling of the interest rate.

(3) I can only afford annual repayments of £11 240 p.a.; how long will the mortgage period be if I borrow £80 000 at 14% interest?

$$\text{annual repayment} = £80\,000 \times \text{factor} = £11\,240$$
$$\text{factor} = 0.1405$$

A search of the annual value tables for the factor 0.1405 in the 14% column shows that the loan period will have to be extended to 43 years! This looks like an unaffordable mortgage.

During the life of a mortgage, as interest rates change, the mortgage lender determines how much of the capital has been repaid, from this the lender calculates the outstanding capital debt and finds the EAV of this sum over the remainder of the period, thus determining the revised annual payments.

Financial planners for companies will carry out similar analyses using the same methods as used by individuals.

Example 15(6)

An engineering company took out a 25 year mortgage for £800 000 one year ago, at an interest rate of 7%. A single annual payment of £68 640[1] has been made. The interest rate now changes to 8.5%; what will be the revised annual repayments?

interest payable in year $1 = 0.07 \times 800\,00 = £56\,000$
capital repaid $= 68\,640 - 56\,000 = £12\,640$
outstanding debt $= 800\,000 - 12\,640 = £787\,360$
EAV of £787 360 over 24 years at 8.5% interest $= 787\,360 \times 0.0990 = £77\,950$
the factor 0.0990 is found in the 8.5% column, row 24 years of the *annual value tables*

The new annual repayments will be £77 950. Alternatively, if the business could not afford this, and if the lender agreed, the mortgage could be extended for a further 45 years, as shown below.

EAV of £787 360 over 45 years at 8.5% interest $= 787\,360 \times 0.0872 = £68\,660$

A modest increase in interest rates combined with an inability to increase repayments can result in a very unpleasant increase in the period of the loan!

15.3.5   Machine replacement

EAVs are particularly useful when deciding upon a replacement policy for machinery or equipment. Where two alternative machines which do a similar job, produce modestly different benefits, have different lives, different capital costs and different scrap values, EAVs can be used to determine which machine is the better investment. Assume for the moment that there is no inflation. Later on, the issue of inflation will be examined.

---

[1]See equivalent annual value tables, 7% column, row 25 years for factor=0.0858, therefore payment=0.0858 × 800 000=68 640.

Example 15(7)

Machine M1

$$\text{initial cost } C_0 = 200 \qquad \text{scrap value} = 80$$
$$\text{annual benefits} = 84 \qquad \text{life} = 3 \text{ years}$$

Machine M2

$$\text{initial cost } C_0 = 270 \qquad \text{scrap value} = 70$$
$$\text{annual benefits} = 90 \qquad \text{life} = 5 \text{ years}$$

It would be wrong to find the NPV of each machine and compare the two values. The stated intention is to repeatedly replace the machines with similar models which will continue to do the job required of them.[2] The obvious approach is to consider the machines over a common period. In this case 15 years is the lowest common multiple of the two lives and could be chosen. The cash flow diagrams are shown in Figures 15.3 and 15.4.

The values of 120 for M1 and 200 for M2 in Figure 15.4 represent the replacement cost minus the scrap value for each 'project'.

The NPV of each scheme at a discount rate of 10% can now be found.

$$\text{M1} \quad \text{NPV} = 84 \times 7.6061 - 120(0.7513 + 0.5645 + 0.4241 + 0.3186)$$
$$+ 80 \times 0.2394 - 200$$
$$= 211.04$$

$$\text{M2} \quad \text{NPV} = 90 \times 7.6061 - 200(0.6209 + 0.3855) + 70 \times 0.2394 - 270$$
$$= 230.03$$

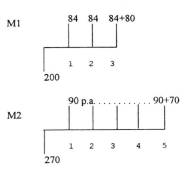

Figure 15.3   Cash flow diagrams for machines M1 and M2

[2]These financial evaluations make no allowance for changing technology. Where such changes are probable, engineers will need to exercise judgement before putting any reliance on calculations. In Chapter 14, section 14.5.3, similar problems arise with depreciation.

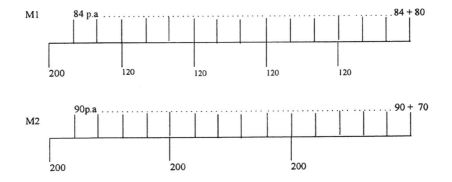

Figure 15.4   15 year cash flow diagrams for machines M1 and M2

Thus M2 is marginally better than M1 at the selected discount rate.

   This method could become a little tedious. If three machines with, say, lives of three years, five years and seven years were being compared, cash flow diagrams of 105 years duration would have to be drawn in order to find the NPVs of each machine! In fact, NPVs do not need to be compared. All that is needed is to compare the EAVs of the three, five and seven year projects.
   The following analysis should show that a comparison of EAVs is sufficient.

   Reconsidering machines M1 and M2: using a discount rate of 10%

M1

$$NPV = 84 \times 2.4869 + 80 \times 0.7513 - 200 = 69.00$$
$$EAV = 69.00 \times 0.4021 = 27.75$$
alternatively,
$$EAV = 84 - 200 \times 0.4021 + 80 \times 0.7513 \times 0.4021 = 27.75$$

M2

$$EAV = 90 - 270 \times 0.2638 + 70 \times 0.6209 \times 0.2638 = 30.24$$

   M2, as before, is marginally better than M1 at the selected interest rate. The reason why this comparison of EAVs is sufficient is as follows:
   Finding an EAV provides a different representation of the cash flow diagram as shown in Figure 15.5.
   If this cash flow diagram is repeated five times the cash flow diagram for the 15 year period (the lowest common multiple) is obtained as shown in Figure 15.6.
   Therefore, finding the EAV of each 'project' gives a direct comparison over the period of the lowest common multiple, or, for that matter, indefinitely. This method should be used for all comparisons of projects having lives of different durations.

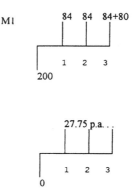

Figure 15.5   Equivalent cash flow diagrams for M1

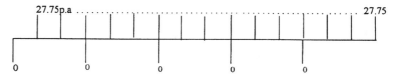

Figure 15.6   15 year equivalent cash flow diagram for M1

15.4   INTERNAL RATE OF RETURN

Another approach to comparing alternative investment projects is by means of their internal rates of return. The *internal rate of return* (IRR) of a project is the rate of interest at which the NPV is zero. This is also known as the *yield*. An investor might decide that the highest yield should be the determining criterion in project selection, rather than NPV or EAV. In most cases the IRR of a project cannot be calculated save by an iterative method. However, it can be found by plotting values of NPV against interest rate as shown in Figure 15.7 below.

There are two ways of looking at the IRR. For the project described in Figure 15.7:

- If £1 million is borrowed at 16.5% the benefits over the six years will completely repay both capital and interest.
- The accumulative benefits over the six years at an interest rate of 16.5% would equal the sum obtained by investing £1 million in a bank to earn 16.5% over a six year period.

In the case in which an investment project has an initial cost followed by a uniform series of annual payments the IRR can be determined quite easily.

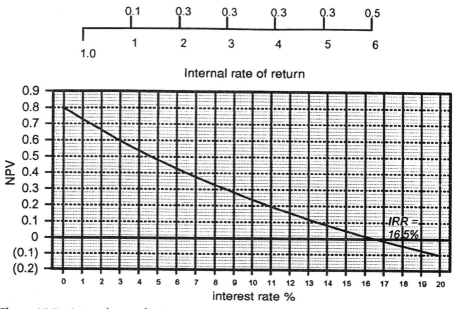

Figure 15.7   Internal rate of return

Example 15(8)

A project has an initial cost of £5 m and equal annual net benefits of £962 000 for 24 years

at the IRR, the present value of the benefits equals the initial cost

$$962\,000 \times factor = 5\,000\,000$$
$$factor = 5.1975$$

examination of the *present value of annuity tables* for a 24 year annuity shows an IRR of approximately 19%.

In Figure 15.8 below the NPVs for three projects, A, B and C have been plotted against interest rate. Observe that the project with the highest yield (IRR) does not necessarily have the highest NPV across the range of interest rates. Observe also, as the interest rates become very high the value of NPV tends toward the initial cost of the project.

$$Ca = initial\ cost\ of\ project\ A$$
$$Cb = initial\ cost\ of\ project\ B$$

In Figure 15.8 the only difference between project B and project C is the initial cost. The initial cost of project C is £4000 less than the initial cost of project B. The distance on the vertical axis between the curves of projects B and C is £4000 at all points along the curve.

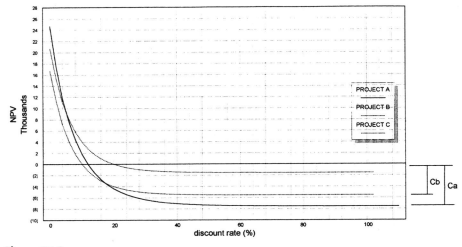

Figure 15.8

The assumption so far has been that the costs and benefits are known. In fact they will always have to be derived. A project evaluation necessitates a determination of the costs and of the benefits. Example 15(9) provides a comprehensive project evaluation.

Example 15(9)

It is proposed to invest £10 million to install a 5000 tonne tri-axis press to replace a line of five 1000 tonne presses. The replaced presses are only five years old and have a total written down value of £2.5m. They can be sold for £1m.

Installation of the tri-axis press will reduce direct labour by 24 employees and indirect labour by 16 employees on each of two shifts. Training will equate to one employee per shift for the first year only. The new press will occupy 2000 sq. ft. less than the old 5-press line. This space will be used to store coil steel for use on the new press, enabling suppliers to deliver JIT and reducing incoming materials inventories by £50 000. Faster die changes on the tri-axis press will allow work-in-progress inventories to be reduced by £50 000. Inventories of emergency spares for the new press will cost £200 000.

Steel for the new press has to be specially heat treated and though scrap rates will be lower there is a net increase in costs of £10 000 p.a.

There will be savings of £2000 p.a. on electricity and £2000 p.a. on operating supplies. Maintenance costs will be £100 000 lower in each of the first three years, and £50 000 lower in subsequent years.

Quality will improve by one repair per 1000 vehicles in operation per 12 months in service. There are no environmental effects.

Use a labour rate of £30 000 p.a.

Use the form provided in Table 15.3 to determine whether the investment is worthwhile.

Calculation

Annual savings

Direct labour: 24 × 2 × 30 000 =1 440 000
Indirect labour: 16 × 2 × 30 000= 960 000
Training: 1 × 1 × (30 000)   = (30 000) yr 1 only
Materials: (10 000)
Utilities: 2000
Operating supplies: 2000
Maintenance: 100 000 for 3 yrs, then 50 000 thereafter

Table 15.3 PCR Engineering Co. plc.
Description of Proposal: New Tri-axis Press to replace five presses.
Planned life of investment: *10 years*

	Year 0–1	Year 1–2	Year 2–3	Year 3–4	Year 4–5	Long term average
Cost Effect +/(−)	£k	£k	£k	£k	£k	£k
Direct labour	1410	1440	1440	1440	1440	1440
Indirect labour	960	960	960	960	960	960
Material	(10)	(10)	(10)	(10)	(10)	(10)
Utilities	2	2	2	2	2	2
Operating supplies	2	2	2	2	2	2
Maintenance	100	100	100	50	50	50
Other overhead	(1500)					
Total Revenue	964	2494	2494	2444	2444	2444
Investment +/(−)	£k	£k	£k	£k	£k	£k
Land and Buildings						
Machinery/Equipment	10 000					
Inventory	200					
Other						
Total investment	10 200					
Net value +/(−)	(9236)	2494	2494	2444	2444	2444

Discount rate used: *8* %   . . .

NPV: *£7253k*   . . . .

IRR: *23.5* %   . . . . .

Notes:
Company assets (the five 1000 tonne presses) valued at £2.5m must be sold for £1m; this represents a book loss of £1.5m and has been entered as such under other overhead (this is the opportunity cost of the investment).

Quality Effect: improves by one repair/1000 vehicles in operation per 12 months in service.

Environmental Effect: nil.

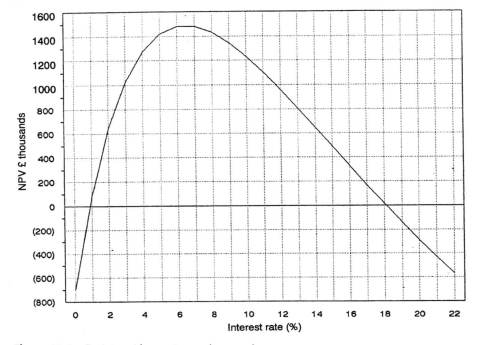

Figure 15.9   Project with two internal rates of return

A project which has a very large late cost, so large that at zero interest rates the total costs exceed the total benefits, can give rise to the curious effect shown in Figure 15.9.

Examples of projects of this nature might include nuclear facilities in which the decommissioning costs can exceed the initial costs and, at a more modest level, refrigeration plant, the disposal costs of which might have to be very high to ensure that no harmful CFC gases leak to the environment.

15.5   COST–BENEFIT ANALYSIS AND LIFE CYCLE COSTING

15.5.1   Benefit-to-cost ratios

Projects may be assessed by comparing their *benefit-to-cost ratios (B/C)*.

> Let B = present value of benefits
> C = present value of costs
> then if *B/C*>1 the investment is worthwhile.

While numerous investments might be worthwhile, there will almost certainly be limits on both the capital available for investment and on revenue available for future annual expenditure. Choices will need to be made between alternative projects. If this is so, then those projects that provide the best value for money will be chosen. The B/C ratio provides one measure of value for money; the higher the ratio the greater the value for money.

Example 15(10)

Consider two projects X and Y, each having an initial cost and each generating a series of benefits over a period, of ten years.

$$\text{let } C_x = 10\,000 \qquad C_y = 12\,000$$

Assume that at a discount rate of 8% the present value of the benefits for each project is as follows:

$$B_x = 15\,000 \qquad B_y = 17\,500$$

$$\text{then } B_x/C_x = 1.5 \text{ and } B_y/C_y = 1.46$$

The B/C ratio for project X is higher than the B/C ratio for project Y, but

$$NPV_x = 5000 \qquad NPV_y = 5500$$

A project with a higher B/C ratio does not necessarily have the higher NPV.

   This can be thought of in a different way by examining the incremental project $Y - X$.

$$\frac{B_{y-x}}{C_{y-x}} = \frac{2500}{2000} = 1.25$$

This shows that for every additional £1 invested in Y over X a benefit of £1.25 is earned. Thus, if a choice were being made between the two projects then Y should be chosen.
   Benefit/cost ratios are not only indicators of value for money, they also provide a good discipline for long term project assessment in that they should ensure that much closer attention is given to future costs as well as to future benefits.

15.5.2   Cost–benefit analysis (CBA) and life-cycle costing (LCC)

Cost–benefit analysis (CBA) examines future annual benefits and future annual costs, not merely the net annual benefits (or costs). For example, a project which earns annual benefits of £1 million p.a. and incurs annual costs of £950 000 could be described by a cash flow diagram as either an annuity of net benefits of

£50 000 p.a., which gives no indication of the costs of operation, or as annuities of £1 million benefits and £950 000 costs, which does.

Cost-benefit analysis is often used in *life-cycle costing* (LCC). LCC is another term for methods of analysis that take into account the whole life cost of a project. For example, if a bridge is to be built, the usual procedure is to receive tenders for the construction (or the design and construction) of the bridge, and let the contract to the lowest bidder. So the decision is made solely on the basis of lowest initial cost. This is how most large public works contracts and contracts for large buildings are let. No account is taken of the maintenance, repair and replacement costs of the project. No account is taken of the decommissioning costs of the project at the end of its life. For many projects this may be perfectly reasonable where running costs are very small in relation to the initial capital cost and/or where the running costs for the alternatives schemes are of the same magnitude. The importance of LCC has in recent years come more to the fore because the physical rates of decay of concrete and steel structures have been in many cases much faster than originally anticipated. Bridge structures with design lives of 120 years have experienced such high levels of deterioration that major components are being replaced after 20 or 30 years. Whilst the direct costs of installing new components may not be particularly high, the indirect costs that arise from delays and rerouting of traffic can be very high indeed. Where this is so, a structure having a much higher capital cost and a far lower frequency of major replacement and repair, could have the lowest LCC and, therefore, should be selected. Similar arguments can be put forward when choosing between alternative building designs in which major elements such as external cladding systems or air-conditioning systems may need replacement after only 25 or 30 years.

The term cost-benefit analysis is more strictly used for public sector projects where government funding is invested in some asset for society, which will not only provide society with economic benefits but may also provide benefits that are not directly quantifiable in monetary terms. When used in this way, CBA attempts to assess non-quantifiable costs as well. The purpose of such analyses is to assist government in choosing between alternative public sector projects. Difficulties arise when CBA is used as an absolute, rather than a comparative measure to determine whether the project selected should be allowed to go ahead or not. For example, it seems quite reasonable to use CBA when comparing alternative highway schemes, but to claim that the analyses provide absolute values of the schemes to the community is highly questionable. Public roads in the UK do not generate income but they do result in savings to the community. Therefore, if the government has limited capital for spending on new highways it makes sense to spend on those highway projects with the highest B/C ratios. Table 15.5 shows the criteria usually used in cost–benefit analysis for highways.

In the UK the Department of Transport uses the COBA program to analyse planned trunk road schemes. This is a very sophisticated program in terms of traffic and accident analyses (although it is not without its critics). However, it is less successful in its provisions for the evaluation of environmental impact.

If traffic flows are heavy, journey time savings and savings in accidents can give rise to very large benefits. In the UK these are usually discounted over a period of

Table 15.5   Cost-benefit analysis for roads

Costs	Benefits
Capital costs	Journey time savings (manhours, vehicle hours)
Maintenance costs	Maintenance costs saved on existing routes
Operating costs	Operating costs saved
	Savings in accidents

30 years at an 8% interest rate. Two further assumptions are often made; these are that traffic volumes will increase and that the national economy will also improve over the period so that the value of journey time savings will increase at some notional annual rate. These two increases are used to offset the relatively high discount rate, thus providing the projects with higher benefit/cost ratios than otherwise.

A criticism of this approach is that certain, very real costs are seldom quantified, since they are only quantifiable in terms of compensation to third parties (e.g. landowners), and such evaluations are notoriously difficult. These costs include: effects of the new highway on non-users and pedestrians and effects on the environment, including:

- noise
- vibration
- pollution
- changes in ground water levels
- visual impact
- community severance.

A further criticism in the UK is that, while CBA is used in this narrow sense to choose between alternative highway schemes, it is not used to choose between alternative transport systems, for example, whether to invest in more railways or in more roads.

Cost–benefit analysis, with the exception of highways, has not been widely used in the UK in recent years. This has been a consequence of both its general unacceptability to the British Government and the very real difficulties facing those who attempt to use it.

This section has provided the reader with a very brief introduction to CBA. Further development of the subject requires a study of economic theory. Those who wish to increase their awareness of the issues should read Mishan [1].

15.6   PERFECT CAPITAL MARKET

The analyses so far have made, implicitly, an underlying assumption, which needs some explanation and justification. The assumption is that the rate of interest payable on a debt is the same as the rate of interest earned on cash in the bank. This situation is known as the perfect capital market. The validity of assuming a perfect capital market for all DCF analyses will be examined later in this section.

First, analyses of a simple project using alternatively DCF and common accounting methods will be made to show that the result will always be the same.

When the net present value of a project is calculated this is done by discounting future benefits to a present value and subtracting the initial cost. This process means that there is no need to calculate the interest earned or the interest paid in each year. DCF gives the value now of a project for a given rate of interest, not the sum of money accrued at the end of the project, or, indeed, the accumulative debts/credits over the life of the project.

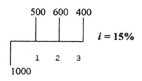

Figure 15.10   Cash flow diagram

Example 15(11)

For the cashflow diagram in Figure 15.10, using a discount rate of 15%, the NPV can be found.

$$NPV = 500 \times 0.8696 + 600 \times 0.7561 + 400 \times 0.6575 - 1000 = 151.46$$

Using normal accounting methods as developed in Table 15.4, the balance in the account after three years is £230.37 as shown. The interest rate of 15% is assumed to apply equally to the debt and to the benefits.

Table 15.4   Future worth

At end of	Accumulative debt	Accumulative benefit
Year 0	1000	0
Year 1	1000×1.15	500
Year 2	1000×1.15^2	$500 \times 1.15 + 600$
Year 3	1000×1.15^3	$500 \times 1.15^2 + 600 \times 1.15 + 400$
	$=1520.88$	$=1751.25$

balance$=1751.25 - 1520.88 = 230.37$

With an interest rate of 15% the sum of

$$\frac{230.37}{1.15^3} = 151.46$$

needs to be invested at year 0 to obtain 230.37 by the end of year 3.

Both methods give the same result. The difference is that DCF compares investment projects in *present value* or *annual value* terms whilst the traditional accounting method looks at the *future* worth.

How can the perfect capital market be justified? Individuals, certainly, do not experience a perfect capital market. When a person borrows from a bank, he/she does so at a higher rate of interest than when he/she deposits savings in the bank. Businesses should also receive similar treatment. When a business borrows money the interest rate applied to the loan is greater than the interest rate which applies to any cash reserves that the business might have. Even so, the assumption of a perfect capital market is a reasonable one as the following analysis attempts to show.

Figure 15.11 below represents two alternative businesses. Assume that the bank pays interest to its account holders of 8% p.a. and charges interest at a rate of 12% on borrowings.

In the first case the business has large reserves of cash (represented here as blocks of gold) deposited in the bank. A substantial investment is made, e.g. buying a factory (this is shown here by the term *initial cost*). This reduces the cash reserves; the effect of this is to lose the 8% interest that would have been earned by the depositor on the money used to buy the factory. As time passes and benefits are paid into the account the benefits will earn interest at 8%, so the one rate of interest applies to both the initial cost and to the benefits.

In the second case the business is already in debt (represented here as a pile of IOU notes) to the bank. A substantial investment is made by increasing this debt,

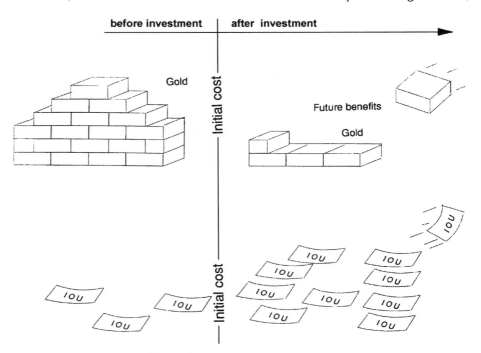

Figure 15.11 Alternative financial arrangement

and interest is paid on this debt at 12%. As benefits are credited to the account, the level of debt falls, so the benefits reduce the amount of interest being paid at 12%, so, once again, the one interest rate (12%) applies to both the initial cost and to the benefits.

Most businesses are net borrowers. That is, their borrowings far exceed their reserves. As time passes, and particular loans are repaid, businesses will seek to expand their operations or sustain them by further loans, thus maintaining a net level of borrowing.

15.7   CAPITAL RATIONING

It has been noted that B/C ratios are indicative of value for money. However, the value of C represents the present value of all the costs of the project, present and future. Most commercial investors will be especially concerned with the initial capital cost. If several projects are available as investment opportunities and the capital available is insufficient for them all, then a simple way to proceed is to select those projects with the highest NPW/C_0 ratio where $C_0 = $ initial cost.

Example 15(12)

Projects P1 to P10 have been analysed at a discount rate of 8%. The results of the analysis are shown in Table 15.7. In the right hand half of the Table the projects have been placed in an order of declining NPW/C_0 ratio.

If the capital is limited to £9400 projects P1, P6, P2, P8, P4, P9 and P5 should be selected.

This simple approach does have its limitations. For example, if the capital limit were £10 000, project P10 could also be included without exceeding the capital limit, but this is not immediately clear from the table. The method works well when the initial costs and NPWs of the projects under review are of the same order. A quick check on the difference between the capital limit and the

Table 15.7   Capital rationing

Project	NPW	C_o	Project	NPW/C_o	$\Sigma\ C_o$
P1	560	1400	P1	0.4	1400
P2	540	1500	P6	0.4	2200
P3	400	2300	P2	0.36	3700
P4	380	1700	P8	0.3	4700
P5	360	1800	P4	0.22	6400
P6	320	800	P9	0.21	7600
P7	320	2000	P5	0.20	9400
P8	300	1000	P3	0.174	11 700
P9	250	1200	P10	0.167	12 300
P10	100	600	P7	0.16	14 300

accumulative cost should always be made to see whether a project further down the list could be included.

15.8   INFLATION

The introduction of the concept of *inflation*, and the matter of handling it, when applying DCF often causes considerable confusion. Confusion arises over the meaning of inflation, how it is taken into account and why, sometimes, apparently, it is not taken into account. First the meaning of inflation itself must be examined.

Inflation in prices is a consequence of a fall in the value of money in relation to the value of the goods being sold. If a new camera costs £100 this year, and exactly one year later the identical model costs £105, then cameras (or this model) are experiencing 5% inflation. The example below shows the relationship between annual interest rate and annual rate of inflation.

Example 15(13)

This year I buy 100 kg of widgets for £103. How many can I buy for £206? Answer: 200 kg

How many can I buy for £112? Answer: $100 \times 112/103 = 108.7$ kg.

One year ago I bought 100 kg of widgets for £100. What has been the annual rate of inflation over the last year? Answer: $(103 - 100)/100 = 0.03 = 3\%$.

Last year I invested £100 in the bank at an interest rate of 12%. How much money do I have in the bank one year later? Answer: £112.

How many widgets will my £112 buy? Answer: 108.7 kg (see above)

By how much has my investment increased in *real terms* (purchasing power)? Answer: $(108.7 - 100)/100 = 0.087 = 8.7\%$.

So, what has been the *real* interest rate? Answer: 8.7%.

$$(1 + r) = \frac{(1 + m)}{(1 + p)}$$

where r = real interest rate
m = money interest rate (what the bank pays)
p = rate of inflation

The most common measure of inflation in the UK is the Retail Price Index (RPI). (See also Chapter 13, section 13.5.2.) This measures the changes in prices over a range of consumer goods and services as well as housing, applying a weighted formula to arrive at a monthly figure. Similar indices operate throughout Europe. The formula by which a RPI is calculated is adjusted from time to time to take into account historic changes in how society spends its money. When domestic coal was an important part of every family budget its price had to be included in the formula, today a RPI might include the price of skiing holidays, with an appropriate weighting, of course. Each time the formula is adjusted a new base date is established and the RPI for the new base date is set at 100.00.

To determine the 'current' rate of inflation, the RPI now is compared with that of 12 months previously, as illustrated below. Thus the 'current' rate of inflation is always a measure of the past!

Example 15(14)

(a)   The RPI now is 142.6, 12 months ago it was 134.5, what has been the rate of inflation?

142.6/134.05 = 1.06   Answer: 6%

(b)   The RPI now is 142.6, four years ago it was 119.6, what has been the average rate of inflation over the last four years?

$$\frac{142.6}{119.6} = 1.1923 = (1+p)^4$$

therefore $p = 0.045 = 4.5\%$

therefore, the average rate of inflation over the last four years has been 4.5%.

Investment projects can be analysed in *real* terms or in *money* terms. Analysis in real terms means in terms of current purchasing power (current prices). Thus, the statement that the real net benefits at the end of year 4 are £1000, means that the net benefits will have the same purchasing power in year 4 as £1000 has today. This carries with it the implicit assumption that future money benefits are expected to keep abreast of the rate of inflation. No long term plan could afford any other provision!

However, if the analysis of a project is conducted in *money* terms, and the net benefits at the end of year 4, say, are stated to be £1000, then this means that £1000 is the actual sum of money that is expected to be earned; that future earnings are 'fixed' and that they will not rise with inflation. This could be a fixed price contract. An analysis for such a project must use money interest rates.

Whether alternative investment projects are analysed in real terms or money terms, a consistent approach is essential. Thus, if the analysis is conducted in money terms, then money costs, money benefits and a money interest rate must be used. If the analysis is in real terms, then real costs, real benefits and real interest rates must be used. What is a real interest rate? In the earlier example the real interest rate was 8.7%. As has been previously observed, the real interest rate is something which is derived, not what the banks advertise; what they advertise is the money interest rate.

When should the analysis be conducted in money terms and when in real terms? If the projects under consideration are relatively short term, i.e. two or three years, they can be analysed in money terms. If the projects are long term, then it is far better to analyse them in real terms. The reason for this is that it is impossible to predict inflation rates over the next say, 20 years, therefore there is no way in which money income for any of the later years can be predicted safely. But engineers can predict operating costs and revenues at current prices for a project, therefore, they can predict income in these terms, i.e. real terms. A good example of this would be a power station, if demand and hence output can be predicted for year 20, or any other year, then it is certainly possible to estimate the net revenue for that year at current prices. So, the only way to analyse this investment is to use real values at real discount rates.

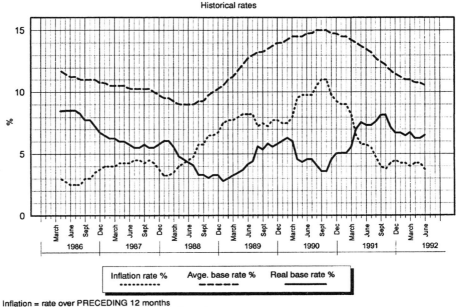

Inflation = rate over PRECEDING 12 months
Avge. base rate = average over PRECEDING 12 months

Figure 15.12   UK interest and inflation rates

There remains the difficulty of selecting a real interest rate for discounting future cash flows. Historically, the UK real (Bank of England) base rates have varied between about 2% and 8% (see Figure 15.12), although in the 1970s negative values occurred when the inflation rate exceeded the interest rates. The cost of borrowing does depend upon the need and the nature of a business, but an assumption that interest rates selected for the purposes of discounting should be about 3% above the base rate does not seem inappropriate for UK projects. Government departments have in the past used 7% or 8% for discounting long term projects which seems reasonable. In Germany, where money interest rates and inflation rates have been far lower, much lower real rates of interest should be applied.

For short-term projects, current (i.e. money) interest rates and current inflation rates should be used.

Example 15(15)

Shown in Table 15.8 are the estimated cash flows for a project at current prices. Assume the current rate of inflation is 5%. The lender advises that the borrowing rate is currently 12% and that it is unlikely to change by much over the three year period. Future benefits in money terms are calculated in Table 15.9.

Table 15.8   Cash flows at current prices

Year	Outflow (cost)	Inflow (benefits)
0	900	
1		500
2		400
3		600

Table 15.9   Cash flows in money

Year	Outflow (cost)	Money inflow (benefits)
0	900	
1		$500 \times 1.05 = 525$
2		$400 \times 1.05^2 = 441$
3		$600 \times 1.05^3 = 695$

From this the NPW is found.

$$NPW = 525 \times 0.8929 + 441 \times 0.7972 + 695 \times 0.7118 - 900 = 415$$

Now, by analysing the project in real terms, using the real rate of interest which is

$$\frac{(1 + 0.12)}{(1 + 0.05)} - 1.00 = 0.067$$

that is 6.7%, the NPW is found:

$$NPW = \frac{500}{1.067} + \frac{400}{1.067^2} + \frac{600}{1.067^3} - 900 = 415$$

NPW(real) = NPW(money)

This is a valuable finding; whether a project is analysed in real terms or in money terms the result will be the same.

15.9   PAST COSTS AND PROJECTS WITH INDEFINITE LIVES

The section explains how past costs should be dealt with, and considers projects with indefinite lives.

15.9.1   Past costs are sunk costs

Two years ago we invested £28k in project A, since then nothing has happened; there have been no earnings, no costs. If we invest £70k *now* in this project it will earn £24k p.a. for the next ten years. Alternatively, if we invest £85k now in project B it will earn £26k p.a. for the same period. If the interest rate is 10% which should we choose? Cash flow diagrams are shown in Figure 15.13.

$$NPW_a = 24 \times 6.1446 - 70 = £77.46k$$
$$NPW_b = 26 \times 6.1446 - 85 = £74.47k$$

The earlier investment of £28k is irrelevant. Past costs are sunk costs, and are common to both projects and, therefore, can be ignored (if we proceed with B we have still incurred the £28k). Choose project A.

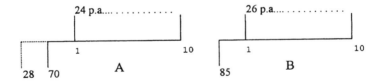

Figure 15.13   Cash flow diagrams

15.9.2   Projects with infinite/indefinite lives

(1) Determine the net equivalent annual value (NEAV) of a project which has an initial cost of 100 monetary units and earns benefits of 20 per annum indefinitely. Use $i = 12\%$.
Assume indefinitely means that the number of years is very large.
Consider the formula

$$\text{EAV of } C_o = C_o \frac{i}{\left(1 - \frac{1}{(1+i)^n}\right)}$$

where C_0 = initial cost

$$\text{when } n \text{ is very large } \frac{1}{(1+i)^n} \text{ tends to zero,}$$

and, therefore,

$$\text{EAV of } C_0 = C_0 \times i = 100 \times 0.12 = 12$$

therefore

$$\text{NEAV} = 20 - 12 = 8$$

(2) Determine the NPW of the project in (1) above. Use $i = 12\%$. In (1) an initial cost of 100 has been converted into equal annual repayments of 12 for an infinite period when $i = 12\%$, that is:

$$\text{annuity payments} = i \times \text{present value (of cost)}$$

therefore,

$$\text{present value} = \frac{(\text{annuity})}{i}$$

$$\text{NPW} = 20/0.12 - 100 = 66.67$$

In short, the present value of an indefinite stream of equal annual benefits or costs is found simply by dividing the annual sum by the interest rate. Conversely, a single sum now can be converted into an annual value for ever by multiplying the sum by the interest rate. Such simplicity is welcome.

15.10   REVIEW

The foregoing sections have covered a considerable amount of material which, although simple in terms of numerical procedures, often gives rise to conceptual difficulties. Because of this, a brief review of the study material is provided in advance of the summary.

An investment involves early costs and later benefits which usually arise at periodic intervals. During its life the investment has a changing value in recognition of the predicted future net benefits.

Payback is a useful but simplistic method of assessing short-term investment projects.

DCF makes the assumption of a perfect capital market. This allows the investor to use NPW as an unambiguous parameter of gain or loss, permitting a set of projects to be considered independently of whether the investing enterprise finances its operations by borrowing or using its own capital.

Projects may be assessed in several ways: NPW, EAV, B/C ratio, IRR, NPW/C_0 ratio. The method adopted will depend upon the priorities of the investor. If the intention is to maximize present worth then NPW should be used. If the intention is to minimize annual costs or to maximize net annual benefits then the use of EAVs would be appropriate. For many long term projects the investor will be far more concerned about the regular (annual) distribution of revenue than about any present value of the investment, therefore the EAVs of such projects will provide far more useful information. If the intention is to take careful account of future costs and benefits, rather than merely net benefits, in order to ascertain value for money or in order to assess the true nature of the costs and benefits then cost-benefit analysis should be used. Where the analyst needs to compare yields, the IRRs of alternative investments can be found, and where the principal criterion for an investment decision is to obtain maximum value for capital employed at a given interest rate, then the NPW/C_0 ratios should be examined.

In drawing up a cash flow diagram the investment analyst is making certain implicit assumptions of which he should be acutely aware. These are:

- certainty about the initial cost
- certainty about future costs and future benefits
- certainty about project life-time
- perfect capital market
- non-variable interest rates
- how inflation will be taken into account.

The following questions should illustrate these points:

(1)   When a builder is asked to tender for the construction of a new factory does the owner really believe that the tender sum is what he will eventually pay for the factory?
(2)   When future operational and maintenance costs for this factory are estimated, how confident can the owner be that these will be the actual costs?
(3)   When future profits/income from a project are estimated, can the owner be confident that these will be achieved?
(4)   Why has a 30 year lifetime for the factory or a 10 year life for a given machine been selected?
(5)   How can the interest rate(s) selected for discounting be justified?

In view of these uncertainties, engineers and investment analysts should avoid evaluating projects to several decimal places (!) and, when the quantitative differences between projects are small they should pay careful heed to the non-quantifiable attributes of the projects.

A method of dealing with these uncertainties is *sensitivity analysis*. Sensitivity analysis examines the effects of changing costs, benefits, project life-times and discount rates to determine how sensitive the decision is to such changes. It may be that a change in life-time from 20 to 30 years has far less effect than a 5% change in initial cost for a given project; if that were the case a careful review of the estimating procedures by which the initial cost has been obtained and/or a review of the contractual arrangements for commissioning the project would be of far greater value than worrying about how long the investment would last. The process of sensitivity analysis will usually involve setting up a spreadsheet for the project by which the effects of changing a variety of parameters can be examined rapidly and thoroughly.

15.11 SUMMARY

This chapter has discussed the utility of payback as a means of investment decision analysis, and studied in some detail discounted cash flow techniques. The concepts of net present value, equivalent annual value, benefit to cost ratio, internal rate of return have been explained. The presumption of a perfect capital market has been justified. Alternative ways of dealing with inflation have been set out: either by analysing projects in money terms or in real terms. The purposes of life-cycle costing and cost-benefit analysis were discussed. Finally methods of dealing with past costs and indefinite lives have been explained. A number of exercises has been included with numerical answers provided; these exercises follow this summary.

15.12 EXERCISES

For the interest rates tabulated and for each of the cashflow diagrams in Figure 15.14 find:

Net present benefit B, B/C ratio, NPV, EAV, and IRR

Ex. 1	Answers				
int. rate %	B	B/C	NPV	EAV	
10	120.34	1.20	20.34	6.42	IRR = 19.5%
15	108.97	1.09	8.97	3.14	
19	101.12	1.01	1.12	0.42	
19.5	100.21	1.00	0.21	0.08	
20	99.31	0.99	−0.69	−0.27	

Ex. 2	Answers				
i	B	B/C	NPV	EAV	
10	114.12	1.14	14.12	4.45	IRR = 16.5%
15	102.78	1.03	2.78	0.97	
16	100.73	1.01	0.73	0.26	
16.5	99.74	1.00	−0.26	−0.09	
20	93.19	0.93	−6.81	−2.63	

Ex. 3	Answers				
i	B	B/C	NPV	EAV	
3	107.06	1.07	7.06	0.47	IRR = 3.5%
3.5	101.55	1.02	1.55	0.11	
4	96.40	0.96	−3.60	−0.26	
5	87.11	0.87	−12.89	−1.03	

Ex. 4	Answers				
i	B	B/C	NPV	EAV	
5	−67.66	−0.45	−217.66	−17.47	no IRR
10	−41.84	−0.28	−191.84	−22.53	
15	−27.85	−0.19	−177.85	−28.41	
20	−19.63	−0.13	−169.63	−34.83	

Ex. 5   Answers

i	B	B/C	NPV	EAV	
5	− 24.77	− 0.14	− 206.77	− 16.59	no IRR
10	− 13.35	− 0.07	− 195.35	− 22.95	
15	− 7.71	− 0.04	− 189.71	− 30.31	
20	− 4.69	− 0.03	− 186.69	− 38.34	

Example 1

Example 2

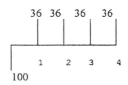

Example 3

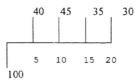

Example 4

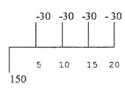

Example 5

Figure 15.14 Cash flow diagrams

General exercises

Ex. 6

(a) What will be the annual repayments for a mortgage of £100 000 over a period of 20 years assuming the lender's interest rate is 10%?
Answer: £11 750

(b) How much of the capital is owed halfway through the period, that is, after the payment for year 10?
Answer: £72 199

(c) Determine the interest charges within the repayments in each of years 1, 11 and 20.
Assume that repayments are made at the end of year 1, year 2, etc.
Answers: £10 000, £7220, £1068
(Note: the answer to this part question can in each case be found by *one line of calculation*).

Ex. 7

A developer has received two tenders for construction of a new building. The tender sums are both equal to £1505k but the monthly expenditures are different over the 16 month contract period. Which tenderer should we choose? Use $i = 1\%$ per month (12.68% p.a.).

Tender No. 1 (payments in £k)

Month	0	1	2	3	4	5	6	7	8	9	10	11	12	13	14	15	16
Payment	0	0	0	40	45	55	100	120	170	210	225	200	180	100	30	20	10

$NPV = £1384k$

Tender No. 2 (payments in £k)

Month	0	1	2	3	4	5	6	7	8	9	10	11	12	13	14	15	16
Payment	0	0	0	48	54	66	120	144	204	230	207	160	144	80	24	16	8

$NPV = £1391k$

Answer: on a 0.5% margin between the two tenders, factors other than NPV (e.g. quality, reputation, etc.) are likely to be far more important.

Ex. 8

Figure 15.15 shows the NPV of a 14 year investment for a range of discount rates. The project has an initial cost and a series of unequal future benefits.
From the graph determine:

  (i) the present value of the benefits (PVB) at $i = 100\%$
 (ii) the PVB at $i = 12\%$
(iii) the PVB at $i = $ zero
(iv) the IRR if the initial cost were to be reduced by £2700.

(b)   From the shape of the curve, comment upon the distribution of benefits along the cash flow diagram.

Answer: (a) (i) zero, (ii) £7600, (iii) £32 200, (iv) 16%
            (b) benefits in first 5 or 6 years are zero or negligible benefits in final
                  years are, therefore, substantial.

Ex. 9

An engineering company owns a fleet of cars. It has been agreed that a replacement policy should be established.
Using the data below and a discount rate of 12% find the optimum replacement period.
Purchase price when new £9000

Assume annual running costs arise at the end of each year.

	yr 1	yr 2	yr 3	yr 4
running costs (£) in year	2000	2500	3200	4100
resale value at end of year	6500	4600	3000	1700

Answer: every two years.

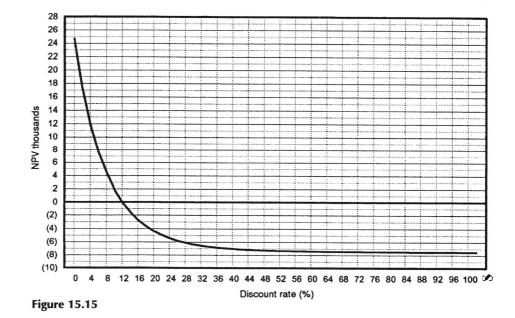

Figure 15.15

REFERENCE

1. Mishan E. J. (1988) *Cost-Benefit Analysis*. Fourth-edition, Unwin Hyman.

BIBLIOGRAPHY

Abelson, P. (1979) *Cost Benefit Analysis and Environmental Problems*. Saxon House. Teakfield Ltd, Farnborough.

Ahmad, Y. J. (ed) (1973) *Environmental Decision-Making*. Vol. 1, Hodder & Stoughton, Sevenoaks.

Ahmad, Y. J., Dasgupta, P. and Maler, K. (1984) *Environmental Decision-Making*. Vol. 2, Hodder & Stoughton, Sevenoaks.

Chapman, C. B., Cooper D. F. and Page M. J. (1987) *Management for Engineers*. Chapter 10, Wiley and Sons, Chichester.

Lanigan, M. (1992) *Engineers in Business*. Chapter 11, Addison-Wesley, Reading.

Layard, R. (ed) (1972) *Cost-Benefit Analysis*, Penguin, Harmondsworth.

Mott, G. (1991) *Management Accounting for Decision Makers*, Chapter 11, Pitman, London.

Mott, G. (1993) *Accounting for Non-Accountants*, Fourth edition, Kogan Page, London.

Pearce, D. W. (1983) *Cost-benefit Analysis*. Second edition, Macmillan, London.

Thuesen, G. J. and Fabrycky, W. J. (1989) *Engineeering Economy*. Seventh edition, Prentice-Hall, London

16

Maintenance management

16.1   INTRODUCTION

In many sectors of industry, maintenance has been regarded as a necessary evil and often has been carried out in an unplanned and reactive way. It has frequently lagged behind other areas of industrial management in the application of formal techniques and/or computing technology. Yet expenditure on maintenance can be a significant factor in a company's profitability. In manufacturing, maintenance typically accounts for between 2 and 10% of income, and in transport of goods by road for up to 24%. Maintenance costs can represent a significant element in the life-cycle costs of some projects, as indicated in Chapter 15. In the UK, national expenditure on maintenance is about 5% of the value of the sales of goods and services and exceeds the amount invested in new plant and equipment.

Modern management practice regards maintenance as an integral function in achieving efficient and productive operations and high quality products, and high levels of equipment reliability are increasingly demanded by 'lean manufacturing' and 'Just-in-Time' operations (see Chapter 20). This chapter outlines the objectives of maintenance, the concept of failure rate, the design of maintenance systems and the provisions for maintenance strategy and maintenance planning.

16.2   OBJECTIVES OF MAINTENANCE

The need for maintenance in most engineering operations is self evident. Without maintenance the plant and equipment used will not survive over the required life of the system without degradation or failure. The design and operation of a maintenance system must usually meet one of two objectives:

- minimize the chance of failure where such a failure would have undesirable consequences (e.g. reduced safety or environmental damage).
- minimize overall cost or maximize overall profit of an operation. This requires striking a balance between the cost of setting up and running the maintenance operation and savings generated by increased efficiency, prevention of downtime, etc.

Maintenance may also take place for other reasons such as corporate image, for example, cleaning the windows of an office building or repainting an aircraft.

The objectives of a maintenance programme may be expressed formally in terms of maximizing plant effectiveness. A total productive maintenance (TPM) strategy attempts to maximize overall plant effectiveness (OPE). This is defined as follows:

OPE   = Availability × Efficiency × Quality

where

Availability = the proportion of time the plant is available to do its job, expressed as a percentage
Efficiency = the 'output' of the plant as a percentage of its maximum output
Quality   = the percentage of products which meet the required specification

In maximizing this measure it is implied that full output of the plant (Availability × Efficiency) is required. If it is not, maximizing OPE may not be cost-effective and the objective of maintenance should then be to achieve the required output and quality in the most cost-effective way.

Maintenance will affect each of the constituents of OPE. Ultimately a balance must be struck between the cost of achieving a high OPE and the benefits it brings. Decisions about directing maintenance efforts to availability, efficiency or quality must be made, again on a cost-effective basis.

16.3 PLANT DETERIORATION AND FAILURE

A knowledge of expected failure rates is fundamental to the design of a maintenance operation. A review of some key concepts is given here. There is an extensive literature on reliability analysis, some titles [1–3] are suggested at the end of this chapter.

16.3.1 Failure rate

The failure rate (or hazard rate, $H(t)$) for components, equipment or plant is normally expressed in failures per hour (or failure per thousand or even per million hours). The figures represent an average for the type of equipment, and the expected number of failures in any time period can only be expressed in terms of probabilities. Failure rates can be used to estimate the number of failures expected in the plant and give an initial indication of the maintenance effort required.

Failure rates are a function of time, typically exhibiting the well known 'bathtub' curve shown in Figure 16.1. This is characteristic of many types of electrical and mechanical engineering equipment, as well as of people!

Three phases may be observed during the life of a component, although in practice the boundaries are often ill-defined.

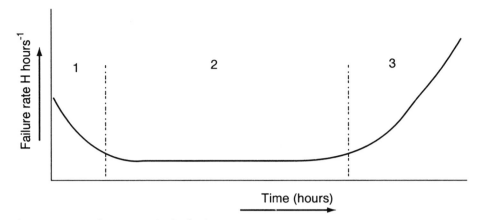

Figure 16.1   Failure rate—the bathtub curve

In *phase 1*, the wear-in phase, the failure rate is initially high but it reduces over a short time. Failures in this phase are due to flaws and weaknesses in materials or faults in manufacture.[1] The wear-in characteristic has implications on the provision of warranties for new equipment, but of greater significance is that it will result in a high initial failure rate. On installations of a critical nature, an initial testing programme, often under severe conditions, should be undertaken to reveal phase 1 failures before the system is put on line. The implication for maintenance is that engineers should be prepared for a heavy maintenance effort on newly commissioned plant. It is also worth noting that wear-in characteristics can be evident after maintenance, perhaps to a less pronounced degree, as a result of new parts being fitted or of faulty workmanship in repair.

In *phase 2*, the useful-life phase, the failure rate is low and approximately constant, representing random failures. The length of this phase, sometimes referred to as durability, will vary with the type of equipment. In this phase the mean time to failure is the reciprocal of the (constant) failure rate.

In *phase 3*, the wear-out phase, the failure rate increases due to ageing, wear, erosion, corrosion and related processes. The rate at which failure rate increases varies with the type of equipment. For much equipment, especially electronics, no wear-out is observed within the working life and there is some debate about whether it occurs. Wear-out has an influence on maintenance policy; if an item has a distinct wear-out characteristic it can be replaced before failure is likely, for example, the brake pads on a car.

16.3.2   Reliability

Reliability $R(t)$ is defined as:

'the probability that an item will perform a required function under stated conditions for a stated period of time.'

---

[1]Use of techniques such as failure mode and effect analysis (FMEA) during simultaneous engineering is aimed at reducing these failures. See Chapter 6, section 6.5.3 and Chapter 4, section 4.4.

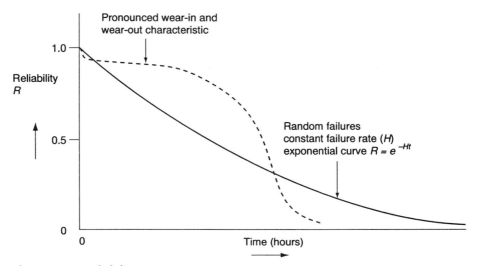

Figure 16.2   Reliability curves

It is related to failure rate by the relationship

$$R = e^{-\int Hdt}$$

Initially the reliability should be 1.0 and eventually it will tend to zero, as all engineering systems will eventually fail or deteriorate to such an extent that they can no longer perform their intended function. Figure 16.2 shows typical reliability functions.

16.3.3   Data sources

Obtaining failure rate data requires testing of many components over long periods of time. This is easy enough for inexpensive items made in large numbers, such as electronic components and ball bearings. For expensive equipment, data are obtained from in-service failure records, since a testing programme could be expensive and would take too long. For components with a very low failure rate, accelerated testing is usually employed; for example, testing of electronic components is often undertaken at a high temperature and the failure rates at normal operating temperatures calculated by means of an empirical relationship (see [1]).

Published data sources generally give failure rate figures for phase 2 of the 'bathtub' curve; some sources are listed in the references [4–6]. In using the data one should be aware of the uncertainty associated with these quoted figures, some sources give an indication of this. Also, the operating conditions under which the data were obtained must correspond to those of the applications being considered. Some sources [4] allow adjustments to be made for different operating conditions. Data on wear-in and wear-out characteristics are often not available.

Information on failure modes is sometimes given if an item can fail in one of several different ways.

16.4   DESIGNING MAINTENANCE SYSTEMS

There is no universally accepted methodology for designing maintenance systems. Sufficient information or time for analysis is generally not available to allow a fully structured approach leading to an optimal solution. Instead, maintenance systems are designed using experience and judgement assisted by a number of formal decision aids. The two sections which follow outline a two-stage approach to the design process:

- Strategy: deciding upon which level within the plant to perform maintenance, and outlining a structure which will support the maintenance.
- Planning: day to day decisions on what maintenance tasks to perform, and providing the resources to undertake these tasks.

Even here it must be emphasized that there is not a once through process, and a degree of feedback and of reiteration will be needed.

16.5   MAINTENANCE STRATEGY

In formulating a maintenance strategy three key points have to be determined:

- At what level within the plant the maintenance is to be performed.
- What structure is needed to support the maintenance.
- What resources are needed.

To illustrate the factors which influence these decisions consider the example of a machine tool shown in Figure 16.3.

Consider the position if a failure of the lubrication system is observed. Judgement will tell the engineers that the replacement of the whole machine (Level 1) or of the whole lubrication system (Level 2) would not be sensible. However, it is not obvious whether maintenance should take place at Level 3, 4 or 5. Factors which affect the decision are summarized below:

- Diagnosis time: the time taken to locate the fault. This will usually be longer at lower levels of the hierarchy. Erratic lubricant flow is a fault of the pump unit which is immediately obvious (Level 3). To determine the cause, say, bearing failure in the motor (Level 5) will take much longer.
- Off-line time: includes shutdown, isolation, removal, repair, replacement, test, start-up. In other words, the total time that the plant is unavailable as a result of the maintenance action. This usually will be lowest for maintenance at middle levels in the hierarchy (e.g. replacing a motor is quicker than replacing one of its bearings or the whole lubrication system). Unavailability of spare parts can be a factor.
- Off-line cost: the loss of income resulting from off-line and diagnostic time.

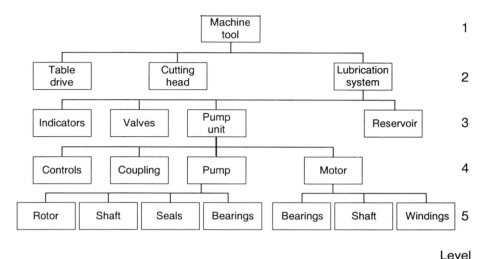

Figure 16.3 Assembly hierarchy for a machine tool

- Repair cost: includes labour and an allowance for the capital cost of diagnostic, repair and test equipment and the space it occupies, and other overhead charges (energy, administration etc.). This cost is usually lower if maintenance is undertaken at middle levels in the hierarchy.
- Spares cost: the cost of spares consumed. This reduces further down the hierarchy (the cost of a bearing is clearly less than the cost of a pump unit), although the associated ordering and storage costs may at some point increase.
- Expected failures: the number of failures increases higher up the hierarchy. The pump unit (Level 3) fails every time a bearing or a seal fails (Level 5).

The decision must also include whether to provide a two (or multi-) level process. It may well be prudent to replace the pump unit quickly to get the machine back in operation, and then dismantle it in a workshop to repair the cause of the failure. For equipment where it is not cost-effective to employ people with the specialist skills to carry out repairs 'in-house' units may be returned to the supplier for repair.

Analysis of the above factors will indicate at which level maintenance is most cost-effective. In practice, such decisions are made, but rarely as a result of a thorough cost analysis. More often it is a case of the application of experience and judgement in the first instance, with adjustments made during the life of the plant. The level at which maintenance is carried out may be:

- at different levels on different branches,
- different for different fault modes at the higher levels,
- different for emergency and planned maintenance.

For a plant of any complexity the analysis clearly involves a significant effort for managers and engineers.

Once decisions on the level of maintenance have been made a structure to support the maintenance operation must be devised. Figure 16.4 indicates a

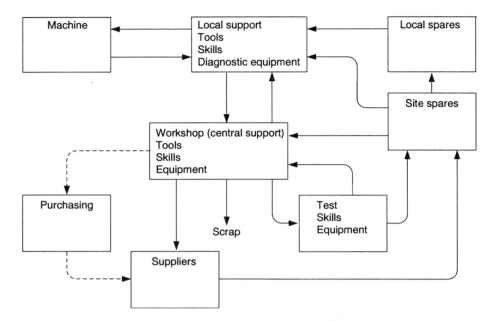

Figure 16.4 Typical maintenance support structure

typical arrangement which may be expanded or reduced depending upon the circumstances. Simple cases will not require the centre layer (workshop); for example, computer systems in small- or medium-sized companies where faulty items are either simply replaced (e.g. a keyboard) or returned to the supplier for repair. Larger operations may have an extra layer (site workshop, main base), especially where there are many operational units remote from the supplier.

Within the structure, resource requirements in terms of people (skills), tools and equipment must be identified. The allocation of tasks to people must be considered. Generally it is better that routine tasks (lubrication, cleaning, adjustment) be made by the operator who knows the machine rather than calling on a separate person. In many industries, efforts are being made to increase the level of maintenance (and repair) carried out by work-area teams rather than by specialist maintenance personnel.

16.6 MAINTENANCE PLANNING

Within the overall maintenance structure the day to day planning of tasks must take place. The starting point for this planning is to decide upon the basis for maintenance which may be one of the following:

- Operate to failure (OTF). Where the consequence of failure is small and the time to failure is difficult to predict, this might be the most appropriate planned method of maintenance (e.g. replacing light bulbs).
- Time based activities. Where maintenance to prevent failure (e.g. painting a bridge) or to replace parts which have deteriorated (spark plugs of a petrol

engine) is undertaken at regular intervals of time or some related variable (miles travelled, in the case of a car). There may be statutory requirements to undertake regular inspections/tests and repairs.

- Condition based activities. Where deterioration can be detected and can be justified financially (e.g. cost of instrumentation), maintenance actions can be based on conditions. This requires condition monitoring.

A planned maintenance programme must be able to respond to unexpected failures which may have to be dealt with immediately (emergency maintenance) or scheduled into the daily plan.

Reliability centred maintenance (RCM) provides the basis for a maintenance plan by considering the failure characteristics of the plant and its components and the cost and consequences of failures. A flow chart summarizing the decision process is shown in Figure 16.5. Clearly all items in the assembly hierarchy cannot be treated independently. If a pump is being taken apart to replace the seals it is sensible to check the bearings. Many activities have to be concentrated into major shutdown periods.

Maintenance planning needs to be a dynamic process. The time based tasks are known well in advance, condition based tasks shortly in advance and emergency tasks will arise with little or zero notice. Flexibility is usually achieved through backlog tasks or by moving forward or back the time based tasks whose timing is not critical. Consideration should be given to this when creating the master schedule for the time based work. Figure 16.6 illustrates the problem.

A further consideration in creating the plan is the availability of 'maintenance windows', possibly evenings or weekends or periods of the year when demand is usually slack. The question of opportunity maintenance also arises; when equipment is shut down and dismantled for a particular repair it may be prudent to undertake other tasks. Such actions may be planned to a limited extent.

The level, strategy, and planning decisions lead in turn to requirements for spare parts, resources, diagnostic equipment and labour. Again, this will generally be reiterative and interactive rather than a once through decision-making process.

Traditionally, control and information systems for the maintenance plan have been paper based, however, today, computer packages are available, the more sophisticated of which are linked to purchasing and stock control functions.

Proper recording of information is the key to the operation of a planned maintenance programme. Analysis of the information can lead to improvements to the programme and greater efficiency in the use of spare parts, equipment and people. Recording is an important aspect of maintenance management, people tend to get the work done and move on to the next task, forgetting the record keeping. Computer based systems have helped record keeping to become more 'user-friendly' but have led to the temptation to record everything — this too must be resisted.

Recorded data can be used for:

- reviewing and updating strategy,
- identifying probable areas where re-design could avoid failures and/or maintenance,
- calculating effectiveness ratios, for example, percentages of unplanned work, or maintenance expenditure as a percentage of income.

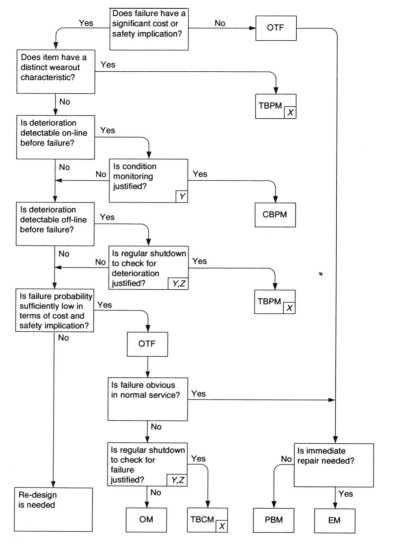

Key:
OTF   Operate to failure
TBPM   Time based preventive maintenance
CBPM   Condition based preventive maintenance
TBCM   Time based corrective maintenance
OM   Opportunity maintenance
EM   Emergency maintenance – repair needed for safety reasons or
        before production can be resumed
PBM   Planned breakdown maintenance

Notes:
X   Time may be replaced by alternative variable eg. number of machine cycles.
Y   Decision should include consequential costs of failure.
Z   May be statutory requirement.

Figure 16.5   Maintenance policy decision chart

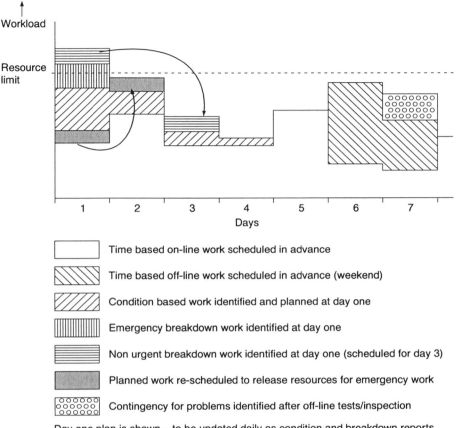

Time based on-line work scheduled in advance

Time based off-line work scheduled in advance (weekend)

Condition based work identified and planned at day one

Emergency breakdown work identified at day one

Non urgent breakdown work identified at day one (scheduled for day 3)

Planned work re-scheduled to release resources for emergency work

Contingency for problems identified after off-line tests/inspection

Day one plan is shown – to be updated daily as condition and breakdown reports are received. A series of integrated plans are required for each resource (people, tests, equipment). Note that resources available may be different at weekends.

Figure 16.6   Typical maintenance resource plan

It is usually beneficial to pre-plan as much maintenance activity as possible and to minimize unplanned work. In this way manpower and resource requirements are largely known in advance although unexpected failures leading to unplanned work can never be entirely eliminated.

The potential benefits of planned maintenance are outlined below.

- reduces maintenance costs in the long term,
- reduces equipment failures,
- significantly reduces disruption caused by failure,
- increases life of equipment,
- improves the performance of equipment,
- improves utilization of people,
- may meet legal requirements (for example, health and safety).

The inhibitors to the implementation of a planned maintenance scheme need to be recognized by management. They are largely concerned with the sometimes considerable effort and costs at start-up. These can include:

- creating an asset inventory by means of a plant survey,
- costs of designing, setting up and installing the system,
- costs of training and supervision,
- increased direct maintenance cost in the short-term, as the backlog of neglect is put right.

16.7 SUMMARY

Planned maintenance will reduce the frequency of failure and the risks of unexpected shutdown to plant. This chapter has outlined the objectives of maintenance, has considered the concepts of failure rate and reliability, and the provisions for maintenance strategy and maintenance planning.

REFERENCES

1. Lewis, E. E. (1987) *Introduction to Reliability Engineering*. Wiley & Sons, Chichester.
2. O'Connor, P. D. T. (1991) *Practical Reliability Engineering*. Third edition, Wiley & Sons, Chichester.
3. Andrew, J. D. and Moss, T. R. (1993) *Reliability and Risk Assessment*. Longman, Harlow.
4. U.S. Department of Defense (1982) MIL-HDBK-217, *Reliability Predictions of Electronic Equipment*. Issue D.
5. International Atomic Energy Agency (1988) TECDOC-478, *Component Reliability Data for Use in Probabilistic Safety Assessment*. Vienna.
6. American Institute of Chemical Engineers (1989) *Process Equipment Reliability Data*.

BIBLIOGRAPHY

Mowbray J. (1991) *Reliability Centred Maintenance*. Butterworth-Heinemann, Oxford.
Kelly, A. *Maintenance and its Management*. Conference Communication, Farnham, Surrey.

17

Project management

17.1 INTRODUCTION

The art of managing large projects preceded managing production processes by more than 4000 years. From the Great Pyramid (2450 BC) to the Languedoc canal (1681), from the Pont du Gard aqueduct (c. 15 BC) to the English railways of the 1840s men and machines and materials were brought together on a massive scale for a time and then disbanded. Yet 'project management' as a recognized intellectual discipline or, more correctly, methodology has only been around for a few decades. Does this mean that the term 'project management' is merely a new name for those past practices which combined common sense and experience? This chapter will show that the formal adoption of project management methods should provide engineering managers with the means to manage large and complex projects working to very tight schedules.

The aims of a project manager today are no different from those in previous centuries, namely to bring together for a finite period of time considerable resources in the form of manpower, machines and materials in order to complete the project on time, to specification and within budget. Today, however, the project manager can use a number of tools that will keep track of a multitude of different parallel tasks and that will allow better informed decisions to be made quickly and with confidence. Complex and concurrent engineering processes need clearly defined relationships between supplier/contractor and purchaser; the project manager must implement policies to this end. It is with these project management tools and a study of alternative relationships between purchaser and supplier that this chapter is concerned.

Although much of the material in this chapter is particularly applicable to the construction of (large) projects, the principles apply equally to manufacturing projects, installation of computer systems or even setting up, say, major one day events for sport or entertainment. Readers will find the concepts of *simultaneous (concurrent) engineering* and *fast track engineering*, previously discussed in Chapter 6, developed further in this chapter.

Project management is a powerful methodology, one with which all engineers should be familiar. By following the methodology, the young engineer should be in a strong position to take on responsibilities that might in earlier times have been assumed by his elders.

17.2   WHAT IS PROJECT MANAGEMENT?

A project is a specific finite task in which the means for its completion must be created for its duration. Each project will be unique. It will be dependent upon parent organizations for its resources, especially people. Each project, almost inevitably, will be subject to change which may mean a departure from plan, programme and from budget. Project management is the overall planning, implementation, control and coordination of the project from inception to completion to meet defined needs to the required standards within time and to budget.

17.2.1   Appointment of the project manager

Historically the term 'project manager' has been used rather loosely. In the USA the person in charge of any construction site, large or small, was usually referred to as the project manager. He was, in fact, the manager of the construction project, and many months of work had been completed by many parties long before he could take up the appointment. The tasks of the project manager concern:

- project definition
- planning
- decision-making structures
- monitoring and controlling.

These are considered in sections 17.2.2 to 17.2.5.

Project management means the management of the whole process, therefore, if continuity is desired, the appointment of the project manager should be for this same period of time. Where the project involves a joint venture, the project manager may be selected from one of the participating companies. Where the future owner of the project is a developer of industrial, commercial or infrastructure projects, the owner may appoint one of his own staff to be project manager. Where the project is a one-off development the future owner will probably hire a project manager specifically to manage that project. In this chapter the term project manager means *the owner's project manager* selected to manage the project on the owner's behalf. However, at the separate and lower levels of a project, the managers who are responsible for planning, implementing and controlling operations at their particular level will be carrying out a project management role too. For large- and medium-sized projects the project manager will be supported by a project management team. In this chapter the term 'project manager' means both the individual and the team.

In view of the considerable responsibility entrusted to the project manager, selection, training and authority are of great importance.[1] The *Latham Report* [2] recommends that the terms of appointment and duties should be clearly defined.

---

[1]See Chapter 3 *The Project Manager* in *Meredith J. R. & Mantel S. J. Project Management A Managerial Approach* [1] for a discussion on the selection of a project manager.

The project manager should be given the necessary authority to ensure the work is carried out satisfactorily through to completion without frequent reference to the owner. In Chapter 19 section 19.8 a form of contract (a cost reimbursement contract) is examined in which such provisions are essential. The *New Engineering Contract* described in Appendix 4 assumes that the project manager has the necessary authority.

17.2.2   Project definition

Morris and Hough [3] assert that a key element in the success of a project is project definition. A project must be properly defined and resources should not be fully committed to the project until the definition is shown to be workable. In this introduction to project management the underlying assumption is that the processes of feasibility studies, financial appraisal and risk assessment have been[2] satisfactorily completed. This is referred to as the proposal stage in some literature. Project definition is more than project specification; project definition contains the objectives of the project as well the physical characteristics and features of the project. For a building or a power scheme the task of project definition should be relatively straightforward and, therefore, pursued with vigour by the project manager. The sooner the project is fully defined the better; an imprecise definition leaves potential for change, and changes are a major cause of delays and extra costs in projects. For an all embracing computer system for a large multidisciplinary company, project definition will be realized in stages and in successive levels of detail; in this case the project manager will maintain continuous pressure on those whose responsibility it is to agree the specification.

17.2.3   Planning

Project planning is often confused with project management. Successful project management requires a well thought out plan, but that is merely the beginning. Project planning must be followed by project control. Project management software is largely planning and monitoring software. Project planning means:

- planning methods,
- choosing between 'in-house' services and external suppliers/contractors,
- deciding on cash flow (the cost plan or budget),
- deciding on the schedule of operations (the timing plan).

Project management software allows an iterative approach to developing the plan. From an initial draft plan, data on the sequence and duration of operations (activities), on resources and on costs are input into the computer. Analysis of the output leads to modification of the plan, for example, to improve resource management, until a satisfactory plan is obtained. This iterative approach is further illustrated in section 17.3.5.

---

[2]See *Chapter 2 Project Evaluation and Selection* in *Meredith & Mantel* for a useful introduction to this subject.

17.2.4   Decision making

The project manager must ensure that decisions are made on time and that they have no adverse effect upon the budget. To achieve this in engineering projects the project manager must establish structures for technical and managerial decision making. This means he must determine by whom and at what level different kinds of technical decisions have to be made and by whom and at what level decisions on expenditure, placing orders, entering into contracts, programming and time limits have to be made.

17.2.5   Monitoring and controlling

As the work proceeds it must be measured against the plan. A computerized plan will permit computerized monitoring, providing extensive data on physical progress, resource use and costs. This is, of course, conditional upon the input of these data. A significant feature of modern project management is the amount of paper work and/or direct data input, often on a weekly basis that must be provided. This is the price for faster projects and more effective control; if these goals are not realized a lot of time and money is being wasted. Monitoring, therefore, needs the wise application of input and careful control over the nature and extent of output and its appropriate distribution to different levels of responsibility. Computerized monitoring should provide the project manager with a measure for any departure from the plan and he will be able to examine the potential effects of any remedial measures such as the reallocation of resources or alternative sequencing before they are implemented.

17.3   PROJECT PLANNING

17.3.1   Method statement

First, of course, the methods of working have to be decided. This is often referred to as a *method statement*. Usually the methods to be used for most of the project will be well known and well tried. The method statement will be based on experience and the technical resources available. Only occasionally will there be alternatives of such a profound difference that the implications for the success or otherwise of the project need rigorous investigation by the project manager. It is not intended in this chapter to pursue this. However, Morris and Hough [3] observed that an important contributor to failure in major projects in the past has been the placing of undue reliance on new technology, on a large scale, when its use and development until then had been on a small scale. The development of Concorde and of the advanced gas cooled reactors in the UK exemplify this. This does not rule out the use of new technologies on a large scale for major projects, but it does suggest that very generous contingency provisions should be allowed for in any plan relying on new technological development.

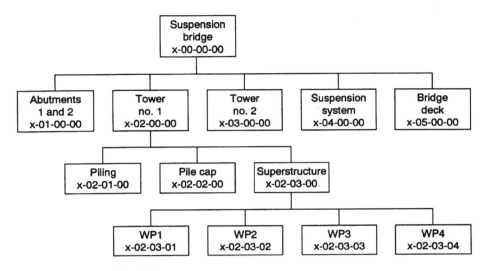

Figure 17.1   Work breakdown structure

17.3.2   Work breakdown structure

The key to the project plan is a *work breakdown structure*. The planner must be able to provide clearly and accurately a statement of the scope of the work. A work breakdown structure (WBS) provides a rational subdivision of the work in hierarchical form down to the lowest level of discrete work packages from which estimates of resource requirements, durations, linkages and costs can be determined.

A WBS can provide the basis for a coding system by which any work package (activity) or any sub-group of activities can be identified. From the WBS a list of activities and precursor activities can be produced for the purposes of network analysis, from which programmes, resource charts and cost plans all flow. Network analysis is dealt with in Chapter 18.

Figure 17.1 shows a WBS for the construction of a suspension bridge. The principle is that all the work at a lower level is contained within the scope of work at the higher level from which it branches. In the USA charts of this form are sometimes referred to as 'gozinto' charts because each lower element 'goes into' the element above it. Thus the scope of work of x-02-00-00 includes each of x-02-01-00, x-02-02-00, and x-02-03-00. An objective of a WBS is clarity, this suggests a maximum subdivision into four or five elements and as many levels. A WBS in which each element at one level was subdivided into four elements at the next level down would result in 256 work packages if there were five levels to the structure!

17.3.3   Cost plan

A WBS provides a useful means of estimating the cost of a project. Estimates of costs are entered at the lowest level and 'rolled up' to successive levels. Once work is in progress the actual costs are entered at the lowest levels and rolled up to the

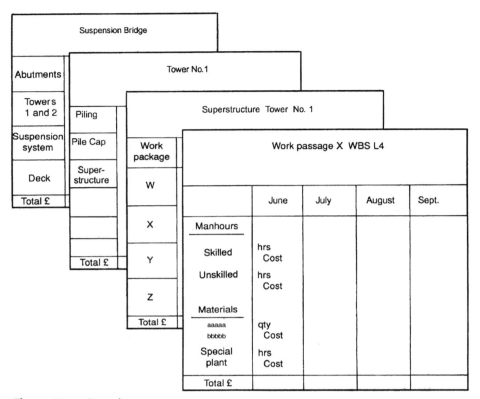

Figure 17.2   Cost plan

higher levels. In presentational terms this works very well. Figure 17.2 shows a typical hierarchy of cost estimates by which a cost plan is obtained or by which actual costs can be measured.

17.3.4   Networks and bar charts

From the WBS a 'milestone' schedule will be produced identifying the several major milestones which must be achieved on the way to completion. With the aid of this schedule and from the WBS, individual activities and sub-activities (work packages) are obtained. From an examination of the relationships between individual activities the whole complex network of relationships between activities can be obtained. (This is developed in Chapter 18, section 18.2 and in Appendix 3 Case Study: Developing a Network.) The planners must then estimate the durations of the individual activities. This can be done either by examining the external time constraints, deciding how long an activity should take and applying the resources to meet that duration, or by examining the resources that are available or would be practicable for that activity and estimating how long it

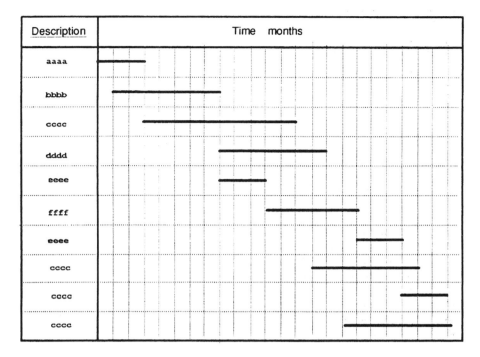

Figure 17.3   Long-term programme

would take to complete. In each case the planners have the problem of estimating the productivity of the resources in the given conditions. Since each project is unique and the problems likely to be encountered will differ from those of previous projects this is where the art (rather than the science) of project planning comes to the fore. Once the durations and linkages of all activities have been estimated a network can be drawn from which a bar chart (or Gantt chart) can be obtained. A bar chart is by far the clearest means of representing a programme of work. Bar charts, too, can be developed for different levels of management showing successive levels of detail, based on the WBS. Figure 17.3 illustrates a long-term programme.

17.3.5   Resource charts and curves

From the bar chart, resource charts can be obtained. For each activity the planners identify the resources needed; for example, manpower per day, cranes per day, quantities of materials. Manpower and cranes are non-consumable resources; that is, using a crane for one day does not prevent its use on the next. Materials are consumable resources. By aggregating resource requirements across all activities shown on the bar chart on each day of the project a daily resource chart for each resource can be obtained. Figure 17.4 illustrates how a resource chart is derived from a bar chart.

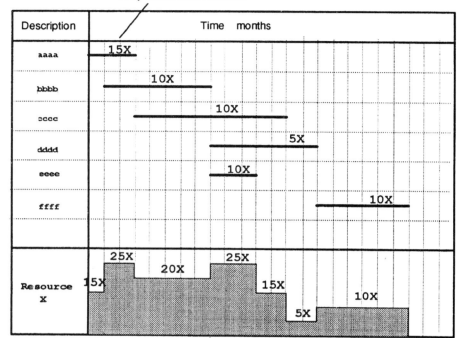

Figure 17.4 Resource chart derived from a bar chart

Resource levelling or resource smoothing is often used to eliminate undesirable peaks in demand for certain resources. If, for example, the daily requirement for welders throughout the project lay between 4 and 6, but for one week the demand rose to 15 because of the concurrence of a number of activities, then the sensible approach would be to reschedule the activities to remove that peak. If any of these activities were not on the *critical path* then rescheduling might have no effect upon the overall duration of the project. The critical path is the sequence of interdependent tasks whose total duration determines the overall length of the project. (See Chapter 18 for a full account of networks and critical path analysis.) If the number of welders could not be reduced sufficiently without rescheduling critical path activities, thus making the project longer, the planner would need to weigh up the comparative disadvantages of bringing in nine extra skilled personnel for one week against the project finishing marginally later. Project planning software usually provides a facility for resource smoothing or resource optimization, which allows the project manager to observe the effect and come to a decision. The ideal resource chart for labour is one in which the labour demand rises to a plateau at which it remains for most of the project, dropping rapidly at the end. This affords a rational recruitment programme followed much later by properly planned reduction. A labour demand chart with peaks then troughs then further peaks and so on, would be highly undesirable, leading to industrial relations problems (as lay-offs were followed by recruitment followed by more lay-offs) or the retention of unnecessary labour, or relocation of some of the workforce for short periods of time, causing much inconvenience. Projects have succeeded in which such fluctuations in labour demand have been experienced but usually only where most of the labour is sub-contracted. Labour-only sub-contractors, serving a range of projects, are better able to move their labour force between projects to suit these fluctuations. For other resources such as plant and equipment it may be possible to hire-in the extra resource for short periods (although short-term hire may be more expensive).

In short, resource charts are of particular value to the project manager in respect of labour, facilitating resource smoothing. A fluctuating demand for materials and/or equipment is of less concern but can be indicative of poor planning, therefore, where such fluctuations arise, a careful examination of the programme should be made.

Since each resource represents a cost, the summation of the costs of all the resources being utilized on a daily basis will provide the project manager with a daily or weekly expenditure curve as shown in Figure 17.5. The shape of the curve is typical of large projects. The low level of expenditure at the end would represent the period of making good, testing and commissioning. Cumulative resource and cost curves may also be obtained, see Figures 17.6 and 17.7.

Generally, cumulative curves are only of value for consumable resources, such as concrete for a construction site, and for controlling costs. The so-called S-curve in Figure 17.7 is typical for large projects. This S-curve is used to analyse progress (in terms of costs and time) as will be seen later in this chapter. An S-curve will also be used by a contractor/supplier to determine the level of borrowing during a project and the anticipated profit at the end. This is illustrated in Figure 17.8.

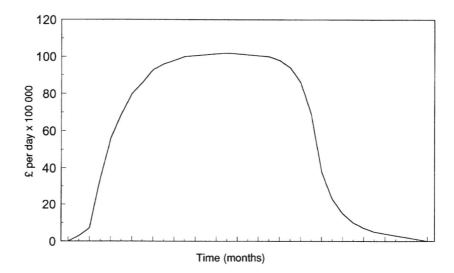

Figure 17.5 A monthly expenditure curve

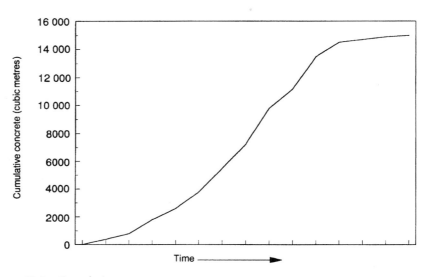

Figure 17.6   Cumulative resources curve

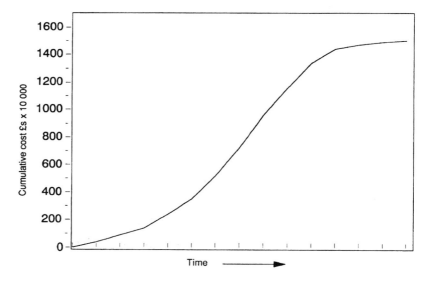

Figure 17.7   The 'S' curve

17.3.6   Summary of project planning

A work breakdown structure (WBS) provides a logical subdivision of the work from which programmes, resource charts and cost plans can be developed and presented at appropriate levels of operation. A primary function of a WBS is to identify the work packages; from the durations, resources and costs of each work

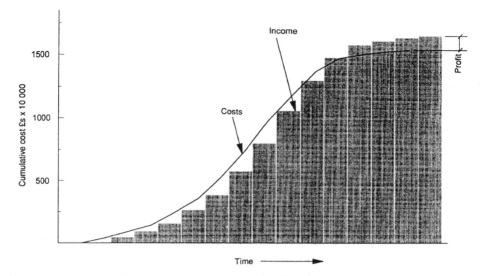

Figure 17.8   Level of borrowing during a project and anticipated profit

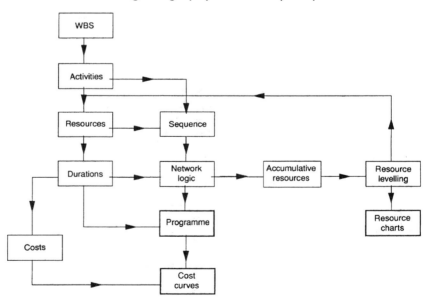

Figure 17.9   Project planning processes

package the programme, resource charts and cost curves for the whole project will be developed. This process is illustrated in Figure 17.9.

17.4   PROJECT MONITORING AND CONTROL

The project manager must:

- measure performance
- control change
- minimize delays
- minimize extra costs
- control and coordinate suppliers/contractors.

The first four of these will be examined in turn; control and coordination of suppliers and contractors will form the final part of this chapter.

17.4.1 Measuring performance

Performance on large projects will be measured at regular intervals; the period chosen is frequently that of a calendar month. *Monthly meetings* attended by the project manager and representatives of the current suppliers/contractors allow coordination problems to be resolved and can be a very effective means of putting pressure on any whose performance in the recent past has been unsatisfactory. Monthly meetings can be the single most effective driving force in a project and their value should not be underrated. A young engineer, responsible for part of a project, attending such a meeting, would be expected to have up-to-date information on progress and costs, be able to explain why there had been any departure from the plan, and be able to predict performance during the coming month(s), making recommendations for remedial measures where necessary.

Performance needs to be measured in terms of time and cost. This is commonly done by monitoring performance against a bar chart and a cumulative cost curve.

Earned value analysis provides a measure of performance in which time and cost form an integral whole. The method also requires that, at each measurement date, forecasts for the expected date of completion and the expected cost at completion be made. The project manager is not merely provided with a rear view mirror to drive by, but a view along the road ahead as well.

In Figure 17.10 the budgeted cost curve (baseline), the actual cumulative costs and the *earned value* of the completed work is recorded. This earned value is the budgeted cost of the work performed (BCWP) to date. From Figure 17.10, measures of the spend-variance and the schedule variance can be read. The spend-variance shows the difference between what should have been spent on that amount of work and what was actually spent. The schedule-variance gives a measure of how far ahead of schedule the project is both in terms of time and in terms of programmed spending. The implications are that for this project getting ahead of schedule has been achieved at a price, the spend-variance.

The following performance ratios are used in earned value analysis.

$$\text{cost performance index} = \frac{\text{ACWP}}{\text{BCWP}} \times 100$$

$$\text{cost variance} = \frac{(\text{ACWP} - \text{BCWP})}{\text{BCWP}} \times 100$$

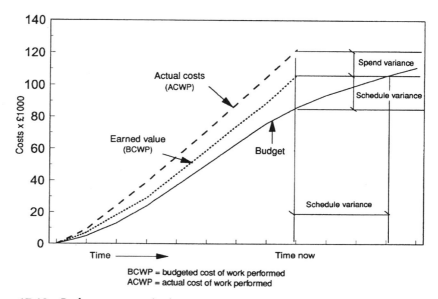

Figure 17.10   Performance monitoring curves

$$\text{schedule variance} = \frac{(\text{BCWP} - \text{BCWS})}{\text{BCWS}} \times 100$$

$$\text{schedule performance index} = \frac{\text{BCWP}}{\text{BCWS}} \times 100$$

$$\text{cash flow variance} = \frac{(\text{ACWP} - \text{BCWS})}{\text{BCWS}} \times 100$$

where   ACWP   is actual cost of work performed
        BCWP   is budgeted cost of work performed
        BCWS   is budgeted cost of work scheduled

The *cost performance index* tells the project manager by how much project costs are above or below budget.

The *cost variance* provides useful information to the estimators. If the cost variance is within 2 or 3% they have done a good job and they can use the same data for estimating costs of new projects. If the cost variance is of the order of 10% or 15% then the estimators will need to re-examine their cost data and decide whether the problem lies with productivity on the current project alone or whether the data need to be revised for future projects.

The *schedule variance* provides similar feedback to the estimators on rates of progress, allowing them to confirm or modify their current data on rates of progress for similar kinds of operation.

The *schedule performance* index tells the project manager by how much the project, in general, is ahead or behind schedule.

The *cash flow variance* tells the project manager how far cash flows have strayed from programme. This is most important as it may mean that the project owner (purchaser) will have to go to his lenders and reschedule the financing of the whole project.

These performance indices need to be used in conjunction with one another; each one taken in isolation is of very limited value. The indices may be used at several levels of a WBS by the managers responsible at a given level. Work package managers should be required at each date of measurement to give two additional pieces of information for that package:

- the estimated cost to completion
- the estimated time to completion.

From this the estimated cost to completion of the whole project can be 'rolled up' through the work breakdown structure, and revised completion date(s) of the project and/or of its several elements can be estimated.

$$\text{estimated cost at completion (EAC)} = \text{ACWP} + \Sigma(\text{ECW})$$

$$\text{where ECW} = \text{estimated cost to completion for each work package}$$

The project manager can provide a further measure of progress toward completion of the project from the equation

$$\frac{\text{ACWP}}{\text{EAC}} \times 100 = \% \text{ complete}$$

Example 17(1)

Sixteen months into a two year £24 m project

$$
\begin{aligned}
\text{actual cost of work performed (ACWP)} &= £17.8\,\text{m} \\
\text{budgeted cost of work performed (BCWP)} &= £18.3\,\text{m} \\
\text{budgeted cost of work scheduled (BCWS)} &= £19.2\,\text{m} \\
\text{estimated cost to completion } \Sigma(\text{ECW}) &= £7.2\text{m}
\end{aligned}
$$

What is the predicted position for completion?

Solution

First the EAC

$$EAC = 17.8 + 7.2 = £25.0 \, m$$

(the project is forecast to overrun by £1.0m), then progress,

$$\text{schedule performance index} = \frac{18.3}{19.2} \times 100 = 95.3\%$$

this shows that progress is unsatisfactory; that the project is behind schedule by 4.7% of 16 months, that is approximately two-thirds of a month behind schedule.

The percentage complete can also be found:

$$\% \text{ complete} = \frac{17.8}{25} \times 100 = 71.2$$

at this stage the project should be

$$\frac{19.2}{24} \times 100 = 80\% \text{ complete}$$

which indicates that progress is far less satisfactory than the schedule performance index would suggest.

The cost performance index appears satisfactory

$$\text{cost performance index} = \frac{17.8}{18.3} \times 100 = 97.3\%$$

but in view of the estimated cost to completion it appears that an underspend to date may be the cause of extra costs for the remainder of the project. The project manager will need to seek further information on the reasons for the revised estimates and, at the same time determine whether progress can be accelerated to bring the project back on schedule.

17.4.2   Controlling change

Probably the greatest single cause of delay and extra expense in most projects is change. Construction contracts very often contain provisions for change. Conditions of contract provide for variations in the scope of work and set out, usually by reference to bills of quantities (see section 17.7.2), the methods by which the extra costs can be valued and charged. Long experience in construction has taught its practitioners that on most projects problems arise which can only be overcome by changes in design and/or construction methods. The unpredictability of ground conditions is one very good reason for this. Since many construction contracts may last for several years it is possible that the owner's/purchaser's needs might change. Unfortunately, a system that facilitates change can have the effect of encouraging change. Many small changes may be authorized by the owner or project manager, the accumulative effect of which is to disturb the regular progress of the work and cause considerable delay and expense. Therefore, the project manager for a large project must establish firm change control procedures. This can be achieved by:

- using *change request forms*
- establishing a *change control board.*

Numbered change request forms, suitably coded to match the WBS, should identify who initiated the request, the nature of the change sought, the reason for the change, an estimate of the cost of the change and any revisions in programme. If, for example, a work package manager made the request, then one would expect him to provide the actual cost of work performed, the budgeted costs of work performed and scheduled and the estimated time and cost to complete the work package. The project manager would define the levels of authority in terms of scope of work and costs. The change control board, which would meet regularly, would monitor all minor changes (having defined the limits of minor change) and would be the sole authority for major changes.

17.4.3 Minimizing delay

The project manager should anticipate the several possible causes of delay and have policies in place to mitigate the effects such delays would have on the overall programme. A major cause of delay is change. Other causes are the late supply of technical information, late deliveries of material and equipment and under-estimation of the time needed for some activities. Rigorous programme controls on the design process should resolve the first, close liaison with suppliers (see Chapter 21) should address the second, and better feedback from projects to estimators and planners might prevent the third. Re-examination of the project network and a re-allocation of resources might be required where a serious underestimation of the time needed has occurred.

The studies of Morris and Hough [3] have shown that 'external forces' have seriously delayed major projects and that, too often, these external forces could have been anticipated, and a contingency strategy put in place. These external forces have, typically, been political, environmental or social influences, the seeds of which were sown during the inception stages of the project. One of the most laudable features of the Thames Barrier Project in London was the extensive consultation with formal and informal bodies to obtain a consensus agreement that would meet the commercial, political, social and environmental needs of a widespread community. At Hartlepool nuclear power station in the early 1970s the Inspectorate of Nuclear Installations required that the reactors be provided with tertiary shutdown facilities at a time when construction work on the reactors was already underway. The direct delays to the programme were of the order of 18 months; the indirect effects of such delays are often incalculable. The decision to introduce a tertiary shutdown facility could not have been totally unexpected; the Inspectorate worked closely with the nuclear power generators; project management strategies could have been prepared which would have mitigated the effects of these changes.

An alternative or complementary approach is to provide incentives for early completion. Bonus payments can be helpful as long as there are strict controls to ensure that the contractor/supplier does not sacrifice quality (or operate unsafely) in order to save time. In the public sector a system of 'lane rental' is used by the Department of Transport in the UK. The principle is that a contractor appointed to carry out repair work or modifications on an existing highway is charged a weekly fee for the 'rental' of the traffic lanes that are out of use. The shorter the duration of the work the more money is saved on the contract cost; in effect a bonus for early completion.

17.4.4 Controlling extra costs

A project may cost more because of additional work, or lower productivity than planned, or inflation. The issue of additional work has already been discussed in the preceding section, low productivity in one area may sometimes be counterbalanced by higher productivity elsewhere. If low productivity is experienced on a major expensive activity, costs inevitably will rise. A change in the budget by reducing later expenditure might help. The estimators, certainly, ought to be advised (see section 17.4.1). A gradual improvement in productivity through learning by experience might mitigate the effects. This is where employing a widely experienced team of engineers is so important.

Experience is important too in those projects where the physical constructs of several engineering disciplines meet to form an integral whole. A design may lack 'buildability'. A lack of buildability is usually a consequence of the designers and detailers having insufficient experience in installation/construction. There is much virtue in employing at the design stages engineers who are experienced in the installation or construction of the work in hand. There is even greater virtue in employing engineers from the companies that are going to install or construct this part of the project. These engineers should be employed both to advise on planning the work (the method statement) and to give advice on 'buildability'. At the design stage the cost of redesign is minimal compared to the costs of delays consequent upon a redesign once the work is underway. At the interface between engineering disciplines there is an even greater risk of such problems. These problems can be avoided if either all drawings are submitted to a working group whose task is to examine, comment upon and approve details at the interface, or computer-aided design (CAD) software with a 'walk through' facility is used, or where 'mock-ups' or prototypes are assembled.

Manufacturers too, (for example the motor industry and the aircraft industry) have experienced similar problems of 'buildability' and incompatibility at the engineering interface. As explained in Chapter 6, the solution has been *simultaneous (concurrent) engineering* in which the designers and suppliers are brought closer (physically and in terms of time and task) to the point of assembly.

The most commonly proffered reason for cost overruns is inflation. Projects of the 1970s and 1980s show costs spiralling uncontrollably upwards. In inflationary times can the project manager exercise any control over rising costs? Does it even matter, since, presumably, the completed facility will reap benefits at inflated prices anyway? The major difficulty is one of confidence. The purchaser will be borrowing from the banks or using up cash reserves at an alarming rate. The banks may lose confidence in the project and threaten to withhold funding. The original estimates (January 1986) for the cost of the Channel Tunnel between Dover and Calais came to a grand total of £5.4 billion including £0.9 billion for inflation and £1 billion for contingencies. In February 1990, by which time the estimated cost to completion had risen to almost £7.5 billion, the group of some 200 bankers funding this project almost withdrew their support from Eurotunnel (the owners and operators) halfway through the project. Thereafter, the performance of the project managers for Eurotunnel was monitored as closely by the bankers as they, the project managers monitored the project. This does not make life easy for the project managers! (The final cost was close to £10 billion.)

Usually the effects of inflation are not uniform. A government's measure of inflation (the Retail Price Index in the UK), in which certain consumer prices are measured and weighted into a formula, is unlikely to reflect the effects of inflation on a project. Wage inflation is usually greater than consumer price inflation, and materials may experience completely different rates of inflation, as in the 1970s when the prices of oil and its derivatives increased five fold in a few months. What strategies should the project manager have in place to counter the effects of inflation? One solution is to enter into fixed price contracts with suppliers and contractors, such that no increased payments will be made where the suppliers' cost increases are a consequence of inflation. This hard-nosed approach places all the risk on the supplier who should, according to this philosophy, be able to control his own costs. Unfortunately, this is seldom the case, particularly in inflationary times when employers will be equally unable to keep wage levels and the prices paid to their suppliers down. Fixed price contracts should only be used for short periods of time, not exceeding two years even when inflation is low. Effective cost control on, say, a four year contract can be exercised by releasing a succession of short fixed price contracts none of which is likely to be put at serious risk by inflation. As tenders are received for each new contract the growing costs can be reviewed, the budget revised and estimates of future income examined in a rational manner; the process will be under control.

The alternative, where short contracts are inappropriate, is to use price fluctuation clauses within the contract by which the sums payable to the supplier/ contractor are adjusted according to a previously agreed formula when the supplier's costs rise or fall. Since most industries monitor the rates of inflation within that industry, the development of a suitable formula or the direct use of an industry formula is a relatively simple matter. This method is reasonably fair to the supplier and means that at the time of tendering he does not have to try to guess the future rates of inflation and build them into his price.

In summary, cost control policies should make provision for:

- minimizing change
- realistic and carefully reviewed estimates of productivity
- reviews of buildability
- interface management
- short-term fixed price contracts
- price fluctuation clause agreements for long-term contracts.

17.5 CONTROLLING AND COORDINATING SUPPLIERS, CONTRACTORS AND SUBCONTRACTORS

Sections 17.5 to 17.9 will consider the management of the relationships between the project owner and his suppliers. (See also Chapter 19 for further examination of types of contract.)

Depending upon the size and nature of the project the following questions may have to be considered.

(1) To what extent should the work be done 'in-house' by the project owner's workforce or by external consultants, suppliers, etc.?
(2) Should design and manufacture/construction be separate activities?
(3) How should suppliers be paid? By fixed price contracts or contracts with price fluctuation clauses (variable price contracts)? By lump sum contracts, measurement contracts, or cost reimbursement contracts?
(4) How should suppliers be selected? By selective or open tendering? By lowest tender? By negotiation? By 'partnering'?

The answers to these questions will influence the procurement strategy adopted by the project manager. Some of the issues are discussed in sections 17.5.1 to 17.5.3.

17.5.1 How should the work be distributed?

Usually the answer to question 1 above should be 'no'. The project owner's business will not normally be that of project management and execution, therefore it is unlikely that he will have the skills to carry out the work. Specialists who have developed their expertise within one field should be in a better position than the project owner to produce the work to specification, on time and at a competitive rate. Even if the project owner has the skills, carrying out the project would mean a substantial reduction in normal business activity which, from the long-term point of view of maintaining and developing one's market might be unwise.

Whether the work should be shared between 'in-house' and external providers will depend upon the skills and availability 'in-house' and, even where these are available, it would be sensible to obtain competitive quotations for the work, as outside businesses may have the competitive edge in the tasks to be done. In the UK, local authorities are required by law to seek competitive tenders from contractors for work for which the local authority has both the resources and the skills. In large companies the decision on how much of the project should be carried out by the project owner must depend upon the intended project management structure, how dependent this structure will be upon the parent organization, and how much dependence can be placed upon the functional departments whose main objectives will be to meet the business needs of the company and not the needs of the project.

17.5.2 Subcontracting

The most common reason for appointing a subcontractor is that the subcontractor has specialist skills not available to the main contractors and suppliers. Generally, contractors should be free to subcontract parts of their work to others if they wish. The project manager can always, by a term in the contract, reserve to himself the right to approve/refuse the contractor's choice of subcontractor. It is not uncommon in the UK to adopt a system of nomination, by which the project manager requires a main contractor to enter into a subcontract with a given supplier or specialist; this can be particularly valuable where the specialist provides a full service from design through manufacture to installation and completion. In law (see Chapter 19 section 19.4.1) the principle of privity of contract applies by which the project owner cannot sue a subcontractor for unsatisfactory performance; it is the contractor who is responsible to the project owner for the work carried out by his subcontractors. Therefore, it is most important that the contract between the project owner and the contractor clearly defines the contractor's obligations and does not release him from any responsibility should the subcontractor default. Because of the principle of privity of contract, nomination has led to some legal/contractual difficulties, especially in the UK construction industry, where it is widely used.

17.5.3 Separation of design and manufacture/construction

Construction projects can provide useful illustrations of project management. Figure 17.11 illustrates how construction projects typically are managed. The project has two phases: the design phase and the construction phase.

The engineer is responsible for design, the contractor for construction. During construction the engineer, on behalf of the promoter (project owner), supervises the contractor's work. The role of the engineer as project manager is not as clear as it might be.

In most construction work the contractor is selected by competitive tender, the successful tenderer being the lowest bidder able to meet all the requirements of time and specification.

If all the design work precedes all the construction work, the project must take longer than if some of the work can be done concurrently. If the contractor has no involvement until all the design is complete there is no check on buildability or project 'interfaces'. If the contractor has no input at the design stage then the overall plan of the work is dictated by decisions made by the engineer; for the nature of the design may determine the project plan. The contractor is usually

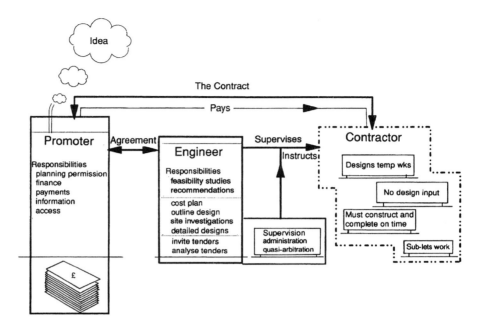

Figure 17.11   Construction project procedures

only given six weeks in which to prepare a tender; in this time he must provide an outline plan of the work and price it. Surely, the planning of a large project of several years duration warrants more attention to planning than this? Shouldn't the planning of the design and of the construction be an integral activity?

What has been demonstrated here is that, in construction and, indeed, for many large projects, 'over the walls' engineering is the norm, when greater consideration might be given to simultaneous engineering. Figure 17.12 provides a graphic

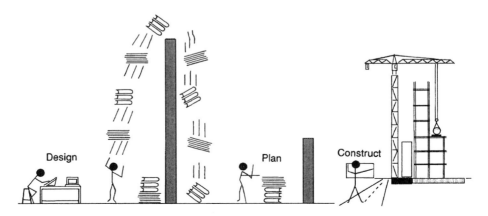

Figure 17.12   Over the wall engineering

illustration of 'over the walls' engineering; section 17.6 will consider some of the alternatives.

17.6   APPROACHES TO SIMULTANEOUS ENGINEERING IN CONSTRUCTION PROJECTS

Alternative methods of project management in the construction industry have become quite widespread in recent years. They have been used largely to overcome the very frequent problem of projects taking far longer than originally estimated with no apparent redress for the owner. The most important of these alternative methods are considered below.

17.6.1   Design-and-construct contracts

In the construction industry, *design-and-construct contracts* have been developed and quite widely used in the UK. Under a design-and-construct contract the contractor carries out the design as well as the construction. This has several advantages:

- the design, almost by definition, will be 'buildable',
- design and construction planning form an integral process,
- construction work can commence long before the design is complete (early start means an early finish).

There are, of course, disadvantages:

- How does the project owner obtain strictly comparable competitive bids?
- Who pays for the expensive tendering process in which contractors have to develop outline designs and price them, knowing that their design may be rejected on grounds of client need, if not on cost?
- Contractors do not employ a wide range of design expertise, therefore this approach only works well where designs are standard, unimaginative and straightforward.
- There is no independent supervision of the contractor's construction work by the engineer/architect.

Design-and-construct contracts have been widely and successfully used in the chemical and oil industries, in the provision of 'turnkey' contracts for power stations, waste water treatment plants, etc. (A turnkey contract is one in which the contractor undertakes full responsibility for the design, procurement, construction, installation, testing and commission of the project.) These are especially successful where the contractor appointed has considerable experience in the field.

Two other methods of project management have been widely used in the building industry in the UK in the last 15 years: *management contracting* (MC) and *contract (or construction) management* (CM). Each has the same objectives, to bring the design process into parallel with the construction process (*simultaneous engineering*), and to shorten the project duration (*fast tracking*).

17.6.2   Management contracting (MC)

In management contracting the promoter (project owner) appoints a firm of contractors to carry out the project management for the construction of the project. The management contractor (MCr) manages the project, does no physical construction work, and usually carries out the supervision normally done by the engineer/architect's representative. A fee plus direct costs is paid for this service. Once authorized by the promoter, the MCr appoints subcontractors progressively for discrete work packages; earthworks, foundations, superstructure, cladding, air-conditioning, lifts, ceilings, etc. The design work, carried out by consulting engineers, architects, subcontractors and suppliers, is also produced in work packages allowing a scheduled release of information to meet the construction programme; there is a phased tendering programme and a progressive appointment of subcontractors. A strong discipline must be exercised over the design process; designers will be put under pressure to meet contractors' deadlines. Where fast tracking is intended, the design process is followed very closely by the supply/manufacture, installation and construction processes. By this means the owner will earn revenue from the facility much sooner. There are risks, however. Any necessary design changes may result in expensive modification of components or even their rejection. Last minute problems may result in expensive delays while incompatibilities at the engineering interfaces are resolved, and genuine mistakes may be made by personnel under pressure.

The total fee payable to the MCr will be between 5% and 10% of the cost of the project. This is a large extra cost and is unlikely to be worthwhile unless completion to time and to budget are critical and the MCr improves considerably the likelihood of completing the project to time and budget. The promoter pays the MCr for all the subcontractors' work, the MCr then pays the subcontractors. This cash flow provides the MCr with useful opportunities for short-term money investments. The proclaimed advantages of MC include:

- completion on time and to budget,
- permits an early start, hence an early finish,
- promoter and contractor do not have an adversarial relationship,
- buildability (the MCr reviews all designs for buildability),
- planning and design decisions can be integrated,
- individual subcontracts are relatively short, so can be fixed price.

Observed disadvantages have been:

- the MCr minimizes contractual risk so that when a subcontractor's performance is unsatisfactory the promoter finds that there is no redress from the MCr and can bring no action against the subcontractor/supplier;
- the price for the whole project is not known until all of the many subcontracts have been let.

17.6.3   Contract/construction management

In contract/construction management the procedures are similar to those of MC. The most important difference is that the contract/construction manager (CMr) does not enter into contracts with the various contractors. The promoter enters into contracts with each contractor whose work is controlled and supervised by the CMr. The CMr only receives a fee plus direct costs. The CMr can be appointed well before any site work begins, to manage the design and planning process. A proclaimed advantage of CM is that all contractors feel part of a team rather than being at the lower level of a project hierarchy. The great advantage that this approach has over MC is that if a contractor's performance is unsatisfactory the promoter can use the contract terms to protect his interests. The risks in fast tracking are the same as those for MC.

CM and MC are, therefore, alternative forms of project management. It is quite possible for a promoter to adopt CM on one contract and MC on another. At No. 1 Canada Square (the tallest building in the UK) in the Canary Wharf development in London, the developers Olympia and York started the tower block under a management contract, but approximately halfway through the contract changed to contract management using the developer's own team of project managers for the contract management. This was not so much a reflection of the developers' view of management contracting as a commentary upon their relationship with their management contractor. The successful transition from MC to CM halfway through the project was a direct consequence of the similarity between the two approaches to project management.

17.7   HOW SHOULD CONTRACTORS/SUPPLIERS BE PAID?

Contractors will usually base their tenders for work either on labour costs per hour (or day or week) plus materials, or all-in costs per unit quantity of the work performed.

17.7.1   Lump sum contracts

A tender for engineering design services usually includes a sum to cover the estimated number of hours to carry out the work, applying different rates for the time spent by engineers, by technicians, and so on. Sums to cover overhead and profit are added. Contracts of this nature are usually *lump sum* contracts in which 'lump sums' are paid according to a schedule as specified work packages are completed. The risk lies with the tenderer who has to estimate how much resources (and time in this case) are needed to meet the objectives.

In large projects different parts of the work may be paid for in different ways. The design, manufacture, installation, commissioning and testing of large mechanical or electrical plant is usually carried out on a lump sum basis, whilst the building and/or structure to house or support the plant could be carried out

Item no.	Description	Unit	Quantity	Rate £/unit	Amount £
	EXCAVATION				
E323	Excavation for foundations 0.5 - 1m max depth	cu. m	450	6.50	2925.00
E532	Disposal of excavated material	cu. m	450	1.50	675.00
	IN SITU CONCRETE				
	Reinforced concrete				
F623	To bases 300 – 500 mm thick	cu. m	100	65.00	6500.00
F642	To walls 150 – 300 mm thick	cu. m	60	75.00	4500.00
	PRECAST CONCRETE				
	Beams				
H136.1	Prestressed post-tensioned 7 – 10 m long Type A1 for central span	nr.	4	5000.00	20 000.00
H136.2	Prestressed post-tensioned 7 – 10 m long Type A2 for north span	nr.	4	7000.00	28 000.00
H136.3	Prestressed post-tensioned 7 – 10 m long Type A3 for south span	nr.	4	8000.00	32 000.00
			page total		

Figure 17.13 Extract from a bill of quantities

using a measurement contract. (See Chapter 19 for analyses of a lump sum contract, a measurement contract and a cost reimbursement contract.)

17.7.2   Measurement contracts

In *measurement contracts*, bills of quantities are drawn up which identify a large range of work items and state the amount of work to be done in terms of a quantity, for example, cubic metres of excavation, or metre lengths of pipe. The contractor enters a rate per unit quantity for each work item (see Figure 17.13 for a typical extract from a bill of quantities). For each item the contractor must include for labour, plant and material costs, as well as for overhead and profit. This might seem difficult at first glance, but the construction industry has traditionally operated in this way and, therefore, has a sophisticated and up-to-date record of costs and prices in this form. As the work proceeds, the contractor is paid, usually on a monthly basis, for the quantities of work carried out. In construction work the final quantities often differ from the original estimated quantities, so the contractor is paid for the work done rather than the work originally estimated.

Measurement contracts are best suited to work in which there is a tradition of measurement, where changes in quantities are anticipated as the work proceeds and the physical characteristics and dimensions of the work are designed in some detail prior to the working being carried out. Lump sum contracts are best suited for work in which the performance of the finished project is all important but where every single detailed dimension is of less consequence. In the USA the use of lump sum contracts for construction work is not uncommon. When so used, there is much less opportunity for change as the work proceeds; the contractor has tendered to the specification and drawings provided, and even small changes will be seen as changes in scope, and new prices will have to be renegotiated or the work paid for at rates which will favour the contractor. This certainly exercises a formidable prejudice against change! The Sears Tower building in Chicago, at that time (1970s) the tallest as well as one of the largest buildings in the world was constructed using, in the main, lump sum contracts. At No. 1 Canada Square, referred to above, most of the separate contracts were let as lump sum contracts.

Both lump sum and measurement contracts require much of the design work to be complete before a contractor can tender for the work. There is one form of contract in which the proportion of design work completed when construction begins can be very small, this is a *cost reimbursement* contract.

17.7.3   Cost reimbursement contracts

A cost reimbursement contract is one in which the contractor is paid his direct costs plus an additional sum for overheads and for profit. As the work proceeds the contractor must provide evidence of his direct costs by invoices for materials and components, records of wages paid, records of plant and equipment hired. Thus, a contractor can be instructed to attend at a given location with certain items of plant and a small labour force, and be put to work immediately. Even if the drawings are insufficient, even if operations are delayed as a result, the contractor will be paid by the hour for plant, labour and materials. The risk lies entirely with the project owner. Why, therefore, should a project owner wish to use this form of contract?

It is ideal for a project in which the nature of the work is far from clear at the start and only gradually becomes clear as the work proceeds. It is especially suitable for projects in which there is a considerable element of risk, in which, until the work is in progress the actual techniques have not been established. An example of this would be the welding of 75 mm thick high strength steel for the lining of a reactor, where very high standards of welding are specified. Until non-destructive tests (and destructive tests) of sample welds and actual welds on the lining have been conducted for a variety of welding techniques the approved procedures cannot be established, therefore neither lump sum nor measurement pricing would be appropriate.

Project owners will only use cost reimbursement contracts where they have to. Where they are used it is most important that the contractor's operations are firmly supervised. The project manager will want assurances that the resources (the manpower and machinery) are being used effectively and efficiently all the time and that all the materials purchased are actually being used on the project! The project managers will take a much closer interest in the contractor's paper work than for other kinds of contract. A difficulty in this kind of contract is to provide the contractor with an incentive to keep costs down. This is certainly not achieved by paying the contractor on the basis of a cost plus a percentage fee, for, in this case, the greater the cost the greater the fee to the contractor.

Alternative approaches include:

- cost plus a fixed fee (as costs rise, the fee as a proportion of total payment falls),
- cost plus a sliding fee (as the costs rise, the fee as a percentage falls, e.g. 7% for first £5 m, 6% for next £1 m, 5% for next £1 m),
- target cost plus fee.

In a target contract, a target cost and a fee are set, for example £100 m cost plus a £10 m fee. If the contractor carries out the work for £98 m then a saving of £2 m has been made on the target; this saving is then shared between contractor and project owner. If the share agreement were 50:50 then the contractor would be paid £99 m plus the £10 m fee. If, however, the contractor carried out the work for £102 m he would have to share the excess with the project owner and would only be paid £101 m plus the £10 m fee. Once the cost of the work carried out reached £120 m the contractor would, in effect, be carrying out the work at cost. Above this level the contractor would not be penalized further and would continue to be paid at cost; his incentive for efficient operations would be gone. There is one difficulty with this method — how is the target cost set? The main reason for using this kind of contract is its ability to cope with projects where the exact scope of work is unknown and hence the cost is unknown. A target contract would be far more effective where the scope of work is fully understood and where the project owner is anxious to save money and prepared to provide the contractor with an appropriate incentive.

17.8 HOW SHOULD SUPPLIERS/CONTRACTORS BE SELECTED?

The alternatives in any project are:

- by open tendering
- by selected tendering
- by negotiation.

In each of the first two there will often be an element of post-tender negotiation. Negotiation, itself, can lead to a number of alternative contractual arrangements.

In competitive tendering, whether 'open' or 'selected', the project manager sends the contract documents (drawings, specifications, conditions of contract, etc.) to interested suppliers/contractors. When a contractor returns the documents, duly completed, this is the tender or offer (see Chapter 19). Once that offer has been accepted a contract has been made.

It is far easier to assess tenders when they are all on exactly the same basis. Parity of tendering is important for publicly accountable bodies, which will have strict procedures for the receipt and analysis of tenders. Some public bodies, as a matter of principle, will not consider tenders which propose alternative solutions for carrying out the project because any alternative is not strictly comparable with tenders conforming to the specified project solution. Whether this approach provides the public with the best service is questionable; certainly there will be occasions when potentially good ideas by suppliers/contractors will not be heard.

Open tendering is when the work is advertised widely and any interested party may apply for the contract documents and then tender. *Selected tendering* is where the project manager invites three or four potential suppliers/contractors to tender. These tenderers will usually have been required to provide evidence of their experience, technical expertise and financial position. In the UK selected tendering has long been favoured for most projects; however, for large public works and for all large infrastructure developments in transport, water, energy and telecommunications, several EU Directives[3] require wider advertisement across the EU for pre-qualification than many purchasers would prefer. The advantages and disadvantages of selected tendering are given below.

Advantages of selective tendering:

- contract documents are only sent to a few contractors,
- recipient contractors know that the chances of being awarded the contract are reasonably high (1 in 5, say) and, therefore, their tendering costs which must be recouped from their customers, are lower than if, say, every tender had a 1 in 20 chance of success,
- analysis of tenders by the project manager does not take long,
- pre-qualification of tenderers ensures they have the technical ability and financial capacity to carry out the work.

The disadvantages of selective tendering are that the process does not test the open market for value or performance or innovation. There is also the risk that a small group of contractors or suppliers might, over a period of time, be encouraged by the system to form a cartel.

The alternative to competitive tendering is *negotiation*. Normally, public bodies will not use negotiation unless the work is so specialized that there is only one known contractor who can do the work. Private companies are usually at liberty to deal with other companies as they wish. There can be some very good reasons for approaching a company, asking it to carry out some work, and in advance of that work, negotiating the methods and rates of payment. Lump sum, measurement or cost reimbursement could be used. Negotiation is likely to be adopted where the two parties have worked well together in the past, have a good working relationship, trust one another, and do not adopt an adversarial stance when problems arise. In the past, negotiation has been quite widely used on an *ad hoc* basis by a range of project owners from building developers to purchasers of high technology advanced weapons systems. For these relationships to work well it is usually important that the project owner has considerable technical expertise in the field, to allow negotiations to proceed with confidence. In the off-shore

---

[3]For example, Directives 93/36/EEC, 93/37/EEC and 93/38/EEC. See also Appendix 1 section A1.4.

industry some customers and suppliers have entered into *alliances* in which the two parties have negotiated a form of target price contract in which there are financial incentives for all parties to work towards a common goal, in which the project management team comprises engineers and managers from customer and suppliers whose aim is to solve problems on the basis of trust rather than by resorting to contractual positions.

Where the project owner has a long-term commitment to project development, for example an oil company with intentions to develop off-shore oil fields around the world, entering into long-term *partnering agreements* with suppliers and contractors may have a number of advantages. The cost of constructing an off-shore platform and its complementary installations is very high and the potential losses that can arise from late provision or unsatisfactory performance within the first few weeks or months of performance are huge. Realistic levels for liquidated damages (see Chapter 19) for late completion, which would provide the purchaser with adequate compensation, would be so great that no contractor could afford to pay them, so the risk of late completion has lain largely with the purchaser. Therefore, historically, the oil companies have taken a close interest in everything that their suppliers/contractors do, yet at the same time insisting that only the lowest bid will be accepted. This has had the effect that even experienced contractors have enjoyed, at the best, only a tenuous relationship with purchasers of their services, inhibiting any long-term investment in skilled personnel, engineering, information systems or plant and equipment which would improve the provision of these services.

In recent years, the oil companies have adopted very different policies with a view to reducing their operating costs by as much as 30%. *Partnering* is one such approach. Partnering is a long term commitment between purchaser and supplier/contractor in which two or more parties work together to reduce their costs in the long term. Partnering has been established in the USA for some years, particularly in the processing and chemical industries, and more recently in Europe in the motor industry where closer customer/supplier relationships have permitted short development times, high quality standards and competitive pricing.[4]

In the off-shore industry, partnering has sometimes given the design, detailed engineering, procurement and construction management services to one company which forms a team with the customer. Formal agreements for four or five years, with the understanding that it is the intention of both parties to extend the agreement, have been entered into. The project management team comprises engineers and managers from customer and contractor. The relationship is based on trust, a dedication to common goals and a mutual understanding of each other's expectations and values. A National Economic Development Council report [4] concluded that the conditions for successful partnering are that there should be:

- a significant long term core programme,
- careful selection of the right partner,

---

[4]A partnering agreement for construction work was recently entered into by the UK Rover Group and building contractor SDC. *New Builder 12 May 1995*

- mutual trust and confidence between partners,
- commitment to a long term relationship,
- preparedness to adopt each other's requirements,
- willingness to accept and learn from each other's mistakes,
- a compatibility of culture between customer and contractor.

Where there is mutual trust and compatibility of culture, the parties are unlikely to adopt adversarial stances and resort to the contract when things go wrong. Sorting the problem out together must be a better way. (See also *When Giants Learn to Dance* [5] for further reading on partnering.)

17.9   SUMMARY

This chapter has examined the role of the project manager in project definition, planning, decision making, monitoring and controlling the project. The importance of work breakdown structures has been identified and earned value analysis has been introduced. Change as a major cause of delay has been discussed and the means of controlling delays and extra costs. Finally the contractual methods by which contractors and suppliers can be appointed and controlled have been discussed.

REFERENCES

1. Meredith, J. R. and Mantel, S. J. (1989) *Project Management*. Second edition, Wiley & Sons, Chichester.
2. Latham, M. (1994) *Constructing the Team*. HMSO, London.
3. Morris, P. and Hough, G. (1987) *The Anatomy of Major Projects*. Wiley & Sons, Chichester.
4. NEDC Construction Industry Sector Group, (1991) *Partnering: Contracting without Conflict*.
5. Moss Kanter, R. (1989) *When Giants Learn to Dance*. Routledge, London.

BIBLIOGRAPHY

1. Burke, R. (1992) *Project Management*. Second edition. Wiley & Sons, Chichester.
2. Lockyer, K. and Gordon, J. (1991) *Critical Path Analysis*. Fifth edition, Pitman, London.
3. Reiss, G. (1992) *Project Management Demystified*. Spon, London.

18

Networks for projects

18.1 INTRODUCTION

It has been shown in Chapter 17 that the bar chart provides an excellent visual representation of a project programme. As a means of communication the bar chart is equally effective whether representing high level programmes for senior management or closely detailed programmes for those who carry out the work.

For simple projects with 20 or 30 activities the production of a bar chart is a relatively straightforward task. A bar chart so constructed will provide a useful means of monitoring progress; late running activities can be identified and the effects on other activities understood, so that measures can be implemented by the project manager to control progress. For complex projects in which many activities are interdependent, possibly across a number of disciplines, it will be difficult to formulate a bar chart which meets all the conditions and dependencies, and interpretation of a bar chart in which several activities are not running on schedule may become very difficult. In these circumstances analytical tools are necessary which will (a) provide a bar chart that meets all the dependencies and (b) facilitate dynamic analyses as the project proceeds. *Network analysis* is just such a tool.

In this chapter the principles of network analysis will be set out and *network diagrams* developed. Two alternative forms of network diagram exist; the activity-on-arrow diagram and the activity-on-node diagram. The *activity-on-node* diagram has been selected for study in preference to the *activity-on-arrow* diagram because of its inherent superiority.

The application of *PERT* (programme evaluation review technique) to networks will be considered in the latter part of the chapter.

18.2 NETWORK DIAGRAMS

The starting point for the construction of a network diagram is a list of activities and their precursor (immediately preceding) activities. The starting point for developing a list of activities is a work breakdown structure as described in Chapter 17. Perhaps the most difficult part is the determination of the precursor activity(ies) for each activity. Too often courses on network analysis give no consideration to this at all. Usually the student starts with a list of activities and precursor activities and is asked to develop the network diagram, and from it determine the critical path. In this chapter the approach will be to take as a starting point lists of activities and precursor activities and to develop and analyse the resulting network diagrams. However in the Appendix 3 Case Study: *Developing a Network* there is a model approach to network analysis, starting with a description of the project activities, from which is developed first a list of activities and precursor activities and finally a network.

18.2.1 Activity-on-Node Diagrams

In this system an activity is represented within a node, usually drawn as a rectangular box. Activities are linked together by arrows to show the order of precedence. Consider the construction of a column comprising three activities:

X — excavate for foundations
F — construct foundations
C — construct column on foundations

the network would be displayed as in Figure 18.1. An activity preceded by two activities and succeeded by two activities would be represented as in Figure 18.2

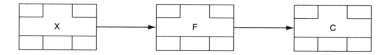

Figure 18.1   Three activities linked by arrows to show order or precedence

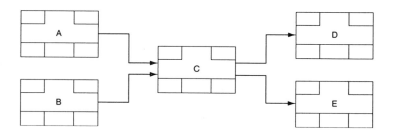

Figure 18.2   An activity preceded by two activities and succeeded by two activities

Example 18(1)

In this example the finish–start (F–S) links have zero duration. A network will be developed for the project represented by the data in Table 18.1.

Some practitioners prefer to show a start node and an end node, others see these as unnecessary. In this chapter they will be included although the authors have no preference in the matter.

Table 18.1

Activity	Duration (weeks)	Precursor activity(ies)
A	4	–
B	3	–
C	6	A, B
D	1	B
E	7	D
F	2	C
G	5	C, E
H	8	E
J	4	G
K	5	F, G
L	6	J, H
M	3	L, K

Thus, the start node will be followed by the nodes for A and B, D will follow B, and C will follow A and B as shown in Figure 18.3.

An activity-on-node network is much easier to construct than an arrow network. There are no dummy arrows and the network can be built up methodically without difficulty. The final network is shown in Figure 18.4, durations of activities are also shown.

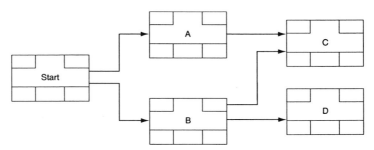

Figure 18.3

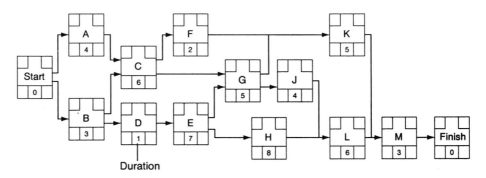

Duration

Figure 18.4

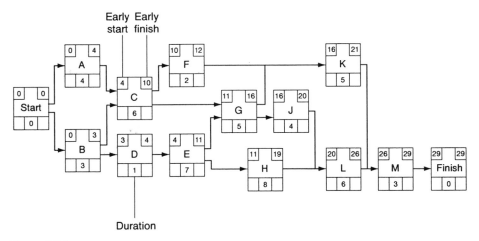

Figure 18.5

The network can now be analysed to determine its duration. On each node there is a space available for the following:

Early start   the earliest time at which the activity can start
Early finish   the earliest time at which the activity can finish
Late start   the latest time at which the activity can start
Late finish   the latest time at which the activity can finish

In Figure 18.5 the earliest start and finish times have been entered. Where an activity is preceded by two activities the larger figure for the early start must be selected. Thus the early start time for activity G is 11 not 10.

The early finish time for activity M is 29 weeks; this therefore is the duration of the project. Therefore the latest date for completion of the project (29 weeks) can now be entered. Once this has been done one can work backwards from the finish to obtain the late finish and late start times for each activity; these have been entered in Figure 18.6.

Where two or more activities follow one, as in the case of J and K both being preceded by G, the lower figure must be selected for the late finish time of G. Thus G cannot finish any later than week 16, otherwise the duration of the project would be extended. The *critical path* is shown by means of a thicker arrow. If the duration of any activity on the critical path is increased then the project duration will be increased by the same amount. Activities not on the critical path have *float*. The float for non-critical activities is given by

Late finish – duration – early start

The values of float for each activity are shown in Table 18.2. Activities with zero float are on the critical path. From this the project manager could observe, say,

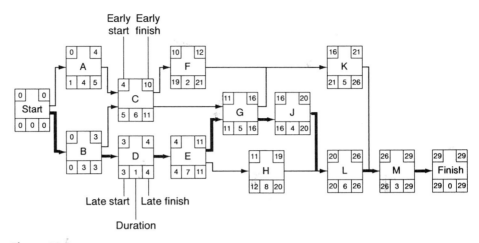

Figure 18.6

that a serious delay of eight weeks on activity F would have no effect on the project duration, nor would speeding up activity H have any useful effect. Likewise, if activities G and J were accelerated to be completed in seven weeks total instead of nine weeks the project duration would only be reduced by one week unless activity H were accelerated by one week also. A delay to any activity on the critical path would delay the project by the same amount.

Table 18.2

Activity	A	B	C	D	E	F	G	H	J	K	L	M
Total float	1	0	1	0	0	9	0	1	0	5	0	0

Activity-on-node diagrams in which finish-to-start (F–S) links have durations, and in which there are start-to-start (S–S) and finish-to-finish (F–F) links will now be considered.

The nature and duration of each link will be shown against each arrow. Figure 18.7 illustrates the case in which activity F cannot start until one week after the finish of activity X, and activity C cannot commence until two weeks after the completion of activity F.

Start-to-start links and finish-to-finish links can be represented in a similar fashion. Where both links exist between a pair of activities both links must be shown as separate arrows. This is because it is possible for the critical path to pass through one link and not the other.

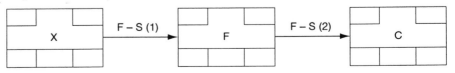

Figure 18.7

Example 18(2)

A project consists of activities A, B and C with links as shown in Table 18.3.

Figure 18.8 is the activity-on-node diagram for the project. The activity times have been entered. The early start time of activity C is 10 because it can start six weeks after the start of activity B; however, the late start time of activity C is week 19, thus the critical path passes through the finish-to-finish link but not through the start-to-start link.

Table 18.3

Activity	Duration (weeks)	Precursor activity	Link type	Link duration
A	4	–		
B	24	A	F–S	0
C	12	B	S–S	6
			F–F	3

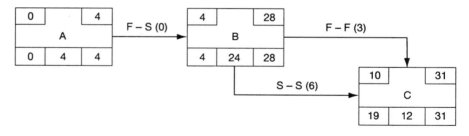

Figure 18.8

Example 18(3)

Table 18.4 provides data on a simpler project. Draw the network and find the critical path.

Figure 18.9 shows the completed network. Construction of the diagram logic is straightforward; the only difficulties that might arise are those concerning some of the activity times. The Early finish time for activity H must be week 27 not week 24, (16+8), because the finish–finish link of two weeks between activity E and activity H imposes this condition. The late finish time for activity D is week 44, for, although the start of this activity is on the critical path, there is no condition placed on its completion at all, other than to finish within the duration of the project. It should be noted that if the start and finish nodes had been omitted from the diagram, activity D would have represented a finish activity as would activity M. This form of network construction, that is, omitting start and finish nodes, allows

Table 18.4

Activity	Duration (weeks)	Precursor activity	Link type	Link duration
A	4	–	F–S	0
B	3	–	F–S	0
C	6	A, B	F–S	0
D	1	B	F–S	6
E	12	D	S–S	4
F	2	C	F–S	0
G	5	E, F	F–S	0
H	8	E	S–S	3
			F–F	2
J	4	G	F–S	1
K	5	F, G	F–S	0
L	6	J, H	F–S	0
M	3	L, K	F–S	0

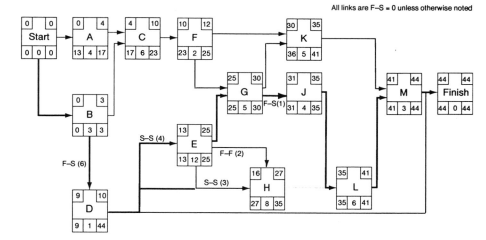

Figure 18.9

sectional completion; the project manager could require activity D to be completed by week 10 and handed over to the owner. In this case the late finish time for activity D would be week 10, not week 44.

The bar chart can now be drawn. It is shown in Figure 18.10. All activities with float have been shown as starting at their earliest start time. Activity D is shown to be on the critical path; this is because its commencement is on the critical path although its finish is not. Since its duration is only one week it would be difficult to show it any other way (on the time scale provided). Activity H is a *stretch* activity, that is it has to take longer than its listed duration.

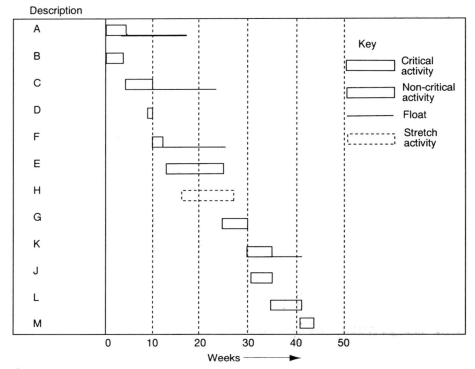

Figure 18.10

18.2.2 Draft networks for large projects

When a large project is being planned, planners and estimators for different parts of the project may provide information on rates of production and on the links between activities which are at odds with one another, although this may not be immediately apparent. Construction and analysis of a first draft network should show the planners these contradictions and allow them to be resolved in the final draft plan.

Example 18(4)

As part of a large project a length of welded steel pipeline is to be installed in a trench. Excavation of the trench will be carried out by a civil engineering group. Placing sections of the pipe into the trench will be carried out by the suppliers of the short lengths of the fabricated pipe. Welding will be carried out by a mechanical engineering group. Non-destructive testing (NDT) of the welds will be carried out by independent assessors for statutory purposes, and, once this has been finished, the civil engineering group will place backfill around the pipe. The different groups have been asked to provide estimates of their rates of progress. The pipeline is 120 km long. Each group assumes that it has one team working,

Table 18.5

Group	Activity	Estimated rate of working (km/day)	Duration (days)
Civil engineering	X – excavation	2	60
Supplier	P – placing	4	30
Mechanical engineering	W – welding	1	120
NDT assessors	N – NDT	2	60
Civil engineering	B – backfilling	4	30

starting at one end and proceeding to the other. The initial plan provides for all operations to be at least 4 km apart. These data have been analysed and are presented in Table 18.5.

The activity-on-node diagram for this sub-project is shown in Figure 18.11. The first thing that should be observed is that the critical path can pass through a S–S link between two activities without passing through the corresponding F–F link and vice versa. Therefore, in constructing an activity-on-node diagram one should always draw the two links, where they arise, separately.

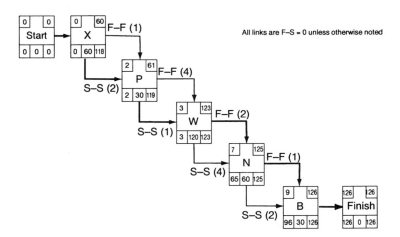

Figure 18.11

Analysis of the network shows an undesirable feature. Activity P (placing) need take only 30 days yet it cannot be completed in less than 59 days. This is because the start of the activity is on the critical path, therefore it cannot be delayed, yet it cannot be completed until after the completion of activity X (excavation). This would be highly undesirable from the supplier's point of view. Either a second draft plan should be prepared in which, for example, the excavation process were accelerated to be completed in 30 days or the suppliers should be consulted to determine whether they would be satisfied with the draft plan. This would be most important in order to avoid any claims by the supplier that his work was being delayed once the work was underway.

It can be seen that production of a draft network is only a first stage in the planning process which can yield useful information. Further development of the plan may be necessary in which the nature of links between activities, their resourcing and, possibly, the method statement may need to be reassessed.

18.3 PROGRAMME EVALUATION AND REVIEW TECHNIQUE (PERT)

A chapter on networks would be incomplete without an introduction to PERT. This technique was developed by the US Navy between about 1958 and 1960 for the Polaris submarine construction programme. PERT takes into account the difficulty of estimating the durations of individual activities. In research and development projects in particular, the estimators may be unwilling to provide a single value for a duration but may be persuaded to provide a *most optimistic duration*, a *most pessimistic duration* and a *most likely duration* for that activity. If these figures are interpreted to be part of a frequency distribution then an expected duration of the activity, and hence of the whole project, can be determined. PERT uses a beta frequency distribution (this is a skewed distribution which, it is claimed, provides a satisfactory model of reality and is easy to use) and from this the *expected mean duration* for an activity and the *standard deviation* of the distribution can be found from the formulae

$$t_e = \frac{a + 4m + b}{6}$$

$$s = \frac{b - a}{6}$$

where

t_e = expected mean duration
a = most optimistic duration
b = most pessimistic duration
m = most likely duration
s = standard deviation of the distribution

A comprehensive explanation of PERT is to be found in Moder and Phillips [1] which remains a fundamental text for this subject. Moder and Phillips recommend that a and b be selected as the lower and upper ten percentiles of the hypothetical performance time distribution.

Expected mean durations are normally calculated to one decimal place of the unit of measurement of time, in order to arrive at an expected duration of the project through the critical path.

Example 18(5)

This uses the activities and links given in Example 18(1) but data on most likely, most pessimistic and most optimistic durations are given in place of the data previously provided.

Table 18.6

Activity	a	m	b	Precursor activity	Link type	Link duration
A	3	5	9	–	F–S	0
B	4	6	8	–	F–S	0
C	5	8	10	A,B	F–S	0
D	3	6	9	B	F–S	6
E	6	9	15	D	S–S	4
F	3	4	5	C	F–S	0
G	8	12	15	E,F	F–S	0
H	2	6	8	E	S–S	3
					F–F	2
J	4	7	9	G	F–S	1
K	3	5	10	F,G	F–S	0
L	7	9	11	J,H	F–S	0
M	10	12	15	L,K	F–S	0

Draw the network, determine the critical path and find the expected mean duration for the sub-project defined by Table 18.6. The value of the expected mean duration for each activity can now be found. For activity A

$$t_e = \frac{3 + 4 \times 5 + 9}{6} = 5.3$$

The value of the expected mean duration (t_e) for each activity has been calculated in like fashion; these are shown in Table 18.7. The standard deviation (s) for each activity has also been calculated using the formula given previously. These figures have also been entered in the table.

The logic of the activity-on-node network will be exactly the same as for Figure 18.9 previously provided. The differences lie in the durations. Figure 18.12 shows the network. The values of t_e have been entered for each activity and all the earliest and latest start and finish times calculated for each activity. The critical path is shown and the expected mean duration of the project is 66.3 weeks, which for planning and programming the work would be taken as 67 weeks.

The standard deviation of the project duration can be determined as follows (in this case a normal distribution is used for summation of variances of activities).

Table 18.7

Activity	A	B	C	D	E	F	G	H	J	K	L	M
t_e	5.3	6.0	7.8	6.0	9.5	4.0	11.8	5.7	6.8	5.5	9.0	12.2
s	1.0	.67	.83	1.0	1.5	.33	1.17	1.0	.83	1.17	0.67	0.83

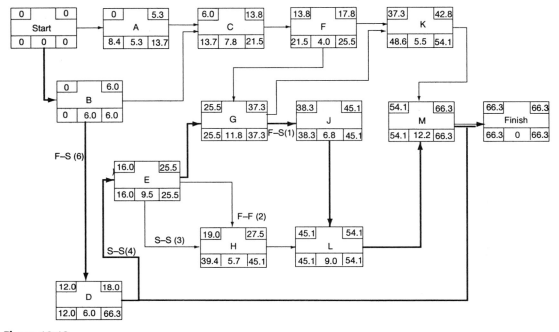

Figure 18.12

The variance for the project duration equals the sum of the variances of the activities along the critical path. The variance for an activity equals the square of the standard deviation for that activity. The standard deviation for the project duration equals the square root of the variance.

Therefore the standard deviation for the duration of the project

$$= \sqrt{0.67^2 + 1.0^2 + 1.5^2 + 1.17^2 + 0.83^2 + 0.67^2 + 0.83^2} = 2.63 \text{ wks}$$

and probabilities can be determined for different project durations from normal distribution curves. For example, the probability that the duration will be greater than

66.3 (the mean) + 2 × 2.63 (2 × standard deviation) = 71.6 weeks, is 2.3%

the probability that the duration will be greater than

66.3 (the mean) + 3 × 2.63 (3 × standard deviation) = 74.2 weeks, is 0.1%

These are attributes of the normal distribution curve and are of some value in determining a range of durations for a project.

18.4   SUMMARY

Two kinds of network diagram are available; activity-on-arrow and activity-on-node. The former are mainly of historical interest and have not been considered. Activity-on-node diagrams are usually straightforward to construct and yield immediately useful data. A first draft network may, upon analysis, allow the planner to perceive potential problems which can only be overcome by challenging some of the assumptions about resources or productivity or the nature of the links between activities. Two or three draft networks may be necessary before the planner can formulate the programme for the project. Network diagrams are the tools by which programmes in bar chart form can be established, and provide a most effective means of observing the effects of delayed/accelerated activities on the overall programme.

PERT is a useful technique for project planning where estimators prefer to state durations for individual activities in terms of a frequency (probability) distribution.

REFERENCE

1. Moder, J. J. and Phillips, C. R. (1964) *Project Management with CPM and PERT*. Reinhold Publishing Corporation, New York.

BIBLIOGRAPHY

Lanigan, M. (1992) *Engineers in Business*. Addison-Wesley, Reading.
Lockyer, K. and Gordon, J. (1991) *Critical Path Analysis*. Fifth edition, Pitman, London.
Pilcher, R. (1992) *Principles of Construction Management*. Third edition, McGraw-Hill, Maidenhead.

19

Project management, contract law and procedures

19.1 INTRODUCTION

This chapter will examine *contract law*[1] and *contract procedures*. Effective project management seeks to control cost, time and quality. Engineering contracts are drafted to encourage the parties to meet these same ends. Therefore they should be of much interest to professional engineers. In large engineering projects the Contract will have special significance for the project manager, as the Contract terms will define the relationships between designer, supplier and client, imposing upon the project a prescribed management structure. Three *Standard Forms of Contract* will be studied. These should be of interest not only to engineers who expect to use them but also to all engineers, in that they provide insights into the user/supplier relationships in engineering projects. This chapter will examine how the *client's and contractor's obligations* are defined, the *supervision and administration of the contract* by the engineer or project manager on behalf of the client, and the provisions for *controlling cash flow, costs and completion*.

Young engineers should not be deterred by the apparent remoteness of such figures as the 'Engineer' or 'project manager'. These terms usually denote teams which are headed by someone with such a title, and many of their duties will be carried out by members of the team, that is, by young engineers.

Appendix 4 provides a brief outline of the *New Engineering Contract* (NEC) [1] first published in 1993, now in its second edition, which, it is hoped by its authors,[2] will become a preferred alternative for project managers to the commonly used Standard Forms.

---

[1]Appendix 6 provides a short introduction to the English legal system which has served as a model for much of the English-speaking world, and is therefore an influence in many engineering contracts.
[2]This hope is shared by *Sir Michael Latham* who, in *Constructing the Team HMSO 1994*, recommends that both public and private sector clients should begin to use the NEC, and that the British Government should use the NEC for one third of its construction contracts within a few years.

19.2 CONTRACTS AND THE ENGINEER

When is a Contract not a Contract? Detailed provisions of engineering contracts will be examined later; first the question of how it is possible for large reputable engineering companies to enter into contracts which are found, when a dispute arises, not to be contracts at all needs to be considered.

19.2.1 Law of contract

A simple (legally binding) contract consists of:

- an OFFER
- an ACCEPTANCE
- plus CONSIDERATION

Consideration is essential for the formation of a simple contract. Paying (or promising to pay) money in return for the supply of services or goods is the usual form of consideration. It is the 'price for which the promise of the other party is bought' [2]. Usually one party provides goods or services whilst the other provides money. Consideration must have economic value, however small. Without consideration the courts will not enforce a *simple* contract. A *specialty* contract, which will be discussed later, does not need consideration.

An *offer* must be definite, that is, clearly defined. An offer to construct a road between A and B would be invalid because it is imprecise and therefore uncertain. An offer to construct a road between A and B in accordance with the specification and drawings would be valid because it is definite. An offer must be communicated to the offeree (the intended recipient of the offer); an offer, for example, lost in the post is no offer at all. An offer is from one party to another and cannot be accepted by another party. An offer may be withdrawn or revoked at any time before acceptance; an offer will lapse after a 'reasonable' time; an offer can include a provision that it is open for a certain period of time, once that time has elapsed and no acceptance has been made the offer is automatically revoked.

Acceptance must be unconditional. A letter of acceptance containing some such phrase as 'we accept your offer on the condition that...' is not an acceptance but a counter offer which cancels the original offer, replacing it with a new offer in the reverse direction. The acceptance must be unambiguous and must correspond to the terms of the offer. Acceptance, though usually by communication, can be by performance. If Company A offers to pay Company B £100 000 (on Company A's conditions of contract) for the provision of machinery, and Company B starts to assemble that machinery, without any further communication between the parties, then this could be viewed as acceptance and a valid contract would be in place. If the post is the proper method of communication between the parties then, exceptionally, acceptance is deemed to have occurred once the letter of acceptance has been *posted*. However, the courts have not interpreted this too narrowly (see *Holwell Securities* v. *Hughes* (1974) [3]. Silence on the part of an offeree can never be taken as acceptance. For example, the recipient of an offer which includes 'if we do not hear from you within the period of 14 days, that will be taken as acceptance of our offer to upgrade your computer system . . .' need not reply if the services offered are not wanted. No contract can be formed in this way.

A *simple contract* can be in writing or formed by oral agreement (or a mixture of both). Where an individual agrees to buy from another, say, some materials for a given sum there is no need for a written document. Some simple contracts must be in writing, for example hire purchase agreements, contracts for the sale of land and contracts of guarantee. Specialty contracts must be in writing.

A *specialty contract* is a contract under seal. A seal is an impression in wax. A small red wafer is usually used in place of wax. A contract under seal is not effective until it is delivered, or, at least, the intention to deliver it has been made known to the recipient. A contract under seal will be signed by both parties and the signatures witnessed; hence the expression 'signed, sealed and delivered'. A contract under seal does not need consideration and can therefore be used for the conveyance of a gift. For the engineer, the significant difference between a simple contract and a specialty contract arises from the Limitations Act 1980. Under this Act, the periods during which actions can be brought to court for breach of contract are limited to six years for a simple contract and 12 years for a specialty contract. If a main contract is under seal, it is important for the contractor that subcontracts are under seal too. Otherwise the contractor could be sued, say, nine years after the breach occurred, by his employer for a fault of the subcontractor, only to find that no suit for damages against the subcontractor is possible. An employer can only sue his contractors or suppliers; no suit against their subcontractors is possible. The doctrine of *privity of contract* is that a contract is between two parties (a party can, of course, consist of more than one body), that only the parties to a contract may sue under it, and that any third parties named in that contract or who benefit from that contract cannot sue or be sued under that contract. There are a number of important exceptions to this doctrine, and there is also the issue of Agency, see Treitel [4].

There have been a number of cases in which, typically, a company has placed an order with a supplier using its own order form, on which the company's contract conditions are set out. The supplier has then issued an acceptance of the order using its own form set of conditions. Neither party has accepted the other's conditions but the goods have been supplied.[3] When one party or the other has defaulted on the contract, either by not paying or by providing unsatisfactory goods only the lawyers have benefited from the attempts to determine what contract has been breached! (See *Butler Machine Tool Co Ltd* v. *Ex-cell-O Corp* (1979) [5]).

Contracts can be found to be void. A contract which included provisions by which one or both parties avoid paying taxes would be illegal and therefore void. A contract can be void because its provisions are seen as inequitable between the parties (see section 19.3) or because they are contrary to public policy. Contracts

---

[3]Recognizing the cost and complexity of resolving disputes about whose conditions apply, buyers and suppliers in some industries, notably the automotive industry, have increasingly sought to establish relationships that reduce reliance on strict legal interpretations, but, instead, emphasize shared interests and the resolution of disputes by negotiation. See sections 22.3 and 22.4 in Chapter 22.

which are in unreasonable restraint of trade can be void for this reason (see *Esso Petroleum Co Ltd* v. *Harper's Garage (Stourport) Ltd* (1968) [6]). A void contract is one which has no legal effect. Uncommonly, a contract can be void because of a mistake. Here, the mistake must be so fundamental that it puts the two parties so seriously at cross-purposes that they cannot be said to have agreed at all (an example of which is *Raffles* v. *Wichelhaus* (1864) [7].

A contract can be voidable; that is, there is something about it which when brought to the attention of one of the parties may allow him to rescind the contract (for example, because of misrepresentation, see below). If, however, despite the problem, the party decides to proceed with the contract, he may do so by affirming the contract, but cannot at a later date withdraw from the contract on the grounds that it is void. A *representation* is a statement of fact made by one party to the other party before the contract is made; a *misrepresentation* is an untrue statement of fact. In the *Institution of Chemical Engineers Conditions of Contract for Process Plant–Reimbursable Contracts* [8], there is a provision in the Form of Agreement that 'any pre-contractual representations and warranties...-shall be of no legal effect...[so that] neither party shall be entitled to found any claim to damages in reliance thereon.' Misrepresentations can be statements that are:

- innocent, that is made honestly but wrongly,
- negligent, that is made wrongly and without due care,
- fraudulent, that is, made wrongly with the intention to mislead.

Engineering firms frequently obtain work by competitive tender. Could an invitation to tender be an offer? If it were, the parties would be bound by the first conforming tender received! There is a general presumption that an invitation to tender is an invitation to treat, but the wording of the invitation needs some care. Phrases such as 'the invitor will not be bound to accept the lowest tender or any tender' will make clear that the invitation to tender is not an offer.

A practice widely used in connection with competitive tendering is to write a letter to the successful bidder informing him that a contract will be entered into in the near future. This is a *letter of intent*. This is not only a matter of courtesy, it also allows the contractor to prepare for the work to be done. Can this letter of intent constitute a contract? If the contractor's preparations involve a considerable amount of work and incur considerable expense, can he obtain any compensation if the employer at the last minute decides not to proceed with the contract? As long as the letter of intent contains no instructions to the recipient to, for example, commence design, order materials, transport goods or equipment, the letter cannot be construed as either an acceptance or, upon performance by the contractor, as a contract in itself.

19.2.2 Written contracts

The purpose of a written contract is to state and provide evidence of the obligations of the parties to the contract. Standard contracts are often entitled 'Conditions of Contract', yet many of the terms of the contract may not, in law, be 'conditions'!

The terms of the contract may be *conditions* or *warranties*. The law makes this distinction because some terms can be of much greater importance than others. A condition is a fundamental obligation under the contract which goes to the root of the contract. A warranty (which is not to be confused with the term warranty used, say, by a manufacturer who gives a warranty against faulty workmanship) is a subsidiary obligation which, if not performed satisfactorily, does not go to the root of the contract. A good example of the latter is the obligation on the contractor under most construction contracts to provide a master programme of his intended operations; if this is not forthcoming but the contractor proceeds with diligence, he would not be viewed as in breach of contract. There are also what are referred to as *innominate terms*; these are terms the breach of which could be serious or not depending upon the facts at the time. These terms will be viewed as conditions if the effects are serious, and as warranties if not.

When a party breaches a condition such that he is in repudiatory breach of the contract, the non-breaching party may elect whether to proceed with the contract or to treat it as repudiated. The discharge of the remaining obligations to perform the contract does not discharge the secondary obligation to pay damages for any loss caused and does not dispense with any exemption clauses. Where damages are awarded, the amount of the award is based on the principle that the injured party should be compensated for damage which arose naturally in the normal course of events from the breach, or was a loss which was reasonably contemplated by the parties at the time of the contract as the probable result of a breach. Damages would not extend to potential losses incurred by missing, say, an unexpected and highly lucrative contract. In cases where monetary damages are inappropriate and performance essential the courts may order the contractor to perform the actual obligation, this is known as *specific performance*; an alternative to this is an *injunction* directing the contractor not to break his contract. In large projects, breach of contract most commonly arises from defective work, late delivery or failure to complete.

A suit for breach of contract must be brought within a limited period of time. This period does not start from the time the contract was made or completed but from the date when such action first became possible, that is, from the time the breach occurs. If the breach is concealed by 'fraud' then the time commences from when the 'fraud' is discovered, or could be reasonably expected to be discovered; this could be years later! 'Fraud', as used in the Limitation Act, does not mean criminal fraud but behaviour which aims to achieve an unfair advantage, for example, deliberately concealing faulty workmanship.

19.3   ENGINEERING CONTRACTS

Contract terms define obligations and determine relationships within a contract. This section examines three well known standard forms of engineering contract to illustrate the management system imposed by the contract. It is the relationships and responsibilities with which this chapter is concerned rather than the legal issues. The forms of contract considered below can and should be used without any recourse to arbitration or the courts of law; usually they are. The standard forms of contract to be considered are:

- *Institution of Civil Engineers Conditions of Contract* (6th edition 1991) [9] (ICE6)
- *Institution of Electrical Engineers and Institution of Mechanical Engineers Model Form of General Conditions of Contract* (1995 Revision) [10] (MF/1)
- *Institution of Chemical Engineers Model Form of Conditions of Contract for Process Plant–Reimbursable Contracts* (1992) [8] (IChemE Green Book).

These are all standard forms of contract, drafted by representatives from all sides of the industries involved; employers, contractors and suppliers. This means that a party to one of these contracts could not claim any of the conditions to be unfair and seek to set aside those conditions by reference to the Unfair Contract Terms Act 1977. When large powerful companies seek to impose onerous contract conditions upon their suppliers, using their own carefully drafted contracts, it is always possible for the courts to declare such conditions to be unfair and release the suppliers from those conditions.

The major difference between the three standard forms is the means by which the contractor is paid. *ICE6* is a measurement contract, *MF/1* a lump sum contract and the *IChemE Green Book* a cost reimbursement contract. These types of contract have been discussed in Chapter 17.

In each form of contract an intermediary is established between the purchaser of the project (known variously as the employer or purchaser) and the provider (known as the Contractor). Under ICE6 and MF/1 the intermediary is known as the Engineer, under the IChemE Green Book the intermediary is called the Project Manager. The Engineer/Project Manager is not a party to the contract but is appointed under a separate agreement by the purchaser. In each case his primary role is to ensure that the project is completed to specification; the Engineer/Project Manager is also responsible for controlling the price paid for the project and for ensuring the Contractor finishes on time. Figure 19.1 shows a typical management structure provided by these forms of contract.

Under ICE6 the Contractor is required to *construct* and *complete to the satisfaction of the Engineer*; under MF/1 and the IChemE Green Book the Contractor must *design, manufacture, construct, complete* and *test* the Works *to the satisfaction of the Engineer*. (In each contract there is provision for sectional or phased completion, such that the Employer or Purchaser may take over part of the Works before the whole Works have been completed, so for 'completion' one can read 'phased completion'.) Under all three contracts the Contract is watched and supervised by the Engineer's or the Project Manager's Representative. As the work proceeds the Engineer/Project Manager issues instructions to the Contractor; it is made quite clear in ICE6 that the purchaser (known as the Employer in this Contract) cannot issue instructions to the Contractor. In all three contracts it is the Engineer/Project Manager who issues variation orders to the Contractor, awards extensions of time, certifies payments to the Contractor and agrees to any additional payments.

Contracts allocate risk. The three contracts broadly allocate the risks of the production processes, such as costs, obtaining resources, and any effects of operations on third parties, to the Contractor. Employer's risks include the site,

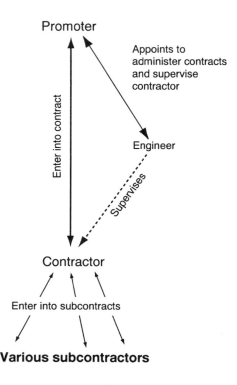

Figure 19.1 Typical management structure for engineering projects

ground conditions, unforeseeable external circumstances and interference by other contractors employed by the Employer.

In some projects several main contracts may be in existence concurrently. For example, in setting up a factory, the purchaser could possibly 'buy' the civil works and buildings from a building contractor, the equipment from a supplier and its installation from a third party. Where this happens the purchaser is responsible for coordinating the operations of the three separate contractors. Each of the conditions of contract below makes provision for the Employer/Purchaser employing other contractors on the given site.

In any contract there is a possibility of a dispute arising between the purchaser and the contractor. In these standard forms it is assumed that the Engineer/ Project Manager will endeavour to resolve any dispute by acting impartially between the two parties. However, it is recognized that this might not always be possible and so each contract makes provision for the appointment of an arbitrator whose decision shall be binding on both parties (ICE6 Clause 66(8) (c); IChemE Green Book Clause 45.4). MF/1 omits stating that the decision will be binding, but in English law the courts will not normally consider a dispute that has already been the subject of arbitration (unless a point of law is at issue), so the parties, in effect, will be bound by the arbitration findings.

Each of the three standard forms will now be studied in turn.

19.4 ICE6

The parties to the contract are the Employer and the Contractor. The Employer plays very little part in the running of the Contract. The Contractor has to construct the Works to the satisfaction of the Engineer. The Engineer, who is responsible for the design and specification of the Permanent Works, issues instructions and directions to the Contractor, monitors progress and administers the Contract. It is the Engineer who authorizes payments by the Employer to the Contractor. During construction the Engineer acts in two separate capacities, as:

(1)   agent for the Employer, acting in the best interests of the Employer,
(2)   quasi-arbitrator, deciding fairly between the interests of the two parties.

The conditions determine the project management structure. A linear programme of operations is assumed. First the design is completed. Next tenders to construct the works described in the drawings and specifications are received from contractors. Then a contract is awarded and the Contractor must complete the works within a stated period of time for sums predetermined by tender rates for measured quantities (the contract is a *measurement contract*). In practice, some 90% of the design is complete by the time of tender; there is little overlap of design and construction, and there is no possibility of Contractor involvement in early planning of the project. Project Management is divided into two distinct phases: the design phase and the construction phase. For the design phase the Employer (promoter of the project) appoints each of the consultants but then requires the Engineer to programme the design work and coordinate the work of the other Consultants up to the time of tender. For building contracts the Architect usually takes on this role.

During the tender period the Engineer will deal with enquiries from tenderers, arrange site visits and so on. The Engineer, in liaison with the other Consultants, will analyse the tenders received and make recommendations to the Employer. Once a contract has been awarded the Engineer supervises the Contractor's operations and administers the Contract.

The major provisions of the Contract can be summarized under the headings:

- Contractor's obligations
- Purchaser's obligations
- supervision and administration by the Engineer
- controlling the Employer's costs
- controlling completion.

19.4.1 The Contractor's obligations

As most of the clauses within ICE6 impose some obligation upon the Contractor, only the most important will be identified.

Cl. 8(1) the Contractor shall 'construct and complete the Works';

this is the very heart of the Contract.

Cl. 8(2) the Contractor 'shall not be responsible for the design...of the Permanent Works...(except as expressly provided in the Contract).'

This makes it very clear that the Contractor has no design responsibility under the Contract unless this responsibility is defined in the Contract documents. This is important where specialist subcontractors are nominated by the Employer or Engineer to be employed by the Contractor. There are many specialist operations today in construction work in which both the design and construction expertise lie with the specialist, so that the specialist subcontractor is responsible for the design of that part of the Permanent Works. If the design work is later found to be defective, the Employer might wish to seek damages from the subcontractor but would be unable to do so because of the doctrine of privity of contract; only an action against the Contractor would be possible. If the Contractor has no design responsibility, as stated in Clause 8(2), then the Employer can take no action at all.

Cl. 8(3) the Contractor 'shall take full responsibility for the adequacy stability and safety of all site operations...'

The Contractor's operations must be the Contractor's responsibility. However, where the stability of an operation is put at risk by unforeseen ground conditions, the Contractor may be able to obtain compensation from the Employer. See *Humber Oil Terminals Trustee Ltd* v. *Harbour and General Works (Stevin) Ltd* (1991) [11] in which, after the collapse of lifting equipment, the Court of Appeal allowed the Contractor to claim under Clause 12 for an extension of time and/or additional payment because the Contractor had encountered 'physical conditions (other than weather conditions...) or artificial obstructions which...could not...have been foreseen by an experienced contractor...'

The Contractor must complete the Works to the satisfaction of the Engineer (Cl. 13(1)) and must comply with the Engineer's instructions. Safety is the Contractor's responsibility (Cl. 19(1)) and he must take proper care of the Works. He must insure the Works in the joint names of the Employer and Contractor (Cl. 21) and will have to put right any insurable damage using insurance monies. The Contractor must also take out insurance against losses and claims by third parties (Cls. 22 and 23). These would be claims in tort for personal injury or damage to property resulting from construction operations.

Delays or extra costs incurred by the Contractor due to any circumstances which could not have been reasonably 'foreseen by an experienced contractor at the time of tender' (Cl. 31(2)) may entitle him to an extension of time and extra costs.

If the Contractor fails to complete within the time prescribed he must pay to the Employer liquidated damages (Cl. 47(2) (b)). The sum stated in the Appendix to the Form of Tender must represent a genuine estimate of the net losses incurred by late completion. This is frequently referred to, wrongly, as a penalty clause. In law, a party to a contract cannot exact a penalty from the other party for poor performance. Damages can only be sought as compensation for losses incurred. The purpose of these liquidated damages is to agree in advance what should be paid by the Contractor to the Employer without imposing a burden of proof at the end of the Contract. Where the Contractor overruns the prescribed time, the Engineer in completing the monthly certificate, deducts liquidated damages at the specified rate from the sums due.

Cl. 49(2) the Contractor 'shall deliver up to the Employer the Works...in the condition required by the Contract (fair wear and tear excepted) to the satisfaction of the Engineer.'

For construction operations which may continue for some years it would be unfair to expect all parts of the Permanent Works to be handed over in pristine condition, hence this provision. It is the Engineer who decides whether the condition is satisfactory, which implies that it is the Engineer who decides what is meant by 'fair wear and tear'.

Cl. 59(3) the Contractor shall normally 'be as responsible for the work executed or goods materials or services supplied by a Nominated Sub-contractor...as if he had himself executed such work....'[4]

This reinforces the points already made about subcontractors and privity of contract.

19.4.2   Purchaser's obligations

These are few and fundamental, namely to provide unhindered access to the site (Cl. 42(2)), to obtain all wayleaves (Cl. 27) and to pay within 28 days the sums certified by the Engineer as interim payments (Clause 60(2)).

19.4.3   Supervision and administration by the Engineer

The Engineer must provide the Contractor with all information and instructions necessary to complete the Works (Cl. 7) and may issue instructions to the Contractor on any matter connected with the Contract (Cl. 13), and all work must be acceptable to the Engineer.

The Engineer may award an extension of time to the Contractor (see 19.4.6 controlling completion) and has a duty to make an assessment of any delay claimed by the Contractor (Cl. 44). In due course the Engineer will issue the Certificate of Substantial Completion (Cl. 48(1)) and the all important Defects Correction Certificate (Cl. 61(1)); (see 19.4.6).

Cl. 51(1) the Engineer 'shall order any variation...that is *in his opinion* (our italics) necessary for the completion of the Works' and '*may* order any variation that...shall *in his opinion be desirable* (our italics again) for the completion and/or improved functioning of the Works.'

This clause provides the Engineer with considerable powers to issue change orders. These are changes within the Contract, that is, changes to the Works. The Engineer has no power to change the contract itself (Cl. 2(1)(c), above); however, what represents a variation within the contract and what represents a variation of the Contract may not always be clear. Adding a second storey to a large one storey building might be viewed as a fundamental change in the nature and purpose of the Works, thus making such a decision a variation of the Contract

---

[4]In each of the contracts under review the parties named in the contract are all referred to as *he*, and he should be taken to mean *he/she* throughout the text and for the remainder of this chapter.

which would require renegotiation by the Employer and Contractor. But, an additional floor for a 97 storey building might well be desirable for the improved functioning of the Works and might be perceived as an admissible variation. Somewhere between these two extremes there lies a grey area! Many contracts, MF/1 included, control variations by limiting their total value to a specified percentage of the Contract Price, not so ICE6. Under ICE6 it is the Engineer who ascertains the value of any variations (Cl. 52), after consultation with the Contractor. Where the Engineer and Contractor disagree, the Engineer decides.

The Engineer may order the Contractor to employ a Nominated Subcontractor (Cl. 58(2)). This is common practice in the UK. Difficulties do arise. The problem of specialist design work carried out by a Nominated Subcontractor has been referred to. Other problems can arise when a subcontractor cannot meet the Contractor's programme (which would have been drawn up prior to the nomination) or when a subcontractor's performance is unsatisfactory despite all the efforts of the Contractor. Is the Contractor bound by Clause 59(3) (see section 19.4.1)? Under ICE6 this would appear to be the case.

The Engineer shall settle disputes between the Employer and the Contractor (Cl. 66(3)). When acting in this capacity the Engineer, whose role will be that of a quasi-arbitrator, must be impartial (Cl. 2(8)). A difficulty here is that in being the designer, the technical adviser and the sole authority for issuing instructions and variation orders, many of the disputes that do arise are actually differences between the Engineer and the Contractor. Even so, most Engineers, when called upon to settle disputes of this nature, do so with an exemplary impartiality, sometimes to the Employer's consternation.

The Engineer has a duty to take action if he receives notice from the Contractor of 'unforeseen physical conditions and artificial obstructions' (Cl. 12(4)). The Contractor may then seek instructions on how to overcome the problem; in addition the Contractor may seek an extension of time and extra payment. The Engineer must take action in all these respects.

On site the Engineer's Representative (ER) watches and supervises the construction of the Works (Cl. 2). The ER may not award extensions of time, issue completion certificates or settle disputes. Typically the ER and his staff will be engaged in checking that the materials and methods conform to specification, supervising tests, keeping daily records of progress, weather, labour, problems encountered, etc., measuring the work for payment purposes, keeping full records when the Contractor gives notice of a claim, giving technical instruction, producing 'as-built' drawings.

It is the Engineer who authorizes payment by the Employer to the Contractor; if the Engineer is not satisfied with the quality of work, or if he disagrees with the Contractor's measurement of the work, then he can certify a lesser sum. The actual payment is always 2% or 3% less than the sum due; this reduction is known as retention money and is held until completion, as an encouragement to complete! The Employer must pay within 28 days of the certificate. The Contractor's monthly statement to the Engineer should show:

- the estimated total contract value of the Permanent Works to the end of the month;

- a list and the value of any goods and materials delivered to the site but not yet incorporated into the Permanent Works (this assists the Contractor's cash flow);
- a list and the value of certain goods identified in the Contract not yet on site (this is usually reserved for expensive machinery or plant that has to be installed on site, which the Contractor has to pay for, and for which storage on site would either be inappropriate or impossible);
- any other entitlements, for example, additional payments agreed by the Engineer.

19.4.4   Controlling the Employer's costs

If the Contractor is required to do anything extra to what was required at the time of tendering he will be entitled to extra payment (Cl52 (4)). Encountering 'unforeseen conditions' (Cl.12), carrying out Engineer's instructions (Cl. 13), experiencing delays caused by late drawings (Cl. 7), late approvals by the Engineer (Cl. 14), suspension of the works by the Engineer (Cl. 40), and delayed access to the site (Cl. 42), may all entitle the Contractor to extra payments for both their direct costs and the indirect costs of any delay (Contractor's overheads). This, after all, is a contract designed to make provision for extensions of time and extra payments. The Engineer in providing technical instruction, in making changes on behalf of the Employer, in adjusting the designs as the work proceeds, may, in pursuit of technical excellence, lose sight of the disruptive effect on the whole project that all these extras might entail, resulting in a project that overruns in terms of time and cost. Successful Project Management is more likely to be achieved where the Engineer appoints separate individuals to oversee Project Management and Project Engineering.

Bad weather often delays construction projects, but, of itself is no reason for awarding extra time or money to a Contractor. The bad weather must be *exceptional*. Under ICE6, exceptionally adverse weather conditions do not entitle the Contractor to extra payments, only to an extension of time (Cl. 44(1)(d)).

19.4.5   Controlling completion

The Contractor must meet the Completion Date (and Sectional Completions if required). How this is achieved is up to the Contractor despite Clause 14 which requires submission of a master programme to the Engineer for approval. Completion occurs on the date on which the Substantial Completion Certificate is signed. Until Substantial Completion (Cl. 48) the Contractor is fully responsible for 'care of the works' and is liable for Liquidated Damages for any delay beyond the Completion Date. Substantial Completion releases half the Retention Money and the Contractor is no longer responsible for insuring the Works. This can be important. If, for example, the Works are seriously damaged by floods one week before the Substantial Completion Certificate is expected then the Contractor, not having completed the Works, must continue on site, repairing the damage using the insurance monies provided. If this damage occurs after Substantial

Completion, the Contractor is not bound by the Contract to stay and make good the damage. If the Employer asks the Contractor to do this work he is free to stay or not, and to negotiate new prices for the work.

Under general law, if one party to a contract delays the other party so that the latter cannot meet the contract requirements then any damages for late completion become unenforceable. The purpose of the extensions of time clause (Cl.44) is to reinstate these damages should the Engineer or Employer delay the Contractor. Under Clause 44(2) the Engineer has an independent duty to make an assessment for an extension of time, whether the Contractor claims extra time or not. When the Engineer awards an extension of time this revises the Completion Date; as long as Substantial Completion occurs before this revised date the Contractor will not have to pay liquidated damages.

Substantial Completion signals the start of the Defects Correction Period; this is usually six months. The Defects Correction Certificate is issued by the Engineer when all outstanding work has been completed to his satisfaction. The issue of this certificate releases the second half of the Retention Money, permits the Contractor to submit the Final Account and signifies that the Works have been completed to the satisfaction of the Engineer. Clause 61(2) states that this does not relieve 'the Contractor or the Employer from any liability ... arising out of ... the Contract.' The Contractor cannot claim as a defence against an action for defective work that the Defects Correction Certificate releases him from liability for quality, standards and performance.

19.4.6   ICE6 and Project Management

It should be clear that the Engineer plays a vital role; as designer of the project, technical adviser to the Employer, Quality Control manager for the Employer, administrator of the Contract, independent authority in respect of claims by the Contractor for extra time or extra money and first line arbitrator in the event of any dispute between Employer and Contractor. Does this provide for the well defined project management which large and complex contracts demand? The Engineer is primarily appointed for his technical expertise and design skills; the Engineer's role during construction can be secondary to the continuing business of an engineering consultancy. ICE6 works extremely well for straightforward civil engineering contracts, it might be less successful where severe technical problems arise and pressures to keep to time and budget are high. Under these circumstances a separate appointment of Project Manager overseeing design, tendering and construction is advisable.

19.5   MF/1

The parties to the Contract are the Purchaser and the Contractor. The Purchaser has a more active role than that assigned to the Employer under ICE6. However, the Purchaser places considerable technical reliance upon the Engineer and the Engineer's Representative. Under MF/1 the Contractor will *design* and *manufacture, erect* and *test* in order to execute the Works, and the terms of payment are those of a *lump sum contract.*

The system of Project Management required by this form of contract is very different from that required by ICE6. The Engineer provides the Contractor with only an outline design of the Works and a performance specification; the management of the design and construction process rests thereafter firmly with the Contractor. This should provide for more effective management of the project. The difficulty occurs at the tender stage. Under ICE6 the Engineer can analyse tenders in great detail, for the tenderers must price every item of work, and comparisons of the rates charged for each work item can be made, and the significance of these differences can be taken into account. But under MF/1 the Engineer will be provided with a very limited schedule of payments for major elements of work such as delivery, installation and testing and will be unable to determine how the prices have been established. The basis of acceptance of a tender is price and the promise to meet performance criteria. Pricing structures cannot be examined and the Engineer is in no position to compare tenders for the effects that any potential changes might have upon the eventual Contract Price.

MF/1 must be accompanied by Special Conditions. These provide information on performance bonds, liquidated damages and the Terms of Payment. Since this is a lump sum contract there must be some means by which the Contractor can obtain progress payments; these Special Conditions allow these provisions to be widely varied to suit the needs of the Contract.

The major provisions are summarized under the headings:

- Contractor's obligations
- Purchaser's obligations
- supervision and administration by the Engineer
- controlling the Purchaser's costs
- controlling completion.

19.5.1   The Contractor's obligations

Only the most important clauses will be identified.

Cl. 2.4 'The Contractor shall proceed with the Contract in accordance with the decisions, instructions and orders given by the Engineer ...'

This comes as no surprise after ICE6.

Cl. 13.1 The Contractor 'shall ... design, manufacture, deliver to Site, erect and test the Plant, execute the Works and carry out the Tests on Completion within the Time for Completion'.

This is the very heart of the Contract.

Although the Engineer's approval is required for the design (Cl. 15.1) and all work must be done to the satisfaction of the Engineer (Cl. 13.2) it is the Contractor who remains responsible for 'any errors, omissions or discrepancies'. (Cl. 16.1)

The Contractor can even be held responsible for detailed design provided by the Purchaser or Engineer unless he disclaims responsibility! The Contractor is required to provide operating and maintenance instructions and as-built drawings so that the Purchaser can 'operate, maintain, dismantle, reassemble and adjust all parts of the Works'. (Cl. 15.6)

Cl. 19.1 'The Contractor shall be responsible for the adequacy, stability and safety of his (sic) operations on Site ... '

This is subtly different from ICE6 in which the Contractor is responsible for *all site* operations. This reflects the fact that often 'the Works' under a MF/1 contract is sited within 'the Works' of a construction contract. The Contractor is 'responsible for the care of the Works ... until the date of taking-over ... ' This leads to Clause 47.1 which requires the Contractor to insure the Works and the Contractor's equipment in the joint names of Contractor and Purchaser. The Contractor is also obliged to take out insurance against claims (in tort) brought against the Purchaser or Contractor by third parties for injuries, death or damage to property (Cl. 47.4).

If the Contractor fails to complete the Works on time he will have to pay to the Purchaser 'the percentage stated in the Appendix of the Contract Value ... ' (Cl. 34.1). The percentage must not be of such a size as to represent a penalty.

After the Works have been taken over by the Purchaser, Performance Tests are usually required by this form of contract. Clause 35.2 requires Performance Tests to be carried out by the Purchaser or Engineer 'under the supervision of the Contractor ...' If the Works fails these tests, the Contractor must modify the Works at his own expense and repeat the tests. Having taken over the Works, the Purchaser will want to put them to use, but with all major plant there needs to be a running-in period; it is during this time that these performance tests can be made. While the Purchaser's operational requirements come first, the Contractor's tests cannot be postponed indefinitely (Cl. 35.5). If the Works continue to fail the Performance Tests within the specified period then either liquidated damages become payable or a reduction in the Contract Price can be agreed by the Purchaser and Contractor or the Contract can even be terminated and the Contractor expelled from the site. This rigorous contractual approach is essential for any major plant.

19.5.2   Purchaser's obligations

The purchaser's obligations include giving the Contractor access to the site, obtaining all consents, wayleaves, etc. and obtaining import permits or licences (Cl. 11). In addition, the Purchaser must:

- provide buildings, structures and foundations,
- operate suitable lifting equipment,[5]

---

[5]In some circumstances permanent lifting equipment may be provided earlier in a contract for the use of the Purchaser once the facility is operational. If this is the case the Purchaser may prefer to retain the responsibility for operating this equipment once it has been installed and handed over.

- make available on site for the Contractor electricity, water, gas, air and other services specified in the Special Conditions,
- provide all facilities for tests.

The assumption is that the Works are to be installed within buildings and on a site already there or to be provided by others, and that the Purchaser's (permanent) lifting equipment will be available. An example of this would be the installation of turbines within the turbine hall of a power station. Here the building could have been constructed using ICE6, an overhead crane installed by a Nominated Subcontractor under ICE6, and the turbines installed within the building using the permanent crane under the provisions of MF/1.

19.5.3   Supervision and administration by the Engineer

The Engineer specifies the parameters for the project and accepts on behalf of the Purchaser 'the Works' which have been designed, manufactured and installed by the Contractor. Project management lies with the Contractor. The Engineer's role is defined in Clause 2. Note, the Engineer may delegate any of his duties to the Engineer's Representative (ER) unlike ICE6. The Engineer or the ER issues 'certificates, decisions, instructions and orders...' Such decisions and instructions include suspension of the Works (Cl. 25.1), and issuing variation orders (Cl. 27). The total value of all variations may not 'involve a net addition to or deduction from the Contract Price of more than 15 per cent ... unless both the Purchaser and Contractor agree. This kind of control on the value of variations is widely adopted in large construction contracts; ICE6 is unusual in not having such a provision. The valuation of variations is reached either by accepting a quotation from the Contractor or shall 'be determined by the Engineer in accordance with the rates specified in the schedules of prices'. If there are no rates then a 'reasonable' sum shall be paid to the Contractor; the Contractor must keep records of cost and time. The underlying assumption is that the Contractor and Engineer will agree a fair price though this is not stated.

The Engineer's Representative 'watches and supervises the Works, and tests and examines any Plant or workmanship.' (Cl. 2.2)

As in ICE6 the Engineer is required to act with independent professional judgement. In making a decision or determining a value 'he shall exercise such discretion fairly ... having regard to all the circumstances.' (Cl. 2.7)

Cl. 23.1 'The Engineer shall be entitled ... during manufacture to inspect, examine and test on the Contractor's premises the materials and workmanship and performances of all Plant ... Such inspection, examination or testing shall not release the Contractor from any obligation under the Contract.'

Cl. 23.4 'When the Engineer is satisfied that any Plant has passed the test of inspection ... he shall ... issue ... a certificate to that effect. Failure results in a notice of rejection and resubmission for testing or inspection.

It is clear that the Engineer's main concern is that the Contractor completes the Works according to specification, and all this watching, supervising, inspecting, examining and testing is to this end.

There is no clause which expressly empowers the Engineer to nominate subcontractors; however, Clause 5.5 allows the Engineer to direct how prime cost sums in the Contract should be expended, and prime costs sums are there for work done by someone other than the Contractor. The Contractor seems to be in a better potential position under MF/1 than he is under ICE6, for 'The Contractor shall have no responsibility for work done or Plant supplied by any other person ... unless the Contractor shall have approved ...' (Cl. 5.6) Certainly, the Contractor has a right to object to a Nominated Subcontractor under ICE6, but the process of objection needs evidence and reasoning, the Contractor has to present a case. Under MF/1 the onus is on the Engineer to convince the Contractor.

Interim payments are paid according to a schedule provided in the Special Conditions; this schedule will be different for every contract. However, in all cases the Contractor must apply to the Engineer for each progress payment. Typically the schedule might include provisions for payment when the value of Plant manufactured reaches 25%, 50%, 75%, and 100% of the Contract Price for manufacture; the sums payable would not be the certified value but a lesser sum. MF/1 provides an example in which the actual payments are only 85% of the certified value. The schedule includes provisions for delivery, work on site and testing.

The Contractor's certificates for payment (Cl. 39) must be accompanied by evidence of the work done, or evidence of delivery or shipment and payment for the same. Clause 39.8 states that no interim certificate of payment 'shall be relied upon as conclusive evidence of any matter ...'; nothing is final until the final certificate, when the Contract goes far beyond the provisions of ICE6 in releasing the Contractor from his obligations; see Clause 39.12 below:

Cl. 39.12 'A final certificate of payment shall be conclusive evidence:
– that the Works ... is in accordance with the Contract;
– that the Contractor has performed all his obligations under the Contract
– of the value of the Works ...
Payment of the amount certified in a final certificate ... shall be conclusive evidence that the Purchaser has performed all his obligations under the Contract ... '

Only where there has been fraud or dishonesty or where disputes or arbitration procedures have been put in hand do these provisions not apply. Contrast this with Clause 61 (2) of ICE6 referred to previously under 19.4.5.

19.5.4   Controlling the Purchaser's costs

Notice of making a claim must be given to the Engineer within 30 days of the circumstances giving rise to the claim. Legitimate reasons for claims include encountering 'conditions or obstructions [which] could not reasonably have been ascertained from an inspection of the Site' (Cl. 5.7), carrying out the Engineer's instructions (Cl. 2.4), experiencing difficulties because of errors in drawings supplied by the Purchaser or Engineer (Cl. 16.2), suspension of the Works by the Engineer (Cl. 25.1), notice of variations (Cl. 27.5) and delayed access to site (Cl. 11.1). Clause 41.2 allows the Contractor to add to the sums claimed a percentage for profit for 15 listed sub-clauses. This is far more generous than ICE6 which allows an addition for profit only for Clause 12 (unforeseen adverse physical conditions and artificial obstructions) claims.

19.5.5 Controlling completion

The 'Time for Completion' is the period in which the work should be done.

Cl. 32.1' ... the Contractor shall so execute the Works that they shall be complete and pass the Tests on Completion (but not the Performance Tests, if any be included) within the Time for Completion.'

Cl. 29.2 'When the Works have passed the Tests on Completion and are complete (except in minor respects that do not affect their use for the purpose for which they are intended) the Engineer shall issue a certificate to the Contractor and to the Purchaser ... '

This certificate is known as the Taking-Over Certificate and, as with the Substantial Completion Certificate in ICE6, releases the Contractor from the risks of loss or damage to the Works, signals the start of the Defects Liability Period (usually 12 months) and releases the Contractor from paying liquidated damages, which in this Contract amount to 'the percentage stated ... of the Contract Value ... for each week between the Time for Completion and the actual date of completion.' (Cl. 34.1). It is the Engineer who decides when completion has taken place but the Tests on Completion are major determinants. Clause 28.4 states that if 'any part of the Works fails to pass the Tests on Completion they shall be repeated within a reasonable time' and Clause 28.5 requires the Contractor to 'take whatever steps may be necessary to enable the Works ... to pass the Tests ...' If the Works cannot pass the tests, Clause 49 (Contractor's Default) comes into force and the Contractor expelled from the site, his equipment seized and a 'Termination Value', which recognizes the lesser value of the Works, certified by the Engineer. Any Performance Tests required by the Contract must be 'carried out as soon as is reasonably practicable ... after the Works ... have been taken over ... (Cl. 35.1). The Special Conditions can specify both a period of time allowed for these tests and liquidated damages for their late completion.

Provisions for extensions of time are found in Clause 33. It is the Engineer who awards such extensions. The reasons include variation orders, 'any act or omission on the part of the Purchaser or the Engineer', any industrial dispute or any 'circumstances beyond the reasonable control of the Contractor'. It is interesting to observe that industrial disputes can be a reason for awarding an extension of time; this is certainly not the case in ICE6. Perhaps it is a reflection of past industrial relations in the UK in the heavy engineering industries. Since industrial disputes are, to a degree, within the control of the Contractor, it seems more appropriate that this risk should be assigned to the Contractor, rather than to the Purchaser.

During the Defects Liability Period the Contractor must 'rectify or complete to the reasonable satisfaction of the Engineer ... any outstanding items of work or Plant ... ' (Cl. 29.4). If any defects or damage appear during this period they must be remedied by the Contractor and the Defects Liability Period extended, save that the Period must not be extended beyond two years after the Taking-Over date (Cl. 36.3). The contractual liability for work done during the Defects Liability Period is very different from liability for work done before the Taking-Over Certificate; the former leaves open the possibility of later claims for breach of contract, the latter does not (Cl. 36.10). This places a special responsibility on the Engineer when issuing the Taking-Over Certificate, clearly the more that has been completed satisfactorily the smaller the risk carried by the Purchaser. Where Latent Defects appear within three years of the Taking-Over date, the Contractor must repair or replace 'at the Contractor's option' (Cl. 36.10).

Unlike ICE6 there is no provision for a Defects Correction Certificate. The Contractor applies for 'the final certificate of payment' once he has completed his 'obligations under Clause 36 (Defects Liability), other than under Clause 36.10 (Latent Defects)...' (Cl. 39.9), and it is the Engineer who issues the final certificate (Clause 39.11). As previously indicated the final certificate is a most important document and, certainly, puts a heavy responsibility upon the Engineer who issues it, for, with the exception of Latent Defects and dishonesty, the Purchaser will be unable to bring a case for breach of contract at a later date against the Contractor.

Unless the Special Conditions provide for earlier payments, the balance of the Contract Price, some 15%, is included in the final certificate. This 15% retention is a formidable incentive for the Contractor to complete to the satisfaction of the Engineer, very different from the 3% in construction contracts.

19.6 IChemE GREEN BOOK

This is a *cost reimbursement contract*. The Contractor supplies goods and/or services required by the Purchaser and, provided he exercises his normal professional skills, is reimbursed all costs incurred. Cost reimbursement contracts are especially suited to projects that are not fully defined at the time the contract is made. Therefore, these contracts can accommodate design by the Contractor, designs gradually developed by others, manufacture, supply, installation, construction and testing by the Contractor or by Nominated Subcontractors. The Contract has provisions for conversion at a later date, if the parties wish, to a lump sum contract. The flexibility of this Contract is such that it has been selected for projects other than process plant installations. (Thames Water have, for example, used it for one of the London Ring Main contracts.) The Contract is unusual in that it is one with which suppliers and purchasers express considerable satisfaction.

The General Conditions must be accompanied by Special Conditions and by a number of Schedules which will be described below.

The major provisions will be examined under five headings:

- Contractor's obligations
- Purchaser's obligations
- supervision and administration by the Project Manager

- controlling the Purchaser's costs
- controlling completion.

19.6.1 Contractor's obligations

Cl. 3.1 'The Contractor shall ... have and maintain resources (including financial resources) adequate to execute the Works and shall execute them in accordance with good engineering practice and to the reasonable satisfaction of the Project Manager. Such execution of the Works ... shall be in accordance with the ... Schedule 1 (Description of Works), the Specification and other provisions of the Contract.'

The Contractor has entered into a contract to do whatever is required, which means to provide all the resources necessary to design or buy or deliver or install, etc. This is the heart of the Contract; the Contractor provides the resources, the Purchaser pays the Contractor. What tasks have to be done will be determined by Schedule 1 — which describes the project and the extent and nature of the Contractor's contribution to the project including engineering services, buying materials, equipment, labour and so on and by the Specification, which is the technical definition and could vary from a brief statement of performance to a detailed description.

If during the Contract, the Contractor believes that 'a change in the design, execution or operation of the Works' is necessary or would be beneficial to the Purchaser then the Contractor should submit for the Project Manager's approval the proposed changes (Cl. 3.2). The Contractor is being encouraged to take the initiative; this is a contract in which confidence in the Contractor's expertise is being firmly expressed.

Cl. 11.1 ' ... the Contractor shall comply with [the Project Manager's instructions] ... within a reasonable period to be agreed ... '

If the Contractor believes that compliance with an instruction constitutes a change in the type or extent of the Works or services to be supplied, or could delay the Works or could prevent the Contractor from fulfilling his obligations then he has to notify the Project Manager (Cl. 11.2); the Contractor may be entitled to payment for work done in justifying why the instruction should not be followed. This clause is necessary in a contract in which the demands upon the Contractor can be wide ranging; there will be some tasks which will be outside 'the Works' as defined by Schedule 1 and the Specification, and which the Contractor should not be expected to do.

Considerable emphasis is placed on staffing the operations. With so much reliance upon the skills and initiative of the Contractor, the Purchaser want to be sure that the right people are employed.

Cl. 12.2 'From the commencement of work at the Site until the whole of the Plant has been accepted by the Purchaser ... [the Contractor] shall ensure that some suitable person is employed ... as Site Manager. ... The Site Manager shall be present at the Site throughout normal working hours ... The Contractor ... shall not make or change such appointment without the ... consent of the Project Manager.'

Cl. 12.3 'The Contractor shall provide such further supervisory staff ... as are specified in the Contract ...'

Cl. 12.4 'The Contractor shall use all reasonable endeavours to ensure that any key personnel named in the Contract shall continue to be employed in their specified capacities ... for so long as ... the Works require.'

Cl. 12.5 'If the Project Manager is of the opinion that the Site Manager or any member of the Contractor's supervisory staff is incompetent or has been guilty of misconduct ... he may ... require such person to leave the site ... The decision by the Project Manager to exercise [this] power ... *shall be the final and binding and not subject to challenge in arbitration or court proceedings*' (our italics).

The validity of this final statement must be debatable!

Cl. 13.2 'The Contractor shall also, if so required ... submit ... with the programme details ... of the personnel of suitable qualifications and experience whom the Contractor proposes to employ ...'

Cl. 27.2 'The Contractor shall at all times conduct his labour relations in close consultation with the Project Manager.'

These provisions go far beyond the requirements of ICE6 and MF/1.

The Contractor will amost certainly be required to carry out a variety of tests.

Cl 19.2 'The Contractor shall carry out such off-site tests as he considers necessary or as the Project Manager instructs ...'

Performance tests may or may not be required and are referred to under 19.6.5 controlling completion.

Provisions for care of the Works and insurance of the Works and in respect of third party claims (Cls. 30 and 31) are similar to the provisions of ICE6 and MF/1 and are not described further. Responsibility for the Works lies with the Contractor until they have been taken over by the Purchaser.

As with ICE6 and MF/1 the Contractor is liable to pay liquidated damages if the work is not completed on time. At the time the Contract is made the completion date or dates may not be known; if so, *Schedule 4 — Times of Completion* must be drawn up by the Contractor, and if the Contractor fails to meet this Schedule with no good cause then liquidated damages become payable at the percentages of the Contract Price stated in Schedules 8 and 9 (Liquidated Damages for delay and Liquidated Damages for failure to pass performance tests), but see later under 19.6.5 controlling completion.

19.6.2 Purchaser's obligations

The fundamental obligations are to give the Contractor possession of the site and ensure that there is appropriate access from the commencement date for the period of the Contract (Cl. 22) and to pay the Contractor within 14 days of certification by the Project Manager (Cl. 39). It is the Project Manager who manages the Contract on behalf of the Purchaser and Clause 10.1(d) states 'the Purchaser shall be responsible for any act, neglect or omission of the Project Manager ... ' which is the same position as ICE6 and MF/1. Since the Contractor and Purchaser may be working alongside one another on the same site it is the Purchaser's responsibility not to interfere with the Contractor's operations (Cl. 4.1). The Purchaser 'may at any time ... order the Contractor to cease the further execution of the Works.' (CL. 42.1).

19.6.3   Supervision and Administration by the Project Manager

Control of the contract is shared between the Contract Manager, for the Contractor, and the Project Manager for the Purchaser. Communication at a higher level is not ruled out.

This Contract recognizes the possibility that the Project Manager is an employee of the Purchaser, that, therefore, he cannot be impartial between Purchaser and Contractor, and so requires that 'where the Project Manager is required ... to exercise a discretion or make a judgement or form an opinion he shall do so to the best of his skill and judgement as a professional engineer.' (Cl. 10.1(e)).

The role of the Project Manager is similar in many respects to the roles of the Engineer under ICE6 and MF/1. The Project Manager has 'full authority to act on behalf of the Purchaser ... an obligation of the Project Manager shall be deemed to be an obligation of the Purchaser' (Cl. 10.1(a) and (c)); 'the Project Manager's Representative shall have authority to condemn any workmanship or materials ... ' (Cl. 10.5); 'the Project Manager may ... authorise the Project Manager's Representative to exercise any of the powers and functions of the Project Manager ... ' (Cl. 10.6), which is not possible under ICE6; 'the Project Manager may at any time instruct the Contractor to execute the Works ... ' (Cl. 11.1). The role ascribed to the Project Manager regarding approval of the Contractor's programme and certification of payments to the Contractor is similar to the Engineer's role under ICE6 and MF/1.

Variations are defined in Clause 17.1 to mean 'any alteration in the Plant or to the type or extent of the Contractor's Services, with special reference to the Specification and to Schedule 1 (Description of Works), which is an amendment, omission or addition but not merely a closer definition, a minor change in detail ... ' This makes clear that any Variation must be within the original scope of 'the Works'. It cannot be something outside the original concept. It also provides that Variation Orders are unnecessary for minor changes. This is in striking and welcome contrast to many construction contracts (for example, the *Standard Form of Building Contract* [12] ('with Quantities' editions) known as JCT80).

A limitation is set on the aggregate value of Variations at the Contractor's discretion.

Cl. 17.5 'The Contractor may object to any Variation order on the grounds that the net effect of compliance therewith and with all other Variation orders [so far] ... would be to decrease or increase the first agreed estimate of the ... value of the Contractor's services by more than twenty five per cent.'

Since this is a cost reimbursement contract, one in which the Contractor's risks are small, he is normally unlikely to object to extra work since both extra time and money will be provided by the Purchaser for any extended services.

This is a Contractor's Contract. The Contractor presents a 'request for payment to the Project Manager towards the end of each month' (CL. 39.2) which provides an estimate of predicted expenditure for the coming month and evidence of what was spent in the preceding month and the amounts certified for that month. The Project Manager issues a certificate within seven days and the Purchaser must pay within 14 days; thus, the Contractor receives his expenses for any one month halfway through that month. Compare that to the 28 days' arrears for ICE6 and the more infrequent schedule of payments under MF/1. The Project Manager may only refuse to certify payment for 'those items about which [he] requires further information.' (Cl. 39.3). Wrong refusal will lead to interest being payable on amounts overdue. There is no provision for refusal where the work is defective. If a defect is due to the failure of the Contractor then it must be remedied at his expense (Cl. 35), but this could be much later in the Contract. There is no provision for retention.

19.6.4   Controlling the Purchaser's Costs

Since all costs are reimbursable, Variation Orders are of little concern for the Contractor. Effective cost control on behalf of the Purchaser requires careful monitoring of payments for all services provided. In a cost reimbursement contract trust and confidence in the Contractor is of paramount importance. Control is exercised by careful scrutiny of each monthly certificate and by close inspection of the Contractor's operations to ensure that all resources are used effectively and economically. In the IChemE Green Book, Guidance Notes are provided on how cost control should be exercised.

Guidance Note Q requires that separate records are kept for Variations. It is recommended that costs are reported on a regular (30 day) basis. The cost records should show:

- the commitment to costs on all orders placed
- costs of engineering
- value of invoices which have been paid
- any milestone payments that have been made
- incentive payments
- forecast of costs of completion.

This latter provision accords with the best principles of Project Management which demand estimates of costs to completion at every payment interval.

Guidance Note DD requires that *Schedule 2* of the Contract lists all cost elements and provides an exhaustive list of typical cost elements; this is reproduced in Appendix 5. For each item the Schedule must indicate the method by which the charges will be debited. The alternatives are:

- directly chargeable at net cost
- directly chargeable at rates quoted in *Schedule 3*
- not directly chargeable, covered by rates for other cost elements
- not directly chargeable, covered by lump sum payments in *Schedule 3*.

Guidance Note EE refers to *Schedule 3* which lists the rates and charges which, when applied to the appropriate cost elements in *Schedule 2* enable that part of the Contract Price to be calculated. Thus every chargeable cost element in *Schedule 2* must have a corresponding entry in *Schedule 3*. The Schedule will consist of a series of tables covering:

- rates per hour for home office personnel
- rates for field personnel
- travelling and subsistence
- rates for reprographics
- computer charges
- tools and plant hire charges
- field labour charges to cover small tools, protective clothing etc.
- charges for procurement
- fees.

There is no recommendation on whether the Contract should be Cost Plus a Percentage Fee, Cost Plus a Fixed Fee or some form of Target Contract; this is left to the Purchaser to decide. These different options were discussed in Chapter 17.

19.6.5   Controlling Completion

For many process plant projects, the end of the construction phase, testing and starting operational life form a continuum; this is usually referred to as 'commissioning'. This Contract provides for orderly controls over substantial completion, take-over, performance tests and acceptance, identifying completion of construction as an important break point.

Cl. 32.1 'As soon as the Plant, or any appropriate part thereof, is in the opinion of the Contractor substantially complete and ready for inspection, the Contractor shall notify the Project Manager by means of a Construction Completion Report. This report shall state which parts of the Plant the Contractor proposes to demonstrate have been completed in accordance with the Specification and have passed ... [any] tests ... included in the Specification.'

Upon successful completion of these 'demonstrations' the Contractor and Project Manager sign the Report with an addendum stating that the demonstrations were satisfactory and that 'the Plant or part thereof is substantially complete ... ' (Cl. 32.2). A note of minor items requiring completion before the issue of a Taking-Over Certificate should be added where necessary.

Since completion is likely to be a gradual process, completion dates for specified sections of the Plant must be set out in *Schedule 4 (Times of Completion)*. Failure to complete any section on time can lead to Liquidated Damages. Those who drafted this Contract recognized that cost reimbursement contracts are used where, at the time of the Contract being formed, the extent of the work required to be done, and hence the time it will take, are uncertain. Guidance Note K provides

'There is an inevitable link between cost and time of completion ... By controlling the expenditure in a reimbursable contract [the Purchaser] can in principle also control its execution ... the Purchaser is often in a position to influence its execution sufficiently to make it impossible for the Contractor to have full responsibility for programme control ... Such considerations show that it could be to the Purchaser's disadvantage to have the terms of Clauses 14 to 16 applied ...'

Therefore, while the provisions for completion by specified dates and for liquidated damages are there, and the accompanying provisions for extensions of time for delays (Cl. 15), it will often be the case that they will not be applied.

After Substantial Completion comes Taking-Over. This, too, may be sectional. Taking-Over usually requires procedures which will be given in *Schedule 5 — Take-over procedures.* This lists activities prior to taking-over tests and the tests themselves. Once these procedures and tests have been concluded to the satisfaction of the Contractor (who must provide the Purchaser and the Project Manager with 'manuals and other documents', (Cl. 19.6)), then the Project Manager issues a Taking-Over Certificate.

Cl. 33.7 'As soon as shall be reasonably possible after the issue of the Taking-Over Certificate the Contractor shall correct, repair, adjust or complete to the satisfaction of the Project Manager all items noted on the ... Certificate as not being complete ... '

After this the Plant 'shall be at the risk of the Purchaser who shall take possession thereof' and he becomes 'responsible for the care, safety, servicing, and maintenance of the Plant, for starting up and operating it and for preparing for and carrying out the performance tests ... ' (Cl. 33.9). Provisions for performance tests are given in Clause 34. The clause only applies if the Contractor is required to make 'specific guarantees in respect of the performance of the Plant, determinable by performance tests ... Otherwise this clause shall form no part of the Contract.' (Cl. 34.1). Guidance Note W observes that 'in the case of a wholly reimbursable contract (to which the Model Form relates), it is difficult to reconcile the Contractor's effective role as an extension of the Purchaser's engineering force ... with the Contractor as an independent body ... taking liability for the plant performance.' This Contract envisages that, usually, there will be no *contractual* performance tests, that any such tests would be part of the taking-over procedures and no penalty would apply in the event that the desired performance criteria could not be attained. Clause 33.8 states that 'Notwithstanding the failure of the Plant to pass any take-over test ... the Project Manager may in his absolute discretion issue a Taking-Over Certificate in respect of the Plant.'

If the Contractor makes no specific guarantees of performance of the Plant then the Taking-Over Certificate 'shall be deemed to be an Acceptance Certificate' (Clause 36.1). Where performance tests are required the Project Manager will issue an Acceptance Certificate upon the satisfactory completion of these tests. The Defects Liability Period of 365 days runs from the date of the Taking-Over Certificate; during this period the Contractor is required to make good all defects brought to his attention. Usually the Contractor will be paid for making good these defects unless the defect is clearly due to some failure of the Contractor. The Final Certificate is not issued until the Defects Liability Period has ended and the defects have been rectified.

This, much more than the other two contracts, is a contract based on trust, in which the Contractor carries out design, construction, testing and commissioning to the Purchaser's directions. Where things go wrong they are sorted out by the two parties concerned, and the Purchaser pays for the use of the Contractor's resources in overcoming the problems; thus provisions for liquidated damages for delay or failure to meet performance criteria are often inappropriate. Provision is, of necessity, made for liquidated damages because large process plants will often include some elements, which could be payable by lump sum provisions, for which contractual controls on time and performance are essential. These provisions are no different in principle from those found in MF/1 and are not considered further.

19.7   REVIEW OF THE ENGINEERING CONTRACTS

Each of the three contracts, ICE6, MF/1, and IChemE Green Book has been examined at some length in order that an engineer intending to use any one of the three will find the section devoted to that contract a useful introduction. The student of one contract form will find much that is familiar in the other contracts, making the task of understanding them much easier.

Major differences arise because ICE6 is a measurement contract, MF/1 a lump sum contract and the IChemE Green Book a cost reimbursement contract. A natural consequence of this is that contractual controls over time, budget and performance with their emphasis on completion dates, liquidated damages, retention and provisions for extra time and extra costs are largely unnecessary when using the IChemE Green Book.

The other fundamental difference is that under ICE6 the Contractor usually will have no design responsibility and therefore has very little input into the planning of the project. This means that the Engineer has a far greater implied responsibility for the successful management of the project than under the other two contracts in which the Contractor can be responsible for design, specification, procurement, installation, testing and commissioning.

What the contracts have in common are:

- the provisions for supervision and administration by the Engineer/Project Manager who will act with professional impartiality,
- provisions for instructions and variation orders by the Engineer/Project Manager
- a minimal role for the Purchaser/Employer,
- a clear requirement that the Contractor be fully responsible for safety on the site and for care of works until completion or take-over, and provisions for insurance of the Works/Plant until that time,
- provisions for regular payments to the Contractor as the work proceeds, although payments under MF/1 will be less frequent than the monthly basis provided for in the other two contracts,
- provisions for substantial completion, taking over by the Purchaser/Employer and the inclusion of defects liability periods of between six and 12 months,

- provision for arbitration in the event of a dispute between the two parties to the contract.

Engineers should find that a careful study of these contracts will be a useful preparation for any set of contract conditions which they are likely to encounter in the future.

19.8   SUMMARY

In this chapter a brief introduction to the English law of Contract has been provided to give engineers a basis for studying engineering contracts. Three widely used standard forms of contract have been examined in some depth. The contracts have been examined from the standpoint of the Project Manager rather than that of the legal representative, hence the emphasis on the obligations of the parties, how the contract is administered, and the control of costs and time.

REFERENCES

1. *The Engineering and Construction Contract* (1995) formerly *The New Engineering Contract, Institution of Civil Engineers*. Second edition, Thomas Telford. London.
2. Keenan, D. (1992) *Smith and Keenan's English Law*. Tenth Edition, Chapter 10, Pitman, London.
3. Keenan, D. *Smith and Keenan's English Law* Case 65. Readers who wish to pursue the issues of communication by telecommunication should read *Entores Ltd.* v *Miles Far Eastern Corporation (1955)* and *Brinkibon* v *Stahag Stahl* (1982), see Keenan Case 63.
4. Treitel G. H. (1991) *The Law of Contract*. Eighth edition, Chapter 15, Sweet & Maxwell/Stevens & Sons, London.
5. *Butler Machine Tool Co Ltd* v *Ex-Cell-O Corporation* (England) [1979] 1 WLR 401.
6. Keenan, D. (1992) *English Law*. Tenth edition, Pitman, London. Case 311.
7. *Raffles* v *Wichelhaus* (1864) 2 H&C 906.
8. *Institution of Chemical Engineers Conditions of Contract for Process Plant — Reimbursable Contracts* (1992). IChemE.
9. *Institution of Civil Engineers Conditions of Contract*. Sixth edition, Thomas Telford.
10. *MF/1 Model Form of General Conditions of Contract Institution of Electrical Engineers and the Institution of Mechanical Engineers* (1995 revision).
11. *Humber Oil Terminals Trustee Ltd* v *Harbour & General Works (Stevin) Ltd.* (1991) 7 *Construction Law Journal* 333.
12. *The Standard Form of Building Contract Private Edition with Quantities* (1980) published by RIBA publications for the Joint Contracts Tribunal (revised 1986).

BIBLIOGRAPHY

Abrahamson, M. W. 1979 *Engineering Law and the ICE Contracts*. Fourth edition, Applied Science Publishers, London.
Betty, J. G. (1993) *Engineering Contracts*. McGraw-Hill, Maidenhead.
Murdoch, J. and Hughes, W. (1992) *Construction Contracts*. Spon, London.

20

Inventory management

20.1 INTRODUCTION

Inventory appears in a company's financial accounts as an asset (see Chapter 14 for further details). It can provide benefits to a business, such as:

- improving availability, to assist sales,
- acting as a regulator to smooth production levels,
- protecting against variations in demand or supply that could interrupt operations,
- providing a hedge against inflation,
- reducing the effects of breakdowns.

Inventory has therefore been regarded as 'a good thing', and techniques have been developed for managing or controlling inventory to provide the benefits while minimizing inventory costs.

The first part of this chapter provides a description of inventory-related costs, and the use of economic order quantity (EOQ) calculations and Pareto analysis. An example of these techniques applied to non production or maintenance, repair and operating (MRO) materials is provided.

Reasons for holding inventory are then examined, and the apparent benefits are questioned. This reveals that, far from being 'a good thing' that improves business performance, inventory is an obstacle to the identification and resolution of fundamental problems. The potential for Just-in-Time (JIT) inventory management is then discussed, using examples from the European automotive industry.

20.2 THE ELEMENTS OF INVENTORY CONTROL

20.2.1 The inventory cycle

In theory, a graph of inventory levels has a saw-tooth profile. The opening stock is reduced by steady usage or demand, and replenished by a delivery, just as stock is exhausted, as shown in Figure 20.1.

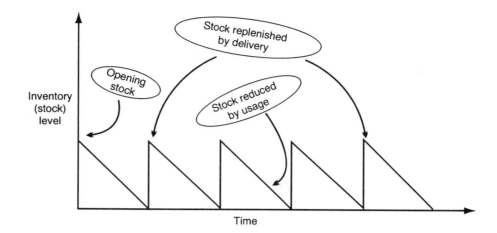

Figure 20.1 The 'saw-tooth' inventory cycle

20.2.2 Performance measures

An inventory or material control system scores a success if the item required is available at the time demanded. Some systems, particularly those serving random or sporadic demand, such as spare parts inventory, are measured in terms of 'first time fill' — that is the percentage of orders filled on demand — with 90% or higher regarded as good performance. The time taken to get the missing 10% is another measure of performance. The inventory management task in retailing is similar to spare parts provisioning, and is covered by Susan Gilchrist in an article 'Stores aim to reclaim buried pots of gold' in *The Times* on 6 September 1994. The article states: 'The principle element of customer service is the availability of the product . . . Marks and Spencer, widely seen as having the best-run supply chain in the industry, has option availability of more than 90 per cent in its stores, significantly above the industry average of about 65 per cent.'

The system scores a failure if a demand cannot be met first time — often termed a 'stock-out'. If the order is held for later supply, the unfilled demand is usually described as a 'back order'. The number and value of back orders, and their age, are also performance measures.

First time fill can be increased, and back orders reduced by holding more stock, but this can be prohibitively expensive. To meet demand between replenishments, the system will contain 'cycle stock', and, to cover variations in demand or delivery, 'buffer stock' or 'safety stock' is added. If demand is random (in statistical terms, normally distributed about the expected mean value), then safety stock would have to be increased by about 20% to raise first time fill from 95% to 96%. Whether this is worthwhile depends on the nature of the demand — if a stock-out were life threatening, it would be worthwhile, and some managers feel the same way about stock-outs that threaten production or construction.

So, another performance measure is needed to gauge whether the first time fill rate is achieved economically. This measure is usually:

- a *turnover rate* (demand or usage during a period, normally a year, divided by inventory held during the period) or
- the *number of days or months stock held* (the reciprocal of a turnover rate, see Chapter 14).

Higher turnover rates are 'good'; higher days' stock are 'bad'.

20.2.3 Acquisition costs and holding costs

The inventory control system requires two basic decisions:

- how much to order or schedule
- when to order or schedule it.

The two factors affecting these decisions are the costs of acquiring more material, and the costs of holding it.

Acquisition costs include the cost of several administrative tasks:

- raising a requisition and getting it approved,
- obtaining quotations from potential suppliers,
- raising an order and getting it approved,
- placing the order, and, possibly, 'chasing' the supplier for delivery,

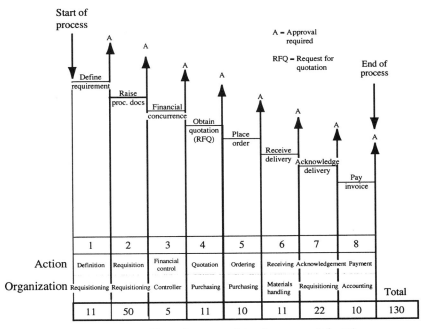

Figure 20.2 The acquisition/procurement process

- processing the receival,
- paying the supplier.

Most of these costs are independent of the quantity ordered, and total acquisition costs can be minimized by minimizing the number of orders and deliveries. In a bureaucratic company, with many checks and controls, such as those shown in Figure 20.2, the administrative costs of acquisition can be as high as £50 per delivery, and even in a company with fewer controls these costs can be between £15 and £20 (UK figures, 1994–5).

Holding costs comprise:

- depreciation on the buildings and equipment used to store the inventory,
- heating, lighting, cleaning and maintaining the storage area,
- security and stock-checking,
- insurance,
- deterioration, damage and obsolescence,
- interest foregone or charged on the cash tied up in stock.

In total, these costs can be between 20% and 30% per annum of the average inventory value — the major element being the interest on the money tied up in stock. Holding costs can be minimized by frequent deliveries of small quantities — but this puts up the acquisition cost.

The balance of acquisition costs and holding costs to minimize total costs can be determined by calculating the 'economic order quantity' (EOQ), as described below.

20.2.4 Economic order quantity

Let A = the total acquisition cost per order
H = the annual cost of holding a unit of inventory
D = the annual demand or usage
Q = the quantity to be ordered

Then:

The number of acquisition cycles a year is D divided by Q, and the yearly acquisition cost is $\frac{A \times D}{Q}$

The average 'cycle' inventory is Q divided by 2 and the cost of holding inventory is $\frac{H \times Q}{2}$

The total annual cost, T, of acquiring and holding inventory can be calculated as

$$T = \frac{A \times D}{Q} + \frac{H \times Q}{2}$$

The value of Q to minimize T can be calculated by setting the first derivative dT/dQ to zero.

$$\frac{dT}{dQ} = \frac{-A \times D}{Q^2} + \frac{H}{2}$$

when this is zero

$$Q^2 = \frac{2A \times D}{H}$$

$$Q = \sqrt{\frac{2A \times D}{H}}$$

This is the economic order quantity (EOQ). The same formula can be used to calculate the 'economic production quantity' to balance set-up costs (a form of acquisition cost) against the cost of holding the quantity produced. In theory, EOQs could be calculated for every item to be held in stock. Alfa Romeo were doing this in the late 1980s to control their MRO inventories. Every Alfa Romeo stock control analyst was given the EOQ matrix shown in Figure 20.3.

The first two left-hand columns show ranges of average monthly usage, for example from 0 to 0.5, from 0.51 to 1 etc. The other columns show the price of the material in lira per unit of measure, for example from 1 to 100, 101 to 200 etc. For any usage up to 7500 per month, and prices ranging up to 2 million lira, the analyst could read off the EOQ. For example, the EOQ for an item with monthly usage of 5001 and price up to 100 lira, is 23 882, as shown in the bottom left-hand corner. The analyst would have rounded this to a quantity that the supplier was willing to ship — say 24 000.

This degree of detail and precision is not effective or efficient. Engineers should beware of such pseudo-scientific systems where spurious accuracy is substituted for sensible analysis and consideration of the business purpose. In this case better overall results can be obtained, and fewer people employed, by using a simpler system that classifies items as fast-moving/high value, medium-moving/medium value and slow-moving/low value, and applies EOQ-like rules to each class, rather than each item. The three classes are normally called A, B and C, and the system is known as ABC inventory control. An example is given in the next section.

20.2.5   An ABC inventory model

ABC inventory control is based on Pareto's Law, that can be roughly interpreted as: 80% of a problem comes from 20% of the possible causes. Pareto was a 19th century Italian engineer who chose to study the distributions of ownership of wealth and receipt of incomes. He found that 80% of wealth was in the hands of 20% of the population. The pattern was the same for incomes — hence Pareto's Law is also known as the 80/20 rule. Although established as a result of studying wealth and incomes, Pareto's Law applies to many materials management

Alfa Romeo
AUTO

PROM INDI

Luglio 1983

Il lotto economico è stato calcolato con la seguente formula:

$$\sqrt{\frac{8 \times consumo\ annuo \times costo\ ordinazione}{prezzo\ del\ materiale \times costo\ di\ giacenza}}$$

assumendo come costo di ordinazione L. 38000 e costo di giacenza 20%.

NB.- Per i lotti economici tratteggiati la quantità richiesta deve essere uguale o ~ sei mesi del consumo mensile o un altro.

17401

LOTTI ECONOMICI

ordine chiuso

Prezzo del materiale   (L. unità di misura)

DA	A	1÷100	101÷200	201÷300	301÷400	401÷500	501÷600	601÷700	701÷800	801÷900	901÷1000	1001÷1200	1201÷1400	1401÷1600	1601÷1800	1801÷2000	2001÷2200	2301÷2600	2601÷3000	3001÷3500
0	0.5	151	17	68	57	50	46	41	39	37	35	33	31	28	26	24	22	22	20	20
0.51	1	263	151	117	98	87	78	72	68	63	59	55	52	48	46	41	39	37	35	33
1.01	1.5	338	196	151	129	113	102	94	87	83	78	72	65	61	59	54	52	48	46	41
1.51	2	400	231	179	153	133	120	111	102	96	92	85	78	72	68	65	61	57	52	48
2.01	2.5	453	262	203	170	150	137	126	116	109	102	96	89	83	78	74	70	65	61	57
2.51	3	501	289	224	190	168	150	140	129	122	116	107	98	92	85	81	76	72	68	61
3.01	4	565	326	253	214	187	170	157	146	137	129	120	111	102	96	92	85	81	76	70
4.01	5	641	370	286	242	214	194	179	166	155	146	137	126	118	109	106	98	92	87	81
5.01	6	708	409	317	268	235	214	196	183	172	161	150	140	129	122	113	107	100	94	84
6.01	7	770	445	344	292	257	231	214	198	187	177	163	150	140	131	124	116	109	102	96
7.01	8	827	477	370	312	275	249	229	214	201	190	177	161	150	142	133	126	118	111	102
8.01	9	880	508	394	334	294	266	244	227	214	203	187	172	161	150	142	133	126	118	109
9.01	10	931	537	416	353	310	281	257	240	227	214	198	183	170	159	150	142	133	124	116
10.1	11	981	566	439	371	325	294	270	253	238	225	209	192	179	168	159	148	140	131	122
11.1	13	1041	605	469	396	349	316	290	270	253	240	222	205	192	179	170	159	148	140	131
13.1	15	1132	654	506	427	377	340	312	292	275	259	240	223	207	194	183	172	161	150	140
15.1	17	1210	699	541	458	403	364	336	312	292	279	257	238	220	207	196	183	172	161	150
17.1	20	1301	751	582	490	434	392	360	336	314	299	277	255	238	222	211	198	185	174	161
20.1	25	1424	821	641	541	477	432	397	371	347	329	305	281	262	246	233	218	205	192	179
25.1	30	1565	915	709	599	528	477	438	410	384	364	338	310	290	270	257	240	227	211	196
30.1	40	1781	1032	800	676	595	538	495	462	434	410	381	349	327	305	290	272	255	240	222
40.1	50	2027	1170	906	765	676	610	562	523	490	464	432	397	371	347	327	307	290	270	251
50.1	75	2388	1379	1068	903	796	719	663	617	580	547	508	469	436	410	386	364	340	318	296
75.1	100	2826	1634	1264	1068	942	852	783	730	685	647	602	554	517	484	458	429	403	377	351
100.1	125	3210	1853	1436	1218	1068	966	889	815	776	735	682	628	584	549	519	486	458	427	392
125.1	150	3548	2048	1587	1339	1182	1068	981	916	859	811	754	693	647	606	573	538	506	473	440
150.1	200	4001	2310	1789	1511	1332	1203	1107	1031	968	916	852	783	730	685	647	608	571	534	495
200.1	300	4780	2760	2138	1805	1591	1439	1323	1234	1158	1091	1018	935	872	820	774	726	682	639	593
300.1	400	5514	3266	2528	2136	1194	1703	1567	1468	1369	1295	1203	1107	1031	968	916	857	807	754	700
400.1	500	6410	3701	2867	2420	2126	1921	1771	1655	1552	1467	1365	1256	1171	1099	1038	974	916	857	796
500.1	750	7553	4361	3379	2856	2485	2267	2093	1949	1831	1731	1609	1478	1380	1286	1223	1119	1079	1009	937
750.1	1000	893	5159	3998	3379	2976	2692	2474	2507	2165	2047	1903	1751	1631	1533	1448	1358	1275	1195	1107
1000.1	1500	10682	6167	4776	4023	3553	3215	2955	2758	2583	2438	2278	2091	1919	1831	1731	1624	1526	1432	1331
1500.1	2000	12637	7296	5653	4774	4207	3815	3562	3359	363	2809	2692	2474	2311	2167	2047	1931	1672	1568	1452
2000.1	3000	15094	8720	6756	5712	5036	4556	4186	5903	2662	3466	3215	2954	2758	2594	2442	2300	2156	2019	1873
3000.1	4000	17872	10318	7992	6758	5951	5395	4872	4623	4327	4091	3815	3619	2370	3052	2899	2714	2551	2381	2215
4000.1	5000	20265	11700	9062	7652	6736	6104	5624	5232	4905	4643	4323	3968	3726	3466	3290	3025	2809	2708	2511
5000.1	7500	23882	13758	10680	9025	7935	7194	6576	6169	5777	5402	5090	4687	4360	4017	3869	3630	3412	3183	3065

Figure 20.3   *(caption opposite)*

Alfa Romeo
AUTO

PROM INDI

Luglio 1983

Il lotto economico è stato calcolato con la seguente formula:

$$\sqrt{\dfrac{2 \times \text{consumo annuo} \times \text{costo ordinazione}}{\text{prezzo del materiale} \times \text{costo di giacenza}}}$$

assumendo come costo di ordinazione L.33000 e costo di giacenza 24%.
N.B.- Per i lotti economici tratteggiati la quantità richiesta deve essere uguale a ~ sei mesi del consumo mensile e non altro.

f.f.2

LOTTI ECONOMICI

ordine chiuso

Consumo medio mensile — Prezzo del materiale (L. unità di misura)

DA	A	3501÷4000	4001÷4500	4501÷5000	5001÷6000	6001÷7000	7001÷8000	8001÷10000	10001÷15000	15001÷20000	20001÷40000	40001÷60000	60001÷80000	80001÷100000	100001÷200000	200001÷400000	400001÷600000	600001÷1000000	1000001÷1500000	1500001÷2000000
0	0,5	17	15	15	16	13	13	11	9	9	7	4	4	4	2	2	2	2	1	1
0,51	1	31	28	26	24	22	22	20	17	15	11	9	7	7	4	2	2	2	2	1
1,01	1,5	39	37	35	33	31	28	24	22	17	13	11	9	7	7	4	2	2	2	2
1,51	2	46	44	41	37	35	33	31	26	22	15	13	11	9	7	4	4	2	3	2
2,01	2,5	52	48	46	44	39	37	33	28	24	17	13	11	11	9	7	4	2	3	2
2,51	3	57	54	50	48	44	41	37	33	26	20	15	13	11	9	7	4	4	3	3
3,01	4	65	61	57	54	50	46	41	35	31	24	17	15	13	11	7	7	4	4	3
4,01	5	74	70	65	61	57	52	48	41	35	26	20	17	15	11	9	7	4	4	3
5,01	6	83	76	72	68	63	57	52	46	37	28	22	20	17	13	9	7	7	5	4
6,01	7	89	83	78	74	68	63	57	48	41	31	24	20	17	13	11	7	7	5	4
7,01	8	96	89	85	78	72	68	61	52	44	35	26	22	20	15	11	9	7	5	4
8,01	9	102	96	89	83	76	72	65	57	48	37	28	24	20	15	11	9	7	6	5
9,01	10	107	100	96	89	83	76	69	59	50	39	31	24	22	17	11	9	7	6	5
10,1	11	113	107	100	94	85	81	74	63	52	41	31	26	24	17	13	9	7	6	5
11,1	13	122	113	107	100	92	85	78	65	57	44	33	28	24	19	13	11	9	7	6
13,1	15	131	122	116	107	98	92	85	72	61	46	35	31	26	19	15	11	9	8	6
15,1	17	140	131	124	116	107	98	89	76	65	50	39	33	28	22	15	13	9	8	7
17,1	20	150	142	133	124	113	107	96	83	70	52	41	35	31	24	17	13	11	9	7
20,1	25	166	155	148	137	126	118	107	92	76	59	46	39	33	26	17	15	11	10	8
25,1	30	183	173	161	150	140	129	118	100	85	65	50	41	37	28	20	15	13	10	9
30,1	40	207	194	183	170	157	146	133	113	96	74	57	48	41	33	22	17	13	12	10
40,1	50	233	220	207	194	177	166	150	129	109	83	63	54	48	37	26	20	15	13	11
50,1	75	277	259	244	227	209	194	179	150	129	98	76	63	57	44	31	24	20	15	13
75,1	100	327	307	290	270	249	231	209	179	150	116	89	76	65	52	37	28	22	18	15
101	125	371	347	339	305	281	262	238	203	172	131	100	85	76	69	41	33	26	20	17
126	150	410	386	364	338	316	290	264	225	190	144	111	94	83	65	46	35	28	22	19
151	200	468	434	410	381	351	327	296	253	214	163	126	107	92	72	52	39	31	25	21
201	300	582	519	490	456	419	390	353	303	255	196	150	129	113	87	61	48	37	30	26
301	400	652	613	580	538	495	462	421	358	301	231	179	150	133	102	72	57	46	36	30
401	500	739	695	654	640	568	523	477	405	342	262	201	170	150	116	81	63	50	41	34
501	750	872	820	774	713	663	617	562	477	403	310	240	201	179	140	98	76	59	48	40
751	1000	1031	970	916	852	783	730	665	565	477	364	283	240	214	163	116	89	72	57	48
1001	1500	1231	1158	1091	1018	935	872	796	676	571	436	328	286	251	196	140	107	85	68	57
1501	2000	1352	1269	1199	1111	1027	955	858	740	626	477	371	313	275	214	150	116	95	80	68
2001	3000	1744	1637	1550	1439	1325	1234	1126	959	807	617	477	403	355	277	196	150	120	95	81
3001	4000	2061	1938	1833	1703	1565	1458	1330	1131	953	730	565	477	419	323	229	179	142	113	95
4001	5000	2335	2202	2071	1929	1777	1653	1506	1280	1081	828	629	538	477	366	259	203	161	128	108
5001	7500	2768	2590	2452	2268	2093	1949	1779	1511	1275	977	754	639	562	436	307	240	190	151	131

Figure 20.3 Alpha Romeo Economic order quantity (EOQ) matrix

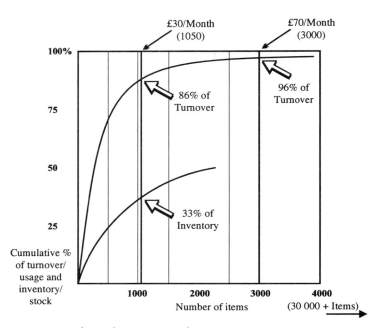

Figure 20.4   Pareto chart of inventory and turnover

situations, and is particularly relevant to inventory management. In most material flows where large numbers of different parts or items are involved, it will be found that about 80% of the value derives from about 20% of the items. This means that inventory control can be exercised efficiently by concentrating on about 20% of the items, and using simple rules to control the other 80% of items.

This is particularly true of MRO items, and since many engineers become involved in the maintenance, repair and operation of plant, equipment, machinery, buildings, ships, planes or other engineering products, an MRO example is described here.

The Pareto chart shown above in Figure 20.4 is based on data from the 1980s for a transmission manufacturing plant which had been operating for over 20 years. It is probably typical of many plants of similar age in many industries, and there are general lessons to be learned from the plant's experience.

The plant stocked just over 30 000 items, which included things like oils and greases, spare parts for machines and equipment, tools for machines, and hand tools, cleaning materials, safety clothing, paint, hardware, building materials, motors, valves etc. In 20 years, a lot of material had been accumulated!

Two Pareto curves are shown. One is the accumulative share of turnover, or usage, plotted against number of items; the other is the accumulative share of inventory. Neither curve complies with the 80/20 rule, but it is clear that relatively few items account for a high percentage of usage — 80% of turnover (or usage) came from less than 1000 items with individual turnover (i.e. units used per month, times unit price) of more than £30 per month, and over 90% from 3000 items with individual turnover of more than £7 per month. From the inventory curve it can be seen that 1000 items generated one-third of the inventory, and 3000 items counted for over 50%. Conversely, almost 50% of inventory resulted from holding 27 000 slow moving (or non-moving) items.

Annual usage was about £4 million, and average stock was about £1.8 million — which means that the turnover rate was 2.2 times per annum, or, using another measure of performance, the plant held 5.5 months' stock.

These were not considered to be 'good' performance measures, and the plant improved them by applying the ABC approach. The ABC approach is to divide the inventory into three classes.

The class A parts warrant continual attention from plant engineers, inventory analysts and purchasing to dissolve the problem. The fastest moving 1000 items accounting for more than 80% of usage were designated as Class A. For these items it is possible to operate with less than one month's stock.

Class B parts deserve some attention, but can be managed with a simple rule, or set of rules based on EOQs, and using reorder point or two-bin systems. For example, the rule could be 'when the reorder point is reached, or the first bin is empty, schedule delivery of two months' usage.' The reorder point can be as simple as a line on the bin or racks — when the physical level of stock falls below the line, it is time to reorder — and the reorder process as simple as pulling a card which carries predetermined instructions and inserting it in a reader, or sending it to the supplier. Figure 20.5 illustrates the use of these two reorder rules. Although simple, these rules are efficient and effective. At their modern manufacturing facility in Montpellier, France, IBM have combined the two-bin system with sophisticated bar-coding and direct electronic links to suppliers as part of a complete update of their operations [1].

It is not necessary to calculate EOQs precisely for each item — the system is very robust, and it may be necessary to simplify materials handling by rounding to

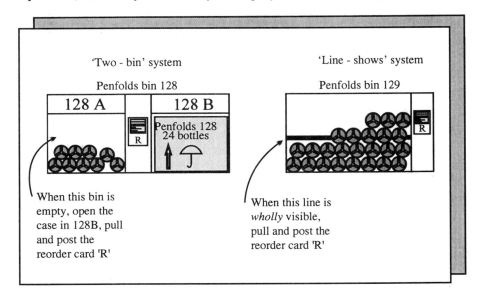

Figure 20.5 Two simple reorder rules

Table 20.1 Stock levels and turn rates before and after ABC control

	Usage p.a. £m	Before		After	
		Stock £m	Turns p.a.	Stock £m	Turns p.a.
Class A (1000 items)	3.44	0.62	5.6	0.21	16.2
Class B (2000 items)	0.42	0.48	0.8	0.14	3.0
Class C (27 000 items)	0.14	0.69	0.2	0.47	0.3
All Stock (30 000 items)	4.00	1.79	2.2	0.82	4.8

the appropriate unit of packing — packs of 10, 12, 100 etc. (The reorder card would show this sort of information.) In the transmission plant under consideration the next 2000 fastest moving items, after Class A, were designated Class B and their stock levels targeted between two and four months.

Class C parts do not repay detailed consideration. A very simple rule, like 'Order one year's supply or £20 worth, whichever is less' will suffice. Like most inventories, the best solution for Class C items is not to have them in the first place, or get rid of them fast if demand has died. In the example plant, the balance of 27 000 items was designated Class C.

A series of actions, by teams with shared values and common goals, resulted in the reductions in stock, and the increased turnover rate, measured as 'turns per annum', shown in Table 20.1. Examples of the actions are given.

Some of the agreed actions were:

Reduce stock levels on high usage items — the mind-set of the old hands (anything better than two turns a year is 'good') meant that 20 days' stock was regarded as 'tight'. Negotiation of faster response from suppliers (e.g. by using blanket orders, using fax or computer links) and a change of attitude often reduced the holding to four or five days' stock. A blanket order commits the user to buy an item, or group of items, from the suppliers for a period of time — normally at least a year. During this time, the user simply issues 'releases' against the order, which can be done by mail, fax or tied line. The order may specify delivery within 24 hours, or 24 hours a day availability. This cuts out the enquiry/order cycle. Chapter 21 describes blanket orders in more detail. Stocks of heating oil were virtually eliminated by changing to gas heating — 'virtually' because some protection against interruption of gas supply was needed. Stocks of hand tools were reduced to two days, by displaying the stock record via a PC link to a local stockist who replenished the plant automatically. Similar schemes were developed for standard bearings and electrical components.

Extend use of consignment stocks — it proved possible to arrange that some commodities, such as oils and greases, protective clothing, and cleaning materials, were delivered to the plant, but remained the suppliers' property until the items were used. Sometimes this involved 'facility management' contracts, e.g. for lubrication systems plant-wide, or plant and equipment cleaning, or parts-inclusive maintenance contracts. In such cases, the supplier provided a service and all the materials required, which meant that the user no longer held them in inventory. (At the start of such schemes, the ideal arrangement is that the contractor takes over existing stocks).

Identify duplication/combine usage — items such as motors and bearings, held as replacement parts for repair of machines and equipment, were often bought initially from the equipment suppliers under the equipment suppliers' part numbers while identical parts were already in stock under the motor makers' or industry numbers. By identifying duplication, sometimes with help from the bearing or motor suppliers, one or more items were deleted.

In the case of motors, the same unit with different mountings — end, top or bottom — was stocked several times, and stock was reduced by deciding to hold one or two motor units and a range of mountings. Also motors with the same ISO specification from three or four different vendors were held, and by standardizing on one manufacturer it was possible to delete the other two or three. Repaired or rewound motors were stocked, but some users always insisted on having the brand new item while hundreds of repaired items gathered dust. Once the plant manager made it clear that he was interested in lower inventories as well as achievement of schedules, the plant managed to reduce significantly stocks of new motors and old motors.

Improve scrap rates/disposals — all that was necessary was to convince the plant controller that his budget provision for obsolescence was not sacrosanct. For years he had refused to sanction disposal of 'usable' stock, which had been identified as obsolete or excess to likely all-time requirements, once the amount allowed in the budget for scrap and obsolescence was approached. This amount had been determined centrally, and the instruction to the plant controller was that the amount must not be exceeded. Additional scrapping would have meant that the budget was exceeded, creating an 'adverse variance' for the plant manager to explain to his boss. Once it was clear that the boss preferred to get rid of the obsolete or surplus material (a shared goal) it was possible to reduce inactive stocks dramatically. For thousands of small value inactive items it was necessary to introduce some rules of thumb implemented by computer programs, since the time taken for review (by engineers) could not be justified. The rules were of the form: if there has been no usage for ten years, scrap all stock; if there has been no usage for five years, scrap 75%, or down to one piece.

These were actions to correct past errors. Other improvements came by *avoiding* inventory, which can only happen if shared goals are established, and communications are improved. It is important that the goal of inventory reduction is shared by production management, who may wish to protect against interruption of operations at almost any cost. Plant managers may fear the agony that follows a missed schedule more than the dull pain that may result from an inventory budget overrun, and will only be able to strike an appropriate balance if senior management heed the eighth of Deming's 14 obligations of top management:

'Reduce fear throughout the organization by encouraging open, two-way communication. The economic loss resulting from fear to ask questions or report trouble is appalling.'

For a full list read *Total Quality Management* [2].

In the transmission plant, it was possible to establish a specification control activity to work towards the shared goal of inventory avoidance. The specification control activity consisted of one person with a PC, and access to a database showing stock and usage information, who could check new requisitions for duplication before the duplicate item was ordered. This person was also able to check the quantity requested by the plant engineer against historical usage of like parts, and had authority to scale down excessive orders. (A better solution would been to have the requisitioning engineer consult the database rather than make a hurried guess at the requirement, or blindly accept the supplier's recommendation.)

Another avoidance action was the determination of plant, machine and equipment maintenance requirements prior to agreement to purchase, and discussing with suppliers ways in which the equipment could be made more reliable. Equipment failure mode and effect analysis (FMEA), and study of mean time between failure (MTBF), and mean time to repair (MTTR) data can eliminate many costly 'investments' in spares [3].

The plant also achieved big savings through a policy of phasing in initial stocks of tooling and parts prone to wear. This was particularly beneficial where something new was being introduced, and usage rates were uncertain — for example tungsten carbide tools instead of high-speed steel tools. There is no point in stocking up with usage-related parts at the level *forecast* to be required to support full production if the climb to full production extends over six months or more. In that time *actual* usage can be determined, and many of the items will be changed. If an item is changed, it may still be good practice to exhaust the replaced item if it is usable, rather than scrap — or, worse, keep the old, and switch to the new.

This review of the ABC approach to inventory management has raised some of the general issues of inventory management, including the question: why hold inventory at all? These issues are examined in the next section.

20.3   WHY HOLD INVENTORY?

The basic reason for holding inventory is to guard against uncertainty. Some of the common areas of uncertainty, and sources of variation in inventory levels are identified in this section, and illustrated in Figure 20.6.

The ideal, or desired situation is shown in section (a) of the graph, where the opening stock is steadily used up and is just exhausted when the replenishment arrives to restore the stock level to its starting point.

Section (b) shows what would happen if usage were greater than expected — maybe because scrap rates somewhere down the line were higher than usual, for example, or a mix of mortar had been allowed to 'go off', and more replacement material had to be called forward, or because the production supervisor thought that a 'good run' was desirable when the operation was running well. Stock would be exhausted before the replenishment delivery. This experience would probably lead to introduction of a buffer, or safety stock just in case future demand again exceeded forecast.

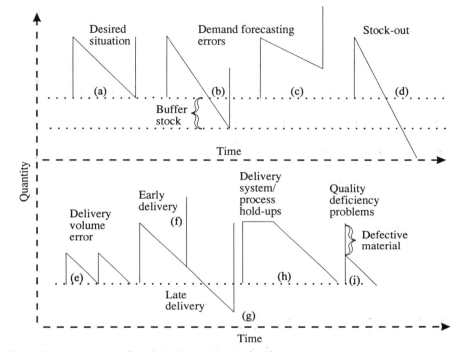

Figure 20.6 Sources of variation in inventory levels

Section (c) shows the stock levels if demand were below forecast, perhaps because operations were slow due to absenteeism, or due to the introduction of inexperienced operators, or because a tooling or die change took longer than expected. The next delivery would push stock levels above the target.

Section (d) illustrates a 'stock-out' due to a sudden surge in usage, which could happen for a variety of reasons — a record error, a production supervisor trying to get ahead of schedule, or an unexpected order could all have this effect.

Section (e) shows the effect of a shortfall in the delivery quantity — in this case it appears that prompt action was taken to secure delivery of the balance, and no stock-out occurred.

Early delivery, as shown in *section (f)* results in excess stock.

Late delivery, as shown in *section (g)* could cause a stock-out (unless the *just in case* buffer stock were still there). In the 1970s, strikes at UK suppliers frequently resulted in late deliveries, which led their customers to hold high levels of safety stock, or to take their business elsewhere. The effects were still evident in the 1990s, in the form of imports and cautious attitudes in inventory management.

Misleading information about stock levels can affect calculation of forward requirements, as shown in *section (h)*. This could result from slow processing of receival or usage information, which would cause over-scheduling or under-scheduling respectively.

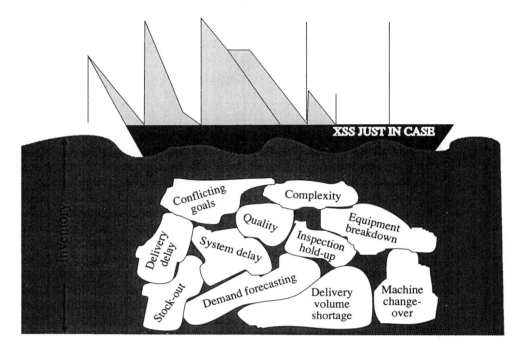

Figure 20.7   Sailing the cruel sea of inventory with its hidden rocks

Section (i) illustrates one of the stock controllers' major problems — materials found to be defective on arrival, or when being processed, not only cause immediate shortages but also lead to extra stock being held so that all subsequent deliveries can be carefully checked, just in case there is something wrong.

The reasons for holding inventory, as just described, are really problems somewhere in the system. The problems do not occur one at a time for one item, as described, but at any time for many items, causing a complex or even chaotic situation for the inventory controller — unless the problems are resolved.

If inventory is continually used to hide problems it will rise to levels that make the business uncompetitive. Funds will be tied up in stock, and allocated to building storage space, instead of being invested in new product development and more efficient equipment.

Far from being 'a good thing', inventory is increasingly seen as an 'evil' or a 'cruel sea', which hides fundamental problems, as illustrated in Figure 20.7.

As long as the rocks (the problems) are there, they are a danger to the ship (the business unit). Rather than build barrages to deepen the water (add inventory), it would be better to remove the rocks (dissolve the problems), and proceed confidently with lower levels of inventory. (Although widely used, this is not a very good analogy, since the captain (manager) does not have control over the sea level (inventory level). In reality, it is nevertheless good business practice to reduce inventories, expose the problems and dissolve them.) Having recognized inventory as an evil, 'management' may decide to eliminate it using

Just-in-Time methods, instead of just-in-case. The next section describes what is involved.

20.4   JUST-IN-TIME INVENTORY MANAGEMENT

It is an appealing idea that if materials can be made to appear at the point of use Just-in-Time (JIT) to be used, then inventory can be dramatically reduced or even eliminated. The idea is so appealing that companies may be tempted to try to instal JIT processes as a sort of overlay to existing systems, and without solving the fundamental problems that have led them to hold so much inventory. The first part of this section gives an indication of the difficulties of this approach to JIT. It is based on a study designed to establish the feasibility of introducing JIT to an established car assembly plant. This is Ford's plant at Saarlouis in Germany, which has a reputation for being one of Europe's best for efficiency and good product quality.

20.4.1   Attempts to 'retrofit' JIT

The study identified some of the preconditions for JIT as:

- stable schedules,
- reduced product complexity,
- record integrity — plant bills of materials exactly the same as the central database; stock records adjusted promptly and with complete accuracy,
- inbound traffic control — the plant needed to know the progress of every incoming truckload, and what it contained,
- container control — the numbers, identity and location of durable containers had to be known, so that they would be available for return to the right supplier,
- local sourcing — suppliers of frequently required parts should be located close to the assembly plant,
- 'parts per million' (ppm) defect rates — that is, suppliers' JIT deliveries had to be 100% usable.

This list is incomplete, and other requirements will be identified later in this section. However, even the incomplete list led to identification of several preparatory tasks, which were:

- completely replace all shipping containers for incoming material,
- substantially modify the assembly building to create more delivery points,
- change in-plant materials handling,
- change plant layouts,
- retrain plant and supplier employees,
- introduce new in-plant information systems,
- introduce new supplier communication systems.

The study identified, but did not resolve another issue:

- how to deal with the engine and transmission plants that were located hundreds of miles away from the assembly plant.

The cost of the changes was estimated at £12m, and the benefits were too small and uncertain to justify the investment, so the plant kept its old practices.

The study report highlighted the concern related to the engine and transmission plants, and prompted another study to determine how these plants could be run on a JIT basis.

This new study team quickly discovered that a wealth of information existed on JIT concept implementation. From this literature and their own discussions with suppliers, competitors and transportation companies, they came up with the following definition of JIT (the emphasis is their own):

'The concept by which the supply and production of *quality parts* is regulated by *next user demand with minimal inventory*

- at the supplier
- in transit
- in plant.'

Their list of key issues was similar to that of the earlier study, but had the following additions or differences of emphasis:

- 'pull' material flow system (see below)
- maximum machine 'up-time' (see below)
- supplier selection
- quality the key to minimal inventory.

The assembler (A) 'pulls' material from producers (P) who 'pull material from suppliers (S), by sending information about their immediate needs

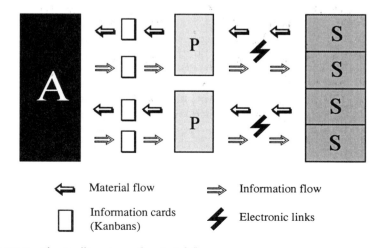

Material flow   ⟹ Information flow

☐ Information cards (Kanbans)   ⚡ Electronic links

Figure 20.8 The 'pull' system of material flow

The concept of a *pull material flow system* is a key part of JIT, which is illustrated in Figure 20.8. By *maximum machine up-time* the study group meant that machines should be reliable, should be fitted with tools that would last at least through a shift, should be flexible and quick to change from one product derivative to another. Another JIT requirement — a flexible workforce — was not listed.

Quick tool changeover or die changeover to make a different part is an essential part of JIT methods. In section 20.2.5 above, it was shown that the EOQ formula can be used to weigh set-up (changeover) costs against holding costs. The JIT approach concentrates on reducing or eliminating the set-up cost. The results are spectacular in press shops or injection moulding or transfer line machining. Set-ups that used to take several hours, leading to 'economic' runs of several days stock, are now performed in minutes, and the economic run is a few hours stock. The reduction in set-up times comes from redesign of tools and machines through cooperation with the equipment suppliers, from assuming that the changeover is right first time, rather than waiting while quality checks are made, from scheduling like parts in sequence, from computer control of changeovers, and from using carefully trained teams of production workers who are already on hand, instead of specialists who have to be called from a remote location.

Despite their clear understanding of JIT requirements, the team was not able to install JIT production even at a new extension to the engine plant in Bridgend, South Wales that was still under construction, because:

- the project was raised without planning for JIT,
- plant layout was not consistent with JIT,
- production lines were not 'balanced' for JIT,
- sourcing actions had storage implications.

Nevertheless, some progress towards JIT was made, and Figure 20.9 shows the plan for one of the major components — the cylinder head. The figure shows Montupey Foundry, Belfast at the bottom, which was the source of castings, from which deliveries of 2500 pieces were to be made once per shift. In phase 1, when annual output was planned to be 550 000 units, the castings were to be machined on Head Line 1, which was equipped with tooling and control systems such that it could produce all derivatives without interruption for changeover. (This is an example of 'flexible machines' as required for JIT.) In phase 2, an additional 300 000 units a year were to be machined on Head Line 2, which was similarly equipped. From the machining lines, the cylinder heads were to be assembled into engines on the Main Assembly Line in both phase 1 and phase 2, supplemented by a Mini Assembly Line in phase 2. The assembled engines were to proceed to the shipping bank, for despatch to the various destinations shown at the top of the chart. The planned numbers of cylinder heads to be stored and in process are shown against each operation. (Note the correspondence with Figure 5.5 in Chapter 5).

The target of five days stock (turnover rate 44 times a year, with 220 working days a year) was a major improvement on past performance, but the location of the plant in Wales, some of its customers in Germany, Belgium and Spain, and

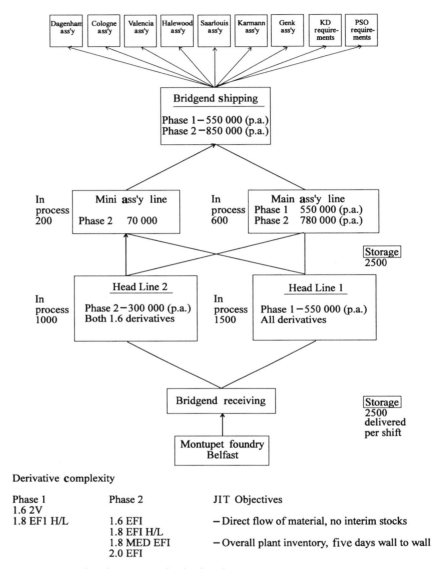

Figure 20.9 JIT plan for ZETA cylinder head

suppliers in Northern Ireland and the USA (not shown), meant that two of the JIT objectives could not be met — 'minimal inventory at suppliers and in transit'. This was one reason why phase 2 was installed not in Bridgend but in Cologne, with castings re-sourced to a nearby foundry, and with customer plants less distant. (This change of plan explains all the 'were to be' phrases in the explanation of Figure 20.9). Building the engine in two plants, each closer to its customers and suppliers, meant that the overall supply system was closer to the JIT concept.

20.4.2   A planned JIT system

This section concludes with an example of a more successful JIT application, where the requirements of JIT were part of the plan from the outset. It relates to the Nissan Manufacturing UK (NMUK) plant at Washington, near Sunderland, UK.

One factor that led Nissan to select the Washington site was its accessibility by road from the Midlands concentration of UK suppliers to the car industry. Even more important was the availability of adjoining sites where key suppliers were able to set up their own new plants. Figure 20.10 is a representation of the location of NMUK's suppliers soon after they began operations in 1986. The 25 suppliers adjoining the plant provide over 50% of the value and volume of NMUK's requirements, (another example of the use of Pareto analysis in materials management). Parts and assemblies from these suppliers are delivered to the point of use in NMUK's plant at less than one hour's notice.

As production at Washington approached 100 000 units a year, NMUK revised their arrangements for deliveries from the Midlands-based suppliers. Shipment by individual suppliers led to congestion, and did not provide the necessary degree of control over delivery. The NMUK plan was to go from scenario one in Figure 20.11, to scenario two, which they achieved by schemes like that shown as pilot area solution.

In scenario one, which has now been superseded, each supplier shipped their own parts, to be offloaded into storage from which there were frequent deliveries of small quantities to the production line, where material was placed 'one step' from the assembly line. In scenario two, which is present practice, small quantities

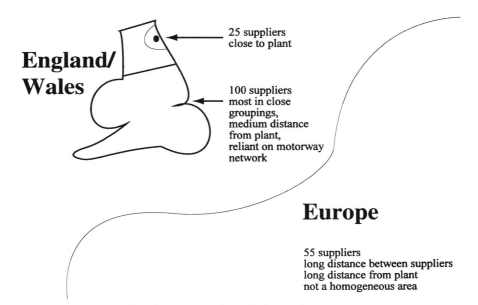

Figure 20.10   Geographic distribution of supply base of NMUK

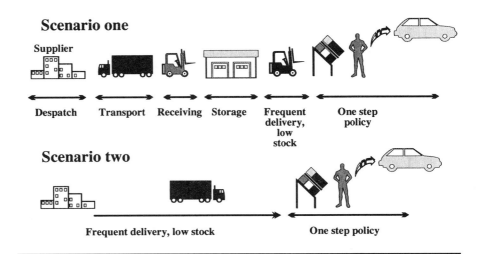

Scenario one

Supplier

| Despatch | Transport | Receiving | Storage | Frequent delivery, low stock | One step policy |

Scenario two

Frequent delivery, low stock   One step policy

Pilot area solution

Simultaneous order transmission

Delivery pre-notification

Cross dock

NMUK

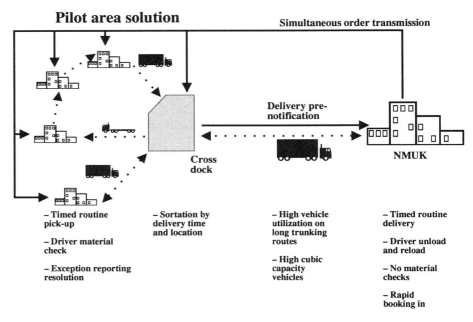

– Timed routine pick-up	– Sortation by delivery time and location	– High vehicle utilization on long trunking routes	– Timed routine delivery
– Driver material check		– High cubic capacity vehicles	– Driver unload and reload
– Exception reporting resolution			– No material checks
			– Rapid booking in

Figure 20.11   Development of NMUK's JIT system

from several suppliers are consolidated for shipment, to arrive *just in time* for offloading and movement direct to the production line.

In the pilot area solution diagram, information flows are shown by solid lines, and material transportation flows by dotted lines. NMUK's requirements are simultaneously transmitted to suppliers through a communications network, so that each supplier can have material ready for a timed pick-up by NMUK contracted transport. The transport contractor's driver is responsible for checking the identity and quantity of the material before it is taken to a 'cross dock'. There

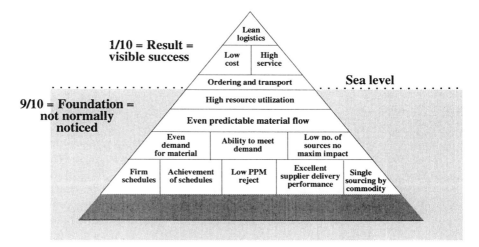

Figure 20.12   Prerequisites of lean logistics–the iceberg principle

it is sorted by required delivery times and separate delivery locations within the NMUK plant. Materials with the same delivery time are loaded to high-capacity vehicles for shipment to NMUK, and the contents of each load are pre-notified via the communications network. This allows 'one touch' booking-in of the complete shipment and unloading without further checks. Small, easy to manhandle quantities of each item are moved to within 'one step' of the production lines.

The siting of NMUK's 25 key suppliers, and their inbound 'lean logistics' operations enable them to manage with about one day's stock of materials (a turnover rate of more than 200 times a year). This is the result of careful, long term planning — and of the opportunity to start at a 'greenfield' site, with all the worldwide experience of the parent corporation to draw on. The extent of the planning is indicated in Figure 20.12.

It is notable that some of the activities shown in the submerged part of the iceberg are 'enabling' actions by NMUK, such as 'firm schedules' and 'even demand for material', which assist supplier reactions such as 'excellent delivery performance'. Others indicate NMUK's sourcing policies, but the foundations of supplier performance are in the unspecified lower area, which includes the building of long term partnerships. It was these partnerships that enabled Nissan to include suppliers in the planning of the Washington plant, and to arrange that 25 of the suppliers established new plants 'next door' to the Nissan site.

Nissan is not alone in this sort of achievement. The Saturn company, established in 1989 — GM's first new car company since 1917 — has similar performance at its integrated facility in Spring Hills near Nashville, USA. There, GM have an in-house foundry, as well as engine, transmission, and injection moulding facilities (yes, injection moulding — all but three body panels are plastic). Most major suppliers have been persuaded to set up nearby and, as a result, the Saturn plant holds less than one day's stock.

As with Nissan Manufacturing UK, the achievement of 'lean logistics' by the Saturn company required long term planning of the entire manufacturing and materials management system.

The selection and development of suppliers is an important element of such long term planning. This is dealt with in Chapter 21.

20.5 SUMMARY

This chapter covered the basics of inventory management. It showed that the questions 'How much should be ordered?' and 'When should it be ordered?' have traditionally been answered in a way that weighs acquisition costs and holding costs to minimize total inventory costs. It also showed that a better question is 'Why hold inventory at all?', since, far from solving problems, inventories often cover up problems and delay their solution. Attempts to introduce Just-in-Time (JIT) methods were described, showing that successful introduction requires long term planning of the materials management system, and the early involvement of suppliers.

REFERENCES

1. Bradshaw, D. (1991) 'An Eastern breeze in the Med', *Financial Times*, Technology page, 25 June.
2. Peratec (1994) *Total Quality Management*. Second edition, Chapman and Hall, London.
3. Moubray, J. (1991) *Reliability-centred Maintenance*. Butterworth-Heinemann, Oxford. Chapters 3 and 4, explain mean time between failures and mean time to repair, together with preventive maintenance and predictive maintenance and other maintenance management techniques.

BIBLIOGRAPHY

Just in Time, a booklet by the consultants A. T. Kearney, written for the Department of Trade and Industry, is a very useful guide to JIT and its benefits. It is available from Mediascene, PO Box 90, Hengoed, Mid Glamorgan CF8 9YE.

Manufacturing resource planning, 'An Executive Guide to MRP II', another DTI booklet, gives an overview of material and production scheduling. This is also available from Mediascene.

The Management of Manufacturing by E. J. Anderson, published by Addison-Wesley (1994), includes an extensive discussion of inventory management in Chapters 4 and 5, and of production planning and scheduling in Chapters 6, 7 and 8.

Optimising plant availability is covered in 'An Executive Guide to Effective Maintenance' published by the DTI. Since reliable equipment is a precondition for JIT, this is a 'companion' to the JIT booklet cited above. It is also available from Mediascene.

Management of the supply system

21.1 Introduction

Chapters 4, 5, 6 and 20 have shown that total quality management (TQM), Just-in-time (JIT) materials management, simultaneous or concurrent engineering (CE) and the management of advanced materials and new technologies all depend on early involvement of suppliers. Chapter 8 listed 'Build close, stable relationships with key suppliers of parts and services' as one of the five common strategies among world-class manufacturers. This chapter describes the interdependence of TQM, JIT and CE and how they all depend on supply system management (SSM). The concepts of a procurement team, and a 'purchasing portfolio' are introduced. 'Old' methods of selecting suppliers are reviewed, and the need to change these practices explained. Features of the 'new' ways of choosing suppliers and building partnerships are then outlined.

21.2 THE SUPPLY SYSTEM

21.2.1 What are suppliers required to supply?

What an organization requires from its suppliers has changed as the nature of competition has changed. In the first half of the 20th century the primary requirement was low-cost supplies, and low cost was achieved by the application of 'Taylorist' methods to the main element of cost, which at that time was the cost of labour (see Chapter 3). By the 1950s, in addition to low cost, suppliers were increasingly required to provide goods and services of consistently high quality. They were encouraged to pursue total quality management (TQM), using the guidance and advice of 'quality gurus' such as Deming, Juran and Taguchi. Customer companies found that the task of introducing their suppliers to TQM, and in particular to the idea of defect prevention, was assisted by designing to a higher level of assembly, and so reducing the number of suppliers required to participate in product and process design (see Chapter 4). This policy of working with fewer suppliers each responsible for assemblies and sub-assemblies rather than with many suppliers providing individual components and materials, also simplified the materials management task, and led to further cost reductions (see Chapter 5). By the late 1970s 'Time' had become an important aspect of competition — the time required to bring new products to market, which was reduced by the avoidance of change using simultaneous (concurrent) engineering (see Chapter 6) — and the time to respond to an order (see Chapter 20). The new challenge of the 1990s is also time-related, but now it is the time to bring new materials and technologies from invention and development in the science base to be incorporated in new products and processes. Suppliers are now called upon to supply revolutionary new ideas and unique new products. This entails the entry of the science base, which includes academic as well as industrial research organizations, as new links in the supply chain. Rather than forming the first link in the chain, feeding forward to materials suppliers, these new participants need to join the concurrent engineering teams made up of members from all parts of the supply chain, and help to supply new low-cost, high-quality products incorporating advanced materials and technologies at a faster rate.

In summary, what suppliers are now expected to supply can be seen in the mirror of customer expectations as stated in the electrical engineering company ABB's 1993 Annual Report:

'In all of ABB's markets, customers now expect more than top quality at a competitive price. They also want a supplier who has an intimate understanding of their business, who can anticipate changing needs and shifting markets, who can deliver *fast, innovative and total system solutions* that help them achieve their business goals.'

21.2.2 Casting off the supply chain

The so-called 'original equipment manufacturers' (OEMs), such as aircraft, oil rig, ship, car or computer producers, have to reach further down the supply chain for their concurrent engineering team partners. In similar ways, suppliers of services need to look further ahead to learn of new enabling technologies that will help them improve their 'products', processes and performance. Civil and construction engineering companies, too, are interested in new materials and new processes to assist them in developing better products that are quicker to build. This drive for innovation entails a new concept of supplier management: since all the members of the development team have to be involved *concurrently*, it is time to abandon the concept of a 'supply chain', which implies sequential links, and substitute the concept of *the supply system*. Management of the supply system is the current key to competitive advantage. Figure 21.1 is a representation of the supply system, showing the interdependencies of the various 'players'. Recognition of the constant and concurrent effects of these interdependencies distinguishes the supply system concept from the supply chain introduced in Chapter 2.

The changes in the nature of competition referred to in section 21.2.1, and the corresponding changes in management focus or themes, are depicted in Figure 21.2.

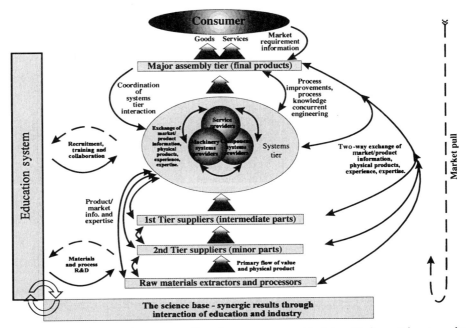

Figure 21.1 The supply system. The figure was provided by Graham Clewer, who developed the idea of the supply system as a replacement for the supply chain as part of his PhD studies at the Engineering Management Centre, City University, and is reproduced with his permission.

The theme 'supply system management' (SSM) is shown overlapping 'concurrent engineering' (CE), since new relationships with suppliers and new ways of selecting them are essential for the success of CE. In this chapter, which deals with 1990s practices, the term 'concurrent engineering' is used, reflecting general usage, rather than 'simultaneous engineering', which was more widely used when the concept was re-introduced in the 1980s.

This is also true of the other contributions that suppliers are expected to 'deliver' to help their customers improve their business performance. All the elements of the primary business performance indicator — return on capital employed (ROCE) — are affected by one or more of total quality (TQ), JIT, and CE, and they all depend on SSM as shown in Figure 21.3.

The links between the elements are as follows:

- Higher sales result from a combination of increased market share, entry to new markets, and premium prices, which all require superior quality at the time of market entry, and market entry of new products ahead of competition — which requires CE, which requires SSM.
- Lower personnel costs depend on better processes — doing things 'right first time' (TQM) — and on having suppliers do more things for their customers (outsourcing), which depends on SSM. Having fewer employees also leads to lower fixed assets — less office space and less equipment are required.

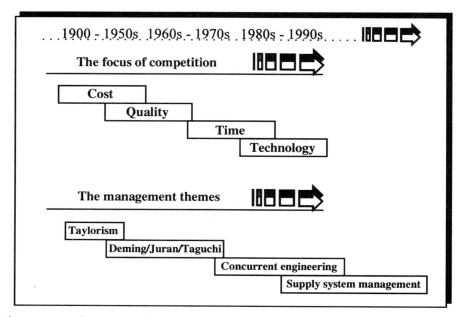

Figure 21.2 The moving edge of competition

- Lower overheads can be achieved by having less inventory and equipment to finance, and smaller buildings to service and finance, see below how this is linked to SSM.
- Lower costs of materials and services depend on suppliers delivering TQ and achieving TQ in their own operations, which depends on CE, which requires SSM.
- Lower debtors can be achieved by applying TQ techniques to debt management, and by partnership-style relations with customers, which is part of SSM.
- Lower inventories depend on JIT, which depends on TQ and CE, which all depend on SSM.
- Less inventory can lead to smaller, lower cost buildings, as can the use of less equipment which is more fully utilized thanks to equipment and materials suppliers' TQ, which depends on CE, which depends on SSM.

Within SSM, the key elements are supplier selection and the development of long term alliances with fewer, better suppliers. The processes of selecting suppliers are dealt with below. Rather than 'purchasing' which has become regarded as a clerical, rubber stamping exercise, the term 'procurement' is used.

21.3 PROCUREMENT — ANOTHER TEAM GAME

Business is a team game. As in all team games, the chances of winning are improved by choosing a good partner or good team-mates, so that among the

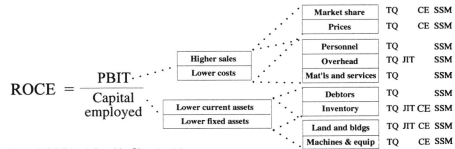

$$ROCE = \frac{PBIT}{Capital\ employed}$$

		TQ		CE	SSM
Market share		TQ		CE	SSM
Prices		TQ		CE	SSM
Personnel		TQ			SSM
Overhead		TQ	JIT		SSM
Mat'ls and services		TQ			SSM
Debtors		TQ			SSM
Inventory		TQ	JIT	CE	SSM
Land and bldgs		TQ	JIT	CE	SSM
Machines & equip		TQ		CE	SSM

Note: ROCE is defined in Chapter 14

Figure 21.3   The dependence of ROCE on SSM

team there are complementary skills, knowledge and experience. The potential of the team is realized through practice, to develop cooperation and collaboration. Throughout this book there have been examples of the need for cooperation between companies, and for collaboration between functions within companies.

This is particularly true for procurement — the process of identifying the best long term suppliers of materials, equipment, goods and services, and forming alliances with them that foster the joint pursuit of shared goals. That is a task very different from the old job of buying from the cheapest source that meets immediate requirements. The new way calls for a new team within the customer company (and in the supplier company). The chart in Figure 21.4 shows the functions involved in procurement of components, materials, equipment or services — it can be used as a generic model.

The specification and requisitioning activities — the internal customers of purchasing — are usually engineers. The interaction between these internal customers and service providers is one of the key factors that determines the team's success.

Not every procurement transaction warrants fielding the top team. Procurement, like all processes, benefits from Pareto analysis in order to apply effort where it will have greatest effect. A 'buy' may be important simply because of its value, (i.e. its effect on life-time cost), or it may have strategic significance. Engineers have a key role in identifying those materials, products and services that have strategic significance because they may be important to the organization in ten or more years' time, as well as those that are required in the next product development cycle. They also are vital members of the team that identifies possible supplier partners. Other team members may be users (shop floor employees), product planners, maintenance and safety personnel.

A 'portfolio' can be compiled, and a plan developed for dealing with each category of 'buy'. Such a portfolio is not static, and has to be updated as the business environment and corporate objectives change. An example for an entirely fictitious company is shown in Figure 21.5.

Some items do not deserve to be in the portfolio. The chart in Figure 21.6 is the typical procurement process introduced in Chapter 20, with an important line of information. It shows across the bottom of the chart the time taken to perform each function. Figures are based on an internal Ford study of the procurement of

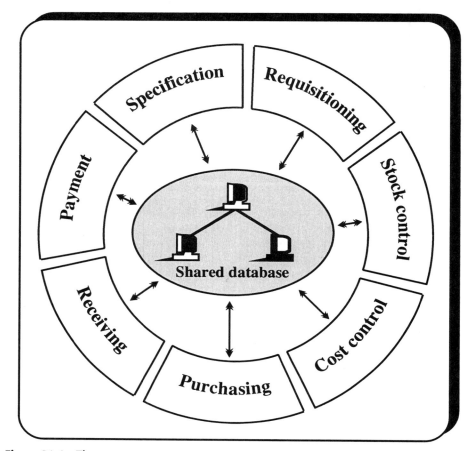

Figure 21.4 The procurement team

non-production materials/goods and services. The number in the bottom right corner (130) is the average time in minutes to perform all the processes — not the elapsed time but the total processing time. In the UK, at average salary and overhead rates, that costs about £30. This far exceeds the saving (15%?) that the most astute buyer could achieve on a high proportion of requisitions — in fact it exceeds the *value* of a high proportion of transactions. Another Ford study of non-production procurement in their UK operations during 1984 showed that the average value of the more than 4000 requisitions per day was £36. Throughout the country, there were over 1000 deliveries per day, some involving more than one item. The average value per item was £153, but 40% had a value below £25, and 70% had a value below £100.

It does not make sense to apply the might of the full procurement process to any requirement with a cost of less than £50, or even a requirement costing £200. These needs can be met from petty cash, or through a company credit card, or through an administratively simple purchasing device — the 'blanket order'. Figure 21.7 illustrates how a blanket order system operates.

Product	Risk		Actions	Information	Method	Responsibility/ timescale
	Operations	Cost				
Strategic Benzol Cyclohexan	H	H	Precise requirements Detailed market research Long term relationships Identify risks	Detailed market knowledge Long term needs	Market analysis Risk analysis Simulation Price forecasts Long term	Purchasing manager Long term
Bottleneck Catalysts Metals	H	L	Volume guarantee (price premiums?) Supplier follow-up Safety stocks	Mid term needs Storage costs Good market knowledge	Negotiated agreements Mid/long term	Purchasing agent Mid/long term
Key DP equipment Motors Heating oil	L	H	Bulk buying Alternative products Spot buys?	Good market knowledge Transport costs Maintenance costs	Competitive bidding leading to extended agreement	Senior buyer
Normal Stationery Office equipment	L	L	Standardization Groupage	Market overview EOQ	Competitive bidding Short term agreement (1 year?)	Buyer short/mid term

H = High risk to operations or cost performance
L = Low risk to operations or cost performance

Figure 21.5 Purchasing portfolio analysis

Once set up, the blanket order enables any authorized user, in any of the several different locations, to obtain what they need by issuing a 'release' direct to the supplier. The supplier ships direct to each user location, and consolidates all transactions covered by the blanket order into a single monthly invoice. This takes time out of actions 2, 3, 4, 5 and 8 shown in the 'procurement process' chart in Figure 21.6. In December 1994, Ford Motor Company held meetings with their leading suppliers to explain their plans to change their purchasing methods and organization on a global basis. One of the major planned method changes was to increase the use of blanket orders since Ford's studies had shown that to process an individual purchase notice (order) cost $280, whereas processing a release against a blanket order cost $190.

Delegated 'local' authority or centrally negotiated blanket orders can take care of many requirements that have low individual value, and no strategic significance. It is the other end of the scale that demands attention. This is the 20% of items that account for 80% of the total value of purchases, or the few items that differentiate the product, or the even fewer number involving new technology and/or long lead times that can make or break a project.

For machinery and equipment purchases, this process of separating the important few from the rest, should include a decision about the need to use the CE approach. Although there are potential benefits in terms of improved quality and savings of time and investment cost, CE requires the application of more human resources than the conventional procurement process. Figure 21.8 shows an algorithm that can help to determine whether a simple request for quotations would be appropriate, or whether the additional efforts involved with CE should be applied.

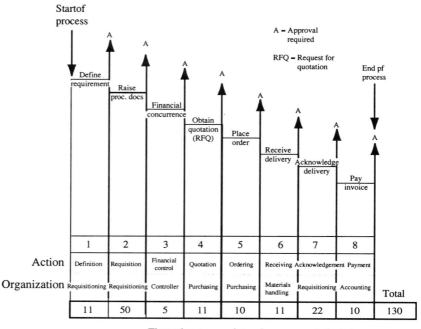

Figure 21.6 The acquisition/procurement process

Successful organizations make these decisions about the use of CE, and the commodities to which CE should be applied, early. This means early enough to involve suppliers in developing concepts, designs and delivery processes (delivery in the sense of meeting all the customers' needs, not deliver by truck, though that may be part of it).

In the automotive industry early involvement means identifying the suppliers of key parts at least four years before production starts. For major changes in materials, or the introduction of radical new features or processes, it may mean ten years. Some other industries, such as pharmaceuticals or aerospace have even longer development spans, and others such as home entertainment equipment or computer peripherals have shorter spans. Since the automotive industry is somewhere in the middle, and has been a leader in making changes to procurement processes, it can provide an insight into methods of supplier selection and management. The following sections describe these methods and how they have been changing.

21.4 PROCUREMENT — THE OLD WAY

The 'old' ways of procurement in the automotive industry are still widely used in other industries, and by some laggard automotive companies. Engineers may therefore find themselves working with or in organizations where these methods are used, and may be assisted by this section on what should be a dying art.

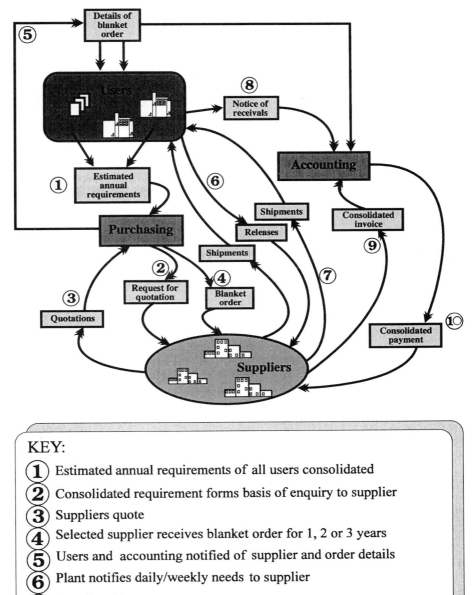

Figure 21.7   Blanket order system

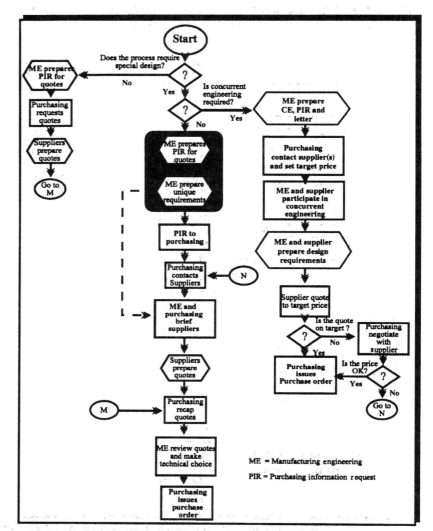

Figure 21.8   Machinery and equipment procurement guidelines

Three criteria have been used to make purchasing decisions in the engineering industries from the time they were founded. These are:

- cost
- quality
- delivery performance.

In many industries, the realization that suppliers' quality management determines their ability to reduce costs, and deliver on time, is fairly recent. In some, the belief that quality can be secured by inspection still persists, but, generally, with a time lag of a few years, supplier quality management has changed in the same ways as

Assessment criterion	Assessed by department....		....on the basis of	
	For components...	For machinery and equipment.....	For components...	For machinery and equipment....
Ability to meet specifications	Purchasing/ quality control Product Development	Purchasing/ manufacturing engineering	Function, laboratory and dimensional tests Development programme	Demonstrations Witness Judgement
Price	Purchasing	Purchasing	Competition and estimates	
Reliability	Purchasing	Purchasing	Delivery, warranty, and performance records financial appraisals and buyer visits	

Figure 21.9   The procurement process—sourcing decisions the old way

their customers'. Management of quality has been covered in Chapter 4, and this section therefore concentrates on the old approach to supplier cost and delivery management, with passing reference to quality.

The table in Figure 21.9 shows the 'old' basis of sourcing decisions, for components (parts) and for machinery and equipment.

The division of responsibilities between purchase, engineering and quality departments, who may all have been pursuing different goals, encouraged 'compartmental' attitudes and 'turf protection', plus time-consuming blame allocation when things went wrong. Conflicts arose, for example, when designers wanted development agreements with suppliers that buyers thought were uncompetitive on price, or had a poor delivery record.

Quality was controlled by issuing detailed specifications, with extensive test requirements, against which suppliers with approved quality control systems were invited to quote. At the quotation stage, suppliers would rarely admit to any difficulty in meeting the specification, so, increasingly, price became the main criterion. This was reinforced by design cost control systems that assigned cost targets to designers as well as by purchase cost control systems that assigned targets to buyers.

Design cost control and purchase cost control systems work in similar ways. By identifying the 20% of 'key' parts that account for 80% of product cost, the cost analysis task can be reduced to a manageable scale. For these key parts it is possible to build up a cost model. This would show what it would cost an efficient producer, using suitable equipment and processes, and paying market labour rates and material prices to make that part or assembly. Profit margins, R&D costs and other overheads can be incorporated. Once the model has been constructed, it is possible to estimate the effect of changes. These include design changes, pay awards, material cost increases, energy cost movements, exchange rate fluctuations etc.

Such systems can be used to measure the cost performance of an individual designer or buyer, or the collective performance of a design group, a manufacturing plant or an outside supplier. In finance-driven companies, this is the principal application, with the added refinement of targeted annual cost reductions. Similarly, estimates can be aggregated to generate total product costs, and to set targets for cost reductions from one design iteration or model to the next.

Even with competitive bidding, the purchase cost estimates can be used by buyers to check each supplier's quotation, and identify opportunities for negotiation. In single bid situations, for example where a supplier has been engaged in a design contract, the estimate may be the only check on their quotation to determine whether it is reasonable or extortionate. If it is extortionate, the only remedy for the buyer is a long memory and carefully-kept records.

The same information can also be used in a more constructive way, to focus *shared* cost reduction effort through value analysis and the highlighting of opportunities to introduce better methods, alternative materials, alternative sources and so on.

The procurement process within which such price control mechanisms were used is illustrated in Figure 21.10. In better run firms, the list of suppliers invited to quote was agreed between users, designers and buyers, but in many organizations commitments were made by designers or users — or worst of all by the boss — and the buyer was expected to negotiate the best deal afterwards. The sequence of actions in this version of the procurement process is as follows.

The stream of releases from product development (design engineering) is divided by pre-production control into two flows of buy parts, and make parts, on the basis of earlier policy decisions or 'integration studies', also conducted previously.

Purchasing receive the information about buy parts, and issue an enquiry, or 'request for quotation' to potential suppliers. The suppliers send in their quotations, purchasing select the 'best' bid, and issue an order to the successful supplier.

Manufacturing engineering receive the information about 'make' parts, and check their capacity and capability to produce the volumes and specifications. If additional equipment or tooling is required, they issue a purchase information request (PIR) to purchasing, who go through an enquiry/quotation process, similar to the buy parts process. However, for equipment there is an added loop, to cover the review of quotations jointly by engineers and buyers — the 'recaps' in the figure. This allows for price and performance trade-offs to be discussed, which are unlikely to be feasible for parts and assemblies. The make parts will also require outside purchases of materials and parts, and the buy parts process is followed for these items. Long-lead requirements of manufacturing — such as a new building, or a major building extension or modification — are bought through a similar process as equipment purchases, but the need for this is identified through the integration studies mentioned earlier, on a time-scale that recognizes construction lead times.

In these 'old' procurement processes it was normally the quoted purchase *price* that was considered when the source was selected. For most purchases, the

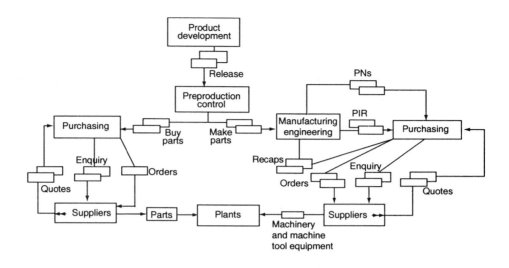

Key to abbreviations:
PN – purchase notice (an order)
PIR – purchase information request (an enquiry)
RECAP – recapitulation (a detailed comparison
of the quotation)

Figure 21.10   The procurement process—purchasing/engineering/supplier links

difference between *price* and *life-time cost*, which recognizes running costs, maintenance costs and disposal costs (see Chapter 15) was not taken into account. This difference can be so great that a decision based on price alone can be a bad one, and, increasingly, purchasing decisions for buildings, manufacturing equipment and transportation equipment are taking note of it. The same should apply to office equipment purchases. For example, the price of a laser printer can be as little as 10% of the cost per page of print over a three year period of printer life [1].

The processes described above are based on manufacturing industry practice, but something similar applied, and still does, in civil engineering. A consultant placed between the user and the constructor would perform the same role of developing very detailed specifications, establishing a list of suitable suppliers, soliciting competitive bids, analysing responses and recommending order placement with the company quoting lowest — providing they met the specification and lead time. The detailed specification was later used to try and control the time and cost effect of changes. (See Chapters 17 and 19).

In the 'old' manufacturing procurement process, extensive buyers' terms and conditions were combined with the detailed specifications to protect the purchasers' interests. These were matched with similarly restrictive terms of offer and sale to protect the sellers' interests. Attempts to negotiate settlements of disputes would start with attempts to determine whose terms and conditions applied. The terms and conditions might include sections designed to assign responsibility for adherence to delivery or completion timing, as well as compliance with specification and price. Graham and Sano in *Beyond Negotiation* [2] note the contrast between western contracts, that may take 100 pages to define buyer rights and supplier responsibilities, and Japanese contracts of a page or two that set out the shared objectives of the agreement. They also observe that the Americans talk of 'concluding business deals', while the Japanese speak of 'establishing business relationships'.

It was common practice in the West to reinforce these contractual arrangements with monitoring — 'chasers', 'follow-up', site engineers, timing analysts, project control engineers or analysts (sometimes working against each other, one to control cost, the other to control timing). Extensive records were kept of back-orders, past dues, slippages and delays, and alleged reasons for them. In many western industries, security of supply of parts and materials was often sought through dual or triple sourcing, as a protection against poor labour relations, quality concerns, transportation difficulties and the like. Where multi-sourcing failed to give this protection, it was supplemented by inventory on the user's site or at a 'neutral' warehouse.

'Transportation difficulties' and 'warehousing' are reminders of the traffic and customs function within 'supply'. (See Chapter 5). They are tagged on here much as they were in the old ways of procurement. After a part or product had been sourced, the materials handling and traffic personnel tried to negotiate packaging and packing modes with the selected supplier, and the traffic or transportation personnel would review in-bound shipping arrangements. This could only be done after the programming and inventory planning group had had their say to determine target inventories, delivery frequencies and quantities. They also needed to know prices, volumes, supplier location and reliability in terms of quality and continuity of operations to do this. Shipping was often the suppliers' responsibility, but there has been a trend to ex-works purchasing for two sets of reasons:

- suppliers fell down on the quality of their packing and delivery performance (under pressure to reduce cost),
- individual suppliers were constantly faced with the task of delivering uneconomic (part) loads, and using common carriers to do this added more delay and risk.

The pressure to introduce JIT concepts forced changes in transportation and packaging, as well as in inventory planning, and was one of the reasons for moving away from a separate procurement process towards integrated purchasing, logistics and planning. Other reasons are included in the next section which describes the 'new' processes of procurement.

21.5   'NEW' PROCESSES OF PROCUREMENT — PARTNERSHIP SOURCING

21.5.1   The 'drivers' for change

As the edge of competition moved from price alone, to include quality, durability, reliability and then time to market, and time to satisfy customers' orders, the old purchasing and follow-up practices were exposed as defective and destructive.

They generated internal conflicts, and conflicts between buyer and seller. Removal of these conflicts required new relationships within companies, and new relationships between companies. All the 'success formulae' identified in Chapter 8, stress the need for long term partnerships with fewer suppliers. Section 21.2.1 summarized the ways in which TQ, JIT, and CE drive to the same conclusion: suppliers have to be involved early in the planning of the product, and the entire production and distribution system. These programmes — TQ, JIT and CE — require 'real-time' communications systems using computerized data exchange (CDX), which, again, is a less difficult task if there are fewer suppliers involved.

So, from many directions there are pressures to change from relationships with many suppliers who bid against each other for short-term contracts, to the practice of early identification of fewer suppliers to be treated as partners pursuing shared goals. This practice precludes the old form of competitive bidding as a means of supplier selection — at the time when suppliers join the CE teams there are no detailed specifications for them to bid against.

The chart in Figure 21.11 shows the timing of 'early sourcing' in the automotive industry in the late 1980s, when alternatives to competitive bidding as a means of supplier selection were being developed. Since then, the 48 month new vehicle development cycle has been reduced to 36 months, and targets as low as 24 months are being pursued. However, these shorter cycles result from the policies and practices developed in the late 1980s, and these are therefore reviewed in the next sections.

21.5.2 New policies and new attitudes towards suppliers

The sourcing policies and attitudes that were widely adopted in the late 1980s had been advocated by Deming some 40 years earlier[1]. The fourth of his 14 responsibilities of management is:

'End the practice of awarding business on the basis of price tag alone. Purchasing must be combined with design of the product, manufacturing and sales to work with the chosen suppliers.'

Acceptance of this advice is evident in policy statements by many of the automotive companies. The following examples are from material supplied by the companies.

Nissan Manufacturing UK:

'The principle of "Partnership" is the key to our supplier relationships. It is, however, not just a purchasing principle — it is a whole company philosophy. To work properly it needs time, patience, trust and full commitment from all parties involved in the buyer/seller relationship on both sides of the partnership... Partnership sourcing is a commitment... to a long-term relationship based on clear mutually agreed objectives to strive for world-class capability and competitiveness.'

The Rover Group:

'Our new standard emphasises strategic issues which are often overlooked and encourages both ownership and flexibility in achieving our common goals . . . This

---

[1]Deming, W. E., *Out of the Crisis*, Cambridge University Press, Cambridge, UK, 1982.

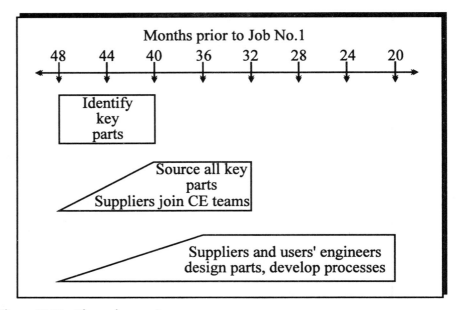

Figure 21.11 The early sourcing process

new standard is an acknowledgement by the Rover Group that we need to form close, lasting partnerships with suppliers to maintain successful, competitive businesses into the next century.'

Chrysler Corporation:

'At Chrysler, we don't view our suppliers as generic interchangeable "vendors" whose only purpose in life is to do what we tell them to do and to never have any ideas of their own. Instead, we view our suppliers as true extensions of our company — as an integral, creative link in the value-added chain, just as we ourselves are merely a link. We call it "the extended enterprise concept." We've totally scrapped the age-old system in the auto industry of auctioning off contracts to the lowest bidder. Instead, we set what we call a "target cost" and then we work closely with trusted, pre-selected supplier partners to arrive at that target. And we don't do that by cutting profit margins, but by encouraging new and innovative ideas, and by rooting out waste and inefficiency — much of it, by the way, in our own systems.'

This last point in the statement by Chrysler is also a part of the Xerox policy (just to get away from the automotive industry for a few lines.) Xerox call it 'cooperative contracting', and it has the same results as Chrysler's approach: lower total costs, but not at the expense of supplier profit margins. The chart in Figure 21.12 illustrates the effect of the Xerox practice.

All these policy statements describe close, long-term relationships with fewer, pre-selected suppliers. The way in which these select few are chosen is described in the next section.

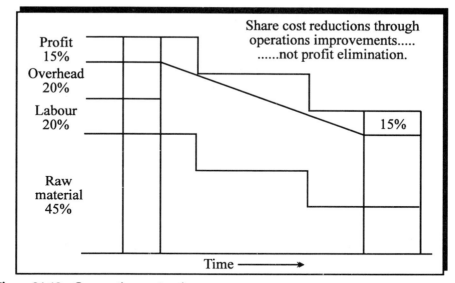

Figure 21.12   Cooperative contracting

21.5.3   Selection criteria for pre-sourcing

History may be 'bunk', as Henry Ford I is alleged to have said, but it nevertheless can be used as a guide to the future. Carefully recorded history, and objective assessment form the basis of most of the supplier selection processes that have been substituted for competitive bidding. The automotive industry generally uses five headings under which supplier history is compiled, and which are used to make an overall assessment of a supplier's capability and potential. These are:

- management ability and attitude
- quality performance
- delivery performance
- technical capability
- commercial performance.

Some schemes incorporate an assessment of management under the other four headings. One of these, the Ford supply base management (SBM) system forms the basis of the following explanation. Figure 21.13 shows the logo from the cover of Ford's SBM booklet, with the four criteria and the activities responsible for rating supplier performance for each of them.

Quality is the overriding criterion. Most producers in the automotive, aerospace, information technology, pharmaceutical and electrical and electronics industries have their own quality management systems and standards for assessment of materials and component suppliers that are more demanding than the international BS/EN/ISO 9000 standards. They have developed comprehensive measures of supplier performance over the years, and many suppliers recognize the value to their own operations of making the continuous improvements

* SQE = supplier quality engineering

Figure 21.13   Supply base management rating criteria

demanded by these quality management systems. Compliance with the customer's quality system requirements is the price of admission to the supplier selection game.

The Ford Q101/Q1 system scores supplier quality performance under three headings with weighting for each. These are:

- supplier management attitude and commitment   20%
- supplier quality management system   30%
- supplier delivered quality performance   50%

Suppliers who consistently score above 80% may petition for the Ford Q1 award, and only suppliers with Q1 status are considered for new business. Based on their scores, suppliers are classified as 'preferred', 'potentially preferred', or 'short-term'. The last category indicates that a supplier will not be used beyond existing contracts.

Objective measurement of equipment suppliers' quality performance is less well developed. The issue is usually clouded by variations in material or rough part quality or tooling quality, by the effectiveness of prior or complementary operations, and by standards of equipment maintenance, and operator training. Nevertheless, by considering process capability (see Chapter 4), mean time between failures, mean time to repair etc., it is possible to reach consensus between equipment users, process designers and purchasing on a ranking of potential suppliers for each type of equipment, and to agree whether quality performance is roughly equal, or markedly different. It should be possible to differentiate between 'acceptable' and 'unacceptable' suppliers, and it is quite likely that one or two 'quality preferred' suppliers can be named.

Current technical capability is a clue to future performance. Since suppliers' participation in the design process is essential for successful CE, their capability in this respect is a vital part of the selection process. The activity best able to make this assessment is the customer company's own technical staff. Purchasing have to ensure that all serious contenders are considered, and that their technical colleagues' opinions are expressed in a rational, measurable way. Scoring or ranking systems can be established to evaluate a supplier's R&D investment and facilities, personnel, rate of innovation, use of CE with their own suppliers, CAD/CAM and CDX capability etc. Absolute precision in ranking is not necessary, and is not meaningful. A useful and sufficient separation between suppliers could be achieved by assessing them as:

- preferrred — frequently provides relevant, tested innovations,
- acceptable — sometimes provides relevant, tested innovations,
- unacceptable — rarely provides relevant, tested innovations.

This approach can be applied equally well to materials suppliers, component suppliers and equipment suppliers. Regular, structured exchange visits between customer and supplier to develop an understanding of each other's operations, with shared, structured reports will enable these evaluations to be built up over an extended period, so that 'off the shelf' selections can be made for new projects.

Measurement of delivery performance and capacity is essential. By systematically measuring supplier delivery performance, and fairly analysing reasons for lateness, it is possible to build up a ranking of suppliers according to this criterion. Rating systems which include measures of supplier responsiveness to change, their planning capability, their management attitudes and commitment etc., can be used to generate scores, and classifications such as:

- preferred
- acceptable
- unacceptable.

Early involvement of preferred or acceptable suppliers in new programmes enables them to improve their delivery performance by planning new processes and capacity in advance. Process capability and capacity, and sub-supplier capability can all be brought to the required levels in good time.

Component, materials and equipment suppliers must have sufficient confidence in their customers to honestly discuss their order backlogs and production and investment plans. It may be necessary for customers to support their suppliers when they make requests from their financiers for investment funds, or to modify their payment terms to assist in the funding of work-in-progress or new facilities.

Continuous exchange of information about current performance, forward requirements and anticipated problems is necessary to maintain deliveries on schedule, or to prepare offsetting measures. It is an important customer responsibility to constantly check demand from all user areas against supplier capacity and commitments. For example service requirements should be included as well as current production needs, or coordinated demands from associate and subsidiary companies around the world.

Supply Base Management

Commodity: wheel bearings   Buyer: A. N. Other   Code: E100

Objective no. suppliers 90 4 91 4 92 4 93 3   Date: April 1991   Division: BAO

Supplier name(s) Ship point	Code	Sales		Ratings								Remarks
		Totals ($ millions)	Commodity ($ millions)	Quality	Date	Tech	Date	Dely*	Date	Comm	Date	
Preferred long term												
W. H. Smith Romford, Essex	A100B	4.8	2.4	Q1	6/89	90	2/90	91	3/90	93	4/90	
E. H. Willis Tipton, W. Midlands	B200A	3.7	1.9	Q1	8/89	91	2/90	89	3/90	85	4/90	
Potential long term												
J. Brown Dudley, W. Midlands	C150B	2.8	2.4	85P	3/90	84	2/90	87	3/90	81		Corrective action plan Available resurvey Q3 1990
Short term												
D. Lete Runcorn, Liverpool	E250A	1.4	1.0	80A	3/90	81	2/90	76	3/90	72	4/90	Deleted with CDW27 1993

*Median Score—of Delivery Ratings

Figure 21.14   Commodity summary

Commercial performance seals the relationship. The 'right price' is essential to both supplier and customer, but may not be known when sourcing commitments are made. CE helps suppliers to improve their efficiency and reduce their costs, so that they can supply at prices that are competitive on a global basis, yet make returns on capital that are sufficient to support their own profitable development. Chrysler's 'target pricing' and Xerox's 'cooperative contracting' are ways of supporting suppliers' efforts in this respect. For 'global' sourcing, these pricing discussions will include projections of supplier productivity improvements and material cost control, taking account of inflation and exchange rate projections. Where design details of the new product are not available, the discussions may be based on 'surrogate' parts, or commodity groups rather than specific parts.

Constructive use of the information is vital for developing partnerships. Evaluation of supplier performance is a continuous process, and the results must be shared regularly with individual suppliers so that opportunities for improvement can be identified. Comparative data should be maintained by the customer's purchasing activity so that supply base capability can be assessed in the light of the purchasing portfolio of long term needs. An example of a Ford summary of quality, delivery, technical and commercial ratings of suppliers in a commodity group is shown in Figure 21.14.

The commodity summary covers the UK only, and shows an objective for the reduction in the number of suppliers from 4 to 3. This is no longer typical. Ford, like many multinational companies, is now buying its most important requirements on a global basis, and a commodity summary would show global supplier ratings, and global supplier reduction plans.

Ford had developed the SBM sourcing process far enough for it to be used in 1989–90 to identify preferred suppliers to participate in the CDW27 programme, which was the codename for the one car eventually marketed as the Mondeo in Europe, and the Contour and Mystique in North America, replacing two separate and different medium car ranges.

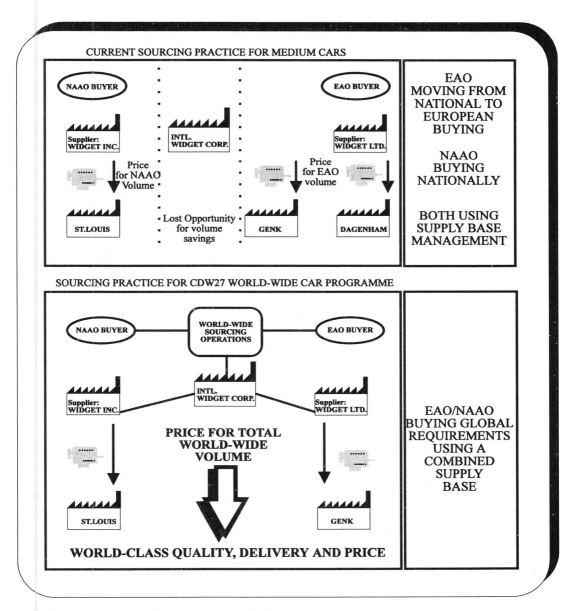

Figure 21.15   The change from regional to global sourcing at Ford

Ford's European Automotive Operations (EAO) had been using the supply base management concept for several years prior to the start of the CDW27 programme. This had enabled EAO to combine their requirements for all their European plants, and to make a 'best buy' using information from the worldwide supply base. Similar sourcing practices had been used by North American Automotive Operations (NAAO) for their total requirements. The CDW27 project was an opportunity to optimize on a global basis, for the combined needs of the CDW27 producer plants in the USA (St Louis) and in Europe (Genk, in Belgium). To do this, Ford established temporary 'worldwide sourcing operations' which coordinated information from EAO and NAAO to compile a single list of preferred suppliers to work with the single CDW27 design and manufacturing team in Europe. Figure 21.15 illustrates the transition from 'regional' to 'global' purchasing. The 'volume savings' referred to in the figure are not economies of manufacturing scale, since most suppliers used separate facilities to serve the St Louis and Genk plants and to apply JIT methods to a limited extent. (Full JIT would have entailed location of the 20 to 30 most important suppliers close to each of the assembly plants, which was not done.) The savings came primarily from combining Ford and supplier design and process engineering capabilities to work on a single, global design and a single best manufacturing process — something the Japanese car producers have always done.

Throughout the CDW27 programme, Ford continued their policy of reducing the number of suppliers with whom they are involved. Despite being assembled in plants in two continents, the CDW27 is supported by less than 300 suppliers — about half the number that EAO and NAAO each used on the superseded models. By the year 2000, Ford will probably be working with only 600 to 800 suppliers of production requirements worldwide, and with about 5000 suppliers for their 'non-production' requirements, instead of something like 50 000. They know that reductions of this sort are possible — Xerox have reduced their supplier base from 5000 to 400 as part of their 'leadership through quality' programme.

21.6 SUMMARY

This chapter described the changes in inter-company relationships that are necessary to achieve world-class levels of business performance. It was noted that the shift of the competitive edge to include faster application of new technologies requires extension of the boundaries within which companies operate. This requires that the whole supply system is managed concurrently, with the science base as well as materials, component and equipment suppliers involved as partners at the early stages of new product and process development. A description of the 'old' methods of supplier selection by competitive bidding showed that these are inadequate for the new competitive environment, and that buyers need to change to methods that promote cooperative rather than confrontational relationships. Sourcing policies of some leading automotive companies were listed to illustrate how assemblers are seeking to establish a sense of partnership with their suppliers, and to take account of quality, delivery and technical ability, as well as price when selecting their partners. Ford's supply base management system was described as an example of these new sourcing processes, and their use to move towards global procurement practices.

REFERENCES

1. Lloyd, C. (1993) 'Hidden costs of running laser printers', *The Sunday Times* 14 December, based on a report by Context, a London UK research company.
2. Graham, J. L. and Sano, Y. (1989) *Smart Bargaining—Doing Business with the Japanese*. Harper & Row, New York. Chapter 7 gives extracts from typical American and Japanese contracts, and comments on the way in which they reflect different attitudes to supplier relationships.

22

Marketing

22.1 INTRODUCTION

Marketing can be defined as:

Marketing is the management process which identifies, anticipates and supplies customer requirements efficiently and profitably. (UK Chartered Institute of Marketing)

Marketing is the process of planning and executing the conception, pricing, promotion and distribution of ideas, goods and services to create exchanges that satisfy individual and organizational objectives. (American Marketing Association)

In order to bridge the 'planning gap' between where an engineering organization is and where it would like to be in terms of its products and the markets in which it operates, a strategy for marketing, engineering practice and corporate planning must be adopted. The organization has to evaluate where it is and predict where current policies and technologies will take it. This projection can leave a gap between where management wishes to be and where it will be unless purposeful action is taken. So the process of strategic management involves a decision about 'where we want to be', a critical evaluation of 'where are we' and the creative process of deciding the policies, products, services and projects that will bridge this planning gap. Success in this process requires a marketing orientation.

Successful marketing is vital to the success of any company and, therefore, is of considerable importance to the success of engineering enterprises and to the engineers who work for them. This chapter will take Figure 22.1, the outline of the business planning process, as its starting point and will consider the concept of *'mission'*, *methods of external and internal analysis*, the *marketing mix*, *marketing tools* and *marketing information systems*.

22.2 BUSINESS PRINCIPLES

Consider the issues that confront an extractor and distributor of natural gas. The organization may define its operation in terms of 'we supply gas'. However, such a company will not survive in the long term as it will not be able to evaluate its environment or serve its customers. The domestic customers may buy gas but they do not want gas, they want the benefits that the gas supplies them. A 100 years ago in a Victorian house the benefit from coal gas was light. In a modern

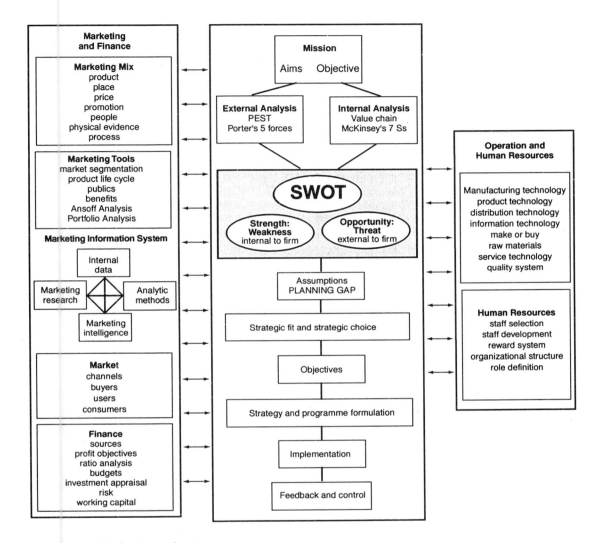

Figure 22.1   The business planning process

household the benefits are reliability (relative freedom from supply cuts), warmth, (central heating), cleanliness (ample supply of hot water) and good food (cooking). As soon as the business is defined in benefit terms it becomes clear that the prime benefit in this case is the supply of energy and that competition can come from many sources. The organization is in direct competition with electricity, and indirectly with organizations and technologies that reduce energy usage such as house insulation. The key concept is that people do not buy products: they have needs, wants and desires for benefits. The gas company would do better to define its business as 'we supply energy for modern living'. Armed with the concept of benefits the strategic planning process can now be considered.

22.3   THE BUSINESS PLANNING PROCESS: MISSION AIMS AND OBJECTIVES

Figure 22.1 shows the outline of the business planning process. The starting point is the definition of the business in marketing orientated terms, the corporate mission. Good mission statements have a number of characteristics:

- A long time-scale — for a power supply company this should be looking well beyond the life of a production unit and needs to project decades rather than years.
- A definition of the business scope — the definition 'we supply gas' is very different to 'we supply energy' which would not preclude the organization entering the electricity supply market.
- A customer orientated perspective — the mission must be defined from the customers' benefit viewpoint.
- It must inspire and motivate — an organization which defines its objective in terms of 'to provide a 20% return on capital', might suggest to both employees and customers that the organization's only concern is what it gets out, not the benefits it supplies.
- It must be realistic — acknowledging the firm's resources and distinctive capabilities.

The mission provides the long term vision for the organization but for effective management it has to be translated into operational terms. Pursuing the example, the energy based mission for the gas company would embrace the possibility of its supplying gas to combined heat and electrical power plants for industrial, commercial and institutional organizations. In this case the mission would be amplified with an aim 'to enter and achieve a significant market share in the supply of combined heat and power'. This provides a specific focus but fails to give the chief project engineer firm targets, specific objectives. These might be to:

- Have a proven marketable system in one year
- Have the first customer installed system within two years.
- Build up to a profitable sales level of ten systems a year within four years.

Objectives are quite different from aims. The relationship is the same as between a vector and direction. The former has direction and magnitude. So a good objective has to have a defined target, quantitative if possible, as well as a timescale for achievement. Armed with this the chief project engineer has specific goals and can proceed to environmental analysis.

22.4   THE BUSINESS PLANNING PROCESS: THE EXTERNAL ENVIRONMENT

Two tools allow the analysis of the external environment: PEST (political, economic, social and technical) and Porter's Five Forces competition analysis [1, 2].

P	E	S	T
Political	Economic	Social	Technical
Legislation Ideology Attitudes	Trends Credits Income Interest rates Tax Exchange rates International trends Gross National Product Wealth distribution	Values Attitudes Work ethic Life styles Demographics Work force Religion Status	Discoveries Developments Substitutes

Figure 22.2 PEST

These are shown in Figure 22.2. The detailed consideration of the marketing aspects is developed in sections 22.7 to 22.11.

22.4.1   PEST

The *political* forces on the organization include the specific demands of legislation as well as the ideology and attitudes within the operating environment. For the supply of combined heat and power, the deregulation of the electrical power industry in the UK has been a major factor. An organization operating such a unit now has the ability to sell excess electrical power, and this of course has changed the economic viability of such installations. The project engineer will be faced with a long list of detailed legal requirements covering the safety of the unit and environmental compliance issues (e.g. noise levels, venting of exhaust gases, etc.). The attitudes and ideology are important as they affect the degree, flexibility and speed with which factors can be resolved. In the present climate of a global commitment to reduce carbon dioxide emissions and to reduce the wasteful use of finite resources, a supportive climate exists for energy efficiency projects.

Note that PEST and competition analysis do not provide a neat set of orthogonal vectors, these do not exist in business. All the elements to some extent interact, but, if the strategist does not consider the differing aspects, critical factors may be neglected and lead to project failure. In the case of energy there is a social concern for 'green' issues and the pressures on energy resources have economic consequences. These two forces result in legislation and changes in political environment. Engineers and scientists will search for innovative technical approaches to the issues. The new technological skills needed might exist in organizations that have not previously been active in the arena and new competition patterns might be established.

Discounted cash flow analysis (see Chapter 15) provides a specific detailed investment appraisal tool but a more general *economic* view has to be exercised at the strategic level. Long term trends in finance sources and interest rates are important for engineering projects with long construction periods and even longer operational lives. Where the engineer is confronted with designing products or production facilities for the manufacture of consumer goods, trends in the shape of the population and life style must be considered. As discussed in Chapter 2, the engineering industries operate in international markets with global procurement and manufacturing operations, and long term trends in relative economic development and exchange rates must be evaluated (also discussed in Chapter 2). In the example, the project engineer will be concerned with the sources and costs of finance for customers who will purchase the units and how these will balance against future energy costs and potential customer savings. In the procurement of production units, long term judgments of relative domestic cost structures against those of overseas suppliers must be considered among the factors affecting the procurement decision.

Social issues impact all aspects of an organization. Attitudes to employment will affect how an organization structures and operates its manufacturing environment. Considerations here include work ethic, demographics and workforce skills. Consumer issues not only affect the manufacturers of consumer products but also major utilities. A general social attitude to safety and quality of life will induce a car manufacturer to introduce air bags into its products to satisfy individual consumers and also to introduce energy efficient methods of manufacture to be able to sustain a positive corporate image such as 'products designed and built with care for people that care'.

Technology provides the ability to supply benefits in entirely new ways with effects which extend far and wide. The invention of microwave ovens provided a new method of cooking which fitted in with the convenience lifestyle demanded by so many consumers. The effect was to bring electronics companies into the kitchen and to drag kitchen appliance manufacturers into electronics. The impact also involved the food industry with the need to produce new products (frozen and chilled microwave specific products), the packaging industry (microwavable packaging) and retailing (new frozen and chilled food display units).

It is only the strategically orientated engineer who can fully evaluate the commercial impact of developments, discoveries and substitutes. The whole business is affected; procurement, manufacturing operations, distribution and marketing. The pace of technology change is such that an organization's competitive position can be quickly changed (see Chapter 6).

22.4.2 Porter's Five Forces of competition

Figure 22.3 shows Porter's Five Forces of competition model [2]. To use this model the strategist has to be clear about the benefit being supplied to the market and the platform from which the analysis is conducted. The results of an analysis

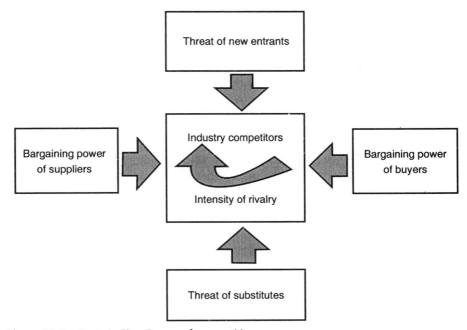

Figure 22.3   Porter's Five Forces of competition

of air travel will be very different for an airline, an aircraft manufacturer, a travel agency or a holiday tour operator. Many engineering technologies have more than one application satisfying differing benefit needs, this is called *segmentation* and the marketing implications are discussed in section 22.7. It is necessary to complete the competition analysis for the differing benefit segments. Gas turbines were developed for air travel but are now used for electricity generation and the powering of warships. Nuclear or coal power stations will compete with gas. Diesel engines may be used to power a ship but not an aircraft. The chief engineer of a turbine manufacturer would have to complete the competition analysis for each sector.

The five forces are in *sector competition* (direct competition), *substitute products, new entrants, supplier power* and *buyer power* (channel and consumer).

The *direct competition* means those organizations that supply the same goods or services in the same way. This does not necessarily mean that they have the same competitive position. Exit and entry costs greatly affect the flexibility and potential for competitive response. For example, three companies produce a similar product. One makes all the components and has a high investment in automated production lines (high entry costs). Another has a simple assembly factory and buys in its components and subassemblies (modest entry costs). The third subcontracts out all its manufacture and concentrates wholly on marketing and distribution. In a recession the latter two companies have greater flexibility for they can reduce their output with much less impact than the fully integrated company, which has to operate at high capacity to cover its fixed and capital costs.

New entrants are organizations that have the potential to supply the goods or services. A continual consideration is the international dimension, where major companies are always looking for new markets and the corporate strategist will be continually alert to such expansionist moves into a given market under appraisal. Shifts and convergence of technology may allow new entrants. IBM defined its business as office efficiency. Providing this benefit took the company into leadership in computing technology. Another company, Hewlett-Packard, was based in advanced scientific instruments and measurement systems. The provision of this benefit moved this company into advanced computer technology. Hewlett-Packard then became a major player in office computer systems in competition with IBM. Again the corporate strategist must scan the external environment for organizations that have moved into positions where they might become a major source of competition. Such entries can come from the most unexpected sources. Banks in the UK had a near monopoly of financial services and now find themselves subject to significant competition from building societies, retail distribution (Marks and Spencer's entry into financial services) and motor manufacturers (credit cards).

In evaluating *supplier power*[1] the relative bargaining power of suppliers vis-à-vis the organization is being appraised. If the organization is large and there are many suppliers then the leverage of the supplier is reduced. If there are only a few suppliers and the organization is a small user, then the positions are reversed. Care must be taken that all the goods, licences (patents, copyrights, etc.) and services (including labour) required by the organization are taken into account. Consider food retailing. When the distribution and retailing of food was highly fragmented the large food processors of branded foods had great supplier power. With the high concentration of retailing power in a few supermarket groups, the roles are now effectively reversed with the supplier power much diminished and the power lying with the retailers.

In evaluating *buyer power* in the engineering context it is usual to consider the power of the channels of supply and the ultimate customers. The direct customers of a manufacturer of consumer electronics are the high street retailers (in the UK, Dixon's, Comet, etc.). However consumers will only purchase a company's products if they provide distinctive benefits (high quality, more useful features etc.) and value for money in a competitive market. It is also wise to consider indirect channel power. A supplier of car engine and transmission lubricants may not have major sales to Ford but will be most concerned if their product is not approved for topping-up Ford vehicles. A supplier of UPS's (un-interruptable power supplies) will have direct sales to computer manufacturers (large customers with high buyer power). The computer manufacturers will also have indirect power since it will be necessary for the UPS supplier to be included in the list of approved power suppliers for customers configuring their own systems. It will be necessary to demonstrate to agents and computer distributors that the system is effective, and will give them an acceptable profit margin and that supply will be

---

[1]This aspect of Porter's analysis is inconsistent with current concepts of supply system management. As shown in Chapter 21, successful engineering companies now seek to establish alliances and partnerships with suppliers. Porter's perspective applied more frequently in the early 1980s when his analysis was developed, but an engineering company's ability to develop partnerships continues to be influenced by the factors identified by Porter.

prompt. The ultimate buyers of these units are knowledgeable and will be able to make accurate performance and cost comparisons. As this analysis demonstrates, this will be a competitive market where the *engineer* will have to ensure extremely good performance with strict control of manufacturing costs for the product to be successful. The *strategist* must consider the external environment in conjunction with the internal environment of the organization.

Example 22(1)

Mini Case Study

PEST and Porter's Analysis for a Division of British Telecom (BT)

Outline External Environment for BT Domestic Services in 1995

PEST

Political issues
Deregulation of the market allowing new competition. Restrictions on BT ability to provide non-speech services (e.g. TV). Deregulation allowing cable TV organizations to offer speech services. General ideology and attitude to deregulation world wide. Requirements to provide a full service, even when not profitable (e.g. rural payboxes).

Economic
Rapidly decreasing costs of bit rate (cost of transmission of a unit of information) compared with consumers disposable income. Decreasing costs of technology and automation compared with labour costs. Seen as the new high ground with many investors prepared to participate, ample funds available for investment. Relatively high penetration to existing households.

Social
Low utilization of lines; UK still to fully develop the telephone habit. Slow uptake of multimedia applications in the domestic sector. Cultural problems in converting from a public service to profit organization, magnified by the need to shed large numbers of staff. Opportunity to exploit teleworking with part time staff (e.g. directory enquiries).

Technical
Broad band ISDN (digital networks based on optical technology), interactive multimedia applications, improved satellite capabilities etc. New microwave technology may allow cableless local connection capability. Mobile telephone technology.

Competition Analysis

Direct
Mercury established as a smaller direct competitor.

New entrants
Local networks being established by cable TV companies. Mobile telephone companies moving into domestic markets. Long distance networks being established by railways and power grid companies. International entry by other telephone companies.

Substitute products
None at present.
Note: in most cases of the use of a model some aspects will not be applicable. It is important to recognize this and not to force the model to fit where it does not have application. Some strategists might prefer to consider mobile telephone technology under this heading rather than new entrants. It is more important to ensure that all potential competition has been identified than to enter long debates as to the most appropriate classification.

Supplier power
BT has few problems with supplier power. There are many suppliers of equipment; even satellite communications are a competitive market place.
Note: a key source of supplier power in the industry in general was the ownership of the long distance land lines. With the entry of new providers the purchase of fibre optic network capacity has become very competitive (this is viewing the situation for organizations that have established local networks such as the new cable TV companies).

Buyer power
Domestic consumers not yet used to price and service competition for telephones. However once a consumer is connected to cable TV the costs of switching to the new supplier may be very low (even zero). There is enormous latent consumer buying power once consumers become more educated.
Note: since BT owns the local distribution network there is no channel power to BT. However a new entry telephone company that wanted to use a local TV company's fibre network for local connection would find that the cable TV company had considerable channel bargaining power.

General competition notes
This is a highly regulated environment and who can compete with what, when and where is still subject to a vast amount of political pressure (both nationally and internationally). The establishment of local fibre networks is an enormous entry cost, and therefore such communications organizations have considerable pressure to maximize their return as soon as possible. Conversely, the establishment of a substantial long distance network, in proportional terms, has allowed organizations that had the rights of way (railways and power supply companies) to establish networks at a modest entry cost. Clearly, in the space of a decade BT has moved from an effective monopoly position to one of extreme competitive pressure and turbulence.

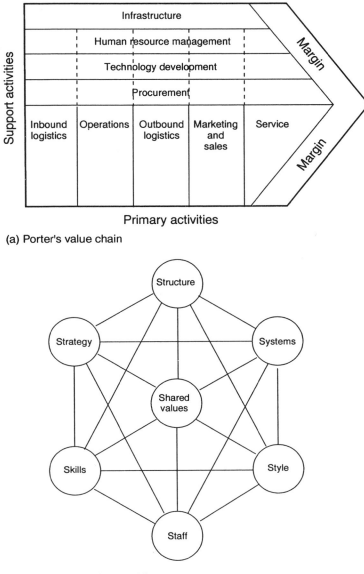

(a) Porter's value chain

(b) McKinsey's 7Ss

Figure 22.4 McKinsey's 7Ss and Porter's value chain

22.5 THE BUSINESS PLANNING PROCESS: THE INTERNAL ENVIRONMENT

Figure 22.4 shows two tools for considering the internal environment, the Porter Value Chain and the 7Ss.

22.5.1   The value chain

The *value chain* is in two parts; primary activities and support activities.[2] The effective and efficient conduct of all the value chain activities produces added value, the margin. The model can be used to audit an existing business or can be used as a framework to consider the facilities that will be needed in a new production location.

Inbound logistics are the activities concerned with the shipping, storage and retrieval of materials for the productive process. Given the need to control working capital in inventory and the high cost of labour this has been an intensive area of engineering management activity with the introduction of Just-in-Time production methods and of materials resource planning computer systems as described in Chapter 20. In any production operation, competitive advantage comes from using superior process technologies that quickly produce first time quality every time with minimum down time. Outbound logistics are the ability to gain advantage by superior packaging and timely distribution to customers. Sales and marketing activities are considered in more detail later in this chapter.

Efficient sales systems are vital. What the customer perceives is the time between ordering and receiving the service or product. It is of no value to have an efficient production system if the *customer's order* takes several weeks to be processed. (Chapter 8 describes how those companies that have 'managed to succeed' have paid attention to reducing the order-produce-deliver cycle.) The engineering manager should carefully audit the complete system from initial customer contact through manufacture to eventual customer receipt of the goods and payment (something which is often neglected). What is the value of a super-efficient distribution system if customers do not receive their bill for weeks? (See Chapter 14, section 14.8 for management of the working capital cycle.) Many engineering products, both in the consumer and industrial sector, require support and field service. The customer will not be very impressed with prompt delivery of a system if installation and commissioning is slow and inefficient.

These primary systems will not remain in good order and adapt to changing conditions without support. An organization should have an appropriate financial structure, good quality physical facilities (buildings and equipment) and, of increasing importance for competitive advantage, effective and efficient information systems. Other elements of the support activities have both general and specific applications, hence the dotted lines. A company will need to run general quality awareness programmes for all staff from the managing director to the new starter. It will also need to provide specialist training — advanced CAM (Computer Aided Management) training for the production department; product training for the sales staff, etc.

Technology development is obviously concerned with the development of the technology of the product and its manufacture. However, all aspects of the value chain system can benefit from the application of engineering style innovation. For

---

[2]Porter's split between 'support' and 'primary' activities is becoming less distinct. For example, as shown in Chapters 20 and 21, procurement is becoming increasingly integrated within logistics and operations.

example, in the service phase, remote diagnostics in a system may allow earlier and more rapid clearing of field failures with consequent less down time for the customer. In some ways this may be more apparent to the customer than super-efficient production (which, of course, is vital) because it is visible, whereas the production process is not. Procurement also applies to all aspects of a firm's purchasing. Effective sourcing of raw materials must include consideration of cost, quality, delivery and technology. However, such a strategy can be completely negated if the same quality, delivery, technology and cost controls are not exercised on the procurement of distribution and communication.

Example 22(2)

Mini Case Study

Outline value chain analysis for a car repair garage

Primary activity — inbound logistics: good delivery bay for components and good store facilities for the rapid retrieval of anything from a bulb to a complete gear box. Part of the process is the collection of the vehicles for repair so good parking with clearly marked bays and good recovery vehicles for the collection of broken down and accident damaged vehicles are required.

Primary activity — operations: good systems for rapid inspection and fault diagnostics, good equipment for the removal and fitting of parts.

Primary activity — outbound logistics: reflection of inbound logistics with good and clearly marked parking bays for completed vehicles. In addition a good system for the disposal of parts and materials is vital, for some of these may be hazardous if disposed of badly (e.g. spent oil).

Primary activity — marketing and sales: Efficient sales system, good telephone booking system, good clear collection of customer fault reports, on-line checking of customer credit status, rapid check out and billing, good electronic point of sale with funds transfer for credit cards, provision of detailed documentation of good quality (e.g. estimates for insurance claims, certificates and itemized bills).

Primary activity — service: Replacement car during service period, possibly additional services such as home car valeting, insurance etc.

Support activity — infrastructure: Good buildings, equipment and workshops. Good computer systems to provide effective parts management and customer service.

Human resource management: Customer care training, recruitment of well qualified staff, continual specialist training (e.g. updates for fitters as new models are released, computer training with new software for sales staff etc.). Effective reward systems to recognize exceptional contributions.

Technology development: Environmental and safety issues important, better systems for the control of exhaust fumes during testing, solvent vapours, etc. New methods of fault detection, systems to maintain advanced auto electronics. Continual attention to improvements to information support systems.

Procurement. Effective purchase of maintenance materials including parts. Good buying for own vehicles, communications and computers. Note: other heavy expenses include insurance etc., and these will need attention.

22.5.2   McKinsey's 7S framework

The 7Ss provide an additional framework for evaluating the 'software' of a company, its people. (See Chapter 3 for a full explanation of the 7Ss.) The company must have a sense of direction, a strategy with mission and objectives and implementation procedures and policies. These must be supported with an organizational structure and systems. This is only possible if the correct staff are recruited and provided with the appropriate range and depth of skills. Two other elements are vital for long term success. All organizations develop their own style and this must be congruent with the industry needs. The other elements can only be successfully orchestrated once a spirit of shared values has been developed. It is no use the production and sales staff having highly customer service orientated attitudes if the accounts take the line 'this is all very well but it costs money'. Organizations only succeed if people pull in the same direction. In a fast moving and complex environment it is not possible to codify all eventualities into a manual. Shared styles and values should ensure that staff will make the right decisions as the shared culture would mean that all understand what the company demands.

22.6   SWOT — FROM ANALYSIS TO DECISION AND ACTION[3]

External and internal analyses involve the consideration of a vast range of issues which may have a potential critical impact on the organization. This expansive process needs to focus on the key issues that, without prompt management action, will result in a loss of competitive advantage. The *strengths, weakness, opportunity* and *threats* (SWOT) analysis is the mechanism for this [3, 4]. Strengths and weakness are internal to the organization. This is not to say that they are taken without reference to the external environment. If staff have been trained to a certain level this can be a either a strength or a weakness depending on how well the competitors' staff are trained. Threats and opportunities are external to the organization. Threats can come from changes in the environment such as legislation. Opportunities are areas where the organization can extend its operations to achieve a profitable expansion.(See Chapter 2 for a more complete review of global threats and opportunities.)

This form of analysis focuses on the firm's key competencies and strategic advantages. This involves a detailed examination of the marketing issues which are covered in the remaining sections of this chapter.

---

[3]See *Johnson J & Scholes K, Exploring Corporate Strategy* 3rd Edition, Prentice Hall 1993 for a useful illustration of SWOT analysis, and chapter 2 (Models of Strategic Planning) of *Mintzberg H, The Rise and Fall of Strategic Planning*, Prentice Hall 1994 for a critical appraisal of this approach.

22.7   MARKET SEGMENTATION

Not all consumers are the same, and to be successful it is essential to match the products or services to the precise needs of different groups of people. A company manufacturing jeans will be concerned with age, sex, height, weight and income to make a range from everyday use to designer products, for the poor student and the affluent fashion conscious. Segmentation is just as important in industrial markets. An analytical instrument manufacturer will be concerned with the type of industry, geography and size of customer as possible variables. The precise variables that should be used depend on the nature of the market and the decisions to be made. In general there need to be six conditions satisfied if segmentation is to be useful.

(1)   *The segments should be accessible.* A company could make computer keyboards for left handed accountants but just how would they be found?
(2)   *The segment should be unique.* The population within the segment is different to the populations outside the segment.
(3)   *The segment should be measurable.* It must be possible to profile the population in the segment and determine its characteristics and the total size and potential value of the segment.
(4)   *The segment should be substantial.* The value of the segment (transaction profit × number of potential customers) should be of sufficient size to make the development of a specific strategy cost-effective. If this is not so the segmentation is of no practical value.
(5)   *The segmentation should be appropriate to the decision in hand.* There are any number of segmentation variables for people (language, colour of the eyes, education, etc.). It is necessary to decide which are the key ones. There are no set rules for this, it is a skill that has to be developed. It may take a page to explain the concept of segmentation, but years of skill to apply it well.
(6)   *The segment should be stable and predictable* so that it is possible to develop and implement a complete marketing plan.

Table 22.1   Major segmentation variables for industrial markets

Variable	Typical breakdown
Type of industry	Manufacturing, service, chemical, etc.
Technology used	Robots, high pressure, clean room operations, etc.
Geographical location	Country, region
Purchasing procedures	Contract arrangements, tendering procedures
Number of sites	1; 2–5; 5–10; 10–50; 50+; global; multinational
Stage of development	New to technology, established user
Size of purchases	Value of product purchased, number of orders, size of delivery (e.g. drums, palettes, small package)
Buying criteria	Price, quality, service, technology
State of R&D	Leader or follower
Organization size	Number of employees, sales revenue, turnover, etc.

Table 22.2 Major segmentation variables for consumer markets

Variable	Typical breakdown
Demographic	
Age	Under 6, 6–11, 12–19, 20–34, 35–49, 50–64, 65+
Sex	male, female
Family size	1–2, 3–4, 5+
Family life cycle	Young, single; young, married, no children; young, married, youngest child under 6; young, married, youngest child 6 or over; older, married, with children; older married, no children under 18; older, single; other
Income	Under £7500; £7500–£12 000; £12 000–£15 000; £15 000–£18 000; £18 000–£25 000; £25 000–£50 000; £50 000 and over
Occupation	Professional and technical; managers, officials and proprietors; clerical, sales; craftspeople, foremen; operatives; farmers; retired; students; housewives; unemployed; military
Education	Fifth form; sixth form; college of further education; technical college; university; NVQs; professional qualifications
Religion	Protestant; Catholic; Muslim; Buddhist; others
Race	White, black, oriental, other
Nationality	British, Chinese, Indian, Pakistani, Japanese, Other Far East, West Indian, French, German, Other European, American, Other
Psychographic	
Social class	Lower lowers, upper lowers, working class, middle class, upper middles, lower uppers, upper uppers
Personality	Compulsive, gregarious, authoritarian, ambitious
Behavioural	
Occasions	Regular occasion, special occasion
Benefits	Quality, service, economy
User status	Non-user, ex-user, potential user, first-time user, regular user
Usage rate	Light user, medium user, heavy user
Loyalty status	None, medium, strong, absolute
Readiness stage	Unware, aware, informed, desirous, intending to buy
Attitude towards product	Enthusiastic, positive, indifferent, negative, hostile
Geographic	
Region	South West, Wales, South, London, Scotland, Northern Ireland, Home Counties, Midlands, North, West
City or town size	Under 5000; 5000–20 000; 20 000-50 000; 50 000–100 000; 100 000–250 000; 250 000–500 000; 500 000–1 million; 1 million–4 million; 4 million or over
Density	Urban, suburban, rural

The precise segmentation variables depend on the decisions to be made. In consumer products, age, sex, lifestyle, income, language and geography might be appropriate. In industrial markets the size of customer, markets served and manufacturing technologies used are potential variables. Tables 22.1 and 22.2 illustrate typical variables for industrial and consumer markets.

22.8   PRODUCT LIFE CYCLE (PLC)

Products have their day, they grow, have their period of ascendancy and then decline. The time for this can vary from a few months for some fashion trend to decades for industrial products (e.g. steam turbines for powering electrical generation). The reproduction of music shows a number of such life cycles: the introduction of the 78 rpm record, the growth of the micro groove record, an extension and extra impetus with the enhancement of stereo and the ultimate decline of records with the introduction of CDs. Part of this product life cycle is shown in Figure 22.5.

In the introduction stage the product may be expensive and may appeal to only a select market. The first group of customers will require much information and advice. This will be provided by specialist outlets. At this stage competition may be rather limited, but the cash flow will be negative as the product will have had high development costs and will require heavy launch marketing communications. In the growth phase many more customers will be drawn to the product, as will some competition. Profits will start to be made but often the cash flow may still be negative. Heavy marketing is still demanded to attract new customers and extra capital will be needed for the new production facilities (and to finance stocks if 'lean' production and logistics have not been introduced). Once the product has reached maturity the competition will become more intense, but the demands for capital will become stabilized. Moreover the learning curve effect will have sharply reduced manufacturing and distribution costs. Thus there will be good profits and strong positive cash flows.

All good things come to an end, and, as new technologies challenge and the competition becomes intense, the weaker producers will exit as the product enters the decline stage. This decline may be fast, given the rapid advancement of new technologies. For example, valves were rapidly overtaken by transistors after more than half a century of being the only technology for weak signal amplification. In engineering markets it is vital to scan the environment for issues that can bring an abrupt decline to the product life cycle.

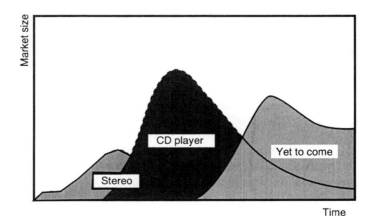

Figure 22.5   Product life cycle

22.9 PORTFOLIO ANALYSIS

It is a major concern to the firm that only in the maturity phase can strong positive cash flows and profits be expected. During the introduction and growth stages, profits may be small and cash flows under great pressure. Failure to exit appropriately may mean that the 'decline' products may also become a drain. However it should be noted that an orderly exit should allow the recovery of working capital. At first sight the firm needs a collection of mature products, but this may only be obtained in a dynamic system by a continual flow of products. This balancing of the products, or business areas, is called *portfolio analysis*. First the company has to classify its products and decide which to promote and which to drop or exit. The simplest such model is the Boston matrix [3] shown in Figure 22.6.

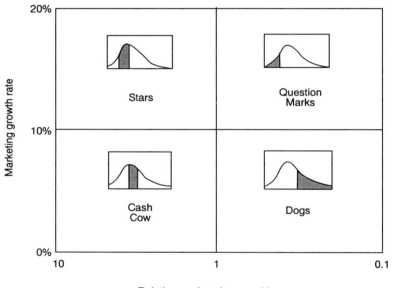

Figure 22.6 Boston matrix

In this model the two key parameters are the relative market share measured on a log scale and the market growth. This yields a 2×2 matrix. A product characterized by a low share and high growth is represented by a question mark. (This would be a product in the introduction phase of the plc.) One with a high growth and a high market share is represented by a star (a product in the growth phase of the plc). This is typical for a new technology where the first entry companies have a strong market share position (there is little or no competition). The 'cash cows' are for mature products where there are strong profits and cash flows as long as manufacturing, distribution and marketing expenses are strictly

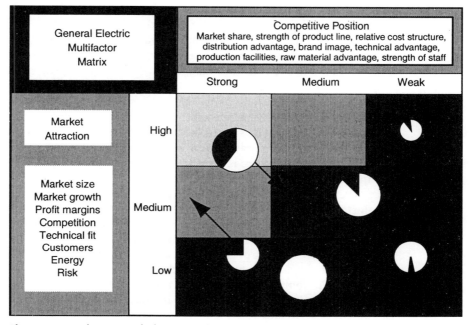

Figure 22.7   The General Electric multifactor matrix

controlled. In the decline phase the 'dogs' can be a continual drain on company resources. Dogs must be driven back to cash cows (sharp reduction in manufacturing costs to recover market share through cost leadership) or an orderly exit. Dogs are a trap for many technical companies. A company may be built up on a product by a founder and it takes strong will to drop a product once equated with the company. At one time IBM made typewriters, they do not do so now. Exit requires firm decisions and skilled management.

The Boston matrix is much discussed in first level marketing books but is a very poor model except in the sphere of fast moving consumer goods where the key parameters for success are market growth and market share. For industrial and technological markets it fails. The GE matrix [4] shown in Figure 22.7 provides a robust and more general framework.

The two key parameters are market attraction (vertical axis) and competitive position (horizontal axis). (The Boston matrix represents a degenerate case of this matrix where competitive advantage is simply measured by market share, and attraction by market growth.) For any particular firm, factors such as technology fit, market size, profit margins and risk can be evaluated and given weighting factors. The fit of products to these factors can also be evaluated and a weighting matrix constructed. Similarly the factors for competitive position for the market can be judged (e.g. strength of product line, cost structure, brand image, patent position, etc.) and the individual product positions judged, and another weighting matrix constructed. It is then possible to construct the GE matrix and position the products. The size of the market is shown by the area of the circle. A firm's market share is indicated by the size of the wedge in the circle.

Such a matrix shows the position at a particular time but markets are dynamic and both market attraction and competitive position will be changing; the direction and speed of this change is indicated by the length and direction of the arrows.

The power of this model is that it allows the consolidation of a range of key parameters and incorporates the best judgements of the marketing engineers for not only the present situation but for the dynamics of the situation. Clearly, products with high attraction and a good competitive position should be developed; where there is little attraction and little competitive advantage, exit is the recommended strategy.

Clearly, both the Boston and the GE models show that the company is in an unstable position, and unable to sustain long term growth and success, unless the design engineers can provide a stream of new successful products, and a decision support model is required to support this activity.

The Ansoff matrix provides a model for this [5]. All the engineer has to decide is what are the existing products and what new potential products the firm could make. To complement this, a decision is required as to what are the existing markets and the potential new markets. This yields the 2×2 matrix and four potential strategies.

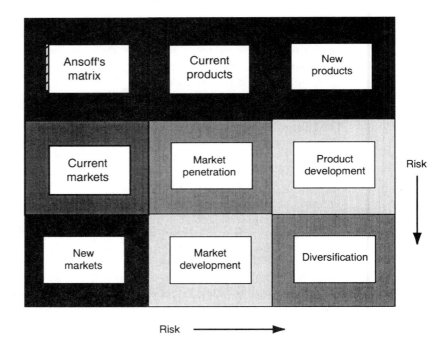

Figure 22.8   Ansoff's matrix

- *Strategy 1: market penetration* (existing markets — existing customers)
  All forms of marketing communications must be expanded to increase market share, encourage more frequent usage and/or alternative usage of the product by existing customers. Given that the marketing engineer understands the product and the customers this represents a strategy of modest risk. Clearly if there is a high market share or the product is in the decline stage this strategy will not be sufficient and alternatives are needed.
- *Strategy 2: product development* (existing markets — new products)
  Here there are two issues: what new products the company can competitively produce and which of these will be of value to existing customers. This is a more risky strategy than simple market penetration. Establishment of new products can be difficult, even in existing markets, where current customers may be resistant to innovation.
- *Strategy 3: market development* (new markets — existing products)
  The product may be of value in new markets, for example by the diffusion of existing technologies into new markets or by moving into new geographic markets. In a mature plc it may be a good strategy to export products to an area where the plc has not reached a decline stage. Again, one parameter will be fully understood, in this case the product, but much less will be known about the other, the markets. So again this is a strategy of increased risk.
- *Strategy 4: diversification* (new products — new markets).
  If strategies 1, 2 and 3 do not provide the expansion required, the company might consider new markets and new products. This is the area of maximum risk where extensive market research is required to reduce that risk. Where conditions are right this can be very profitable.

In the telecommunications field in the UK, in the mid 1990s, companies are using all these strategies. BT had a large group of domestic customers who made minimal use of their lines which represented a large fixed cost. This is a classic market penetration strategy need, and heavy advertising on television and other media is the required strategy. BT could also provide other services over these lines, and video on demand is an example of a BT product development strategy for their existing customers. The cable TV companies have a similar strategy offering telephones as a new service to their TV customers. BT evaluates itself to be a technical leader in competitive telecommunications technology and the expansion of BT into international markets was a clearly expected strategy. It is not so clear when diversification strategies may be appropriate. However consider the immense training tasks faced by BT during all these changes. The skills developed in training may be a marketable skill in their own right in areas outside traditional BT markets and could represent a profitable diversification. Likewise, the entry of the electrical power grid companies into fibre optic super-highways represents a potentially very profitable diversification strategy.

Successful Ansoff analysis for technical markets needs imaginative interpretation of both the technological possibilities and the developing market benefit needs. It is only the engineer with a marketing knowledge who has a sufficiently complete understanding to conduct this structured but very creative process.

There is no set formula for devising new products or for providing the insight to recognize a new attractive market.

Once these business ideas have been evaluated they can be fed into the GE matrix for a decision as to which product to accept. In an innovative company the above process should generate far more opportunities than can be commercially realized. A rational decision process to focus on the best prospects is vital.

22.10 THE MARKETING MIX

The marketing mix is the lever of marketing power, it is the way an organization reacts and positions its offerings in the market place. The marketing mix structure is given in Figure 22.9. It is divided into two parts — the traditional marketing mix:

- product
- place (distribution)
- price
- promotion (marketing communication)

and the service extended marketing mix:

- people
- process
- physical evidence
- period (time).

Services differ from products in that they are intangible. If an engineer consults a patent agent on how to protect an invention, the advice is critical but no tangible object changes hands. This is completely different from the purchase of a new computer where an object changes ownership. However, the purchasers of objects too have intangible feelings, and these are important factors in the purchase decision.

Feelings of security and confidence are intangible but apply as much to industrial purchases as consumer products. A safety engineer installing a new fire detection system will have these feelings. In analysing the product offering required, the marketing engineer must consider the intangible benefits the customers may have. These intangibles will be supported by tangible features. For a fire detection system, it might be self-checking diagnostics to report fault conditions. This list of tangible benefits provides the engineer with a 'wish list' that the design process must develop in terms of specific features.[4] In many cases the resulting product can be relatively featureless in appearance. Alongside functionality, it may be essential to provide some way of communicating the product's appeal. So, with consumer products, functionality must be reflected in an innovative style of design which is not only functional but attractive, and also

---

[4]The way in which a 'wish list' is translated into specific features is described in Chapter 6. Section 6.5.3 outlines QFD which is one of the 'tools' of this process.

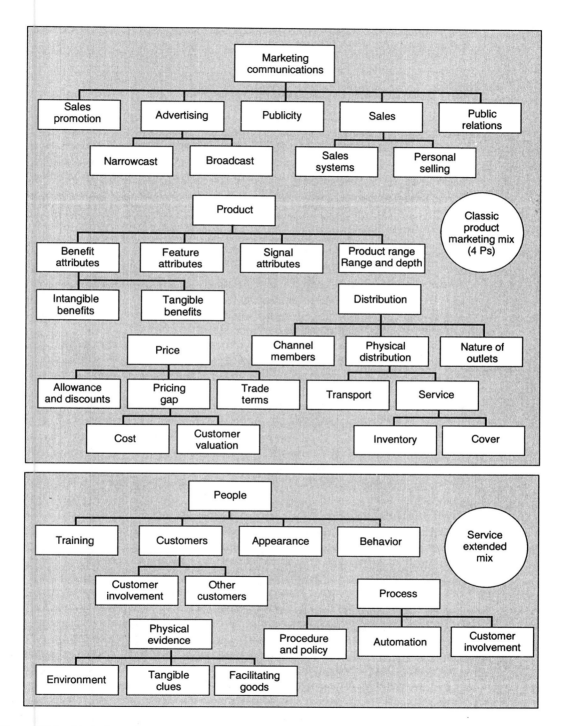

Figure 22.9   Marketing mix

communicates the quality of the product. (See Chapter 6, section 6.3.4 for more information about this aspect of design.)

22.10.1 Product

The collection of products or services a company offers should not be an accident but a specific strategic decision resulting from the portfolio analysis and the Ansoff analysis of the market needs. There are two vectors to this decision: the depth of the product range (the number of variants of a given product) and the breadth of the range (the number of different types of related products which should be included in the portfolio).

Example 22(3)

Attribute Analysis for a Small Office Photocopier

- *Target market*: Small offices such as solicitors, architects, sole traders where there is little or no technical support.
- *Intangible benefits*: Feeling of being up to date, security, empowerment (copies when you want them, how you want them).
- *Tangible benefits*: Low cost, (life-cycle costs, purchase, maintenance, power, toner, paper etc. must be less than bureau service), ease of use, low heat output, small foot-print (space often limited), low service needs, short warm-up, jam free, etc.
- *Feature attributes*: The precise design features such as simple paper path, micro toner in easy replace cartridge, not-in-use detection with switch to stand by power levels etc.
- *Signal attributes*: Stylish design to fit in with modern office furniture, possibly available in different colours.
- *Product range and depth*: Product depth — range of speeds, A4 only, A3 and A4 etc. Product range — plain paper fax, laser printers (all you need for office printing?).

One aspect of product that must not be neglected is *packaging*. For industrial products it should be robust enough to fully protect the product during extended transport and handling. In many countries it must be easy to recycle. Packaging is even more important for consumer goods which have to be sold off-the-shelf, and in such situations should be considered as part of the marketing communication aspects of the marketing mix.

There are two key aspects to *distribution*, the physical distribution of the goods or services, and the nature of outlets and intermediaries the firm needs to use. Physical distribution is where marketing links in with the subject of operations. The best possible configuration for an electricity grid, or the most economical distribution of frozen chickens are approachable with techniques such as linear programming. Wholesalers, distributors and retailers are vital and provide essential value chain links. Typically they break bulk and provide an assortment of goods. A supermarket takes deliveries of pallet loads of goods from a wide range of manufacturers, and consumers can then buy small quantities of a wide assortment of products that they require.[5] However, in the marketing of technical products, distributors and agents also provide other functions such as the supply of consumable items (paper, oil etc.), installation, field service and staff training. The value chain links between the firm and its outlets must be excellent. For consumer goods, electronic point of sale (laser check-outs) provide an aid to excellent stock control and vital feedback on marketing performance of a product. Similar links for improving stock control of industrial goods are discussed in Chapter 20.

22.10.2   Price

Price is a vital part of the market positioning of the product. Again, the company should view the customer's perception of pricing in benefit-orientated terms. Often in technology-driven (product orientated) organizations there is a temptation for an accountant to say the cost of a product is x and so the price should be $(x + y\%)$, where y is the typical industry mark up. This process will work for a stable industry with free competition but most definitely will not work for rapidly changing markets. (See Chapter 13 for further discussion on pricing and costing.) Certainly cost control is vital to ensure maximum competitive advantage. However, given a strategic cost advantage, the firm may decide to maintain high profit margins at small volumes, or pass the benefits onto the customers and gain market share. Whatever the policy, it is essential that the firm has a clear understanding of the customer's benefit valuation. The Porter five forces of competition analysis is one tool for appraising this situation. Further information can be gained by market research. The difference between the firm's cost structures and the market benefit valuation is known as the *strategic pricing gap*. If it is large the firm has lots of options, if it is small it has few and if it is negative it does not have a business!

Given that there is a good pricing gap, the firm may operate a number of different pricing policies to reflect different objectives. If the objective is to maximize the short-term profits the marketing engineers need to estimate the volumes that would be sold at different prices. At low prices the volumes may be high but the margins will be small, and the total profit will be small. If the price is very high the margins will be very good, but the very small volumes will again yield a small total profit. What must be found is the combination of margin and volume that will yield the maximum profit in the period (see Chapter 13 Example 13(11). This is only one policy. If the objective is to build market share, low margins may be acceptable. A low pricing policy is a market penetration policy, a high pricing policy is a market skimming policy.

In technical markets a variation of the skimming strategy may be used. New technology tends to be expensive at first with costs dropping in later years through

---

[5]Chapter 20 describes how large industrial customers are taking over these inbound logistics tasks as well as their own outbound logistics. Linear programming is one of the mathematical techniques used by such companies to optimize, among other things, vehicle routing.

the learning curve effect. (The use of simultaneous engineering, as described in Chapter 6 and Appendix 6, may compress the learning period to months rather than years.) The technology will have applications in differing market areas with different benefit valuations. In such a situation the company can skim the first market and then, once the profits have been maximized in that market, drop the prices to bring in the next level of benefit valuation and repeat this process. This strategy will maximize total profit over the product life cycle and is particularly applicable where the company has some substantial patented technical advantage.

The other aspects of pricing are the normal ones of deciding what discounts should be given to the trade, what price breaks will be given to volume purchasers and what trade-in allowances may be appropriate. In fast moving areas where equipment may become obsolete before its physical life is reached the firm may find it desirable to offer 'migration packages' to encourage earlier upgrades. Increasingly customers are not simply concerned with the purchase costs of items but with life cycle costs.[6] Life cycle costs include the costs of capital purchase, installation, training, servicing, insurance, energy, consumables (e.g. toner, paper), labour costs in operation and costs of ultimate decommissioning and disposal. In pricing policy it is often only the engineer with an understanding of the technology and with marketing and accountancy skills to calculate paybacks etc., who can make the appropriate strategic judgements. These considerations also have to be weighed by the design engineer, as discussed in Chapter 6.

22.10.3 Promotion

Promotion is the aspect of marketing with which people are most familiar, and of this communication mix, advertising in its many forms surrounds us all. Before considering the actual methods of communication it is essential to evaluate the underlying strategies. Maslow's and Herzberg's ideas of motivation (as described in Chapter 9) are applicable to purchase motivation. Moreover the subject has to be taken through a number of stages. One general model for this process is the 'hierarchy of effects' model where the consumer has to be taken through 6 stages (awareness, knowledge, liking, preference, conviction and purchase). In the industrial situation the model should be extended to cover the post purchase experience (e.g. training, and servicing) as the ultimate objective is to become a preferred supplier with many repeat purchases.

In industrial buying, as discussed in Chapter 21, more than one person may be involved in the decision. In marketing some new software, the computer managers (the users) as well as the buyer will be involved. The great skill in marketing is to decide who is in this decision making unit (DMU), what their agendas are and devising communications that answer their different needs (e.g. one person may be more concerned with ease of use, another with total costs).

It is possible to promote products either by a push strategy, a pull strategy or a combination push-pull strategy. In a push strategy, the firm uses its marketing

---

[6]See Chapter 14, section 14.5.3 for a discussion of depreciation, Chapter 15, section 15.5 for more on life cycle costing, and Chapter 21 for the buyer's perspective.

budget to promote and communicate with the distributors and outlets and relies on these to complete the process with the customer. In the pull policy the company advertises and communicates with the customers to create a general market demand that distributors need to satisfy (i.e. a pull through the channels strategy). The most generally used strategy is the combination strategy where the channels are primed with a 'push' communication strategy before a 'pull' advertising campaign.

Sales promotion may be of value in both strategies. Competitions can be run for agents with the best results and incentive offers given to customers (e.g. 10% extra free). Sales promotion efforts are usually intended to stimulate purchase in a short period. So, in the launch of a new product, the producer might offer free installation and service for the first three months of introduction to encourage rapid take up and induce trial.

Advertising is in some ways the most simple method of communication in the sense that the media are paid for and are largely under the control of the firm. Advertising needs to be efficient and effective. To be effective, advertising needs the right message delivered to all the desired customers at the right time. To be efficient, advertising must be provided at a minimum cost and with the minimum of wastage. This is why direct mail and database marketing are becoming so important. No matter what selection of media is made (TV, press) the chances are that advertising will not reach all potential customers. In attempting to reach them, the company could waste much of its effort in placing the advertisement before people who are of no interest to the firm at all. A simple measure is a cost per thousand of potential customers. While consumer advertising is all around us, many engineers will be concerned with company-to-company marketing of technical products. Here the 'narrowcast' media is much more important, this is most commonly in the form of specialist journals. However, as shown below, advertising by any medium is a relatively minor part of industrial marketing.

Advertising is where the media are paid for. Publicity is where a company gets the media to print information on its products but does not pay for it. This is why companies issue press releases on innovative products and why trade journalists are provided with prototype products to evaluate. *Public relations* may be used to provide events that will attract the press. A specialist aspect of public relations is disaster limitation where adverse publicity needs to be managed. This aspect is of special relevance to engineers, as in the event of an accident, it is often the technically competent staff that must meet the media.

In consumer markets the firm has to communicate with large numbers of customers and therefore broadcast advertising is effective and efficient. In industrial markets complex products are being sold to complex decision making units. Here advertising is much less important and the key role is that of the sales engineer who can enter into direct contact with the individuals in the decision making unit. The process of personal selling is simple but needs skill to implement. The stages are:

- research to identify the targets and assemble information,
- relationship building through listening,
- presentation (show and tell),
- meeting objections (e.g., 'this will need a lot of training', etc.),

- closing the sale,
- after-sales follow up to generate repeat sales.

Sales systems are vital to customer satisfaction. A customer may be delighted with a capital purchase, but if the ordering systems for spare parts is slow this all may be lost. In many markets with customers operating EDI and JIT policies, the firm's sales systems may become an outright source of competitive advantage.

22.10.4   Service extended mix

In services, the benefits to be communicated are something intangible. Often people are the most important element of the marketing effort. They must be well trained, have an appropriate appearance and behave in a customer-responsive way. The way a company delivers a service may be important and clear policy guidance should be given to sales staff. The degree of service delivery automation should be part of the strategic marketing policy. Where the customer comes into the firm's premises for training, the physical environment is physical evidence of the quality of the service. The quality of manuals will provide tangible clues to service quality. For many services the sale of supporting goods (e.g. textbooks for a professional institution) will not only be a statement of the service quality, but also a source of additional revenue. (These aspects of quality are discussed under total quality management in Chapter 4.)

22.11   MARKETING INFORMATION SYSTEMS

To develop and market a product, a continual flow of information is needed. This is provided by the marketing information system which has four elements: *research, intelligence, internal data*, and *analytic systems*.

22.11.1   Market research

In the launch of a new product the firm will need to know the size of the potential market, and how people will find out about the proposed product. There are two types of marketing research: expensive secondary research, and very expensive primary research. Secondary research is where the marketing engineers review published information from industry surveys etc., on the products and markets. Then, and only then, the much more expensive market research can be considered. Here, marketing staff actively go out into the market place and conduct experiments and surveys. This is a very expensive process and even a modest and restricted survey may cost £10 000. Typical research methods are customer preference trials, questionnaires, surveys and interviews. The information collected can be divided into quantitative and qualitative (e.g. what price will a consumer be prepared to pay (quantitative), and their attitudes (qualitative)). Both types of information are required for effective marketing.

22.11.2   Marketing intelligence and internal data

Market intelligence is vital to long term success. For technical products it involves tracking competitors' activities such as new promotional campaigns and product launches. Competitors' products may be purchased for retro-engineering to see how they are built and to evaluate their technical performance, strengths and weaknesses. A firm has vast amounts of information which arise in its normal day to day business. This should be examined for its marketing information content. So, sales figures should be analysed to see which accounts are more profitable, which areas have smaller margins, etc. Long term trends should be looked for — declining sales may indicate new competition in a given sector. Apart from the accountancy information, care should be taken to capture and use other sources of data such as field service reports and customer complaints. These can often provide useful insights that will help to develop competitive new products. This area is vital in developing market driven quality (MDQ) programmes, and provides marketing input for the simultaneous/concurrent engineering process.

22.11.3   Analytic methods

Much of the information is hidden in vast amounts of data points. A firm can use statistical and modelling systems to convert a flood of data into specific information. Sales may have seasonal characteristics and month by month comparisons may not be helpful. Various methods of forecasting from basic (simple moving average) to more complex seasonally adjusted trend detecting models (exponential smoothing) may be appropriate.

With these four elements (research, intelligence, internal and analytic) the firm has the ability to adjust its marketing plans and marketing mix to changing market conditions — an essential requirement for long term competitive advantage which is discussed in the next section.

22.12   SUMMARY — INTEGRATED MARKETING PLANS

This chapter began with the business planning process, as described in Figure 22.1. The figure shows that marketing must form an integral part of the management of any organization. The secret of long term competitive advantage is not just excellence in the achievement of any single parameter in the business development process. Technological leadership may be essential, but if integration with the planning process is lacking, the battle in the market may be lost.

Integrated plans start with clear statements of mission, aims and objectives which must be shared with all within the business team. It is not possible to move to action without completing the marketing audit. If you are lost in a strange city the first thing you have to do is to find where you are. The external analysis (PEST and Porter competition analysis) and the internal analysis (value chain) will provide the raw data, and the SWOT analysis will focus it into information and provide the bridge from analysis to the action agenda. At this stage the integrated plan can be outlined giving operating objectives for each element of the plan. Production targets can be set in terms of volumes, timescales and cost structures. The market needs should be firmly linked to the product design specification through product attribute analysis for each of the target market segments. Other elements of the marketing strategy need to be evolved. What will be the strategic pricing gap? Will this be exploited with a penetration or a skimming pricing strategy? What field and distribution service will be required (what outlets will be needed, what physical methods of distribution will be appropriate)? Will the communication strategy be push, pull or push-pull? Who are the communication publics, what is the nature of the DMU's in the market segments. What media will be efficient and effective in making targets aware and thence converting these targets into active, long term accounts?

Once answers to these questions have been agreed within the team, the integrated plan can be drawn up in critical path planning format with milestones and budgets set. These two elements provide the mechanism of control, and feedback. Continual effort is needed to make certain that each element is on schedule and within budget and that where deviations occur corrective actions are taken. The marketing information management system is vital in providing the feedback and control information from the market place. Profits flow by satisfying customer benefit needs and wants more effectively and efficiently than the competition. Only with a strategically integrated marketing approach from the whole organization will this be achieved consistently.

REFERENCES

1. Curtis, T. (1994) *Business and Marketing for Engineers and Scientists.* McGraw-Hill, Maidenhead. Chapter 2 for further discussion on PEST analysis.
2. Porter, M. (1985) *Competitive Advantage, Creating and Sustaining Superior Performance.* The Free Press, London.
3. Hedley, B. (1977) *Long Range Planning.* Pergammon Press, Oxford.
4. Day, G. S. (1986) *Analysis for Strategic Marketing Decisions.* West Publishing, St Paul.
5. Ansoff, I. H. (1957) *Strategies for Diversification.* McGraw-Hill, Maidenhead.

BIBLIOGRAPHY

Cowell, D. (1989) *The Marketing of Services.* Heinemann, London.
Kotler, P. (1991) *Marketing Management, Analysis, Planning, Implementation and Control.* Seventh Edition, Prentice-Hall International, London.
Lancaster, G. and Messingham, L. (1993) *Marketing Management.* McGraw-Hill, Maidenhead.
McDonald, M. (1990) *Marketing Plans, How to Prepare them, How to Use Them.* Second edition, Heinemann, London.
Moore, W. L. (1993) *Product Planning and Management, Design and Delivering Value.* McGraw-Hill, Maidenhead.

Managing people — Employment law and health and safety at work in the UK

23.1 INTRODUCTION

In the developed industrial nations employment law plays a major role in determining the relationships between the employer and his workforce, individually and collectively. Nowhere is this role more important than in engineering. Engineering managers need to be aware of how their actions can be restrained by law, and, as individuals, they should also be aware of their rights *à propos* their employer. In this chapter the most important provisions of United Kingdom employment law are outlined, including the influences of European law.

The chapter will examine the *contract of employment between employer and employee*, the *provisions for health and safety at work*, the expansion of *anti-discrimination and equal pay law*, the *payment of employees, statutory employment protection rights* especially regarding *unfair dismissal* and *redundancy*, and *collective bargaining*.

23.2 DEVELOPMENT OF EMPLOYMENT LAW IN THE UK

Until the beginning of the 1970s the scope of employment law was relatively limited. Industrial relations between employer and employee were regarded as voluntary in which the law should play little part. The common law, moulded by the judges, conditioned and influenced contracts of employment. As regards statute, in 1970 there existed the Contracts of Employment Act 1963, multifarious legislation for health and safety purposes (e.g. the Offices, Shops and Railway Premises Act 1963), the newly arrived Redundancy Payments Act 1965, and the emergence of anti-discrimination legislation. There was little more, other than certain statutory immunities from legal liability in the event of industrial disputes.

The UK's relative economic decline, the civil rights movement imported from the USA, increasing industrial unrest, and a newly elected Conservative government led to Parliament enacting the ill-fated Industrial Relations Act

1971. The aftermath of this legislation eventually led to the downfall of this government in 1974. Between 1974 and 1979 the Labour government produced a thick overlay of statutory provisions relating to employment protection for individual employees and enhancing the position of trade unions. Meanwhile, in 1974 the far-reaching Health and Safety at Work Act had been passed. When the Conservative government returned to power in 1979, it began a process of deregulation where individual employment rights were concerned, and set out to reduce trade union power. The Conservative government sought by statute to make trade unions more accountable and democratic, and to some effect at a time when trade unions were experiencing socio-economic decline. From 1980 onwards there were few years when employment or trade union affairs were not the subject of parliamentary activity, whether in the form of new or amending legislation.

Of growing significance is the UK's membership of the European Union. The impact of regulation from Europe, generally having supremacy over UK domestic law, has been especially penetrating and liberally developed. The effects are most noticeable in the areas of equal pay and sex discrimination legislation, the transfer of businesses, the collective handling of redundancies and, latterly, health and safety at work.

23.3 THE CONTRACT OF EMPLOYMENT

The main legal focus of the employment relationship is the contract of employment. Despite its specialist nature, this contract is no different, in general terms, from other contracts. It represents a private 'legislative' arrangement or agreement between the parties, the employer and the employee. However, initially, the vital question is who is an employee? In this connection, courts and tribunals have made a distinction between a contract *of* service which is a contract of employment involving an employee and a contract *for* services which refers to a self-employed person or independent contractor. For example, a chauffeur might be regarded as an employee whereas a taxi driver would probably be self-employed. The distinction is important for a number of reasons. Preferentially, the contract of employment gives rise to a number of common law obligations and duties and attracts statutory employment protection rights and certain health and safety at work measures. It also has an enhanced position where National Insurance provision and Statutory Sick Pay are concerned. Furthermore, the income tax of an employee is handled on a different basis from that of a self-employed person.

The common law has developed a series of tests to establish who is an employee, which are not necessarily mutually exclusive. The earliest test was that of *control*, which suggested the employer's economic and managerial domination of the employee (*Yewens* v. *Noakes* (1880)). In this century an *organizational* test was established (*Stevenson, Jordan and Harrison Ltd* v. *MacDonald and Evans* (1952)). In essence an employee could be identified if he were integrated into or part of the business. The employer might control the employee's work but not how he performed his tasks. This was obviously more relevant the more skilled an employee was. It would hardly be suitable for a local health authority to instruct a surgeon in its employ *how* to perform an operation although it might well control *when* he would do so. By the late 1960s a more *economic* or *realistic* approach was being adopted. So in *Ready Mixed Concrete (South East) Ltd* v. *Minister of Pensions and National Insurance (1968)* a *multiple* test was propounded. For a contract of employment (contract of service) to exist it was necessary to establish that

(i)   the employee agreed to provide his own work and skill in the performance of a service for his employer ('the wage-work bargain'),
(ii) there was some element of control exercisable by the employer, and
(iii) other terms of the contract were not inconsistent with the existence of a contract of employment.

The subsequent shift to an *entrepreneurial*, or *'in business on one's own account'* test, sought to provide criteria to identify whether or not a person was self-employed, viewed from a private enterprise perspective, rather than under a contract of employment (see, e.g. *Market Investigations Ltd* v. *Minister of Social Security (1969)*). The current approach is a pragmatic one in which a whole range of factors is considered relevant. This is especially pertinent given a flexible labour market. For instance, *Nethermere (St. Neots) Ltd* v. *Taverna and Gardiner (1984)* illustrates the problems presented by marginal workers. In recent times mutuality of obligation as a test has emphasized the obligation of the employer to provide work and the employee to do it (*O'Kelly* v. *Trusthouse Forte plc (1984)*). Overall, discerning whether or not there is a contract of employment is like painting a picture; it is not a matter of operating a checklist (*Hall (HM Inspector of Taxes)* v. *Lorimer (1994)*). Furthermore, a self-description as employee or as self-employed, or as both for different reasons, does not necessarily suffice as a test, especially if there is an attempt to gain unfair advantage, or to avoid fiscal measures or modern protective legislation (*Massey* v. *Crown Life Insurance (1978)* and *Young and Woods Ltd* v. *West (1980)*).

    In practice, the contract of employment will be formed after the stages of advertisement and interview (*invitation to treat*) as illustrated in *Deeley* v. *British Rail Engineering (1980)* and thereafter by *offer* and *acceptance*, which may be subject to conditions as in *Wishart* v. *National Association of Citizens Advice Bureaux Ltd (1990)*. The contract of employment is a creature of the common law, with its general principles as to the formation of contract being judicially developed to serve the social and commercial needs of the times. Consequently, the requirements of *consideration*, *privity*, and *the intention to create legal relations* must be fulfilled. Equally, there must be no vitiating factors such as misrepresentation, mistake, illegality, duress, undue influence and incapacity. There are also collateral contracts, which support the existence of the main contract of employment (*Gill* v. *Cape Contracts Ltd (1985)*), and, less successfully, there have been attempts to manufacture a global contract out of a series of independent but separate employment arrangements (*Hellyer Bros Ltd* v. *McLeod (1987)*).

    Providing that there is a viable contract of employment, the heartland will be its contents. The terms of a contract may be incorporated, expressly or impliedly. Primacy is given to express terms where terms are agreed, orally or in writing, between the contractual parties. Nevertheless, the terms will be subject to the normal canons of construction applicable to contracts generally (*Hooper* v. *British Railways Board (1988)*) and the restrictive interpretation of exclusion clauses whether by the common law or by statute, for example the Unfair Contract Terms Act 1977, s.2. Contracts of employment are in any case extensively overlaid by various statutory provisions. There is a formidable array of employment protection rights, the first of which concerns the right of the employee to be provided with written particulars of his terms of employment within two months of starting work in accordance with the Employment Protection (Consolidation) Act (EPCA) 1978, s.1 including strict requirements concerning access to this information (s.2) and disciplinary procedures (s.3). This is not necessarily the contract of employment, being a unilateral statement by the employer, although in practice it often will be (see *System Floors (UK) Ltd* v. *Daniel (1981)*). (See further European Community (EC) Directive 91/533.) Remedial provisions involving an industrial tribunal are in s.11 (see also *Construction Industry Training Board* v. *Leighton (1978)* and *Eagland* v. *British Telecommunications plc (1992)*).

Despite the fact that the courts and tribunals may construe implied terms in a contract of employment, they will not rewrite inadequate contracts, nor will they modify terms which are clear in a contract on the basis that one party, usually the employee, has ended up with a 'bad bargain', nor will they accord the status of a legally binding contract to an agreement which is either vague or insufficiently certain. However, a variety of methods have been robustly used at common law to imply terms into a contract on the basis of actual or presumed intentions in fact or imposing obligations by law, the purpose being to clarify the content of the contract concerned.

The implied term is first and foremost represented by the '*business efficacy*' test (*The Moorcock (1889)*). This aims to inject into a contract a term without which the contract simply would not function, in short an indispensable requirement. What the parties may well have intended may be blindingly obvious. That it may not have been included in the contract has led to the '*officious bystander*' or '*oh, of course*' test (*Shirlaw* v. *Southern Foundries Ltd (1939)*). *Custom and practice* have also had a considerable role to play by way of implication, particularly with contracts of employment (*Mears* v. *Safecar Security Ltd (1982)*). Finally, the exigencies of a situation may require a court or tribunal to search for *what must be implied in the circumstances into the contract as a matter of necessity or, arguably, of reasonableness* (*Liverpool CC* v. *Irwin (1976)* and *Scally* v. *Southern Health and Social Services Board (1992)*). Terms can also be derived by statute. The best example in the employment area is the so called 'equality clause', which forms a compulsory part of all contracts of employment by virtue of the Equal Pay Act (Eq PA) 1970, s.l(1).

As a special area of contract, terms in the form of duties, reciprocal or otherwise, can be automatically implied into a contract of employment as a matter of law. First, the common law has never recognized a general right to work providing wages are paid (*Collier* v. *Sunday Referee Publishing Co. (1940)*). There are some exceptions such as where commission is being paid for work (*Turner* v. *Goldsmith (1891)*), piece-work is involved (*Devonald* v. *Rosser (1906)*), or a reputation needs to be maintained (*Clayton & Waller* v. *Oliver (1930)*). The fact that an employee was appointed to a particular office (*Breach* v. *Epsylon Industries Ltd (1976)*) or needs to maintain certain skills (*Provident Financial Group plc* v. *Hayward (1989)*) has remained controversial regarding whether or not a right to work exists. Exceptionally, this right was advanced to counter the abuse of trade union power in *Langston* v. *AUEW (1974)*. Secondly, a duty to maintain mutual trust and confidence fosters the personal nature of the contract of employment (*Woods* v. *WM Car Services (Peterborough) Ltd (1982)*). Thirdly, an employee has a duty to obey reasonable and lawful orders (*Laws* v. *London Chronicle (1959)*) and, fourthly, there is a duty to provide faithful service (*Secretary of State for Employment* v. *ASLEF (No.2) (1972)*, *Cresswell* v. *Board of Inland Revenue (1984)*, *Ticehurst* v. *British Telecommunications plc (1992)*) and probably a duty to cooperate (*Sim* v. *Rotherham BC (1986)*). Fifthly, a duty of fidelity is strongly imposed on employees in respect of accounting for secret profits (*Devis W. & Sons Ltd* v. *Atkins (1977)*), disclosing misconduct (*Sybron Corp.* v. *Rochem Ltd (1983)*), and not assisting competitors (*Hivac Ltd* v. *Park Royal Scientific Instruments Ltd (1946)* and *Laughton* v. *Bapp Supplies Ltd (1986)*). However, covenants in restraint of trade cannot prevent ex-employees entering into competition with their former employers, unless the restrictions are reasonable regarding their time, place and extent. Confidential information obtained from an employer is similarly protected, unless it is against the public interest (*Initial Services Ltd* v. *Putterill (1968)*). But there are restrictions depending on the type of information involved, its relation to the skill of the employee, and whether the employee has left the employment concerned (*Faccenda Chicken Ltd* v. *Fowler (1986)*). Sixthly, there is a duty on the employer to take reasonable care of his employees, an important matter to be considered shortly. These then are the main implied terms, yet they are by no means exhaustive.

While express terms in a contract of employment take priority over implied terms (*Nelson* v. *BBC (1977)*), courts and tribunals have recently endeavoured to ensure that employers, in particular, implement express terms reasonably which in spirit support implied terms to the benefit of the employee (*United Bank Ltd* v. *Akhtar (1989)*). Nor should it be overlooked how job descriptions, grievance and disciplinary procedures, union membership and, very importantly, collective agreements influence and control the employment relationship whether or not these industrial phenomena are incorporated into the contract of employment (expressly or impliedly).

A contract of employment is dynamic in the sense that it responds to the changing needs of the parties. Common law requires agreement before any term can be varied and consideration for the variation. In practice, the employee's continued working under the new terms is taken to represent both assent and consideration for an amended contract of employment. Whereas there is no need at common law for any variation to be in writing, EPCA 1978, s.4 requires the employer to give written notice within one month of such occurrence. Furthermore, the mere signing of a standard contract of employment does not necessarily constitute an effective variation (see *Hawker Siddeley Power Engineering Ltd* v. *Rump (1979)*). However, providing there is a consensual variation of a contract of employment, this should be trouble-free. A unilateral variation, where either the employer or the employee seeks to alter the contract of employment without the other's agreement, will constitute a breach of contract which may lead to termination of the contract. For instance, an employer has no right to vary a contract of employment unilaterally by reducing wages or salaries (*Miller* v. *Hamworthy Engineering Ltd (1986)*).

23.4   HEALTH AND SAFETY AT WORK

23.4.1   Negligence and Breach of Statutory Duty: The Common Law Position

As has already been seen the employer's responsibility to take care of his employee at work can arise in a contractual context as an implied term (cf. *Johnstone* v. *Bloomsbury Health Authority (1991)*). However, the common law has also imposed a primary liability in *tort* (civil wrong) on an employer for negligence should an employee be injured at work. In general terms, negligence consists of a breach of the duty of care owed by the employer which causes reasonably foreseeable damage (injury) to the employee. For any breach of this duty, the remedy is damages, i.e. monetary compensation, to the extent of the harm caused. An action for damages for negligence must be brought in the county court or High Court within three years from the date when the cause of the action accrued, or from the date when there was knowledge of the injury (Limitation Act 1980). In the employment context the *employer's duty of care* is *personal* and *non-delegable* as established in *Wilsons & Clyde Coal Co. Ltd* v. *English (1938)*. This duty requires the employer to provide:

  (i)   safe plant and appliances (*Taylor* v. *Rover Car Co. (1966)*),
 (ii)   a safe system of work (*General Cleaning Contractors Ltd* v. *Christmas (1953)*),
(iii)   adequate supervision, and
(iv)   reasonably competent fellow employees (*Hudson* v. *Ridge Manufacturing Co. Ltd (1957)*).

It has also recently been established that an employer's duty to take reasonable care not to injure an employee's health not only involves physical but also mental health (*Walker* v. *Northumberland CC (1995)*.

To some extent Parliament has intervened in this area of employers' liability. Thus there is the Employers' Liability (Defective Equipment) Act 1969 and the Employers' Liability (Compulsory Insurance) Act 1969. Indeed employers should now be adequately covered by insurance, if only to counter the technical and impractical position of the negligent employee's common law duty to indemnify his employer (*Lister* v. *Romford Ice and Cold Storage Ltd (1957)*). More generally, there is the statutory duty of care owed towards all invitees on premises (with certain qualifications) imposed by the Occupiers' Liability Act 1957, and the statutory duty of common humanity towards trespassers under the Occupiers' Liability Act 1984. These provisions obviously cover both employees and others whenever they are on employers' premises.

The tort of negligence and its duty of care embrace *the standard of care* required. The employer should take reasonable precautions to protect his employee from harm (*Latimer* v. *AEC Ltd (1953)*). It is not an absolute responsibility without financial limit. Furthermore, if fault is to be attributed to the employer there is a degree of risk allocation involved. The more vulnerable the employee, the greater the care that is needed (*Paris* v. *Stepney BC (1951)*), and the less obvious the risk, the greater the need for warning (*Pape* v. *Cumbria CC (1991)*). Notionally, the safety of the employee is paramount whatever the employee's predisposition (*Page* v. *Freight Hire (Tank Haulage) Ltd (1981)*).

The burden of proof (which in civil law is 'on the balance of probabilities') lies upon the employee in an action which he may bring against his employer for injuries sustained at work. A crucial issue, and one on which many actions fail, is to establish that there was an unbroken chain of causation between the acts and omissions of the employer which resulted in the injuries suffered by the employee. Scientific and medical evidence may be essential for this purpose. In fact and in law it must be proved that the employer directly caused the employee's injuries. No new factor must have intervened (*novus actus interveniens*) to break this chain of causation, whether by a third party or otherwise. Sometimes it may be that the thing speaks for itself (*res ipsa loquitur*), namely that the employer's causing the employee harm is so apparent that there can be no other explanation (*Scott* v. *London and St. Katherine Docks Co. (1865)*).

The employer may have certain defences. First of all, negligence may be denied where appropriate care had been taken, for instance in *Latimer* v. *AEC Ltd (1953)*. Secondly, the injury may be the sole fault of the employee (*Brophy* v. *Bradfield & Co. (1955)*). A variant of this defence is *volenti non fit injuria* (that to which a man consents cannot be considered an injury). It is rare for this defence to succeed in the employment field, even if the employee has knowledge of the situation (*Smith* v. *Baker & Sons (1891)*).This is because it is the employer who has put the employee in a position confronting hazards or dangers at work (cf. *ICI Ltd* v. *Shatwell (1965)*). Unlike the previous defences, *contributory negligence* — under the Law Reform (Contributory Negligence) Act 1945 — is a partial defence. Here the amount of damages an employee can claim for negligence can be reduced by, or apportioned to, the extent that he is responsible for his own injury, in that he has failed to take proper or adequate care at work.

If an employee, by tortious act or omission, in the course of his employment causes injury or damage to a third party (which can include a fellow employee), the employer will have vicarious liability for the employee's conduct (*Limpus* v. *London General Omnibus Co. (1862)*). Vicarious liability may arise even though the employee is acting incorrectly but is still acting within the scope of employment (*Rose* v. *Plenty (1976)*). The employee will also be personally liable to the victim. But it is more likely than not that the employee will be unable to pay compensation to the victim. However, both the employer and employee (and any other parties responsible) may be treated as jointly responsible in tort under the Civil Liability (Contribution) Act 1978. The employer is not usually liable for the actions of independent contractors, unless the employer requests the performance of actions known to be tortious or particularly dangerous. But the employer cannot escape personal liability for the safety of his employees just because they are under the control of independent contractors (*McDermid* v. *Nash Dredging & Reclamation Co. (1987)*). In certain circumstances an employer can be strictly liable in tort for any acts or omissions of an independent contractor, as in *Rylands*

v. *Fletcher (1868)* for allowing dangerous things to escape from land because of its non-natural use.

Breach of statutory duty, while primarily involving criminal liability, has sometimes given rise to civil liability in tort as well. It must have been intended by Parliament that this breach would also confer a right to sue in tort for compensation (*Groves* v. *Lord Wimborne (1898)*). The best example is probably the requirement to fence dangerous machinery under the Factories Act 1961. Tortious liability only arises if the statutory duty is specifically imposed on the employer in respect of the employee, the employer is in breach, and the employee suffers harm or damage which is not too remote a consequence of the breach (*Close* v. *Steel Co. of Wales (1962)*). Actions for negligence, where employers' liability is concerned, are often pursued in tandem with actions for the tort of breach of statutory duty. The ambit of the latter tort is often narrower and stricter than the former because of the statutory and common law requirements already indicated. The issues of causation, vicarious liability and defences, in respect of the tort of breach of statutory duty, are similar to those for the tort of negligence, providing they remain within and do not contravene any statutory prescription.

23.4.2   Health and Safety at Work Act 1974: the statutory position

The Health and Safety at Work Act (HASAWA) 1974 was the result of the Robens Committee report. The committee was critical of the haphazard nature of existing legislation which targeted specific theatres of work rather than imposing responsibilities on particular actors the consequences of whose activities might well extend beyond the workplace. There was a need to raise the level of consciousness in the prevention of industrial accidents. Consequently, research, advice and enforcement simply had to become more effective. Thus the new legislation was meant to be preventative rather than punitive, being predominantly aimed to exhort and promote safety at work. To this end the Health and Safety Commission and the Health and Safety Executive were established.

The Commission makes policy. It issues Codes of Practice (s.16), for instance in connection with making regulations providing for Safety Representatives, Safety Committees and for Time Off for Training of Safety Representatives, and has been responsible for regulations on health and safety and welfare at work, e.g. the Control of Substances Hazardous to Health Regulations 1988. The Executive's role is enforcement by such means as Improvement and Prohibition Notices (ss.21-24) issued by the Factories Inspectorate, and, of course, ultimately by criminal prosecution (s.33) for breach of any relevant statutory provisions (see, e.g., *R.* v. *Swan Hunter Shipbuilders and Telemeter Installations Ltd (1982)*). Here the burden of proof in respect of criminal liability lies on the prosecution to prove the case 'beyond reasonable doubt'.

The general duties are set out in ss.2–9 (see below) of the HASAWA 1974. Most follow the common law duty of care in the tort of negligence as far as employers and (with some modifications) others are concerned. Yet there is no civil liability but criminal liability for breach of these provisions (s.47(1)).

S.2 The employer must ensure the health, safety and welfare of all employees. This specifically includes a safe system of work, safe equipment, and a safe working environment. It also involves provision of information, training and supervision to ensure safety.

S.3 Employers and independent contractors must ensure that they conduct their undertakings to ensure the safety of third parties (employees of another employer, independent contractors, subcontractors, and the general public).

S.4 This covers the general duties of persons concerned with premises to persons other than their employees.

S.5 This imposes a general duty on persons in control of certain premises in relation to harmful emissions into the atmosphere.

S.6 Designers, manufacturers, importers, and suppliers of articles for use at work must ensure that these articles will be safe.

S.7 Employees have a general duty to take reasonable care for their own safety and for the safety of others who may be affected by their acts or omissions at work, and must cooperate with their employer to those ends.

S.8 This imposes a duty not to interfere with or misuse — intentionally or recklessly — items provided for health, safety and welfare at work.

S.9 An employer must not charge an employee for the provision of any safety measure or equipment.

With the exceptions of s.5, s.8 and s.9 the duties mentioned generally speak of reasonably practicable means being used.

23.4.3   The European Union position

The domestic provision for delegated statutory regulation in the health and safety at work area is likely to be enveloped by recent regulations made in response to previous EC Directives (especially 89/391) under Article 118A of the Treaty of Rome (pursuant to the Single European Act 1986). The regulations, which have been or are being implemented, concern:

(i)   Management of Health and Safety at Work,
(ii) Provision and Use of Work Equipment,
(iii) Manual Handling Operations,
(iv) Workplace (Health and Safety at Work),
(v)   Personal Protective Equipment at Work, and
(vi) Display Screen Equipment (Health and Safety at Work).

23.5   DISCRIMINATION IN THE WORKPLACE

There is no general law prohibiting discrimination. At common law the employer has the freedom whether or not to select an employee (*Allen* v. *Flood (1898)*). The most important statutory restraints are mainly in the form of the Sex Discrimination Act (SDA) 1975, subsequently extended by SDA 1986, and the Race Relations Act (RRA) 1976. Age, religion and sexual preference are not directly controlled by these Acts. Discrimination on grounds relating to membership or non-membership of a trade union *is* unlawful under the Trade Union and Labour Relations (Consolidation) Act (TULRCA) 1992, ss.137–143. Limited but positive assistance is, in theory, given to the disabled under the Disabled Persons (Employment) Acts 1944 and 1958, but new legislation is now pending in this area which will considerably improve the position. The effects of removal of restrictions on employment by the Rehabilitation of Offenders Act 1974 should be noted, as should the freedom of movement of workers within the European Union.

23.5.1   Sex and race discrimination

With very few exceptions anti-discrimination law is a matter for civil and not criminal liability. Discrimination in employment is unlawful on the grounds of sex (SDA 1975, s.l), which includes marital status, but not being single (s.3(1)). It is also unlawful on racial grounds (RRA 1976, s.1), which includes colour, race, nationality, ethnic or national origins (s.3(1)), and encompasses segregation (s.1(2)).

Direct discrimination is defined by SDA 1975 and RRA 1976 as less favourable treatment on the grounds of sex (s.l(1)(a) and s.3(1)(a)) or racial grounds (s.1(1)(a)). In the employment field, the forms of discrimination which are unlawful are defined by SDA 1975, s.6 and RRA 1976, s.4. The provisions are almost identical. They cover discrimination in respect of selection, terms of employment, refusal or deliberate omission to offer employment or access to opportunities for promotion, transfer, training, benefits, facilities or services, dismissal and any other detriment. The fact of discrimination occurring is fundamental: intention, motive and purpose are irrelevant (*James* v. *Eastleigh BC (1990)*). Discrimination can be transferred (*Showboat Entertainment Centre Ltd* v. *Owens (1984)*) and has embraced racial insults (*De Souza* v. *AA (1986)*) and sexual harassment (*Porcelli* v. *Strathclyde RC (1986)*). Pregnancy is, controversially, within the remit of sex discrimination (*Webb* v. *EMO Air Cargo (UK) Ltd (1995)*).

Indirect discrimination is somewhat more insidious. The statutory provisions here are designed to deal with situations where discrimination is arguably unintentional. Some social engineering seems to be involved. Prohibition is extended to requirements applied to all persons, but which have a disproportionate effect on members of a particular sex, marital status or racial group (SDA 1975, s.l(1)(b) and s.3(1)(b) and RRA 1976, s.1(1)(b)). The references below are to indirect sex discrimination but there is equal applicability to discrimination on marital and racial grounds. Indirect discrimination occurs when a person applies a requirement or condition equally to a person of the opposite sex (*Price* v. *Civil Service Commission (1978)*), but:

(i)   which is such that a proportion of persons from one sex who can comply with that condition or requirement is considerably smaller (*Jones* v. *University of Manchester (1993)*), and

(ii)   it cannot be shown that the condition or requirement is justified by objective determination irrespective of the sex of the person to whom it is applied (cf

Bilka Kaufhaus v. *Weber von Hartz (1986)* and *Enderby* v. *Frenchay Area Health Authority (1993)*), and

(iii) it is to that person's detriment because he or she cannot comply.

Discrimination can occur by victimization (SDA 1975, s.4 and RRA 1976, s.2). This concerns less favourable treatment of someone because he or she has done a 'protected act'. Broadly, a protected act concerns being involved in bringing proceedings or making a complaint under these Acts. Other unlawful acts under SDA 1975 Part IV and RRA 1976 Part IV include provisions regarding discriminatory practices, discriminatory advertisements, instructions to discriminate, pressure to discriminate, liability of employers and principals, and aiding any unlawful acts.

There are many exceptions within the legislation. Thus, genuine occupational qualifications provide exemption. SDA 1975, s.7(2) is extensive, covering physiology, decency, privacy, lack of separate sleeping accommodation, single-sex institutions, personal services, legal restrictions, and where a job is one of two held by a married couple. RRA 1976, s.5(2) only provides such exemption in relation to authenticity in dramatic performances, modelling, ethnic restaurants, and effective personal services. Other exceptions relate to acts done to safeguard national security (SDA 1975, s.52; RRA 1976, s.42), charitable trusts (SDA 1975, s.43; RRA 1976, s.34) and acts done under statutory authority (SDA 1975, s.57; RRA 1976, s.41). With regard to the SDA 1975, there are dispensations concerning Ministers of Religion (s.19), Police and Police Cadets in respect of height, uniform, equipment, pregnancy and pensions (s.17), Prison Officers in respect of height (s.18) and generally where death or retirement are involved (s.6(4)). RRA 1976 does not apply to immigration rules, or Civil Service regulations which restrict Crown employment on grounds of birth, nationality, descent or residence. The only special occupation exception for RRA 1976 relates to seamen recruited abroad. There are provisions regarding the special needs of racial groups as regards education, training or welfare (RRA 1976, s.35), education or training for persons not ordinarily resident in Great Britain (s.36) and sports and competitions (s.39).

To a very limited extent, SDA 1975, ss.47 and 48 and RRA 1976, ss.37 and 38 permit positive (reverse) discrimination. In effect, this allows preferential treatment of one group at the expense of others. This only relates to training. Employers or training bodies may offer training to one sex only, or to one racial group only, in order to equip them for a job, if no one, or very few, of that sex or racial group have been doing that work in the previous 12 months.

Proof of discrimination can be very difficult. To that end the Equal Opportunities Commission (EOC) has issued a Code of Practice on the Elimination of Discrimination. The Commission for Racial Equality (CRE) has likewise issued a Code of Practice on the Promotion of Equal Opportunities in Employment. Statistics and ethnic monitoring have played a great part in discrimination cases (see e.g., *West Midlands PTE* v. *Singh (1988)*), as has the Questions and Replies Procedure provided by statutory regulations under SDA 1975, s.74 and RRA 1976, s.65. Ultimately, the information on discrimination (if it exists) may be peculiarly within the preserve of the employer. A difficult balance may have to be struck between extracting that information whilst at the same time respecting confidentiality (*Science Research Council* v. *Nassé (1980)*). Whereas the burden of proof remains on the employee (or prospective employee) alleging discrimination, the absence of an adequate explanation from the employer can lead to adverse inferences being drawn. Support for this approach has been given in sex discrimination cases in *Baker* v. *Cornwall CC (1990)* and racial discrimination cases in *King* v. *Great Britain China Centre (1991)*. Finally, it should be noted that discrimination which continues does not cease to be discrimination (*Barclays Bank plc* v. *Kapur (1991)*).

As for remedies, industrial tribunals have jurisdiction to deal with claims of sex discrimination in employment (SDA1975, s.63) and racial discrimination in employment (RRA 1976, s.54). Claims must be made within three months of the alleged act of discrimination (SDA 1975, s.76(1); RRA 1976, s.68(1)). Complainants need have no contract of employment relationship with the employer complained against; thus discrimination in recruitment and against any self-employed person are covered. The remedies available (SDA 1975, s.65; RRA 1976, s.56) are:

(i)   an order declaring the rights of the parties,
(ii) compensation which can include an amount for injury to feelings (in the case of indirect discrimination, discriminatory intention must be proved), and
(iii) a recommendation for action to remove discrimination.

Assistance and, in appropriate cases, enforcement and remedies may be available from the EOC and the CRE. This can include conducting formal investigations (SDA 1975, ss.57–61; RRA 1976, ss.48–52) and issuing non-discrimination notices (SDA 1975, ss.67-70; RRA 1976, ss.58–61) to curb and cure discriminatory practices.

23.5.2   Equal pay

Equal pay and sex discrimination legislation in essence forms a single charter. The Equal Pay Act (Eq PA) 1970 is concerned with the establishment of equal terms and conditions of employment (including pay) between men and women. Its provisions are not restricted to employees (s.1(6)(a)), and it applies equally to men and women (s.1(13)), although it is predominantly women (many of them being part-timers) who, in socio-economic terms, suffer disadvantage. The development and interpretation of Eq PA 1970 have been considerably influenced by EC provisions, especially Article 119 of the Treaty of Rome, the Equal Pay Directive 75/117 and the Equal Treatment Directive 76/207, and the intervention of the European Court of Justice. The point of departure is that Eq PA 1970 requires that the contracts of employment of all women (and men) shall be deemed to include an equality clause (s.l(1)), in effect a statutory implied term.

Three distinct situations are envisaged in treating any disparity. First, like work (s.l(2)(a) and s.1(4)) is work which is the same or broadly similar requiring equal treatment on terms and conditions of employment (*Capper Pass* v. *Lawton (1977)*). Secondly, the work is rated as equivalent (s.l(2)(b) and s.1(5)) effectively after a job evaluation study which must be rational and scientific (*Bromley* v. *H & J Quick Ltd (1988)*). Thirdly, the work is of equal value (s.1(2)(c) and see *Pickstone* v. *Freemans plc (1989)* and *Dibro Ltd* v. *Hore (1990)*). The last two categories are not without their conceptual difficulties. Basically, job A is being compared with job B and possibly others. The claimant may choose his or her comparator without any restriction (*Pickstone* v. *Freemans plc (1989)*), who may be at a different establishment providing the terms and conditions of employment are generally common (*Leverton* v. *Clwyd CC (1989)*), or who may be a predecessor (*Macarthys Ltd* v. *Smith (1980)*).

The employer can, nonetheless, defend any claim for equal pay on the basis that the variation was 'genuinely due to a material factor which is not the difference of sex' (s.1(3)). This area has produced considerable litigation. There clearly has to be an objective and rational justification (*Bilka Kaufhaus* v. *Weber von Hartz (1986)*). Market forces have been accepted for this purpose (*Rainey* v. *Greater Glasgow Health Board (1987)*). Part-time workers compared with full-time workers have been, in principle, accorded protection (in *Jenkins* v. *Kingsgate (Clothing Productions) Ltd (1981)* and in the *Rinner-Kühn* case (1989)), and discriminatory pay structures (*Danfoss* case (1989)) and separate collective bargaining structures (*Enderby* v. *Frenchay Area Health Authority (1993)*) have been attacked when they have sought to hide behind this defence. It is a volatile area as *Ratcliffe* v. *North Yorkshire C C* (1995) has indicated.

A term by term approach is adopted under Eq PA 1970; it is not a question of looking at the contract of employment as a whole (*Hayward* v. *Cammell Laird Shipbuilders Ltd (1988)*). In many of these cases resort has been made to European Union law at the expense of domestic law. The direct effect of Article 119 on 'pay' and its liberal and purposive interpretation are especially evident in the revolutionary decision on the equalization of occupational pension ages between men and women in *Barber* v. *Guardian Royal Exchange Assurance Group (1991)*. The complex ramifications of this historic decision are still being felt.

For remedies under Eq PA 1970, a complaint regarding contravention of an equality clause, including a claim for arrears of remuneration or damages, may be made to an industrial tribunal, and an employer may similarly refer a dispute there (s.2). An employee must have been employed for at least six months (s.2(4)), and an award can only be made in respect of two years prior to the commencement of proceedings (s.2(5)).

23.6   PAYMEN OF EMPLOYEES

Legislation regulates the circumstances in which employers may make deductions from the wages of their employees. In accordance with the Wages Act (WA) 1986, s.l, deductions may only be made when authorized by statute, contractually in writing, or through written consent by the employee. However, deductions will not contravene this Act (s.1(5)) in the following situations:

(i)   overpayment of wages, providing the power to recoup exists at common law,
(ii) in respect of disciplinary proceedings which have a statutory base,
(iii) statutory requirement,

(iv) the employee has agreed a deduction in favour of a third party, e.g. subscription to a trade union,

(v) industrial action, or

(vi) the employee has agreed that a court or tribunal order may be so satisfied.

Special provisions exist for retail workers (ss.2–4). Claims brought within three months under WA 1986 are subject to industrial tribunal jurisdiction. A tribunal may make an appropriate declaration and may order repayment or other financial adjustment. The most significant decision in this area has been in *Delaney* v. *Staples (1992)* when the House of Lords finally ruled that a payment in lieu of notice on termination of a contract of employment (see EPCA 1978, s.49(3)) was tantamount to damages and was therefore not 'wages' within WA 1986. The county court (and not the industrial tribunal) therefore had jurisdiction to deal with such a claim. This led to renewed calls for the jurisdiction of the industrial tribunals to be widened under EPCA 1978, s.131 so that they could receive these claims which would be more practical. Change here seems likely and some legislative steps have already been taken.

With the Trade Union Reform and Employment Rights Act (TURERA) 1993, s.35, the remaining Wages Councils have been abolished. This means that there is now no legislative support where collective bargaining by trade unions is largely absent. Consequently, workers on low pay receive little, if any, protection or assistance, despite the debate which has continued regarding a national minimum wage. Many workers in this category lie below 'the decency threshold' of the European Union.

So far as sick pay is concerned, at common law a contract of employment will either make express provision or there will be an implied term often fed largely by custom and practice that sick pay is or is not paid (see *Mears* v. *Safecar Security Ltd (1982)*). There is currently a minimum provision for employees off work sick to be covered by Statutory Sick Pay for 28 weeks (Social Security Contributions and Benefits Act 1992, ss.151–163). The Statutory Sick Pay Act 1994 abolished the 80 per cent reimbursement of employers' costs under the statutory sick pay scheme (counter-balanced by a reduction in employers' National Insurance contributions). Also, under this Act women will be able to receive Statutory Sick Pay until the age of 65, placing them on a par with men.

23.7 STATUTORY EMPLOYMENT PROTECTION RIGHTS — DURING EMPLOYMENT

The right of employees to receive written particulars of their terms of employment (EPCA 1978, ss.1–11), including the right to receive an itemized pay statement, has already been mentioned.

23.7.1 Guarantee payments (EPCA 1978, ss.12–18)

This is to provide employees with a minimum payment for a maximum of five days in any three month period, where they are laid off work through no fault of their own. However, the employer must have the contractual right to lay off employees. Otherwise the employer will have breached the contract of employment. A lay-off exceeding four weeks could give rise to the redundancy payment provisions being triggered. The employer may avoid making a guarantee payment if the employee has either been offered suitable alternative employment during the lay-off and unreasonably refuses, or has been involved in any industrial action. The qualification period for this employment protection right is one month in employment. Recourse for non-payment of a guarantee payment is to an industrial tribunal. Where a collective agreement already provides for guarantee payments, the employer and other parties can apply for statutory exemption.

23.7.2 Suspension from work on medical grounds and the right not to suffer detriment in health and safety cases (EPCA 1978, ss.19–22C and sch.1)

Under Health and Safety legislation a business might be required to close. Unless the employer has a contractual right to suspend employees they are entitled to be paid for a maximum of 26 weeks, even if they are unable to work. The employer has a defence, once again, where the employee unreasonably refuses suitable alternative employment during the suspension period or is unfit to work during that time. The employee need only be employed for one month (similarly in unfair dismissal cases) to be entitled to this right. An industrial tribunal will order payment of the requisite amount. Compensation will also be awarded if an employee has suffered detriment in a health and safety case where action was being taken in an official capacity by the employee or in a personal capacity to warn of, or to prevent, dangerous situations, and this was impeded or sanctioned by the employer.

23.7.3 Time off for trade union duties and activities (TULRCA 1992, ss.168–175; ACAS Code of Practice No. 3)

Officials of recognized trade unions are entitled to paid time off during working hours for (i) performance of duties and (ii) undertaking training. The duties must relate to negotiations with an employer, be related to collective bargaining matters, and where the employer recognizes the trade union involved (*London Ambulance Service* v. *Charlton (1992)*). Such training must pertain to industrial relations matters and must be approved by the independent trade union concerned or the TUC. All members of recognized trade unions are entitled to unpaid time off during working hours for trade union activities which include acting as a representative (*Luce* v. *Bexley LBC (1990)*).

While participating in industrial action is proscribed, there is no statutory stipulation as to how much paid and unpaid time off trade union officials and members are permitted. It is that which is 'reasonable in all the circumstances' (*Wignall* v. *British Gas (1984)*) and (*Hairsine* v. *Hull CC (1992)*). In the event of default, declarations can be obtained from an industrial tribunal. If relevant, pay can be obtained and also just and equitable compensation where time off is refused.

Finally, it is unlawful to take action short of dismissal on grounds involving trade union membership or activities (TULRCA 1992, s.146). This could, for example, focus on a particular trade union and involve actions such as blocking promotion or refusing a pay rise as in *National Coal Board* v. *Ridgway (1987)*. It does not include derecognition of a trade union (s.148(3)). The remedy from an industrial tribunal is just and equitable compensation.

23.7.4   Time off for public duties (EPCA 1978, ss.29 and 30)

An employee is entitled to reasonable time off if he is a magistrate, a member of a local authority, Broads Authority, health authority of any kind or hospital trust, a governor of a school, college or university, a member of a statutory tribunal, or a member of the National Rivers Authority or a river purification board, or a member of a Board of Visitors for a prison. There is no provision for pay. Should time off not be granted, an industrial tribunal cannot stipulate what this provision should be but it can give guidance (*Borders RC* v. *Maule (1993)*). Remedies are a declaration and compensation. (Time off for jury service is covered by the Juries Act 1974).

23.7.5   Time off to look for work (EPCA 1978, s.31)

An employee who is given notice of dismissal for redundancy is entitled to reasonable time off work to look for new employment or to make arrangements for retraining. To qualify the employee must have been continuously employed for two years. Recourse is to an industrial tribunal which can order the employer to pay compensation equal to the pay the employee would have got if he had been allowed the time off. Arbitrarily, this is subject to a maximum of two-fifths of a week's pay.

23.7.6   Maternity provisions

Paid time off for ante-natal care (EPCA 1978, s.31A)

A pregnant employee under medical supervision is entitled to reasonable paid time off to attend ante-natal appointments.

Maternity leave (EPCA 1978, ss.33–38A) and maternity (compulsory leave) regulations 1994

Any employee who is pregnant, regardless of length or type of service, is entitled to 14 weeks' maternity leave (EPCA 1978, s.35). The period commences on the first day's absence or the start of the 11th week before confinement (whichever is the later). Where the birth takes place more than 11 weeks before the expected week of confinement the leave period starts with the date of the birth. During this period a woman is entitled to all contractual benefits other than pay, and is entitled to be paid at the level of Statutory Sick Pay until Statutory Maternity Pay cover is reached. In order to receive these benefits a woman should, where practicable, give 21 days' notice with medical certification (EPCA 1978, ss.36 and 37). If the employee wishes to return to work during her maternity leave, she must give her employer at least seven days' notice of the date upon which she intends to return. The employer can postpone her return by up to seven days (EPCA 1978, s.37A).

In addition under the Maternity (Compulsory Leave) Regulations 1994 any woman statutorily entitled to maternity leave must not work or be permitted to work by her employer during the period of two weeks starting on the day when the baby is born.

Right to return to work (EPCA 1978, ss.39–44)

A female employee who has been absent from work due to pregnancy or confinement is entitled to return to work in certain circumstances. A woman must have two years' continuous service 11 weeks before the expected week of confinement. She must give three weeks' notice of her intention to leave, where practicable, with medical documentation as to the expected week of confinement.

A woman who ceased to work no more than 11 weeks before the expected week of confinement may return to work at any time before 29 weeks after the actual date of birth (EPCA 1978, s.39(1)). Three weeks' notice of this intention must be given to the employer (EPCA 1978, s.42). Either party may postpone the date of return to a maximum of four weeks. If the employee does this, medical documentation must support the reason for the postponement.

Providing all requirements have been fulfilled, a refusal to allow a woman to return in these circumstances will be treated as a dismissal (EPCA 1978, s.56 and sch.2). If five or fewer employees (a small business) are involved, the employer is exempt where it is not reasonably practicable to permit the woman to return (or to offer suitable alternative employment which is not substantially less favourable) (EPCA 1978, s.56A).

The employer may request written confirmation whether the employee still intends returning to work within 21 days of the expiry of her maternity leave period. The employee must normally give written confirmation within 14 days after receiving this request (EPCA 1978, s.40(2)).

Where it is not practical for a woman to return to her previous job, she may be offered suitable alternative employment with her own or an associated employer which is appropriate and on terms which are not substantially less favourable (EPCA 1978, s.39(2)).

Maternity pay (Social Security Contributions and Benefits Act 1992, ss.164–171, the Maternity Allowance and Statutory Maternity Pay Regulations 1994 and the Statutory Maternity Pay (Compensation of Employers) Regulations 1995)

Any woman who has been continuously employed with the same employer for 26 weeks will be entitled to Statutory Maternity Pay. All women who qualify for

Statutory Maternity Pay will receive the higher level (90% of their normal weekly earnings) for the first six weeks of their maternity leave, and the standard rate of Statutory Maternity Pay for the remaining 12 weeks. Maternity leave and pay can begin at any time after the start of the 11th week before the baby is due. However, if a woman is on sick leave because of her pregnancy and there are fewer than six weeks, she will be deemed to be on maternity leave and entitled to maternity pay. These and other provisions fulfil the requirements of EC Directive 92/85.

Suspension from work on maternity grounds (EPCA 1978, ss.45–7)

A woman may be suspended from work by her employer because she is pregnant or has recently given birth to a child or is breast-feeding a child (see also EC Directive 92/85), and the suspension is due to any statutory requirement or to any recommendation contained in a Code of Practice issued under HASAWA 1974. Such a woman is entitled to be offered suitable alternative employment before being suspended, which must not be substantially less favourable than her normal terms and conditions of employment and must be appropriate to her circumstances. Failure to make such an offer may be remedied by an industrial tribunal awarding just and equitable compensation.

A woman who is suspended from work on maternity grounds is entitled to be paid a week's pay in respect of each week of suspension (or pro rata). An industrial tribunal may remedy any deficiency in this respect.

23.7.7   General points

Before considering unfair dismissal and redundancy as statutory employment protection rights, it is important to remember two points:

(1)   All these statutory employment protection rights represent a minimum floor of employees' rights which may promote better or enhanced provision in any contract of employment.

(2)   Attempts to avoid statutory employment protection provisions are generally prohibited under EPCA 1978, s.140. But TURERA 1993, s.39 has introduced the phenomenon of compromise agreements, whereby proceedings are not taken before an industrial tribunal.

23.8   TERMINATION OF EMPLOYMENT AT COMMON LAW

If the employer terminates the employee's contract of employment without notice or with inadequate notice and which is not justified as a summary dismissal for gross misconduct (see *Pepper* v. *Webb (1969)*), there will be a *wrongful dismissal*. If reasonable notice is given by the employer (cf. *Hill* v. *C. A. Parsons & Co. Ltd (1972)*) a contract of employment will be terminated lawfully. While a contract of employment may provide for longer notice, EPCA 1978, s.49 stipulates minimum periods of notice as follows. An employee with between one month and two years' continuous employment must be given at least one week's notice; between two and 12 years one week's notice for each complete year of service; and beyond 12 years at least 12 weeks' notice (cf. one week's notice required from the employee to the employer regardless of length of service). The remedy for any breach of contract caused by wrongful dismissal is damages, but not for injured feelings (*Addis* v. *Gramophone Co. Ltd (1909)* and *Bliss* v. *S. E. Thames Regional Health Authority (1985)* or stigma (*Malik* v. *BCCI* (1995)). The employee must endeavour to mitigate his loss. Given the limits to compensation for unfair dismissal, a claim for wrongful dismissal, although more formal, costly, and time-consuming through the County Court or High Court, will be of greater benefit to the highly paid employee who is successful (see e.g., *Shove* v. *Downs Surgical plc (1984)*). Litigation must be commenced within six years of the date of dismissal, otherwise it will be time-barred (Limitation Act 1980).

Neither resignation (*Sheffield* v. *Oxford Controls Co. (1979)*) nor termination by mutual agreement (*Birch* v. *University of Liverpool (1985)*) will, in essence, constitute dismissal at common law. Much will depend on the circumstances, the conduct of the parties and what is said or written. Indeed, while resignation in response to a fundamental breach of contract could constitute a dismissal, 'constructive resignation' — where the employer is entitled to terminate the contract because of the employee's repudiatory conduct — does not do so (*London Transport Executive* v. *Clarke (1981)*). A contract of employment can come to an end by performance, for instance with the expiry of a fixed term contract or a contract for a specific purpose or contingent on a particular event (cf. *Igbo* v. *Johnson Matthey Chemicals Ltd (1986)*). Remedies may also be available where there has been partial performance of a contract of employment (see e.g., *Miles* v. *Wakefield MDC (1987)* and *Wiluszynski* v. *Tower Hamlets LBC (1989)*). If a contract of employment is *frustrated* because its termination arises through no fault of the parties, there is no dismissal at common law (*Egg Stores (Stamford Hill) Ltd* v. *Leibovici (1976)*, *Notcutt* v. *Universal Equipment Ltd (1986)*, and *F. C. Shepherd* v. *Jerrom (1986)*). Death of an individual employer or compulsory liquidation of a company would constitute frustration of a contract of employment (cf. the statutory position in Part VII and sch.12 of the EPCA 1978 and the Insolvency Acts 1986 and 1994).

The personal nature of the contract of employment has meant that the common law has shied away from enforcement, a position reinforced by statute: TULRCA 1992, s.236. However, there have been exceptions and subtle distinctions have been made in using the equitable remedies of specific performance and injunction (see e.g., *Warner Bros Pictures Inc.* v. *Nelson (1937)*). As a general point where there is a breach of a contract of employment the innocent party can accept the repudiation and rescind the contract (*Rigby* v. *Ferodo Ltd (1987)*) or waive the breach and affirm the contract thereby continuing with it, reserving the right to sue for a declaration and damages (*Burdett-Coutts* v. *Hertfordshire CC (1984)*). An employer's power to terminate may be contractually fettered, for instance where there is first the requirement to follow a disciplinary procedure (*Irani* v. *Southampton & S W Hampshire Area Health Authority (1985)*). Damages, injunctions and declarations may be available in such a situation. Whilst the contract of employment is normally within the realm of private law, public law remedies, such as judicial review, have been pursued in appropriate cases, usually where the contract has had a statutory base (see e.g., *R* v. *Secretary of State for the Home Department ex parte Benwell (1985)*).

23.9 UNFAIR DISMISSAL AND REDUNDANCY: Statutory Employment Protection for the Termination of Employment (Parts V and VI of the EPCA 1978 as amended and modified by TULRCA 1992 and TURERA 1993)

Overshadowing the common law in this area, unfair dismissal is undoubtedly the most important aspect of employment protection legislation. Despite voluminous case law, statute is the primary source. The focus is essentially on reasons and the manner and mode of dismissal, whether or not a breach of contract is involved. Public awareness and the persistent influence on personnel practices have been marked where unfair dismissal is concerned. Originally intended for collective purposes, unfair dismissal appeared on the industrial horizon in 1971. Although its impact may not now be so great, it still concerns job security and the notion that a job is in some sense a person's property. Provision for redundancy payments, originating from the Redundancy Payments Act 1965, interacts with unfair dismissal. Apart from the fatuous hope of promoting mobility of labour, its principal aim was to compensate for the loss of a job and not to provide unemployment benefit (*Lloyd* v. *Brassey (1969)*).

The basic right is that an employee under a contract of employment shall not be unfairly dismissed by his employer (EPCA 1978, s.54). Sensibly, a dismissed employee should seek written reasons for dismissal (EPCA 1978, s.53). There are a number of exclusions from unfair dismissal protection. Unless the dismissal is automatically unfair (see below) an employee must be continuously employed for at least two years (EPCA 1978, s.64(1)(a) which is now subject to legal challenge) and must not be over the normal retirement age or 65 (EPCA 1978, s.64(1)(b)) on the effective date of termination which is determined under EPCA 1978, s.55. There is a legal presumption in EPCA 1978, sch. 13 that continuity of employment exists. Because of legislative change to sch. 13 consequent upon *R* v. *Secretary of State for Employment ex parte EOC (1994)* the number of hours worked by an employee each week is irrelevant. Furthermore, in the following situations continuity will be preserved despite any actual break in employment, and in all cases except the last will count in computing length of service: sickness or injury, temporary cessation of work, absence by arrangement or custom, and strike or lock-out. Particular provision has also been made in this context when there is a transfer of business and the employee moves immediately before the transfer from one employer to another (*Litster* v. *Forth Dry Dock & Engineering Co. Ltd (1990)*), domestic legislation being supplemented by the Transfer of Undertakings (Protection of Employment) (TUPE) Regulations 1981 in fulfilment of EC Directive 77/187.

23.9.1 Unfair dismissal

In the first place there must be a dismissal and this is a question of law. This can occur under EPCA 1978, s.55:

(i) on termination of employment by the employer (actual dismissal with or without notice),

(ii) upon expiry of a fixed term contract without renewal (*Dixon* v. *BBC (1979)*), or

(iii) in constructive dismissal (*Western Excavating (ECC) Ltd* v. *Sharp (1978)*), where the employee resigns when entitled to do so by reason of the employer's conduct, that conduct constituting a repudiation of the contract of employment (because it goes to its root) which the employee accepts by resigning.

While the employee must prove that he has been dismissed, the employer has the burden of proving the reason for dismissal (*Maund* v. *Penwith DC (1984)* and *Smith* v. *Glasgow CDC (1987)*). If the employer cannot prove the reason for dismissal, the dismissal is automatically unfair (*Adams* v. *Derby CC (1985)*). The industrial tribunal must, therefore, determine whether or not the employer's reason for dismissal is fair on the set of facts known to the employer or the belief held by the employer at the time of the dismissal which actually caused the employer to dismiss the employee (*Devis W. & Sons Ltd* v. *Atkins (1977)* cf. *National Heart and Chest Hospitals Board of Governors* v. *Nambiar (1981)*). It is then necessary to establish the substantive reason (or principal reason if more than one) for dismissal and that it falls within one of the following categories of *prima facie* fair dismissal (EPCA 1978, s.57).

(i) It was related to capability or qualifications of the employee for performing his work (*Davison* v. *Kent Meters Ltd (1975)*).

(ii) It was related to the conduct of the employee (*Alidair* v. *Taylor (1978)*).

(iii) The employee was redundant (*Williams* v. *Compair Maxam Ltd (1982)*).

(iv) The employee could not continue to work in the position without contravention of a statutory provision or restriction (*Sandhu* v. *Department of Education and Science (1978)*).

(v) There was some other substantial reason of a kind such as to justify the dismissal of an employee holding the position which that employee held (*Hollister* v. *NFU (1979)*, *Dobie* v. *Burns International Security Services (UK) Ltd (1984)*, and *St John of God (Care Services) Ltd* v. *Brooks (1992)*).

Thereafter the industrial tribunal has to determine whether the dismissal was fair or unfair, having regard to the reason shown by the employer, which will depend on whether in the circumstances (including the size and administrative resources of the employer's undertaking) the employer acted reasonably or unreasonably in treating it as a sufficient reason for dismissing the employee, and whether this was in accordance with equity and the substantial merits of the case (EPCA 1978, s.57(3)). The employer has to act, substantively and procedurally, 'within the band of reasonable responses'. The industrial tribunal does not have to establish how it would have acted in the circumstances (*Iceland Frozen Foods Ltd* v. *Jones (1982)*). Whether or not the dismissal is fair has to be judged by what the employer did — for example dismissing an employee straightaway without following correct procedure — not by what might have been done. If a dismissal is unfair because of any procedural defect, compensation may be reduced to take account of the fact that the employee may still have lost his employment in any event (*Polkey* v. *A. E. Dayton Services Ltd (1988)*).

Procedural unfairness can raise issues of natural justice and has led to extensive litigation where dismissals from employment have occurred. In situations of misconduct or incapability it may be first a matter of warning and giving the employee the chance to improve rather than dispensing with his services forthwith. Sensible employers will adopt the ACAS Code of Practice No. 1 on Disciplinary Practice and Procedures in Employment. Infringement of these provisions does not give rise to legal sanction (TULRCA 1992, s.207(1)) but may be evidentially important: the greater the departure the more likely that there will be legal liability for the employer (*Lewis Shops Group* v. *Wiggins (1973)*). Very sound guidance on a fair approach to disciplinary hearings against employees and appeals by employees is to be found in *Clark* v. *Civil Aviation Authority (1991)*, *Stoker* v. *Lancashire CC (1992)*, and *Paul* v. *East Surrey District Health Authority (1995)*.

So far the mainstream of unfair dismissal has been considered. There are, however, a growing number of specific grounds for unfair dismissal which require some attention.

Dismissal for trade union membership or non-membership

Participation or otherwise in trade union activities is an automatically unfair reason for dismissal (TULRCA 1992, s.152). No qualification period therefore is required. Although not outlawing the post-entry closed shop directly, it has substantially eroded this phenomenon. It is also unlawful to refuse a person employment on grounds related to trade union membership (TULRCA 1992, s.137), thereby effectively removing pre-closed shop restrictions.

Selection for redundancy

This is now automatically unfair in the following specific situations (TULRCA 1992, s.153 and EPCA 1978, s.59 as amended):

(i) Where there is the reason that the person has been selected because of union membership/activities/non-membership.
(ii) Where selection was because the person exercised his functions in health and safety cases.
(iii) Where either pregnancy or childbirth was the basis for selection.

Protection from dismissals in relation to statutory maternity rights and pregnancy

EPCA 1978, ss.56, 56A, 60, and sch.2 has now been expanded. It will be recalled that a refusal by an employer to allow a woman the right to return to work after having a baby is normally an unfair dismissal. The dismissal of a female employee in such a situation is thus an automatically unfair reason, with no qualification period needed. Dismissal will be automatically unfair where:

(i)   the dismissal is due to or connected with pregnancy;
(ii) maternity leave is ended by dismissal which is connected with childbirth;
(iii) dismissal occurs after the maternity leave period as a result of the employee taking such leave;
(iv) an employee is dismissed within a period when she has been covered by a medical certificate stating she is incapable of work;
(v)   the dismissal is in connection with a statutory restriction or recommendation in a Code of Practice issued under the HASAWA 1974; or
(vi) the employee is dismissed by reason of redundancy and no attempt is made to find or offer her alternative employment where a suitable vacancy is available.

The selective dismissal or re-engagement of employees involved in a lock-out or strike or other industrial action

This can lead to successful unfair dismissal claims from those who are victimized within a three month period of the 'relevant employees' not being dismissed or being re-engaged (TULRCA 1992, s. 238).

Dismissal due to industrial pressure

In considering whether the employer acted reasonably, under EPCA 1978, s. 63 no account shall be taken of any industrial pressure on the employer to dismiss the employee (involving calling, organizing, procuring or financing a strike or other industrial action, or threatening to do so). Pressure might come from a trade union or its members. In that case an employer would be entitled to join the union as a third party to seek reimbursement, in whole or in part, of any compensation awarded to an employee (TULRCA 1992, s.160).

The TUPE Regulations 1981

If there is a 'relevant transfer' under these regulations and if any job is lost, this will be regarded as an automatically unfair dismissal (reg.8(1)). This does not apply if the reason (or principal reason) is an 'economic, technical or organizational reason' entailing changes in the workforce as a whole (reg. 8(2)). This would be tantamount to a fair dismissal for 'some other substantial reason' in accordance with EPCA 1978, s.57(1)(b). It could lead to a redundancy payment as *Gorictree Ltd* v. *Jenkinson (1984)* demonstrates.

There are recently enacted provisions regarding unfair dismissal in health and safety cases (EPCA 1978, s.57A) and for asserting a statutory right in the context of employment (EPCA 1978, s.60A).

23.9.2   Remedies for unfair dismissal

These normally should be sought within three months (EPCA 1978, s.67(2)), and are primarily re-instatement and re-engagement (EPCA 1978, ss. 68 and 69) when an industrial tribunal will endeavour to establish whether the dismissed employee wishes to be re-employed respectively in his old job or in a similar job. For practical reasons, these remedies are rarely ordered (*Port of London Authority* v. *Payne (1994)*). Consequently, it is usually a matter of compensation (EPCA 1978, s.72). This is in the form of a basic award (EPCA 1978, s.73) calculated on the basis of an employee's age, length of service (subject to a maximum) and gross weekly pay (subject to a maximum). There is a minimum where the dismissal involves trade union membership (or non-membership). This is followed by a compensatory award (EPCA 1978, s.74 and see *Norton Tool Co.* v. *Tewson (1973)*) aimed at compensating the employee for the loss caused by the dismissal which includes expenses incurred and remuneration and benefits lost. Both awards can be reduced by such matters as failure to mitigate, contributory fault and the receipt of other relevant payments. An additional award of compensation (EPCA 1978, s.71) is made where reinstatement or re-engagement has been ordered but not implemented with provision, in particular, for contributory fault on the part of the employee. The special award of compensation (EPCA 1978, s.75A) is reserved for dismissals in trade union membership (or non-membership) cases and where re-employment has been sought. There is also provision for interim relief pending determination of unfair dismissal claims in trade union cases (TULRCA 1992, ss.161–166), including official representation on matters involving health and safety at work or membership of a safety committee (EPCA 1978, ss.77–79).

23.9.3   Redundancy

Redundancy payments are modelled on the basic award for compensation in unfair dismissal cases. Claims for payment, normally to be made within six months, are handled by industrial tribunals. Their calculation is governed by EPCA 1978, sch.4. A redundancy payment would usually be made in a genuine situation of redundancy and where the dismissal for redundancy is fair. An employer can challenge a claim for redundancy if it was not a genuine one (*O'Hare* v. *Rotaprint Ltd (1980)*). If the reason is other than redundancy, it is for the employer to prove. Should the employer do so, there will be no liability for redundancy pay. Otherwise, the statutory presumption of redundancy will prevail (EPCA 1978, s.91(2)), but this is not applicable in an unfair dismissal claim (*Midland Foot Comfort Centre* v. *Moppett (1973)*). An employee must have been continuously employed for at least two years under a contract of employment (EPCA 1978, s.81(4)) excluding any week which began before the employee was 18 (s.151(4)). Otherwise, broadly similar considerations (with some minor differences) apply to exceptions and to types and the occurrence of dismissal where redundancy payments are concerned, as are applied to unfair dismissal provision.

Under EPCA 1978, s.81(2), a dismissal is because of redundancy if it is wholly or mainly attributable to certain factors. It could be that the employer has ceased, or intends to cease, carrying on business for the purposes of which the employee was employed (*Moon* v. *Homeworthy (Northern) Furniture Ltd (1976)*), or that the employer has ceased or intends to cease carrying on business in the place where the employee was employed (*O'Brien* v. *Associated Fire Alarms Ltd (1968)*). Alternatively, it may be a case of surplus labour. The needs of a business for employees to carry out work of a particular kind, or that work in the place where they were employed, may cease or diminish, or be expected to do so (*Bass Leisure Ltd* v. *Thomas (1994)*). This may occur through reorganization or rationalization of a business (cf. *Lesney Products Ltd* v. *Nolan (1977)*). It could be that fewer employees are needed for existing work (*Carry All Motors Ltd* v. *Pennington (1980)*), or that there is less work for existing employees (*Chapman* v. *Goonvean & Rostowrack China Clay Co. Ltd (1973)*).

The employer may raise certain defences to a claim for a redundancy payment. In the first place the employer may deny that there was a dismissal or that it was for redundancy or indeed both. Misconduct may disentitle an employee to a redundancy payment (EPCA 1978, s.82(2)) as the employer might well be able to terminate the contract of employment on that basis alone. Yet the redundancy payment may be saved if the misconduct takes place after notice of redundancy in response to that fact, say in the form of a strike (EPCA 1978, s.92).

Another step the employer may take to avoid having to make a redundancy payment is to offer the employee a renewal of contract on similar terms and conditions or suitable alternative employment before the conclusion of the old contract of employment (EPCA 1978, s.82(3)). If the employee unreasonably refuses either offer, then he will be disentitled to a redundancy payment (s.82(5)). However, the entitlement to a redundancy payment will be kept alive if his refusal is subjectively 'reasonable' (*Cambridge & District Co-operative Society* v. *Ruse (1993)*). A statutory trial period of four weeks is provided as a minimum for any new employment arrangement (EPCA 1978, s.84) in addition to any common law trial period (*Air Canada* v. *Lee (1978)*). If the employee unreasonably terminates the new contract, this will disentitle him to a redundancy payment in respect of the previous contract (EPCA 1978, s.82(6)). Termination by either party could leave open the issue of whether the previous dismissal under the old contract was fair or unfair in respect of any dismissal during the trial periods (*Hempell* v. *W. H. Smith & Sons Ltd (1986)*). Finally, transfer of a business as opposed to its assets under EPCA 1978, sch.13 para.17(2), or the TUPE Regs. 1981, will normally preserve continuity of employment. Therefore employees so transferred (cf. the common law position in *Nokes* v. *Doncaster Amalgamated Collieries Ltd (1940)*) would not be entitled to a redundancy payment.

Provision is also made for lay-off and short-time which may escalate into redundancy (EPCA 1978, ss.87–89). There is also provision for collective handling of redundancies in response to EC Directive 75/129 (as amended by EC Directive 92/56) under TULRCA 1992, ss.188–192 and 195–198, whereby an employer must consult any independent trade union which it recognizes over any intended redundancies. Extensive information and periods of time involving this matter and the process of redundancy are entailed. Unless there are special circumstances which excuse the employer from compliance, consultation must not only take place, but, if representations by the trade union are rejected, the reasons for doing so must be stated in writing. Failure to comply may result in an industrial tribunal awarding just and equitable compensation in the form of a protective award to individual employees (whether union members or not), if the trade union concerned makes a complaint.

23.10   COLLECTIVE BARGAINING

Collective agreements between trade unions and employers have been the major source of terms and conditions of employment for the majority of workers in the UK. A principal purpose of trade union activity is to redress the unequal position experienced by an individual employee by providing a collective force to which an employer is more likely to respond. Collective bargaining is not essentially about legal regulation, but is an exercise of countervailing social and economic power. Collective agreements can be classified in a number of different ways, but these are not mutually exclusive and may interconnect. Often collective agreements will be substantive and affect individual employees, e.g. provision for performance-related pay. They may also be procedural (in a collective or individual sense). Thus the contents of these agreements can cover a multitude of matters, for instance, terms and conditions of employment, disciplinary procedures, disputes procedures over industrial action, and redundancy arrangements. An agreement may be at national, regional, plant or local level. In the UK the process of collective bargaining is always dynamic and its techniques and period of operation can vary. All of this can complicate any legal involvement. With the reduction of trade union power in the late 1980s and early 1990s, the impact of collective bargaining is now less than it was. The tendency is for single union deals to be more frequent, for collective bargaining to become more decentralized from national to plant level, and for there to be a re-emergence of individual bargaining.

At common law (*Ford* v. *AUEFW (1969)*) and by statute (TULRCA 1992, s.179) collective agreements are not normally regarded as legally enforceable as between the collective parties, e.g. an employer and a trade union, although there are exceptions. If a collective agreement were a legally enforceable contract or were deemed to be so, because of privity of contract (*Dunlop Pneumatic Tyre Co. Ltd* v. *Selfridge (1915)*) individual employees, being third parties, could not, strictly speaking, benefit whether or not they were union members. There are, of course, difficulties in regarding the trade union acting as agent in this context (*Holland* v. *London Society of Compositors (1924)*). It seems that a union can only really act as an agent on behalf of employees generally insofar as they are actually union members, if a specific agency is created for a particular purpose to effect legal transactions, say on a local basis (*Burton Group* v. *Smith (1977)*).

Notwithstanding any indication to the contrary, a collective agreement can still be incorporated into an individual contract of employment (see *Marley* v. *Forward Trust Group Ltd (1986)*), and therefore become legally binding, providing the terms of the collective agreement are appropriate and suitable for this purpose (*Alexander* v. *Standard Telephones and Cables plc (No.2) (1991)*). Once this threshold of 'individuation' has been crossed, it will be a matter of express incorporation (*NCB* v. *Galley (1958)*) or implied incorporation (*MacLea* v. *Essex Line Ltd (1933)*). There can, limitedly, be statutory incorporation through 'no strike' clauses (TULRCA 1992, s.180) and where an independent and recognized trade union successfully triggers the disclosure of information machinery for more effective collective bargaining under TULRCA 1992, ss.181–5 (see further ACAS Code of Practice No. 2 and *R* v. *Central Arbitration Committee ex parte BTP Tioxide Ltd (1982)*). Viewed from another dimension, terms in collective agreements which discriminate on grounds of sex may now be statutorily challenged in a court or industrial tribunal in that they contravene the European Union principle of equal treatment (SDA 1986, s.6 as amended).

23.11   SUMMARY

In this chapter the common law position of the employee in a contract of employment has been considered with the duties and obligations which arise from this relationship with the employer. Increasingly there has been statutory intervention in the world of work. This has been examined in connection with health and safety at work, the prevention of racial and sexual discrimination, the regulation of pay and the broad foundation of employment protection rights which eventually concentrate on unfair dismissal and redundancy provision. However, the individual employee cannot be viewed in isolation, and has thus been also considered in the context of collective bargaining.

BIBLIOGRAPHY

Anderman, S. (1993) *Labour Law: Management Decisions and Workers' Rights.* Second edition, Butterworths, London.

Bourn, C. and Whitmore, J. (1993) *Discrimination and Equal Pay.* Second edition, Sweet and Maxwell, London.

Bowers, J. (1994) *Employment Law.* Fourth edition, Blackstone Press, London.

Downes, T. A. (1995) *Textbook on Contract.* Fourth edition, Blackstone Press, London. This book deals in general with an essential understanding of the law of contract, but not specifically from an employment perspective. Furthermore, Part 1 on legal method gives a basic and very useful introduction to legal structure (Chapter 1), sources of law (Chapter 2) and the impact of the European Union (Chapter 3).

Goodman, M. (1993) *Health and Safety at Work: Law and Practice.* Sweet and Maxwell, London.

Morris, G. S. and Archer, T. J. (1993) *Trade Unions, Employers and the Law.* Second edition, Butterworths, London.

Pitt, G. (1995) *Employment Law.* Second edition, Sweet and Maxwell, London.

Pitt, G. (1993) *Cases and Materials on Employment Law.* Pitman, London.

Selwyn, N. M. (1993) *Law of Employment.* Eighth edition, Butterworths, London.

Smith, I. T. and Wood, J. C. (1993) *Industrial Law.* Fifth edition, Butterworths, London.

Wallington, P. (ed.) (1993) *Butterworths Employment Law Handbook.* Sixth edition, Butterworths, London. Essentially this is a source book for statutory and related materials.

Wedderburn, Lord (1993) *Worker and the Law.* Fourth edition, Penguin, Harmondsworth.

Appendices

Appendix 1
The single European market

A1.1 INTRODUCTION

This appendix starts with a brief history of the European Union (EU), formerly known as the European Community (EC). The scale of Europe is illustrated by comparison with the USA and Japan, using the measures of population and Gross National Product (GNP), and figures for selected industries. The objectives, and official estimates of the benefits of the Single European Market (SEM) are described, and the validity of these estimates challenged by questioning some of the linkages in the official economic model, and by cross-checking the theory against the actions of business organizations. This challenge is developed in more detail through an analysis of the European automotive industry. The appendix concludes with a section on Eastern Europe.

A1.2 THE EUROPEAN UNION

The origins of the EU lie in an agreement, made in 1952, to form the European Coal and Steel Community (ECSC). This agreement was between France, West Germany, Italy, and the three 'Benelux' countries, Belgium, The Netherlands and Luxembourg, under the Treaty of Paris. The coal and steel industries of these six countries were placed under joint control with the twin aims of economic recovery and the prevention of war. This meant that, from the outset, there was a political as well as an economic dimension to the plans of 'The Six'. Five years later, the same six countries formed the European Economic Community (EEC), with the same objectives, and the European Atomic Energy Community, (EURATOM), under the Treaty of Rome. In 1965, administration of the ECSC, EEC and EURATOM was revised within a single structure that included the European Council, the European Commission, the European Parliament and the European Court of Justice. This structure, was continued as the Community of 'The Six' expanded to 12 by 1986, and 15 by 1995. The roles of the institutions are described in a booklet *Working Together — The Institutions of the European Community* [1].

A1.3 THE SCALE OF THE EUROPEAN COMMUNITY AND ITS ASSOCIATES

The EC is significantly larger than the USA or Japan by most measures of economic activity. Cooperation with the EFTA countries and the democratized Eastern European states will extend the lead of 'Europe' as a market and a producer for most manufactured goods. Some indicators of relative size are given in Table A1.1. The figures for Gross Domestic Product (GDP) are sensitive to exchange rates. For example, the Japanese yen appreciated markedly against the US dollar between 1991 and 1993, from about 150 Yen/$ to just over 100 Yen/$, so the same 1991 level of economic activity in Japan would have

Table A1.1   Europe, USA and Japan some comparative figures (1991)

	EU	EFTA	EU+EFTA	USA	Japan
Population (millions)	344	33	377	246	122
GDP ($ billion)	6300	900	7200	4400	3250
Car Production (m units)	13	1	14	8	8
Steel Production (m tonnes)	137	24	161	84	106
Machine Tool Production ($bn)	16	3	19	3	12

been valued at $4875 billion when the SEM came into effect. The basic point is that European GDP is greater than that of the USA or Japan.

The sheer size of Europe, in economic terms, has attracted inward investment, particularly from the USA and Japan, and particularly in the car, electronics, computer, home entertainment and oil industries. The opportunities for high volume sales of the products from these and other industries has also made Europe an interesting market for imports. However, the summary market figures can be misleading for several product sectors, as there are major differences between the products sold in the individual European countries. Some of the differences are due to consumer preferences, but others are due to legislation or history. For example, electrical power supplies are at different voltages and electrical connectors are of various designs — as most travellers have come to realize. Differences such as these have meant that for many products it was necessary to develop different specifications to meet individual national requirements. As a result, there was not a truly European market in many goods and services. This led to waste, and added cost on such a scale that by the mid 1980s efforts were made to create the conditions for a single market. These efforts are outlined in the next section.

A1.4   THE SINGLE EUROPEAN MARKET (SEM) OR '1992'

A 1985 EC summit meeting endorsed the *White Paper on Completing the Internal Market*, which set out a programme to remove the 'non-tariff' barriers to trade within the EC — the 'tariff' barriers having been removed by membership of the EEC. This new programme required over 300 pieces of legislation to be enacted by each of the 12 national governments by the end of 1992. This gave the programme its '1992' title, which was slightly misleading since the single market was to be created from 1 January 1993. Political support for the programme was confirmed by the 1987 Single European Act, which, with other agreements, reduced the legislative burden to about 280 acts — still a formidable task.

As a result of this legislation it was anticipated that there would be free movement of labour, goods and services and capital within the SEM. In turn, it was forecast that this freedom of movement would reduce costs by removal of non-value-added controls, and would increase competition by simplifying and easing access to other countries in the Community.

In 1986, the European Commission initiated a study into 'the costs of non-Europe'. The results were published in 1988, and are presented by Cecchini *et al.* in *The European Challenge 1992* [2]. This describes the benefits of the SEM created by the removal of the three types of barrier that are listed below:

'• *physical barriers* — like intra-EC border stoppages, customs controls and associated paperwork;

- *technical barriers* — for example, meeting divergent national product standards, technical regulations and conflicting business laws; entering nationally protected public procurement markets;
- *fiscal barriers* — especially differing rates of VAT and excise duties.'

The costs of non-Europe were estimated by 13 sub-studies dealing with multi-sectoral barriers (four reports), the service sector (three reports) and manufacturing (six reports). The six manufacturing reports covered telecommunications equipment, automobiles, foodstuffs, building materials, textiles and clothing and pharmaceuticals.

As a result of these studies, it was estimated that removal of the three sets of non-tariff barriers would achieve savings valued at more than Ecu 200 billions — about £133 billion [2]. This was expected to convert into GDP growth of between 6.5% and 7.5%, and employment increases of between four million and six million jobs.

The mechanisms by which these gains were to be achieved are shown in the two figures Figure A1.1 and A1.2, both reproduced from *The European Challenge 1992*. The first chart suggests that removal of barriers will lower costs, leading to lower prices and higher demand, and will increase competitive pressures which will also reduce costs and improve margins — which will lead to lower prices, and the creation of a 'virtuous circle'. Some of the linkages in this cycle are challenged in section A1.5.1.

In the second model, the four sets of measures grouped under 'market integration' are shown collectively to result in lower costs, which lead to lower prices, more investment,

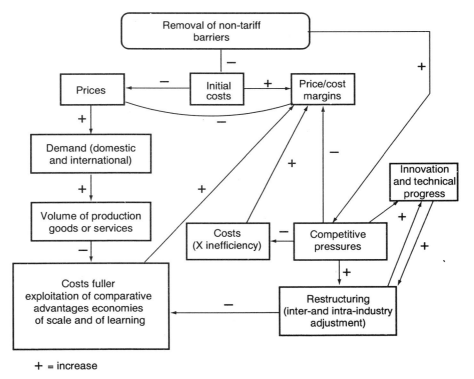

+ = increase

− = decrease

Figure A1.1   Flow chart of micro-economic effects triggered by EC market integration

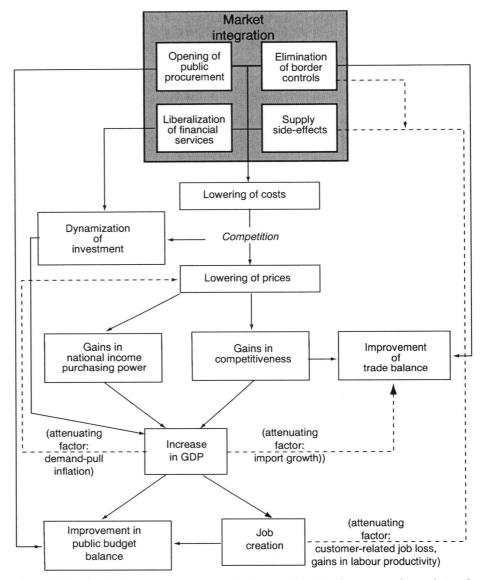

Figure A1.2 Principal macro-economic mechanisms activated in the course of completing the internal market

higher GDP and job creation. Separately, some of the sets of measures were expected to reinforce some of the collective effects, creating another virtuous circle. The scope and expected benefits of actions in each of the four areas are summarized below.

Opening of public procurement relates to supplies (of goods), works (building and civil engineering projects) and services (such as maintenance and repair of equipment, transport of mail, telecommunications, and architectural and engineering property management services). Regulations extend beyond the purchases of central and local government to include provision of goods, works and services to other bodies such as National Health

Services, and the police. Energy, water, transport and the telecommunications sectors are generally excluded from the general provisions, but are subject to the Utilities Directive which has broadly similar effects. In total, the procurement activities that are covered constitute about 15% (or £500 billion annually) of the Community's gross domestic product.

Purchasers are required to publish their annual procurement plans for supplies in each product area where expenditure is likely to exceed about £500 000, and each individual contract has to be advertised if it exceeds about £130 000 for local government or £90 000 for central government agencies. Intention to place works contracts above about £3.3 m have to be advertised, and the contract award must be published. The limits are different under the Utilities Directive — for example, the level above which all supplies and services contracts must be put out to tender is rather higher at about £300 000 — but the principles are the same. (Values in sterling are approximate because the limits are set in European Currency Units (ECUs).)

Contracts may be awarded according to three sets of procedures. It should be noted that the general thrust of these procedures is in conflict with partnership sourcing and the intimate long term relationships necessary for concurrent/simultaneous engineering. The processes appear to be rather bureaucratic, and likely to be slow moving — which is inconsistent with the vision of a revitalized, dynamic public procurement activity. These are:

- open procedures where any supplier may tender
- restricted procedures where any supplier may apply to be considered, but only selected suppliers are invited to tender
- negotiated procedures where direct discussions take place with one or more suppliers of the purchasers choice.

Purchasers may award contracts either to the supplier submitting the lowest price, or on the basis of a combination of factors, which are considered economically advantageous.

Many of the '1992' rules on public purchasing are not new, and are similar to the Government Purchasing Agreement terms within the General Agreement on Tariffs and Trade. Nevertheless, it was expected [2] that there would be three direct beneficial effects:

- a 'static trade effect' — buying from the cheapest source,
- a 'competition effect' — prices driven down by foreign competition,
- a 'restructuring effect' — through economies of scale.

The total savings from these three effects were estimated to be in the range from ECU 8 billion to ECU 19 billion (£6 billion to £15 billion) annually.

Elimination of border controls was expected to have a downward effect on prices through avoidance of border delays and red tape. However, the macro-economic effects were expected to be relatively small, (as opposed to micro-economic effects of this change which were expected to reduce costs by 2%).

Liberalization of financial services — banking, insurance and stockbroking, for example — was expected to have significant effects through reducing the costs of these services, and by lowering the cost of credit to domestic and business borrowers. These effects were estimated to be:

- 1.4% reduction in consumer prices,
- 1.0% reduction in public finances,
- 1.5% growth in Community GDP.

Since all the major banks and insurance companies have been operating internationally for many years, or centuries, prior to 1993, it is difficult to share the analysts' expectations of the SEM financial services measures. Large institutions had developed efficient ways of competing and dealing across national borders. Smaller companies, who may have expected to benefit, were still experiencing long delays and high costs at the end of 1994 — almost two years into the SEM. If benefits had accrued, they were being retained within the financial institutions, and were not providing smaller companies with a stimulus to export.

Supply side-effects were expected as a result of price reductions following from cost reductions, and from productivity gains from more efficient allocation of resources, industrial restructuring and improved internal business organization. These effects were estimated to produce 2% growth in Community GDP, and a 'steep drop in prices' (2%).

Together, as stated earlier, the macro-economic and micro-economic effects of the SEM were expected to create between four and six million jobs, and to increase the level of economic activity in the Community by between 6.5% and 7.5%. These benefits were expected to flow from lower costs, which would lead to lower prices; from increased competition, which would also lead to lower prices; and from economies of scale as a result of the higher demand generated by the lower prices.

Although the analysis leading to these conclusions was detailed and sophisticated, the assumptions about cost/price linkages and the scope for increased competition are naive. Similarly, there is a lack of realism in the expectation that more legislation will change what Cecchini *et al.* call 'almost hermetically sealed procurement practices' in the public sector, particularly since they note that 'the Community legislature has up to now proved no match for national and local purchasing bureaucracies' [2].

It is hard to name a major industry or branch of commerce where competition in Europe was not already fierce before 1993 — so fierce that all the major companies were engaged in desperate cost-reduction actions that make the SEM effects look puny. These actions had broken the link between output growth and employment growth. Almost all industries had been producing more output with fewer employees in the years leading up to '1992' and continued in the same way afterwards. Competition had broken, or reversed the cost/price linkage too — prices were reduced first, and drove the search for cost reductions to restore profit margins.

Most branches of financial services, and many major manufacturing industries, were already operating on a global scale before the SEM came into being, and were dominated by companies (e.g. Nomura, Merrill Lynch, Siemens, General Electric, General Motors, Ford, Hoechst, Bayer, Glaxo, Du Pont, IBM, Exxon) to whom the national frontiers of Europe were almost transparent. Driven by the already-existing competition, these transnational companies had adopted strategies and taken actions that anticipated the SEM, and pre-empted the benefits.

This was true of all the major engineering industries. Civil engineering has been an international industry for 150 years; the major companies operated throughout Europe and the rest of the free world (and some other parts) prior to 1992. Aerospace is a global industry, and, in Europe, both military and civil aircraft as well as missiles and space vehicles have been developed and produced by international consortia for sale throughout the world. Oil and petrochemicals are also global businesses, with non-European companies long-established in Europe, and European companies such as Royal Dutch/ Shell and British Petroleum operating worldwide. Pharmaceuticals, bio-pharmaceuticals, the electrical and electronic industries, machine tools and surface transportation are all industries conducted on an international scale, and dominated by transnational or multinational companies, many of whom are European.

Engineering managers, and others, in such companies have been striving to improve corporate performance in existing and predicted business environments. They have sought to overcome tariff and non-tariff barriers, and in Europe had achieved widespread success in these endeavours prior to 1992. This was particularly true in the automobile industry, which is examined in more detail in section A1.5. The examination is in the context of the

SEM, but much of the information should be of interest more generally, since this is the largest engineering industry and the test-bed for many engineering management skills.

A1.5   '1992' AND THE AUTOMOBILE INDUSTRY

A1.5.1   Overview of the European automobile industry pre-1992

In many respects, the Single European Market had been anticipated by the motor industry since the late 1960s — for example, Ford of Europe was created in 1967 to coordinate all the activities of the Ford companies in Europe. Consequently, some of the predicted benefits had already been secured, or the post 1993 effects were muted, by actions taken in the preceding 20 years or more.

The following sections cover the size, structure, complexity and recent growth of the European car industry. They show that competition was intense, cost reduction was a constant task, and that buying and selling across frontiers was commonplace.

Size and structure

The European vehicle industry prior to 1993 had production of 13 to 15 million units a year, and capacity rather greater than this, depending somewhat on how a vehicle is defined and how Europe is defined. Whichever definitions are used, Europe was the largest car market in the world in 1993, and had been since 1986. (See Figure A1.3). These volumes, together with the associated supply and distribution activities, translated into something like 10% of European GNP.

Apart from being bigger, the European industry differed from North America and Japan in several ways. Three of the most important ways were:

- There were six major car suppliers or groups of suppliers, all capable of moving their volume or market share rank within the six by a place or two within a few years, plus the Japanese, who together were about equal to one of the six 'Europeans' (see Figure A 1.4). The long-standing competition between these seven groups was so fierce that '1992' made it more intense in only one respect — by exposing the 'national champions' to Japanese competition. Peugeot Group, which includes Citroen are one of 'the big six' and one of the national champions. (Cecchini *et al.* erroneously show Volvo as one of the six, instead of Peugeot [2].)
- It was not one market in the same sense as Japan or the USA, but the six major players had all been operating on an international basis for many years, and had become skilled in living with the diversities and obstacles that existed.
- Europe's truck market was relatively small — 1.5 to 2 million units a year compared with 4 to 5 million in the US, where light utility vehicles, classified as trucks, were, and continue to be a popular form of personal transportation.

The chart in Figure A.1.4 shows that Fiat was the market leader up to 1989, though they shared this position with Volkswagen-Audi (VAG) in 1988–9. From 1989, Fiat's share declined, but VAG became clear leaders by the acquisition of the Spanish company SEAT, and the Czech company Skoda. Peugeot moved from fourth place in 1984 to third in 1988, but their lead over General Motors was eroded by 1992. Ford fell from joint second in 1984 to sixth in 1992. Renault lost one percentage point of market share between 1984 and 1988, and were unable to recover it.

None of the producers would give up market share lightly, and they would all go to extraordinary lengths to gain even one percentage point.

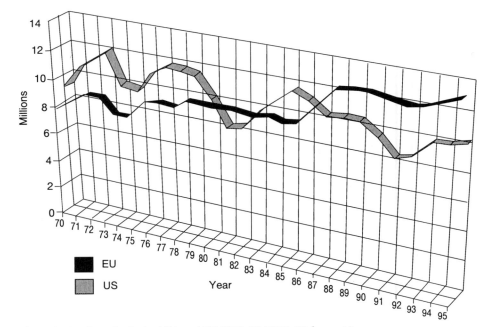

Figure A1.3   Car sales in the USA and EU 1970–95 (1992–95 forecasts)

Short-term variations in a producer's position were achieved by measures such as aggressive pricing or discounting, heavy advertising and promotional campaigns or more frequent 'facelifts'. Strategies for longer term gain in market share included more investment in new products and facilities, and acquisitions. All these actions, both short and long term, have proved damaging to profitability, and there have been few years when the European industry in total was profitable. With the seven groups constantly striving for extra market share, and for lower production costs to fund their marketing effort and restore profit margins, intense competition already existed before 1993. Therefore, the benefits to society, and to the European economy, which economists claim to be a natural consequence of intense competition, must also have existed before 1993.

Complexity

For more than 20 years prior to the SEM, the long-established European producers supplied almost 90% of the market, and almost half their product was sold in countries other than the one in which it was produced. There was thus the anomalous situation that the industry and market were large in global terms, but both production and sales volumes were fragmented by customer requirements and the structure of the manufacturing base. Complex patterns of inter-company and intra-company shipments across national frontiers developed long before 1992.

The major supplier companies are also pan-European in their operations. In the 1960s and 1970s UK companies such as GKN and Lucas, and US groups such as ITT and Allied were investing on the European mainland partly to escape the labour relations and quality problems of the UK, and partly to improve the logistics of supplying the French, German and even the Italian automobile companies. The entry of GM and Ford into Spain brought a surge of foreign investment there, largely due to conditions attached to investment grants.

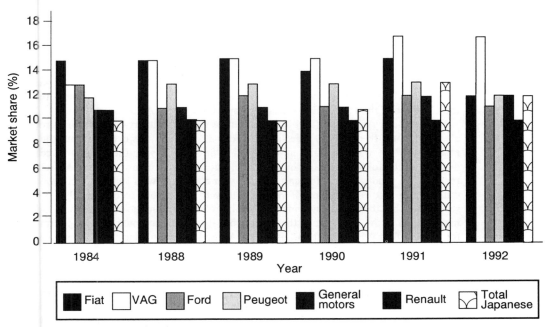

Figure A1.4   European car market shares 1984–92

And in the five years running up to 1993, the strengthening of the German mark combined with the improved reputation of the UK as a manufacturing base, led to new plants or acquisitions in the UK by firms such as Bosch, Magnetti Marelli, Fischer, Schlegel etc., from which they could ship lower cost parts to supplement their continental European output.

This well-developed supply base enabled the 'big six' vehicle producers to source over 95% of their purchases in Europe. The vehicle producers and their suppliers were constantly looking for opportunities to reduce costs by changes in the allocation of schedules between manufacturing locations in Europe, and by improvements in their distribution systems. Specially designed ships, trains and trucks moved materials and vehicles across and around Europe, sometimes through 'roll-on/roll-off' harbour facilities especially constructed for automotive industry traffic. Using dedicated consolidation and break-bulk depots the vehicle producers were able to simplify the shipping task for smaller suppliers. All they had to do was to deliver to a local centre, or have their products available for collection by a common carrier. This left the large suppliers and the automotive companies themselves with the task of crossing borders, and they became very skilled at it. The total cost of all the transport activities of a vehicle producer: bringing materials from suppliers into plants, moving products between plants, and delivering products to dealers, was in the order of 2.5% of the company's sales revenue. Somewhere in that 2.5% was the cost of crossing borders, but it was not the 2% of sales estimated for all industries by the EC Commission's study.

Growth of demand and capacity

Throughout the 1980s and through to the end of the century, the predictions of motor industry market size have suggested that it would grow at a rate of about 2% per annum.

However, there have been ups and downs along the way, and short-term variations around the trend will continue to occur — often to the surprise of those involved most closely, and often at more than 2%. Motor industry experts are as poor as any other group of forecasters, and a look at past performance will help put the SEM effects in context. Figure A1.5 shows forecasts made in 1985 for the USA and Europe.

The 1985 forecasts for European and US demand over the following five years were both wrong, and in opposite ways — the European forecast was too low, and the forecast for the USA too high. This can be seen by comparing Figures A1.3 and A1.5.

Later 'industry' forecasts (that is the consensus view of industry experts) for Europe were also erroneous. In mid 1986 a decline of about 3% in 1987 was expected, but the market rose in 1987. It was the same in 1987 and 1988 — each year the experts forecast that demand in the following year would decline, but each year it rose. Even in March 1989 a reduction in total sales was forecast for that year compared with 1988. In fact, 1989 turned out to be a record high, and 1989 was followed by another record in 1990. It is now recognized that there was a step increase of about 20%, or 2 million units, in the underlying market level in the later half of the decade, but it was not accepted as a long-term change for three or four years after it had occurred. Annual variations since 1987 have been up and down around this higher underlying market size.

The step increase in demand did not absorb surplus production capacity, which was still around 2 million units and growing as '1992' approached. This 2 million units was Europe's share of world surplus capacity of about 8 million. Despite this, all the producers in Europe were adding to capacity one way or another. Some, notably the Japanese producers who selected the UK as their main European manufacturing base, were building new assembly plants, which was good news for construction companies. Others built extensions to existing assembly plants, for example VW added 100 000 units of assembly capacity in Spain to expand their SEAT acquisition. This form of expansion was moderately good news for construction companies. Most producers, however, expanded capacity by using the brainpower and experience of their engineers (and others) to break bottlenecks and improve productivity, which may be more subtle, but it does have spectacular results. For example, Ford's European operations produced 1.4 million vehicles in 1979 with 150 000 employees, and in 1989, without any added assembly plant, they made 1.8 million units with less than 100 000 employees. That's almost twice as many vehicles per employee. The key, of course, was quality improvement — doing things right first time — which was the major concern of European car makers in that decade. The quality drive entailed new styles of management, and employee and supplier involvement, which had an important effect on capacity. Team problem solving, leading to method changes, increased machine utilization on press lines and transfer lines from below 50% to over 90% in some cases. This was another way of getting 50% more capacity with little or no investment. (This was bad news for construction companies, who faced a substantially different task in serving their automotive industry customers. The new task was refurbishment, rearrangement and maintenance, rather than new building.)

The new UK assembly plants of Nissan, Toyota and Honda will have added 600 000 units of capacity by the end of the century, and the efforts of the longer established producers to match or beat Japanese productivity will increase their capacity. This is simply a continuation of trends that were established well before 1992. With production capacity consistently growing faster than market size, there was already fierce competition on product, quality, service and price.

For more than ten years before the SEM, the benchmark in each of these areas of competition was Japanese performance, which was superior to the Europeans' in almost every respect. Recognition of this led to a whole range of attempts at cooperative ventures between European vehicle producers, and between the producers and their suppliers. By the

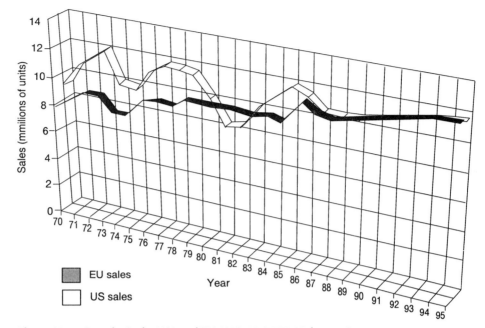

Figure A1.5   Car sales in the USA and EU 1970–95 (1985–95 forecasts)

launch of the SEM, it had also meant a change in relationships between the car assembly companies and their suppliers.

Initially this was prompted by joint efforts to improve quality, but this was reinforced by the consequent development into simultaneous engineering (joint new product and process development), Just-in-Time materials management and CDX/EDI (computer links). Almost the only aspect of competition which remained to be influenced by the SEM was the protection of some national markets from the Japanese producers, and the assistance given to 'national champions' — the domestic producers favoured by national governments. This is covered in the next section.

National champions and the Japanese

In the three major (biggest) national markets, there are interesting differences in the performances of the 'national champions' prior to the SEM. These are shown in Table A1.2.

France and Italy had restrictions on Japanese imports which predated the EC, and which were allowed to continue, limiting Japanese market share to 3%. Germany did not have any volume or share restrictions, and the Japanese took 16% market share despite the presence of very powerful domestic producers, which is a good indication of their capability in unprotected EU markets. There were also restraints on the Japanese in the next two largest markets — the UK and Spain — as well as in Portugal.

The SEM did away with the national restrictions, and substituted a total European agreement with Japan, allowing their overall share to rise to 17% by the year 2000 — but all the growth had to come from expansion of Japanese 'transplant' activities in Europe. The effect of the SEM legislation was therefore to expose the French and Italian markets to the full force of the Japanese producers, both from production within the EU, and from imports of vehicles from Japan. The Japanese, like the Americans, were free to import as many vehicles as they wished from their plants in the USA.

Distribution and pricing

Vehicles are distributed through tied dealerships that enable producers to determine specifications and prices in each national market, subject to local legislation. Some dealer chains are owned by the producers, others by separate companies, and many dealerships are independent companies in their own right. These arrangements have come under EC/ EU scrutiny from time to time, due to concern that they may not be in the consumers' best interests. However, for the start-up of the SEM the arrangements were allowed to continue under a 'block exemption' which was to be reviewed in 1995.

Several factors led to wide national variations in retail list prices in the EC:

- dealer margins were 15–20% in the UK, 6–10% elsewhere,
- specifications differed because of sales policy, safety and other legislation,
- special car and registration taxes ranged from 15% to 200%,
- short-term currency fluctuations affected international differentials,
- periods of price control in some countries distorted international comparisons.

The European Commission for Competition tried to restrict the range of international price variation for the same model to 15%, but one or more of the factors listed above usually acted faster than the Commission's enforcement.

Summary of automotive industry overview

The pre '1992' European vehicle market was big — around 13 million units — but was growing only slowly, apart from a step change in 1986–1988, with annual variations greater than the trend growth rate. (That is, a trend growth of 2%, but annual variations of between 3 and 7%). Production capacity was significantly bigger than sales volumes, and was growing quite fast. Consequently there was fierce competition.

Over 90% of production, and almost 90% of sales was in the hands of six major groups. There had been some mergers and joint ventures, but all six groups looked likely to persist as separate entities.

The long-established producers had made dramatic improvements in quality and productivity in the previous ten years, and had changed their relationships with their suppliers. However, the Japanese remained ahead in these respects, both with their imports and with their local production.

The market was fragmented by customer preferences and diverse national legislation, and distorted by tax policies and import restrictions that predated EC membership.

Prices and costs were subject to the effects of currency fluctuations. Distribution arrangements were constantly scrutinized.

Slow growth, excess capacity and the resultant competition had caused most of the producers to be unprofitable, or to make inadequate returns on their huge investments in facilities and new products.

Table A1.2 A comparison of Japanese and national champions' unit sales volumes and domestic market shares (1991)

	France			Italy			Germany	
	Sales (000)			Sales (000)			Sales (000)	
Citroen	240		Alfa	114		VW	688	
Peugeot	433		Lancia	200		Audi	204	
Total PSA	673		Fiat	762				
Renault	541							
		Share %			Share %			Share %
Champions' total	1214	61	Champions' total	1076	46	Champions' total	892	26
Japanese	60	3	Japanese	70	3	Japanese	548	16

A1.5.2 '1992' and its impact on the automotive industry

The motor industry was one of six examined in detail to arrive at the estimated total effect of the SEM — 7% increase in GNP and 5 million extra jobs. The expected effect of the planned measures on the motor industry was summarized as:

- removal of physical barriers: 2% cost reduction
- removal of technical barriers: 2% cost reduction
- increased competition: 1% cost reduction.

This total 5% cost reduction was expected to lead to price cuts, which would stimulate demand, and in turn result in additional sales of 500 000 units.

There was within this the expectation of greater cooperation between producers to share vehicle platforms and hence reduce development costs. A vehicle 'platform' is the underbody, plus possibly the chassis parts and even some of the powertrain parts, onto which a variety of different bodies may be fitted. Some minibus bodies or pick-up van bodies, for example, are fitted to the same underbody and mechanical assemblies as very different-looking passenger car bodies — they all share the same platform.

These theoretical results can be checked against the reality of the European motor industry prior to the SEM. Referring back to earlier sections, it can be seen that much of this analysis was fallacious.

The vehicle makers and their major suppliers had been crossing borders for years, and had applied some of their talents to make this a routine affair, involving computerized submission and clearance of 'documentation', and the selection of routes with minimum risk of delay. The actual cost of these processes was probably nearer to 0.5% of total cost than 2%.

Harmonization of technical specifications certainly provided an advantage, particularly with acceptance of single type approval. (That is, approval by one national authority became sufficient to demonstrate compliance and allow sale in any member state.) The persistence, until 1993, of variations in lighting, braking, crash impact and exhaust emission regulations certainly complicated the designers' task. The example of emissions shows how simplification of this task did not automatically reduce costs. Years of uncertainty preceding the eventual agreement on Community-wide emission controls led to vast expenditure on what became unacceptable developments. However, the means of meeting the most demanding emission requirements had long existed, and the diversity of approaches was very much the result of vehicle makers trying to offer lower cost solutions in whichever markets would tolerate them. The new single standards may therefore have reduced development costs without an overall cost reduction, since the cost of standardizing on three-way catalytic converters (which the new regulations require) may for most buyers exceed the saving in design duplication. More generally, much of the variety was due to factors that will not change, such as right-hand drive in the UK, or producers' interpretations of customer wishes, manifested in a typical popular car range by 128 different body, trim, and finish levels to be combined with six different engines and three different transmissions.

Economies of scale through added demand, which was one of Cecchini *et al.*'s forecasts, are unlikely to have a significant effect [2]. As shown earlier, the sort of volume growth that may result from the 1992 actions is within the industry's annual forecasting error. No changes in facilities or processes would be required to deal with it. Nor would there be productivity or component cost savings. All the vehicle companies and their suppliers have been bending their backs and their minds for many years to make annual savings of the level estimated to come from the 1992 measures. This has not resulted in consumer price reductions. For example, Jacques Nasser, when chairman of Ford of Europe, announced that the Dagenham UK plant had reduced the man-hours required to build a car by 45% between 1989 and 1993, and that the total cost of manufacturing the Fiesta model there had fallen by 23%. Over the same period, the retail price of Fiestas in the UK increased more than the retail price index, production of Fiestas increased, and employment at the Dagenham plant went down. That is, the cost/price and sales/employment relationships were the reverse of those in the EC Commission's economic model.

What of the benefits from tax harmonization and competition? The most distorting taxes remain unaffected, such as Denmark's sales tax and Italy's engine displacement tax differentials. Currency fluctuations will continue to add to price variations.

Competitive restraints, if they exist, within the dealer and distributor agreements will continue beyond 1995, and the removal of national limitations on Japanese market share is not having much effect. Whether produced in the UK or Spain, or imported from Japan or the USA, Japanese cars have not flooded into France, Italy, UK, Spain and Portugal. The Japanese are more subtle, and have used the new overall quotas to boost profits, not volume for the sake of it. Imports were moved more towards the high specification, high margin market segments, and Japanese volume products from European plants have been priced at whatever the local market would bear. Competition in all the national markets was already severe — there was worldwide surplus capacity, with up to 3 million of that in Europe — and it is this competition that determines prices, not the cost of production (see Chapter 13, section 13.5.1). This is the basic '1992' fallacy, illustrated in Figure A1.6. The 'system' breaks down at the asterisks.

The overstatement of cost reductions can be viewed as normal political hyperbole, but some of the inferences ignore the reality of the automotive industry. Whatever the cost reductions may be, they will not automatically lead to price reductions. Further, the task facing the established European vehicle and parts producers is to handle any increase in demand with fewer employees. The assumed series of links between increased demand/more jobs, more jobs/increased demand, increased demand/lower costs, lower costs/lower prices, breaks down where the two asterisks are shown.

A1.5.3   The automotive industry beyond the SEM

Having challenged the extent of the impact of the SEM on the motor industry, it may be worth reflecting on an implicit assumption — that there is such a thing as the European motor industry. If the Japanese are regarded as one group, then three of the major vehicle

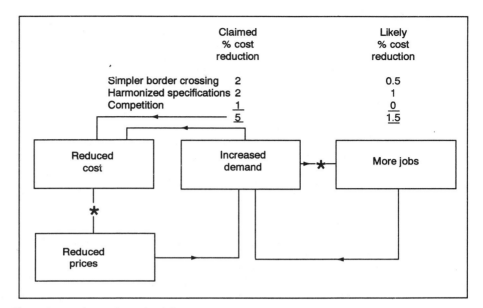

	Claimed % cost reduction	Likely % cost reduction
Simpler border crossing	2	0.5
Harmonized specifications	2	1
Competition	<u>1</u>	<u>0</u>
	5	1.5

Figure A1.6 The single market fallacy

suppliers in Europe are in fact the local representatives of global players — Ford and GM being the other two. (Some of the other four producer groups have operations outside Europe, but they are not global players.) The Japanese design in one place, to make and sell throughout the world, often using components and sub-assemblies made in Japan. GM and Ford have been trying to do the same thing for some years, with more success than is generally acknowledged, and with failures, widely publicized, due more to inept implementation than faulty conceptualization.

Clinging to the idea that there was a British industry, serving a British market, was one of the causes of the decline of the UK motor industry. The revival of production in that country is due to the efforts of companies that take a wider view. The same may be true on a European scale. Many people have come round to thinking 'European' as a result of the SEM, but this may not be enough, since the automotive industry is increasingly 'global'.

Asked on the eve of the SEM 'What is your company's strategy for 1992?', Lindsey Halstead, who retired in January 1993 as Chairman of Ford of Europe, replied:

'To supply the highest quality products and services providing the greatest customer satisfaction at the most competitive costs. These three considerations — Quality, Customer Satisfaction and Competitive Costs — are behind every decision we take . . . and will continue to be.' [3]

What he did not say is that that had been the company's strategy worldwide for years. In other words — no change for 1992. That summarizes the impact of the SEM on the motor industry. As far as the producers are concerned, it is 'business as usual'. The management of these engineering companies have studied the business environment, developed strategies and acted faster than the legislators — though no doubt influenced by what they expected the legislators to do.

A1.6   EASTERN EUROPE

Measured data about the former Communist Bloc countries are unreliable, and this section is therefore largely descriptive. The only reliable measure of size is a figure for their population — about 360 million. Economic data were distorted by inclusion of fictitious output, and by official exchange rates which overstated the value of some of the local currencies.

There is enormous variety in the experience of individual Eastern European states following the overthrow of their Communist regimes. Some, such as Poland, Hungary, and the Czech and Slovak republics moved towards democracy and the introduction of market economies relatively smoothly, and have formal associations with the EU. Others, including some of the former members of the USSR, have had serious economic, social and political problems, and the former Yugoslavia has been almost destroyed by war between ethnic factions.

The countries which achieved some sort of social stability presented immediate opportunities for western companies, and the others offer longer term potential. They all had a need for the technological and managerial skills of the West, as well as a demand for products. One engineering company, Asea Brown Boveri (ABB), considered the opportunities to be the equal of those around the Pacific Rim, and expansion into Eastern Europe has been part of their global strategy. In two years to mid 1994, ABB set up more than 60 companies or joint ventures in former Communist Bloc countries, and hired 25 000 employees there, at a time when, worldwide, they were reducing staffing levels.

ABB and other engineering companies found a pool of young people with good technical training, willing to learn, and used to very low rates of pay. This has enabled them to undertake major projects, such as new power stations, at low cost and in record quick time. They have also been able to set up design offices to do work for projects in the West at a fraction of western costs.

Around their new ventures, however, they found low levels of productivity, no understanding of industrial buying and selling, and no supply chain. It has therefore been necessary for ABB (and other western companies) to set up training and educational schemes, in cooperation with local institutions and in their own centres, and to locate their personnel in supplier companies to improve availability of materials and components.

Information obtained during Ford's study of a possible joint venture to assemble cars in Gorky, then in the USSR, gives an illustration of these supply difficulties. Materials for the Gorky Automobile Plant (GAZ) were allocated by a central agency in Moscow, said to employ some 30 000 people. There was no agreed price for the material, nor any quality standard, and no schedule of deliveries. Body steel, for example, arrived with little if any advanced notice twice a year, and had to be accepted whatever its condition, and however much was shipped. Unused, and largely unusable, stocks of steel sufficient for more than a year's production were piled up around the site. With such inputs it is difficult to generate outputs that will delight customers, though some may be surprised. Private buyers of cars from Gorky would have been surprised to get a car at all. Most of the output was supplied to middle-ranking officials, and private buyers, despite paying in full at the time of ordering, had to wait years for their car to be delivered — in whatever colour the plant was producing on their lucky day. It is also impossible to know whether an operation will be profitable — the concept of 'profit', until recently, was completely foreign.

Crude as they were, the supply and 'sales' schemes for plants such as GAZ, were part of an overall system which worked, though badly. The system has now been disrupted by fragmentation of the USSR, and scarcely works at all. The effects of this are also felt by other Eastern Bloc countries for whom the USSR was their major market, since many of their former customers are unable to pay for further deliveries. Finding new customers in the West is difficult, since product designs and quality frequently fall short of western standards.

A measure of the task involved in bringing western industrial performance to Eastern Europe can be obtained from employment levels in the DDR (East German) states when they were reunited with the FDR (West Germany). According to articles in *The Times*, [4] almost four million people — about half the 'working' population — were unemployed in the terms used by West Germany, but this level of unemployment was disguised by various 'training', 'work creation' or part-time working schemes. *The Times* articles also compared actual numbers of employees in 1989 for the major industrial sectors with a projection of the number of employees that would be required in these major industries if West German levels of productivity were to be introduced. Unemployment would then rise to over five million — over 60% of the 1989 'workforce'.

These figures for Germany alone show how significantly the expected post '1992' position was changed by events in Eastern Europe. Between the 1986 forecast of a two to five million '1992' jobs boost, and the time the SEM was established, unemployment in the EC had already increased by two million. Reunification of Germany pushed this increase immediately to nearly five million, dwarfing the effects of the SEM, and creating new social, political and economic problems within the Community.

Handling these internal problems, and at the same time providing financial and managerial assistance to Eastern Europe, has presented major challenges as well as opportunities for the EU. The same challenges and opportunities face engineering companies and individual engineers.

Restoring infrastructures that have decayed through more than 40 years of neglect and mismanagement is a huge engineering task in which Western European companies can share. Raising the performance of East European organizations to western levels is an even greater task for engineering management. Competition from the improving Eastern European engineering organizations will add to the pressures on engineers and engineering managers in the West. Integrating the restored countries in an expanded European Union will require engineers to work closely and constructively with other professionals of many kinds, which is probably the biggest challenge of all.

REFERENCES

1. *Working Together — the Institutions of the European Community*. Office for Official Publications of the EC, Jean Monnet House, 8 Storey's Gate, London SW1P 3AT. Other titles covering Community affairs are also available.
2. Cecchini, P. Catinat, M. and Jacquemin, A. (1988) *The European Challenge 1992*. Wildwood House, Aldershot, UK.
3. Halstead, L. L. (1990) *European Industrial Integration — an Industrialist's View*. A speech delivered at the launch of new models of Escort and Orion cars, September 1990. Re-issued by Public Affairs, Ford of Europe as Number 3 in a collection of four speeches under the title *Ford and the New Europe of '1992'*.
4. Muenchau, W. (1991) 'Chemical industry faces dilution in Germany's unified economy.' *The Times* 1 October. 'Statistics that disguise the size of Germany's army of unemployed'. *The Times* 2 October.

Appendix 2
Quality management tools

A2.1   INTRODUCTION

This appendix presents some of the forms and processes that are used in 'planning for quality', and 'managing for quality'. Two of them are 'generic' — the eight disciplines (8D) or team oriented problem solving (TOPS) approach, and the cause and effect (fishbone) diagram can be used in many problem-solving situations, as well as in the context of quality management.

The descriptions of the three 'tools' have been provided by the Ford Motor Company, and are reproduced with their permission from publications which the company provides free to all suppliers.

The fourth document lists the subject headings against which companies seeking recognition of compliance with the BS/ISO 9000 quality standard are assessed.

A2.2   8D TEAM ORIENTED PROBLEM SOLVING

The eight disciplines (8D) approach, also known as team oriented problem solving (TOPS), is the Ford method for addressing concerns including those issues concerning capability indices that are below desired values.

The 8D approach to problem solving:

- Provides an orderly team-oriented method for solving problems using facts rather than personal bias. Creative, permanent solutions usually require input from many activities.
- Applies to any problem or activity and assists in achieving effective communication between departments which share a common objective.
- Requires documentation through the concern analysis report. A typical report form is shown on the following pages.
- Provides the missing link between SPC and realized quality improvement.

The eight disciplines are identified and defined on the following page, and diagramed with a flow chart.

While the documentation of each problem is essential, the order of steps taken for resolution may vary depending on the degree of difficulty or complexity of a particular problem. For example, by the time a problem is reported and a team formed, interim action may have been taken already by the manufacturing personnel but the permanent solution may require subsequent team involvement.

The eight disciplines are:

(1) Use team approach
Establish a small group of people with the process/ product knowledge, allocated time, authority, and skill in the required technical disciplines to solve the problem and implement corrective actions. The group must have a designated champion.

(2) Describe the problem
Specify the internal/external customer problem by identifying in quantifiable terms the who, what, when, where, why, how, how many (5W2H) for the problem.

(3) Implement and verify interim (containment) actions
Define and implement containment actions to isolate the effect of problem from any internal/ external customer until corrective action is implemented. Verify the effectiveness of the containment action.

(4) Define and verify root causes
Identify all potential causes which could explain why the problem occurred. Isolate and verify the root cause by testing each potential cause against the problem description and test data. Identify alternative corrective actions to eliminate root cause.

(5) Verify corrective actions
Through pre-production test programmes quantitatively confirm that the selected corrective actions will resolve the problem for the customer, and will not cause undesirable side effects. Define contingency actions, if necessary, based on risk assessment.

(6) Implement permanent corrective actions
Define and implement the best permanent corrective actions. Choose ongoing controls to ensure the root cause is eliminated. Once in production, monitor the long term effects and implement contingency actions, if necessary.

(7) Prevent recurrence
Modify the management systems, operating systems, practices, and procedures to prevent recurrence of this and all similar problems.

(8) Congratulate your team
Recognize the collective efforts of the team.

These steps do not have to be followed in the order given. They can vary with each problem. For example, by the time a problem is reported and a team formed, the interim action may have been taken by the foreman or operator.

PROBLEM SOLVING PROCESS

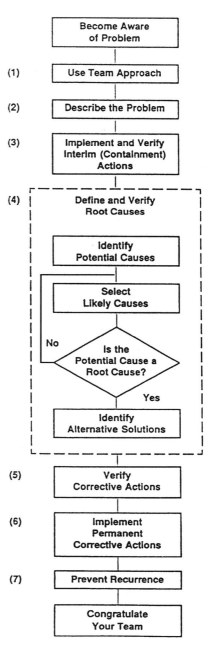

PROBLEM SOLVING DISCIPLINES — CONCERN ANALYSIS REPORT

Status Date:

Concern/RFR No.	CS No	Concern Title		Date Opened	Assigned To

(2) Describe Concern	Date Completed	Concern Code	Vehicle	Engine/Trans/Axle
			Build Date	Build Date
			(1) Team/Activity—Phone	

(3) Containment/ (6) Corrective Actions (Des Manut B&A Ser)	% Effect	Effective Date	
		Supply	B&A

PCR SREA TSL/TSB Number—

(4) Define Root Causes	Root Cause Code	Commit Date	Completion Date
		Transfer Code	% Contribution (each cause)

If additional analysis is required indicate completion dates.

(5) Verification of Containment/Corrective Actions

(7) Action to Prevent Recurrence

	Containment Action Date			Corrective Action Dates	
	Committed	Completion		Committed	Completion
Define			Define		
Verify			Verify		
Implement			Implement		

Reporting Engineer	Date Status/Closed		Concurrence Supervisor	Date

(8) CONGRATULATE YOUR TEAM

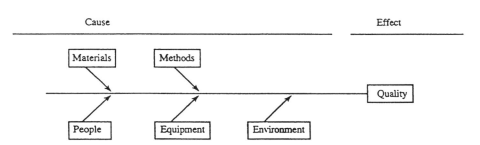

Figure A2.1   Cause and effect

A2.3   CAUSE AND EFFECT DIAGRAMS

The cause and effect diagram was developed to represent the relationship between some 'effect' and all possible 'causes' influencing it. This relationship is shown in Figure A2.1.

A2.3.1   Making cause and effect diagrams

The possible causes of dispersion in the quality characteristic (effect) are arranged in the cause and effect diagram in such a way that all relationships are clearly shown.

Step 1.   Decide the quality characteristic (e.g. wobble during machine rotation). This is something you may want to improve and control. In this case you may have found that most of the defectives were due to wobble during rotating. To eliminate this wobble, you must identify its causes.

Step 2.   Construct the diagram by boxing in the quality characteristic (e.g. wobble) on the right side. Draw an arrow extending from the left to the box. Then, write the main factors which may be causing the wobble directing a branch arrow to the main arrow. Group the main possible causes of dispersion into such items as materials, equipment, methods, people and environment. Each individual group will form a branch. See Figure A2.2.

Step 3.   Onto each of these branches, write in the detailed factors which may be regarded as the causes. And onto each of these, write in even more detailed causes. See Figure A2.3.

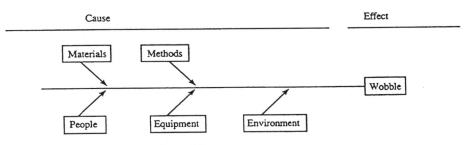

Figure A2.2   Cause and effect with 'wobble'

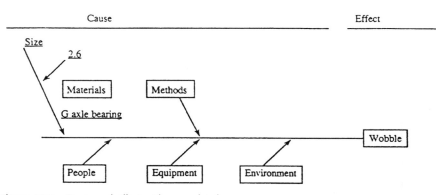

Figure A2.3 Cause and effect with more detail

If you pursue the following thought process, you will eventually identify all possible causes of the problem.

(1)   Why do production process defects occur?
Because of machine wobble (dispersion), therefore, machine wobble is a quality characteristic (effect).

(2)   Why does the machine wobble (dispersion) occur?
Because of the dispersion in the materials, 'Materials' is illustrated on the diagram as a branch.

(3)   Why does dispersion in the materials occur?
Because of the dispersion in the G axle bearing, the G axle bearing becomes a cause.

(4)   Why does the dispersion in the G axle bearing occur?
Because of the dispersion in the size of the G axle bearing, size becomes a cause.

(5)   Why does the dispersion in the size of the G axle bearing occur?
Because of the dispersion at the 2.6 mm point, the 2.6 mm point becomes a cause.

In this way you add to a cause and effect diagram until it clearly shows the causes of the dispersion.

Step 4.   Finally check to make certain that all factors that may be causing dispersion are included in the diagram. If they are, and the relationships of causes to effect are properly illustrated, then the diagram is complete.

Step 5.   From this well-defined diagram of possible causes, identify and select the most likely causes for further analysis. When examining each cause, search for things that have changed, and deviations from the norm or patterns. Seek to cure the causes and not the symptoms of the problem

A2.3.1 SUMMARY

Your aim is to get results. A cause and effect diagram is an aid to clearly show the relationship between the causes and effect of a problem. After the causes of the problem have been identified, corrective actions can be taken.

A2.4   POTENTIAL FAILURE MODE AND EFFECTS ANALYSIS

POTENTIAL FAILURE MODE
AND
EFFECTS ANALYSIS
(FMEA)

AN INSTRUCTION MANUAL
Revised September 1988

DESIGN FMEA

INTRODUCTION

A Design potential FMEA is an analytical technique utilized by Product Engineers as a means to assure that, to the extent possible, potential failure modes and their associated causes have been considered and addressed. End items, along with every related subassembly and detail part, should be evaluated. In its most rigorous form, an FMEA is a summary of the engineer's thoughts (including an analysis of items that could go wrong based on experience and past concerns) as a component or system is designed. This systematic approach parallels and formalizes the mental discipline that an engineer normally goes through in any design process.

The Design potential FMEA supports the design process in reducing the risk of failures by:

- Aiding in the objective evaluation of design requirements and design alternatives.

- Increasing the probability that potential failure modes and their effects on system operation have been considered in the design/development process.

- Providing additional information to aid in the planning of thorough and efficient design test and development programs.

- Developing a list of potential failure modes ranked according to their effect on the "customer," thus establishing a priority system for design improvements and development testing.

- Providing an open issue format for recommending and tracking risk reducing actions.

- Providing future reference to aid in analyzing field concerns, evaluating design changes, and developing advanced designs.

Customer Defined

The definition of "CUSTOMER" for a Design FMEA should normally be seen as the "END USER." However, the design engineer's customers are also the design engineers of the vehicle or higher level assemblies, and/or the manufacturing process engineers in activities such as Manufacturing, Assembly, and Service, who require a clearly defined, manufacturable and service-friendly design.

When fully implemented, the FMEA discipline requires a Design FMEA for all new parts, changed parts, and carryover parts in new applications. It is initiated by an engineer from the responsible design activity, which for a proprietary design (black/gray box) may be the supplier.

Team Effort

During the preparation of the Design potential FMEA, the responsible engineer is expected to seek input from such areas as Manufacturing, Quality, and Service, as well as from the Design area responsible for next assembly. In addition, for any black/gray box items, the responsible Ford Product Engineer should be consulted. The FMEA should be a catalyst to stimulate the interchange of ideas between the functions affected and thus promote a team approach.

The Design FMEA is a living document and should be initiated at or by design concept finalization, be continually updated as changes occur throughout the phases of product development, and be fundamentally completed along with the final drawings.

DESIGN FMEA

INTRODUCTION (Continued)

Team Effort (cont'd)

The Design FMEA addresses the design intent and assumes the design will be manufactured/assembled to this intent. Potential failure modes/causes which can occur during the manufacturing or assembly process should not be included in a Design FMEA, as their identification, effect and control are covered by the Process FMEA. However, potential manufacturing/assembly concerns known by the design engineer should be conveyed to the manufacturing/assembly source, using means such as team meetings.

The Design FMEA does not rely on process controls to overcome potential weaknesses in the design, but it does take the technical/physical limits of a manufacturing/assembly process into consideration, e.g.:

- necessary mold drafts
- limited surface finish
- assembling space/access for tooling
- limited hardenability of steels
- process capability

DEVELOPMENT OF A DESIGN FMEA

The design engineer has at his or her disposal a number of documents that will be of use in preparing the Design potential FMEA. The process begins by developing a listing of what the design is expected to do, and what it is expected not to do, i.e., the design intent. Customer wants and needs, as may be determined from sources such as Quality Function Deployment (QFD), Corporate Vehicle Requirements Manual (CVRM), known product requirements and/or manufacturing wants, should be incorporated. The better the definition of the wanted characteristics, the easier it is to identify potential failure modes for corrective action.

In order to facilitate documentation of the analysis of potential failures and their consequences, form No. 1695, shown in the Design FMEA Appendix, was developed for use in Ford Motor Company.

Application of the form is described below; points are numbered according to the numbers encircled on the form (as shown in Appendix).

1) Subsystem/Name

Enter the number and name of the subsystem.

2) Design Responsibility

Enter the name of the area responsible for the design of the component, assembly or system.

3) Other Areas Involved

Enter any areas/departments or organizations affected by or involved in the design or function of the component(s).

DESIGN FMEA

DEVELOPMENT OF A DESIGN FMEA (Continued)

4) Suppliers and Plants Affected

List any supplier(s) or manufacturing plants involved in the design or manufacture of components or assemblies being analyzed.

5) Model Years/ Vehicle(s)

Enter the model year and all car lines that will utilize the design being analyzed.

6) Scheduled Engineering Release Date

Indicate the date the component or assembly is scheduled to be released.

7) Prepared By

Indicate the name, telephone number, address and company of the engineer preparing the FMEA.

8) FMEA Date

Show the date the original FMEA was compiled, and then show the latest FMEA revision date.

9) Part Name and Number/Function

Enter the name and number of the part or assembly being analyzed. Use suffixes, change letters and/or Concern Report/Change Request (CR/CR) numbers, as appropriate. Prior to initial release, experimental part numbers should be used. In the space below the part name and number, indicate as concisely as possible the function of the part or assembly being analyzed. Where the assembly has numerous functions with different potential modes of failure, it may be desirable to list the functions separately.

10) Potential Failure Mode

Potential Failure Mode is defined as the manner in which a part or assembly could potentially fail to meet the design intent, performance requirements, and/or customer expectations. The potential failure mode may also be the cause of a potential failure mode in a higher level assembly, or be the effect of one in a lower level part.

List each potential failure mode for the particular part and part function. The assumption is made that the failure could occur, but will not necessarily occur. A recommended starting point is a review of past FMEAs, test reports, quality, warranty, durability and reliability concerns, things-gone-wrong, concern reports, and group "brainstorming" on similar components.

Potential failure modes that would only occur under certain operating conditions (i.e., hot, cold, wet, dry, dusty, etc.) and under certain usage conditions (i.e., above average mileage, rough terrain, only city driving, etc.) shall be considered. Typical failure modes could be:

Cracked	Sticking
Deformed	Short Circuited (electrical)
Worn	Open Circuited (electrical)
Corroded	Oxidized
Loosened	Vibrating
Leaking	Fractured

Note: Potential failure modes should be described in "physical" or technical terms, not as a symptom noticeable by the customer.

DESIGN FMEA

DEVELOPMENT OF A DESIGN FMEA (Continued)

11) Potential Effect(s) of Failure

Potential Effects of Failure are defined as the effects of the failure mode on the customer.

Describe the effects of the failure in terms of what the customer might notice or experience. These should always be stated in terms of vehicle or system performance. Typical failure effects could be:

Noise	Rough
Erratic Operation	Excessive Effort Required
Inoperative	Unpleasant Odor
Unstable	Operation Impaired
Intermittent Operation	Draft
Vehicle Control Impaired	Poor Appearance

If the effect of failure could potentially affect safe vehicle operation, or involves potential noncompliance with government regulations, it must be so indicated, e.g., "may not comply with FMVSS #XXX."

12) Severity

Severity is an assessment of the seriousness of the effect (listed in the previous column) of the potential failure mode to the next assembly, the vehicle, or the customer. Severity applies to the effect and to the effect only. A reduction in Severity Ranking index can be effected only through a design change. Severity should be estimated on a "1 to 10" scale.

Evaluation Criteria:

Severity of Effect	Ranking
Minor: Unreasonable to expect that the minor nature of this failure would cause any real effect on the vehicle or system performance. Customer will probably not even notice the failure.	1
Low: Low severity ranking due to nature of failure causing only a slight customer annoyance. Customer will probably only notice a slight deterioration of the system or vehicle performance.	2 3
Moderate: Moderate ranking because failure causes some customer dissatisfaction. Customer is made uncomfortable or is annoyed by the failure (e.g., engine misfire, compressor rumble, sunroof leak). Customer will notice some subsystem or vehicle performance deterioration.	4 5 6
High: High degree of customer dissatisfaction due to the nature of the failure such as an inoperable vehicle (e.g., engine fails to start) or an inoperable convenience subsystem (e.g., air conditioning system, power sunroof). Does not involve vehicle safety or noncompliance to government regulations.	7 8
Very High: Very high severity ranking when a potential failure mode affects safe vehicle operation and/or involves noncompliance with government regulations.	9 10

13) Critical Characteristics (∇)

Critical Characteristics should be identified by entering an inverted delta (∇) in this column. Determine if the inverted delta should be assigned by following the flow chart in Engineering Practice 5 (shown in Reference section of this manual) whenever the severity ranking is 9 or 10 and the occurrence (Step 15) and detection (Step 17) are both greater than 1.

DESIGN FMEA

DEVELOPMENT OF A DESIGN FMEA (Continued)

14) Potential Cause(s) of Failure

Potential Cause of Failure is defined as an indication of a design weakness, the consequence of which is the failure mode.

List, to the extent possible, every conceivable failure cause assignable to each failure mode. The causes should be listed as concisely and completely as possible so that remedial efforts can be aimed at pertinent causes. Typical failure causes could be:

Incorrect Material Specified	Inappropriate Material Specified
Incorrect Assembling Instruction	Inadequate Design Life Assumption
Incorrect Torque Specified	Over-stressing
Insufficient Lubrication Capability	Overload
Permissible Material Impurity Level	Inadequate Maintenance
Poor Mold Form	Instructions
Incorrect Material Thickness	Imbalance
Specified	Poor Environment Protection

15) Occurrence

Occurrence is the likelihood that a specific cause (listed in the previous column) will result in the failure mode. The occurrence ranking number has a meaning rather than a value. Removing or controlling one or more of the causes of the failure mode through a design change is the only way a reduction in the occurrence ranking can be effected.

Estimate the likelihood of the occurrence of potential failure modes on a "1 to 10" scale. In determining this estimate, questions such as the following should be considered:
- How adequate is the proposed Design Verification (DV) program?
- Is part carryover or similar to previous level part or assembly?
- How significant are changes from previous level part or assembly?
- Is part radically different from previous level part?
- Is part completely new?
- What are the environmental changes?
- What is the service history/field experience with similar parts or assemblies?

The following occurrence ranking system should be used to ensure consistency. The "Design Life Possible Failure Rates" are based on the number of failures which are anticipated during the design life of the part or assembly.

Evaluation Criteria:

Probability of Failure	Ranking	Design Life Possible Failure Rates
Remote: Failure is unlikely.	1	<1 in 10^6
Low: Relatively few failures.	2	1 in 20000
	3	1 in 4000
Moderate: Occasional failures.	4	1 in 1000
	5	1 in 400
	6	1 in 80
High: Repeated failures.	7	1 in 40
	8	1 in 20
Very High: Failure is almost inevitable.	9	1 in 8
	10	1 in 2

DESIGN FMEA

DEVELOPMENT OF A DESIGN FMEA (Continued)

16) Design Verification (DV)

List all current DVs which are intended to prevent the design cause(s) of potential failure from occurring or are intended to detect the design cause(s) of the potential failure or the resultant failure mode.

Current DVs (e.g., road testing, design reviews, mathematical studies rig/lab testing, feasibility reviews, prototype tests, fleet testing) are those that have been or are being used with the same or similar designs. The initial occurrence and detection rankings will be based on these DV controls, considering the representatives of the prototypes and models being used. The DV controls listed should be directly related to the prevention or detection of specific causes of failure.

If any other specific DVs, such as those for a radically new design, are necessary, they should be listed in the Recommended Action column.

17) Detection

Detection is an assessment of the ability of the proposed design program (listed in the previous column) to identify a potential design weakness before the part or assembly is released for production. In order to achieve a lower ranking, generally the planned verification program has to be improved.

Evaluation Criteria:

Likelihood of Detection by D V Program	Ranking
Very High: D V Program will almost certainly detect a potential design weakness	1
	2
High: D V Program has a good chance of detecting a potential design weakness	3
	4
Moderate: D V Program may detect a potential design weakness	5
	6
Low: D V Program not likely to detect a potential design weakness	7
	8
Very Low: D V Program probably will not detect a potential design weakness	9
Absolute Certainty of Non-Detection: D V Program will/can not detect a potential design weakness, or there is no D V Program	10

18) Risk Priority Number (RPN)

The Risk Priority Number is the product of the occurrence, severity and detection rankings. This value should be used to rank order the concerns in the design (e.g., in Pareto fashion). In themselves, RPNs have no other value or meaning.

DESIGN FMEA

DEVELOPMENT OF A DESIGN FMEA (Continued)

19) Recommended Action(s)

When the failure modes have been rank ordered by RPN, corrective action should be first directed at the highest ranked concerns and critical items. The intent of any recommended action is to reduce any one or all of the occurrence, severity and/or detection rankings. An increase in design verification actions will result in a reduction in the detection ranking only. A reduction in the occurrence ranking can only be effected by removing or controlling one or more of the causes of the failure mode through a design revision. Only a design revision can bring about a reduction in the severity ranking. Actions such as the following could be considered.

- Design of Experiments (particularly when multiple or interactive causes are present)
- Revised Test Plan
- Revised Design
- Revised Material Specification

If no actions are recommended for a specific cause, then this should be indicated.

20) Area/Engineer Responsible (for the Recommended Action)

Enter the area and engineer responsible for the recommended action as well as the target completion date.

21) Actions Taken:

After an action has been completed, enter a brief description of the actual action and effective or completion date.

22) Resulting RPN:

After the corrective action has been identified, estimate and record the resulting occurrence, severity, and detection rankings. Calculate and record the resulting RPN. If no actions are taken, leave the "Resulting RPN" and related ranking columns blank.

All Resulting RPN(s) should be reviewed and if further action is considered necessary repeat Steps 19 through 22.

Follow-Up: The design engineer is responsible for assuring that all actions recommended have been implemented or adequately addressed. The FMEA is a living document and should always reflect the latest design level, as well as the latest relevant actions, including those occurring post Job #1.

The design engineer has several means of assuring that concerns are identified and that recommended actions are implemented. They include the following:

- Engineering drawings and specifications: These show design changes, critical characteristics and supplier and/or manufacturing test requirements.
- Sign-off responsibility for Manufacturing Installation Drawings: Installation Drawings specify such items as critical torques, assembly sequences and part positioning. Verify that assembly concerns identified by the Design FMEA are addressed by the installation drawings.
- Review of Process FMEAs and Manufacturing Control Plans.

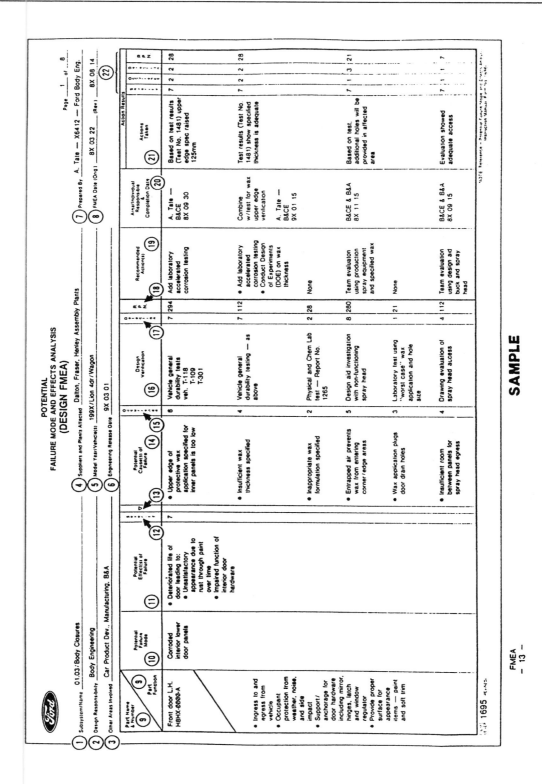

POTENTIAL
FAILURE MODE AND EFFECTS ANALYSIS
(DESIGN FMEA)

SAMPLE

A2.5   BS 5750

The following three paragraphs are the British Standards Institute's description of BS 5750. Although superseded in 1994 by a slightly modified standard (BS/EN/ISO 9000), BS 5750 is the Standard to which some 30 000 UK firms were assessed prior to the change. Until they are re-assessed, companies describing themselves as 'BS 5750/ISO 9000 approved' conform to the Standard described here.

What is BS 5750?

The BS 5750 series are the national standards which promulgate, for use by UK suppliers and purchasers, the ISO 9000 series international standards and the EN 29000 series European standards for quality systems respectively. They tell suppliers and manufacturers what is required of a quality-oriented system. They do not set out extra special requirements which only a very few firms can — or need — comply with, but are practical standards for quality systems which can be used by all UK industry.

The principles of BS5750 are applicable whether you employ 10 people or 10 000. They identify the basic disciplines and specify the procedures and criteria to ensure that products or services meet the customers' requirements.

The benefits of applying BS 5750 are real; it will save you money — because your procedures will be more soundly based and more efficient; it will ensure satisfied customers — because you will have built in quality at every stage; it will reduce waste and time-consuming re-working of designs and procedures.

How do we define quality?

Quality has a number of different meanings but BS 5750 looks at it in the fitness for purpose and safe in use sense; is the service provided or product designed and constructed to satisfy the customer's needs?

What are the constituent parts of BS 5750/ISO 9000/EN 29000?

- BS 5750:Part 0: Section 0.1/ISO 9000/EN 29000 is a guide to the selection and use of the appropriate part of the BS 5750/ISO 9000/EN 29000 series.
- BS 5750:Part 0: Section 0.2/ISO 9004/EN 29000 is a guide to overall quality management and the quality system elements within the BS 5750/ISO 9000/EN 29000 series.
- BS 5750:Part 1/ISO 9001/EN 29001 (the part dealt with in this booklet) relates to quality specifications for design/development, production, installation and servicing when the requirements of goods or services are specified by the customer in terms of how they must perform and which are then provided by the supplier.
- BS 5750:Part 2/ISO 9002/EN 29002 sets out requirements where a firm is manufacturing goods or offering a service to a published specification or to the customer's specification.
- BS 5750:Part 3/ISO 9003/EN 29003 specifies the quality system to be used in final inspection and test procedures.

The table shows the 20 headings under which BS 5750 assessments were made, with an indication of the coverage of Part 1, Part 2 and Part 3 of the Standard. When considering potential suppliers' 'quality' qualifications it is important to discern the level to which each company was assessed.

Table A2.1   Cross-reference list of quality system elements. (This annex is given for information purposes and does not form an integral part of the standard.)

Clause (or sub-clause) No. in BS 5750:Pt 0, 0.2/ISO 9004	Title	BS 5750:Pt1/ ISO 9001	BS 5750:Pt2/ ISO 9002	BS 5750:Pt 3/ ISO 9003
4	Management responsibility	4.1 ●	4.1 ◐	4.1 ○
5	Quality system principles	4.2 ●	4.2 ●	4.2 ◐
5.4	Auditing the quality system (internal)	4.17 ●	4.16 ◐	—
6	Economics — Quality-related cost considerations	—	—	—
7	Quality in marketing (Contract review)	4.3 ●	4.3 ●	—
8	Quality in specification and design (Design control)	4.4 ●	—	—
9	Quality in procurement (Purchasing)	4.6 ●	4.5 ●	—
10	Quality in production (Process control)	4.9 ●	4.8 ●	—
11	Control of production	4.9 ●	4.8 ●	—
11.2	Material control and traceability (Product identification and traceability)	4.8 ●	4.7 ●	4.4 ◐
11.7	Control of verification status (Inspection and test status)	4.12 ●	4.11 ●	4.7 ◐
12	Product verification (Inspection and testing)	4.10 ●	4.9 ●	4.5 ◐
13	Control of measuring and test equipment (Inspection, measuring and test equipment)	4.11 ●	4.10 ●	4.6 ◐
14	Nonconformity (Control of non-conforming product)	4.13 ●	4.12 ●	4.8 ◐
15	Corrective action	4.14 ●	4.13 ●	—
16	Handling and post-production functions (Handling, storage, packaging and delivery)	4.15 ●	4.14 ●	4.9 ◐
16.2	After-sales servicing	4.19 ●	—	—
17	Quality documentation and records (Document control)	4.5 ●	4.4 ●	4.3 ◐
17.3	Quality records	4.16 ●	4.15 ●	4.10 ◐
18	Personnel (Training)	4.18 ●	4.17 ◐	4.11 ○
19	Product safety and liability	—	—	—
20	Use of statistical methods (Statistical techniques)	4.20 ●	4.18 ●	4.12 ◐
—	Purchaser supplied product	4.7 ●	4.6 ●	—

Key:
● Full requirement
◐ Less stringent than BS 5750: Part 1/ISO 9001
○ Less stringent than BS 5750: Part 2/ISO 9002
— Element not present
Notes
1. The clause (or sub-clause) titles quoted in the table above have been taken from BS 5750: Pt 0: Section 0.2/ISO 9004; the titles given in parentheses have been taken from the corresponding clauses and sub-clauses in BS 5750: Pt 1/ISO 9001, BS 5750: Pt 2/ISO 9002 and BS 5750: Pt 3/ISO 9003.
2. Attention is drawn to the fact that the quality system element requirements in BS 5750: Pt 1/ISO 9001, BS 5750: Pt 2/ISO 9002 and BS 5750: Pt 3/ISO 9003 are in many cases, but not in every case, identical.

Appendix 3

Case study:
Developing a network

A3.1 INTRODUCTION

The objective of this case study is to illustrate the manner in which a *precedence list* can be developed for the purposes of producing a first draft network and carrying out *critical path analysis*. The analysis itself is not carried out. However, for the precedence list which is eventually developed there is only one possible solution, and the duration of the project for that solution and some comments on the solution are given at the end of the case study for those who wish to complete the whole exercise. The methods of critical path analysis are described in Chapter 17.

A3.2 GENERAL DATA

An irrigation scheme is to be built. It will consist of a pump house on a river and 17 km of 500 mm diameter steel pipeline to which are connected, at 4 km intervals, 3 km lengths of 100 mm diameter PVC pipeline, which feed surface networks of 25 mm diameter PVC pipes. The 500 mm and 100 mm pipeline are placed in trenches which are then backfilled. The 25 mm surface pipes are connected by means of standpipes to the 100 mm pipes.

At one location the 500 mm pipeline crosses a valley. This is achieved by means of a 1 km long bridge which will be built as part of the project. The bridge will provide a single lane vehicle crossing for local traffic.

Figure A3.1 shows a schematic diagram of the project, Figure A3.2 provides details of the pump house and Figure A3.3 shows details of the bridge.

A3.3 ACTIVITIES LISTS

The main activities are listed in Tables A3.1 to A3.3 below. Activities are not necessarily listed in chronological order.

A3.4 ACTIVITIES DESCRIPTIONS

Some of the activities may require a little explanation. This is provided as briefly as possible.

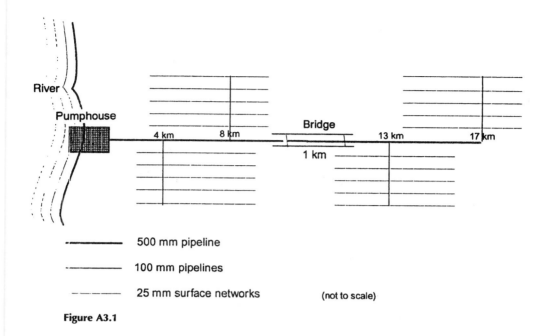

Figure A3.1

Pump house

The pumps are to be installed below river surface level. This is achieved by constructing in the river a watertight caisson from which the water is pumped. A concrete substructure chamber is then built in which the pumps are installed. When the caisson is dismantled the pump chamber can be flooded and the system tested. The pumps have to be installed before the roof is constructed as they are lifted into position using a crane.

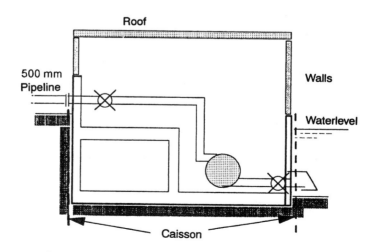

Figure A3.2   Pump house

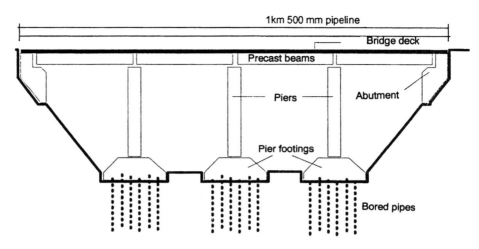

Figure A3.3   Bridge

Table A3.1   Pump house activities

Pump house	Duration (days)
PH1 Order pumps and deliver	85
PH2 Order pipework and valves and deliver	50
PH3 Construct caisson	10
PH4 Excavate within caisson	10
PH5 Concrete substructure	15
PH6 Install pumps, pipework and valves	20
PH7 Dismantle caisson	5
PH8 Build walls	10
PH9 Build roof	10
PH10 Test and commission	10

Table A3.2   Bridge activities

Bridge	Duration (days)
B1 Order precast beams and deliver	50
B2 Bore one set of piles	20
B3 Construct one footing	10
B4 Construct one pier	20
B5 Construct one abutment	15
B6 Place one span of precast beams	5
B7 Lay bridge deck	7

Bridge

The construction of each footing and pier is an independent operation. A span of precast beams cannot be placed until the piers and abutments for supporting that span are complete. The bridge deck cannot be laid until all precast beams have been placed.

Table A3.3 Pipeline activities

Pipelines	Duration (days)	Work rate (km/day)
500 mm		
P51 Order 17 km of pipes and fittings and deliver	50	
P52 Clear 16 km route for pipeline		1
P53 Dig trench		0.5
P54 Place pipe in trench and join		0.5
P55 Backfill around pipe, and complete to surface		1
P56 Place 1 km length across bridge	2	
100 mm		
P11 Order 12 km of pipes and fittings and deliver	40	
P12 Clear route for 3 km pipeline ($\times 4$)		1
P13 Dig trench for 3 km pipeline ($\times 4$)		0.5
P14 Place pipe in trench and join (includes all standpipes for connecting to 25 mm pipes) ($\times 4$)		0.25
P15 Backfill around pipe, and complete to surface ($\times 4$)		1
P16 Join 100 mm pipe to 500 mm pipe (each)	3	
25 mm		
PN1 Order all pipes and fittings, and deliver	30	
PN2 Clear area for each of the four surface networks ($\times 4$)	20	
PN3 Install each surface network ($\times 4$)	60	
PC1 Commission and hand over all pipelines	10	

Pipelines

Work on the different pipelines and on the surface networks are independent operations which can be carried out in parallel or series. At each connection between the 500 mm and 100 mm pipes a short length of trench will be left open until the pipes have been joined. The activity 'Join 100 mm pipe to 500 mm pipe' includes backfilling around the completed connection. For the 500 mm and 100 mm pipe lines, *backfilling* will follow *placing* (and joining) the pipes at a practical distance, and *placing* will follow *trenching* in a similar fashion.

A3.5 DEVELOPING THE PRECEDENCE LIST

The task is to determine the linkages between activities. Two questions will need to be asked of each activity in turn, they are:

1. Which activities must be completed/started to allow the given activity to proceed and finish?
2. Should there be any minimum duration prescribed for the linkage?

The linkages between activities are determined by:

- logic
- resources
- method

Logic is the most important determinant of precedence. A pier cannot be constructed until its foundation is complete. That is logic. There is no logical linkage between one pier and another. A decision that one pier should precede another can only be justified on the grounds of *resources*, for example, because only one team of workers and/or equipment is available for pier construction, or *method*, because, for example, the equipment used for the construction of one pier would interfere with the equipment and operations on the other pier.

It should be borne in mind that the objective of the precedence list is to produce a *first draft network*. The fewer conditions that are imposed in the form of dependencies (linkages) between activities the greater the freedom for the contractor in planning the operations. Links which are determined on the basis 'it would be a good idea to complete *X* before *Y*' should be avoided because the consequence of this is that, logically, *Y* cannot proceed until *X* is complete. What would happen if *X* was delayed indefinitely because of supply problems? Obviously, in practice, the contractor would ignore the network linkage and precede with *Y*, but a properly constructed network should work just as well when activities are delayed as when work proceeds according to programme. Indeed, an essential purpose of a network is to provide information on new critical paths and on which activities might need to be accelerated when activities are held up, so each link should be an expression of necessary dependency not of arbitrary choice. This should lead to a greater degree of float on a greater number of activities, allowing the contractor more options when producing the programme bar chart. In developing the precedence list, question 1 and question 2 will be asked of each activity in turn, in the order presented. Where the answer to question 1 is that no activity needs be completed/started to allow the activity to proceed, an activity 'START', of zero duration, will be entered.

The analyses are presented in Tables A3.4 to A3.7.

Pump house

Table A3.4

Activity	Answer to question 1	Answer to question 2
PH1 Order pumps etc.	START	nil
PH2 Order pipework etc.	START	nil
PH3 Construct caisson	START	nil
PH4 Excavation in caisson	PH3 — logic	nil
PH5 Concrete substructure	PH4 — logic	nil
PH6 Install pumps etc.	PH1 and PH2 — logic	nil
	PH5 — logic	7 days to cure concrete
PH7 Dismantle caisson	PH5 and PH6 — method	nil
PH8 Build walls	PH5 — logic	nil
PH9 Build roof	PH8 — logic	nil
	PH6 — method	nil
PH10 Test etc.	PH6 — logic	nil
	PH9–optional	nil

Bridge

Before a precedence list can be developed for the bridge certain decisions have to be made. Should it be assumed that there are sufficient resources for working on the piers concurrently or not? In practice this would be determined by a number of factors including the anticipated size of the labour force, the types of equipment to be used, the materials lead times and delivery rates and the ground conditions. However, maintaining the view that the fewer dependencies that are imposed the better, it is assumed for the purpose of this case study that sufficient resources could be provided to allow independent and parallel operations at any of the pier locations, except for boring the piles where it is assumed that a single subcontractor will carry out this work using a single team which will move across the site from pier 1 to pier 2 to pier 3. It may be the case, once the whole network has been developed that there will be sufficient float on the independent pier operations to allow them to be constructed in series. Instead of predetermining the position, this approach allows network analysis to provide a solution. For the precast beams it is assumed that sequential working will take place from span to span.

In Table A3.5, B21 indicates activity B2 at pier 1, B32 indicates activity B3 at pier 2, and so on.

Table A3.5

Activity	Answer to question 1	Answer to question 2
Bridge		
B1 Order beams etc.	START	nil
B21 Bore piles 1	START	nil
B22 Bore piles 2	B21 — resources	nil
B23 Bore piles 3	B22 — resources	nil
B31 Construct footing 1	B21 — logic	nil
B32 Construct footing 2	B22 — logic	nil
B33 Construct footing 3	B23 — logic	nil
B41 Construct pier 1	B31 — logic	nil
B42 Construct pier 2	B32 — logic	nil
B43 Construct pier 3	B33 — logic	nil
B51 Abutment 1	START	nil
B52 Abutment 2	START	nil
B61 Precast span 1	B1, B51 and B41 — logic	nil
B62 Precast span 2	B61 — method	nil
	B41 and B42 — logic	nil
B63 Precast span 3	B62 — method	nil
	B42 and B43 — logic	nil
B64 Precast span 4	B63 — method	nil
	B43 and B52 — logic	nil
B7 Bridge deck	B61, B62, B63, B64 — method	nil

Pipelines

Similarly, decisions need to be made with respect to the methods of constructing the pipelines. The question of resources must be considered.

For the construction of the 16 km of 500 mm pipeline there are many alternatives:

- starting from one end and proceeding to the other,
- working on the sections either side of the bridge concurrently,
- having three or more operational sections concurrently.

For the construction of the four 3 km lengths of 100 mm pipeline the alternatives could be:

- using one team to proceed from one 3 km length to another,
- working concurrently on all four lengths,
- using two teams, each to work on two 3 km lengths.

For the four 25 mm surface networks similar alternatives to those above present themselves. For the purposes of this case study the following assumptions have been made.

500 mm pipeline — one team
100 mm pipeline — one team
25 mm networks — four teams could be available if necessary

In Table A3.7, PN21 indicates activity PN2 at network 1, PN32 indicates activity PN3 at network 2, and so on.

A3.6   FINALIZING THE PRECEDENCE LISTS

One further check must be made. Which activities in the left-hand columns of Tables A3.4 to A3.7 do not appear in the middle column? All activities except those which are the final tasks of the project must appear at least once as a preceding activity, that is, in the middle column. The following activities have not been found in the middle column:

PH7 Dismantle caisson
PH10 Test and commission pumps
PC1 Commission and handover pipelines

It is arguable that PH7 should have preceded PH10, but it has been left as shown. Thus the final activity on the network FINISH, is preceded by PH7, PH10, PC1.

The finalized precedence list is given in Table A3.8. All links are F-S (0) unless otherwise shown.

Network

Analysis of the network shows a project duration of 125 days. The critical path passes through activities PH1 — PH6 — PH9 — PH10. What makes the pump house work critical is the long lead time required for ordering and delivering the pumps (PH1).

Operations on the bridge piers were set up to be independent of one another. In fact an examination of the network shows that construction of the bridge footings B31 to B33 and of the bridge piers B41 to B43 could be done sequentially without putting them on the critical path. The project manager is likely to select this option.

Work on the surface networks was also assumed to be a series of independent operations. Clearing can take place in the period from day 0 to day 105; the network shows that this could be done sequentially for the first three areas (activities PN21 to PN23) but that the final area (activity PN24) must not start later than day 50 which would be halfway through activity PN23, so, unless the project manager decides that the project should take 135 days instead of 125 days, there will have to be some overlap between PN23 and PN24 and extra resources will be needed.

Installation of the surface pipe is a different matter. The four surface networks must be installed in the period from day 30 until day 115, each takes 60 days; these activities cannot be programmed sequentially and all four surface networks will be worked at the same time although their start dates could be staggered by seven or eight days.

Table A3.6

Activity	Answer to question 1	Answer to question 2
P51 Order 500 mm	START	nil
P52 Clear 500 mm	START	nil
P53 Dig 500 mm	P52 — logic	S-S (1 day) this allows P52 a 1 km start F-F (2 days) this keeps P53 1 km behind P52
P54 Place 500 mm	P51 — logic P53 — logic	nil S-S (2 days) this allows P53 a 1 km start F-F (2 days) this keeps P54 1 km behind P53
P55 Backfill 500 mm	P54 — logic	S-S (2 days) this allows P54 a 1 km start F-F (1 day) this keeps P55 1 km behind P54
P56 500 mm on bridge	B7 — logic P54 — method	7 days — to cure concrete S-S (16 days) assumes 8 km of pipeline have been placed
P11 Order 100 mm	START	nil
P12 Clear 100 mm	START	nil
P13 Dig 100 mm	P12 — logic	S-S (1 day) this allows P12 a 1 km start F-F (2 days) this keeps P13 1 km behind P12
P14 Place 100 mm	P11 — logic P13 — logic	nil S-S (2 days) this allows P13 a 1 km start F-F (4 days) this keeps P14 1 km behind P13
P15 Backfill 100 mm	P14 — logic	S-S (4 days) this allows P14 a 1 km start F-F (1 day) this keeps P15 1 km behind P14
P16 Join 100 mm to 500 mm	P14 and P54 — method (assumes that a separate team does this work)	nil

Table A3.7

Activity	Answer to question 1	Answer to question 2
PN1 Order 25 mm	START	nil
PN21 Clear 25 mm	START	nil
PN22 Clear 25 mm	START	nil
PN23 Clear 25 mm	START	nil
PN24 Clear 25 mm	START	nil
PN31 Place 25 mm	PN1 PN21	nil (and for P32, P33, P34) for PN3 following PN2 S-S (5
PN32 Place 25 mm	PN1 PN22	days) and F-F (10 days), this allows PN3 to start after one
PN33 Place 25 mm	PN1 PN23	quarter of PN2 has been completed and keeps PN3
PN34 Place 25 mm	PN1 PN24	behind PN2 by one quarter of the area.
PC1	PN31 to PN34 P15, P16 P55, P56	nil nil nil

Table A3.8

Activity	duration days	Precursor Activity	Link type and duration
PH1	85	START	
PH2	50	START	
PH3	10	START	
PH4	10	PH3	
PH5	15	PH4	
PH6	20	PH1, PH2,	
		PH5	F-S (7)
PH7	5	PH5, PH6	
PH8	10	PH5	
PH9	10	PH8, PH6	
PH10	10	PH6, PH9	
B1	50	START	
B21	20	START	
B22	20	B21	
B23	20	B22	
B31	10	B21	
B32	10	B22	
B33	10	B23	
B41	20	B31	
B42	20	B32	
B43	20	B33	
B51	15	START	
B52	15	START	
B61	5	B1, B51, B41	
B62	5	B61, B41, B42	
B63	5	B62, B42, B43	
B64	5	B63, B43, B52	
B7	7	B61, B62, B63, B64	
P51	50	START	
P52	16	START	
P53	32	P52	S-S(1), F-F(2)
P54	32	P51	
		P53	S-S(2), F-F(2)
P55	16	P54	S-S(2), F-F(1)
P56	2	B7	
		P54	S-S(16)
P11	40	START	
P12	12	START	
P13	24	P12	S-S(1), F-F(2)
P14	48	P11	
		P13	S-S(2), F-F(4)
P15	12	P14	S-S(4), F-F(1)
P16	12	P14, P54	
PN1	30	START	
PN21	20	START	
PN22	20	START	
PN23	20	START	
PN24	20	START	
PN31	60	PN1	
		PN21	S-S(5), F-F(10)
PN32	60	PN1	
		PN22	S-S(5), F-F(10)
PN33	60	PN1	
		PN23	S-S(5), F-F(10)
PN34	60	PN1	
		PN24	S-S(5), F-F(10)
PC1	10	PN31, PN32, PN33,	
		PN34, P15, P16, P55, P56	
FINISH		PH7, PH10, PC1	

Appendix 4
The New Engineering Contract

A4.1 INTRODUCTION

The New Engineering Contract (NEC) has been drafted for use in construction projects where any or all of the disciplines of civil, mechanical and electrical engineering play a part. This new standard form is written clearly and simply, provides flexibility, and stimulates good management. The second edition, now known as the *Engineering and Construction Contract*, provides for minor revisions only [1].

Ordinary language and short sentences are used so that laymen and engineers can readily understand it, and for ease of translation into other languages. At the time of publication of this book none of the terms of the NEC has been tested in the courts, so its degree of success in respect of clarity and simplicity remains in question. Simple words, which engineers and lay people take for granted, may not have been 'judiciously defined' and, therefore, remain open to interpretation by the courts.

The NEC can be used for any engineering construction/installation project whether the Contractor has full responsibility, some responsibility, or no responsibility for design. The six options available allow the Employer (the purchaser of the facility) to select between lump sum, measurement, cost reimbursement and management contracts.

The roles and responsibilities of the parties are closely defined, the work to be done is set out under Works Information, and a Schedule of Cost Components identifies the recognized components of any cost so that, when changes occur, the cost (and time) impact of these changes can be easily established. The intention is that where a problem arises which could lead to delay or extra costs the Contractor and Employer act together to resolve the problem rather than adopting adversarial roles.

As noted in section 19.1 of Chapter 19, *Latham* commends the use of the NEC. Whether this strong endorsement will have much effect remains to be seen.

A4.2 THE NEC

The NEC consists of ten booklets which are outlined below.

The six booklets A to F are separate contracts, entire in themselves, needing no cross referencing with other documents. Each of these contains the nine core clauses common to all options, and each has its own main option clauses plus additional secondary option clauses to be used at the Employer's discretion.

The contract options are:

Option A: priced contract with activity schedule

Option B: priced contract with bill of quantities
Option C: target contract with activity schedule
Option D: target contract with bill of quantities
Option E: cost reimbursable contract
Option F: management contract

The black booklet, the *new engineering contract*, contains options A to F but presented in a different fashion. The nine core clauses followed by the main option clauses for each of A to F; the secondary option clauses G to U follow and where they should be used identified.

The three remaining booklets are:

Guidance Notes
New Engineering Subcontract
Flow Charts

The purpose of the first two of these should be self explanatory. The flow charts are diagrammatic representations of the relationships and responsibilities under the different options and are intended to assist Employer, Project Manager and Contractor when using a given option for the first time.

The NEC does not include a standard form of tender. The assumption is made that Employers will have their own.

In this appendix the major differences between the NEC and the standard contracts are identified and the purpose of each of the six options explained.

A4.2.1 Core provisions

Each booklet begins with contract data providing such information as the starting date and completion date.

The structure of the core clauses, holds no surprises:

Section 1 General
Section 2 The Contractor's responsibilities
Section 3 Time
Section 4 Quality
Section 5 Payment
Section 6 Compensation events
Section 7 Property
Section 8 Risks and insurance
Section 9 Disputes and termination

Distinctive features of the NEC are:

the provision of Works Information
the roles of Project Manager, Supervisor and Adjudicator
the provision for Compensation Events
the Schedule of Cost Components

Section 1 requires the Contractor to do the work described in the Works Information. This will include schedules of work to be designed by the Contractor, performance specifications, procedures for submitting designs and gaining consents, schedules of key dates and sequences of work, testing procedures, requirements for delivery and storage and so on.

The Project Manager manages the project on behalf of the Employer. The NEC assumes that he has the Employer's authority to make decisions and act as required by the Contract. Only the Project Manager has authority to change the Works Information.

The Supervisor's main function is quality management, to ensure that all work complies with the Works Information. He will eventually be responsible for certifying that the Works have been completed satisfactorily.

All disputes between the Project Manager and the Contractor should be resolved by an Adjudicator. Normally the Adjudicator will be named in the tender documents. This is a joint appointment by the Employer and Contractor; his fees are shared equally by the two parties irrespective of the decision. A dispute can only be referred to arbitration after going through the adjudication process; this should only happen in the most intractable cases.

Compensation Events are events which can lead either to extra payment or delay; where these arise the Contractor prepares proposals and quotations on how to proceed, and the Project Manager decides how to proceed on the basis of these quotations. Variations orders are effected by changing the Works Information. A variation will be a Compensation Event. The Contractor's quotation must be based upon his forecast of the impact which the change will have upon the actual cost of carrying out the work. The quotation must use the Schedule of Cost Components as its starting point.

A4.2.2 Options A to F

Options A and C use *activity schedules*. An activity schedule has some similarity to a bill of quantities, but the effect is a lump sum contract. The tenderer provides and prices a list of all the activities which he believes necessary to complete the work described in the Works Information. The prices are lump sums not unit rates as in a bill of quantities. As the work proceeds, payments become due upon completion of an activity.

Option A is a conventional contract, of a type commonly used in the USA, although unusual for UK construction contracts. It is not dissimilar to MF/1. Option C is a target contract and will be used where the potential for change as the work proceeds is considerable. The Contractor tenders a price which is a summation of lump sum prices (for the activities listed in the activity schedule) plus a fee for profit and overhead. The Contractor is paid actual costs plus fee (this is called the price of work done to date (PWDD)). Quotations will be made (based on actual costs) by the Contractor for Compensation Events, and the target price adjusted. At the end of the contract, the Contractor is paid his share of the difference between the final total of the target price and the final PWDD. If the PWDD is greater than the price the Contractor pays his share of the difference.

Options B and D are measurement contracts. Option B is a traditional measurement contract using a bill of quantities. Option D is a target contract similar to Option C but using a bill of quantities instead of an activity schedule.

Option E is a traditional cost reimbursement contract in which the Contractor is paid actual costs plus tendered fee.

Option F is a management contract in which the Management Contractor tenders a fee and an estimated total of the prices of the subcontractors. All subcontracts are direct contracts with the Management Contractor. The subcontract prices are paid to the Management Contractor as actual cost.

A4.3 SUMMARY

This appendix has outlined the structure and key provisions of the NEC. The NEC is intended to replace traditional construction contract forms. The drafting committee believes that it provides for better project management; this is achieved by a clearer definition of the roles of the parties, by a more precise definition of the work to be done, and by providing clearer and less contentious procedures for dealing with changes.

The most important measure of the success of this Contract will be the extent of its use in the future; this will depend upon whether Employers are satisfied with its operation, whether they are prepared to use it again, and whether they are prepared to recommend its use to other Employers.

REFERENCE

1. *The Engineering and Construction Contract* (1995) Second edition, Institution of Civil Engineers, Thomas Telford.

IChemE guidance note DD

DD. SCHEDULE OF COST ELEMENTS (SCHEDULE 2)

In any reimbursable contract, a schedule of cost elements is a necessity. This Schedule (i.e. Schedule 2) should list all the elements of cost that the Contractor may incur and against each item or natural group of items should be shown the method by which the charge will be debited to the Purchaser.

The degree to which the cost elements are detailed can range from an exhaustive list of everything and everybody to broad headings and explanatory texts and is a matter for contractual agreement, but it is evident that the greater the detail the less the chance of a misunderstanding during the course of the Contract.

Whichever way it is carried out, it is important to ensure that a heading is available for the allocation of all and any cost elements and that every cost element listed in the Schedule is identified as being one of the following:

(1) Directly chargeable to the Purchaser at net cost.
(2) Directly chargeable to the Purchaser at quoted rates (in which case corresponding rates must be set out in Schedule 3).
(3) Not directly chargeable to the Purchaser but covered by rates charged for other cost elements.
(4) Not directly chargeable to the Purchaser but covered by lump sum payment(s) (in which case the corresponding payment(s) must be set out in Schedule 3).

Any project, irrespective of size or nature, can be subdivided into main cost groups under which all costs can be allocated, e.g.:

- Home office costs (engineering and engineering subcontracts, procurement services (including expediting and inspection), construction and commissioning, general administration and business support facilities generally).
- Materials and freight (materials, equipment, freight, insurance and import duties).
- Field costs (field office, construction, labour and subcontracts, construction costs including tools and equipment, commissioning).

Each activity involving staff may be further subdivided for charging purposes to take account of man-hours booked, payroll burden, accommodation, overheads, expenses and other related costs.

In itself the payroll burden element can be expanded to indicate the main items that are usually included, e.g. statutory holidays and vacation pay, luncheon vouchers, national health insurance, pension contributions, sickness pay, employers' portion of company superannuation and life assurance schemes, training levies, etc.

Accommodation and fixed overheads would normally include rates, rents, light, heating, maintenance, depreciation and building services.

General Administration covers such items as legal, accounting, marketing, R & D, royalties and patent charges, consultant fees, insurances, etc.

Miscellaneous administrative facilities would include communication costs, stationery, reprographic charges, fees and expenses incurred in the execution of the contract, etc.

Construction labour should identify the known bases for payment, e.g. wages, incentives, overtime and premium pay, vacation pay, severance pay, radius and lodging allowances, travelling time and other wage elements introduced by statutory regulation and/or union agreement for all weekly or hourly paid site staff, statutory payroll taxes, pension contributions, etc.

Construction costs must account for all miscellaneous charges relating to the construction including temporary facilities, power, water and fuel supplies, security, recruitment, transportation, small tools and consumables, etc.

Examples of items that should be covered under Schedule 2 are shown in the following list of main cost elements for a reimbursable contract. Against each element the cost allocation should be shown by appropriate indication to indicate clearly to the Purchaser where his financial commitment will lie (this could be quantified in part by information given in Schedule 3).

Typical list of main cost elements

Home Office

- Salaries — net cost (permanent or agency).
- Payroll burden (permanent staff only).
- Accommodation.
- Overheads for agency staff.
- Expenses — net cost.
- Insurance.
- Independent consultants or inspectors.
- Accounting for specified site personnel.
- Computer time.
- Communications.
- Stationery.
- Prints, reprographic services.
- Provisions for client's staff.
- Marketing and sales.
- Licence fees and know-how.
- Accounts in general.
- Laboratory work.
- Legal.
- Advertising.
- General administration and overheads.
- Model building.
- Financial items — bank charges, exchange rates, VAT, etc.

Construction equipment and tools

- Hired construction equipment (rent and maintenance)
- Contractor-owned construction equipment.

- Small tools.
- Consumables.
- Oils, fuels, and greases.
- Equipment transportation.
- Licences, duty and tax.
- Insurance.

Materials and subcontract materials

- Materials and plant.
- Spare parts.
- Subcontract materials.
- Transportation.
- Insurance.
- Licences, duty and tax.
- Inspection materials.

Field office

- Salaries — net cost (permanent and agency).
- Payroll burden (permanent staff).
- Overheads for agency staff.
- Expenses.
- Insurance.
- General overheads, e.g. advertising.
- Administration, etc.
- Buildings and contents.
- Fuel, electricity, etc to offices.
- Communications.
- Stationery, reprographic services.
- Vehicles.

Field labour

- Wages, including all additional payments.
- Payroll taxes, insurance, pensions, etc.
- Payroll accounting, including computer time.
- Training levies, etc.
- Insurance.
- Specialist labour.

Field costs

- Recruitment.
- Qualifying tests.
- Temporary facilities.
- Power, fuel and water.
- Transportation.
- Storage of materials.
- Insurance.
- Security.
- Site services, canteen, medical.
- Local services for field offices.

Field commissioning

- Salaries — net cost (permanent and agency).
- Payroll burden.
- Overheads for agency staff.
- Expenses.
- Insurance.
- General administrative overheads.
- Vendor's/subcontractor's staff.
- Feedstock, steam, etc.
- Spare parts (commissioning only).

Appendix 6
The English legal system

A6.1 INTRODUCTION

The English legal system serves England and Wales; in Scotland the system is different in some important respects and some minor ones, and will not be considered here. The English legal system has served as a model or as a basis for the legal systems of British Commonwealth countries as well as the USA and, therefore, a study of the system and its provisions should be of value to a wide community of professional people.

A6.2 SOURCES OF ENGLISH LAW

English law evolved by gradually distilling local customary rules into a set of rules common to all parts of the land. This law became known as Common Law. Application of Common Law by the courts could lead to injustice where the court adhered strictly to 'the letter of the law'. As a consequence, a parallel system of fairness or 'Equity' arose in the Court of Chancery. In the late 19th century the Common Law and Chancery Courts merged so that Common Law and Equity were available in the same court. The principle had also been established at an early stage that where there was a conflict between the rules of Common Law and Equity the rules of Equity should prevail.

In modern times, while custom still exists as a very limited source of law, the main sources are:

- Common Law and Equity developed in the form of judicial precedent ('stare decisis'),
- Legislation in the form of Statutes, essentially Acts of Parliament.

Judicial precedent is also referred to as case law and, sometimes, as unwritten law. The courts in deciding upon a case will examine previous cases to determine the principles that should be applied. A judge's decision may consist of three elements. The first is 'res judicata'; the actual decision on the facts of the case. The second is the 'ratio decidendi', the most important element, which is his (legal) reason for arriving at his decision. The third, optional, element might be either a statement of what the decision could have been if the facts had been somewhat different, or, possibly, a statement of rules which, although having no direct bearing on the case, would apply in a related situation. This is known as an 'obiter dictum'. A ratio decidendi can be binding upon future cases, depending upon the authority of the court; the higher the court, the more binding the decision. The obiter dictum is never binding in later cases but can be used as 'persuasive authority'. Every decision of a court develops or distinguishes the law to some degree, and can provide a reference point for subsequent cases.

Legislation or Statute Law is the other major source of English law. Acts of Parliament, unless they provide otherwise, will always prevail over both Common Law and Equity. However, whilst Parliament drafts new laws it is the independent judiciary in the courts who interpret statute, and do so sometimes in a way in which Parliament had not perhaps intended! Furthermore, domestic (UK) law is now subject, where appropriate, to the law of the European Union.

A6.3   LEGISLATION AND DELEGATED LEGISLATION

It is necessary to distinguish between *legislation*, which is law made by Acts of Parliament, and *delegated legislation* made by some person or body which has been given authority by an Act of Parliament to make orders, regulations and bye-laws on specified matters, under that enabling or parent Act. These measures are known as delegated (or subordinate or secondary) legislation and are often in the form of Statutory Instruments. Examples are safety regulations made under the Health and Safety at Work Act 1974, and the Building Regulations made under the Public Health Act 1936 and its successors.

A6.4   THE LAW AND THE ENGINEER

The law can be divided into Criminal Law and Civil Law. This book will only consider Civil Law, that is, disputes between private citizens, businesses, associations, etc. The honest engineer is unlikely to appear in the criminal courts, save in one important respect; contraventions of the Health and Safety at Work Act 1974 (including its safety regulations) can be considered criminal acts or omissions which can lead to heavy personal fines and/or imprisonment.

Many engineers find themselves concerned with one area of Civil Law, namely, the Law of Contract. A contract is an agreement between two parties which is intended to be legally binding. Certain rules determine whether a contract is valid, but, generally, the parties are free to enter into any kind of legitimate contractual arrangement they desire.

Cases of breaches of contract are likely to be heard in the Queen's Bench Division of the High Court of Justice (known as the High Court); cases of lesser monetary value may be heard in the County Court. Subject to its statutory jurisdiction, disputes between employer and employee are considered by Industrial Tribunal. Appeals on any point of law are to the Employment Appeal Tribunal which is on a par with the Queen's Bench Division of the High Court. Appeals from the County Courts, High Court and the Employment Appeal Tribunal are heard in the Court of Appeal (Civil Division), which can uphold, reverse or modify the decision of the lower court. This court usually consists of three Lord Justices of Appeal. Superior to the Court of Appeal is the House of Lords sitting as a Court which usually comprises five senior judges known as Lords of Appeal in Ordinary, but generally referred to as the 'Law Lords'. The Law Lords will only hear appeals from the Court of Appeal where any point of law in the case is seen to be of general public importance. The precedent to be set by their judgement will usually have far-reaching significance for the future.

In addition, the European Court of Justice ensures that the Law of the European Union is observed by member states. Generally, the national courts concerned interpret the Treaty of Rome, its successors and provisions made thereunder (such as Regulations which are 'directly applicable' where member states have implemented Directives, or where such Directives already have 'direct effect') for their own country. However, the Court of Appeal in particular may refer cases to the European Court of Justice.

Appendix 7
Table of cases, statutes etc.

TABLE OF CASES

Adams v. Derby CC (1985) IRLR 163
Addis v. Gramophone Co Ltd (1909) AC 488
Air Canada v. Lee (1978) IRLR 392
Alexander v. Standard Telephones and Cables Ltd (No. 2) (1991) IRLR 286
Alidair v. Taylor (1978) ICR 445
Allen v. Flood (1898) AC 1
Baker v. Cornwall CC (1990) IRLR 194
Barber v. Guardian Royal Exchange Assurance Group (1991) 2 WLR 72
Barclays Bank plc v. Kapur (1991) 1 AllER 646
Bass Leisure Ltd v. Thomas (1994) IRLR 104
Bilka Kaufhaus v. Weber von Hartz (1986) IRLR 317
Birch v. University of Liverpool (1985) IRLR 165
Bliss v. S. E. Thames Regional Health Authority (1985) IRLR 308
Borders RC v. Maule (1993) IRLR 199
Breach v. Epsylon Industries Ltd (1976) IRLR 180
Brinkibon v. Stahag Stahl (1982) AllER 293
Bromley v. H & J Quick Ltd (1988) IRLR 249
Brook v. Haringey LBC (1992) IRLR 478
Brophy v. Bradfield & Co (1955) 1 WLR 1148
Burdett-Coutts v. Hertfordshire CC (1984) IRLR 91
Burton Group v. Smith (1977) IRLR 357
Butler Machine Tool Co Ltd v. Ex-Cell-O Corp (England) (1979) 1WLR 401
Cambridge and District Co-operative Society v. Ruse (1993) IRLR 156
Capper Pass Ltd v. Lawton (1977) QB 852
Carry All Motors Ltd v. Pennington (1980) IRLR 455
Chapman v. Goonvean Rostowrack China Clay Co Ltd (1973) 1 WLR 678
Clark v. Civil Aviation Authority (1991) IRLR 412
Clarke v. Eley (IMI) Kynoch Ltd (1982) IRLR 482
Clayton (Herbert) & Waller (Jack) Ltd v. Oliver (1930) AC 209
Close v. Steel Co of Wales (1962) AC 367
Collier v. Sunday Referee Publishing Co (1940) 2 KB 647
Construction Industry Training Board v. Leighton (1978) 1 AllER 723
Cresswell v. Board of Inland Revenue (1984) 2 AllER 713
Danfoss case (see Handels–Og etc.)
Davison v. Kent Meters Ltd (1975) IRLR 145

De Souza v. AA (1986) IRLR 103

Deeley v. British Rail Engineering Ltd (1980) IRLR 147

Delaney v. Staples (1992) IRLR 86

Devis W. & Sons v. Atkins (1977) AC 931

Devonald v. Rosser & Sons (1906) 2 KB 728

Dibro Ltd v. Hore (1990) IRLR 129

Dixon v. BBC (1979) 2AllER 112

Dobie v. Burns International Security Services (UK) Ltd (1985) 1 WLR 43

Dunlop Pneumatic Tyre Co Ltd v. Selfridge & Co Ltd (1915) AC 847

Eagland v. British Telecommunications plc (1992) IRLR 323

Egg Stores (Stamford Hill) Ltd v. Leibovici (1976) IRLR 376

Enderby v. Frenchay Area Health Authority (1993) IRLR 591

Entores Ltd v. Miles Far Eastern Corporation (1955) 2QB 327

Faccenda Chicken Ltd v. Fowler (1986) 3 WLR 288

Ford v. AUEFW (1969) 2 QB 303

General Cleaning Contractors Ltd v. Christmas (1953) AC 180

Gill v. Cape Contracts Ltd (1985) IRLR 499

Gorictree Ltd v. Jenkinson (1984) IRLR 391

Groves v. Lord Wimborne (1898) 2 QB 402

Hairsine v. Hull CC (1992) IRLR 211

Hall (HM Inspector of Taxes) v. Lorimer (1994) IRLR171

Handels-Og Kontorfunktionaerernes Forbund i Danmark v. Dansk Arbejdsgiverforening (acting for Danfoss) (1989) IRLR 532

Hawker Siddeley Power Engineering Ltd v. Rump (1979) IRLR 425

Hayward v. Cammell Laird Shipbuilders Ltd (1988) AC 894

Hellyer Bros Ltd v. McLeod (1987) 1 WLR 728

Hempell v. W H Smith & Sons Ltd (1986) IRLR 95

Hill v. C A Parsons & Co Ltd (1972) 1 Ch 305

Hivac Ltd v Park Royal Scientific Instruments Ltd (1946) Ch 169

Holland v. London Society of Compositors (1924) TLR 404

Hollister v. NFU (1979) IRLR 238

Holwell Securities Ltd v. Hughes (1974) AllER 161

Hooper v. British Railways (1988) IRLR 517

Hudson v. Ridge Manufacturing Co Ltd (1957) 2 QB 348

Iceland Frozen Foods Ltd v. Jones (1982) IRLR 439

ICI Ltd v. Shatwell (1965) AC 656

Igbo v. Johnson Matthey Chemicals Ltd (1986) IRLR 215

Initial Services Ltd v. Putterill (1968) 1 QB 396

Irani v. Southampton and S W Hampshire Area Health Authority (1985) IRLR 203

James v. Eastleigh BC (1990) AC 751

Jenkins v. Kingsgate (Clothing Productions) Ltd (1981) 1 WLR 1485

Johnstone v. Bloomsbury Health Authority (1991) IRLR 118

Jones v. University of Manchester (1993) IRLR 218

King v. Great Britain China Centre (1991) IRLR 513

Langston v. AUEW (1974) 1 WLR 185

Latimer v. AEC Ltd (1953) AC 643

Laughton v. Bapp Industrial Supplies Ltd (1986) IRLR 245

Laws v. London Chronicle (1959) 1 WLR 698

Lesney Products & Co v. Nolan (1977) IRLR 77

Leverton v. Clwyd CC (1989) AC 706

Lewis Shops Group v. Wiggins (1973) IRLR 205

Limpus v. London General Omnibus Co (1862) 1 H&C 526
Lister v. Romford Ice and Cold Storage Ltd (1957) AC 555
Litster v. Forth Dry Dock and Engineering Co Ltd (1990) AC 546
Liverpool C.C. v. Irwin (1976) 2 WLR 562
Lloyd v. Brassey (1969) 2 QB 98
London Ambulance Service v. Charlton (1992) IRLR 510
London Transport Executive v. Clarke (1981) IRLR 215
Luce v. Bexley LBC (1990) IRLR 422
Macarthys Ltd v. Smith (1980) ICR 672
MacLea v. Essex Line Ltd (1933) 45 LILRep 254
Malik v. BCCI (1995) IRLR 375
Market Investigations Ltd v. Minister of Social Security (1969) 2 QB 173
Marley v. Forward Trust Group Ltd (1986) IRLR 389
Massey v. Crown Life Insurance Co (1978) 1 WLR 676
Maund v. Penwith DC (1984) IRLR 24
McDermid v. Nash Dredging & Reclamation Co (1987) AC 906
Mears v. Safecar Security Ltd (1982) 3 WLR 366
Midland Foot Comfort Centre v. Moppett (1973) 2 AllER 294
Miles v. Wakefield MDC (1987) AC 539
Miller v. Hamworthy Engineering Ltd (1986) IRLR 461
Moon v. Homeworthy Furniture (Northern) Ltd (1976) IRLR 298
The Moorcock (1889) 14 PD 64
National Coal Board v. Galley (1958) 1 WLR 16
National Coal Board v. Ridgway (1987) 3 AllER 582
National Heart and Chest Hospitals Board of Governors v. Nambiar (1981) ICR 441
Nelson v. BBC (1977) IRLR 148
Nethermere (St Neots) Ltd v. Gardiner and Taverna (1984) IRLR 103
Nokes v. Doncaster Amalgamated Collieries (1940) AC 1014
Norton Tool Co v. Tewson (1973) 1 AllER 183
Nottcutt v. Universal Equipment Co (1986) 1 WLR 641
NUGSAT v. Albury Bros Ltd (1977) IRLR 173
O'Brien v. Associated Fire Alarms Ltd (1968) 1 WLR 1916
O'Hare v. Rotaprint Ltd (1980) IRLR 47
O'Kelly v. Trusthouse Forte plc (1984) QB 90
Page v. Freight Hire (Tank) Haulage Ltd (1981) 1 AllER 394
Pape v. Cumbria CC (1991) IRLR 463
Paris v. Stepney BC (1951) AC 367
Paul v. East Surrey District Health Authority (1995) IRLR 305
Pepper v. Webb (1969) 1 WLR 514
Pickstone v. Freemans plc (1989) 3 WLR 265
Polkey v. A E Dayton Services Ltd (1988) AC 344
Porcelli v. Strathclyde RC (1986) ICR 564
Port of London Authority v. Payne (1994) IRLR 9
Price v. Civil Service Commission (1978) 1 AllER 1228
Provident Financial Group plc v. Hayward (1989) 3 AllER 298
R v. Central Arbitration Committee ex parte BTP Tioxide Ltd (1982) IRLR 60
R v. Secretary of State for Employment ex parte Benwell (1985) QB 554
R v. Secretary of State for Employment ex parte Equal Opportunities Commission (1994)
    IRLR 204
R v. Swan Hunter Shipbuilders and Telemeter Installations Ltd (1982) 1 AllER 264
Raffles v. Wichelhaus (1864) 2H&C 906

Rainey v. Greater Glasgow Health Board (1987) AC 224
Ratcliffe v. North Yorkshire CC (1995) IRLR 439
Ready Mixed Concrete (South East) Ltd v. Minister of Pensions and National Insurance (1968) 2 QB 497
Rigby v. Ferodo Ltd (1987) IRLR 516
Rinner-Kühn v. FWW Spezial-Gebaudereinigung GmbH & Co KG (1989) IRLR 493
Rose v. Plenty (1976) 1 WLR 141
Rylands v. Fletcher (1868) LR 3 HL 330
Sandhu v. Department of Education and Science (1978) IRLR 208
Scally v. Southern Health and Social Services Board (1992) 1AC 294
Science Research Council v. Nassé (1980) AC 1028
Scott v. London and St Katherine Docks Co (1865) 3 H&C 596
Secretary of State for Employment v. ASLEF (No. 2) (1972) 2 QB 455
Sheffield v. Oxford Controls Co (1979) IRLR 133
Shepherd FC v. Jerrom (1986) IRLR 275
Shirlaw v. Southern Foundries Ltd (1939) 2 KB 206
Shove v. Downs Surgical plc (1984) 1 AllER 7
Showboat Entertainment Centre v. Owens (1984) 1 WLR 384
Sim v. Rotherham B.C. (1986) 3 WLR 851
Smith v. Baker & Sons (1891) AC 325
Smith v. Glasgow CDC (1987) IRLR 326
St John of God (Care Services) Ltd v. Brooks (1992) IRLR 546
Stevenson, Jordan and Harrison Ltd v. MacDonald and Evans (1952) 1 TLR 101
Stoker v. Lancashire CC (1992) IRLR 75
Sybron Corp v. Rochem Ltd (1983) 3 WLR 713
Systems Floors (UK) Ltd v. Daniel (1981) IRLR 475
Taylor v. Rover Car Co (1966) 1 WLR 1491
Ticehurst v. British Telecommunications plc (1992) IRLR 204
Turner v. Goldsmith (1891) 1 QB 544
United Bank Ltd v. Akhtar (1989) IRLR 507
Walker v. Northumberland CC (1995) IRLR 35
Warner Bros Pictures Inc v. Nelson (1937) 1 KB 209
Webb v. EMO Air Cargo (UK) Ltd (1994) QB718 and HL 19/10/95
West Midlands PTE v. Singh (1988) 1 WLR 730
Western Excavating (ECC) Ltd v. Sharp (1978) QB 761
Wignall v. British Gas (1984) IRLR 493
Williams v. Compair Maxam Ltd (1982) IRLR 82
Wilsons & Clyde Coal Co v. English (1938) AC 57
Wiluszynski v. Tower Hamlets LBC (1989) IRLR 259
Wishart v. National Association of Citizens Advice Bureaux Ltd (1990) IRLR 393
Woods v. WM Car Services (Peterborough) Ltd (1982) IRLR 413
Yewens v. Noakes (1880) 6 QBD 530
Young & Woods Ltd v. West (1980) IRLR 201

TABLE OF STATUTES

Civil Liability (Contribution) Act 1978
Contracts of Employment Act 1963
Disabled Persons (Employment) Acts 1944 and 1958
Employers' Liability (Compulsory Insurance) Act 1969

Employers' Liability (Defective Equipment) Act 1969
Employment Protection (Consolidation) Act 1978
Equal Pay Act 1970
Factories Act 1961
Health and Safety at Work Act 1974
Industrial Relations Act 1971
Insolvency Acts 1986 and 1994
Juries Act 1974
Law Reform (Contributory Negligence) Act 1945
Limitation Act 1980
Occupiers' Liability Act 1957
Occupiers' Liability Act 1984
Offices, Shops and Railways Premises Act 1963
Race Relations Act 1976
Redundancy Payments Act 1965
Rehabilitation of Offenders Act 1974
Sex Discrimination Acts 1975 and 1986
Single European Act 1986
Social Security Contributions and Benefits Act 1992
Statutory Sick Pay Act 1994
Trade Union and Labour Relations (Consolidation) Act 1992
Trade Union Reform and Employment Rights Act 1993
Unfair Contract Terms Act 1977
Wages Act 1986

TABLE OF STATUTORY INSTRUMENTS

Control of Substances Hazardous to Health Regulations 1988 (SI 1988/1657)
Health and Safety (Display Screen Equipment) Regulations 1992 (SI 1992/2792)
Health and Safety Information for Employees Regulations 1989 (SI 1989/682)
Management of Health and Safety at Work Regulations 1992 (SI 1992/2051)
Management of Health and Safety at Work (Amendment) Regulations 1994 (SI 1994/2865)
Manual Handling Operations Regulations 1992 (SI 1992/2793)
Maternity Allowance and Statutory Maternity Pay Regulations 1994 (SI 1994/1230)
Maternity (Compulsory Leave) Regulations 1994 (SI 1994/2479)
Personal Protective Equipment at Work Regulations 1992 (SI 1992/2966)
Provision and Use of Work Equipment Regulations 1992 (SI 1992/2932)
Race Relations (Questions and Replies) Order 1977 (SI 1977/842)
Race Relations (Formal Investigations) Regulations 1977 (SI 1977/841)
Safety Representatives and Safety Committees Regulations 1977 (SI 1977/500)
Sex Discrimination (Questions and Replies) Order 1975 (SI 1975/2048)
Sex Discrimination (Formal Investigations) Regulations 1975 (SI 1975/1993)
Statutory Maternity Pay (Compensation of Employers) Regulations 1995 (SI 1995/566)
Suspension from Work (on Maternity Grounds) Order 1994 (SI 1994/2930
Transfer of Undertakings (Protection of Employment) Regulations 1981 (SI 1981/1794)
Workplace (Health, Safety and Welfare) Regulations 1992 (SI 1992/3004)

TABLE OF STATUTORY CODES OF PRACTICE

ACAS Code of Practice 1: Disciplinary Practice and Procedures in Employment (1977)

ACAS Code of Practice 2: Disclosure of Information to Trade Unions for Collective Bargaining Purposes (1977)

Health and Safety Commission Code of Practice: Safety Representatives and Safety Committees (1978)

Health and Safety Commission Code of Practice: Time Off for the Training of Safety Representatives (1978)

Commission for Racial Equality: Code of Practice for the Elimination of Racial Discrimination and the Promotion of Equality of Opportunity in Employment (1983)

Equal Opportunities Commission : Code of Practice for the Elimination of Discrimination on the Grounds of Sex and Marriage and the Promotion of Equality of Opportunity in Employment (1985)

ACAS Code of Practice 3: Time Off for Trade Union Duties and Activities (as revised in 1991)

TABLE OF EUROPEAN COMMUNITY/EUROPEAN UNION MEASURES

Treaty establishing the European Community (1957) (Treaty of Rome), Articles 118, 118A, and 119.

Council Directive 75/117/EEC on the approximation of the laws of the member states relating to the application of the principle of equal pay for men and women.

Council Directive 75/129 EEC on the approximation of the laws of the member states relating to collective redundancies.

Council Directive 76/207/EEC on the implementation of the principle of equal treatment for men and women as regards access to employment, vocational training and promotion, and working conditions.

Council Directive 77/187/EEC on the approximation of the laws of the member states relating to the safeguarding of employees' rights in the event of transfer of undertakings, businesses or parts of businesses.

Council Directive 89/391/EEC on the introduction of measures to encourage improvement in health and safety of workers at work.

Council Directive 91/533 EEC on an employer's obligation to inform employees of the conditions applicable to the contract of employment relationship.

Council Directive 92/56/EEC amending Directive 75/129/EEC on the approximation of the laws of the member states relating to collective redundancies.

Council Directive 92/85 EEC on the introduction of measures to encourage improvements in the safety and health at work of pregnant workers who had recently given birth or were breast-feeding.

Appendix 8
DCF Tables

A8.1 PRESENT VALUE TABLES

i / n	0.5	1	1.5	2	2.5	3	3.5	4	4.5	5
1	0.9950	0.9901	0.9852	0.9804	0.9756	0.9709	0.9662	0.9615	0.9569	0.9524
2	0.9901	0.9803	0.9707	0.9612	0.9518	0.9426	0.9335	0.9246	0.9157	0.9070
3	0.9851	0.9706	0.9563	0.9423	0.9286	0.9151	0.9019	0.8890	0.8763	0.8638
4	0.9802	0.9610	0.9422	0.9238	0.9060	0.8885	0.8714	0.8548	0.8386	0.8227
5	0.9754	0.9515	0.9283	0.9057	0.8839	0.8626	0.8420	0.8219	0.8025	0.7835
6	0.9705	0.9420	0.9145	0.8880	0.8623	0.8375	0.8135	0.7903	0.7679	0.7462
7	0.9657	0.9327	0.9010	0.8706	0.8413	0.8131	0.7860	0.7599	0.7348	0.7107
8	0.9609	0.9235	0.8877	0.8535	0.8207	0.7894	0.7594	0.7307	0.7032	0.6768
9	0.9561	0.9143	0.8746	0.8368	0.8007	0.7664	0.7337	0.7026	0.6729	0.6446
10	0.9513	0.9053	0.8617	0.8203	0.7812	0.7441	0.7089	0.6756	0.6439	0.6139
11	0.9466	0.8963	0.8489	0.8043	0.7621	0.7224	0.6849	0.6496	0.6162	0.5847
12	0.9419	0.8874	0.8364	0.7885	0.7436	0.7014	0.6618	0.6246	0.5897	0.5568
13	0.9372	0.8787	0.8240	0.7730	0.7254	0.6810	0.6394	0.6006	0.5643	0.5303
14	0.9326	0.8700	0.8118	0.7579	0.7077	0.6611	0.6178	0.5775	0.5400	0.5051
15	0.9279	0.8613	0.7999	0.7430	0.6905	0.6419	0.5969	0.5553	0.5167	0.4810
16	0.9233	0.8528	0.7880	0.7284	0.6736	0.6232	0.5767	0.5339	0.4945	0.4581
17	0.9187	0.8444	0.7764	0.7142	0.6572	0.6050	0.5572	0.5134	0.4732	0.4363
18	0.9141	0.8360	0.7649	0.7002	0.6412	0.5874	0.5384	0.4936	0.4528	0.4155
19	0.9096	0.8277	0.7536	0.6864	0.6255	0.5703	0.5202	0.4746	0.4333	0.3957
20	0.9051	0.8195	0.7425	0.6730	0.6103	0.5537	0.5026	0.4564	0.4146	0.3769
21	0.9006	0.8114	0.7315	0.6598	0.5954	0.5375	0.4856	0.4388	0.3968	0.3589
22	0.8961	0.8034	0.7207	0.6468	0.5809	0.5219	0.4692	0.4220	0.3797	0.3418
23	0.8916	0.7954	0.7100	0.6342	0.5667	0.5067	0.4533	0.4057	0.3634	0.3256
24	0.8872	0.7876	0.6995	0.6217	0.5529	0.4919	0.4380	0.3901	0.3477	0.3101
25	0.8828	0.7798	0.6892	0.6095	0.5394	0.4776	0.4231	0.3751	0.3327	0.2953
26	0.8784	0.7720	0.6790	0.5976	0.5262	0.4637	0.4088	0.3607	0.3184	0.2812
27	0.8740	0.7644	0.6690	0.5859	0.5134	0.4502	0.3950	0.3468	0.3047	0.2678
28	0.8697	0.7568	0.6591	0.5744	0.5009	0.4371	0.3817	0.3335	0.2916	0.2551
29	0.8653	0.7493	0.6494	0.5631	0.4887	0.4243	0.3687	0.3207	0.2790	0.2429
30	0.8610	0.7419	0.6398	0.5521	0.4767	0.4120	0.3563	0.3083	0.2670	0.2314
31	0.8567	0.7346	0.6303	0.5412	0.4651	0.4000	0.3442	0.2965	0.2555	0.2204
32	0.8525	0.7273	0.6210	0.5306	0.4538	0.3883	0.3326	0.2851	0.2445	0.2099
33	0.8482	0.7201	0.6118	0.5202	0.4427	0.3770	0.3213	0.2741	0.2340	0.1999
34	0.8440	0.7130	0.6028	0.5100	0.4319	0.3660	0.3105	0.2636	0.2239	0.1904
35	0.8398	0.7059	0.5939	0.5000	0.4214	0.3554	0.3000	0.2534	0.2143	0.1813
36	0.8356	0.6989	0.5851	0.4902	0.4111	0.3450	0.2898	0.2437	0.2050	0.1727
37	0.8315	0.6920	0.5764	0.4806	0.4011	0.3350	0.2800	0.2343	0.1962	0.1644
38	0.8274	0.6852	0.5679	0.4712	0.3913	0.3252	0.2706	0.2253	0.1878	0.1566
39	0.8232	0.6784	0.5595	0.4619	0.3817	0.3158	0.2614	0.2166	0.1797	0.1491
40	0.8191	0.6717	0.5513	0.4529	0.3724	0.3066	0.2526	0.2083	0.1719	0.1420
50	0.7793	0.6080	0.4750	0.3715	0.2909	0.2281	0.1791	0.1407	0.1107	0.0872
60	0.7414	0.5504	0.4093	0.3048	0.2273	0.1697	0.1269	0.0951	0.0713	0.0535
80	0.6710	0.4511	0.3039	0.2051	0.1387	0.0940	0.0638	0.0434	0.0296	0.0202
100	0.6073	0.3697	0.2256	0.1380	0.0846	0.0520	0.0321	0.0198	0.0123	0.0076
120	0.5496	0.3030	0.1675	0.0929	0.0517	0.0288	0.0161	0.0090	0.0051	0.0029

A8.1 PRESENT VALUE TABLES (cont'd)

i n	5.5	6	6.5	7	7.5	8	8.5	9	9.5	10
1	0.9479	0.9434	0.9390	0.9346	0.9302	0.9259	0.9217	0.9174	0.9132	0.9091
2	0.8985	0.8900	0.8817	0.8734	0.8653	0.8573	0.8495	0.8417	0.8340	0.8264
3	0.8516	0.8396	0.8278	0.8163	0.8050	0.7938	0.7829	0.7722	0.7617	0.7513
4	0.8072	0.7921	0.7773	0.7629	0.7488	0.7350	0.7216	0.7084	0.6956	0.6830
5	0.7651	0.7473	0.7299	0.7130	0.6966	0.6806	0.6650	0.6499	0.6352	0.6209
6	0.7252	0.7050	0.6853	0.6663	0.6480	0.6302	0.6129	0.5963	0.5801	0.5645
7	0.6874	0.6651	0.6435	0.6227	0.6028	0.5835	0.5649	0.5470	0.5298	0.5132
8	0.6516	0.6274	0.6042	0.5820	0.5607	0.5403	0.5207	0.5019	0.4838	0.4665
9	0.6176	0.5919	0.5674	0.5439	0.5216	0.5002	0.4799	0.4604	0.4418	0.4241
10	0.5854	0.5584	0.5327	0.5083	0.4852	0.4632	0.4423	0.4224	0.4035	0.3855
11	0.5549	0.5268	0.5002	0.4751	0.4513	0.4289	0.4076	0.3875	0.3685	0.3505
12	0.5260	0.4970	0.4697	0.4440	0.4199	0.3971	0.3757	0.3555	0.3365	0.3186
13	0.4986	0.4688	0.4410	0.4150	0.3906	0.3677	0.3463	0.3262	0.3073	0.2897
14	0.4726	0.4423	0.4141	0.3878	0.3633	0.3405	0.3191	0.2992	0.2807	0.2633
15	0.4479	0.4173	0.3888	0.3624	0.3380	0.3152	0.2941	0.2745	0.2563	0.2394
16	0.4246	0.3936	0.3651	0.3387	0.3144	0.2919	0.2711	0.2519	0.2341	0.2176
17	0.4024	0.3714	0.3428	0.3166	0.2925	0.2703	0.2499	0.2311	0.2138	0.1978
18	0.3815	0.3503	0.3219	0.2959	0.2720	0.2502	0.2303	0.2120	0.1952	0.1799
19	0.3616	0.3305	0.3022	0.2765	0.2531	0.2317	0.2122	0.1945	0.1783	0.1635
20	0.3427	0.3118	0.2838	0.2584	0.2354	0.2145	0.1956	0.1784	0.1628	0.1486
21	0.3249	0.2942	0.2665	0.2415	0.2190	0.1987	0.1803	0.1637	0.1487	0.1351
22	0.3079	0.2775	0.2502	0.2257	0.2037	0.1839	0.1662	0.1502	0.1358	0.1228
23	0.2919	0.2618	0.2349	0.2109	0.1895	0.1703	0.1531	0.1378	0.1240	0.1117
24	0.2767	0.2470	0.2206	0.1971	0.1763	0.1577	0.1412	0.1264	0.1133	0.1015
25	0.2622	0.2330	0.2071	0.1842	0.1640	0.1460	0.1301	0.1160	0.1034	0.0923
26	0.2486	0.2198	0.1945	0.1722	0.1525	0.1352	0.1199	0.1064	0.0945	0.0839
27	0.2356	0.2074	0.1826	0.1609	0.1419	0.1252	0.1105	0.0976	0.0863	0.0763
28	0.2233	0.1956	0.1715	0.1504	0.1320	0.1159	0.1019	0.0895	0.0788	0.0693
29	0.2117	0.1846	0.1610	0.1406	0.1228	0.1073	0.0939	0.0822	0.0719	0.0630
30	0.2006	0.1741	0.1512	0.1314	0.1142	0.0994	0.0865	0.0754	0.0657	0.0573
31	0.1902	0.1643	0.1420	0.1228	0.1063	0.0920	0.0797	0.0691	0.0600	0.0521
32	0.1803	0.1550	0.1333	0.1147	0.0988	0.0852	0.0735	0.0634	0.0548	0.0474
33	0.1709	0.1462	0.1252	0.1072	0.0919	0.0789	0.0677	0.0582	0.0500	0.0431
34	0.1620	0.1379	0.1175	0.1002	0.0855	0.0730	0.0624	0.0534	0.0457	0.0391
35	0.1535	0.1301	0.1103	0.0937	0.0796	0.0676	0.0575	0.0490	0.0417	0.0356
36	0.1455	0.1227	0.1036	0.0875	0.0740	0.0626	0.0530	0.0449	0.0381	0.0323
37	0.1379	0.1158	0.0973	0.0818	0.0688	0.0580	0.0489	0.0412	0.0348	0.0294
38	0.1307	0.1092	0.0914	0.0765	0.0640	0.0537	0.0450	0.0378	0.0318	0.0267
39	0.1239	0.1031	0.0858	0.0715	0.0596	0.0497	0.0415	0.0347	0.0290	0.0243
40	0.1175	0.0972	0.0805	0.0668	0.0554	0.0460	0.0383	0.0318	0.0265	0.0221
50	0.0688	0.0543	0.0429	0.0339	0.0269	0.0213	0.0169	0.0134	0.0107	0.0085
60	0.0403	0.0303	0.0229	0.0173	0.0130	0.0099	0.0075	0.0057	0.0043	0.0033
80	0.0138	0.0095	0.0065	0.0045	0.0031	0.0021	0.0015	0.0010	0.0007	0.0005
100	0.0047	0.0029	0.0018	0.0012	0.0007	0.0005	0.0003	0.0002	0.0001	0.0001
120	0.0016	0.0009	0.0005	0.0003	0.0002	0.0001	0.0001	0.0000	0.0000	0.0000

A8.1 PRESENT VALUE TABLES (cont'd)

n \ i	10.5	11	11.5	12	12.5	13	13.5	14	14.5	15
1	0.9050	0.9009	0.8969	0.8929	0.8889	0.8850	0.8811	0.8772	0.8734	0.8696
2	0.8190	0.8116	0.8044	0.7972	0.7901	0.7831	0.7763	0.7695	0.7628	0.7561
3	0.7412	0.7312	0.7214	0.7118	0.7023	0.6931	0.6839	0.6750	0.6662	0.6575
4	0.6707	0.6587	0.6470	0.6355	0.6243	0.6133	0.6026	0.5921	0.5818	0.5718
5	0.6070	0.5935	0.5803	0.5674	0.5549	0.5428	0.5309	0.5194	0.5081	0.4972
6	0.5493	0.5346	0.5204	0.5066	0.4933	0.4803	0.4678	0.4556	0.4438	0.4323
7	0.4971	0.4817	0.4667	0.4523	0.4385	0.4251	0.4121	0.3996	0.3876	0.3759
8	0.4499	0.4339	0.4186	0.4039	0.3897	0.3762	0.3631	0.3506	0.3385	0.3269
9	0.4071	0.3909	0.3754	0.3606	0.3464	0.3329	0.3199	0.3075	0.2956	0.2843
10	0.3684	0.3522	0.3367	0.3220	0.3079	0.2946	0.2819	0.2697	0.2582	0.2472
11	0.3334	0.3173	0.3020	0.2875	0.2737	0.2607	0.2483	0.2366	0.2255	0.2149
12	0.3018	0.2858	0.2708	0.2567	0.2433	0.2307	0.2188	0.2076	0.1969	0.1869
13	0.2731	0.2575	0.2429	0.2292	0.2163	0.2042	0.1928	0.1821	0.1720	0.1625
14	0.2471	0.2320	0.2178	0.2046	0.1922	0.1807	0.1698	0.1597	0.1502	0.1413
15	0.2236	0.2090	0.1954	0.1827	0.1709	0.1599	0.1496	0.1401	0.1312	0.1229
16	0.2024	0.1883	0.1752	0.1631	0.1519	0.1415	0.1318	0.1229	0.1146	0.1069
17	0.1832	0.1696	0.1572	0.1456	0.1350	0.1252	0.1162	0.1078	0.1001	0.0929
18	0.1658	0.1528	0.1409	0.1300	0.1200	0.1108	0.1023	0.0946	0.0874	0.0808
19	0.1500	0.1377	0.1264	0.1161	0.1067	0.0981	0.0902	0.0829	0.0763	0.0703
20	0.1358	0.1240	0.1134	0.1037	0.0948	0.0868	0.0794	0.0728	0.0667	0.0611
21	0.1229	0.1117	0.1017	0.0926	0.0843	0.0768	0.0700	0.0638	0.0582	0.0531
22	0.1112	0.1007	0.0912	0.0826	0.0749	0.0680	0.0617	0.0560	0.0508	0.0462
23	0.1006	0.0907	0.0818	0.0738	0.0666	0.0601	0.0543	0.0491	0.0444	0.0402
24	0.0911	0.0817	0.0734	0.0659	0.0592	0.0532	0.0479	0.0431	0.0388	0.0349
25	0.0824	0.0736	0.0658	0.0588	0.0526	0.0471	0.0422	0.0378	0.0339	0.0304
26	0.0746	0.0663	0.0590	0.0525	0.0468	0.0417	0.0372	0.0331	0.0296	0.0264
27	0.0675	0.0597	0.0529	0.0469	0.0416	0.0369	0.0327	0.0291	0.0258	0.0230
28	0.0611	0.0538	0.0475	0.0419	0.0370	0.0326	0.0288	0.0255	0.0226	0.0200
29	0.0553	0.0485	0.0426	0.0374	0.0329	0.0289	0.0254	0.0224	0.0197	0.0174
30	0.0500	0.0437	0.0382	0.0334	0.0292	0.0256	0.0224	0.0196	0.0172	0.0151
31	0.0453	0.0394	0.0342	0.0298	0.0260	0.0226	0.0197	0.0172	0.0150	0.0131
32	0.0410	0.0355	0.0307	0.0266	0.0231	0.0200	0.0174	0.0151	0.0131	0.0114
33	0.0371	0.0319	0.0275	0.0238	0.0205	0.0177	0.0153	0.0132	0.0115	0.0099
34	0.0335	0.0288	0.0247	0.0212	0.0182	0.0157	0.0135	0.0116	0.0100	0.0086
35	0.0304	0.0259	0.0222	0.0189	0.0162	0.0139	0.0119	0.0102	0.0087	0.0075
36	0.0275	0.0234	0.0199	0.0169	0.0144	0.0123	0.0105	0.0089	0.0076	0.0065
37	0.0249	0.0210	0.0178	0.0151	0.0128	0.0109	0.0092	0.0078	0.0067	0.0057
38	0.0225	0.0190	0.0160	0.0135	0.0114	0.0096	0.0081	0.0069	0.0058	0.0049
39	0.0204	0.0171	0.0143	0.0120	0.0101	0.0085	0.0072	0.0060	0.0051	0.0043
40	0.0184	0.0154	0.0129	0.0107	0.0090	0.0075	0.0063	0.0053	0.0044	0.0037
50	0.0068	0.0054	0.0043	0.0035	0.0028	0.0022	0.0018	0.0014	0.0011	0.0009
60	0.0025	0.0019	0.0015	0.0011	0.0009	0.0007	0.0005	0.0004	0.0003	0.0002
80	0.0003	0.0002	0.0002	0.0001	0.0001	0.0001	0.0000	0.0000	0.0000	0.0000
100	0.0000	0.0000	0.0000	0.0000	0.0000	0.0000	0.0000	0.0000	0.0000	0.0000
120	0.0000	0.0000	0.0000	0.0000	0.0000	0.0000	0.0000	0.0000	0.0000	0.0000

A8.1 PRESENT VALUE TABLES (cont'd)

i / n	15.5	16	16.5	17	17.5	18	18.5	19	19.5	20
1	0.8658	0.8621	0.8584	0.8547	0.8511	0.8475	0.8439	0.8403	0.8368	0.8333
2	0.7496	0.7432	0.7368	0.7305	0.7243	0.7182	0.7121	0.7062	0.7003	0.6944
3	0.6490	0.6407	0.6324	0.6244	0.6164	0.6086	0.6010	0.5934	0.5860	0.5787
4	0.5619	0.5523	0.5429	0.5337	0.5246	0.5158	0.5071	0.4987	0.4904	0.4823
5	0.4865	0.4761	0.4660	0.4561	0.4465	0.4371	0.4280	0.4190	0.4104	0.4019
6	0.4212	0.4104	0.4000	0.3898	0.3800	0.3704	0.3612	0.3521	0.3434	0.3349
7	0.3647	0.3538	0.3433	0.3332	0.3234	0.3139	0.3048	0.2959	0.2874	0.2791
8	0.3158	0.3050	0.2947	0.2848	0.2752	0.2660	0.2572	0.2487	0.2405	0.2326
9	0.2734	0.2630	0.2530	0.2434	0.2342	0.2255	0.2170	0.2090	0.2012	0.1938
10	0.2367	0.2267	0.2171	0.2080	0.1994	0.1911	0.1832	0.1756	0.1684	0.1615
11	0.2049	0.1954	0.1864	0.1778	0.1697	0.1619	0.1546	0.1476	0.1409	0.1346
12	0.1774	0.1685	0.1600	0.1520	0.1444	0.1372	0.1304	0.1240	0.1179	0.1122
13	0.1536	0.1452	0.1373	0.1299	0.1229	0.1163	0.1101	0.1042	0.0987	0.0935
14	0.1330	0.1252	0.1179	0.1110	0.1046	0.0985	0.0929	0.0876	0.0826	0.0779
15	0.1152	0.1079	0.1012	0.0949	0.0890	0.0835	0.0784	0.0736	0.0691	0.0649
16	0.0997	0.0930	0.0869	0.0811	0.0758	0.0708	0.0661	0.0618	0.0578	0.0541
17	0.0863	0.0802	0.0746	0.0693	0.0645	0.0600	0.0558	0.0520	0.0484	0.0451
18	0.0747	0.0691	0.0640	0.0592	0.0549	0.0508	0.0471	0.0437	0.0405	0.0376
19	0.0647	0.0596	0.0549	0.0506	0.0467	0.0431	0.0398	0.0367	0.0339	0.0313
20	0.0560	0.0514	0.0471	0.0433	0.0397	0.0365	0.0335	0.0308	0.0284	0.0261
21	0.0485	0.0443	0.0405	0.0370	0.0338	0.0309	0.0283	0.0259	0.0237	0.0217
22	0.0420	0.0382	0.0347	0.0316	0.0288	0.0262	0.0239	0.0218	0.0199	0.0181
23	0.0364	0.0329	0.0298	0.0270	0.0245	0.0222	0.0202	0.0183	0.0166	0.0151
24	0.0315	0.0284	0.0256	0.0231	0.0208	0.0188	0.0170	0.0154	0.0139	0.0126
25	0.0273	0.0245	0.0220	0.0197	0.0177	0.0160	0.0144	0.0129	0.0116	0.0105
26	0.0236	0.0211	0.0189	0.0169	0.0151	0.0135	0.0121	0.0109	0.0097	0.0087
27	0.0204	0.0182	0.0162	0.0144	0.0129	0.0115	0.0102	0.0091	0.0081	0.0073
28	0.0177	0.0157	0.0139	0.0123	0.0109	0.0097	0.0086	0.0077	0.0068	0.0061
29	0.0153	0.0135	0.0119	0.0105	0.0093	0.0082	0.0073	0.0064	0.0057	0.0051
30	0.0133	0.0116	0.0102	0.0090	0.0079	0.0070	0.0061	0.0054	0.0048	0.0042
31	0.0115	0.0100	0.0088	0.0077	0.0067	0.0059	0.0052	0.0046	0.0040	0.0035
32	0.0099	0.0087	0.0075	0.0066	0.0057	0.0050	0.0044	0.0038	0.0033	0.0029
33	0.0086	0.0075	0.0065	0.0056	0.0049	0.0042	0.0037	0.0032	0.0028	0.0024
34	0.0075	0.0064	0.0056	0.0048	0.0042	0.0036	0.0031	0.0027	0.0023	0.0020
35	0.0065	0.0055	0.0048	0.0041	0.0035	0.0030	0.0026	0.0023	0.0020	0.0017
36	0.0056	0.0048	0.0041	0.0035	0.0030	0.0026	0.0022	0.0019	0.0016	0.0014
37	0.0048	0.0041	0.0035	0.0030	0.0026	0.0022	0.0019	0.0016	0.0014	0.0012
38	0.0042	0.0036	0.0030	0.0026	0.0022	0.0019	0.0016	0.0013	0.0011	0.0010
39	0.0036	0.0031	0.0026	0.0022	0.0019	0.0016	0.0013	0.0011	0.0010	0.0008
40	0.0031	0.0026	0.0022	0.0019	0.0016	0.0013	0.0011	0.0010	0.0008	0.0007
50	0.0007	0.0006	0.0005	0.0004	0.0003	0.0003	0.0002	0.0002	0.0001	0.0001
60	0.0002	0.0001	0.0001	0.0001	0.0001	0.0000	0.0000	0.0000	0.0000	0.0000
80	0.0000	0.0000	0.0000	0.0000	0.0000	0.0000	0.0000	0.0000	0.0000	0.0000
100	0.0000	0.0000	0.0000	0.0000	0.0000	0.0000	0.0000	0.0000	0.0000	0.0000
120	0.0000	0.0000	0.0000	0.0000	0.0000	0.0000	0.0000	0.0000	0.0000	0.0000

A8.1 PRESENT VALUE TABLES (cont'd)

i / n	21	22	23	24	25	30	35	40	50	100
1	0.8264	0.8197	0.8130	0.8065	0.8000	0.7692	0.7407	0.7143	0.6667	0.5000
2	0.6830	0.6719	0.6610	0.6504	0.6400	0.5917	0.5487	0.5102	0.4444	0.2500
3	0.5645	0.5507	0.5374	0.5245	0.5120	0.4552	0.4064	0.3644	0.2963	0.1250
4	0.4665	0.4514	0.4369	0.4230	0.4096	0.3501	0.3011	0.2603	0.1975	0.0625
5	0.3855	0.3700	0.3552	0.3411	0.3277	0.2693	0.2230	0.1859	0.1317	0.0313
6	0.3186	0.3033	0.2888	0.2751	0.2621	0.2072	0.1652	0.1328	0.0878	0.0156
7	0.2633	0.2486	0.2348	0.2218	0.2097	0.1594	0.1224	0.0949	0.0585	0.0078
8	0.2176	0.2038	0.1909	0.1789	0.1678	0.1226	0.0906	0.0678	0.0390	0.0039
9	0.1799	0.1670	0.1552	0.1443	0.1342	0.0943	0.0671	0.0484	0.0260	0.0020
10	0.1486	0.1369	0.1262	0.1164	0.1074	0.0725	0.0497	0.0346	0.0173	0.0010
11	0.1228	0.1122	0.1026	0.0938	0.0859	0.0558	0.0368	0.0247	0.0116	0.0005
12	0.1015	0.0920	0.0834	0.0757	0.0687	0.0429	0.0273	0.0176	0.0077	0.0002
13	0.0839	0.0754	0.0678	0.0610	0.0550	0.0330	0.0202	0.0126	0.0051	0.0001
14	0.0693	0.0618	0.0551	0.0492	0.0440	0.0254	0.0150	0.0090	0.0034	0.0001
15	0.0573	0.0507	0.0448	0.0397	0.0352	0.0195	0.0111	0.0064	0.0023	0.0000
16	0.0474	0.0415	0.0364	0.0320	0.0281	0.0150	0.0082	0.0046	0.0015	0.0000
17	0.0391	0.0340	0.0296	0.0258	0.0225	0.0116	0.0061	0.0033	0.0010	0.0000
18	0.0323	0.0279	0.0241	0.0208	0.0180	0.0089	0.0045	0.0023	0.0007	0.0000
19	0.0267	0.0229	0.0196	0.0168	0.0144	0.0068	0.0033	0.0017	0.0005	0.0000
20	0.0221	0.0187	0.0159	0.0135	0.0115	0.0053	0.0025	0.0012	0.0003	0.0000
21	0.0183	0.0154	0.0129	0.0109	0.0092	0.0040	0.0018	0.0009	0.0002	0.0000
22	0.0151	0.0126	0.0105	0.0088	0.0074	0.0031	0.0014	0.0006	0.0001	0.0000
23	0.0125	0.0103	0.0086	0.0071	0.0059	0.0024	0.0010	0.0004	0.0001	0.0000
24	0.0103	0.0085	0.0070	0.0057	0.0047	0.0018	0.0007	0.0003	0.0001	0.0000
25	0.0085	0.0069	0.0057	0.0046	0.0038	0.0014	0.0006	0.0002	0.0000	0.0000
26	0.0070	0.0057	0.0046	0.0037	0.0030	0.0011	0.0004	0.0002	0.0000	0.0000
27	0.0058	0.0047	0.0037	0.0030	0.0024	0.0008	0.0003	0.0001	0.0000	0.0000
28	0.0048	0.0038	0.0030	0.0024	0.0019	0.0006	0.0002	0.0001	0.0000	0.0000
29	0.0040	0.0031	0.0025	0.0020	0.0015	0.0005	0.0002	0.0001	0.0000	0.0000
30	0.0033	0.0026	0.0020	0.0016	0.0012	0.0004	0.0001	0.0000	0.0000	0.0000
31	0.0027	0.0021	0.0016	0.0013	0.0010	0.0003	0.0001	0.0000	0.0000	0.0000
32	0.0022	0.0017	0.0013	0.0010	0.0008	0.0002	0.0001	0.0000	0.0000	0.0000
33	0.0019	0.0014	0.0011	0.0008	0.0006	0.0002	0.0001	0.0000	0.0000	0.0000
34	0.0015	0.0012	0.0009	0.0007	0.0005	0.0001	0.0000	0.0000	0.0000	0.0000
35	0.0013	0.0009	0.0007	0.0005	0.0004	0.0001	0.0001	0.0000	0.0000	0.0000
36	0.0010	0.0008	0.0006	0.0004	0.0003	0.0001	0.0000	0.0000	0.0000	0.0000
37	0.0009	0.0006	0.0005	0.0003	0.0003	0.0001	0.0000	0.0000	0.0000	0.0000
38	0.0007	0.0005	0.0004	0.0003	0.0002	0.0000	0.0000	0.0000	0.0000	0.0000
39	0.0006	0.0004	0.0003	0.0002	0.0002	0.0000	0.0000	0.0000	0.0000	0.0000
40	0.0005	0.0004	0.0003	0.0002	0.0001	0.0000	0.0000	0.0000	0.0000	0.0000
50	0.0001	0.0000	0.0000	0.0000	0.0000	0.0000	0.0000	0.0000	0.0000	0.0000
60	0.0000	0.0000	0.0000	0.0000	0.0000	0.0000	0.0000	0.0000	0.0000	0.0000
80	0.0000	0.0000	0.0000	0.0000	0.0000	0.0000	0.0000	0.0000	0.0000	0.0000
100	0.0000	0.0000	0.0000	0.0000	0.0000	0.0000	0.0000	0.0000	0.0000	0.0000
120	0.0000	0.0000	0.0000	0.0000	0.0000	0.0000	0.0000	0.0000	0.0000	0.0000

A8.2 PRESENT VALUE OF ANNUITY TABLES

i	0.5	1	1.5	2	2.5	3	3.5	4	4.5	5
n										
1	0.9950	0.9901	0.9852	0.9804	0.9756	0.9709	0.9662	0.9615	0.9569	0.9524
2	1.9851	1.9704	1.9559	1.9416	1.9274	1.9135	1.8997	1.8861	1.8727	1.8594
3	2.9702	2.9410	2.9122	2.8839	2.8560	2.8286	2.8016	2.7751	2.7490	2.7232
4	3.9505	3.9020	3.8544	3.8077	3.7260	3.7171	3.6731	3.6299	3.5875	3.5460
5	4.9259	4.8534	4.7826	4.7135	4.6458	4.5797	4.5151	4.4518	4.3900	4.3295
6	5.8964	5.7955	5.6972	5.6014	5.5081	5.4172	5.3286	5.2421	5.1579	5.0757
7	6.8621	6.7282	6.5982	6.4720	6.3494	6.2303	6.1145	6.0021	5.8927	5.7864
8	7.8230	7.6517	7.4859	7.3255	7.1701	7.0197	6.8740	6.7327	6.5959	6.4632
9	8.7791	8.5660	8.3605	8.1622	7.9709	7.7861	7.6077	7.4353	7.2688	7.1078
10	9.7304	9.4713	9.2222	8.9826	8.7251	8.5302	8.3166	8.1109	7.9127	7.7217
11	10.6770	10.3676	10.0711	9.7868	9.5142	9.2526	9.0016	8.7605	8.5289	8.3064
12	11.6189	11.2551	10.9075	10.5753	10.2578	9.9540	9.6633	9.3851	9.1186	8.8633
13	12.5562	12.1337	11.7315	11.3484	10.9832	10.6350	10.3027	9.9856	9.6829	9.3936
14	13.4887	13.0037	12.5434	12.1062	11.6909	11.2961	10.9205	10.5631	10.2228	9.8986
15	14.4166	13.8651	13.3432	12.8493	12.3814	11.9379	11.5174	11.1184	10.7395	10.3797
16	15.3399	14.7179	14.1313	13.5777	13.0550	12.5611	12.0941	11.6523	11.2340	10.8378
17	16.2586	15.5623	14.9076	14.2919	13.7122	13.1661	12.6513	12.1657	11.7072	11.2741
18	17.1728	16.3983	15.6726	14.9920	14.3534	13.7535	13.1897	12.6593	12.1600	11.6896
19	18.0824	17.2260	16.4262	15.6785	14.9789	14.3238	13.7098	13.1339	12.5933	12.0853
20	18.9874	18.0456	17.1686	16.3514	15.5892	14.8775	14.2124	13.5903	13.0079	12.4622
21	19.8880	18.8570	17.9001	17.0112	16.1845	15.4150	14.6980	14.0292	13.4047	12.8212
22	20.7841	19.6604	18.6208	17.6580	16.7654	15.9369	15.1671	14.4511	13.7844	13.1630
23	21.6757	20.4558	19.3309	18.2922	17.3321	16.4436	15.6204	14.8568	14.1478	13.4886
24	22.5629	21.2434	20.0304	18.9139	17.8850	16.9355	16.0584	15.2470	14.4955	13.7986
25	23.4456	22.0232	20.7196	19.5235	18.4244	17.4131	16.4815	15.6221	14.8282	14.0939
26	24.3240	22.7952	21.3986	20.1210	18.9506	17.8768	16.8904	15.9828	15.1466	14.3752
27	25.1980	23.5596	22.0676	20.7069	19.4640	18.3270	17.2854	16.3296	15.4513	14.6430
28	26.0677	24.3164	22.7267	21.2813	19.9649	18.7641	17.6670	16.6631	15.7429	14.8981
29	26.9330	25.0658	23.3761	21.8444	20.4535	19.1885	18.0358	16.9837	16.0219	15.1411
30	27.7941	25.8077	24.0158	22.3965	20.9303	19.6004	18.3920	17.2920	16.2889	15.3725
31	28.6508	26.5423	24.6461	22.9377	21.3954	20.0004	18.7363	17.5885	16.5444	15.5928
32	29.5033	27.2696	25.2671	23.4683	21.8492	20.3888	19.0689	17.8736	16.7889	15.8027
33	30.3515	27.9897	25.8790	23.9886	22.2919	20.7658	19.3902	18.1476	17.0229	16.0025
34	31.1955	28.7027	26.4817	24.4986	22.7238	21.1318	19.7007	18.4112	17.2468	16.1929
35	32.0354	29.4086	27.0756	24.9986	23.1452	21.4872	20.0007	18.6646	17.4610	16.3742
36	32.8710	30.1075	27.6607	25.4888	23.5563	21.8323	20.2905	18.9083	17.6660	16.5469
37	33.7025	30.7995	28.2371	25.9695	23.9573	22.1672	20.5705	19.1426	17.8622	16.7113
38	34.5299	31.4847	28.8051	26.4406	24.3486	22.4925	20.8411	19.3679	18.0500	16.8679
39	35.3531	32.1630	29.3646	26.9026	24.7303	22.8082	21.1025	19.5845	18.2297	17.0170
40	36.1722	32.8347	29.9158	27.3555	25.1028	23.1148	21.3551	19.7928	18.4016	17.1591
50	44.1428	39.1961	34.9997	31.4236	28.3623	25.7298	23.4556	21.4822	19.7620	18.2559
60	51.7256	44.9550	39.3803	34.7609	30.9087	27.6756	24.9447	22.6235	20.6380	18.9293
80	65.8023	54.8882	46.4073	39.7445	34.4518	30.2008	26.7488	23.9154	21.5653	19.5965
100	78.5426	63.0289	51.6247	43.0984	36.6141	31.5989	27.6554	24.5050	21.9499	19.8479
120	90.0735	69.7005	55.4985	45.3554	37.9337	32.3730	28.1111	24.7741	22.1093	19.9427

A8.2 PRESENT VALUE OF ANNUITY TABLES (cont'd)

n \ i	5.5	6	6.5	7	7.5	8	8.5	9	9.5	10
1	0.9479	0.9434	0.9390	0.9346	0.9302	0.9259	0.9217	0.9174	0.9132	0.9091
2	1.8463	1.8334	1.8206	1.8080	1.7956	1.7833	1.7711	1.7591	1.7473	1.7355
3	2.6979	2.6730	2.6485	2.6243	2.6005	2.5771	2.5540	2.5313	2.5089	2.4869
4	3.5052	3.4651	3.4258	3.3872	3.3493	3.3121	3.2756	3.2397	3.2045	3.1699
5	4.2703	4.2124	4.1557	4.1002	4.0459	3.9927	3.9406	3.8897	3.8397	3.7908
6	4.9955	4.9173	4.8410	4.7665	4.6938	4.6229	4.5536	4.4859	4.4198	4.3553
7	5.6830	5.5824	5.4845	5.3893	5.2966	5.2064	5.1185	5.0330	4.9496	4.8684
8	6.3346	6.2098	6.0888	5.9713	5.8573	5.7466	5.6392	5.5348	5.4334	5.3349
9	6.9522	6.8017	6.6561	6.5152	6.3789	6.2469	6.1191	5.9952	5.8753	5.7590
10	7.5376	7.3601	7.1888	7.0236	6.8641	6.7101	6.5613	6.4177	6.2788	6.1446
11	8.0925	7.8869	7.6890	7.4987	7.3154	7.1390	6.9690	6.8052	6.6473	6.4951
12	8.6185	8.3838	8.1587	7.9427	7.7353	7.5361	7.3447	7.1607	6.9838	6.8137
13	9.1171	8.8527	8.5997	8.3577	8.1258	7.9038	7.6910	7.4869	7.2912	7.1034
14	9.5896	9.2950	9.0138	8.7455	8.4892	8.2442	8.0101	7.7862	7.5719	7.3667
15	10.0376	9.7122	9.4027	9.1079	8.8271	8.5595	8.3042	8.0607	7.8282	7.6061
16	10.4622	10.1059	9.7678	9.4466	9.1415	8.8514	8.5753	8.3126	8.0623	7.8237
17	10.8646	10.4773	10.1106	9.7632	9.4340	9.1216	8.8252	8.5436	8.2760	8.0216
18	11.2461	10.8276	10.4325	10.0591	9.7060	9.3719	9.0555	8.7556	8.4713	8.2014
19	11.6077	11.1581	10.7347	10.3356	9.9591	9.6036	9.2677	8.9501	8.6496	8.3649
20	11.9504	11.4699	11.0185	10.5940	10.1945	9.8181	9.4633	9.1285	8.8124	8.5136
21	12.2752	11.7641	11.2850	10.8355	10.4135	10.0168	9.6436	9.2922	8.9611	8.6487
22	12.5832	12.0416	11.5352	11.0612	10.6172	10.2007	9.8098	9.4424	9.0969	8.7715
23	12.8750	12.3034	11.7701	11.2722	10.8067	10.3711	9.9629	9.5802	9.2209	8.8832
24	13.1517	12.5504	11.9907	11.4693	10.9830	10.5288	10.1041	9.7066	9.3341	8.9847
25	13.4139	12.7834	12.1979	11.6536	11.1469	10.6748	10.2342	9.8226	9.4376	9.0770
26	13.6625	13.0032	12.3924	11.8258	11.2995	10.8100	10.3541	9.9290	9.5320	9.1609
27	13.8981	13.2105	12.5750	11.9867	11.4414	10.9352	10.4646	10.0266	9.6183	9.2372
28	14.1214	13.4062	12.7465	12.1371	11.5734	11.0511	10.5665	10.1161	9.6971	9.3066
29	14.3331	13.5907	12.9075	12.2777	11.6962	11.1584	10.6603	10.1983	9.7690	9.3696
30	14.5337	13.7648	13.0587	12.4090	11.8104	11.2578	10.7468	10.2737	9.8347	9.4269
31	14.7239	13.9291	13.2006	12.5318	11.9166	11.3498	10.8266	10.3428	9.8947	9.4790
32	14.9042	14.0840	13.3339	12.6466	12.0155	11.4350	10.9001	10.4062	9.9495	9.5264
33	15.0751	14.2302	13.4591	12.7538	12.1074	11.5139	10.9678	10.4644	9.9996	9.5694
34	15.2370	14.3681	13.5766	12.8540	12.1929	11.5869	11.0302	10.5178	10.0453	9.6086
35	15.3906	14.4982	13.6870	12.9477	12.2725	11.6546	11.0878	10.5668	10.0870	9.6442
36	15.5361	14.6210	13.7906	13.0352	12.3465	11.7172	11.1408	10.6118	10.1251	9.6765
37	15.6740	14.7368	13.8879	13.1170	12.4154	11.7752	11.1897	10.6530	10.1599	9.7059
38	15.8047	14.8460	13.9792	13.1935	12.4794	11.8289	11.2347	10.6908	10.1917	9.7327
39	15.9287	14.9491	14.0650	13.2649	12.5390	11.8786	11.2763	10.7255	10.2207	9.7570
40	16.0461	15.0463	14.1455	13.3317	12.5944	11.9246	11.3145	10.7574	10.2472	9.7791
50	16.9315	15.7619	14.7245	13.8007	12.9748	12.2335	11.5656	10.9617	10.4137	9.9148
60	17.4499	16.1614	15.0330	14.0392	13.1594	12.3766	11.6766	11.0480	10.4809	9.9672
80	17.9310	16.5091	15.2848	14.2220	13.2924	12.4735	11.7475	11.0998	10.5189	9.9951
100	18.0958	16.6175	15.3563	14.2693	13.3237	12.4943	11.7613	11.1091	10.5251	9.9993
120	18.1524	16.6514	15.3766	14.2815	13.3311	12.4988	11.7640	11.1108	10.5261	9.9999

A8.2 PRESENT VALUE OF ANNUITY TABLES (cont'd)

i	10.5	11	11.5	12	12.5	13	13.5	14	14.5	15
n										
1	0.9050	0.9009	0.8969	0.8929	0.8889	0.8850	0.8811	0.8772	0.8734	0.8696
2	1.7240	1.7125	1.7012	1.6901	1.6790	1.6681	1.6573	1.6467	1.6361	1.6257
3	2.4651	2.4437	2.4226	2.4018	2.3813	2.3612	2.3413	2.3216	2.3023	2.2832
4	3.1359	3.1024	3.0696	3.0373	3.0056	2.9745	2.9438	2.9137	2.8841	2.8550
5	3.7429	3.6959	3.6499	3.6048	3.5606	3.5172	3.4747	3.4331	3.3922	3.3522
6	4.2922	4.2305	4.1703	4.1114	4.0538	3.9975	3.9425	3.8887	3.8360	3.7845
7	4.7893	4.7122	4.6370	4.5638	4.4923	4.4226	4.3546	4.2883	4.2236	4.1604
8	5.2392	5.1461	5.0556	4.9676	4.8820	4.7988	4.7177	4.6389	4.5621	4.4873
9	5.6463	5.5370	5.4311	5.3282	5.2285	5.1317	5.0377	4.9464	4.8577	4.7716
10	6.0148	5.8892	5.7678	5.6502	5.5364	5.4262	5.3195	5.2161	5.1159	5.0188
11	6.3482	6.2065	6.0697	5.9377	5.8102	5.6869	5.5679	5.4527	5.3414	5.2337
12	6.6500	6.4924	6.3406	6.1944	6.0535	5.9176	5.7867	5.6603	5.5383	5.4206
13	6.9230	6.7499	6.5835	6.4235	6.2698	6.1218	5.9794	5.8424	5.7103	5.5831
14	7.1702	6.9819	6.8013	6.6282	6.4620	6.3025	6.1493	6.0021	5.8606	5.7245
15	7.3938	7.1909	6.9967	6.8109	6.6329	6.4624	6.2989	6.1422	5.9918	5.8474
16	7.5962	7.3792	7.1719	6.9740	6.7848	6.6039	6.4308	6.2651	6.1063	5.9542
17	7.7794	7.5488	7.3291	7.1196	6.9198	6.7291	6.5469	6.3729	6.2064	6.0472
18	7.9451	7.7016	7.4700	7.2497	7.0398	6.8399	6.6493	6.4674	6.2938	6.1280
19	8.0952	7.8393	7.5964	7.3658	7.1465	6.9380	6.7395	6.5504	6.3701	6.1982
20	8.2309	7.9633	7.7098	7.4694	7.2414	7.0248	6.8189	6.6231	6.4368	6.2593
21	8.3538	8.0751	7.8115	7.5620	7.3256	7.1016	6.8889	6.6870	6.4950	6.3125
22	8.4649	8.1757	7.9027	7.6446	7.4006	7.1695	6.9506	6.7429	6.5459	6.3587
23	8.5656	8.2664	7.9845	7.7184	7.4672	7.2297	7.0049	6.7921	6.5903	6.3988
24	8.6566	8.3481	8.0578	7.7843	7.5264	7.2829	7.0528	6.8351	6.6291	6.4338
25	8.7390	8.4217	8.1236	7.8431	7.5790	7.3300	7.0950	6.8729	6.6629	6.4641
26	8.8136	8.4881	8.1826	7.8957	7.6258	7.3717	7.1321	6.9061	6.6925	6.4906
27	8.8811	8.5478	8.2355	7.9426	7.6674	7.4086	7.1649	6.9352	6.7184	6.5135
28	8.9422	8.6016	8.2830	7.9844	7.7043	7.4412	7.1937	6.9607	6.7409	6.5335
29	8.9974	8.6501	8.3255	8.0218	7.7372	7.4701	7.2191	6.9830	6.7606	6.5509
30	9.0474	8.6938	8.3637	8.0552	7.7664	7.4957	7.2415	7.0027	6.7778	6.5660
31	9.0927	8.7331	8.3980	8.0850	7.7923	7.5183	7.2613	7.0199	6.7929	6.5791
32	9.1337	8.7686	8.4287	8.1116	7.8154	7.5383	7.2786	7.0350	6.8060	6.5905
33	9.1707	8.8005	8.4562	8.1354	7.8359	7.5560	7.2940	7.0482	6.8175	6.6005
34	9.2043	8.8293	8.4809	8.1566	7.8542	7.5717	7.3075	7.0599	6.8275	6.6091
35	9.2347	8.8552	8.5030	8.1755	7.8704	7.5856	7.3193	7.0700	6.8362	6.6166
36	9.2621	8.8786	8.5229	8.1924	7.8848	7.5979	7.3298	7.0790	6.8439	6.6231
37	9.2870	8.8996	8.5407	8.2075	7.8976	7.6087	7.3390	7.0868	6.8505	6.6288
38	9.3095	8.9186	8.5567	8.2210	7.9089	7.6183	7.3472	7.0937	6.8564	6.6338
39	9.3299	8.9357	8.5710	8.2330	7.9191	7.6268	7.3543	7.0997	6.8615	6.6380
40	9.3483	8.9511	8.5839	8.2438	7.9281	7.6344	7.3607	7.1050	6.8659	6.6418
50	9.4591	9.0417	8.6580	8.3045	7.9778	7.6752	7.3942	7.1327	6.8886	6.6605
60	9.5000	9.0736	8.6830	8.3240	7.9932	7.6873	7.4037	7.1401	6.8945	6.6651
80	9.5206	9.0888	8.6942	8.3324	7.9994	7.6919	7.4071	7.1427	6.8964	6.6666
100	9.5234	9.0906	8.6955	8.3332	7.9999	7.6923	7.4074	7.1428	6.8965	6.6667
120	9.5237	9.0909	8.6956	8.3333	8.0000	7.6923	7.4074	7.1429	6.8966	6.6667

A8.2 PRESENT VALUE OF ANNUITY TABLES (cont'd)

n \ i	15.5	16	16.5	17	17.5	18	18.5	19	19.5	20
1	0.8658	0.8621	0.8584	0.8547	0.8511	0.8475	0.8439	0.8403	0.8368	0.8333
2	1.6154	1.6052	1.5952	1.5852	1.5754	1.5656	1.5560	1.5465	1.5371	1.5278
3	2.2644	2.2459	2.2276	2.2096	2.1918	2.1743	2.1570	2.1399	2.1231	2.1065
4	2.8263	2.7982	2.7705	2.7432	2.7164	2.6901	2.6641	2.6386	2.6135	2.5887
5	3.3129	3.2743	3.2365	3.1993	3.1629	3.1272	3.0921	3.0576	3.0238	2.9906
6	3.7341	3.6847	3.6365	3.5892	3.5429	3.4976	3.4532	3.4098	3.3672	3.3255
7	4.0988	4.0386	3.9798	3.9224	3.8663	3.8115	3.7580	3.7057	3.6546	3.6046
8	4.4145	4.3436	4.2745	4.2072	4.1415	4.0776	4.0152	3.9544	3.8950	3.8372
9	4.6879	4.6065	4.5275	4.4506	4.3758	4.3030	4.2322	4.1633	4.0963	4.0310
10	4.9246	4.8332	4.7446	4.6586	4.5751	4.4941	4.4154	4.3389	4.2647	4.1925
11	5.1295	5.0286	4.9310	4.8364	4.7448	4.6560	4.5699	4.4865	4.4056	4.3271
12	5.3069	5.1971	5.0910	4.9884	4.8892	4.7932	4.7004	4.6105	4.5235	4.4392
13	5.4605	5.3423	5.2283	5.1183	5.0121	4.9095	4.8104	4.7147	4.6222	4.5327
14	5.5935	5.4675	5.3462	5.2293	5.1167	5.0081	4.9033	4.8023	4.7047	4.6106
15	5.7087	5.5755	5.4474	5.3242	5.2057	5.0916	4.9817	4.8759	4.7738	4.6755
16	5.8084	5.6685	5.5342	5.4053	5.2814	5.1624	5.0479	4.9377	4.8317	4.7296
17	5.8947	5.7487	5.6088	5.4746	5.3459	5.2223	5.1037	4.9897	4.8801	4.7746
18	5.9695	5.8178	5.6728	5.5339	5.4008	5.2732	5.1508	5.0333	4.9205	4.8122
19	6.0342	5.8775	5.7277	5.5845	5.4475	5.3162	5.1905	5.0700	4.9544	4.8435
20	6.0902	5.9288	5.7748	5.6278	5.4872	5.3527	5.2241	5.1009	4.9828	4.8696
21	6.1387	5.9731	5.8153	5.6648	5.5210	5.3837	5.2524	5.1268	5.0065	4.8913
22	6.1807	6.0113	5.8501	5.6964	5.5498	5.4099	5.2763	5.1486	5.0264	4.9094
23	6.2170	6.0442	5.8799	5.7234	5.5743	5.4321	5.2964	5.1668	5.0430	4.9245
24	6.2485	6.0726	5.9055	5.7465	5.5951	5.4509	5.3134	5.1822	5.0569	4.9371
25	6.2758	6.0971	5.9274	5.7662	5.6129	5.4669	5.3278	5.1951	5.0685	4.9476
26	6.2994	6.1182	5.9463	5.7831	5.6280	5.4804	5.3399	5.2060	5.0783	4.9563
27	6.3198	6.1364	5.9625	5.7975	5.6408	5.4919	5.3501	5.2151	5.0864	4.9636
28	6.3375	6.1520	5.9764	5.8099	5.6518	5.5016	5.3588	5.2228	5.0932	4.9697
29	6.3528	6.1656	5.9883	5.8204	5.6611	5.5098	5.3661	5.2292	5.0989	4.9747
30	6.3661	6.1772	5.9986	5.8294	5.6690	5.5168	5.3722	5.2347	5.1037	4.9789
31	6.3775	6.1872	6.0073	5.8371	5.6758	5.5227	5.3774	5.2392	5.1077	4.9824
32	6.3875	6.1959	6.0149	5.8437	5.6815	5.5277	5.3818	5.2430	5.1111	4.9854
33	6.3961	6.2034	6.0214	5.8493	5.6864	5.5320	5.3854	5.2462	5.1139	4.9878
34	6.4035	6.2098	6.0269	5.8541	5.6905	5.5356	5.3886	5.2489	5.1162	4.9898
35	6.4100	6.2153	6.0317	5.8582	5.6941	5.5386	5.3912	5.2512	5.1182	4.9915
36	6.4156	6.2201	6.0358	5.8617	5.6971	5.5412	5.3934	5.2531	5.1198	4.9929
37	6.4204	6.2242	6.0393	5.8647	5.6996	5.5434	5.3953	5.2547	5.1212	4.9941
38	6.4246	6.2278	6.0423	5.8673	5.7018	5.5452	5.3969	5.2561	5.1223	4.9951
39	6.4282	6.2309	6.0449	5.8695	5.7037	5.5468	5.3982	5.2572	5.1233	4.9959
40	6.4314	6.2335	6.0471	5.8713	5.7053	5.5482	5.3993	5.2582	5.1241	4.9966
50	6.4468	6.2463	6.0577	5.8801	5.7125	5.5541	5.4043	5.2623	5.1275	4.9995
60	6.4505	6.2492	6.0600	5.8819	5.7139	5.5553	5.4052	5.2630	5.1281	4.9999
80	6.4515	6.2500	6.0606	5.8823	5.7143	5.5555	5.4054	5.2632	5.1282	5.0000
100	6.4516	6.2500	6.0606	5.8824	5.7143	5.5556	5.4054	5.2632	5.1282	5.0000
120	6.4516	6.2500	6.0606	5.8824	5.7143	5.5556	5.4054	5.2632	5.1282	5.0000

A8.2 PRESENT VALUE OF ANNUITY TABLES (cont'd)

i n	21	22	23	24	25	30	35	40	50	100
1	0.8264	0.8197	0.8130	0.8065	0.8000	0.7692	0.7407	0.7143	0.6667	0.5000
2	1.5095	1.4915	1.4740	1.4568	1.4400	1.3609	1.2894	1.2245	1.1111	0.7500
3	2.0739	2.0422	2.0114	1.9813	1.9520	1.8161	1.6959	1.5889	1.4074	0.8750
4	2.5404	2.4936	2.4483	2.4043	2.3616	2.1662	1.9969	1.8492	1.6049	0.9375
5	2.9260	2.8636	2.8035	2.7454	2.6893	2.4356	2.2200	2.0352	1.7366	1.9688
6	3.2446	3.1669	3.0923	3.0205	2.9514	2.6427	2.3852	2.1680	1.8244	1.9844
7	3.5079	3.4155	3.3270	3.2423	3.1611	2.8021	2.5075	2.2628	1.8829	0.9922
8	3.7256	3.6193	3.5179	3.4212	3.3289	2.9247	2.5982	2.3306	1.9220	0.9961
9	3.9054	3.7863	3.6731	3.5655	3.4631	3.0190	2.6653	2.3790	1.9480	0.9980
10	4.0541	3.9232	3.7993	3.6819	3.5705	3.0915	2.7150	2.4136	1.9653	0.9990
11	4.1769	4.0354	3.9018	3.7757	3.6564	3.1473	2.7519	2.4383	1.9769	0.9995
12	4.2784	4.1274	3.9852	3.8514	3.7251	3.1903	2.7792	2.4559	1.9846	0.9998
13	4.3624	4.2028	4.0530	3.9124	3.7801	3.2233	2.7994	2.4685	1.9897	0.9999
14	4.4317	4.2646	4.1082	3.9616	3.8241	3.2487	2.8144	2.4775	1.9931	0.9999
15	4.4890	4.3152	4.1530	4.0013	3.8593	3.2682	2.8255	2.4839	1.9954	1.0000
16	4.5364	4.3567	4.1894	4.0333	3.8874	3.2832	2.8337	2.4885	1.9970	1.0000
17	4.5755	4.3908	4.2190	4.0591	3.9099	3.2948	2.8398	2.4918	1.9980	1.0000
18	4.6079	4.4187	4.2431	4.0799	3.9279	3.3037	2.8443	2.4941	1.9986	1.0000
19	4.6346	4.4415	4.2627	4.0967	3.9424	3.3105	2.8476	2.4958	1.9991	1.0000
20	4.6567	4.4603	4.2786	4.1103	3.9539	3.3158	2.8501	2.4970	1.9994	1.0000
21	4.6750	4.4756	4.2916	4.1212	3.9631	3.3198	2.8519	2.4979	1.9996	1.0000
22	4.6900	4.4882	4.3021	4.1300	3.9705	3.3230	2.8533	2.4985	1.9997	1.0000
23	4.7025	4.4985	4.3106	4.1371	3.9764	3.3254	2.8543	2.4989	1.9998	1.0000
24	4.7128	4.5070	4.3176	4.1428	3.9811	3.3272	2.8550	2.4992	1.9999	1.0000
25	4.7213	4.5139	4.3232	4.1474	3.9849	3.3286	2.8556	2.4994	1.9999	1.0000
26	4.7284	4.5196	4.3278	4.1511	3.9879	3.3297	2.8560	2.4996	1.9999	1.0000
27	4.7342	4.5243	4.3316	4.1542	3.9903	3.3305	2.8563	2.4997	2.0000	1.0000
28	4.7390	4.5281	4.3346	4.1566	3.9923	3.3312	2.8565	2.4998	2.0000	1.0000
29	4.7430	4.5312	4.3371	4.1585	3.9938	3.3317	2.8567	2.4999	2.0000	1.0000
30	4.7463	4.5338	4.3391	4.1601	3.9950	3.3321	2.8568	2.4999	2.0000	1.0000
31	4.7490	4.5359	4.3407	4.1614	3.9960	3.3324	2.8569	2.4999	2.0000	1.0000
32	4.7512	4.5376	4.3421	4.1624	3.9968	3.3326	2.8569	2.4999	2.0000	1.0000
33	4.7531	4.5390	4.3431	4.1632	3.9975	3.3328	2.8570	2.5000	2.0000	1.0000
34	4.7546	4.5402	4.3440	4.1639	3.9980	3.3329	2.8570	2.5000	2.0000	1.0000
35	4.7559	4.5411	4.3447	4.1644	3.9984	3.3330	2.8571	2.5000	2.0000	1.0000
36	4.7569	4.5419	4.3453	4.1649	3.9987	3.3331	2.8571	2.5000	2.0000	1.0000
37	4.7578	4.5426	4.3458	4.1652	3.9990	3.3331	2.8571	2.5000	2.0000	1.0000
38	4.7585	4.5431	4.3462	4.1655	3.9992	3.3332	2.8571	2.5000	2.0000	1.0000
39	4.7591	4.5435	4.3465	4.1657	3.9993	3.3332	2.8571	2.5000	2.0000	1.0000
40	4.7596	4.5439	4.3467	4.1659	3.9995	3.3332	2.8571	2.5000	2.0000	1.0000
50	4.7616	4.5452	4.3477	4.1666	3.9999	3.3333	2.8571	2.5000	2.0000	1.0000
60	4.7619	4.5454	4.3478	4.1667	4.0000	3.3333	2.8571	2.5000	2.0000	1.0000
80	4.7619	4.5455	4.3478	4.1667	4.0000	3.3333	2.8571	2.5000	2.0000	1.0000
100	4.7619	4.5455	4.3478	4.1667	4.0000	3.3333	2.8571	2.5000	2.0000	1.0000
120	4.7619	4.5455	4.3478	4.1667	4.0000	3.3333	2.8571	2.5000	2.0000	1.0000

A8.3   ANNUAL VALUE TABLES

(for intermediate values use the inverse of Table A8.2 values)

i / n	1	2	3	4	5	6	7	8	9	10
1	1.0100	1.0200	1.0300	1.0400	1.0500	1.0600	1.0700	1.0800	1.0900	1.1000
2	0.5075	0.5150	0.5226	0.5302	0.5378	0.5454	0.5531	0.5608	0.5685	0.5762
3	0.3400	0.3468	0.3535	0.3603	0.3672	0.3741	0.3811	0.3880	0.3951	0.4021
4	0.2563	0.2626	0.2690	0.2755	0.2820	0.2886	0.2952	0.3019	0.3087	0.3155
5	0.2060	0.2122	0.2184	0.2246	0.2310	0.2374	0.2439	0.2505	0.2571	0.2638
6	0.1725	0.1785	0.1846	0.1908	0.1970	0.2034	0.2098	0.2163	0.2229	0.2296
7	0.1486	0.1545	0.1605	0.1666	0.1728	0.1791	0.1856	0.1921	0.1987	0.2054
8	0.1307	0.1365	0.1425	0.1485	0.1547	0.1610	0.1675	0.1740	0.1807	0.1874
9	0.1167	0.1225	0.1284	0.1345	0.1407	0.1470	0.1535	0.1601	0.1668	0.1736
10	0.1056	0.1113	0.1172	0.1233	0.1295	0.1359	0.1424	0.1490	0.1558	0.1627
11	0.0965	0.1022	0.1081	0.1141	0.1204	0.1268	0.1334	0.1401	0.1469	0.1540
12	0.0888	0.0946	0.1005	0.1066	0.1128	0.1193	0.1259	0.1327	0.1397	0.1468
13	0.0824	0.0881	0.0940	0.1001	0.1065	0.1130	0.1197	0.1265	0.1336	0.1408
14	0.0769	0.0826	0.0885	0.0947	0.1010	0.1076	0.1143	0.1213	0.1284	0.1357
15	0.0721	0.0778	0.0838	0.0899	0.0963	0.1030	0.1098	0.1168	0.1241	0.1315
16	0.0679	0.0737	0.0796	0.0858	0.0923	0.0990	0.1059	0.1130	0.1203	0.1278
17	0.0643	0.0700	0.0760	0.0822	0.0887	0.0954	0.1024	0.1096	0.1170	0.1247
18	0.0610	0.0667	0.0727	0.0790	0.0855	0.0924	0.0994	0.1067	0.1142	0.1219
19	0.0581	0.0638	0.0698	0.0761	0.0827	0.0896	0.0968	0.1041	0.1117	0.1195
20	0.0554	0.0612	0.0672	0.0736	0.0802	0.0872	0.0944	0.1019	0.1095	0.1175
21	0.0530	0.0588	0.0649	0.0713	0.0780	0.0850	0.0923	0.0998	0.1076	0.1156
22	0.0509	0.0566	0.0627	0.0692	0.0760	0.0830	0.0904	0.0980	0.1059	0.1140
23	0.0489	0.0547	0.0608	0.0673	0.0741	0.0813	0.0887	0.0964	0.1044	0.1126
24	0.0471	0.0529	0.0590	0.0656	0.0725	0.0797	0.0872	0.0950	0.1030	0.1113
25	0.0454	0.0512	0.0574	0.0640	0.0710	0.0782	0.0858	0.0937	0.1018	0.1102
26	0.0439	0.0497	0.0559	0.0626	0.0696	0.0769	0.0846	0.0925	0.1007	0.1092
27	0.0424	0.0483	0.0546	0.0612	0.0683	0.0757	0.0834	0.0914	0.0997	0.1083
28	0.0411	0.0470	0.0533	0.0600	0.0671	0.0746	0.0824	0.0905	0.0989	0.1075
29	0.0399	0.0458	0.0521	0.0589	0.0660	0.0736	0.0814	0.0896	0.0981	0.1067
30	0.0387	0.0446	0.0510	0.0578	0.0651	0.0726	0.0806	0.0888	0.0973	0.1061
31	0.0377	0.0436	0.0500	0.0569	0.0641	0.0718	0.0798	0.0881	0.0967	0.1055
32	0.0367	0.0426	0.0490	0.0559	0.0633	0.0710	0.0791	0.0875	0.0961	0.1050
33	0.0357	0.0417	0.0482	0.0551	0.0625	0.0703	0.0784	0.0869	0.0956	0.1045
34	0.0348	0.0408	0.0473	0.0543	0.0618	0.0696	0.0778	0.0863	0.0951	0.1041
35	0.0340	0.0400	0.0465	0.0536	0.0611	0.0690	0.0772	0.0858	0.0946	0.1037
36	0.0332	0.0392	0.0458	0.0529	0.0604	0.0684	0.0767	0.0853	0.0942	0.1033
37	0.0325	0.0385	0.0451	0.0522	0.0598	0.0679	0.0762	0.0849	0.0939	0.1030
38	0.0318	0.0378	0.0445	0.0516	0.0593	0.0674	0.0758	0.0845	0.0935	0.1027
39	0.0311	0.0372	0.0438	0.0511	0.0588	0.0669	0.0754	0.0842	0.0932	0.1025
40	0.0305	0.0366	0.0433	0.0505	0.0583	0.0665	0.0750	0.0839	0.0930	0.1023
50	0.0255	0.0318	0.0389	0.0466	0.0548	0.0634	0.0725	0.0817	0.0912	0.1009
60	0.0222	0.0288	0.0361	0.0442	0.0528	0.0619	0.0712	0.0808	0.0905	0.1003
80	0.0182	0.0252	0.0331	0.0418	0.0510	0.0606	0.0703	0.0802	0.0901	0.1000
100	0.0159	0.0232	0.0316	0.0408	0.0504	0.0602	0.0701	0.0800	0.0900	0.1000
120	0.0143	0.0220	0.0309	0.0404	0.0501	0.0601	0.0700	0.0800	0.0900	0.1000

A8.3 ANNUAL VALUE TABLES (cont'd)

(for intermediate values use the inverse of Table A8.2 values)

i \ n	11	12	13	14	15	20	25	30	40	50
1	1.1100	1.1200	1.1300	1.1400	1.1500	1.2000	1.2500	1.3000	1.4000	1.5000
2	0.5839	0.5917	0.5995	0.6073	0.6151	0.6545	0.6944	0.7348	0.8167	0.9000
3	0.4092	0.4163	0.4235	0.4307	0.4380	0.4747	0.5123	0.5506	0.6294	0.7105
4	0.3223	0.3292	0.3362	0.3432	0.3503	0.3863	0.4234	0.4616	0.5408	0.6231
5	0.2706	0.2774	0.2843	0.2913	0.2983	0.3344	0.3718	0.4106	0.4914	0.5758
6	0.2364	0.2432	0.2502	0.2572	0.2642	0.3007	0.3388	0.3784	0.4613	0.5481
7	0.2122	0.2191	0.2261	0.2332	0.2404	0.2774	0.3163	0.3569	0.4419	0.5311
8	0.1943	0.2013	0.2084	0.2156	0.2229	0.2606	0.3004	0.3419	0.4291	0.5203
9	0.1806	0.1877	0.1949	0.2022	0.2096	0.2481	0.2888	0.3312	0.4203	0.5134
10	0.1698	0.1770	0.1843	0.1917	0.1993	0.2385	0.2801	0.3235	0.4143	0.5088
11	0.1611	0.1684	0.1758	0.1834	0.1911	0.2311	0.2735	0.3177	0.4101	0.5058
12	0.1540	0.1614	0.1690	0.1767	0.1845	0.2253	0.2684	0.3135	0.4072	0.5039
13	0.1482	0.1557	0.1634	0.1712	0.1791	0.2206	0.2645	0.3102	0.4051	0.5026
14	0.1432	0.1509	0.1587	0.1666	0.1747	0.2169	0.2615	0.3078	0.4036	0.5017
15	0.1391	0.1468	0.1547	0.1628	0.1710	0.2139	0.2591	0.3060	0.4026	0.5011
16	0.1355	0.1434	0.1514	0.1596	0.1679	0.2114	0.2572	0.3046	0.4018	0.5008
17	0.1325	0.1405	0.1486	0.1569	0.1654	0.2094	0.2558	0.3035	0.4013	0.5005
18	0.1298	0.1379	0.1462	0.1546	0.1632	0.2078	0.2546	0.3027	0.4009	0.5003
19	0.1276	0.1358	0.1441	0.1527	0.1613	0.2065	0.2537	0.3021	0.4007	0.5002
20	0.1256	0.1339	0.1424	0.1510	0.1598	0.2054	0.2529	0.3016	0.4005	0.5002
21	0.1238	0.1322	0.1408	0.1495	0.1584	0.2044	0.2523	0.3012	0.4003	0.5001
22	0.1223	0.1308	0.1395	0.1483	0.1573	0.2037	0.2519	0.3009	0.4002	0.5001
23	0.1210	0.1296	0.1383	0.1472	0.1563	0.2031	0.2515	0.3007	0.4002	0.5000
24	0.1198	0.1285	0.1373	0.1463	0.1554	0.2025	0.2512	0.3006	0.4001	0.5000
25	0.1187	0.1275	0.1364	0.1455	0.1547	0.2021	0.2509	0.3004	0.4001	0.5000
26	0.1178	0.1267	0.1357	0.1448	0.1541	0.2018	0.2508	0.3003	0.4001	0.5000
27	0.1170	0.1259	0.1350	0.1442	0.1535	0.2015	0.2506	0.3003	0.4000	0.5000
28	0.1163	0.1252	0.1344	0.1437	0.1531	0.2012	0.2505	0.3002	0.4000	0.5000
29	0.1156	0.1247	0.1339	0.1432	0.1527	0.2010	0.2504	0.3001	0.4000	0.5000
30	0.1150	0.1241	0.1334	0.1428	0.1523	0.2008	0.2503	0.3001	0.4000	0.5000
31	0.1145	0.1237	0.1330	0.1425	0.1520	0.2007	0.2502	0.3001	0.4000	0.5000
32	0.1140	0.1233	0.1327	0.1421	0.1517	0.2006	0.2502	0.3001	0.4000	0.5000
33	0.1136	0.1229	0.1323	0.1419	0.1515	0.2005	0.2502	0.3001	0.4000	0.5000
34	0.1133	0.1226	0.1321	0.1416	0.1513	0.2004	0.2501	0.3000	0.4000	0.5000
35	0.1129	0.1223	0.1318	0.1414	0.1511	0.2003	0.2501	0.3000	0.4000	0.5000
36	0.1126	0.1221	0.1316	0.1413	0.1510	0.2003	0.2501	0.3000	0.4000	0.5000
37	0.1124	0.1218	0.1314	0.1411	0.1509	0.2002	0.2501	0.3000	0.4000	0.5000
38	0.1121	0.1216	0.1313	0.1410	0.1507	0.2002	0.2501	0.3000	0.4000	0.5000
39	0.1119	0.1215	0.1311	0.1409	0.1506	0.2002	0.2500	0.3000	0.4000	0.5000
40	0.1117	0.1213	0.1310	0.1407	0.1506	0.2001	0.2500	0.3000	0.4000	0.5000
50	0.1106	0.1204	0.1303	0.1402	0.1501	0.2000	0.2500	0.3000	0.4000	0.5000
60	0.1102	0.1201	0.1301	0.1401	0.1500	0.2000	0.2500	0.3000	0.4000	0.5000
80	0.1100	0.1200	0.1300	0.1400	0.1500	0.2000	0.2500	0.3000	0.4000	0.5000
100	0.1100	0.1200	0.1300	0.1400	0.1500	0.2000	0.2500	0.3000	0.4000	0.5000
120	0.1100	0.1200	0.1300	0.1400	0.1500	0.2000	0.2500	0.3000	0.4000	0.5000

Appendix 9
Academic credits

ACADEMIC CREDITS

John V. Chelsom   City University
Preface
Chapters 1–8
Chapters 20, 21
Andrew C. Payne   City University
Chapters 12–13
Chapter 15
Chapter 17–19

Lawrence R. P. Reavill   City University
Chapters 9–11

Additional Chapters Edited by A. C. Payne
Chapter 14 by Diane Campbell — Stoy Hayward
Chapter 16 by F. J. Charlwood — City University
Chapter 22 by Tony Curtis — Plymouth Business School
Chapter 23 by David Telling — Council of Legal Education

INDEX